second canadian edition

retailing management

MICHAEL LEVY, Ph.D
Babson College

BARTON A. WEITZ, Ph.D
University of Florida

SHERYN BEATTIE, MA.Ed
Humber Institute of
Technology & Advanced Learning

McGraw-Hill Ryerson

Toronto Montréal Boston Burr Ridge, IL Dubuque, IA Madison, WI
New York San Francisco St. Louis Bangkok Bogotá Caracas
Kuala Lumpur Lisbon London Madrid Mexico City Milan
New Delhi Santiago Seoul Singapore Sydney Taipei

The McGraw-Hill Companies

McGraw-Hill
Ryerson

Retailing Management
Second Canadian Edition

ISBN-13: 978-0-07-097424-1
ISBN-10: 0-07-097424-1

1 2 3 4 5 6 7 8 9 10 CTPS 0 9 8

Printed and bound in China

Editorial Director: Joanna Cotton
Executive Sponsoring Editor: Leanna MacLean
Senior Marketing Manager: Joy Armitage Taylor
Developmental Editor: Marcia Luke
Editorial Associate: Stephanie Hess
Permissions Editor: Alison Derry
Supervising Editor: Elizabeth Priest
Copy Editor: Jim Zimmerman
Senior Production Coordinator: Jennifer Hall
Cover and Interior Design: Liz Harasymczuk
Cover Image: © Martin Poole/Digital Vision/Getty Images
Page Layout: Liz Harasymczuk
Printer: China Translation & Printing Services Limited

Library and Archives Canada Cataloguing in Publication

Levy, Michael
    Retailing management / Michael Levy, Barton A. Weitz, Sheryn Beattie. -- 2nd Canadian ed.

Includes bibliographical references and index. ISBN 978-0-07-097424-1

    1. Retail trade--Management--Textbooks. 2. Retail trade--Canada-- Textbooks. I. Weitz, Barton A.
II. Beattie, Sheryn III. Title.

HF5429.L47 2008   658.8'7   C2007-906798-0

To Norman and Jacquie Levy, whose enduring
love for each other is an inspiration to all.
Michael Levy

To Shirley Weitz, whose love, patience,
and understanding support are cherished.
Barton A. Weitz

To Peter Schoppel, the love and spirit of my life.
Sheryn Beattie

About the Authors

Michael Levy, PhD, is the Charles Clarke Reynolds Professor of Marketing at Babson College and co-editor of *Journal of Retailing*. He received his PhD in business administration from The Ohio State University and his undergraduate and MS degrees in business administration from the University of Colorado at Boulder. He taught at Southern Methodist University before joining the faculty as professor and chair of the marketing department at the University of Miami. He has taught retailing management for 25 years.

Professor Levy has developed a strong stream of research in retailing, business logistics, financial retailing strategy, pricing, and sales management that has been published in over 45 articles in leading marketing and logistics journals, including the *Journal of Retailing, Journal of Marketing,* and *Journal of Marketing Research*. He currently serves on the editorial review board of the *Journal of Retailing, Journal of the Academy of Marketing Science, International Journal of Logistics Management, International Journal of Logistics and Materials Management, ECR Journal,* and *European Business Review*.

Professor Levy has worked in retailing and related disciplines throughout his professional life. Prior to his academic career, he worked for several retailers and a housewares distributor in Colorado. He has performed research projects with many retailers and retail technology firms, including Accenture, Burdines Department Stores, Khimetrics, Mervyn's, Neiman Marcus, ProfitLogic, and Zale Corporation.

Barton A. Weitz, PhD, received an undergraduate degree in electrical engineering from MIT and an MBA and a PhD in business administration from Stanford University. He has been a member of the faculty at the UCLA Graduate School of Business and the Wharton School at the University of Pennsylvania and is presently the JCPenney Eminent Scholar Chair in Retail Management in the Warrington College of Business Administration at the University of Florida.

Professor Weitz is the executive director of the David F. Miller Center for Retailing Education and Research at the University of Florida. The activities of the centre are supported by contributions from 30 national and regional retailers, including JCPenney, Sears, Macy's, Wal-Mart, Famous Footwear, Build-A-Bear, Bealls, City Furniture, and Office Depot. Each year the centre places over 200 undergraduates in paid summer internships and management trainee positions with retail firms and funds research on retailing issues and problems.

Professor Weitz has won awards for teaching excellence and has made numerous presentations to industry and academic groups. He has published over 50 articles in leading academic journals on channel relationships, electronic retailing, store design, salesperson effectiveness, and sales force and human resource management. He is on the editorial review boards of the *Journal of Retailing, Journal of Marketing, International Journal of Research in Marketing, Marketing Science,* and *Journal of Marketing Research*. He is a former editor of the *Journal of Marketing Research* and is presently co-editor of *Marketing Letters*.

Professor Weitz was the chair of the American Marketing Association and a member of the board of directors of the National Retail Federation, the National Retail Foundation, and the American Marketing Association. In 1989 he was honoured as the AMA/Irwin Educator of the Year in recognition of his contributions to the marketing discipline.

Sheryn Beattie, MA.Ed, has been a faculty member at Humber Institute of Technology & Advanced Learning in Toronto, Ontario, for 24 years. As a professor and program coordinator in the retail management program, she was actively involved in planning and implementing an integrated learning project that linked the retail industry to student outcomes. Professor Beattie took undergraduate courses at Ryerson and the University of Toronto and received her MA in Education from Central Michigan University. She is a winner of numerous teaching awards including the NISOD (National Institute for Staff and Organizational Development) Excellence Award from the University of Texas at Austin. Professor Beattie also received the Distinguished Faculty Award and was named Innovator of the Year by Humber. Teaching has always been her passion, and in 1999 Professor Beattie received the heartfelt Student Appreciation Award for dedication to international students in the learning environment.

Professor Beattie participated in the Ontario Retail Sector Study, 1999, and as a member of the Education Subcommittee identified gaps in retail education in Ontario and made recommendations for retail curriculum in the province. She uses much of her extensive experience as a retail consultant and industry presenter to fuel classroom discussion and seeks to empower students to assume responsibility for their own learning. The hands-on experience she gained through The Main Street Renewal Project, a Heritage Canada venture, and the day-to-day realities of owning a retail business in Toronto add vitality to her classroom. Professor Beattie believes that the success of any business course must involve the three major stakeholders: the students, sector leaders, and faculty members.

Professor Beattie participates in international assignments, including in Ningbo (China) and Zimbabwe, Lesotho, and Swaziland (Africa); extensive personal travel has also added an expanded dimension to her understanding of global issues in retailing.

Brief Contents

Contents

CHAPTER 6   RETAIL LOCATIONS STRATEGY—TRADE AREA DECISIONS AND SITE ASSESSMENT, 124

CHAPTER 7   STORE DESIGN, LAYOUT, AND VISUAL MERCHANDISING STRATEGY, 162

CHAPTER 8   INTERNATIONAL RETAILING STRATEGY, 194

SECTION III   FINANCIAL MANAGEMENT, 218

CHAPTER 9   FINANCIAL STRATEGY, 220

CHAPTER 16   APPEALING TO THE CUSTOMER: RETAIL COMMUNICATION MIX, 466

SECTION V   CASES, 498

Preface

In the Second Canadian Edition of *Retailing Management* our focus has been to increase currency and Canadian content, while structuring the text around the three important developments in retailing that were integral to the First Canadian Edition: the increasing sophistication of retail operations and decision-making tools for the supply chain, buying merchandise, and managing store operations; the growth of retailing into international markets; and, continuing investment in the Internet channel to communicate with and sell merchandise and services to customers.

In addition, we have made a number of changes to reflect the evolving nature of retailing, including up-to-date data and statistics, current and Canadian examples, and cutting edge information on new technology and trends in retailing.

Our objective is to stimulate student interest in retailing courses and careers by capturing the exciting and challenging opportunities facing the retailing industry, an industry that plays a vital economic role in society.

basic philosophy

The Second Canadian Edition of *Retailing Management* continues to focus on the broad spectrum of retailers, both large and small, that sell merchandise or services. The text examines key strategic issues with an emphasis on the financial considerations and store management issues. We include descriptive, how-to, and conceptual material.

Broad Spectrum of Retailing   In this text, we define retailing as the set of business activities that add value to the products and services sold to consumers for their personal or family use. Thus, in addition to products in stores, this text examines the issues facing service retailers such as Starbucks and nonstore retailers such as eBay, Lands' End, and Avon.

Strategic Perspective   The entire textbook is organized around a model of strategic decision making. Each section and chapter are related back to this overarching strategic framework. In addition, the book focuses on critical strategic decisions such as selecting target markets, developing a sustainable competitive advantage, and building an organizational structure and information and distribution systems to support the strategic direction.

Financial Analysis   The financial aspects of retailing are becoming increasingly important. The financial problems experienced by some of the largest retail firms highlight the need for a thorough understanding of the financial implications of retail decisions. Financial analysis is emphasized in selected chapters. Financial issues are also raised in the sections on negotiating leases, bargaining with suppliers, pricing merchandise, developing a communication budget, and compensating salespeople.

Operations and Store Management   Traditionally, retailers have exalted the merchant prince—the buyer who knew what the hot trends were going to be. This text, by devoting an entire chapter to information systems and supply chain management and an entire section to store management, reflects the changes that have occurred over the past 10 years—the shift in emphasis from merchandise management to the block and tackling of getting merchandise to the stores and customers and providing excellent customer services and an exciting shopping experience. Due to this shift toward store management, most students embarking on retail careers now go into store management rather than merchandise buying.

balanced approach

The Second Canadian Edition continues to offer a balanced approach to teaching an introductory retailing course by including descriptive, how-to, and conceptual information in a highly readable format.

Descriptive Information   Students can learn about the vocabulary and practice of retailing from the descriptive information throughout the text. Examples of this material are:

- Leading North American and international retailers
- Management decisions made by retailers
- Types of store-based and nonstore retailers
- Approaches to entering international markets
- Issues concerning retail locations
- Organizational structure of typical retailers
- Flow of information and merchandise
- Branding strategies
- Methods for communicating with customers
- Store layout options and merchandise display equipment

How-To Information   *Retailing Management* goes beyond this descriptive information to illustrate how and why retailers, large and small, make decisions. Step-by-step procedures with examples are provided for making the following decisions:

- Comparison shopping
- Managing a multichannel outreach to customers
- Scanning the environment and developing a retail strategy
- Analyzing the financial implications of retail strategy
- Evaluating location decisions
- Developing a merchandise assortment and budget plan
- Negotiating with vendors
- Pricing merchandise
- Recruiting, selecting, training, evaluating, and compensating sales associates
- Designing the layout for a store

Conceptual Information   *Retailing Management* also includes conceptual information that enables students to understand why decisions are made as outlined in the text. As Mark Twain said, "There is nothing as practical as a good theory." Students need to know these basic concepts so they can make effective decisions in new situations. Examples of this conceptual information in the Second Canadian Edition are:

- Retail evolution theories
- Customers' decision-making process
- Market attractiveness/competitive position matrix for evaluating strategic alternatives
- Activity-based costing analysis of merchandise categories
- The strategic profit model
- Price theory and marginal analysis
- The gaps model for service quality management

unique aspects of *retailing management*, 2nd canadian edition

Chapter on Customer Relationship Management   Chapter 15 examines how retailers are using customer databases to build repeat business and realize a greater share of wallet from key customers. These customer relationship management activities exploit the 80-20 rule—20 percent of the customers account for 80 percent of the sales and profits. In this chapter, we discuss how retailers identify their best customers and target these customers with special promotions and customer services. Some topics covered in this chapter are:

- Why retailers want to provide special services to their best customers
- How retailers use customer databases to determine who are their best customers
- How retailers build loyalty from their best customers
- What retailers do to increase their share of wallet
- How retailers balance customer privacy concerns with the provision of personalized promotions and services

Superior Coverage on Multichannel Retailing   This coverage includes the opportunities and challenges retailers face interacting with customers through multiple channels—stores, catalogues, and the Internet. Although the e-commerce bubble has burst for e-tailing entrepreneurs, traditional retailers are investing in using the Internet to complement their stores. We discuss the unique issues that store-based retailers face when communicating with and selling merchandise to customers over the Internet, and address issues such as:

- The distinctive customer benefits offered to customers by the different channels—stores, catalogues, and the Internet
- How multichannel retailers provide more value to their customers
- Factors that will affect the growth of the Internet channel
- The key success factors in multichannel retailing
- How technology might affect the future shopping experience

Expanded Treatment of Brand Development Issues   To differentiate their offerings and build a competitive advantage, retailers are placing more emphasis on developing their brand image, building a strong image for their private-label merchandise, and extending their image to new retail formats. Issues related to the development of brand images and private-label merchandise are discussed in more detail from both a merchandise management and a communication perspective.

Emphasis on International Retailing   We examine international retailing strategies ranging from those used to enter new international markets to the global sourcing of merchandise. Each of the expanded number of international retail examples is designated by a special global icon. As retailing evolves into a global industry, it is imperative that students understand how firms adapt their business practices to the cultural and infrastructural differences in international markets.

Active Learning and Application   Twenty-five percent of the end-of-chapter questions including Get Out & Do It! activities and Discussion Questions and Problems are new to the Second Canadian Edition.

The Get Out & Do It! exercises suggest projects that students can undertake by either visiting local retail stores or using the Internet. The exercises are designed to provide a hands-on learning experience for students. The Discussion Questions and Problems allow the student to critically analyze the chapter material in a particular scenario or context.

End-of-text cases and video cases provide discussion questions for a comprehensive examination of a scenario or case covering multiple topics and chapters. These use current and exciting examples of retailers students see every day. New cases in this edition include companies like Lululemon, Sephora, and Spence Diamonds.

new features in the second canadian edition

Up-to-Date and Cutting Edge!   Over 40% of the Executive Briefings and Retailing Views have been replaced with new examples and photos to help put the text material into a real-world context. The Refacts, cases at the end of the text, and the video cases available online, have all been updated for currency. New in-text examples such as Craig's List, Winners, and Mango have been included.

Also, new or expanded content on these retailing innovations and trends includes:

- U.S.-owned Canadian companies
- Regional focus issues in Canada
- Updated StatsCan information and Financial Post Markets
- Low-scale retailers in upscale venues/locations
- Teenage and young boys as an up-and-coming target market
- Multichannel strategies including direct mail and catalogue retailing
- Radio Frequency Identification (RFID) Technology and biometrics

Chapter-by-Chapter Updates   In addition to reorganization within some chapters to improve flow and structure, the following changes have been made for the Second Canadian Edition:

- New exhibit in Chapter 1: "Retail Sales by Sector."
- Added content in Chapter 1 on Ethical and Legal Considerations.
- Retail Strategy model in Chapter 5 is used also in Chapter 1 to ensure consistency of coverage.

- New material in Chapter 2 on pop-up stores.
- Expanded content in Chapter 3 including blogging, online shopping, e-commerce, and multichannel retailing.
- Appendix to Chapter 3: "Shopping in the Future."
- New information in Chapter 4 on teen shopping and tweens, plus-size audiences, male vs. female shoppers, and geodemographics.
- New exhibit in Chapter 4: "Canada Post's Snapshot Segmentation System."
- New section in Chapter 6 on Location and Retail Strategy.
- New content in Chapter 8 on the world's largest shopping district, Bawadi, Dubai.
- New section in Chapter 8 on Costs Associated with Global Sourcing Decisions.
- New section in Chapter 8 on counterfeiting.
- New section in Chapter 9 on Retailing Objectives and Goals.
- Updated Exhibit in Chapter 10: "Variations in Category Life Cycles."
- New section in Chapter 10 on Market Research.
- Additional explanation in Chapter 10 on Economic Order Quantity.
- New exhibit in Chapter 11: "Inventory Levels for Staple Merchandise."
- Revised Beginning of Month and Calculating Open-to-Buy sections in Chapter 11.
- New information on Radio Frequency Identification (RFID) Technology, including diagram in Chapter 11.
- New section in Chapter 12 on Support Services for the Buying Process, including Internet Exchanges.
- Additional section in Chapter 13 on the Difference between Initial Markup and Maintained Markup.
- Updated section in Chapter 13 on calculating Break-Even Analysis.
- Added definition in Chapter 13 for Zone Pricing.
- New section in Chapter 13 on The Internet and Price Competition.
- Expanded content on Store Management Responsibilities in Chapter 14, including a new exhibit.
- New section in Chapter 14 on Compensating and Rewarding Store Employees.
- Updated content in Chapter 14 on identity theft and payment fraud.
- Updated content in Chapter 15 to reflect new customer points systems such as key tags.
- New example in Chapter 15 on Harry Rosen's use of PDAs.
- Expanded section in Chapter 16 on branding.
- New exhibit in Chapter 16: "Steps to Implementing an Advertising Communications Strategy."
- Updated exhibit in Chapter 16: "Communications Methods."

about *retailing management*: guided tour

Executive Briefing: Each chapter opens with a brief profile of a manager or industry expert whose job or expertise is related to the material in the chapter. These profiles illustrate how senior executives view the industry and provide students with firsthand information about what people in retailing do and their successes and challenges.

refact

Hudson's Bay Company, the oldest retailer in North America, conquered the Canadian wilderness by trading furs over 300 years ago. Today, one of its divisions, Zellers, is one of the largest full-line discount chains in Canada.[3]

Refacts: Highlighted boxes in the margin of each chapter contain interesting facts about retailing. For instance, did you know that a Montgomery Ward buyer created Rudolph the Red-Nosed Reindeer as a Christmas promotion in 1939? Or that "Dollar Store" retailing is the fastest growing sector in Canadian retailing?

Retailing Views: The textbook contains new and updated vignettes called Retailing Views to relate concepts to activities and decisions made by retailers. The vignettes look at major retailers such as Wal-Mart, Canadian Tire, Shoppers Drug Mart, and Home Depot. They also discuss innovative retailers including Harry Rosen, Mountain Equipment Co-op, and Running Room.

exhibit 1–5
Retail Strategy

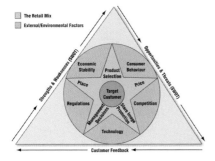

Exhibits: Charts, illustrations, and tables give visual meaning to complex subject matter and provide easy reference for students.

International Retailing Icon: This icon appears in the margin to indicate an international retailing example.

Summary and Key Terms: Recap of the chapter content—a great tool for studying!

Get Out and Do It!: At the end of each chapter, these exercises suggest hands-on projects that students can complete either by visiting a local retailer or using the Internet.

Discussion Questions and Problems: These questions propose thoughtful questions and encourage analysis and application of the text material.

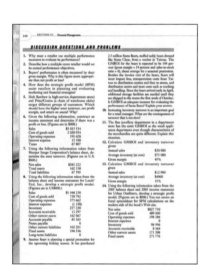

End-of-Text Cases: There are 24 of these longer, comprehensive cases and accompanying discussion questions.

acknowledgements

The support, expertise, and occasional coercion from Executive Sponsoring Editor, Leanna MacLean, and Developmental Editor, Marcia Luke, are greatly appreciated. The book also would never have come together without the editorial and production staff at McGraw-Hill Ryerson.

The Second Canadian Edition of *Retailing Management* was greatly supported by the reviews, suggestions, and direction from the following Canadian instructors on both the first and second editions:

Richard Appleby, Okanagan University College
D. Wesley Balderson, University of Lethbridge
Ed Brooker, Conestoga College
Pat Browne, Kwantlen University College
Terri Champion, Niagara College
Scott Colwell, University of Guelph
Lorrisa Dilay, Ryerson University
Charlene Hill, Capilano College
Charles J. Ireland, Centennial College
Suzanne Ivey, College of the North Atlantic
Philip Jones, Algonquin College
Paul Messinger, University of Alberta
Norma Ouellette, George Brown College
Cheryl Pollmuller, Lethbridge College
Jeff Schissler, Durham College
Robert Shustack, Concordia University
Donna M. Stapleton, Memorial University of Newfoundland
Barb Tooth, York University
Robert Warren, University of Manitoba
Brian Wrightson, Northern Alberta Institute of Technology

And finally, grateful acknowledgement goes to:

Dr. Peter Schoppel, the love and spirit of my life, and the most amazingly creative and innovative person that I have ever known, whose caring perspective has always been an inspiration and whose guiding philosophy "do no harm" should be a mantra for all.

Nancy Epner, a colleague and dear friend whose patience, dedication, and experience in the retail industry provided invaluable insight in the financial management sections in this textbook.

Sheryn Beattie

supplements for students

Online Learning Centre (www.mcgrawhill.ca/olc/levy) Numerous resources are available on this text-specific Web site, including:

- Additional content and appendices
- Tutorials and modules
- *Globe and Mail* headlines
- Self-assessment quizzes
- Suggested readings
- Glossary

supplements for instructors

Instructor's CD-ROM The following instructor supplements are available on the Instructor's Resource CD-ROM. Most are downloadable from the Online Learning Centre:

Instructor's Manual and Video Notes, containing an annotated outline and notes, answers to Discussion Questions and Problems, ancillary lectures and exercises, and notes to the end-of-text and video cases.

Computerized Test Bank, multiple-choice, essay, fill-in-the-blank, and short answer questions. Professors may use this software to create, edit, and print a variety of tests.

PowerPoint® Presentations to support and organize lectures.

Instructor's Online Learning Centre The OLC content is flexible enough to be used with any course management platform currently available. If your department or school is already using a platform, we can help. The OLC also includes a password-protected Web site for instructors; visit us at www.mcgrawhill.ca/olc/levy. The site offers downloadable supplements and PageOut, the McGraw-Hill Ryerson course Web site development centre. For information, contact your *i*Learning Sales Specialist.

SUPERIOR SERVICE

_i_Learning Sales Specialist Your Integrated Learning Sales Specialist is a McGraw-Hill Ryerson representative who has the experience, product knowledge, training, and support to help you assess and integrate any of the following products, technology, and services into your course for optimum teaching and learning performance. Whether it's helping your students improve their grades, or putting your entire course online, your *i*Learning Sales Specialist is there to help you. Contact your local *i*Learning Sales Specialist today to learn how to maximize all of McGraw-Hill Ryerson's resources!

_i_Learning Services McGraw-Hill Ryerson offers a unique *i*Learning Services package designed for Canadian faculty. Our mission is to equip providers of higher education with the superior tools and resources required for excellence in teaching. For additional information visit www.mcgrawhill.ca/highereducation/iservices/.

Teaching, Learning, & Technology Conference Series The educational environment has changed tremendously in recent years, and McGraw-Hill Ryerson continues to be committed to helping you acquire the skills you need to succeed in this new milieu. Our innovative Teaching, Learning, & Technology Conference Series brings faculty together from across Canada with 3M Teaching Excellence award winners to share teaching and learning best practices in a collaborative and stimulating environment. Pre-conference workshops on general topics, such as teaching large classes and technology integration, will be offered. We will also work with you at your own institution to customize workshops that best suit the needs of your faculty.

PageOut McGraw-Hill Ryerson's course management system, PageOut, is the easiest way to create a Web site for your retailing management course. There is no need for HTML coding, graphic design, or a thick how-to book. Just fill in a series of boxes in plain English and click on one of our professional designs. In no time, your course is online!

Course Management For the integrated instructor, we offer *Retailing Management* content for complete online courses. Whatever your needs, you can customize the *Retailing Management* Online Learning Centre content and author your own online course materials. It is entirely up to you. You can offer online discussion and message boards that will complement your office hours and reduce the lines outside your door. Content cartridges are also available for course management systems, such as WebCT and Blackboard. Ask your *i*Learning Sales Specialist for details.

the world of retailing

CHAPTER ONE
INTRODUCTION TO THE WORLD OF RETAILING

CHAPTER TWO
TYPES OF RETAILERS

CHAPTER THREE
E-TAILING ISSUES— CONNECTING TO THE CUSTOMER

CHAPTER FOUR
CUSTOMER BUYING BEHAVIOUR

The chapters in Section I provide background information about retail customers and competitors that is needed to understand retailing and develop and effectively implement a retail strategy.

Chapter 1 describes the role of retailing as a keystone to the Canadian economy, the functions retailers perform, and the variety of decisions they make to satisfy customers' needs in the rapidly changing, highly competitive Canadian marketplace.

Chapter 2 describes the different types of retailers and how retailers are using the multichannel approach to attract customers.

Chapter 3 discusses the impact of electronic retailing and examines the strategies of successful e-tailers.

Chapter 4 discusses factors consumers consider when choosing stores and buying merchandise and explores trends in consumer demographic segments.

Section II outlines the strategic decisions retailers make.

Sections III and IV explore tactical decisions concerning merchandise and store management.

Section V provides 24 longer comprehensive cases.

introduction to the world of retailing

Executive Briefing

Chip Wilson—Canada's Marketing and Fashion Retail Visionary

Chip Wilson, creator of Lululemon Athletica Inc., is described by his peers as Western Canada's marketing and fashion retail visionary, and is credited with helping to start the surf and snowboard fashion trend in Vancouver almost two decades ago.

The Lululemon brand, launched in 1999, has created a buzz with yoga-inspired apparel. Lululemon isn't just a yoga store in British Columbia, it's a cultural icon. The stretchy pants and colourful tops match function with fashion and have helped the company become a national retailing powerhouse valued at more than $225 million in 2006 with a staff of 700.

Since opening its first retail outlet, Lululemon has launched 27 stores in Canada, plus another nine stores abroad. Revenue has doubled every year for the past four years. Growth was achieved without any traditional advertising—no television commercials, radio ads, or national newspaper campaigns. The in-house marketing group called the Community Relations Team and store managers are funded to run their own local marketing initiatives.

Chip Wilson's business model is based on a corporate philosophy which includes a few fundamental principles: encouraging a healthy lifestyle for employees; treating salespeople as educators; and a hands-on approach to management where everyone works one day a week in the store.

QUESTIONS

What is retailing?

What do retailers do?

Why is retailing important in our society?

What career and entrepreneurial opportunities does retailing offer?

What types of decisions do retail managers make?

To facilitate expansion, Wilson made an alliance with two Massachusetts-based venture capital firms, selling a 48% stake in Lululemon in 2006. As part of the new business strategy, a new experienced CEO, Robert Meers, has been challenged with building Lululemon into a successful global brand.

The ambitious expansion plan includes additional stores in Los Angeles, San Francisco, and Seattle, as well as multiple openings in New York City and Boston and four more stores in Tokyo. In 2007, further expansion into the U.S. and Asia and a dramatic move to Europe. Lululemon's greatest challenge now is making sure their manufacturing, sourcing, logistics, and distribution systems are capable of supplying these expansion goals.

Chip Wilson, always the marketing and fashion retail visionary, has launched a new clothing line. The Oqoqo label is committed to using a minimum of 75% natural organic and/or sustainable fibres such as soy, bamboo, hemp, and cotton. Wilson aims to provide a threshold demand for sustainable textiles, making use of fabrics economically feasible all along the supply chain, from farms to fabric mills to manufacturers and retailers.

What's next for this retail visionary?

Retailing is a global high-tech industry. Wal-mart is the world's largest corporation, with retail sales of $245 billion and stores in 11 countries worldwide. French-based Carrefour, the world's second largest retailer, operates hypermarkets in 24 countries. The largest retailer in Canada, Loblaw, with annual sales of $25.2 billion, sources unique non-food product lines in overseas markets; Canadian Tire has offices in Asia to facilitate business transactions.

Retailing in Canada is a vibrant industry, with total retail sales in 2005 of $367.8 billion (representing a positive growth of 6.1 percent from 2004). The retail sector is the second-largest employer nationally, with approximately two million Canadians in the workforce. See the Canadian Retailer article, "Retail is Your Career" at www.mcgrawhill.ca/olc/levy.

Success in retailing is about understanding and engaging your customer. Retailers use sophisticated technologies and information systems to improve their customers' shopping experience, reduce costs, and provide better value. Small local retailers such as Toad Hall in Winnipeg offer customers the opportunity to shop in their store as well as online, thus expanding their market share. Customers today want to interact with retailers as they seek information and buy merchandise ranging from concert tickets to a new iPod, shopping through multiple channels, such as PDAs, computers, Web-enabled kiosks, telephone lines to call centres, and retail stores. In addition to selling merchandise, retailers use the Internet to build brand images, provide customer service, and manage their employees. Retailers such as Amazon.com use advanced analytical techniques and data warehousing to customize

refact

Quebec had 57 190 retail establishments in 2003, representing 11.4 percent of the province's total number of businesses.[2]

approaches to online customers, suggesting books and products that might be of interest based on previous sales. According to a study released by the Retail Council of Canada in 2006, the key issues impacting the retail industry in Canada are:

- Canadian consumers are bombarded with choices.
- The lines between mass merchandisers, grocery and drugstores, club stores and warehouses, and dollar stores are blurring.
- Globalization in the retail industry is increasing.
- Retailers are consolidating.
- Pop-up or temporary stores are more prevalent.

The key to failure in the Canadian retail marketplace is trying to please everyone!

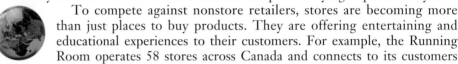

To compete against nonstore retailers, stores are becoming more than just places to buy products. They are offering entertaining and educational experiences to their customers. For example, the Running Room operates 58 stores across Canada and connects to its customers with a Learn to Run Program that offers advice to the novice runner. As well, the Running Room produces a free magazine to advise 130 000 customers of new products and community runs.[1] These features enhance customers' visual experiences, provide them with educational information, and enhance sales potential by enabling them to "try before they buy."

Retailing is such a part of our everyday lives that it's often taken for granted. Customers often aren't aware of the sophisticated business decisions retail managers make and the technologies they use to provide goods and services. Retail managers must make complex decisions in selecting target markets and retail locations, determining what merchandise and services to offer, negotiating with suppliers and distributing merchandise to stores, training and motivating sales associates, and deciding how to price, promote, and present merchandise. Considerable skill and knowledge are required to make these decisions effectively. Working in this highly competitive, rapidly changing environment is challenging and exciting and offers significant financial rewards.

This book describes the world of retailing and provides principles for effectively managing businesses in this challenging environment. Knowledge of retailing principles and practices will help you develop management skills you can apply in many business contexts. For example, Procter & Gamble and Hewlett-Packard managers need to have a thorough understanding of how retailers operate and make money so they can get their products on retail shelves and work with retailers to sell them to consumers. Financial and health care institutions use retail principles to develop assortments of services, improve customer service, and make their offerings available at convenient locations.

what is retailing?

Retailing is the set of business activities that add value to the products and services sold to consumers for their personal or family use. Often people think of retailing only as the sale of products in stores, but retailing also involves the sale of services: overnight lodging in a motel, a doctor's exam, a haircut, a movie rental, or a home-delivered pizza. Not all retailing is done in stores. Examples of nonstore retailing are Internet sales of CDs, direct sales of cosmetics by Avon, and catalogue sales by Canadian Tire.

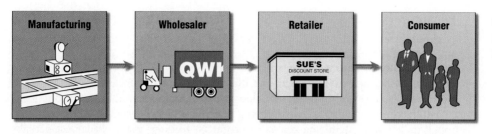

exhibit 1–1
Example of a
Distribution Channel

A RETAILER'S ROLE IN A DISTRIBUTION CHANNEL

A **retailer** is a business that sells products or services, or both, to consumers for their personal or family use. Retailers attempt to satisfy consumer needs by having the *right merchandise*, at the *right price*, at the *right place*, in the *right quantities*, at the *right time* when the consumer wants it. Retailers also provide markets for producers to sell their merchandise. Retailers are the final business in a distribution channel that links manufacturers to consumers. A **distribution channel** is a set of firms that facilitate the movement of products from the point of production to the point of sale to the ultimate consumer. Exhibit 1–1 shows the retailer's position within a distribution channel.[3]

Manufacturers typically make products and sell them to retailers or wholesalers. When manufacturers such as Roots and Dell Computers sell directly to consumers, they are performing both the production and retailing business activities. Wholesalers buy products from manufacturers and resell these products to retailers, and retailers resell products to consumers. Wholesalers and retailers may perform many of the same functions, but wholesalers satisfy retailers' needs, whereas retailers direct their efforts to satisfying the needs of ultimate consumers. Some retail chains, such as Rona and Costco, are both retailers and wholesalers. They're performing retailing activities when they sell to consumers and wholesaling activities when they sell to other businesses such as building contractors or restaurant owners.

In some distribution channels, the manufacturing, wholesaling, and retailing activities are performed by independent firms. But most distribution channels have some vertical integration.

Vertical integration means that a firm performs more than one set of activities in the channel. For example, most large retailers—such as Wal-Mart and Staples Business Depot—do both wholesaling and retailing activities. They buy directly from manufacturers, have merchandise shipped to their warehouses for storage, and then distribute the merchandise to their stores. Other retailers, such as The Gap, La Senza, and Roots, are even more vertically integrated. They design the merchandise they sell and then contract with manufacturers to produce it exclusively for them.

FUNCTIONS PERFORMED BY RETAILERS

Why bother with retailers? After all, wouldn't it be easier and cheaper to buy directly from those who produce the products? The answer is, generally no. Although there are situations where it is easier and cheaper to buy directly from manufacturers, such as at a farmer's market or from Dell Computer, retailers provide important functions that increase the value of the products and services they sell to consumers and facilitate the distribution of those products and services for those who produce them. These functions are:

- Providing an assortment of products and services.
- Breaking bulk.

- Holding inventory.
- Providing services.

Providing Assortments   Supermarkets typically carry 20 000 to 30 000 different items made by over 500 companies. Offering an assortment enables customers to choose from a wide selection of brands, designs, sizes, colours, and prices in one location. Manufacturers specialize in producing specific types of products. For example, Campbell makes soup, Kraft makes dairy products, Kellogg makes breakfast cereals, and McCormick makes spices. If each of these manufacturers had its own stores that sold only its own products, consumers would have to go to many different stores to buy groceries to prepare a single meal.

All retailers offer assortments of products, but they specialize in the assortments they offer. Supermarkets provide assortments of food, health and beauty care, and household products; Club Monaco provides assortments of clothing and accessories. Most consumers are well aware of the product assortments retailers offer. But new types of retailers offering unique assortments appear each year, such as Play It Again Sports (used sporting goods) and Molly Maid (home cleaning services).

Breaking Bulk   To reduce transportation costs, manufacturers and wholesalers typically ship cases of frozen dinners or cartons of shirts to retailers. Retailers then offer the products in smaller quantities tailored to the individual consumer's and household's consumption patterns. This is called **breaking bulk.** Breaking bulk is important to both manufacturers and consumers. It is cost-effective for manufacturers to package and ship merchandise in larger rather than smaller quantities. It is also easier for consumers to purchase merchandise in smaller, more manageable quantities.

Holding Inventory   A major function of retailers is to keep inventory that is already broken into user-friendly sizes so that products will be available when consumers want them. By maintaining an inventory, retailers provide a benefit to consumers—they reduce the consumer's cost of storing products. This is particularly important to consumers with limited storage space and when purchasing perishable merchandise such as meat and produce.

Providing Services   Retailers provide services that make it easier for customers to buy and use products. They offer various methods of payment, including debit, direct and credit payment, as well as various payment plans so that customers can have a product now and pay for it later, thus encouraging sales. Retailers display products so that consumers can see and test them before buying. Increasingly, retailers must have knowledgeable sales staff on hand to answer questions and provide information about products. Multichannel retailers offer flexibility to the customer by answering questions online and enabling buying anytime, day or night.

By providing assortments, breaking bulk, holding inventory, and providing services, retailers increase the value consumers receive from their products and services. To illustrate, consider a closet door in a shipping crate in a manufacturer's warehouse. The door won't satisfy the needs of a do-it-yourselfer who wants to replace a closet door today. For the customer, a conveniently located home improvement centre such as Rona sells one door which is available when the customer wants it. The home improvement centre helps the customer select the door by displaying doors so they can be examined before they're purchased. An employee is available to explain which door is best for closets and how the door should be hung. The centre has an assortment of hardware, paint, and tools that the customer will need for the job. Thus, retailers can increase the value of products and services bought by their customers.

exhibit 1–2
Retail Employment by Province

Region	Total, All Industries (in 000s)	Manufacturing (in 000s)	Retail Trade (in 000s)	Percentage of Provincial Labour Force	Rank in Labour Force
Canada	17 046.8	2 440.2	1 988.9	11.7%	3rd
British Columbia	2 202.1	219.8	258.3	11.7%	1st
Alberta	1 814.9	153.6	205.1	11.3%	1st
Saskatchewan	515.8	29.8	63	12.2%	1st
Manitoba	598.6	71.9	66.5	11.1%	3rd
Ontario	6 694.1	1 148.6	748.8	11.2%	2nd
Quebec	4 016.5	687.1	493.6	12.3%	2nd
New Brunswick	385.8	47.5	45.7	11.8%	3rd
Nova Scotia	480.1	53.5	63.5	13.2%	1st
Prince Edward Island	77.5	7.7	9.6	12.4%	1st
Newfoundland & Labrador	261.4	20.8	34.7	13.3%	1st (tied)

Source: Adapted from Statistics Canada, Canadian Business Patterns, June 2003.

* Labour force data are not provided for Nunavut, Yukon, or the Northwest Territories.

economic significance of retailing

RETAIL SALES IN CANADA

Retailing affects every facet of life. Just think of how many contacts you have with retailers when you eat meals, furnish your apartment, have your car fixed, or buy clothing for a party or job interview. In Canada 2005, the retail sector was the second largest employer nationally, providing jobs for approximately 12 percent of those employed, and had the largest labour force in six provinces. In 2005, total retail sales amounted to $368 billion, up 6.1 percent from 2004. Ontario and Quebec contributed the largest share of retail sales in 2005, followed by the Prairies, British Columbia, and Atlantic Canada. Albertans experienced the largest increase in sales from 2004 to 2005, with an annual increase of 12.1 percent.

Retail establishments retain a major presence in the Canada marketplace, representing a 9.4 percent share of all business in Canada, with 227 222 retail establishments. Roughly one out of every 10 business establishments in Canada is a retail store.

Retail tend to have somewhat smaller businesses than other sectors; a dominant characteristic of the retail sector in Canada is the small size of many of the establishments—72 percent of all retail businesses employ fewer than five persons. Exhibit 1–2 shows the retail employment representation by province. The retail sector focuses on stores. Statistics Canada identified 199 952 store locations, of which 41 498 were chain stores (four or more locations under one owner). Broadly speaking, there are roughly six store locations for every 1000 persons in Canada. There are relatively fewer stores in northern communities, suggesting a greater dependence on nonstore catalogue formats. The largest sectors in terms of retail sales are food and automotive, occupying roughly half of the retail landscape (see Exhibit 1-3). Although the retail sector is characterized by many businesses in many locations, large retail chains dominate many segments. Statistics Canada conducts a monthly survey to track sales of 80 large retailers (non-automotive) accounting for 35% of retail sales in Canada. This group of large

exhibit 1–3   Retail Commodity Sales 2004

Retail Sales by Sector (unadjusted in millions of dollars)

Year to date Sales	2004 ($ in millions)	2005 ($ in millions)	2004– 2005 % Change
All Stores	346 722	367 829	6.1%
Automotive	116 064	125 687	8.3%
Food and Beverage Stores	82 358	86 313	4.8%
Drug	22 769	23 951	5.2%
General Merchandise Stores	42 123	N/A*	N/A*
Furniture, Home Furnishings and Electronic Stores	23 970	25 525	6.5%
Clothing and Accessories Stores	20 188	21 080	4.4%
Sporting Goods, Hobby, Music, and Book Stores	8831	9464	7.2%
Building and Outdoor Home Supplies Stores	20 971	22 706	8.3%
Miscellaneous Store Retailers	9446	9398	(0.5%)

Average Consumer Spending per $100

- Food & beverages
- Motor vehicles, parts & additives
- Automotive fuels, oils & additives
- Furniture, home furnishings & electronics
- Clothing, footwear & accessories
- Health & personal care products
- Hardware, lawn & garden products
- Other

Source: Statistics Canada, Retail Trade Annual Sales. *Statistucs Canada is no longer publishing separate figures for department stores and other (general merchandise stores due to confidentiality constraints. Instead, "Department Stores" sales are combined with "Other General Merchandise Stores" sales and will be published in the near future under the grouping "General Merchandise Stores."

retailers, identified by their relative dominance of market segments, includes Loblaws, Canadian Tire, Home Depot, and Chapters/Indigo Books. In many commodity groups these retailers account for more than 50% of the retail sales in their product group. Although several trade groups (car dealerships, grocery stores) measure their annual sales per store in the millions of dollars, for most trade groups the average annual revenue per store is less than $800 000.

opportunities in retailing

MANAGEMENT OPPORTUNITIES

To cope with a highly competitive and challenging environment, retailers are hiring and promoting people with a wide range of skills and interests. Students often view retailing as a part of marketing because management of distribution channels is part of a manufacturer's marketing function. Retailers undertake most of the traditional business activities. Retailers raise capital from financial institutions; purchase goods and services; develop accounting and management information systems to control operations; manage warehouses and distribution systems; and design and develop new products as well as undertake marketing activities such as advertising, promotions, sales force management, and market research. Thus, retailers employ people with expertise and interest in finance, accounting, human resource management, logistics, and computer systems as well as marketing.

Retail managers often are given considerable responsibility early in their careers. Retail management is also financially rewarding. After completing a management training program in retailing, managers can increase their starting salary in three to five years if they perform well.

refact

Since 1945, London Drugs (with annual sales of $1.5 billion) has prospered in Western Canada and was named Distinguished Canadian Retailer of the Year by the Retail Council of Canada in 2003.[5]

ENTREPRENEURIAL OPPORTUNITIES

Retailing also provides opportunities for people wishing to start their own businesses. Some of the most successful people are retail entrepreneurs, such as Canada's John Forzani. Some are household names because their names appear over the stores' doors; these include Tim Horton (Tim Hortons), Eddie Black (Black's Cameras), and John Holt and G.R. Renfrew (Holt Renfrew).

While playing pro football 30 years ago for the Calgary Stampeders, *John Forzani*, frustrated by the inability to buy high-quality Canadian athletic footwear, envisioned a retail opportunity. John Forzani became Canada's largest sporting goods retailer, and in 2001 was named Retailer of the Year by the Retail Council of Canada, with revenues in excess of $681 million and net earnings of $12.5 million. Today the Forzani Group Ltd. operates under a number of banners selling

retailing view

JOHN STANTON, FOUNDER AND PRESIDENT OF RUNNING ROOM INC.

1.1

"My philosophy is built on a triple win: a win for the customer, for the Running Room, and for the community where we operate."

Twenty years ago, John Stanton of Edmonton, Alberta, Canada, weighing in at 105 kilograms and smoking two packs of cigarettes a day, experienced a life-changing event. Agreeing to join his son on a three-kilometre run, Stanton struggled through the course and was barely able to make it to the finish line. Embarrassed by his lack of physical fitness, Stanton embarked upon a personal goal to "get fit." Success was achieved within a few months: "The little chubby guy" managed to shed 27 kilograms and became a committed runner.

Taking his newfound passion to a business opportunity, Stanton decided to open the Running Room in Edmonton in 1983. He envisioned "an information clubhouse" atmosphere supported by the sale of T-shirts and running shoes where runners could meet and share their passion for running. The idea was embraced by runners in the Edmonton area and, within a year, the Running Room outgrew its one-room location and relocated to a 186 square metre store.

Today the Running Room operates 58 stores across Canada with locations in Calgary, Vancouver, and Toronto, and two stores in the U.S. in Minneapolis-St. Paul, Minnesota. Operating in a competitive marketplace, the Running Room has managed to maintain the original clubhouse atmosphere through group practice runs and information sessions in the Run Club Clinics organized

by the store's enthusiastic staff. Stanton, understanding the importance of a team approach to encouraging a fitness program, interacts with his customers, connecting to 150 000 customers via the Running Room Web site, working tirelessly at communicating the "you can do it" approach to fitness. His tips on "How to Go from Running on Empty to Fit and Fabulous" encourage the novice walker or runner to stay on course. As well, the Running Room produces a free magazine that reaches 130 000 customers with information on new products and community runs.

Giving back to the community is a philosophy that Stanton believes in. The Running Room sponsors over 400 events annually, producing millions in donations to local charities. The Running Room sponsors races such as the CIBC Run for the Cure in support of the Canadian Breast Cancer Society and the Do It for Dad Run for prostrate cancer research. Other commitments include the Canadian Diabetes Association, Salvation Army Santa Shuffle run before Christmas to help the needy, and the YMCA's Resolution Run to raise money for youth programs.

The success of the Running Room is due to the committed passion of Stanton: He is passionate about people, about running, and about being successful. But John Stanton never loses sight of the fact that it is his proactive team of dedicated staff that makes the retail difference and brings his dream to reality.

There are entrepreneurial opportunities in retailing. Jeff Bezos, founder of Amazon.com, came up with a business plan for his new company in 1994 while driving across the U.S. with his wife.

sporting goods, footwear, and apparel in 300 corporate and franchised stores across Canada. The company developed several store concepts that cater to different segments of the population: The Sports Mart banner is directed to the value shopper; Sport Chek aims toward the mid-market sports and leisure customer; and Coast Mountain Sports is focused as a higher-end concept. In the battle to maintain market share and stay ahead of the competition, the Forzani Group acquired Toronto-based inventory liquidator Gen-X Sports Ltd. in 2004. This strategic move is an attempt to source goods cheaply from overstocked or distressed suppliers anywhere in the world to expand Forzani's ability to compete on price without hurting profits.[6]

the retail management decision process

UNDERSTANDING THE WORLD OF RETAILING

The first step in the retail management decision process is understanding the world of retailing. Retail managers need to understand their environment, especially their customers and competition, before they can develop and implement effective strategies. The first section of this book provides a general overview of the retailing industry and its customers.

The critical environmental factors in the world of retailing are the macro-environment and the micro-environment. The impacts of the macroenvironment—including technological, social, and ethical/legal/political factors on retailing—are discussed throughout the book. The successful retailer will react to changes in the macro-environment. Huge technological changes in the macro-environment are having significant impact on retailers, enabling database marketing to provide information about consumers, the Internet to connect to customers, and RFID technology to increase retail efficiencies.

Competitors   At first glance, identifying competitors appears easy. A retailer's primary competitors are those with the same format. Thus, department stores compete against other department stores and supermarkets against other supermarkets. This competition between retailers of the same type is called **intratype competition**.

To appeal to a broader group of consumers and provide one-stop shopping, many retailers are increasing their variety of merchandise. **Variety** is the number of different merchandise categories within a store or department. By offering greater variety in one store, retailers can offer one-stop shopping to satisfy more of the needs of their target market. For example, clothing and food are now available in grocery, department, and discount stores and drugstores. Fast food is available at McDonald's and convenience stores. The offering of merchandise not typically associated with the store type, such as clothing in a drugstore, is called **scrambled merchandising.** Scrambled merchandising increases **intertype competition**—competition between retailers that sell similar merchandise using different formats, such as discount and department stores.

Increasingly intertype competition has made it harder for retailers to identify and monitor their competition. In one sense, all retailers compete against each other for the dollars consumers spend on goods and services. But the intensity of competition is greatest among retailers located close together with retail offerings that are viewed as very similar, such as in a shopping mall.

Since convenience of location is important in store choice, a store's proximity to competitors is a critical factor in identifying competition. Consider two DVD rental retailers, Blockbuster and Harry's Video, in two suburbs 10 kilometres apart. The stores are the only specialty DVD rental retailers within 50 kilometres, but a grocery store also rents a more limited selection of movies in the same strip mall as Blockbuster. Due to the distance between Blockbuster and Harry's Video, they probably don't compete against each other intensely. Customers who live near Harry's Video will rent DVDs there, whereas customers close to Blockbuster will rent movies at Blockbuster or the grocery store. In this case, Harry's major competition may actually be movie theatres and cable TV, because it's too inconvenient for customers close to Harry's to rent DVDs elsewhere. On the other hand, Blockbuster competes most intensely with the grocery store.

Retailing is intensely competitive. Understanding the different types of retailers and how they compete with each other is critical to developing and implementing a retail strategy.

Customers   The second factor in the microenvironment is customers. Customer needs are changing at an ever-increasing rate. Retailers are responding to broad demographic and lifestyle trends in our society, such as the growth in the elderly and minority segments of Canadian population and the increasing importance of shopping convenience to the rising number of two-income families. To develop and implement an effective strategy, retailers need to understand why customers shop, how they select a store, and how they select among that store's merchandise.

DEVELOPING A RETAIL STRATEGY

The next stages in the retail management decision-making process, formulating and implementing a retail strategy, are based on an understanding of the macro- and microenvironments. Section II in this book focuses on decisions related to developing a retail strategy.

The **retail strategy** indicates how the firm plans to focus its resources to accomplish its objectives. It identifies:

- the target market, or markets, toward which the retailer will direct its efforts
- the nature of the merchandise and/or services the retailer will offer to satisfy needs of the target market
- how the retailer will build a long-term advantage over competitors

The nature of a retail strategy can be illustrated by comparing strategies of Wal-Mart and Toys "R" Us. Wal-Mart offers name-brand merchandise at low prices in a broad array of categories, ranging from laundry detergent to girls' dresses. Although Wal-Mart stores have many different categories of merchandise, selection in each category is limited. A store might have only three brands of detergents in two sizes, while a supermarket carries eight brands in five sizes.

In contrast, Toys "R" Us identified its target as consumers living in suburban areas of large cities. Rather than carrying a broad array of merchandise categories, Toys "R" Us stores specialize in toys, games, bicycles, and furniture for children.

Although Toys "R" Us has limited categories of merchandise, it has almost all the different types and brands of toys and games currently available in the market.

Both Wal-Mart and Toys "R" Us emphasize self-service. Customers select their merchandise, bring it to the checkout line, and then carry it to their cars. Customers may even assemble the merchandise at home.

Since Wal-Mart and Toys "R" Us emphasize low price, they've made strategic decisions to develop a cost advantage over competitors. Both firms have sophisticated distribution and management information systems to manage inventory. Their strong relationships with suppliers enable them to buy merchandise at low prices.

Strategic Decision Areas   The key strategic decision areas for a retailer involve determining a market strategy, financial strategy, location strategy, organizational structure and human resource strategy, information systems and supply chain strategies, and customer relationship management strategies.

The selection of a retail market strategy is based on analyzing the environment and the firm's strengths and weaknesses. When major environmental changes occur, the current strategy and the reasoning behind it are reexamined. The retailer then decides what, if any, strategy changes are needed to take advantage of new opportunities or avoid new threats in the environment.

The retailer's market strategy must be consistent with the firm's *financial objectives*. Financial variables such as sales, costs, expenses, profits, assets, liabilities, and owner's equity are used to evaluate the market strategy and its implementation.

Decisions concerning *location strategy* are important for both consumer and competitive reasons. First, location is typically consumers' top consideration when selecting a store. Generally, consumers buy gas at the closest service station and patronize the shopping mall that's most convenient to their home or office. Second, location offers an opportunity to gain long-term advantage over competition. When a retailer has the best location, a competing retailer has to settle for the second-best location.

A retailer's *organization design and human resource management strategy* are intimately related to its market strategy. For example, retailers that attempt to serve national or regional markets must make trade-offs between the efficiency of centralized buying and the need to tailor merchandise and services to local needs. Retailers that focus on customer segments seeking high-quality customer service must motivate and enable sales associates to provide the expected levels of service. The organization structure and human resources policies coordinate the implementation of the retailing strategy by buyers, store managers, and sales associates.

Retail information and supply chain management systems will offer a significant opportunity for retailers to gain strategic advantage in the coming decade. Retailers are developing sophisticated computer and distribution systems to monitor flows of information and merchandise from vendors to retail distribution centres to retail stores. Point-of-sale (POS) terminals read price and product information that's coded into Universal Product Codes (UPCs) affixed to the merchandise. This information is then transmitted to distribution centres or directly to vendors electronically, computer to computer. These technologies are part of an overall inventory management system that enables retailers:

• to give customers a more complete selection of merchandise

• to increase awareness of inventory levels

• to decrease inventory investment

Basic to any strategy is understanding the customers in order to provide them with the goods and services they want. And even more important is to understand and cater to the wants of the retailer's most-valued customers. After all, these customers account for the major share of a retailer's sales and profits. **Customer relationship management (CRM)** is a business philosophy and set of strategies, programs, and systems that focus on identifying and building loyalty with a firm's most-valued customers. Data analysis is used by retailers to identify their most-valued customers. Once these customers are identified, special programs are designed to build their loyalty.

ETHICAL AND LEGAL CONSIDERATIONS

When making the strategic and tactical decisions discussed previously, managers need to consider the ethical and legal implications of their decisions in addition to the effects those decisions have on the profitability of their firms and the satisfaction of their customers. **Ethics** are the principles governing the behaviour of individuals and companies to establish appropriate behaviour and indicate what is right and wrong. Defining the term is easy, but determining what the principles are is difficult. What one person thinks is right another may consider wrong.

What is ethical can vary from country to country and from industry to industry. For example, offering bribes to overcome bureaucratic roadblocks is an accepted practice in some countries, but is considered unethical, and even illegal, in Canada. An ethical principle also can change over time. For example, some years ago, doctors and lawyers who advertised their services were considered unethical. Today such advertising is accepted.

Some examples of difficult situations that retail managers face are:

- Should a retailer sell merchandise it suspects was made using child labour?
- Should a retailer advertise that its prices are the lowest available in the market even though some items are not?
- Should a retail buyer accept an expensive gift from a vendor?
- Should retail salespeople use a high-pressure sales approach when they know the product is not the best for the customer's needs?
- Should a retailer give preference to minorities when making promotion decisions?
- Should a retailer treat some customers better than others?

Laws dictate which activities society has deemed to be clearly wrong, those activities for which retailers and their employee will be punished through the federal or provincial legal systems. However, most business decisions are not regulated by laws. Often retail managers have to rely on their firms' and industries' codes of ethics and/or their own codes of ethics to determine the right thing to do.

Many companies have codes of ethics to provide guidelines for their employees in making their ethical decisions. These ethical policies provide a clear sense of right and wrong so that companies and their customers can depend on their employees when questionable situations arise. However, in many situations, retail managers need to rely on their personal code of ethics—their personal sense of what is right or wrong.

Exhibit 1.4 lists some questions you can ask yourself to determine whether a behaviour or activity is unethical. The questions emphasize that ethical behaviour is determined by widely accepted views of what is right and wrong. Thus, you should engage only in activities about which you would be proud to tell your family, friends, employer, and customers.

If the answer to any of these questions is yes, the behaviour or activity is probably unethical, and you should not do it.

exhibit 1–4
Checklist for Making Ethical Decisions

1. Would I be embarrassed if a customer found out about this behaviour?
2. Would my supervisor disapprove of this behaviour?
3. Would most co-workers feel that this behaviour is unusual?
4. Am I about to do this because I think I can get away with it?
5. Would I be upset if a company did this to me?
6. Would my family or friends think less of me if I told them about engaging in this activity?
7. Am I concerned about the possible consequences of this behaviour?
8. Would I be upset if this behaviour or activity were publicized in a newspaper article?
9. Would society be worse off if everyone engaged in this behaviour or activity?

Your firm can strongly affect the ethical choices you will have to make. When you view your firm's polices or requests as improper, you have three choices:

1. Ignore your personal values and do what your company asks you to do. Self-respect suffers when you have to compromise your principles to please an employer. If you take this path, you will probably feel guilty and be dissatisfied with your job in the long run.

2. Take a stand and tell your employer what you think. Try to influence the decisions and policies of your company and supervisors.

3. Refuse to compromise your principles. Taking this path may mean you will get fired or be forced to quit.

You should not take a job with a company whose products, policies, and conduct conflict with your standards. Before taking a job, investigate the company's procedures and selling approach to see if they conflict with your personal ethical standards. In this text, we will highlight the legal and ethical issues associated with the retail decisions made by managers.

The **retail strategy** (see Exhibit 1–5) provides the direction retailers need to take to deal effectively with the business and economic environment, the macro-

exhibit 1–5
Retail Strategy

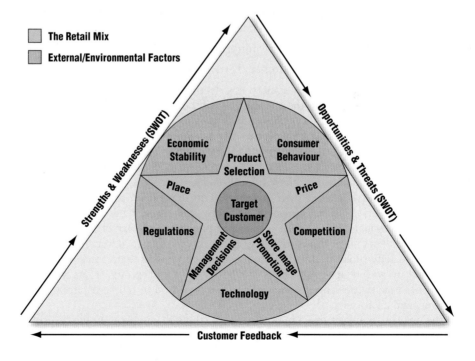

environment and the micro-environment. It considers how to attract customers, exceed expectations, and identify direct competitors. A retail strategy is a plan identifying the retailer's target market, the format the retailer plans to use to satisfy the target market, and the bases upon which the retailer plans to build a sustainable competitive advantage. For details, see Chapter 5.

Retailers must differentiate themselves from their competitors if they are to succeed in a marketplace that is characterized by a blurring of retail channels, increasing retail competition, and changing customer preferences.

SUMMARY

This chapter provides an overview of the importance of the retailing sector to the Canadian economy. The retailing process is the final stage in the distribution of merchandise and is one of the most important sectors of the Canadian economy, providing approximately 12 percent of employment in Canada and producing annual retail sales of approximately $330 billion in 2003.

A dominant characteristic of the sector is the small size of many of the retail establishments, with 72 percent of all retail businesses in Canada employing fewer than five persons.

The Canadian retail industry has witnessed a number of dramatic changes in recent years as big box stores and power centres hit our landscape, and information and communication technology grow in sophistication. Retailing in Canada has responded with diversity, with many types of stores compet-

ing in this dynamic marketplace: specialty retailers compete against category killers, and traditional department stores battle for market share with mass merchandisers. The examples in this chapter provide real-life glimpses of what is happening.

There is no doubt that the nature of retailing has changed, as sophisticated technologies create efficiency of product distribution and improve daily operations to satisfy customer needs.

The key to successful retailing is offering the right product, at the right price, in the right place, in the right quantities, at the right time, and making a profit. To accomplish all this, retailers must understand what customers want and what competitors are offering now and in the future. Retailers' wide range of decisions extends from setting a sweater's price to determining whether a new multimillion-dollar store should be built in a mall.

KEY TERMS

breaking bulk, *8*
customer relationship
    management (CRM), *15*
distribution channel, *7*
ethics, *15*

intertype competition, *12*
intratype competition, *12*
retailer, *7*
retailing, *6*
retail strategy, *13, 16*

scrambled merchandising, *12*
variety, *12*
vertical integration, *7*

Get Out & Do It!

1. **GO SHOPPING** Visit your favourite multichannel retailer by going to a store and going to its Internet site. Evaluate how well the company has integrated these channels into one seamless strategy.

DISCUSSION QUESTIONS AND PROBLEMS

1. Read the profile of Chip Wilson, Lululemon.
   a) Describe Wilson's entrepreneurial traits.
   b) What factors contributed to the success of Lululemon?

2. Choose one clearly identifiable item (e.g., a pair of jeans, a white shirt). Visit one big box retailer (e.g., Costco, Wal-Mart) or a department store, one specialty chain retailer, and one online retailer.
   a) Conduct a price comparison and determine which is the better buy.
   b) Observe customers in the store. Take notes.
   Be prepared to discuss your research.

3. Does Wal-Mart contribute to or detract from the communities in which it operates stores?

4. How might managers at different levels of a retail organization define their competition?

5. Explain the strategy used by your favourite retailer.

6. You are familiar with the GAP as a retailer currently undergoing changes to attract more customers. You have been given $150.00 to go shopping. Go to GAP online (www.gap.com) and go through the process of picking your product. Describe your experience.

APPENDIX 1A   Sam Walton, Founder of Wal-Mart (1918–1992)

"Like Henry Ford with his Model T," said a professor of rural sociology at the University of Missouri, "Sam Walton and his Wal-Marts, for better or for worse, transformed small-town America." Others think he transformed the entire nation.

After graduating from the University of Missouri in 1940, Walton began working at a JCPenney store in Des Moines, Iowa. After serving in the Army during World War II, he purchased a Ben Franklin variety store franchise in Newport, Arkansas. He boosted sales by finding offbeat suppliers who would sell to him lower than he could buy from Ben Franklin.

Walton lost his store, however, in 1950 when the landlord refused to renew the lease. He then moved to Bentonville, Arkansas, where he and a younger brother franchised another Ben Franklin store. Walton employed a new self-service system, one he had discovered at two Ben Franklin stores in Minnesota: no clerks or cash registers around the store, only checkout lanes in the front. By 1960, Walton had 15 stores in Arkansas and Missouri and had laid the foundation for his own discount chain.

By the early 1960s, retailers had developed the discount superstore concept using self-service, large inventories, and massive parking lots. Walton joined them in 1962 when he opened his first Wal-Mart Discount City in Rogers, Arkansas. At least one observer called it a mess—with donkey rides and watermelons mixed together outside under the boiling sun and merchandise haphazardly arranged inside.

But Walton quickly brought order to his enterprise and pursued an important new concept: large discount stores in small towns. Walton saw cities saturated with retailers and believed he could prosper in towns that the larger companies had written off. By the 1980s, Walton started building stores in larger suburbs. Walton then started Sam's Clubs, warehouse-style stores that sold merchandise at discount prices in bulk. Next came Wal-Mart Supercenters, ranging from 97,000 to 211,000 square feet, that featured a supermarket and a regular Wal-Mart under one roof. As a result of their success, Wal-Mart is now the largest food retailer in the United States.

Walton often visited his stores, dropping in unannounced to check the layouts and books and talk to his "associates." He prided himself on a profit-sharing program and a friendly, open atmosphere. He often led his workers in a cheer—some called corny, others uplifting. He once described it: "Give me a W! Give me an A! Give me an L! Give me a Squiggly! (Here, everybody sort of does the twist.) Give me an M! Give me an A! Give me an R! Give me a T! What's that spell? Wal-Mart! What's that spell? Wal-Mart! Who's number one? THE CUSTOMER!"

He offered his own formula for how a large company must operate: "Think one store at a time. That sounds easy enough, but it's something we've constantly had to stay on top of. Communicate, communicate, communicate: What good is figuring out a better way to sell beach towels if you aren't going to tell everybody in your company about it?

Keep your ear to the ground: A computer is not—and will never be—a substitute for getting out in your stores and learning what's going on."

In 1991, Walton reached a pinnacle as America's wealthiest person. He died of leukemia in 1992. Wal-Mart is now the world's largest corporation.

Source: "Sam Walton," *American Business Leaders*, January 1, 2001. Reprinted by permission.

CHAPTER 2

types of retailers

Executive Briefing
Winners, Buy Low, Win Big

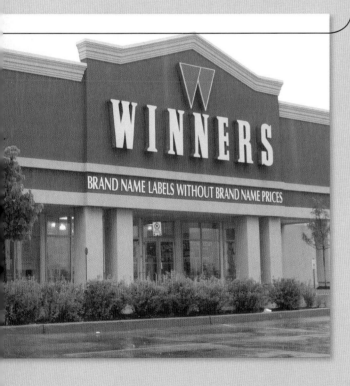

Winners, Canada's largest discount fashion retailer, has hit the mark with price-reduced designer brands. The concept has won applause from happy customers who return for the thrill of a bargain. Hard-core Winners shoppers not only visit the stores regularly, they spend an average of 60 to 90 minutes per visit and brag about their finds.

The buzz about Winners has been growing for over a decade as word-of-mouth praise spreads. Opened in 1982, it was acquired in 1990 as a five-store Canadian discount chain by TJX Companies, the company behind successful U.S. discounters T.J. Maxx and Marshalls and remains a wholly owned Canadian subsidiary. The winning strategy was to buy superfluous merchandise from suppliers resulting from cancelled or returned orders, brand-name seconds, and designer ends-of-lines. Often it is the same merchandise you might find in a department store—but much cheaper, which usually means that it is a season late and without services such as attentive sales staff and neat and orderly merchandise displays. Winners sells their merchandise at 20 to 60 percent off regular retail prices.

QUESTIONS

What trends are shaping today's retailers?

What are the different types of retailers?

How do retailers differ in terms of how they meet the needs of their customers?

How do services retailers differ from merchandise retailers?

What are the types of ownership for retail firms?

How do multichannel retailers provide more value to their customers?

What are the key success factors in multichannel retailing?

Winners continues to increase its position in the marketplace. In 2005 the retailer opened a 3720 square metre store in the prestigious Yorkville area of Toronto. The store is the 160th outlet for the chain. To fit in with the esthetics of the Bloor Street West location, Winners has played down its brash outlet-style lighting, added stylish signage throughout the store, introduced a new shopping bag, and is selling fine jewellery. The neighbours include Holt Renfrew, Chanel, and Tiffany.

Winners has managed to gain a growing share of the women's apparel market, a market that hasn't grown in years. Winners and Home Sense (60 locations, discount home décor store, part of the Canadian company) saw revenues grow to $1.7 billion in 2005. Winners' increased appeal to the Canadian shopper has come at the expense of traditional department stores. It seems consumers' only complaint about Winners is that it's now so popular that it's no longer their little secret.

To develop and implement a retail strategy, retailers need to understand the nature of competition in the retail marketplace. This chapter describes the different types of retailers—both store- and nonstore-based retailers. Retailers differ in terms of the types of merchandise and services they offer to customers, the nature of the retail mix used to satisfy customer needs, the degree to which their offerings emphasize services versus merchandise, and the ownership of the firm.

trends in the retail industry

As discussed in the first chapter, the retail industry is changing rapidly. Some of the most important changes involve:

- changing consumer preferences
- increasing industry concentration
- globalization of retail
- the use of multiple channels to interact with customers
- increasing competition in the Canadian marketplace
- the growing importance of the Internet to retail success
- the blurring of retail channels

As consumer needs and competition have changed, new retail formats have been created and continue to evolve. Consider the theory of natural selection and its relevance for explaining change in retailing. It follows Charles Darwin's view that organisms evolve and grow on the basis of the *survival of the fittest*. In retailing, those businesses best able to adapt to change in customer demands, technological advances, and increased competition have the greatest chance of success. For example, the growth of the one-stop shopping environment has become firmly established as a success strategy that appeals to busy, time-stressed working women. Department stores are challenged as consumers demand ever-lower prices combined with extended services; in response, department stores have added specialty boutiques within their stores to cater to specific market segments.

Video stores appeared in virtually every neighbourhood in Canada soon after videocassette recorder technology was developed. Today these stores have evolved to offer DVD technology, but as more and more consumers move to movies and programming on-demand, the DVD retail rental stores will have to reinvent themselves. Blu-ray is now thought to be the next generation DVD format, as endorsed by Global Video. Rental chain Blockbuster Inc. operates 8000 rental stores worldwide, commanding 45 percent of the North American home market.

There are more than 12.6 million pets in Canada, of which 7.7 million are cats and 4.9 million dogs. This is a growing, lucrative market opportunity for grocery and niche market pet stores that recognize the exploding pet market (55% of Canadian households have a pet). See *Canadian Grocer*, "Retail Intelligence," on the Online Learning Centre at www.mcgrawhill.ca/olc/levy.

GROWING DIVERSITY OF RETAIL FORMATS

Over the past 20 years, many new retail formats have been developed. Consumers now can purchase the same merchandise from a wide variety of retailers. The initial category specialists in toys, consumer electronics, and home improvement supplies have been joined by a host of new specialists including Sport Chek (sports wear), Bed Bath & Beyond (home decor), and PETsMART (pet supplies). Grocery stores such as Loblaws are adding pharmacies, as well as clothing and home decor products to expand their retail mix; Shoppers Drug Mart has added shelves full of grocery products to the traditional health and beauty options. The Internet has spawned a new set of retailers offering consumers the opportunity to buy merchandise and services (www.amazon.com), participate in auctions (www.ebay.com), or submit "take-it-or-leave-it" bids (www.priceline.com).

Many new types of retailers coexist with traditional retailers. Each type of retailer offers a different set of benefits. Thus, consumers patronize different retailers for different purchase occasions. For example, a consumer might purchase a pair of pants from a catalogue as a gift for a friend in another city and then visit a local store to try on and buy the same pants for himself. The greater diversity of retail formats increases competition in the industry and also enables consumers to buy merchandise and services from a retailer that better satisfies their needs for the specific purchase.

INCREASING INDUSTRY CONCENTRATION

Although the number of different types of retailers has grown, the number of competitors within each format is decreasing. The Canadian marketplace is powered by a small number of large retailers who dominate in their specific retail category. For example, Wal-Mart (which entered the Canadian market in 1994) and Zellers are the major mass merchandisers, and Shoppers Drug Mart is the largest drugstore chain. In Canada, the consumer electronics specialists are Future Shop and Best Buy (both owned by Best Buy parent company in the U.S.). The dominant warehouse club is Costco, but Sam's Club (open fall 2003) will rival for position. Two major department stores dominate the Canadian retail landscape: The Bay and Sears (a subsidiary of

Sears Roebuck and Co. in the U.S.). Loblaw Cos. Ltd. (including Loblaws, Fortino's, No Frills, and Provigo chains) is Canada's largest grocery chain, with sales of $25.2 billion. Loblaw owns the successful President's Choice house brand label. Dominant in home improvement retailing are Canadian Tire, which differentiates itself from competitors with an extremely successful, long-running customer loyalty program, "Canadian Tire Money," and a popular automotive centre. The purchase of Mark's Work Wearhouse in 2004 has been a positive move for Canadian Tire, widening the assortment mix of product to include the popular casual clothing line for men and women. Canadian Tire faces stiff competition from American giant Home Depot and Quebec retailer Reno. Both have had rapid growth across Canada.

The trend toward a blurring of retail channels will continue: Drug stores have moved into high-end cosmetics, traditionally the territory of the department stores; grocery stores have invaded the pharmacy business. Meanwhile, banks have a problem—more and more customers are not coming into their branches. Banking online or by phone is now the norm. In addition, there is competition from retailers (including Loblaws and Canadian Tire) offering banking services that include mortgages and loans that extend the customer relationship. In response, progressive banks are luring customers with plasma TVs, plants, and comfy chairs to attract more profitable clients to invest in financial advisory services. Ultimately it will be the customer who makes the retail decisions.

retailer characteristics

Store-based retailers range from street vendors selling hot dogs to large corporations such as Sears that have become an integral part of North American culture.[1] Each retailer survives and prospers by satisfying a group of consumers' needs more effectively than its competitors. Over time, different types of retailers have emerged and prospered because they have attracted and maintained a significant customer base.

The most basic characteristic of a retailer is its retail mix—the elements used by a retailer to satisfy its customers' needs (see Exhibit 1–3). Four elements of the retail mix are particularly useful for classifying retailers:

- the type of merchandise sold
- the variety and assortment of merchandise sold
- the level of customer service
- the price of the merchandise

Retailers should shop at their competitors' stores to compare their retail offering with the competition.

PRICE–COST TRADE-OFF

As you read about the different types of retailers, notice how patterns among retail mix elements arise. For example, department stores appeal to consumers looking for fashionable apparel and home furnishings. Typically, department stores have higher prices because they have higher costs due to stocking a lot of fashionable merchandise, discounting merchandise when errors are made in forecasting consumer tastes, providing some personal sales service, and having convenient but expensive mall locations. On the other hand, discount stores appeal to customers who are looking for lower prices, and are less interested in services, and are satisfied with limited of merchandise sizes and colours.

This difference between the retail mixes of department and discount stores illustrates the trade-off retailers make between the price and assortment of merchandise they sell and the services they offer to their customers. Offering more sizes, colours, and brands, making the store atmosphere more attractive and entertaining, and increasing the staff of knowledgeable sales associates all raise the retailer's costs. To make a profit and provide these additional benefits to their customers, department stores have to increase the prices of their merchandise to cover the additional costs.

TYPE OF MERCHANDISE

The degree to which retailers compete against each other isn't simply based on the similarity of their merchandise. The variety and assortment of merchandise offered and the services they provide must also be considered. For example, sports clothing can be purchased in specialty sporting goods stores, department stores, and warehouse clubs, as well as electronic shopping and catalogue shopping. Although these stores all sell sports clothing, they satisfy different consumer needs and thus appeal to different market segments. Sporting goods stores have a large variety of sports clothing at relatively high prices and knowledgeable sales assistance. Department stores are equally expensive and service-oriented, but they don't offer the same broad assortment of sporting goods. Warehouse clubs may have a narrow assortment of relatively inexpensive clothing but provide no services.

VARIETY AND ASSORTMENT

Variety is the number of merchandise categories a retailer offers. **Assortment** is the number of different items in a merchandise category. Each different item of merchandise is called a **SKU (stock keeping unit).** For example, a 3.7 kg box of Tide laundry detergent and a white, long-sleeved, button-down-collar Tommy Hilfiger shirt, size 16–33, are both SKUs.

Warehouse club stores, discount stores, and toy stores all sell toys. However, warehouse clubs and discount stores sell many other categories of merchandise in addition to toys. (They have greater variety.) Stores specializing in toys stock more types of toys (more SKUs). For each type of toy, such as dolls, the specialty toy retailer offers more assortment (more models, sizes, and brands, and deeper assortment) than general merchants such as warehouse clubs or discount stores.

Variety of merchandise is often referred to as the **breadth of stock** carried by a retailer; assortment is referred to as the **depth of stock.** Exhibit 2–1 shows the breadth and depth of bicycles carried in a local bicycle shop called Bikes and Boards (a specialty store), in Toys "R" Us (a category specialist), and in Zellers (a discount store). Toys "R" Us carries three basic types and has a narrower variety than the Bikes and Boards store, which carries four types; but Toys "R" Us has the greatest depth of assortment in children's bicycles. Zellers has the lowest number of total SKUs (34) compared to Toys "R" Us (142) and Bikes and Boards (253). Note that Zellers and Toys "R" Us have some of the same brands, but the Bikes and Boards store offers a mix of brands for the discriminating cyclist.

CUSTOMER SERVICES

Retailers differ in the services they offer customers. For example, the bicycle shop Bikes and Boards offers assistance in selecting the appropriate bicycle, adjusting bicycles to fit the individual, and repairing bicycles. Toys "R" Us and Zellers don't provide any of these services. Customers expect retailers to provide some services:

Bikes and Boards (left) offers the deepest assortment of bicycles. Toys "R" Us (right) is in the middle of the assortment/variety dimension.

exhibit 2–1
Variety and
Assortment of Bicycles
in Different Retail
Outlets

	Adult Road	Adult Hybrid	Mountain	Child
Bikes and Boards	Trek, Bianchi, Specialized, Lemond, Klein, Litespeed, Merlin	Gary Fisher, Trek 800, Specialized, Bianchi, Lemond	Gary Fisher, Trek, Klein Attitude, Specialized	Gary Fisher, Trek, Specialized, Haro
	80 SKUs	44 SKUs	99 SKUs	30 SKUs
	$599–5405	$239.99–1299.99	$219–4900	$109–349.99
Toys "R" Us	Mongoose, Huffy Bicycles, Pacific Cycle, Kent International		Pacific Cycle, Dynacraft	Mongoose, AMX/Patriot, Pacific Cycle, Gravity Games, Dynacraft, Rand International, Koncept, Hyper, Cosmic, Huffy Bicycles, Girl Power, Fisher Price, Barbie, Girls Starbright, Blossom Girls' Mountain Bike, Power Wheels, Magna, Rallye Bikes, Kent International, Murray Cycle
	16 SKUs		28 SKUs	98 SKUs
	$99.99–149.97		$59.98–399.98	$29.98–119.98
Wal-Mart	Tri-Fecta		Mongoose, RoadMaster, Next	RoadMaster, Mongoose, Next, Barbie
	13 SKUs		8 SKUs	13 SKUs
	$89.68–269.96		$89.96–149.96	$48.88–129.78

accepting credit and debit payment, providing parking, and being open at convenient hours. Some retailers charge customers for additional services, such as home delivery and gift wrapping. Retailers that cater to service-oriented consumers offer most of these services at no charge.

COST OF OFFERING BREADTH AND DEPTH OF MERCHANDISE AND SERVICES

Stocking a deep assortment like the Toys "R" Us offering in bicycles is appealing to customers but costly for retailers. When a retailer offers customers many SKUs, inventory investment increases because the retailer must have backup stock for each SKU.

Similarly, services attract customers to the retailer, but they're also costly. More salespeople are needed to provide information and assist customers, to alter merchandise to meet customers' needs, and to demonstrate merchandise. Child care facilities, rest rooms, dressing rooms, and check rooms take up valuable store space that could be used to stock and display merchandise. Offering delayed billing, credit, and installment payments requires a financial investment that could be used to buy more merchandise.

A critical retail decision involves the trade-off between costs and benefits of maintaining additional inventory or providing additional services.

general merchandise retailers

Types of general merchandise retailers include discount stores, specialty stores, category specialists, department stores, home improvement centres, off-price retailers, and value retailers. Exhibit 2–2 summarizes characteristics of general merchandise retailers that sell through stores. Many of these general merchandise retailers sell through multichannels, such as the Internet and catalogues.

DISCOUNT STORES

A **discount store** is a retailer that offers a broad variety of merchandise, limited service, and low prices. Discount stores offer both private labels and national brands, but these brands are typically less fashion-oriented than brands in department stores. Disount stores can also be referred to as **mass merchandisers**. Examples include Zellers and Wal-Mart.

refact

Hudson's Bay Company, the oldest retailer in North America, conquered the Canadian wilderness by trading furs over 300 years ago. Today, one of its divisions, Zellers, is one of the largest full-line discount chains in Canada.[3]

Issues in Discount Store Retailing[2]   The most significant trend in discount store retailing is the Wal-Mart–led push toward supercentres that carry grocery items. Additionally, discount stores face intense competition from specialty stores that focus on a single category of merchandise, such as Future Shop, Sport Chek, and Home Depot. They also compete with Old Navy and The Bay for apparel, Sears for home furnishings, and Shoppers Drug Mart for health and beauty products. To respond to this competitive environment, discount stores have created more attractive shopping environments, placed more emphasis on apparel, and developed strong private-label merchandise programs.

Wal-Mart pioneered the everyday low price concept. And its efficient operations have allowed it to offer the lowest-priced basket of merchandise in every market in which it competes. This doesn't mean that Wal-Mart has the lowest price on every item in every market. But it tries to be the lowest across a wide variety of things. Many scholars of business believe Wal-Mart has the best and most sophisticated supply chain and information systems in the industry, allowing for retail efficiency and lower prices.

There is no doubt that Wal-Mart's global success has been a matter of efficiency and timing. Target, in the U.S., on the other hand, wins with merchandising. Opting for quality and style, Target has even developed a certain cult quality among fashion hipsters with its private labels. Target has also successfully read several important

exhibit 2–2   Characteristics of Different General Merchandise Retailers

Type	Variety	Assortment	Service	Prices	Size (sq. m)	SKUs (000)	Location
Discount stores	Broad	Average to shallow	Low	Low	5580–7440	30	Stand alone, power strip centre
Specialty stores	Narrow	Deep	High	High	372–1016	5	Regional malls
Category specialists	Narrow	Very deep	Low to high	Low	4650–11 160	20–40	Stand alone, power strip centre
Home improvement centres	Narrow	Very deep	Low to high	Low	7440–11 160	20–40	Stand alone, power strip centre
Department stores	Broad	Deep to average	Average to high	Average to high	9300–18 600	100	Regional malls
Drugstores	Narrow	Very deep	Average	Average to high	279–1395	10–20	Stand alone, strip centre
Off-price stores	Average	Deep but varying	Low	Low	1860–2790	50	Outlet malls
Value retailers	Average	Average and varying	Low	Low	651–1395	3–4	Urban, strip

broad consumer trends: Americans are looking for a good value, but that doesn't mean the same thing as cheap. It has also realized that consumers who are farther up the economic ladder than typical discount shoppers will become customers if the merchandise is well designed and of high quality.

SPECIALTY STORES

A **specialty store** concentrates on a limited number of complementary merchandise categories and provides a high level of service in an area typically under 744 square metres.

Issues in Specialty Store Retailing   Specialty stores tailor their retail strategy toward a very specific market segment by offering deep but narrow assortments along with knowledgeable sales staff. For example, West 49 retails action sports clothing that had its origins with young skateboard enthusiasts. West 49 has very specific strategies to make sure that it appeals to the under-16 demographic. For example, the mall is a perfect location for this retailer because the target age group does not drive and usually relies on mom to drop them off at the shopping centre.

Sephora, France's leading cosmetic chain and a division of the luxury goods conglomerate LVMH (Louis Vuitton–Moet Hennessy), is another example of an innovative specialty store concept. In Canada, prestige cosmetics are typically sold in department stores and increasingly also at Shoppers Drug Mart. In contrast, Sephora is a cosmetic and perfume specialty store offering a deep assortment of merchandise in a 465 square metre self-serve retail environment. Each cosmetic brand has a separate counter with testers and sales staff available to answer questions. The concept is extremely popular with customers who are encouraged to browse and experiment in a friendly environment.

Because specialty retailers focus on specific market segments, they are vulnerable to shifts in consumer tastes and preferences. For example, mall-based specialty retailers are affected by consumers who prefer the convenience of shopping in retail locations outside of the mall. Ease of parking and time-saving are two factors that influence the consumer. Apparel and footwear specialty retailers are capturing fewer consumers' dollars because consumers are spending more on necessities such as rent or mortgage, school expenses, and transportation costs and enjoying eating out, a concert, or club.

 Europe-based apparel specialty stores Zara (Spain) and H&M (short for Hennes & Mauritz, in Sweden) are very successful in Europe, and are expanding into Canada. Zara's philosophy is "fashion on demand." At the end of every day in each of the chain's more than 1000 shops around the world, the manager goes online to company headquarters in Spain and describes which items were moving and which weren't. Using this simple method as a guide, designers can get a newly created item on the racks within little more than a week, compared to as long as six months for The Gap. In the fickle and fast-changing world of fashion, agility means success. Zara produces more than half of its own clothes and makes 40 percent of its own fabric. H&M also responds quickly to fashion trends. In contrast, however, H&M has 900 suppliers and does not own factories.[4] H&M also competes at lower price points than both Zara and The Gap. Its philosophy is "disposable chic," and its merchandise is so inexpensive that it doesn't matter if it goes out of style quickly.[5]

CATEGORY SPECIALIST/CATEGORY KILLER

A **category specialist** is a retailer that offers a narrow variety but deep assortment of merchandise. Most category specialists use a self-service approach, but some specialists in consumer durables offer assistance to customers. For example, Staples Business Depot stores have a warehouse atmosphere, with cartons of copying paper stacked on pallets plus equipment in boxes on shelves. However, some merchandise, such as computers, are displayed in the middle of the store, and salespeople in the display area are available to answer questions and make suggestions.

By offering a complete assortment in a category at low prices, category specialists can "kill" a category of merchandise for other retailers and thus are frequently called **category killers.** Because category specialists dominate a category of merchandise, they can use their buying power to negotiate low prices and are assured of supply when items are scarce. Department stores and full-line discount stores located near category specialists often have to reduce their offerings in the category because consumers are drawn to the deep assortment and low prices at the category killer.

Many of these category killers are operating in a big-box format. These large format stores typically range in size from approximately 1860 to 13 950 square metres. But it must be realized that it is the size of the store in comparison to its competitors that would qualify it as a big-box category killer, as shown in Exhibit 2–3. For example, the Body Shop Canada, with 124 stores primarily located in shopping malls across Canada, opened its first big-box store of 279 square metres in a power centre in 2001. The Body Shop wanted to be part of the trend that sees customers increasingly turning to clusters of big-box outlets located on the fringe of urban centres that offer convenience and expanded selection.[6]

One of the largest and most successful types of category specialist is the home improvement centre. A **home improvement centre** is a category specialist offering equipment and material used by do-it-yourselfers and contractors to make home improvements. Rona, the Quebec-based home improvement retailer with 530 stores and 60 big-box stores across Canada, understands the competitive nature of the market. The company's expansion strategies include opening a 27 900 square metre distribution centre in Calgary, recruiting dealers, and buying up small regional chains. With 65 percent of Canadian homes being older than 20 years, and low interest rates at Canadian banks, the home renovation market is set to enjoy strong growth over the next few decades. Rona held 12.2 percent of the Canadian home

- Superstores three times the traditional supermarket
- Home Depot 18 times the traditional hardware store
- Chapters 12 times the traditional book store
- Winners six times the traditional fashion store
- Staples Business Depot five times the traditional office supply store
- Michaels Craft Stores nine times the traditional arts and crafts store
- Sport Chek six times the traditional sporting goods store

exhibit 2–3
Big-Box Comparative
Size Advantage

improvement retailing market in 2004, compared with Home Depot at a 14 percent share and Home Hardware with 12 percent.[7]

refact
Women make over 50 percent of the purchases at home improvement centres.[9]

Issues for Category Specialists   Most category specialist chains started in one region of the country and saturated that region before expanding to other regions. During this period of expansion, competition between specialists in a category was limited.

Competition between specialists in each category becomes intense as firms expand into regions originally dominated by another firm. In many merchandise categories, the major firms are now in direct competition across the country. This direct competition focuses on price, resulting in reduced profits because the competitors have difficulty differentiating themselves on other elements of the retail mix. All the competitors in a category provide similar assortments since they have similar access to national brands. These sophisticated big-box, category killer venues are often grouped together in power centres, dominating the industry with their low prices, extensive product offerings, and ample customer parking.[8]

In response to this increasing competitive intensity, the category killers continue to concentrate on reducing costs by increasing operating efficiency and acquiring smaller chains to gain scale economies. Where appropriate, category specialists have attempted to differentiate themselves with service.

DEPARTMENT STORES

Department stores are retailers that carry a broad variety and deep assortment of stock, offer some customer services, and are organized into separate departments for displaying merchandise. The largest department store chains in Canada are Sears Canada and The Bay, bought in 2006 by Jerry Zucker, U.S. billionaire investor.[10] Department store chains are very diverse. There are those that carry relatively inexpensive products and compete closely with discount stores, such as Sears and The Bay, and there is Holt Renfrew that sells expensive, exclusive merchandise that competes with high-end specialty store chains, such as Alfred Sung and Your Choice.

Each department within the store has a specific selling space allocated to it, a POS terminal to transact and record sales, and salespeople to assist customers. The department store often resembles a collection of specialty shops. The major departments are: women's, men's, and children's clothing and accessories; home furnishings and furniture; kitchenware and small appliances; and cosmetics and fragrances.

In some situations, departments in a department store or discount store are leased and operated by an independent company. A **leased department** is an area in a retail store that is leased or rented to an independent firm. The lease holder is typically responsible for all retail mix decisions involved in operating the department and pays the store a percentage of its sales as rent. Retailers lease departments when they feel they lack expertise to operate the department efficiently. Commonly leased departments in Canadian stores are beauty salons, pharmacies, shoes, jewellery, furs, photography studios, and repair services.

Department stores are unique in terms of the shopping experience they offer, the services they provide, and the atmosphere of the store. They offer a full range of services from altering clothing to home delivery. To create excitement, apparel is displayed on mannequins; attention is drawn to displays with theatrical lighting; and sales associates are frequently stationed throughout the store demonstrating products. Department stores also emphasize special promotions such as elaborate displays during the Christmas season.

Issues in Department Store Retailing   Department stores' overall sales have stagnated and market share has fallen in recent years due to increased competition from discount stores and specialty stores, as well as a decline in perceived value for merchandise and services. Department stores, which started in the nineteenth century, attracted consumers by offering them ambience, attentive service, and a wide variety of merchandise under one roof. They still account for some of retailing's romance—its parades, its Santa Claus lands, and its holiday windows. Department stores also offer designer brands that are not available at other retailers.

Unfortunately, many consumers believe that department stores are no longer romantic or convenient. Many believe that they are difficult to get to because they are located in large malls, that it is difficult to find specific merchandise because the same category is often located in several designer departments, and that it is difficult to get professional sales assistance because of labour cutbacks. At the same time, department stores typically charge higher prices than their discount and specialty store competitors.

Department store retailers work closely with their vendors to ensure better in-stock positions for fashion merchandise and reduce average inventory levels. These initiatives are referred to as quick response (QR). For example, at the beginning of a season, a department store chain that has a QR relationship with a vendor will commit to buying 120 000 sweaters, but will specify the sizes and colours for only the initial shipment of 2500 sweaters. The vendor and retailer will closely monitor initial sales and use this information to knit and dye the sweaters in sizes and colours that will match customer demand for the rest of the season.

DRUGSTORES

Drugstores are specialty stores that concentrate on health and personal grooming merchandise. Pharmaceuticals often represent over 50 percent of drugstore sales and an even greater percentage of their profits. The largest drugstore chain in Canada is Shoppers Drug Mart.

Issues in Drugstore Retailing   Drugstores, particularly the national chains, are experiencing sustained sales growth because the aging population requires more prescription drugs and the profit margins for prescription pharmaceuticals are higher than for other drugstore merchandise. The nonprescription side of drugstores is also being squeezed by considerable competition from pharmacies in discount stores and supermarkets, as well as from prescription mail-order retailers.

In response, the major drugstore chains are building larger stand-alone stores offering a wider assortment of merchandise, more frequently purchased food items, and drive-through windows for picking up prescriptions.[13] To build customer loyalty, the chains are also changing the role of their pharmacists from dispensing pills (referred

refact

Department stores' share of the apparel market has fallen to 40 percent from 70 percent two decades ago. Over the same period, their share has fallen to about 5 percent of the home electronics market from 25 percent, and to less than 5 percent of the furniture market from 40 percent. Discounters and specialty stores have taken up much of the slack.[11]

refact

Although not considered a drugstore per se, Wal-Mart is the third-largest pharmacy operator in the United States.[12]

to as count, pour, lick, and stick) to providing health care assistance.

Shoppers Drug Mart, Canada's largest pharmacy, operates 856 drugstores plus 46 Shoppers Health Care stores, with 2001 sales of $4.5 billion or $10 578 per square metre. Shoppers has launched beauty boutiques by adding prestige cosmetics and fragrance brands. Following suit, London Drugs and Jean Coutu are also giving their cosmetics sections a major makeover, borrowing ideas from the department stores to chase new revenue opportunities.

Sephora offers a unique shopping experience, differentiating it from other specialty stores selling beauty products.

OFF-PRICE RETAILERS

Off-price retailers offer an inconsistent assortment of brand-name, fashion-oriented soft goods at low prices. Winners—launched in Canada in 1982—had grown to 150 stores across the country by 2004. The company, which is owned by TJ Maxx, U.S., has 70 buyers worldwide in Canada, Hong Kong, New York, Los Angeles, and London searching for the best buys in fashion. The flagship store, which opened in 2003 at the College Park location in Toronto, receives about 10 000 new items a week and is a shopper's dream. [15] [16] In 2005 Winners arrived on fashionable Bloor Street in Toronto not far from Tiffany, Chanel, and Holt Renfrew.

Off-price retailers can sell brand-name and even designer-label merchandise at low prices due to their unique buying and merchandising practices. Most merchandise is bought opportunistically from manufacturers or other retailers with excess inventory at the end of the season. This merchandise might be in odd sizes or unpopular colours and styles, or it might be irregulars (having minor mistakes in construction). Typically, merchandise is purchased at one-fifth to one-fourth of the original wholesale price. Off-price retailers can buy at low prices because they don't ask suppliers for advertising allowances, return privileges, markdown adjustments, or delayed payments.

Due to this pattern of opportunistic buying, customers can't be confident that the same type of merchandise will be in stock each time they visit the store. Different bargains will be available on each visit. To improve their offerings' consistency, some off-price retailers complement opportunistically bought merchandise with merchandise purchased at regular wholesale prices. Two special types of off-price retailers are closeout and outlet stores.

- **Closeout retailers** are off-price retailers that sell a broad but inconsistent assortment of merchandise usually obtained from a store closing or bankruptcy, consisting of general merchandise, apparel, and home furnishings.

- **Outlet stores** are off-price retailers owned by manufacturers or retailers. Outlet stores owned by manufacturers are referred to as **factory outlets**. Outlet stores can be found clustered together in a geographic area, such as in Cambridge, Ontario; maps are distributed to shoppers indicating outlet locations. The outlet mall provides a shopping location that includes added services such as food and beverages, parking, and a climate controlled environment, along with the bargains of off-price merchandise.

Manufacturers view outlet stores as an opportunity to sell irregulars, production overruns, and merchandise returned by retailers. Outlet stores also allow manufacturers some control over where their branded merchandise is sold at discount prices.

refact

North Americans rate pharmacists as the most trusted profession. [14]

Retailers with strong brand names such as Holt Renfrew (LastCall) operate outlet stores. By selling excess merchandise in outlet stores rather than selling it at markdown prices in their primary stores, these department and specialty store chains can maintain an image of offering desirable merchandise at full price.

Canadian retailers operating outlet stores include Roots outdoor apparel, Club Monaco trendy urban apparel, and Danier Leather. Problems occur as traditional mall landlords dispute with tenants who are opening branches in power centres located close to their shopping centres. Fashion retailers are selling identical merchandise and price points of clothes at their power centre stores and their mall locations. The end result: The consumer is confused, assumes there are higher prices at the mall, and thus avoids shopping at the traditional shopping centre.

VALUE RETAILERS

Value retailers are general merchandise discount stores that are found in either lower-income urban, or middle-income suburbs, or in rural areas and are much smaller than traditional discount stores (less than 837 square metres). Value retailers are the fastest-growing segment in Canadian retailing.[18] Many value retailers target low-income consumers, whose shopping behaviour differs from typical discount store or warehouse club customers. For instance, although these consumers demand well-known national brands, they often can't afford to buy large-size packages. Since this segment of the retail industry is growing rapidly and is known to pay its bills on time, vendors are creating special smaller packages for these people.

Value retailers follow a variety of business models. Although most cater to low-income groups, some draw from multiple-income groups and are generally located in suburban strip malls. They specialize in giftware, party, and craft items rather than consumables. Despite some of these chains' names, few just sell merchandise for a dollar. The $1 price is the focus, but the chains carry many different price points, all rounded off in even dollars. Your Dollar Store With More, a Kelowna, BC, franchise chain, has grown to 150 stores in five years and incorporates a similar pricing strategy. Dollar stores are attracting the "tween" market with low cost, trendy cosmetics and jewellery for girls ages 8 to 13. The names imply a *good value*, while not limiting the customer to the arbitrary dollar price point.

POP-UP STORES

So-called pop-up stores—temporary stores—are creating retail buzz as they respond to customers by reaching out in non-traditional ways and locations such as unfinished space. These stores pop up unexpectedly for hours, days or months, draw word-of-mouth crowds, then vanish and may resurface someplace else. Subscribers are usually given notice via e-mail as to time and place of the event. Smart retailers must be prepared to cater aggressively to their customers anywhere/anytime.

It is not enough for retailers to build a store and expect customers will find them. Strong retailers are reaching customers through touch points. Pop-up stores can also act as an effective promotional medium. These stores most often exist for a defined period of time in a place where the target customer will be focused. For example, a garden centre may open a temporary site to attract customers during the spring months to capture additional sales. Mobile wireless technology allows retailers to provide a full range of POS services to their non-permanent locations.

Pop-up stores are the perfect embodiment of a here today, replaced tomorrow retail ethic, and has built-in obsolescence at the core of the consumer dynamic. Brands and retailers love them because they create buzz, provide an incubator for new ideas, and permit targeted market research. Pop-ups can also provide benefits to a community, turning a forgotten neighbourhood into a destination or, like old fashion craft shows, allowing market exposure for those who can't afford the retail infrastructure.

food retailers

Ten years ago, people purchased food primarily at conventional supermarkets. Today, however, discount stores and warehouse clubs are significantly changing consumers' food purchasing patterns because they also sell food. At the same time, traditional food retailers carry many nonfood items, plus many have pharmacies, photo processing centres, banks, and cafés.

Surprisingly, the world's largest food retailer is Wal-Mart, with supermarket-type sales of US$77 billion in 2000. Yet supermarket-type products still generate only 40 percent of its revenue.[19]

Loblaws, Canada's largest grocery chain, continues to achieve success with the President's Choice brand and build convenience convergence by forming strategic alliances with coffee shops, fitness studios, photo marts, wine shops, dry cleaners, and other companies to provide its customers with the convenience of one-stop shopping. The addition of a "community room" that is available to local groups and charities, and which can be used for cooking classes by local chefs, is a popular community connection in Loblaws' new stores. The experiences are all designed to build loyalty and stimulate sales.[20]

It is now easy to see that one can't easily answer the question, When is a food retailer really not a food retailer? Nonetheless, our discussion of food and **combination stores** will include conventional supermarkets, big-box food retailers, and convenience stores. Exhibit 2–4 shows the sales revenues and retail mixes for different types of food retailers.

CONVENTIONAL SUPERMARKETS

A **conventional supermarket** is a self-service food store offering groceries, meat, and produce with limited sales of nonfood items, such as health and beauty aids and general merchandise. **Superstores** are larger conventional supermarkets (1860 to 4650 square metres) with expanded service deli, bakery, seafood and nonfood sections.[21]

In Canada, about half of the conventional supermarkets are considered to be very promotional. One day each week, they advertise that week's sale items in local papers. These promotion-oriented supermarkets also offer their own coupons and may agree to reimburse customers double or triple the face value of manufacturer coupons. This is called a *high–low pricing strategy*.

	Conventional Supermarket	Supercentre	Hypermarket	Warehouse Club	Convenience Store
Percentage food	70–90	30–40	60–70	60	90
Size (sq. m)	1860–4650	13 950–20 460	9300–27 900	9300–13 950	186–279
SKUs (000s)	20–30	100–150	40–60	20	2–3
Variety	Average	Broad	Average	Broad	Narrow
Assortment	Average	Deep	Deep	Shallow	Shallow
No. of checkout lines	6–10	20–30	40–60	10–15	1–2
Prices	Average	Low	Low	Low	High

exhibit 2–4
Types of Food Retailers

The other half of conventional supermarkets use very few promotions and sell almost all merchandise at the same price every day. This is called an *everyday low pricing (EDLP) policy.* Typically, everyday prices in these supermarkets are lower than regular prices in promotional supermarkets. For example, Food Basics uses an EDLP strategy and keeps costs low by offering a "no-frills" shopping experience. By adopting everyday low pricing, Food Basics reduces advertising costs to 25 percent of typical advertising expenses for a supermarket. Currently, Loblaws in Canada employs a hybrid pricing strategy consisting of EDLP for approximately 500 of the most shopped items and high–low pricing on the remainder of the items that are featured in weekly flyers. High–low and EDLP strategies are discussed in detail later in the text.

BIG-BOX FOOD RETAILERS

Over the past 25 years, supermarkets have increased in size and have begun to sell a broader variety of merchandise.

Supercentres are 13 950 to 20 460 square metre stores that offer a wide variety of food (30–40 percent) and nonfood merchandise (60–70 percent).[23] They are the fastest-growing retail category. Supercentres stock between 100 000 and 150 000 individual items (SKUs). With the popularity of the superstore concept in Canada in the 1990s, Loblaws expanded its product offering by including clothing, pharmaceuticals, and other nonfood items. By maintaining its quality and position through a three-part strategy of innovation, market domination, and reduction of costs, Loblaws remains relatively unchallenged in the Canadian grocery retail marketplace.[24]

By offering broad assortments of grocery and general merchandise under one roof, supercentres provide a one-stop shopping experience. Customers will typically drive farther to shop at these stores than to visit conventional supermarkets (which offer a smaller selection). General merchandise items (nonfood items) are often purchased on impulse when customers' primary reason for coming to the store is to buy groceries. The general merchandise has higher margins, enabling the supercentres to price food items more aggressively. However, since supercentres are very large, some customers find them frustrating because it can take a long time to find the items they want.

Hypermarkets are also large (9300 to 27 900 square metres) combination food (60–70 percent) and general merchandise (30–40 percent) retailers. Hypermarkets typically stock less than supercentres, between 40 000 and 60 000 items ranging from groceries, hardware, and sports equipment, to furniture and appliances, computers, and electronics.[25]

Hypermarkets were created in France after the Second World War. By building large stores on the outskirts of metropolitan areas, French retailers could attract customers and not violate strict land-use laws. They have spread throughout Europe and are popular in some South American countries such as Argentina and Brazil.

Consider, for instance, France-based Auchan. It is a hypermarket chain with a workforce of 145 000 operating in 14 countries, including Taiwan, China, Argentina, the United States, Mexico, and most European countries. A typical store is 22 320 square metres and has 60 checkout counters, more than 100 000 food and nonfood items, and 2000 shopping carts. Auchan offers everything from fresh produce to groceries to housewares to electronics.

Supercentres versus Hypermarkets Hypermarkets, per se, are not prevalent in North America,[27] although the differences between a French hypermarket and a Wal-Mart or Target supercentre are sometimes difficult to distinguish. Both hypermarkets and supercentres are large, carry grocery and general merchandise categories, are self-service, and are located in warehouse-type structures with large parking facilities.

Hypermarkets are often larger, but they carry fewer items. The merchandise mix is different as well. Hypermarkets carry a larger proportion of food items than supercentres: fresh food—produce, meat, fish, and so forth—is their specialty, provides a profit centre, and is the primary reason why many people shop there. Supercentres, on the other hand, have a larger percentage of nonfood items. Furthermore, on the food side, their specialty is dry grocery, such as breakfast cereal and canned goods, instead of fresh items.

Warehouse Club   A **warehouse club** is a retailer that offers a limited assortment of food and general merchandise with little service at low prices to ultimate consumers and small businesses. Stores are large (at least 9300 square metres, with some over 13 950[28]) and located in low-rent districts. They have simple interiors and concrete floors. Aisles are wide so forklifts can pick up pallets of merchandise and arrange them on the selling floor. Little service is offered. Customers pick merchandise off shipping pallets, take it to checkout lines in the front of the store, and pay with cash, credit, or debit. The largest warehouse club chains are Costco and Sam's Club, a division of Wal-Mart (both with 2000 sales of over US$26 billion).

Costco lures its more affluent clientele with warehouse prices for gourmet foods and upscale brands such as Waterford crystal, Raymond Weil watches, and Ralph Lauren clothing.

Merchandise in warehouse clubs is about half food and half general merchandise. Specific brands and items may differ from time to time because the stores buy merchandise available on special promotions from manufacturers. Warehouse clubs reduce prices by using low-cost locations and store designs. They reduce inventory holding costs by carrying a limited assortment of fast-selling items. Merchandise usually is sold before the clubs need to pay for it.

Most warehouse clubs have two types of members: wholesale members who own small businesses, and individual members who purchase for their own use. For example, many small restaurants are wholesale customers who buy their supplies, food ingredients, and desserts from a warehouse club rather than from food distributors.

Typically, members must pay an annual fee of $35 to $45. In some stores, individual members pay no fee but pay 5 percent over an item's ticketed price. Wholesale members typically represent less than 30 percent of the customer base but account for over 70 percent of sales. The membership fee-driven warehouse club is a U.S.-based phenomenon.

CONVENIENCE STORES

Convenience stores provide a limited variety and assortment of merchandise at a convenient location in a 186 to 279 square metre store with speedy checkout. They are the modern version of the neighbourhood mom-and-pop grocery/general store.

Convenience stores enable consumers to make purchases quickly, without having to search through a large store and wait in a long checkout line. Over half the items bought are consumed within 30 minutes of purchase. Due to their small size and high sales, convenience stores typically receive deliveries every day.

Convenience stores offer a limited assortment and variety, and they charge higher prices than supermarkets. Milk, eggs, and bread once represented the majority of their sales. Now almost all convenience stores in nonurban areas sell gasoline, which accounts for over 55 percent of annual sales.

Traditional food retailers are competing with convenience stores for customers who want gourmet prepared meals.

U.K.-based apparel retailer Marks & Spencer competes directly with supermarkets and restaurants by offering a wide assortment of prepared foods. For instance, it sells more than 7 million cake slices over the holiday season—that's one for almost every person living in London.[33]

Although the convenience store concept has stagnated a bit in Canada and Europe, it has been growing throughout Japan, the rest of Asia, and in parts of Latin America. The reason is that they are so convenient. In many Asian countries, consumers face space constraints at home so, they prefer buying in smaller quantities at neighbourhood locations. Additionally, many e-tailers in Asia use convenience stores as distribution points. Customers buy online and pick up at the store.[29]

ISSUES IN FOOD RETAILING

The primary issue facing food retailers in general, and supermarket and convenience store retailers in particular, is the increasing level of competition from other types of retailers. As mentioned earlier, supercentres in North America and hypermarkets in the rest of the world are growing at a rapid pace. In Canada, this growth has been spurred by Wal-Mart's aggressive strategy. Competition is coming from other sources as well. Drug chains such as Shoppers Drug Mart carry many grocery essentials found in convenience stores. Fast-food restaurants such as Subway sandwich shops have positioned themselves as a healthy food alternative.

Convenience stores are also developing new concepts emphasizing prepared meals. For example, Mac's combines a convenience store and takeout restaurant. Mac's has ready-to-heat meals, a sandwich bar, salads, and a ready-to-eat section. It also offers fresh produce, beverages, snacks, and other food. Customers can park, walk in, pick up tonight's dinner and tomorrow's breakfast, and be back in their cars in 10 minutes.[30]

Traditional grocery chains are fighting back by making significant investments in providing meal solutions, either hot food or partially cooked entrées. The market for prepared foods can be quite profitable. Profit margins on prepared foods are higher than most other grocery categories. Also, although shoppers rarely visit a supermarket in search of prepared foods alone, those who do spend almost 40 percent more than those who seldom or never purchase prepared foods.[31] Imagine being greeted by chefs in white hats tossing fresh pasta, with a dining area in the grocery store. The store could offer an extensive variety of prepared meals ranging from Caesar salads to Chinese food made by chefs in full view of its customers, and a satisfied customer saying, "They have the drama. I ask for a fresh salmon sautéed with a little lemon, browse 10 minutes in the store, and take it home for dinner."[32]

nonstore retail formats

By 2010, it is expected that 12 percent of all North American retail sales will be through catalogues, direct mail, interactive television, and the Internet.[34]

In the preceding sections, we have examined retailers whose *primary* modes of operation are bricks-and-mortar stores. In this section, we will discuss types of retailers that operate primarily in nonstore environments. The major types of nonstore retailers are electronic retailers, catalogue and direct-mail retailers, direct selling, television home shopping, and vending machines.

ELECTRONIC RETAILING

Electronic retailing (also called **e-tailing** and **Internet retailing**) is a retail format in which the retailers communicate with customers and offer products and services for sale over the Internet. The rapid diffusion of Internet access and usage and the perceived low cost of entry stimulated the creation of over 10 000 entrepreneurial electronic retailing ventures during the last five years of the twentieth century. These electronic retailers ranged in size from Amazon.com, with over $3 billion in annual sales, to niche retailers such as Dilmah's, which sells teas from the plantations in the highlands of Ceylon (www.dilmahtea.com), and Steel of the Night, which offers a complete line of steel drums (www.steelofthenight.com).

One famous Internet listing site to find/post what you want, or read reviews and testimonials is craigslist (www.craiglist.org). This site is a centralized network of online urban communities, featuring classified advertisements. On craigslist you can find jobs, internships, housing, personal, for sale/barter or wanted items, cheap offers such as travel, services, community happenings, gigs, resume categories, and forums sorted by various topics.

The continued consumer interest in buying electronically is the result of traditional store-based and catalogue retailers beginning to offer merchandise through an electronic channel. Although the electronic retail innovators had superior skills in using the new technology, they lacked retailing expertise and a deep understanding of customer needs.[35] Traditional retailers have incorporated an Internet channel into a multichannel offering that provides more value to customers. The success of multichannel retailing is reflected in the rating of retail Web sites. Each year, *Internet Retailer* selects the best Internet sites. In 2002, only 4 of the top 25 Web sites were pure electronic retailers, whereas in 2001, 14 were pure electronic retailers.[36] E-tailing issues are discussed in Chapter 3.

CATALOGUE AND DIRECT-MAIL RETAILING

Catalogue retailing is a nonstore retail format in which the retail offering is communicated to a customer through a catalogue, whereas **direct-mail retailers** communicate with their customers using letters and brochures. Historically, catalogue and direct-mail retailing were most successful with rural consumers, who lacked ready access to retail stores. Today's customers enjoy the convenience of shopping by catalogue. The major catalogue retailers have embraced a multichannel strategy by integrating the Internet into their catalogue operations. Customers often get a catalogue in the mail, look it over, and go to the Internet for more information and to place an order.[37]

Canadian Tire, which was founded in 1922, began producing its catalogue in 1928 and became a household name in Canada for auto parts and service, sports and leisure products, and hardware goods. In 2001, Canadian Tire had 443 stores and sales of $4.3 billion. The store has also built its reputation on a strong loyalty program, which gives consumers just over 1 percent of the purchase price of goods back in Canadian Tire money.

Types of Catalogue and Direct-Mail Retailers   Two types of firms selling products through the mail are general merchandise, specialty catalogue retailers, and direct-mail retailers. **General merchandise catalogue retailers** offer a broad variety of merchandise in catalogues that are periodically mailed to their customers. **Specialty catalogue retailers** focus on specific categories of merchandise, such as fruit (Harry and David), gardening tools (Smith & Hawken), and seeds and plants (Burpee).

Direct-mail retailers typically mail brochures and pamphlets to sell a specific product or service to customers at one point in time. For example, American Express sells a broad array of financial services targeted to the consumer. In addition to the focus on a specific product or service, most direct-mail retailers are primarily interested in making a single sale from a specific mailing, whereas catalogue retailers typically maintain relationships with customers over time.

Specialty catalogue retailers focus on specific categories of merchandise such as fruit (Harry and David), sporting goods (REI and Bass Pro Shops), seeds (Burpee), and home furnishings (Restoration Hardware).

Issues in Catalogue Retailing Catalogue retailing can be an attractive business opportunity because the start-up costs are relatively low. On the other hand, catalogue retailing can be very challenging.

- It is difficult for smaller catalogue and direct-mail retailers to compete with large, well-established firms that have embraced a multichannel strategy. The Internet has become a natural extension to most cataloguers' selling strategy: 95 percent of cataloguers describe themselves as multichannel retailers, with 53 percent defining their companies as catalogue/Internet/retail and 42 percent as catalogue/Internet.[38]

- The mailing and printing costs are high and increasing.

- It is difficult to get consumers' attention as they are mailed so many direct-mail promotions.

- The length of time required to design, develop, and distribute catalogues makes it difficult for catalogue and direct-mail retailers to respond quickly to new trends and fashions.

Most analysts believe that the future will bring a seamless multichannel offering that integrates catalogues, the Internet, and often bricks-and-mortar stores.

DIRECT SELLING

Direct selling is a retail format in which a salesperson, frequently an independent businessperson, contacts a customer directly in a convenient location, either at the customer's home or at work, and demonstrates merchandise benefits, takes an order, and delivers the merchandise to the customer. Direct selling is a highly interactive form of retailing in which considerable information is conveyed to customers through face-to-face discussions with a salesperson. Home parties organized by associates of the Pampered Chef are a method used to sell kitchenware.

Almost three-quarters of all direct sales are made through multilevel sales networks. In a **multilevel network,** people serve as master distributors, recruiting other people to become distributors in their network. The master distributors either buy merchandise from the firm and resell it to their distributors or receive a commission on all merchandise purchased by the distributors in their network. In addition to selling merchandise themselves, the master distributors are involved in recruiting and training other distributors.

Some multilevel direct-selling firms are illegal pyramid schemes. A **pyramid scheme** develops when the firm and its program are designed to sell merchandise and services to other distributors rather than to end users. The founders and initial distributors in pyramid schemes profit from the inventory bought by later participants, but little merchandise is sold to consumers who use it.

TELEVISION HOME SHOPPING

Television home shopping is a retail format in which customers watch a TV program demonstrating merchandise and then place orders for the merchandise by telephone. The three forms of electronic home shopping retailing are:

- cable channels dedicated to television shopping

- infomercials

- direct-response advertising

Infomercials are TV programs, typically 30 minutes long, that mix entertainment with product demonstrations and then solicit orders placed by telephone. **Direct-response advertising** includes advertisements on TV and radio that describe products and provide an opportunity for consumers to order them.

The Shopping Channel is located in Mississauga, Ontario, and on any given day the business can move thousands of units of a single item; for example, a necklace. The potential sales volume of the daily show stopper—the station's version of a door crasher—is staggering. For example, the company moved $4 million in Dell computers in one day. The Shopping Channel broadcasts 18 hours of live broadcasting a day. This is a multi-channel retailer offering up bargains through TV cable/satellite households, The Shopping Channel Web site, catalogue, and soon via interactive television that combines television with a computer.

The logistical issues connected with television retailing are apparent when you consider 10 000 products in stock and between 200 to 1000 new items arriving each week. Every item must be photographed, videotaped, catalogued, and made ready for television and to accommodate their online sales through the www.theshoppingchannel.com.

Competitors to the Canadian Shopping Channel are home shopping networks out of the U.S. which broadcast through infomercials and online and as well Amazon and eBay, and Sears Canada which offers a department store selection.

The major advantage of TV home shopping compared to catalogue retailing is that customers can see the merchandise demonstrated on the TV screen. However, customers can't examine a particular type of merchandise or a specific item when they want to, as they can with catalogues. They have to wait for the time when the merchandise shows up on the screen. To address this limitation, home shopping networks schedule categories of merchandise for specific times so customers looking for specific merchandise can plan their viewing time.

VENDING MACHINE RETAILING

Vending machine retailing is a nonstore format in which merchandise or services are stored in a machine and dispensed to customers when they deposit cash or use a credit card. Vending machines are placed at convenient, high-traffic locations such as in the workplace, the airport, or on university campuses, and primarily contain snacks or drinks.

Although $25.6 billion in goods is sold annually through vending machines in North America, vending machine sales growth is relatively slow, less than 5 percent, and closely mirrors the growth in the economy.[39]

Technological developments in vending machine design may result in long-term sales growth. New video kiosk vending machines enable consumers to see the merchandise in use, get information about it, and use their credit cards to make a purchase.

The new vending machine designs also enable the retailers to increase the productivity of the machines. Electronic systems in the machine keep track of inventory, cash, and other operating conditions. Then radio devices transmit data back to a host computer. These data are analyzed, and communications are sent to route drivers telling them when stockouts and malfunctions occur.[40]

refact

There are 5.4 million vending machines in Japan—one machine for every 23 people. Unlike the packaged-food and soft-drink offerings in North America, products in Japan range from rice crackers and eyebrow shapers, to micro radios and condoms.[41]

services retailing

The retail firms discussed in the previous sections sell products to consumers. However, **services retailers**, firms selling primarily services rather than merchandise, are a large and growing part of the retail industry. Consider a typical Saturday. After a bagel and cup of coffee at a nearby Tim Hortons, you go to the laundromat to

These are retailers, too. You start the day with a bagel, go to the bank, and then burn off the calories at the fitness centre.

wash and dry your clothes, drop a suit off at a dry cleaner, leave film to be developed at a Shoppers Drug Mart, and make your way to the Jiffy Lube to have your car's oil changed. Since you are in a hurry, you drive through a Taco Bell so you can eat lunch quickly and not be late for your haircut at 1 P.M. By midafternoon, you're ready for a swim at your health club. After stopping at home for a change of clothes, you're off to dinner, a movie, and dancing with a friend. Finally, you end your day with a caffe latte at Starbucks, having interacted with 10 different services retailers during the day.

There are several trends that suggest considerable future growth in services retailing. For example, the aging of the population will increase demand for health services. Younger people too are spending increasing amounts of time and money on health and fitness. Parents in two-income families are willing to pay to have their homes cleaned, lawns maintained, clothes washed and pressed, and meals prepared so they can spend more time with their families.

There is a wide variety of services retailers. These companies are retailers because they sell goods and services to consumers. However, some of these companies are not just retailers. For example, airlines, banks, hotels, and insurance and express mail companies sell their services to businesses as well as consumers. Also, a large number of services retailers such as lawyers, doctors, and dry cleaners focus on local markets and do not have a Canada-wide presence.

Many organizations—such as banks, hospitals, health spas, legal clinics, entertainment firms, and universities—that offer services to consumers traditionally haven't considered themselves as retailers. Due to increased competition, these organizations are adopting retailing principles to attract customers and satisfy their needs.

All retailers provide goods and services for their customers. However, the emphasis placed on the merchandise versus the services differs across retail formats, as Exhibit 2–5 shows. On the left side of the exhibit are supermarkets and warehouse clubs. These retail formats consist of self-service stores that offer very few services. However, these formats do offer a few services, such as cheque cashing and some assistance from store employees. Moving along the continuum from left to right, we find category specialists, which also emphasize self-service but have employees who can answer questions, demonstrate merchandise, and make recommendations. Next, department and specialty stores provide even higher levels of service. In addition to assistance from sales associates, these stores offer services such as gift wrapping, bridal registries, and alterations.

Optical centres and restaurants lie somewhere in the middle of the merchandise/service continuum. In addition to selling frames, eyeglasses, and contact lenses,

exhibit 2–5   Merchandise/Service Continuum

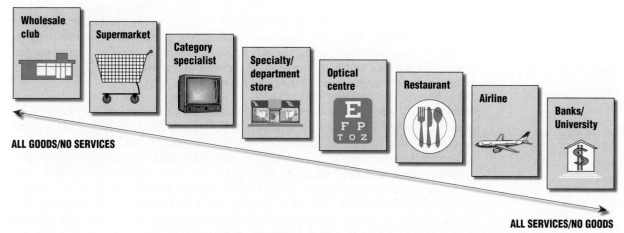

ALL GOODS/NO SERVICES

ALL SERVICES/NO GOODS

optical centres also provide important services such as eye examinations and eyeglass fittings. Similarly, restaurants offer food plus a place to eat, music in the background, a pleasant ambience, and table service. As we move to the right end of the continuum, we encounter retailers whose offering is primarily services. However, even these retailers have some products associated with the services offered, such as a meal on the airplane or a chequebook at a bank. Services retailers are defined as retailers for which the major aspect of their offerings is services versus merchandise.

DIFFERENCES BETWEEN SERVICES AND MERCHANDISE RETAILERS

As a retailer falls more to the right on the merchandise/service continuum, services become a more important aspect of the retailer's offering. Four important differences in the nature of the offering provided by services and merchandise retailers are:

- intangibility
- simultaneous production and consumption
- perishability
- inconsistency of the offering to customers[42]

Intangibility   Services are generally intangible—customers cannot see, touch, or feel them. They are performances or actions rather than objects. For example, health care services cannot be seen or touched by a patient. Even after diagnosis and treatment, the patient may not realize the full extent of the service that has been performed.

Services retailers also have difficulty in evaluating the quality of services they are providing. To evaluate the quality of their offering, services retailers emphasize soliciting customer evaluations and complaints.

Simultaneous Production and Consumption   Products are typically made in a factory, stored and sold by a retailer, and then used by consumers in their homes. Service providers, on the other hand, create and deliver the service as the customer is consuming it. For example, when you eat at a restaurant, the meal is prepared and consumed almost at the same time.

Because services are produced and consumed at the same time, it is difficult to reduce costs through mass production. For this reason, most services retailers are small, local firms. Large national retailers are able to reduce costs by "industrializing" the services they offer. They make substantial investments in equipment and training to provide a uniform service. For example, McDonald's has a detailed procedure for cooking french fries and hamburgers to make sure they come out the same whether cooked in Paris, France, Paris, Ontario, or Paris, Illinois.

Perishability   Because the creation and consumption of services are inseparable, services are perishable. They can't be saved, stored, or resold. This is in contrast to merchandise that can be held in inventory until a customer is ready to buy it.

Due to the perishability of services, an important aspect of services retailing is matching supply and demand. Most services retailers have a capacity constraint, and the capacity cannot be changed easily. There is a fixed number of tables in a restaurant, seats in a classroom, beds in a hospital, and a finite amount of electricity that can be generated by a power plant. To increase capacity, services retailers need to make major investments such as buying more airplanes.

In addition, demand for service varies considerably over time. Consumers are most likely to fly on airplanes during holidays and the summer, and eat in restaurants at lunch and dinner time. Thus, services retailers often have times when their services are underutilized and other times when they have to turn customers away because they can't accommodate them.

Services retailers use a variety of programs to match demand and supply. For example, airlines and hotels set lower prices on weekends when they have excess capacity because businesspeople aren't travelling.

Inconsistency   Merchandise is often produced by machines with very tight quality control so customers are reasonably assured that, for example, all boxes of a cereal will be identical. Because services are performances produced by people (employees and customers), no two services will be identical. The waiter at a restaurant can be in a bad mood and make your dining experience a disaster.

Thus, an important challenge for services retailers is to provide consistently high-quality services. Services retailers expend considerable time and effort selecting, training, managing, and motivating their service providers.

types of ownership

Previous sections of this chapter discussed how retailers are classified in terms of their retail mix (the variety and depth of merchandise and services offered to customers) and the merchandise and services they sell (food, general merchandise, and services). Another way to classify retailers is by their ownership. The major classifications of retail ownership are:

* independent, single-store establishments
* corporate chains
* franchises

INDEPENDENT, SINGLE-STORE ESTABLISHMENTS

Retailing is one of the few sectors in our economy where entrepreneurial activity is extensive. Over 60 000 new retail businesses are started in North America each year.[43] Many such stores are owner-managed. Thus, management has direct contact with customers and can respond quickly to their needs. Small retailers are also very flexible and can therefore react quickly to market changes and customer needs. They aren't bound by bureaucracies inherent in large retail organizations.

Although single-store retailers can tailor their offerings to their customers' needs, corporate chains can more effectively negotiate lower prices for merchandise and advertising due to their larger size. In addition, corporate chains have a broader management base, with people who specialize in specific retail activities. Single-store retailers typically have to rely on owner–managers' capabilities to make the broad range of necessary retail decisions.

To better compete against corporate chains, some independent retailers join a **wholesale-sponsored voluntary cooperative group,** which is an organization operated by a wholesaler offering a merchandising program to small, independent retailers on a voluntary basis. Independent Grocers Alliance (IGA) is an example of a wholesale-sponsored voluntary cooperative group. In addition to buying, warehousing, and distribution, these groups offer members services such as store design and layout, site selection, bookkeeping and inventory management systems, and employee training programs.

CORPORATE RETAIL CHAINS

A **retail chain** is a company operating multiple retail units under common ownership and usually has centralized decision making for defining and implementing its strategy. Retail chains can range in size from a drugstore with two stores to retailers with many stores such as The Bay and Zellers. Some retail chains are divisions of larger corporations or holding companies. For example, Venator owns Foot Locker, Lady Foot Locker, Kids Foot Locker, Foot Locker International, Champs Sports, and Footlocker.com/Eastbay.Champs; Intimate Brands owns Victoria's Secret, Bath & Body Works, and The White Barn Candle Co.

There has been considerable concern that corporate retail chains drive independent retailers out of business. For example, Wal-Mart has pursued a strategy of opening full-line discount stores and supercentres on the outskirts of small towns.[44] These stores offer a broader selection of merchandise at much lower prices than previously available from local retailers. Due to scale economies and an efficient distribution system, corporate chains can sell at low prices. This forces some directly competing local retailers out of business and alters the community fabric.

On the other hand, local retailers offering complementary merchandise and services can prosper. When large chain stores open, more consumers are attracted to the community from surrounding areas. Thus, the market for the local stores expands. Although chain stores may have cost advantages over local retailers, large retail chains can be very bureaucratic, stifling managers' creativity with excessive rules and procedures. Often, all stores in the chain have the same merchandise and services, whereas local retailers can provide merchandise compatible with local market needs.

FRANCHISING

Franchising is a contractual agreement between a franchisor and a franchisee that allows the franchisee to operate a retail outlet using a name and format developed and supported by the franchisor. Approximately one-third of all North American retail sales are made by franchisees.

In a franchise contract, the franchisee pays a lump sum plus a royalty on all sales for the right to operate a store in a specific location. The franchisee also agrees to operate the outlet in accordance with procedures prescribed by the franchisor. The franchisor provides assistance in locating and building the store, developing the

Approximately one-third of all North American retail sales are made by franchisees like these.

products or services sold, management training, and advertising. To maintain the franchisee's reputation, the franchisor also makes sure that all outlets provide the same quality of services and products.

The franchise ownership format attempts to combine advantages of owner-managed businesses with efficiencies of centralized decision making in chain store operations. Franchisees are motivated to make their store successful because they receive the profits (after the royalty is paid). The franchisor is motivated to develop new products and systems and to promote the franchise because it receives a royalty on all sales. Advertising, product development, and system development are efficiently done by the franchisor, with costs shared by all franchisees.

multichannel retailing

Retailers were classified either as store-based or nonstore (electronic, catalogue/direct mail, direct selling, TV home shopping, and vending machine) retailers. However, many retail firms use more than one channel to reach their customers. For example, Gateway started as an electronic retailer and has opened up stores; Amazon.com now distributes a catalogue; Eddie Bauer and Sears interface with customers through their stores, catalogues, and Web sites.

A **multichannel retailer** is a retailer that sells merchandise or services through more than one channel. Single-channel retailers are evolving into multichannel retailers to attract and satisfy more customers. By using a combination of channels, retailers can exploit the unique benefits provided by each channel.

Exhibit 2–6 lists the unique benefits of stores, catalogues, and the Internet. These benefits illustrate how the channels can be used to complement each other.[45]

STORE CHANNEL

Stores offer a number of benefits to customers that they cannot get when shopping through catalogues and the Internet.

Browsing　Although many consumers surf the Internet and look through catalogues for ideas, most consumers still prefer browsing in stores.

Stores	Catalogue	Internet
• Browsing • Touching and feeling products • Personal service • Cash payment • Immediate gratification • Entertainment and social interaction	• Convenience • Portability; easily accessible • Safety • Visual presentation	• Convenience • Safety • Broad selection • Detailed information • Personalization • Problem-solving information

exhibit 2–6
Channel Benefits

Touching and Feeling Products   Perhaps the greatest benefit offered by stores is the opportunity for customers to use all of their senses when examining products—touching, smelling, tasting, seeing, and hearing.

Personal Service   Although shoppers can be critical of the personal service they get in stores, sales associates still have the capability of providing meaningful, personalized information.

Cash Payment   Stores are the only channel that accepts cash payments.

The climbing wall in a Mountain Equipment Co-op store provides an exciting, entertaining experience for customers that cannot be matched by the retailer's catalogue and Internet offerings.

In some situations, catalogues are much more convenient than shopping in stores or over the Internet.

Immediate Gratification   Stores have the advantage of allowing customers to get the merchandise immediately after they buy it.

Entertainment and Social Experience   In-store shopping can be a stimulating experience for some people, providing a break in their daily routine and enabling them to interact with friends. Paco Underhill, author of *How We Shop*, points out, "Stores are a social experience. I don't care how many chat rooms there are on a site, they will never provide what the experience of brick-and-mortar shopping provides for all five senses, if not six or seven."[48]

Convenience   All nonstore formats offer the convenience of looking at merchandise and placing an order any day at any time from almost anywhere.

Safety   Nonstore retail formats have an advantage over store-based retailers by enabling customers to review merchandise and place orders from a safe environment—their homes.[49]

Quality of Visual Presentation   The photographs of merchandise in catalogues, although not as useful as in-store presentations, are superior to the visual information that can be displayed on a CRT screen.

SUMMARY

This chapter reviews the types of retailers and ownership classifications. This is an excellent resource for students and highlights strategies for success in a competitive retail marketplace. Definitions of the retail formats and the examples explain the diversity and innovation within the retail sector.

Many different types of retailers now offer multichannel approaches to their retail customers in an attempt to gain loyalty. Multichannel is not a format in itself but rather an additional way of reaching the customer and increasing revenue.

This chapter explained different types of retailers and how they compete with different retail mixes to sell merchandise and services to customers. To collect statistics about retailing, the federal government classifies retailers by type of merchandise and services sold. But this classification method may not be useful in determining a retailer's major competitors. A more useful approach for understanding the retail marketplace is classifying retailers on the basis of their retail mix, the merchandise variety and assortment, services, location, pricing, and promotion decisions made to attract customers.

Over the past 30 years, North American retail markets have been characterized by the emergence of many new retail institutions. Traditional institutions (supermarkets, convenience, department, discount, and specialty stores) have been joined by category specialists, superstores, hypermarkets, convenience stores, warehouse clubs, off-price retailers, catalogue showrooms, and hypermarkets. In addition, there has been substantial growth in services retailing. The inherent differences between services and merchandise result in services retailers emphasizing store management while merchandise retailers emphasize inventory control issues.

Traditional retail institutions have changed in response to these new retailers. For example, department stores have increased their emphasis on fashion-oriented apparel and improved the services they offer. Supermarkets are focusing more attention on meal solutions and perishables.

Although the bubble burst for most pure electronic retailers, traditional store-based and catalogue retailers are adding an electronic channel and evolving into being integrated, customer-centric, multichannel retailers. This evolution toward multichannel retailing is driven by the increasing desire of customers to communicate with retailers anytime, anywhere, anyplace.

Each of the channels (stores, catalogues, and Web sites) offers unique benefits to customers. The store channel enables customers to touch and feel merchandise and use the products shortly after they are purchased. Catalogues enable customers to browse through a retailer's offering anytime and anyplace. A unique benefit offered by the electronic channel is the opportunity for consumers to search across a broad range of alternatives, develop a smaller set of alternatives based on their needs, and get specific information about the alternatives they want.

By offering multiple channels, retailers overcome the limitations of each channel. Web sites can be used to extend the geographical presence and assortment offered by the store channel. Web sites also can be used to update the information provided in catalogues. Stores can be used to provide a multisensory experience and an economical distribution capability supporting the electronic channel.

Providing a seamless interface across channels is very challenging for multichannel retailers. Meeting customer expectations will require the development and use of common customer databases and integrated systems. In addition, multichannel retailers will have to make decisions about how to use the different channels to support the retailer's brand image and how to present consistent merchandise assortments and pricing across channels.

KEY TERMS

assortment, *24*	electronic retailing, *36*	pyramid scheme, *38*
breadth of stock, *24*	e-tailing, *36*	retail chain, *43*
catalogue retailing, *37*	factory outlet, *31*	services retailer, *39*
category killers, *28*	franchising, *43*	SKU (stock keeping unit), *24*
category specialist, *28*	general merchandise catalogue retailers, *37*	specialty catalogue retailers, *37*
closeout retailer, *31*		specialty store, *27*
combination store, *33*	home improvement centre, *28*	supercentre, *34*
convenience store, *35*	hypermarket, *34*	superstore, *33*
conventional supermarket, *33*	infomercials, *39*	television home shopping, *38*
department store, *29*	Internet retailing, *36*	value retailers, *32*
depth of stock, *24*	leased department, *29*	variety, *24*
direct-mail retailers, *37*	mass merchandiser, *26*	vending machine retailing, *39*
direct-response advertising, *39*	multichannel retailer, *44*	warehouse club, *35*
direct selling, *38*	multilevel network, *38*	wholesale-sponsored voluntary cooperative group, *43*
discount store, *26*	off-price retailer, *31*	
drugstore, *30*	outlet store, *31*	

Get Out & Do It!

1. **GO SHOPPING** Go to an athletic footwear specialty store such as Foot Locker, a department store, and a discount store. Analyze their variety and assortment of athletic footwear by creating a table similar to Exhibit 2–1 on page 25.

2. **GO SHOPPING** Keep a diary of where you shop, what you buy, and how much you spend for two weeks. Tabulate your results by type of retailer. Are your shopping habits significantly different from your parents'? Do your and your parents' shopping habits coincide with the trends discussed in this chapter? Why or why not?

3. **INTERNET EXERCISE** Two large associations of retailers are the National Retail Federation (www.nrf.org) and the Retail Council of Canada (www.retailcouncil.org). Visit these sites and report the latest retail developments and issues confronting the industry.

4. **INTERNET EXERCISE** Go to www.walmart.com. Scroll to the bottom of the page and click on "Wal-Mart Stores Info." Look for "About Wal-Mart," and click on "Divisions." Look for "Retail Divisions," and click on "Supercenters." Now go to www.auchanhypermarket.com. See if you can determine the differences between a Wal-Mart supercentre and an Auchan hypermarket.

5. **INTERNET EXERCISE** Check out Mark's Work Wearhouse at www2.marks.com/. Explain why Mark's retail product is a successful addition to Canadian Tire's assortments, broadening the product mix for consumers.

6. **INTERNET EXERCISE** Do an online search for "Craig's List." Explain the popularity of this unique site.

DISCUSSION QUESTIONS AND PROBLEMS

1. Distinguish between variety and assortment. Why are these important elements of retail market structure?

2. How can small independent retailers compete against the large national chains?

3. What do off-price retailers need to do to compete against other formats in the future?

4. Compare and contrast the retail mixes of convenience stores, traditional supermarkets, supercentres, hypermarkets, and warehouse stores. Can all of these food retail institutions survive over the long run? Why?

5. Why haven't hypermarkets been successful in North America? Do you believe they will be successful in the future?

6. The same brand and model personal computer is sold in specialty computer stores, discount stores, category specialists, and warehouse stores. Why would a customer choose one store over the others?

7. Choose a product category that both you and your parents purchase (e.g., clothing, CDs, electronic equipment). In which type of store do you typically purchase this merchandise? What about your parents? Explain why there is, or is not, a difference in your store choices.

8. At many optical stores you can get your eyes checked *and* purchase glasses or contact lenses. How is the shopping experience different for the service as compared to the product? Design a strategy to get customers to purchase both the service and the product. In so doing, delineate specific actions that should be taken to acquire and retain optical customers.

9. Many experts believe that customer service is one of retailing's most important issues in the new millennium. How can retailers that emphasize price (such as discount stores, category specialists, and off-price retailers) improve customer service without increasing costs and, thus, prices?

10. Should a multichannel retailer offer the same assortment of merchandise for sale on its Web site at the same price as it sells in its stores? Explain why, or why not.

CHAPTER 3

e-tailing issues—connecting to the customer

Executive Briefing

Fred Pritchard and Howard Goldstein, Owners, Golda's Kitchen

Golda's Kitchen, the leading Canadian online shopping site for quality kitchenware, is a retail venture that was designed by entrepreneurs Fred Pritchard and Howard Goldstein with two types of customers in mind: those who take cooking seriously and those who like to bake. Golda's Kitchen has been honoured as *Retailer of the Year* by the Canadian Gift and Tableware Association and declared one of the best cookware stores by the *Toronto Star*. The concept was originally designed to be an e-tailing Web site with a store rather than a store supported by a Web site.

Entrepreneurs Pritchard and Goldstein bring diverse personal backgrounds to the business. Fred Pritchard has his CGA designation and Howard Goldstein, who manages the online retail functions, has a degree in computer science and engineering. The two manage the retail functions by means of a distinct division of authority that matches their individual skills and personalities: online sales, Web site management, and purchasing are Goldstein's domain; the people part of the bricks-and-mortar business along with the store's accounting and marketing belong to Pritchard.

Golda's has been selling quality kitchenware online at http://shopping.netsuite.com/goldaskitchen since 1999 and at the retail store in Mississauga, Ontario, which opened in September 2001. In addition to a successful online business and a retail store, the entrepreneurs have connected to their customers with a fully equipped kitchen that features classes in creative cooking and cake decorating demonstrations at the Mississauga store. The only advertising that they do is Google ads in the U.S., where a large percentage of their business originates.

QUESTIONS What factors will affect the growth of electronic retailing?

Why did most pure electronic retailers fail?

How do multichannel retailers provide more value to their customers?

What are the key success factors in multichannel retailing?

How might technology affect the future shopping experience?

In the midst of fierce competition in the kitchenware business, Pritchard and Goldstein find themselves working long days, but the hard work has paid off. Golda's has become a booming business where two-thirds of their sales are generated through the Web site that features 6000 items for sale, ranging from pricey espresso machines to inexpensive cookie cutters. The pair attribute much of Golda's success to the niche market created by carrying specialty items for the serious cook that are hard to find. They stress that the key is to offer unique items that the competition does not sell. Howard Goldstein manages the extensive inventory by carefully analyzing sales trends, checking the availability of products and shipping times from suppliers, and satisfying customers' requests immediately. He admits that an essential success strategy is forging strong relationships with suppliers who, because of strong loyalty, hold some of the extensive inventory for Golda's e-tailing business.

The need for companies to have effective Web sites that convert hits to sales dominates Golda's online growth. Goldstein searched for an e-commerce software vendor to redesign and enhance their Web site. Software glitches are a disaster for a retailer like Golda's. "I can't afford to have hiccups," Pritchard says. After an exhaustive search, they finally selected NetSuite Inc., created by a former Oracle executive with the aim of providing small businesses with online economies of scale in Web development. Rapid growth of online sales has necessitated the expansion of Golda's warehouse capabilities. In 2008, to ensure efficiency of future growth in online sales, larger premises were opened.

In a world where dot.com retailers fail in large numbers, Golda's is thriving.

What a difference a few years make! E-commerce is very big and is going to get much bigger. Internet sales in Canada are growing at a rate of 30 to 40 percent a year, and are expected to represent 6 percent of total retail sales by 2008. Although this appears to be a small percentage of total sales, the Internet is profoundly changing consumer behaviour.

The actual value of transactions currently concluded online is dwarfed by the huge influence the Internet is exerting over purchases carried out at retail locations. A retailer's Web site is increasingly becoming the gateway to a company's brand, products, and services, providing customers price transparency and information. The Internet has become a place to shop, gather information, and browse for new ideas. For retailers it provides an opportunity to connect to the consumer anytime, anyplace, and provide personalization benefits to engage consumers in the retail experience.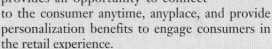

Averaging 2.4 million unique visitors per month annually, the Canadian Tire Web site ranked ninth among Web sites visited by Canadians (behind Ebay, Amazon, and Ticketmaster). Canadian Tire views its Web site as a research tool for customers, helping them make the right purchasing decisions. According to Caroline Casselman, Canadian Tire's spokesperson, "It is really helpful to our customers to browse; it helps drive a lot of customers to the store." A tool frequently used by Canadian Tire shoppers is one that tells the customer whether a product is in stock at the store closest to them.

Super cyber Craig Newark began posting e-mail messages to dozens of friends about local art and technology events in the San Francisco area and continued to update and expand content until craigslist took on a life of its own. The widely popular www.craigslist.org is a combination of classified ads, dating sites, and garage sales, all rolled into one. Jobs and housing listings receive the most page views, followed by items for sale, personals, and forums on everything from haiku and weddings to transgender issues and philosophy. The site has attracted more than 6.5 million posts per month, with over 700 hits per second during peak periods. The New York Times described Craigslist as a marketplace in the ancient style: chaotic, unruly, and vividly human.

E-commerce is analogous to a marketplace on the Internet. E-commerce primarily consists of the distributing, buying, selling, marketing, and servicing of products over the Internet. It also encompasses a very wide range of business activities and processes, from e-banking to e-logistics. The growth of supporting systems that are part of e-commerce activities include supply-chain management software, customer relationship management (CRM) software, inventory control systems, and financial accounting software—all essential to business success. E-tailing is a growing aspect of e-commerce activity.

In this chapter, we take a strategic perspective in discussion of the Internet. The Internet has become the place to shop, gather information, and browse for new ideas. For retailers it provides an opportunity to connect to the customer anytime, anyplace. Using new technologies provides personalization benefits to engage consumers in the retail experience.

3.1 retailing view
TRYING ON CLOTHES IN VIRTUAL REALITY AT THE LANDS' END WEB SITE

At the Lands' End Web site (www.landsend.com), women can enter information about their body types, including hair colour, height, weight, and shoulder and waist descriptions, such as narrow or generous. Based on their responses, a three-dimensional model resembling their body type appears on the screen. Then customers are provided with suggestions of appropriate apparel for their body type. These suggestions are offered for four apparel styles: dressy office attire, casual office, after-work, and very casual. Using a click-and-drag interface, customers can electronically "try on" different outfits and accessories and see how they look.

In the future, this virtual shopping experience will be made even more realistic by enabling customers to see clothing on their actual body and view the fit from all angles by rotating the three-dimensional picture.

The use of virtual models at some Web sites lets customers "try on" the merchandise.

Sources: Jonathan Boorstein, "Online Mini-Me: 3-D Modeling Enhances E-Commerce Sites," *Direct*, June 2000, p. 101; and Mary Wagner, "Picture This: E-Retailers Aim to Zoom, Spin and Model Their Way to Higher Sales," *Internet Retailer*, May 2000, pp. 56, 58–60.

electronic retailing (e-tailing)

An **e-tailer** is a retailer that primarily uses the Internet as a medium for customers to shop for goods or services for their personal use. According to Forrester Research www.forrester.com, "Nontravel online retail revenues (worldwide) will top the quarter-trillion-dollar mark by 2011. The driver of this growth is a segment of the most active Web shopping households that is approximately 8 million strong. This group of consumers is extremely comfortable with technology and values convenience above all else in the online experience. As retailers begin to wade through their copious data warehouses and understand the who, when, where, why and how of this segment, they will benefit from targeting these customers."

TYPES OF E-TAILERS

There are two distinct types of e-tailers. The categories of e-tailers are pure plays and bricks and clicks. A **pure play e-tailer** uses the Internet as its primary means of retailing. Examples of pure play retailers are Dell and Ebay. A **brick and click e-tailer** uses the Internet to promote its goods and services but also maintains a traditional physical retail storefront available to its customers. A popular example of a brick and click e-tailer is Mountain Equipment Co-op (MEC). This popular outdoor camping equipment and sportswear retailer has an interactive e-tail site that encourages customer interaction and facilitates trading used equipment between customers online.

ADVANTAGES OF E-TAILING

E-tailers who are designated pure play type of businesses have the opportunity to turn higher profit margins, due in part to the fact that many of the overhead expenses are associated with a physical retail space. The expenses involved in rent for retail space, costs associated with designing and fixturing the store, inventory costs for merchandise, and, of course, labour costs to staff the store are significantly alleviated. Pure play allows for the e-tailer to reach customers worldwide while still maintaining only one location for each and every customer to visit, 24 hours a day and seven days a week.

DISADVANTAGES OF E-TAILING

Research indicates that many e-tailers are failing to meet the needs of online customers and that they generally only have one chance to make a good impression if they want their customer's loyalty. In this competitive online world it is said that the three most important things that an e-tailer must work on to ensure retail profitability are "search, support, and promotion."

CUSTOMER EXPERIENCE

Retailers with electronic channels are using technology to convert touch-and-feel information into look-and-see information that can be communicated through the Internet. E-tail sites are going beyond posting pictures: Using 3D imaging and/or zoom technology, customers have the opportunity to view merchandise from different angles and perspectives. The use of these image-enhancing technologies has increased conversion rates (the percentage of consumers who buy the product after viewing it) and reduced returns. Visit www.bombayco.com for a 3D tour of The Bombay Company using technology from www.livepicture.com.

To overcome the limitations for trying on clothing, apparel e-tailers use virtual models on their Web sites. These virtual models enable consumers to see how selected merchandise looks on a virtual model with similar proportions to their own and then rotate the image to see the "fit" from all angles. The virtual models are either selected from a set of pre-built models or constructed on the basis of the shopper's response to questions about his or her height, weight, and other characteristics. For example, at www.landsend.com shoppers choose a model that looks like them and, using a click and drag interface, try on clothes in a virtual environment. Research showed that customers using a virtual model were 28 percent more likely to make a purchase and spent 13 percent more on their average purchases.

Online Shopper Categories According to the Consumer Electronics Manufacturing Association Web shoppers fall into four categories:

* Money Savers
* Smarter Shoppers
* Selection Seekers
* Convenience Lovers

According to Esearch, www.esearch.com, more than half of online shoppers expect a 20 to 30 percent discount from the retail price when buying an item that would normally be priced at between $30.00 and $500.00 at the traditional retail store.

Customer Benefits The two obvious personal benefits are convenience and personal security. Shopping online from home at any time is increasingly attractive to busy consumers who are often time-strapped and security-conscious in light of perceived danger in our society. Another advantage to the consumer is the benefit of a greater selection of products and more personalized information and services. For example, a customer is not likely to buy a new car on the Internet, but research indicates that e-tail influences on retail shopping amongst Canadians tops 60 percent in the auto, appliance, furniture, and garden categories, and that 51 percent of Canadian online shoppers indicate that comparison shopping at multiple e-tailers' Web sites influenced their e-tail purchase decision. Consumers rarely visit more than two e-tailers, even when buying expensive consumer durables.

Customer benefits are outlined as follows:

Broader Selection Consumers can shop electronically at Harrod's in London in less time than it takes them to visit the local grocery store. The Internet provides opportunities for customers and retailers to connect in a global marketplace.

More Information to Evaluate Merchandise E-tailers have the capability of providing more information than the customer can get through store and catalogue channels.[1] The e-tailer can respond to customers' inquiries just like a sales associate would. The information on the Web site database can be frequently updated and will always be available, whereas retaining knowledgeable sales associates is often difficult. The cost of adding information to a Web site is less than the cost of continually training sales associates.

Expanded Web search capabilities make it easier for customers to find the types of goods they are looking for, and, at the same time, to communicate with a retail representative concerning product features.

Personalization The most significant potential benefit of the Internet is the ability to economically personalize information for each customer.

refact

28% of all online shoppers are age 25 to 34.

An **electronic agent** is a computer program that locates and selects alternatives based on some predetermined characteristics.[2] The electronic agent can learn about a consumer's tastes by asking questions when the customer goes to the retailer's Web site.

These agents function as a super sales associate, helping customers locate merchandise they might like. For example, Amazon.com has an electronic agent that recommends books based on the customer's previous purchases. This type of product placement based on previous purchases will increase the visibility of goods that the customer is likely to buy. For example, by customizing the Web pages to highlight products at appropriate price points based on previous purchases, the e-tailer will increase sales and encourage loyalty.

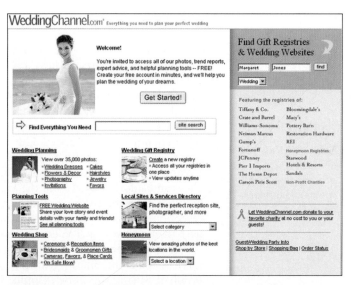

WeddingChannel.com offers merchandise, services, and information for couples planning a wedding.

retailing view
RETAILERS USE CUSTOMERS TO DELIVER SERVICES
3.2

Retailers use message boards and chat rooms on their Web sites to provide a valuable service by enabling customers to communicate with each other. **Message boards** are locations in an Internet site at which customers can post comments; **chat rooms** are locations at which customers can engage in interactive, real-time, text-based discussions. For example, Tomboy Tools (www.tomboytools.com) sells tools and provides home improvement information to women. Its Web site has bulletin boards, called Tool Talk, on which customers can post home improvement questions to which other customers offer solutions.

Authors and visitors to Amazon.com post comments and book reviews. Visitors to electronic travel retail sites frequently post messages inquiring about hotels, restaurants, and tourist attractions at places they will be visiting. Other customers who are familiar with the places respond to these inquiries with their suggestions.

Many electronic retailers offer public chat rooms. At The Knot site (www.theknot.com) people can enter a public chat room and have a real-time discussion about their experiences planning their weddings, seven days a week, 24 hours a day. In addition to the public chat room, The Knot also offers moderated chat rooms in which a staff member or a well-known expert on an issue leads an electronic discussion at specific times during the day.

Sources: Lorrie Grant, "Tomboy Tools Caters to Handy Women," *USA Today*, June 13, 2002, p. D3; Mary C. Hickey, "Click, Click, and a Way!" *Business Week*, March 29, 1999, p. 188; and Rochelle Rafter, "Can We Talk?" *The Industry Standard*, February 8, 1999, pp. 12–13.

Problem-Solving Information   The electronic channel also offers an opportunity to go beyond the traditional product information offered in stores to provide tools and information for solving customer problems. For example, the typical engagement/wedding planning process lasts for 14 months and costs almost $20 000. The process involves many emotional decisions such as how many people and whom to invite, what print style to use on the invitations, where to hold the reception, what music to play during the ceremony, and what gifts to list in a registry.

E-tail wedding sites offer couples planning guides and an opportunity to chat with other couples getting married. Gift registries are created at different retailers and then sent to guests through e-mail. Alternatives for the reception location can be assessed by looking at photos on the Web site and instead of going to hear different bands, audio clips can be downloaded from the Web. Hotel reservations for out-of-town guests can be made over the Internet, and maps created showing the location of the hotel and reception by using mapquest, www.mapquest.com. Post-wedding, happy couples can have their own personal Web site on which they can post wedding pictures.[3]

Virtual communities, networks of people who seek information, products, and services and communicate with each other about specific issues, are examples of these problem-solving sites. For example, iVillage (www.ivillage.com) is a virtual community for women with subcommunities for pregnant women, women with babies, and working women. The site offers information and advice as well as books and apparel for pregnant women and chat rooms in which community members can express their views and ask questions. The Internet is part of a business's service strategy. High-profile private golf clubs, for example, St. Georges, allow their memebers to book tee times via their Web site, and check tournament results and upcoming events. The Internet is also an excellent tool for sports fans to participate in chats (see frontstalk and ohlnoof chat lines). Retailers are ideally suited to offer these problem-solving sites for customers. Retailers have the capability to put together merchandise assortments, services, and information to attract members.

Blogging   A **blog** is a Web site where entries are written in chronological order and displayed. Blogs provide commentary or news on a particular subject such as retailing issues www.retailstore.blogspot.com. Bloggers sometimes lead the way in bringing key information to public light, with mainstream media following their lead. A typical blog combines text, images (photos=photoblog; video=vlog) and links to other blogs, Web pages (weblog), and other media related to its topic. The ability for readers to leave comments in an interactive format is an important part of many blogs. In 2007, blog search engine Technorati was tracking more than 71 million blogs.

Usability Web Design   In an interview, Dr Jakob Nielsen, the Web's usability czar, discusses designing Web usability strategies. Visual appearance is the first thing that the customer will see, but the most important thing is to discover the three main reasons users come to your site and make these things fast and obvious to do. Content should be written to the requirements of the reader: very short and with liberal use of bulleted lists and highlighted words. All pages must download as quickly as possible and assist consumers to feel comfortable buying. Sites lose money because they design poor shopping carts, check out procedures, or handling fees. See www.useit.com for "Top Ten Mistakes in Web Design."

WILL SALES THROUGH THE INTERNET CONTINUE TO GROW?

The electronic channel accounts for about 1 percent of retail sales in North America and Europe and an even smaller percentage of retail sales in Asia. However, the annual growth rate of electronic retail sales is four to five times greater than sales in retail stores.[5] Three critical factors affecting the adoption of a new innovation such as shopping electronically are the ease with which customers can try the innovation, the perceived risks in adopting the innovation, and the advantages of the innovation compared to the present alternatives.[6]

Canadian Online Marketplace   Canadians are taking advantage of the convenience and affordability of buying on the Internet. According to an Ipsos-Reid study, 75 percent of all Canadians use the Internet and 46 percent of those have made a purchase of goods or services online. The most popular e-commerce sites in Canada in 2006 were Amazon.ca, followed by Sears in second place, eBay in third, and Chapters/Indigo in fourth place. Ticketmaster is a popular Web site for online purchases of tickets for concerts, events, and plays. Younger Canadians are more likely to buy online than older Canadians (46 percent of people aged 18–34, 49 percent of people aged 35–54, and 35 percent of people aged 55+ have bought online). It was also noted that there is regional variation in online spending behaviour. The study indicated that 33 percent of Internet users in Quebec shop online, whereas 60 percent of Internet users in British Columbia have made an e-tail purchase.[8] More and more consumers are getting an opportunity to experience electronic shopping. In 2002, over 544 million people globally had Internet access at home or work, with 181 million in North America, 171 million in Europe, and 157 million in Asia.[9] In North America, 66 percent of all primary household shoppers own a home computer and 63 percent have personal access to the Internet at home, school, or work. About one-quarter of the households with Internet access have broadband, high-speed connection.

Mainstream Canadian shoppers are adapting to the online channel:

- Online influences 60% of Canadian purchase decisions for automobile, appliances, and furniture/home and garden categories.

- 33% of Canadian online shoppers indicate that using a search engine to find online stores selling a product influenced their online purchase decision.

- 63% of money that Canadians spend online goes to online merchants in the U.S. (remember there are no borders on the Internet).

- 51% of Canadian online shoppers are information-driven and will comparison shop at multiple online stores.

- 87% of online shoppers are happy with the online retail experience, whereas only 46% were satisfied with the store visit to make a purchase.

- 73% of Canadian online shoppers prefer to pay with their credit card, Visa being the most popular.

- 42% of Canadians are worried about using a credit card online and 36% worry about disclosing private information.

www.fastcompany.com provides the ability to connect with business professionals, share ideas, and join local interest groups. Read *The Experienced Customer* by P. Kelly Mooney, who considers herself to be one click-happy, online-shopaholic.

The substantial Internet usage by young people suggests a bright future for electronic retailing. Teenagers and children constitute one of the fastest-growing Internet populations, with 77 million people under age 18 online globally in 2006. Surfing the Internet is a highly regarded activity by this age group. As one would expect, entertainment products such as games, music, tickets, and videos are the most common purchases by these young consumers.[10]

refact
71 percent of Canadian adults (16 million) accessed the Internet in 2003, making Canadians the leading users of Internet, compared with 70 percent of Koreans and 68 percent of Americans.[7]

refact
North American teenagers make less than 1 percent of their annual US$155 billion purchases online, even though 80 percent have online access.[11]

The fastest-growing segment of Internet users is people over 50 years old.

Several e-tail Web sites now let parents establish an account for their children using a credit card to set the initial balance. The teenager logs onto the site using a password, browses the site's electronic retailer partners, selects desired merchandise, and puts it in an electronic shopping cart. The shopping site takes care of the payment. Using their own passwords, parents can check up on the teen's buying habits and balance.[12]

But it's not just teenagers and young adults surfing the Web. In Canada, adults over 50 years old are the fastest-growing market going online, now comprising almost 20 percent of the Internet users. Seventy percent of Canadians in this age group have home access to the Internet. Studies have found that older people are receptive to new technology and have the time, money, and enthusiasm to surf the Web regularly. They spend an average of 130 minutes a day online, almost 50 percent more than any other age group. Their primary attraction to the Internet is the use of e-mail to stay in touch with long-distance family and friends.

Perceived Risks in Electronic Shopping   Although most consumers have the opportunity to try out electronic shopping, they also have some concerns about buying products through an electronic channel. The two critical perceived risks are:

- the security of credit card transactions on the Internet
- potential privacy violations

Because many consumers are concerned about credit card security, almost all e-tailers use sophisticated technologies to encrypt communications. The perception of risk also is diminishing as credit card companies promote the use of their cards on the Internet and inform consumers that customers will not be responsible for security lapses.[13]

Consumers are still concerned about the ability of e-tailers to collect information about their purchase history, personal information, and search behaviour on the Internet.

WHAT TYPES OF MERCHANDISE WILL BE SOLD EFFECTIVELY THROUGH THE ELECTRONIC CHANNEL?

When you purchase apparel, some critical information might be "look-and-see" attributes such as colour and style, as well as "touch-and-feel" attributes such as how the fabric feels. It is impossible to feel the fabric in a dress, taste a sample of chocolate, or smell a perfume before buying the product through an e-tailer. Customers' ability even to assess colour electronically depends on the adjustment of a computer monitor, and fit can only be predicted well if the apparel has consistent sizing and the consumer has learned over time what size to buy for a particular brand.

Consider branded merchandise such as Nautica perfume or Levi's 501 jeans. Even though you can't smell a sample of the perfume before buying it, you know that it will smell like your last bottle when you buy it electronically because the manufacturer of Nautica makes sure each bottle smells the same. Similarly, if you wear size 30-inch waist/32-inch inseam Levi's 501 jeans, you know they will fit when you buy them electronically.

In some situations, the electronic channel might even be able to provide superior information to stores, for example a picture on the side of the box containing a toy. Shopping online can often provide detailed information and full-motion video clips showing the product in use.

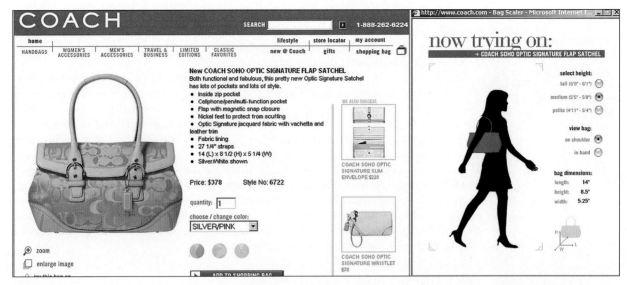

Using 3-D and zoom technology, Coach.com converts "touch and feel" into "look and see" information.

Gifts   Buying gifts electronically offers the benefit of saving you time and effort in packing and sending the gift. For this reason, gifts represent a substantial portion of sales made online because they are sent directly to the recipient.

Services   Some services retailers have been very successful over the Internet. You go to an Internet travel planning service and fill in an online form indicating your destination and preferred departure time, and the electronic agent locates the lowest-cost fare for the flight. To purchase a ticket, you simply click on the purchase ticket icon, enter your credit card information, and get an e-ticket confirmation number. Travel service providers include detailed information about destinations, such as the locations of hotels on a map. Chat rooms provide an opportunity for travellers to share their experiences of hotels and restaurants.[15] Due to the appeal of the Internet for providing services, most banks provide banking services online.[16] Canadian national banks all offer 24/7 online banking as well as credit card and debit card services. Canadians' preference for direct payment is evident: 43 percent of Canadian shoppers prefer using a debit card; 30 percent use credit cards.[17]

Thus, the critical issue determining what types of merchandise can be sold successfully by e-tailers is whether the Web site can provide enough information prior to the purchase to make sure customers will be satisfied with the merchandise once they get it. There are many buying situations where e-tailers can provide sufficient information even though the merchandise has important touch-and-feel attributes.

WILL OFFERING AN E-TAIL SITE LEAD TO MORE PRICE COMPETITION?

Searching for the lowest prices is facilitated by shopping bots. **Shopping bots** or **search engines** are computer programs that search for and provide a list of all Internet sites selling a product category or price of specific brands offered.

While consumers shopping electronically can collect price information with little effort, they can get a lot of other information about the quality and performance of products at a low cost. For instance, an electronic channel offering custom-made oriental rugs can clearly show real differences in patterns and materials used for con-

refact

Travel services, apparel, CDs, video, and computer software are the best-selling product categories on the Internet.[18]

refact

Orvis, a catalogue retailer, had a 60–70 percent increase in sales after adding 3-D technology to display merchandise on its Web site.[21]

struction. Electronic grocery services allow customers to sort cereals by nutritional content, thus making it easier to use that attribute in decision making. The additional information about product quality might lead customers to pay more for high-quality products, thus decreasing the importance of price.[19]

Bricks-and-clicks retailers can reduce the emphasis on price by providing better services and information. Customers might be willing to pay higher prices for merchandise providing exceptional service and reliability. For example, Amazon.com provides a customer with the table of contents and synopsis of a book, as well as reviews and comments by the author and by people who have read the book. When the customer finds an interesting book, Amazon's system is programmed to suggest other books by the same author or of the same genre. Finally, customers can tell Amazon about their favourite authors and subjects and then receive e-mail on new books that might be of interest. The classic response to the question, "What are the three most important things in retailing?" was "Location, location, location." In the world of electronic retailing, the answer will be "information, information, information."[20]

WHY DID SO MANY ELECTRONIC RETAILER ENTREPRENEURS FAIL?

In light of the immense potential for selling merchandise and services over the Internet, one can understand the initial enthusiasm of entrepreneurial companies to get online. However, some of these ventures have not been successful.

Resources Needed to Successfully Operate an E-tail Site To understand why so many of these entrepreneurs failed, and the reason for the evolution to multichannel retailing, you must consider the critical resources needed to profitably sell merchandise over the Internet. The capabilities needed to be successfully sell merchandise online are outlined in Exhibit 3–1 on page 62.

Well-Known Brand Name and Trustworthy Image Brand name and image are important for two reasons. First, a retailer's Web site competes with over 100 000 alternative URLs that consumers can visit. Thus, it is important for a retailer operating an e-tailing site to be well known.

Second, a trustworthy reputation is important because buying merchandise over the Internet is risky. Online shoppers need to believe the retailer will provide secure credit card transactions, deliver the quality of merchandise described on its Web pages, and maintain the privacy of any information revealed by the customer.

Customer Information To tailor merchandise and recommendations, retailers operating an e-tail site need information about the preferences and past purchase behaviour of their customers.

Providing and Managing Assortments of Complementary Merchandise and Services The opportunity to make multiple-item sales of complementary merchandise through an e-tailer is important for two reasons. First, when making multiple-item purchases through an e-tailer, customers reduce their shipping costs. Second, the e-tailer is ideally suited for making recommendations for additional purchase to the customer.

Offering Unique Merchandise Due to the low search cost, price comparisons are made easily for merchandise sold online. By offering unique merchandise through
refact

Merchandise returns can be as high as 40 percent for sales made through an electronic channel, compared to 6 percent for catalogues and even less for store sales.[22]

an e-tail Web site retailers can differentiate themselves and reduce the potential for price competition. Three approaches for offering unique merchandise are:

- private-label merchandise
- branded variants or co-branded merchandise
- prepackaged assortments

Bricks-and-click e-tailers can differentiate themselves by developing their own private-label merchandise that they sell exclusively. For example, the merchandise sold at The Gap and Victoria's Secret can be bought only from these retailers.

Presenting Merchandise and Information Electronically The design of Web sites in terms of the download time, ease of navigating through the site, and sensory experiences plays an important role in stimulating purchases, promoting multi-item purchases, and encouraging repeat visits.[24]

refact
CDNOW, an electronic retailer selling recorded music, spent 79 percent of its revenue to build traffic at its Web site before declaring bankruptcy.[23]

retailing view

DAN AYSAN, TOAD HALL

3.3

Toad Hall, an award-winning family business, had its beginning in 1977. Well known for its heritage retail location in downtown Winnipeg, Toad Hall has become a tourist attraction selling quality toys.

This is not just an ordinary toy store: Toad Hall is among Canada's largest independent toy retailers, offering the widest variety of product with 22 000 SKUs. The product mix contains many hard-to-find items from Europe, including toys, books, and hobby items such as diecast cars, magic supplies, and model trains. Amazingly, an additional 40 000 SKUs can be ordered and delivered, usually in one week. Toad Hall is in a class of its own, as it does not stock popular Nintendo, Disney, or Barbie; instead, it has unique products that one might find in a museum gift shop.

In response to increased competition from big-box retailers, Toad Hall made a strategic move in 1990 to develop an e-tail site. The online sales channel was designed to complement existing mail order and retail store business, as a cost-effective alternative to establishing and maintaining a traditional mail order catalogue. According to Dan Aysan, former financial officer and Internet operations manager, Toad Hall saved itself headaches by outsourcing the e-tailing back-end technologies. The Web site was designed in-house, but the servers and payment processing were outsourced. To expand customer service, the company adopted a database-driven Web site with standardized templates for pages that offered flexibility for customers to search for specialized items. Aysan concludes that, due to the level of security necessary, the sophistication of equipment, and the software needed, it made good business sense to outsource these services.

What makes Toad Hall unique in today's competitive toy marketplace? As Dan Aysan explains, Toad Hall offers merchandise that is hard to find elsewhere, it has prices that are stable, and its reliable supply chain management allows for quick response on orders. Management never underestimates that critical to the store's success is the consistent respectful personal care from staff, whether to an e-tail customer or to a traditional store shopper. Toad Hall is a successful small business with 12 dedicated employees that sells unusual toys.

Sources: Jonathan Andrews, "E-business Drops the 'E'," *CA Magazine*, Toronto, May 2002; Jackie Johnson, "Profiles of Success: Kari England," *Manitoba Business*, Winnipeg: September 1, 2001; Andrew Allentuck, "Toy Story: Find a Niche," *E Business Journal*, Toronto: September 2002.

It is very costly to deliver merchandise to homes, but customers typically bear most of these costs.

Efficient Fulfillment   Fulfillment costs and systems play a particularly important role in the growth of online grocery shopping. Since many items sold in grocery stores are perishable, deliveries must be made when someone is at home to put the perishables in a refrigerator or freezer. Some online grocery retailers avoid the problem by selling only nonperishable merchandise and shipping it via standard package delivery firms. Others are committed to making deliveries within a 30-to-120-minute window and charge extra for this service. To address delivery problems, refrigerated storage boxes with touch-pad security have been installed, enabling deliveries to garages and other secure locations outside the home. Due to the difficulty of passing the high fulfillment costs along to customers, most of the pure play grocery retailers went bankrupt.

Grocery Gateway Inc. of Ontario invested $80 million worth of venture capital funding in the creation of a complex supply chain that allows consumers to electronically purchase everything from bread to beer over the Web. Strategic partnerships have been developed with Longo's supermarket chain and the Liquor Control Board of Ontario. The delivery fee is a flat rate of $8 for groceries for a required minimum order of $60. Staff pick from a 2604 square metre market centre, pack, and deliver to the customer. Selling online means delivering the right product, at the right time, every time to ensure that the customer is not forced to go back to the store to shop.[25] Grocery Gateway was acquired by Longo Brothers Fruit Markets in August 2004.

Developing an E-tail Site   As indicated in Exhibit 3–1, catalogue retailers are best positioned to exploit an electronic retail channel. They have very efficient systems for taking orders from individual customers, packaging the merchandise ordered for shipping, delivering it to homes, and handling returned merchandise. They also have extensive information about their customers and database management strategies to effectively personalize service. Finally, the visual merchandising skills necessary for preparing catalogues are similar to those needed in setting up an effective Web site. Retailing View 3.5 gives Web site design advice that follows from tried-and-true store design methods.

exhibit 3–1   Capabilities Needed to Successfully Sell Merchandise Online

Capabilities	Electronic-Only Retailers	Catalogue Retailers	Store-Based Retailers	Merchandise Manufacturers
Strong brand name and image to build traffic and reduce customers' perceived risk	Low	Medium to high	High	Medium to high
Availability of customer information to tailor presentations	Medium to high	High	Medium to high	Low
Providing and managing complementary merchandise and services	High	High	High	Medium
Offering unique merchandise	Low	Medium to high	Medium to high	High
Presenting merchandise and information in electronic format	High	High	Medium to high	Medium
Efficient distribution system to deliver merchandise to homes and accept returns	Low	Medium to high	High	Low

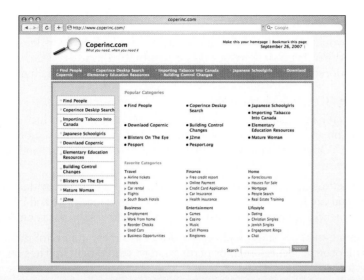

The homepage of this company is an example of services for information management that are available on the Internet.

retailing view
MOUNTAIN EQUIPMENT CO-OP

3.4

Mountain Equipment Co-op (MEC) is a Vancouver-based retailer that strives to make a difference. MEC is a well-recognized brand that has become synonymous with high quality outdoor clothing and gear for cyclists, hikers, mountain bikers, and active everyday users.

The company, founded in 1971, has evolved from a business run out of the back of a Volkswagen van into a successful company with stores across Canada. Much of their success can be attributed to participation by Canadians in a more active lifestyle and the appeal of the company's unshakeable ethical philosophy. Peter Robinson, the company's chief executive officer and former park ranger, explains: The "core purpose is to offer high-quality outdoor gear to our members at the lowest possible price, and we believe in trying to achieve the leading edge on issues that affect social and environmental responsibility."

MEC is Canada's biggest consumer co-operative, with 2.5 million members and 2007 sales of a quarter of a billion dollars. By 2009 MEC will have 12 stores across Canada. According to Robinson, "as a non-profit organization, MEC budgets for a yearly surplus of $2 million to $3 million, a prudent financial cushion." Customers must be members to shop at Mountain Equipment Co-op; a lifetime membership is $5 for one share which enables the customer to vote at the annual shareholder's meeting.

Private label merchandise has become a hallmark of MEC's success and makes up about half of the store's soft goods, including clothing, sleeping bags, tents, and backpacks. Traditionally, in-house brands have the capability of producing higher profit margins for the retailer, but MEC maintains a lower markup on the private label merchandise, and therefore is able to pass the savings on to the consumer. According to Peter Robinson, "We don't

want to have a high margin; we want to offer our gear at good prices." Profit is not the motivator for business growth at MEC.

Mountain Equipment Co-op's philosophy is all about connecting; from connecting to the customer at www.mec.ca, connecting to ethical sourcing for products, to connecting to the planet by building green solutions. Robinson explains that it is essential to connect in a meaningful way to the customer who has "a serious passion for outdoor activity" and to strive to exceed customer expectations.

Suggestions include:

- A retailer would never open up a new store and not let customers know where to find it. When Web sites are not properly promoted, this is essentially what happens. All retail communications, faxes, and mailings should include your Web site URL.

  Your Web site is a product. What can you offer your customers that is of value to them? For example, if you are a travel agent, you might include packing tips or, if you are a fashion store, you could include a list of the season's fashion "essentials." Offer something extra that is related to your product and update it as appropriate.

- Consider setting up a newsgroup on your site for like-minded individuals to connect; you can learn about your customers (see www.mec.ca). Send newsletters to a niche audience, include a "forward to a friend" button (see www.runningroom.ca).

- Permission e-mail is a smart strategy for your customers in light of the invasion of junk mail; provide a check box for permission to send e-mail updates on products and services.

- When considering a search engine, remember that studies indicate that 90 percent of Internet users find Web sites through a search engine, but users rarely look beyond the first page of results. Knowledge of metatags (key words used to describe what your site is about) is vital; you will have a better chance of ranking well in search engines when you use specific phrases in the metatags.

- Keep in mind also that most associations feature a page with links to members' Web sites (e.g., Retail Council of Canada); connect your site also to industry-specific directories (e.g., Office Supplies) and directories of local businesses (e.g., Downtown Business Association).

- Remember that the Internet is a community; the opportunity exists to create a list of businesses with complementary services. [28]

  The top 20 retail Web site designs in 2004 as selected by *Internet Retailer* are shown in Exhibit 3–2.

exhibit 3–2
Top 20 Web Site Designs

Amazon.com
BestBuy.com
Blockbuster.com
Bombaycompany.com
CircuitCity.com
Dell.com
eBay.com
EddieBauer.com
LandsEnd.com
Lego.com
LLBean.com
NeimanMarcus.com
Netflix.com
Nordstrom.com
OfficeDepot.com
Overstock.com
PotteryBarnKids.com
Saks.com
Sears.com
Williams-Sonoma.com

Source: Adapted from "Internet Retailer Best of the Web: The Top 50 Retailing Sites," www.internetretailer.com, December 2004 (accessed July 16, 2007).

WILL MANUFACTURERS USE E-COMMERCE TO SELL THEIR PRODUCTS?

Disintermediation occurs when a manufacturer sells directly to consumers, bypassing retailers. Retailers are concerned about disintermediation because manufacturers can get direct access to consumers by establishing an e-tail site. But as indicated in Exhibit 3–1, manufacturers lack some of the critical resources to sell merchandise on-line. Retailers are more efficient dealing with customers directly than manufacturers are. They have considerably more experience than manufacturers in distributing merchandise directly to customers, providing complementary assortments, and collecting and using information about customers. Retailers also have an advantage since they can provide a broader array of products and services to satisfy customers. For example, if consumers want to buy a dress shirt and tie directly from the manufacturers, they

retailing view
DESIGNING A WEB SITE: LESSONS FROM STORE DESIGN

3.5

Superficially, nothing could be more different. A Web site is virtual and a store is physical. In many but not all cases, good design components appear to transcend the physical world to the virtual world. In other cases, the Web requires a different approach. Consider the following examples:

Simplicity matters. A good store design allows shoppers to move freely, unencumbered by clutter. There is a fine line between providing customers with a good assortment and confusing them with too much merchandise.

Similarly in a Web site, it is not necessary to mention all the merchandise available at a site on each page. It is better to present a limited selection tailored to the customer's needs and then provide a few links to related merchandise and alternative assortments. It is also important to have a search feature on each page in case a customer gets lost. Note: The search feature in the virtual world is similar to having sales associates readily available in the physical world. Also, less is more. Having a small number of standard links on every page makes it more likely that users will learn the navigation scheme for the site.

Getting around. When a store is properly designed, customers should be able to easily find what they are looking for. The products that customers purchase together are merchandised together—umbrellas are with raincoats, soft drinks are with snack foods.

One way to help customers get around a Web site is by using *local links*—links that are internal to a Web site. When establishing local links, Web sites should link

- Products that are close in price, both higher and lower. If you link only to higher-priced merchandise, you might lose customer trust
- Complementary products
- Products that differ from the current product in some important dimension (for example, link to a colour printer if the user is looking at a black-and-white printer)
- Different versions of the current product (for example, the same blouse in yellow)

Let them see it. Stores are designed so customers can easily view the merchandise and read the signs. But in a store, if the lighting isn't good or a sign is too small to read, the customer can always move around to get a better view. Customers don't have this flexibility on the Internet. Web designers should assume that all potential viewers don't have perfect vision. They should strive for realistic colours and sharpness. Some retailers who use the Internet channel have developed interesting ways of viewing merchandise in multiple dimensions (see, for instance, www.landsend.com).

Blend the Web site with the store. It is important to visually reassure customers that they're going to have the same satisfactory experience on the Web site that they have in stores. So even if the electronic store is designed

for navigation efficiency, there should still be some design elements that are common to both channels. For instance, although very different store types, www.tiffany.com and www.officedepot.com have a similar look and feel to their stores.

Prioritize. Stores become annoying if everything jumps out at you as if to say, "Buy me, no buy me." Other stores are so bland that the merchandise appears boring.

Setting priorities for merchandise displays and locations is just as important on the Web site as it is in a physical store. A common mistake on many Internet sites is that everything is too prominent: overuse of colours, animation, blinking, and graphics. If everything is equally prominent, then *nothing* is prominent. Being too bland is equally troublesome.

The site should be designed to advise the customers and guide them to the most important or most promising choices, while at the same time ensuring their freedom to go anywhere they please. As in a newspaper, the most important items or categories should be given the bigger headlines and more prominent placement.

Type of layout. Some stores are laid out to be functional. They use a grid design to make it easy to locate merchandise. Other stores, such as department stores or bookstores, use a more relaxed layout to encourage browsing. The trick is to pick the appropriate layout that matches the typical motives of the shopper.

Here is where store layout and Web site layout differ. Although many higher-end multiple-channel retailers experimented with fancy and complex designs in their early years on the Internet, most have become much simpler and utilitarian than their bricks-and-mortar counterparts (see, for instance, www.polo.com, www.neimanmarcus.com, and www.bloomingdales.com). When shopping on the Web, customers are interested in speed, convenience, and ease of navigation—not necessarily fancy graphics.

Store designers also strive to make their stores different, to stand out in the crowd. A Web site, on the other hand, must strive for a balance between keeping the customers' interest and providing them with a comfort level based on convention. Users spend most of their time on *other* sites, so that's where they form their expectations about how most sites work. So when trying to make a decision about Web site design, good designers look at the most-visited sites on the Internet to see how they do it. If 90 percent or more of the big sites do things in a single way, then this is the de facto standard.

Source: Jakob Nielsen's *Alertbox*, www.useit.com; and "Communicating with Your Customers on the Web," *Harvard Management Communication Letter*, article reprint no. COOO8A, 2000.

must go to two different Internet sites and still can't be sure that the shirt and tie will go together.

Finally, if manufacturers start selling direct, they risk losing the support of the retailers they bypass. For example, when Levi Strauss & Co. experimented with selling custom fit jeans directly over the Internet, it angered many retailers who sold Levi's jeans. Home Depot issued a warning to its vendors indicating that any one attempting to sell directly to its customers would be treated as a competitor.[29]

the evolution toward multichannel retailing

REASONS FOR BECOMING A MULTICHANNEL RETAILER

Traditional retail stores and catalogue retailers are placing more emphasis on their Web sites and evolving into multichannel retailers for five reasons:

- **The Internet gives them an opportunity to reach new markets.** Adding an e-tail site is particularly attractive to firms with strong brand names but limited locations and distribution.

- **They can leverage their skills and assets to grow revenues and profits.** They have a well-known brand name, customer information, vendor relationships, buying power, supply chain systems, and advertising that can include a Web site URL. The stores can also be used as "warehouses" for gathering merchandise to fill e-tailing orders, and the store can provide the customer a convenient pick-up location.

- **An e-tail site overcomes some limitations of their traditional formats.** By adding an e-tailing option to the retail store, retailers can dramatically expand the assortment offered to the customer and the product information that is available.

- **An e-tailing site enables retailers to gain valuable insights into their customers' shopping behaviour.** The e-tail site offers the opportunity to collect detailed customer information and recommend personalized preferences for brand, size, colour, or price. An e-tail site can also be used to get both positive and negative feedback from customers.

- **They have an opportunity for increasing their "share of wallet."** They can increase the percentage of total purchases made by a customer in the store. The e-tail site drives more purchases from the stores, and the stores drive more purchases from the Web site.

When Levi Strauss & Co. experimented with selling custom fit jeans directly over the Internet, it angered many retailers who sold Levi's jeans.

TUNING INTO THE MULTICHANNEL UNIVERSE

The Shopping Channel is based in Mississauga, Ontario, and can be seen on television, in the stores that you frequent, and on the Internet. It is one of the most effective multichannel retailers in Canada. Sales efforts are directed to 7.5 million cable/satellite households, catalogue and direct mail, as well as www.theshoppingchannel. com which draws 500 000 visitors per month. The concept is successful because it delivers what customers want and prides itself on exceeding customer expectations.

The Shopping Channel broadcasts 18 hours of live television each day. This logistics of this are enormous. The retailer carries more than 10 000 products at one time, having between 200 and 1000 items enter the inventory each week. Each item must be photographed, videotaped, catalogued, and made ready for Web sales and for television.

Behind the scenes there is a massive support system operating in a 2790 square metre warehouse and shipping to 10 000 customers a day. A call system manages thousands of calls a day, and if a product does not generate a specified number of dollars a minute it is dropped from inventory. The infrastructure and attention to detail have allowed the Shopping Channel to venture into many different selling channels.

IN-STORE ELECTRONIC KIOSKS

Another multichannel approach to retailing is the addition of the electronic kiosk. **In-store kiosks** are spaces located within stores containing a computer connected to the store's central offices or to the Internet. In-store kiosks can be used by customers or salespeople to order merchandise through a retailer's electronic channel, check on product availability at distribution centres or other stores, get more information about the merchandise, and scan bar codes to check the prices. Retailers are interested in installing these kiosks because they create a synergy between the store and the Internet site. Kiosks provide additional assortment choices that aren't available in stores. For instance, The Source by Circuit City makes slower-moving electronic accessories available at its kiosks so it doesn't have to carry them in the stores.[31] The typical Staples store has 9000 SKUs, compared to 100 000 offered via in-store kiosks.[32]

Do kiosks cannibalize store sales? Yes, but only initially. Shoppers who purchase in stores and online from an in-store kiosk tend to buy more. When REI installed in-store kiosks, it found that customers who shop both online and in the store spend 22 percent more than those who buy only from traditional stores.[33] Staples provided an incentive to store managers to push the use of kiosks. Online sales are credited to the stores from which they're placed.[34]

> refact
>
> Eighty percent of all major retailers plan to install kiosks in their stores.[35]

The Sears kiosk (left) allows customers to look up bridal, baby, or engagement registry and then purchase the item in the store or place an order. The Chapters kiosk (right) also helps customers find specific merchandise in the store by indicating the section where it is located and how many are in stock.

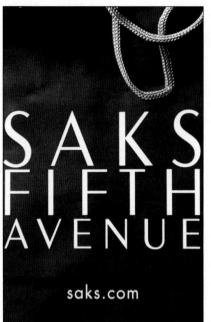

Saks Fifth Avenue, a multichannel retailer, uses its shopping bags to promote its Internet channel.

There are downsides to making investments in these kiosks, however. First, they can be expensive—anywhere from $3000 to $25 000 per kiosk.[36] Second, once the investment is made, there is no guarantee that customers will use them. Gap Inc. abandoned its program because shoppers didn't use them enough.[37] Finally, there are significant costs in maintaining the kiosks—making sure they are working properly.

Customer Service Using Technology Many retailers are installing kiosks with broadband Internet access in the stores. In addition to offering customers the opportunity to order merchandise not available in the store, kiosks can provide routine customer service, freeing employees to deal with more demanding customer requests and problems. For example, customers can use kiosks to locate merchandise in the store and to inquire whether specific products, brands, and sizes are available in the store. Kiosks can also be used to automate existing store services such as gift registry management, rain checks, film drop-off, and credit applications, and to preorder service for bakeries and delicatessens.

Customers can use a kiosk to find out more information about products and how they are used. A Best Buy customer can use a kiosk to provide side-by-side comparisons of two DVD players and to find more detailed information than is available from the shelf tag or from a sales associate. The customer can also access evaluations of the models as reported by *Consumer Reports*. The information provided by the kiosk could be tailored to specific customers by accessing the retailer's customer database. For example, a customer who is considering a new set of speakers might not remember the preamplifier purchased previously from Best Buy. This customer might not know whether the speakers are compatible with the preamplifier or what cables are needed to connect the new speakers. These concerns could be addressed by accessing the retailer's customer database through the kiosk.

Kiosks can also be used to provide customized solutions. For example, a customer, perhaps with the assistance of a salesperson, wants to design a home entertainment system. A kiosk could allow the customer to see what the system would look like after setup. Music store customers could use a kiosk to review and select tracks and make a custom compact disc. Finally, customers could use a kiosk to see how different colour cosmetics would look on them without having to apply the cosmetics. These types of applications could complement the efforts of salespeople and improve the service they can offer to customers.[38]

Customers want to be recognized by a retailer whether they interact with a sales associate or kiosk in a store, log on to the retailer's Web site, or contact the retailer's call centre by telephone.

Integrated Concept In summary, to provide this same face to a customer across multiple channels, retailers need to integrate their customer databases and systems used to support each channel.[39] In addition to the information technology issues, other critical issues facing retailers that desire to provide an integrated, customer-centric offering involve:

- brand image
- merchandise assortment
- pricing[40]

Brand Image   Multichannel retailers need to project the same image to their customers through all channels. For example, Talbots reinforces its image of classic-style apparel and excellent customer service in its stores, catalogues, and Web site. Customers enter the Web site through an image of the red doors used in its stores and are greeted by "Always classic, never closed." At the Web site, customers can consult an online style guide offering seasonal fashion tips and articles about how to buy the right size swimsuit, the art of layering, and petite sizing. Talbots' commitment to "friendly" service is reinforced by the availability of 24/7 personal service.

Merchandise Assortment   Typically, customers expect that everything they see in a retailer's store will also be available on its Web site. A significant product overlap across channels reinforces the one-brand image in the customer's mind. The trend now is to integrate the merchandise offerings across channels.

Other multichannel retailers use the Internet to increase revenues by expanding the assortment they can offer to customers. For example, Gap.com sells more colours and sizes for some merchandise categories than are available in Gap stores.

Pricing   Pricing is another difficult decision for a multichannel retailer. Customers expect pricing consistency across channels (excluding shipping charges and sales tax). However, in some cases, retailers need to adjust their pricing strategy because of the competition they face in different channels. For example, Barnes & Noble.com offers lower prices over its electronic channel to compete effectively against Amazon.com.

Retailers with stores in multiple markets often set different prices for the same merchandise to deal with differences in local competition. Typical customers do not notice these price differences because they are only exposed to the prices in their local markets. Multichannel retailers may have difficulties sustaining these regional price differences when customers can easily check prices on the Internet.

Multichannel retailers are beginning to offer new types of pricing, such as auctions, that take advantage of the unique properties of the Internet.

Customization Approach   The **customization approach** encourages retailers to tailor services to meet each customer's personal needs. For example, sales associates in specialty stores help individual customers locate appropriate apparel and accessories.

Some retailers are introducing a human element into their electronic channel. At Lands' End, customers can simply click on a button and chat—referred to as *instant messaging*—with a service provider. Lands' End was one of the first retailers to offer live chats with service representatives on its Web site. Sales representatives respond within 20 seconds when a customer clicks the Help button. Over 200 of Lands' End's 2500 service representatives are dedicated to providing the service. Lands' End has found that the average order increases 8 percent when customers use the instant messaging service.[43]

There is a growing expectation among customers to interact with retailers anytime, anywhere, anyplace, and to have the retailer recognize them and their transaction history independent of the channel used to contact the retailer. Multichannel retail is no longer a buzzword, but a reality that retailers must recognize in order to sustain market competitiveness. Adding a direct sales channel (mail-order, telephone, or e-commerce) requires a fundamental shift in mindset of a traditional store-focused retailer. The new retail model should be treated as an enterprisewide initiative that must be led by a clearly defined retail strategy based on exceeding customer expectations.

refact
Future Shop has one of the most successful e-tailing sites in Canada. In January 2004, www.futureshop.ca shut down due to a promotion error that offered $200 discounts off electronic purchases; several hundred orders had to be declined.[42]

refact
Canadian retail online site visits grew 16.3 percent from October 2002 to December 2003, and time spent on a site per visitor per month grew 86.5 percent, although online sales account for only 1 to 2 percent of overall sales.[44]

SUMMARY

The chapter "E-tailing Issues—Connecting to the Customer" has been created as a separate chapter within "The World of Retailing" because of the growing significance of e-tailing as an emerging influence on retail revenues.

The Internet and its vast capabilities will enable retailers to gain competitive advantage through developing new strategies. This relatively new form of retailing is evolving to meet the needs of a new generation of technology-savvy consumers: the net generation, aged 8 to 13, who are wired for the future. Canadian online retail sales are growing rapidly at an average annual growth rate of 79 percent.

E-tailing offers expanded capabilities of reaching large new global markets and at the same time developing a one-to-one personal relationship with each customer.

The type of merchandise sold effectively through the electronic channel depends on delivery costs, the consumer's need for immediacy, and the degree to which electronic retailers can provide prepurchase information that helps customers determine whether they will be satisfied with the merchandise. Successful use of an electronic channel overcomes the limitations of collecting touch-and-feel data by offering testimonials from other buyers, providing video information about the experience with the merchandise, or using information about brand–size combinations that fit specific members of the household. For consumers who have previously purchased a branded product, brand name alone may be enough information to predict satisfaction with the purchase decision.

Some critical resources needed to successfully sell merchandise electronically are: (1) strong brand name and image, (2) customer information, (3) skills in providing and managing complementary merchandise assortments and services, (4) unique merchandise, (5) ability to present information on Web pages, and (6) a distribution system to efficiently ship merchandise to homes and receive and process returns. Traditional store-based and catalogue retailers possess most of these assets and thus are better positioned to evolve into multichannel retailers than the entrepreneurial electronic retailers that first started using an electronic channel to reach customers. Disintermediation by manufacturers is unlikely because most manufacturers do not have the capability to efficiently distribute merchandise to individual consumers, provide assortments, and use information about specific consumers to develop individual catalogues for specific customers.

KEY TERMS

blog, *56*

brick and click e-tailer, *53*

chat rooms, *55*

customization approach, *69*

disintermediation, *64*

e-commerce, *52*

electronic agent, *55*

e-tailer, *53*

in-store kiosks, *67*

message boards, *55*

multichanner retailers, *66*

pure play e-tailer, *53*

search engines, *59*

share of wallet, *66*

shopping bots, *59*

virtual communities, *56*

Get Out & Do It!

1. **GO SHOPPING AND INTERNET EXERCISE** Compare the merchandise assortment offered and the prices in your favourite store and on the store's Web site. If there are differences, what is the reason for these differences?

2. **INTERNET EXERCISE** Go to The Gap (www.gap.com), Sears (www.sears.ca), and Lands' End (www.landsend.com) and shop for a pair of pants. Evaluate your shopping experience at each site. Compare the sites and experience on characteristics you think are important to consumers.
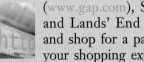

3. INTERNET EXERCISE Examine a variety of online stores. Explain what works for you and what doesn't work for you.

4. INTERNET EXERCISE Visit Toad Hall at www.toadhalltoys.ca
a) Check out the testimonials in the Q&A section.
b) Describe the retailer's philosophy.

5 INTERNET EXERCISE Visit www.bombay.ca and take a virtual tour of the store. Describe the experience.

6. INTERNET EXERCISE Check out www.useit.com, "About Jakob Nielsen," and identify the Top Ten Mistakes in Web Design.

7. INTERNET EXERCISE Visit the retail and e-commerce blogging site www.getelastic.com and take notes of comments on the e-commerce checkout report blog.

8. INTERNET EXERCISE Conduct a Google search for Golda's Kitchen. What did you find in your search for information about Golda's Kitchen?

9. INTERNET EXERCISE Attempt to plan a vacation on the Internet for your next school break. Describe the experience. Did you find that your vacation goals were achievable?

10. INTERNET EXERCISE Shop for a luxury used vehicle on www.autotrader.ca. What did you experience in doing this exercise?

11. INTERNET EXERCISE Go to www.frontstalk.com and www.ohl.ca, noof chat lines. What are the significant marketing implications?

12. INTERNET EXERCISE Go to www.forrester.com. Describe the contents of this site. What services does Forrester offer? Explain.

DISCUSSION QUESTIONS AND PROBLEMS

1. Why are store-based retailers aggressively pursuing sales through an e-tailing site?

2. Why did most of the pure play e-tail entrepreneurs fail?

3. Do you think sales through an e-tail site will eventually have annual values greater than catalogue sales? Why or why not?

4. Why are e-tail and catalogue channels frequently patronized for gift giving?

5. Which of the following categories of merchandise do you think could be sold effectively through an e-tail site: jewellery, TV sets, computer software, high-fashion apparel, pharmaceuticals, and health care products such as toothpaste, shampoo, and cold remedies? Why?

6. What is an electronic agent? What benefit does it offer to consumers?

7. Assume you are interested in investing in a virtual community targeting people interested in active outdoor recreation such as hiking, rock climbing, and kayaking. What merchandise and information would you offer on the site? What type of a company do you think would be most effective in running the site: a well-known outdoorsperson, a magazine targeting outdoor activity, or a retailer selling outdoor merchandise? Why?

8. Outline a strategy for pure play e-tail business that is involved in selling merchandise or services in your town. Outline your strategy in terms of your target market and the offering available at your Internet site. Who are your competitors in providing the merchandise or service? What advantages and disadvantages do you have over your competitors?

APPENDIX 3A   Shopping in the Future

The following scenario illustrates the seamless interface across channels that customers in the future may experience.

SHOPPING EXPERIENCE

It's Tuesday morning, and Judy Jamison is reviewing her calendar. She notices that she will be going to a cocktail party and dinner for the Cancer Society this Friday night. The event is being held at the Ritz Carlton hotel and will be attended by a lot of movers and shakers in town. Judy decides she needs to buy a new dress for the party. She goes to look at some dresses displayed on the Web sites of local department stores. She finds some dresses she likes at one of her favourite stores and decides to go to the store after work.

Shortly after Judy walks into the store, a chip on her credit card signals her presence and her status as a frequent shopper to a PDA (personal digital assistant) held by the store sales associate responsible for preferred clients. Information about items that Judy might be interested in, including the items she viewed on the Web site earlier in the day, is downloaded from the store server to Judy's and the sales associate's PDAs.

A sales associate approaches Judy and says, "Hello Ms. Jamison. My name is Joan Bradford. How can I help you?" Judy tells the associate she needs to buy a dress for a cocktail party. She has seen some dresses on the store's Web site and would like to look at them in the store. The sales associate takes Judy to a virtual dressing room.

In the dressing room, Judy sits in a comfortable chair and sees the dresses displayed on her image. Judy's image is drawn from a body scan stored in Judy's customer file. Information about Judy's recent visit to the retailer's Web site and past purchases is used to select the dresses displayed.

Using her PDA, Judy is able to share this personalized viewing with her friend who is still at work in California. They discuss which dress looks best on Judy. Then using her PDA, Judy searches more information about the dress—the fabrication,

cleaning instructions, and so forth. Finally she selects a dress and purchases the dress with one click.

Using information displayed on her PDA, Joan, the sales associate helping Judy, suggests a handbag and scarf that would complement the dress. These accessories are displayed on the image of Judy in the dress. Judy decides to buy the scarf but not the handbag. Finally, Judy is told about the minor alterations needed to make the dress a perfect fit. She can check the retailer's Web site to find out when the alterations are completed and then indicate whether she wants the dress delivered to her home or if she will pick it up at the store.

As Judy passes through the cosmetics department on her way to her car, she sees an appealing new lipstick shade. She takes the lipstick and a three-ounce bottle of her favourite perfume and walks out of the store. The store systems sense her departure, and the merchandise she has selected is automatically charged to her account through the use of RFID (radio frequency identification).

SUPPORTING THE SHOPPING EXPERIENCE

This scenario illustrates the advantages of having a customer database shared by all channels and integrated systems. The sales associate and the store systems are able to draw on this database for information about Judy's body scan image, her interaction with the retailer's Web site, and her past purchases and preferences. Judy can use the retailer's Web site to review the available merchandise before she goes to the store, to check the status of her alterations, and to decide about having the merchandise delivered to her home.

The scenario also includes some new technologies that will be in the store of the future, such as RFID, self-checkout, and personalized virtual reality displays.

> **refact**
> Less than 3 percent of the consumers visiting a retailer's Web site purchase merchandise.[45]

customer buying behaviour

Executive Briefing

West 49, Exclusively Youth Culture

West 49 knows skateboarders and supports their youth culture exclusively. Sam Bio created the concept dedicated to tweens and young teens and learned that knowing your market intimately is not only good business, it is exactly why he is so successful.

West 49 is a twelve-year-old company that targets the Generation Y market of action sports lovers. Riding the youth market wave, the company has multiplied its sales eightfold since 2000 and has grown from 59 stores to more than 100 outlets in nine Canadian provinces. (Banners include West 49, Billabong, Off the Wall, Arsenic, Amnesia, D-Tox, and Duke's Northshore, www.boardzone.com).

Concern could be that the demographic age 8 to 15 is historically fickle about fashion choices and also about sporting trends. So the big question to Sam Bio is: How do you remain sustainable? West 49 seems to have a finger on the pulse on the evolving needs of the youth segment who strive for a "live big with friends lifestyle." West 49 does not see their business as selling to a specific age group—rather they are selling a dream and a lifestyle, and then the product sales just come naturally.

QUESTIONS How do customers make decisions about whether to patronize a retailer and buy merchandise?

What social and personal factors affect customer purchase decisions?

How can retailers get customers to visit their stores more frequently and buy more merchandise during each visit?

Why and how do retailers group customers into market segments?

West 49 has very specific strategies to sell to tweens and young teens. The tween-friendly environment is a media-soaked retail space devoted to "the brotherhood of the board." At the store, boarders play Nintendo for free and talk easily to young staff who are all sports enthusiasts. Part of this strategy involves their store locations—almost all are in a mall. When appealing to an under-16 demographic, it is important to be in a shopping centre because kids do not drive. The mall is an acceptable and convenient location for most parents to drop off and pick up kids.

The future bodes well for West 49. It is estimated that about one in five teenage boys own skateboards and/or snowboards and, although girls are less active in the boarding trend, many take their style cues from boarding wear. The boarding culture has also moved into mainstream media, and virtually every mountain resort worldwide has snowboarding. Once limited to fringe participation, snowboarding is now a high-tech industry and an extremely competitive sport where top athletes become legends participating in the Olympic Dream.

An effective retail strategy satisfies customer needs better than competitors' strategies. Thus, understanding customer needs and buying behaviour is critical for effective retail decision making. We're not all the same. This is a mistake many marketers make when going after a demographic group, particularly the boomer segment, a population segment that has over half of the country's discretionary spending potential. Consider the teen population: Not all teens are the same. Some are jocks, others are geeks; some like rap music, others like punk rock. Retailers are beginning to realize the importance of understanding the subgroups in the marketplace in order to connect with the customer. You cannot be all things to all customers.

This chapter focuses on the needs and buying behaviour of customers and market segments. It describes the stages customers go through to purchase merchandise and the factors that influence the buying process. We then use the information about the buying process to discuss how consumers can be grouped into market segments.[1] The Canadian marketplace exhibits some general consumer trends:

- Value-oriented consumer; price sensitivity is an issue and consumers will shop around for best price.

- Bigger is better; big-box stores and power centres are popular.

- Consumers are time-stressed; looking for time-saving products and easy to-shop-stores.

- Women are the dominant consumers, with 52 percent of the population and 81 percent of the buying power.

- Tweens (2.7 million kids aged 8 to 13) have money, and influence parents' spending.

- Ethnic markets are growing in Canada, providing retail opportunity.
- Loyalty: What's in it for me?
- Customer satisfaction is a challenging issue; how to retain customer loyalty, adding services becomes a challenge
- Shopping centres need to re-invent; develop a niche image to keep customers returning
- Technology is embraced by most consumers; retailers need to get online
- Aging Canadian population (boomers) will create new challenges for retailers; by 2016 there will be more seniors than children aged 14 and under.[2]

market segmentation

The preceding discussion focused on how individual customers evaluate and select stores and merchandise and factors affecting their decision making. To increase their efficiency, retailers identify groups of customers (market segments) and target their offerings to meet the needs of typical customers in that segment rather than the needs of a specific customer. A **retail market segment** is a group of customers whose needs are satisfied by the same retail mix because they have similar needs. For example, families travelling on a vacation have different needs than do executives on business trips. Thus, Marriott offers hotels with different retail mixes for each of these segments.

The Internet enables retailers to efficiently target individual customers and market products to them on a one-to-one basis.

CRITERIA FOR EVALUATING MARKET SEGMENTS

Customers are grouped into segments in many different ways. For example, customers can be grouped on the basis that they live in the same city, have similar incomes and education, or barbecue at their homes twice a week or more. Exhibit 4–1 shows different methods for segmenting retail markets. There's no simple way to determine which method is best. Four criteria for evaluating whether a retail segment is a viable target market are actionability, identifiability, accessibility, and size.

Actionability   The fundamental criteria for evaluating a retail market segment are:

- customers in the segment must have similar needs, seek similar benefits, and be satisfied by a similar retail offering, and
- those customers' needs must be different from the needs of customers in other segments

Actionability means that the definition of a segment must clearly indicate what the retailer should do to satisfy its needs. According to this criterion, it makes sense for Addition Elle (which caters to full-figured women) to segment the apparel market on the basis of the demographic characteristic, physical size of women. Customers who wear large sizes have different needs than those who wear small sizes, so they are attracted to a store offering a unique merchandise mix. Plus-size retailers have been striving to offer fashion to this consumer group that wants more than just clothing that fits—they insist on style. The plus-size market has been a growing segment of the women's apparel market over the last few years.

On the other hand, it wouldn't make sense for a supermarket to segment its market on the basis of the customer size. Large and small men and women probably have

exhibit 4–1

Methods for
Segmenting Retail
Markets

Segmentation Descriptor	Example of Categories
GEOGRAPHIC	
Region	Pacific, Mountain, Central, South, Mid-Atlantic, Northeast
Population density	Rural, suburban, urban
Climate	Cold, warm
DEMOGRAPHIC	
Age	Under 6, 6–12, 13–19, 20–29, 30–49, 50–65, over 65
Gender	Male, female
Family life cycle	Single; married with no children; married with youngest child under 6; married with youngest child over 6; married with children no longer living at home; widowed
Family income	Under $19 999; $20 000–29 999; $30 000–49 999; $50 000–$74 999; over $75 000
Occupation	Professional, clerical sales, craftsperson, retired, student, homemaker
Education	Some high school, high school graduate, some university, university graduate, graduate degree
Religion	Catholic, Protestant, Jewish, Muslim
Race	Caucasian, African American, Hispanic, Asian
Nationality	American, Japanese, British, French, German, Italian, Chinese
PSYCHOSOCIAL	
Social class	Lower, middle, upper
Lifestyle	Striver, driver, devoté, intimate, altruist, fun seeker, creative
Personality	Aggressive, shy, emotional
FEELINGS AND BEHAVIOURS	
Attitudes	Positive, neutral, negative
Benefit sought	Convenience, economy, prestige
Stage in decision process	Unaware, aware, informed, interested, intend to buy, bought previously
Perceived risk	High, medium, low
Innovativeness	Innovator, early adopter, early majority, late majority, laggard
Loyalty	None, some, complete
Usage rate	None, light, medium, heavy
Usage situation	Home, work, vacation, leisure
User status	Nonuser, ex-user, potential user, current user

the same needs, seek the same benefits, and go through the same buying process for groceries. This segmentation approach wouldn't be actionable for a supermarket retailer because the retailer couldn't develop unique mixes for large and small customers. Thus, supermarkets usually segment markets using demographics such as income or ethnic origin to develop their retail mix.

Identifiability   Retailers must be able to identify the customers in a target segment. **Identifiability** is important because it permits the retailer to determine:

- the segment's size
- with whom the retailer should communicate when promoting its retail offering

Accessibility   **Accessibility** is the ability of the retailer to deliver the appropriate retail mix to the customers in the segment. Customers for Marriott convention hotels and resort hotels are accessed in different ways because they use different sources to collect information about products and services. Convention hotel customers are best reached through newspapers such as the *National Post* and the *Globe and Mail*, whereas resort hotel customers are best reached through ads on TV and in travel and leisure magazines.

Size   A target segment must be large enough to support a unique retailing mix. For example, in the past, health food and vitamins were found primarily in small, owner-operated stores that catered to a relatively small market. In the wake of higher consciousness about exercise and nutrition, health food stores such as Whole Foods have gained customer loyalty. Supermarkets have also expanded their offering of health foods, vitamins, and organic produce to meet this substantial market segment's needs.

On the other hand, the number of consumers in a target segment may not be a good indicator of potential sales. For example, international retailers are very interested in China because it has 1.2 billion consumers. Although many consumers in China's coastal cities have considerable disposable income, 70 percent of all Chinese live in rural areas with minimal incomes. Even in the urban areas, many Chinese consumers are in their twenties and live with their parents in an apartment.[4]

APPROACHES FOR SEGMENTING MARKETS

There is a wide variety of approaches to segmenting retail markets. No single approach is best for all retailers. They must explore various factors that affect customer buying behaviour and determine which factors are most important. Now we'll discuss methods for segmenting retail markets.

Geographic Segmentation   **Geographic segmentation** groups customers by where they live. A retail market can be segmented by countries (Japan, Mexico) and by areas within a country such as provinces, cities, and neighbourhoods. Since customers typically shop at stores convenient to where they live and work, individual retail outlets usually focus on the customer segment reasonably close to the outlet.

In the United States, many food retailers concentrate on regions of the country. For example, HEB concentrates on Texas; Wegmans concentrates on Western New York. However, in the U.K., supermarket retailing is dominated by national firms such as Sainsbury and Tesco. The Canadian grocery industry is dominated by George Weston Ltd., the country's largest food processor and distributor and owner of Loblaws, the country's biggest grocery chain.

Even though national retailers such as The Gap and Sears have no geographic focus, they do tailor their merchandise selections to different regions of North America. Snow sleds don't sell well in Florida, and surfboards don't sell well in Alberta. Even within a metropolitan area, stores in a chain must adjust to the unique needs of customers in different neighbourhoods. For example, supermarkets in affluent neighbourhoods typically have more gourmet foods than stores in less affluent neighbourhoods.

Segments based on geography are identifiable, accessible, and substantial. It's easy to determine who lives in a geographic segment such as the Paris metropolitan area and to target communications and locate retail outlets for customers in Paris. When customers in different geographic segments have similar needs, it would be inappropriate to develop unique retail offerings by geographic markets. For example, a fast-food customer in Toronto probably seeks the same benefits as a fast-food customer in Vancouver. Thus, it wouldn't be useful to segment the fast-food market geographically. Even though The Bay and The Gap vary some merchandise assortments geographically, the majority of their merchandise is identical in all of their stores because customers who buy basic clothing (underwear, slacks, shirts, and blouses) have many of the same needs in all regions of North America. On the other hand, Home Depot and many supermarket chains have significantly different assortments in stores located in the same city.

Demographic Segmentation   Demographics are numbers about people, and this information on the population is collected through a census of the population every four years in Canada by Statistics Canada and in the United States by the U.S. Census Bureau. The law requires that all people living in the country complete the questionnaire accurately. The general demographic information collected is available to all researchers, businesspeople, and students to assist in decision making. **Demographic segmentation** groups consumers on the basis of easily measured, objective characteristics such as age, gender, income, and education. Demographic variables are the most common means to define segments because consumers in these segments can be easily identified and accessed. The media used by retailers to communicate with customers are defined in terms of demographic profiles. Demographics such as gender are related to differences in shopping behaviour.

Who Is the Male Shopper?   It does appear that men are from Mars and women are from Venus when the sexes go shopping. *Men* show little ability or interest in honing their shopping skills, whereas women view the supermarket as a place where they can demonstrate their expertise in getting the most value for their money. Rather than looking for items on sale or making price comparisons, men tend to select well-known brands. They also tend not to pay attention at the checkout register, whereas women watch the cashier to be sure they're charged the right price. Men and women even buy different merchandise. Women buy more health-oriented foods (such as cottage cheese and refrigerated yogurt) and household essentials (such as cleaning and personal health products). Men's shopping baskets contain more beer, cupcakes, ice cream, and hot dogs. Men also do less planning and make numerous last-minute grocery trips. Single men visit supermarkets 99 times a year; single women make 80 trips a year. These eleventh-hour trips make men more susceptible to impulse purchases such as potato chips and cookies.[5]

The Power of Women.   *Women* comprise 52 percent of the North American population and have significant buying power, making 81 percent of all retail and service purchases ($3.7 trillion), and buying 51 percent of consumer electronics, 51 percent of all cars (and influencing 85 percent of all auto purchases), 50 percent of computers, and 51 percent of all travel (EVEolution, Faith Popcorn). Women bring in half or more of the income in most North American households. Unlike their male counterparts, who rely on promotions to make a purchasing decision, women will seek out a product's credibility or discuss the product's attributes with a friend. Well-known retailers such as Home Depot are aware of the importance of understanding gender difference in marketing to both sexes. The big-box stores are recognizing that women are wearing the overalls and are designing stores with wider aisles, detailed signage, samples of finished projects, and lots of helpful staff to assist with decisions. Even men's clothier Harry Rosen understands the influence of women in closing a sale; you talk to the men but sell to their wives. Women are rapidly surpassing men in starting to use online services, and nearly half of first-time Web buyers are women (WiredNews.com). According to GenderMark International, up to 70 percent of women ignore marketing campaigns that don't speak to them and if they have a bad experience with a product or service, on average women will tell 28 people. The bottom line is that women want a more intelligent, more honest approach to retailing. Women make up 80 percent of The Shopping Channel's paying customers, and 50 percent of online shoppers are women ages 35 to 54. It seems that women want it all—make them feel special please online and offline, but when it comes right down to it, they show no loyalty because price matters more than brand.

Knowledge of Demographics Is Critical.   Demographics is critical to understanding product demand and defining a retailer's strategy. Demographics can explain the growth of specialty beers and skin care creams, the demand for healthy food, the trends in real estate, and golf memberships. "A Handy Guide to the Male Shopper," in *Business Week* 2006 identified five profiles: *The Metrosexual*, this affluent urban sophisticate aged 20 to 50, absolutely shops on; *The Maturiteen*, is savvy, responsible, mature, pragmatic, and a technology master; *The Modern Man*, neither retro nor metro in his 20s or 30s, is comfortable with women but doesn't find shopping with them much fun; *The Dad*, ignored by retailers, often shops for family necessities and is in peak earning years; *The Retrosexual*, happy in traditional male behaviour, rejects feminism and moisturizers for men.

4.1   retailing view DAVID FOOT, UNIVERSITY OF TORONTO PROFESSOR & AUTHOR OF "BOOM BUST AND ECHO" AND "BOOM BUST AND ECHO 2000."

David Foot is a best-selling author and controversial guru who predicts the future based on demographics, the study of human populations. According to Foot, demographic factors such as gender, age, and ethnicity can explain two-thirds of everything.

By studying the demographic profile of different generations in Canada, Foot claims to have a window on the future. The essence of Foot's theory is that people at certain ages will engage in predictable activity, and by understanding the population numbers in each age group you can then determine trends in retail, real estate, the stock market, and sports and leisure activities. Although age may not be the most important thing about people, it is the most revealing. Certainly every person is unique, but each individual within an age cohort acts according to a behavioural pattern typical of that age group. Examine the size of the various age groups and it becomes obvious how to predict human behaviour. It is true that many skeptics are opposed to Foot's philosophy and believe that blind adherence to the fad of demographics could be risky.

In the world of retailing, market share can often be predicted based on demographics, but other factors may come into play. For example, attractive demographics may spur a rush of entrants into the marketplace to follow a trend. The result may be intense retail competition and possibly diminished financial returns. Unfavourable demographics in the kid's cohort may indicate a tough time for a children's toy store. Further research will show that although there may be fewer children to demand toys, there are many grandparents to spoil children with toy purchases. As well, the high incidence of divorce means that many children have two homes and therefore two sets of toys.

Demographics, according to Foot, indicate that Canada's population is aging. The drop in the birth rate is one factor; the other is that Canadians are living longer. On average, men live to 75 years and women to 81 years. The reality is that the number of deaths will increase over time as the baby boom (1947 to 1966), eventually becomes a "seniors boom." As a result, it is predicted that after the year 2020 deaths in Canada will exceed births and Canada's population will cease to grow through natural means. However, Canada's population will continue to expand through immigration. This predicted shift in demographics will have a profound effect on all aspects of business and society.

Demographics will not likely be a useful tool for short-term gain, suggests Foot, but if you are planning for five years and beyond, demographics are a powerful planning technique essential to formulating business strategy to recognize opportunities and threats in the marketplace. Marketers and manufacturers count on demographics to take the guesswork out of what new products and services to provide.

Harley Davidson Motorcycles knows about the importance of demographics: In 1990, the company's best customer was 32; in 1998, he was 38; and in 2001, he was even older, at 46. Harley's reputation as the tough guy's bike of choice prevailed when the boomers were young, but as time marched on the company's marketing strategy turned its focus to the middle-aged white-collar boomers. The marketing strategy was a success story in the mid-1980s, but future demographics point to a maturing North American population in which the aging boomer may be too old to buy motorcycles. Harley's new strategy is positioned to develop less expensive bikes and market to women. It was estimated that by 2005, people aged 50 to 59 would control 25 percent of household income in North America.

Harley Davidson's best customer has gone from 32 years old in 1998 to 46 years old in 2001.

David Foot—demographer, professor at the University of Toronto, and author of *Boom, Bust & Echo* (followed by *Boom, Bust & Echo 2000*)—has discussed the impact of demographics on Canadian life. For example, he explains that one-third of the North American population was born after the Second World War. Known as the Boomers (born from 1946 to 1960), by sheer numbers this large group has had immense impact on every aspect of social and economic life.

Tween Consumers In *Growing Up Digital* (1998), author Don Tapscott describes the impact of the Net generation—88 million people in Canada and the U.S. between the ages of 2 and 22—which is imposing its culture and reshaping how society and individuals interact. This new youth culture is smart, savvy, and the first generation to grow up surrounded by digital media: the Internet, computer games, DVDs, MP3, and digital cameras. Food retailers are watching pre-teens under age 14 as they wield incredible purchasing power in North America, spending an estimated $35 billion on food annually. This will certainly influence the move to develop innovative snack options marketed to this age group.

RETAILING TO TWEENS

Tweens, those between the ages of 8 and 13 years, are the fastest growing segment in Canada. The 2.5 million tweens spend $2.9 million annually on candy, clothing, shoes, games, and toys, using money from allowances and birthday and holiday gifts, and also influence the $20 billion their parents spend. This phenomenon is known as *kidfluence*, the influence that kids have over the family's purchase decisions.

The tweens of today are very sophisticated for their young years, primarily because they have been exposed to so much knowledge and information through various media. In fact, television is the number one place that tweens learn about new brands and products. Check out www.ytvmedia.com and learn more about tweens through an annual survey, the YTV Tween Report of activities, attitudes, and lifestyles.

Female tweens spend $700 million a year on retail items, more than double that of boys at the same age. This group has tremendous retail power and is a huge influence on parents' purchases of consumer electronics, computers, home entertainment systems, restaurant meals, and holidays. According to *YTV Kid & Tween Report*, Canada's 2.5 million tweens are given on average $74 of birthday money each year, and a regular allowance of $7.70 a week. Research by YTV also revealed that one in six have a part-time job, babysitting, walking a dog, or shovelling snow, for which they are paid on average $5.60 an hour. It is estimated that Canadian parents spend $800 million each fall on back-to-school clothing and books for tween children. This young consumer is often catered to as working parents compensate for their absence at home by buying whatever their kids want. Shopkeepers often ignore kids, but it is wise to remember that they are the consumers of tomorrow and will long remember poor shopping experiences.[6]

However, demographics may not be useful for defining segments for some retailers. For example, demographics are poor predictors of users of active wear such as jogging suits and running shoes. At one time, retailers assumed that active wear would be purchased exclusively by young people, but the health and fitness lifestyle trend has led people of all ages to buy this merchandise. Relatively inactive consumers find active wear to be comfortable. Initially, retailers felt that DVDs would be a luxury product purchased mainly by wealthy customers. But retailers found that low-income customers and families with young children were strongly attracted to DVDs because they offered low-cost, convenient entertainment.

Geodemographic Segmentation   **Geodemographic segmentation** uses both geographic and demographic characteristics to classify consumers. This segmentation scheme is based on the principle that "birds of a feather flock together."[7] Consumers in the same neighbourhoods tend to buy the same types of cars, appliances, and apparel and shop at the same types of retailers.

The busy staffers at geodemographics are busy tracking consumer habits across Canada postal code by postal code. This is the business of data mining. They tabulate and map information from surveys and census data and then fit together a picture of Canadians. Based on information gathered, they are able to formulate a statistical prediction of the likely behaviour the next time someone picks a movie or a restaurant, or hands over a credit card at the shopping mall.

Geodemographers do not know you by name, but from juggling postal codes and probabilities they have a good idea of your lifestyle and spending habits.

Environics Analytics specializes in data mining. They break the country down into recognizable clusters of consumer habits, by region, city, and even neighbourhood. They have clients who pay to know what consumers want, how to track them down, and how to get their attention. Environics can advise on retail locations, best products to succeed in specific markets, and appropriate advertising strategies.

With each retail transaction, consumers give valuable data that will provide insight into buying behaviour. Retail stores want to track where their customers live and what they purchase, in order to target the biggest-spending potential buyers. Privacy laws in Canada prevent companies from trading customers' names, so they collect information based on customers' postal codes. The idea is based on the premise that people live and act more or less like their neighbours.

Geodemographers group people into clusters, using census data to determine factors such as age, income, education, and ethnicity, and overlay the findings with consumer purchasing and attitudinal data. In Canada 66 consumer clusters were identified, for example, the wealthiest—the *Cosmopolitan Elite*—represents those earning in excess of $330 000 annually, and accounts for only 0.21 percent of the population. They can be found in Toronto's Forest Hill and Montreal's Westmount. The cluster profiles also make a strong case for cultural influences. Environics was able to determine that there were 15 clusters that were unique to Quebec. Quebeckers shop differently than other Canadians, and Quebec cities appear as almost uniform groupings, enjoying good wine, fine restaurants, and high fashion. Research also indicated that Quebeckers and New Yorkers were more fashion conscious than the rest of the country. Only 16 Canadian clusters were similar to clusters found in the United States, leaving 50 clusters unique to Canada.

Some interesting tidbits: There are more coffee addicts per capita in Medicine Hat than anywhere else in Canada; more wine connoisseurs in Quebec; more bottle blondes in Oshawa, Ontario; more dieters in Barrie, Ontario; and more gadget-mad consumers in Vancouver.

Geodemographic segmentation is particularly appealing to store-based retailers, because customers typically patronize stores close to their neighbourhood. Thus, retailers can use geodemographic segmentation to select locations for their stores and tailor assortment in the stores to the preferences of the local community.

Lifestyle Segmentation   **Lifestyle** or **psychographics** refers to how people live, how they spend their time and money, what activities they pursue, and their attitudes and opinions about the world in which they live. When you are conducting market research, you want more information than basic market size and growth. You need to understand your market's attitudes, interests, and opinions. The aim is to narrowly define your target market so that you can effectively sell to the customers with the most potential for sales. Retailers today are placing more emphasis on lifestyles than on demographics to define a target segment.

Although psychographics can provide revealing information about your market, they can also be the most difficult to access. In Canada, the most readily available psychographics information is in the publication *FP Markets—Canadian Demographics* by the *Financial Post*. This annual publication has two sets of consumer "PSYTE" categories. The first examines lifestyle patterns and segments the population into 60 different categories. For example, The Affluents are educated middle-aged executive and professional families with older children and teenagers who live in expensive lightly mortgaged houses in stable, older, executive sections of larger cities. The second set of PSYTE categories provides segmentation based on financial psychographics, for example the Mortgages and Minivans category is a large family with young children. The average household income is above average, but dwelling values are significantly below average. Dual incomes predominate in this group, and jobs are a mix of the white- and grey-collar categories. The tendency towards larger families results in significant expenditures on child care, toys, and sports equipment.

FP Markets (www.financialpost.com/product/prodframe.htm) provides you with the number and percentage of households that fall into a specific category by city or town. Conducting larger scale research can be very expensive, but a suggested affordable option for collecting secondary data is GDSourcing (www.gdsourcing.com). Sometimes it is possible to uncover detailed data free of charge. Check the following: Ipsos-Reid (www.ipsosreid.com), Leger Marketing (www.legermarketing.com), Pollara (www.pollara.ca), Decima Research (www.decima.ca), and Environics (www.environics.ca).

Michael Adams is a social scientist, the president of Environics Research Group, and a bestselling author. In his second book, *Better Happy Than Rich* (2000), Adams looks at money and its changing meaning in the lives of Canadians. He makes the point that today money has achieved an unprecedented primacy as a lens through which we see ourselves and others. Instead of eroding our values, money is becoming the primary manifestation of our values. The way Canadians earn, spend, invest, and give away their money expresses how they think the world works—and how they would like to see it work. [8]

Loblaws caters to the needs of various types of customers and can quickly adapt to changing customer preferences. The Loblaws grocery chain continues to develop

exhibit 4–2
Canada Post's Snapshot
Segmentation System

Canada is an extremely diverse multicultural society of more than 32 million people. Canada Post's Snapshot Segmentation System segments Canada 's population into five major spending categories: Big Spenders, Beyond Basics, Wannabe Shoppers, Smart Shoppers, and Penny Pinchers. This system is designed to provide information to:

- Build direct mail circulation based on target market
- Increase relevance of product offerings
- Customize marketing according to target market's lifestyle and preferences

BIG SPENDERS

Income: $80 000 plus
High maintenance lifestyle
Purchase goods to enhance their status
Respond to direct mail
Use Internet for purchases
Hot Spends: home decor, clothing, garden supplies, sporting goods, toys/games/ novelties

SMART SHOPPERS

Income: $50 000 to $75 000
Work–life balance important
Respond to direct mail
Shop by catalogue
Look for quality, family-oriented products
Shop around for the best deal
Shop online
Hot Spends: household tools, appliances, home decor, digital camera, garden supplies

BEYOND BASICS

Income: $40 000 to $65 000
Empty nesters
Own their home
Enjoy dining and theatre
More disposable income than other segments
Respond to direct mail
Shop by catalogue
Hot Spends: garden supplies, jewellery, flowers

PENNY PINCHERS

Income: $ 30 000 to $ 50 000
Low income/high aspirations
Like to buy for their children
Respond to direct mail
Spend conservatively
Hot Spends: electronics, kids stuff, household tools, computer, sporting goods

WANNABE SHOPPERS

Income: $35 000 to $50 000
"It's all about me"
Impulsive, want to lead glamorous life
Early adopters of technology and new trends
Shop online
Hot Spends: clothing, DVD equipment and home electronics, computer, music/CDs

the President's Choice brand of products by focusing on niche food markets such as organic, ethnic, and prepared food offerings. Under its Fortino's banner, Loblaws is capitalizing on Canada's ethnic mosaic and a growing appetite for international foods.

Lifestyle segmentation is useful because it identifies what motivates buying behaviour. However, it is difficult to identify and access consumers in specific lifestyle segments.

Buying Situation Segmentation   Buying behaviour of customers with the same demographics or lifestyle can differ depending on their buying situation. Thus, retailers may use **buying situation segmentation** such as fill-in versus weekly shopping to segment a market. For example, a parent with four children prefers the supercentre to the Internet grocer or supermarket for weekly grocery purchases. But if the parent ran out of milk during the week, he or she would probably go to the convenience store rather than the wholesale club for this fill-in shopping. Convenience would be more important than assortment in the fill-in shopping situation. Similarly, an executive will stay at a convention hotel on a business trip and a resort on a family vacation.

Benefit Segmentation   Another approach to defining a target segment is to group customers seeking similar benefits; this is called **benefit segmentation**. In the multiattribute attitude model, customers in the same benefit segment would attach a similar set of importance weights to the attributes of a store or a product. For example, customers who place high importance on fashion and style and low importance on price would form a fashion segment, whereas customers who place more importance on price would form a price segment.

Benefit segments are very actionable. Benefits sought by customers in the target segment clearly indicate how retailers should design their offerings to appeal to the segment. But customers in benefit segments aren't easily identified or accessed. It's hard to look at a person and determine what benefits he or she is seeking. Typically, the audience for media used by retailers is described by demographics rather than by the benefits sought.

COMPOSITE SEGMENTATION APPROACHES

As we've seen, no one approach meets all the criteria for useful customer segmentation. For example, segmenting by demographics and geography is ideal for identifying and accessing customers, but these characteristics often are unrelated to customers' needs. Thus, these approaches may not indicate the actions necessary to attract customers in these segments. On the other hand, knowing what benefits customers are seeking is useful for designing an effective retail offering; the problem is identifying which customers are seeking these benefits. For these reasons, **composite segmentation** plans use multiple variables to identify customers in the target segment. They define target customers by benefits sought, lifestyles, and demographics.

social factors influencing buying decisions

Exhibit 4–3 illustrates that a customer's buying decisions are influenced by both the customer's beliefs, attitudes, and values and factors in the customer's social environment. In this section, we discuss how buying decisions are affected by the customer's social environment—the customer's family, reference groups, and culture.

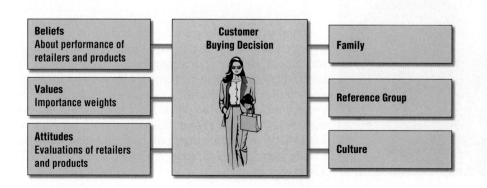

exhibit 4–3
Factors Affecting
Buying Decisions

Many purchase decisions consider the needs of family members other than the shopper.

FAMILY

Many purchase decisions are made for products that the entire family will consume or use. Thus, retailers must understand how families make purchase decisions and how various family members influence these decisions.

Family Decision Making   When families make purchase decisions, they often consider the needs of all family members.[9] In a situation such as choosing a vacation site, all family members may participate in the decision making. In other situations, one member of the family may assume the role of making the purchase decision. For example, the husband might buy the groceries, the wife uses them to prepare their child's lunch, and the child consumes the lunch in school. In this situation, the store choice decision might be made by the husband, but the brand choice decision might be made by the wife, though greatly influenced by the child.

Children play an important role in family buying decisions.[10] Satisfying the needs of children is particularly important for many baby boomers who decide to have children late in life. They often have high disposable income and want to stay in luxury resorts, but they still want to take their children on vacations. Resort hotels now realize they must satisfy children's needs as well as adults'. For example, Hyatt hotels greet families by offering books and games tailored to the children's ages. Parents checking in with infants receive a first-day supply of baby food or formula and diapers at no charge. Baby-sitting and escort services to attractions for children are offered.[11]

Retailers can attract consumers who shop with other family members by satisfying the needs of all family members. For example, IKEA, a Swedish furniture store chain, has a "ball pit" in which children can play while their parents shop. By accommodating the needs of children who might not be interested in shopping, the family stays in the stores longer and buys more merchandise.[12]

REFERENCE GROUPS

A **reference group** is composed of two or more people whom a person uses as a basis of comparison for beliefs, feelings, and behaviours. A consumer might have a number of different reference groups, although the most important reference group is the family. These reference groups affect buying decisions by:

- offering information
- providing rewards for specific purchasing behaviours
- enhancing a consumer's self-image

Reference groups provide information to consumers directly through conversation or indirectly through observation. Celebrity sports people can capture the hearts and wallets of consumers through product endorsements and retailer relationships. Examples include: Canadian professional golfer Mike Weir has a business relationship with Sears. Female golfers might look to Lori Kane or Michelle Wei to guide their purchase decisions. Canadian hockey hero Wayne Gretzky has added his face to Ford's advertising campaign.

Some reference groups influence purchase behaviours by rewarding behaviour that meets with their approval. For example, the reference group of employees in a company might define the appropriate dress style and criticize fellow workers who violate this standard.

CANADA'S MULTICULTURAL MARKET

Visible minorities in Canada have grown threefold over the last two decades and now make up 13 percent of the population. It is predicted that visible minorities will make up 20 percent of Canada's population and 18 percent of the labour force by 2016. Today more than eight out of ten visible minorities are first-generation immigrants. More than 48 percent of Toronto's population is now foreign-born, making Toronto the most ethnically diverse city in the world, and Vancouver is more ethnically diverse than any city in the United States. According to Statistics Canada, in another few years Toronto's population will be more than half foreign-born. Almost a quarter of Southern Ontario residents, 37 percent of Vancouver citizens, and approximately 20 percent of people living in Calgary and Montreal are first-generation immigrants. Across Canada, 5.4 million people are first-generation immigrant Canadians. According to Statistics Canada, immigrants from India, Pakistan, South China, the Philippines, and other south Asian countries will represent the largest proportion of new Canadians by 2017.

Canada has evolving societal issues; no one comes here and discards his **culture** (values shared by most members of a society). These people bring unique culture and world views to Canada, and they also bring unique shopping preferences: They like to shop around, haggle with shop owners, and if they don't feel like they can negotiate a better price, they will shop somewhere else. Haggling is about building a relationship. It is all about learning about the product, talking to a shop owner, and negotiating a special price; think of it as a shopping ritual. For South Asians it is a way of gaining respect. This aspect of Canada's new cultural influx is going to be a challenge for many retailers.

For Canada's large retailers with centralized pricing and buying it will be difficult to adjust prices and product to meet the needs of individual markets. It may be important to connect to community leaders who can talk to people from their population and find out about retail preferences of the ethnic market. Show the market that you are talking to them by acknowledging special times, for example, Chinese New Year.

The one thing that ethnic consumers and aging boomers have in common is their desire for quality service. They know the value of a dollar and they will not trade away quality.

Marketers must understand how new immigrants think before they can market to them, because the solution is not simply to take a commercial and add a voiceover in another language. The way to optimize the multicultural market is to build relationships. It is not just about selling to the market, but rather about serving the market. For example, General Motors Canada capitalizes on the fact that the Chinese culture considers 2, 8, and 9 to be lucky numbers by trying to help customers obtain licence plates reflecting this preference.

In this changing marketplace you cannot afford not to invest in research. Retailers need to keep their research up-to-date and look at their product mix, fashion sizes, and service and match them to the market preferences. Hiring an ethnically diverse staff will also assist retailers to understand the market. The reality is, if you don't keep up with the market someone else will. Two important points to remember:

- Immigrants often arrive in Canada with only money and a suitcase. They will need to buy necessary supplies and household items to set up a home.

- Immigrants are often used to sophisticated marketing from their home country and will look to advertising for information, store product, price, and location.

Wal-Mart began airing ethnic ads in 1998 in Toronto, featuring customers of different ethnicities speaking in their own language.

In addition, not only does retailing have to differ for Canadian and foreign-born market segments, but differences can arise among groups of native Canadians as well. What appeals to the rest of Canada may not work in Quebec. The needs and tastes of the Quebec market are particular to its culture and its self-contained nature. Quebeckers differ in their shopping behaviour; retailers who are not of Quebec origin generally have a tough time becoming successful in this marketplace. Many non-Quebec retailers who have entered the market have had limited success and subsequently have left the market. Quebeckers are loyal to Quebec-based retailers whether they are francophone or not. Quebec represents its own media universe that is unique in Canada; the province has more beauty and fashion publications than the rest of Canada combined. Tween girls have a strong cultural background where pop icons and cultural references are different; for example, when Britney Spears is hot, she's hot in Quebec too, but most of the Quebec pop icons are francophones. It is good to tie your product to a spokesperson, but make sure that you know the market to find the best match for your product. Young Quebeckers watch French-language movies and reality shows, and are not fond of clothes displaying big logos and brand names that may be popular in the rest of Canada. Language is responsible for fundamental cultural distinctions.[13]

Subcultures are distinctive groups of people within a culture. Members of a subculture share some customs and norms with the overall society but also have some unique perspectives.[14] Subcultures can be based on geography (southerners), age (baby boomers), ethnicity (Asian Canadians), or lifestyle (punks).

IMPACT OF THE EXTERNAL ENVIRONMENT

Environmental segmentation may occur through external forces that a retailer can neither foresee nor control. For example, SARS (Severe Acute Respiratory Syndrome) in Toronto in the spring of 2003 had an immense impact on retail sales. Toronto shoppers were reluctant to mingle in stores and malls and avoided public places, and the drop in retail sales hit most retail sectors in the city, with one exception: supermarkets and grocery stores. Consumers avoiding restaurants made the move to home-cooked meals during the outbreak, and grocery stores benefited. The effect of the first outbreak of SARS during April 2003 saw retail sales in Toronto fall 3.8 percent while dropping only 0.1 percent in the rest of Canada. It is important to understand that Toronto retail sales account for about 40 percent of Ontario sales, and 15 percent of all Canadian retail sales. The impact of SARS was compounded as tourists avoided not only Toronto, but also resort and entertainment offerings throughout Ontario.

Another example of a disastrous, uncontrollable environmental segmentation occurred with BSE (Bovine Spongiform Encephalopathy) in Western Canada in the spring of 2003. The deadly BSE scare resulted in the systematic destruction of valuable herds of cattle and, at the same time, the destruction of farm livelihoods. The impact on the beef industry was felt across the country as Canadians avoided eating beef and the Canadian beef export market closed. Although only one BSE-infected cow was found, the lingering impact to the beef industry ($7.8 billion to the Canadian economy) will have long-term consequences.

The external environment in the context of a global concern may pressure consumer buying decisions. For example, a negative psychological impact on the consumer occurred as the effect of 9/11 sent shivers of fear throughout the North American marketplace and had a negative impact on airline sales to resort destinations.[15] Restrictions on carry-on luggage on major airlines had a devastating impact on duty-free sales at airports around the world in 2006.

consumer behaviour toward fashion

Many retailers, particularly department and specialty stores, sell fashionable merchandise. To profitably sell this type of merchandise, retailers need to:

- understand how fashions develop and diffuse through the marketplace
- use operating systems that enable them to match supply and demand for this volatile merchandise

Fashion is a type of product or a way of behaving that is temporarily adopted by a large number of consumers because the product or behaviour is considered to be socially appropriate for the time and place.[16] For example, in some social groups, it is or was fashionable to have brightly coloured hair, play golf, wear a coat made from animal fur, have a beard, or go to an expensive health spa for a vacation. In many retail environments, however, the term *fashion* is typically associated with apparel and accessories.

CUSTOMER NEEDS SATISFIED BY FASHION

Fashion gives people an opportunity to satisfy many emotional and practical needs. Through fashions, people develop their own identity. They can use fashions to manage their appearance, express their self-image and feelings, enhance their egos, and make an impression on others. Through the years, fashions have become associated with specific lifestyles or roles people play. You wear different clothing styles when you are attending class, going out on a date, or interviewing for a job.

Fashion also can be used to communicate with others. For example, you might wear a classic business suit when interviewing for a job at Sears but more informal attire when interviewing for a job with Abercrombie & Fitch. These different dress styles would indicate your appreciation and understanding of the differences in the cultures of these firms.

People use fashions both to develop their own identity and to gain acceptance from others. These two benefits of fashion can be opposing forces. If you choose to wear something radically different, you will achieve recognition for your individuality but might not be accepted by your peers. To satisfy these conflicting needs, manufacturers and retailers offer a variety of designs and combinations of designs that are fashionable and still enable consumers to express their individuality.

WHAT CREATES FASHION?

Fashion is affected by economic, sociological, and psychological factors.

Economic Factors Fashion merchandise is a luxury. It includes design details that go beyond satisfying basic functional needs. Thus, demand for fashion merchandise is greatest in countries with a high level of economic development and in market segments with the greatest disposable income.

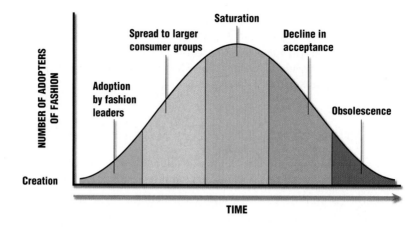

exhibit 4–4
Stages in the Fashion Life Cycle

Sociological Factors   Fashion changes reflect changes in our social environment, our feelings about class structure, the roles of women and men, and the structure of the family. For example, time pressures arising from the increased number of women in the workforce have led to the acceptance of low-maintenance, wrinkle-resistant fabrics. Rising concern for the environment has resulted in natural fibres becoming fashionable and fur coats going out of fashion. Interest in health and fitness has made it fashionable to exercise and wear jogging clothes, leotards, and running shoes.

Psychological Factors   Consumers adopt fashions to overcome boredom. People get tired of wearing the same clothing and seeing the same furniture in their living room. They seek changes in their lifestyles by buying new clothes or redecorating their houses.

HOW DO FASHIONS DEVELOP AND SPREAD?

Fashions are not universal. A fashion can be accepted in one geographic region, country, or age group and not in another. In the 1970s, the fashion among young women was ankle-length skirts, argyle socks, and platform shoes, while older women were wearing pantsuits, double-breasted blazers, and midheeled shoes. During the 1970s, natural hairstyles were fashionable among African Americans, whereas cornrow hairstyles became fashionable in the early 1980s.

   The stages in the fashion life cycle are shown in Exhibit 4–4. The cycle begins with the creation of a new design or style. Then some consumers recognized as fashion leaders or innovators adopt the fashion and start a trend in their social group. The fashion spreads from the leaders to others and is accepted widely as a fashion. Eventually, the fashion is accepted by most people in the social group and can become overused. Saturation and overuse set the stage for a decline in popularity and the creation of new fashions.

Creation   New fashions arise from a number of sources. Couture fashion designers are only one source of creative inspiration. Fashions are also developed by creative consumers, celebrities, and even retailers. Courteney Cox and Jennifer Aniston, two actors in the TV program *Friends*, created an interest in wearing hair accessories such as banana clips and scrunchies. Britney Spears popularized low-rider jeans. The Sungil baby carrier was designed by American Ann Moore based on slings she saw African women use.[17]

refact

The bikini was designed by a former civil engineer, Louis Reard, in 1947.[18]

Celebrities such as Avril Lavigne played a major role in creating the low-rider fashion.

The trickle-down theory suggests that new fashions start with upper-class people buying the latest fashions presented at designer shows.

Adoption by Fashion Leaders   The fashion life cycle really starts when the fashion is adopted by leading consumers. These initial adopters of a new fashion are called *fashion leaders* or *innovators*. They are the first people to display the new fashion in their social group. If the fashion is too innovative or very different from currently accepted fashion, the style might not be accepted by the social group, thus prematurely ending the life cycle.

Three theories have been proposed to explain how fashion spreads within a society. The **trickle-down theory** suggests that the fashion leaders are consumers with the highest social status—wealthy, well-educated consumers. After they adopt a fashion, the fashion trickles down to consumers in lower social classes. When the fashion is accepted by the lowest social class, it is no longer acceptable to the fashion leaders in the highest social class.

Manufacturers and retailers stimulate this trickle-down process by copying the latest styles displayed at designer fashion shows and sold in exclusive specialty stores. These copies, referred to as **knock-offs**, are sold at lower prices through retailers targeting a broader market. For example, shortly after the models walk down the runway at Prada's annual fashion show in Milan, Italy, displaying the latest designs using pajama prints and gold lamé, sewing machines are whirring 10 000 km away in Hong Kong, churning out men's cotton "medallion" print shirts. Six month later, these shirts, which look a lot like Prada's pajama designs, appear in H & M stores selling for $44.[19]

The second theory, the **mass-market theory**, suggests that fashions spread across social classes. Each social class has its own fashion leaders who play a key role in their own social networks. Fashion information "trickles across" social classes rather than down from the upper classes to the lower classes. Department stores use teen boards to stimulate diffusion of fashion across social classes. Social leaders are selected to be members of the board and promote the retailer and the merchandise sold in its stores.

However, consumers often can distinguish between hype and buzz. **Buzz** is genuine, street-level excitement about a hot new product; **hype** is artificially generated word of mouth, manufactured by public relations people. Sometimes hype and buzz converge. For example, shortly after the launch of the "Yo Quiero Taco Bell!" advertising campaign featuring the talking Latino Chihuahua, the dog started showing up on skateboards in Venice Beach, California, and on black-market T-shirts.[20]

The third theory, the **subculture theory**, is based on the development of recent fashions. Subcultures of mostly young and less affluent consumers, such as motorcycle riders and urban rappers, started fashions for such things as colourful fabrics, T-shirts, sneakers, jeans, black leather jackets, and surplus military clothing. These fashions started with people in lower-income consumer groups and "trickled up" to mainstream consumer classes. Nike employs "cool-hunters" to canvass subcultures to find out what will be the next hot sneaker.

The goth scene is an example of a subculture that has developed a unique style. It revolves around dark fashion and even darker, moody music performed by artists such as Marilyn Manson. Hot Topics, a Pomona, California–based mall retailer, is the goth Gap, selling clothing and accessories to hip-hop kids, punks, and lounge rats. Some goth fashions are black lipstick, nail polish, and eyeliner as well as silver bracelets and earrings, black rubber pants, hooded capes, black fishnet leggings, and fitted, square-neck velvet gowns. Popular items at Hot Topics are two dolls, Misery and Tragedy, dressed in goth fashion—the Ken and Barbie dolls of goth.[21]

These theories of fashion development indicate that fashion leaders can come from many different places and social groups. In our diverse society, many types of consumers have the opportunity to be the leaders in setting fashion trends.

SPREAD TO LARGE CONSUMER GROUPS

During this stage, the fashion is accepted by a wider group of consumers referred to as early adopters. The fashion becomes increasingly visible, receives greater publicity and media attention, and is readily available in retail stores.

The relative advantage, compatibility, complexity, trialability, and observability of a fashion affect the time it takes the fashion to spread through a social group. New fashions that provide more benefits have a higher relative advantage compared to existing fashions, and these new fashions spread faster. Fashions are often adopted by consumers because they make people feel special. Thus, more exclusive fashions such as expensive clothing are adopted more quickly in an affluent target market. On a more utilitarian level, clothing that is easy to maintain, such as wrinkle-free pants, will diffuse quickly in the general population.

Compatibility is the degree to which the fashion is consistent with existing norms, values, and behaviours. When new fashions aren't consistent with existing norms, the number of adopters and the speed of adoption are lower. Since the mid-1960s, the fashion industry has repeatedly attempted to revive the miniskirt. It has had only moderate success because the group of women with the most disposable income to spend on fashion are baby boomers, many of whom no longer find the miniskirt a relevant fashion for their family-oriented lifestyles.

Complexity refers to how easy it is to understand and use the new fashion. Consumers have to learn how to incorporate a new fashion into their lifestyle. For example, at times, tie manufacturers have tried to stimulate sales of bow ties but were unsuccessful because men had difficulty tying the knot.

Trialability refers to the costs and commitment required to initially adopt the fashion. For example, when consumers need to spend a lot of money buying a new type of expensive jewellery to be in fashion, the rate of adoption is slower than if the fashion simply requires wearing jewellery that the consumer already owns on a different part of the body.

Observability is the degree to which the new fashion is visible and easily communicated to others in the social group. Clothing fashions are very observable compared to fashions for the home, such as sheets and towels. It is therefore likely that a fashion in clothing will spread more quickly than a new colour scheme or style for the bedroom.

Fashion retailers engage in many activities to increase the adoption and spread of a new fashion through their target market. Compatibility is increased and complexity is decreased by showing consumers how to coordinate a new article of fashion clothing with other items the consumer already owns. Trialability is increased by providing dressing rooms so customers can try on clothing and see how it looks on them. Providing opportunities for customers to return merchandise also increases trialability. Retailers increase observability by displaying fashion merchandise in their stores and advertising it in newspapers.

SATURATION

In this stage, the fashion achieves its highest level of social acceptance. Almost all consumers in the target market are aware of the fashion and have decided either to accept or to reject it. At this point, the fashion has become old and boring to many people.

DECLINE IN ACCEPTANCE AND OBSOLESCENCE

When fashions reach saturation, they have become less appealing to consumers. Because most people have already adopted the fashion, it no longer provides an opportunity for people to express their individuality. Fashion creators and leaders are beginning to experiment with new fashions. The introduction of a new fashion speeds the decline of the preceding fashion.

SUMMARY

This chapter takes a look at trends that are impacting consumer buying decisions. Based on life stage and lifestyle influences, dominant market segments are emerging to reshape the retail environment; for example, the influential tween market and the time-starved working woman. The very nature of our multitasking lifestyles will influence how and where we choose to shop in the future.

Understanding consumer buying behaviour is essential to describing a retailer's target market. Awareness of the consumer's needs will assist the retailer in developing a strategic plan that includes the right product, at the right price, and available at a desired retailer.

To satisfy customer needs, retailers must thoroughly understand how customers make store choice and purchase decisions and the factors they consider when deciding. This chapter describes the six stages in the buying process (need recognition, information search, evaluation of alternatives, choice of alternatives, purchase, and postpurchase evaluations) and

how retailers can influence their customers at each stage. The importance of the stages depends on the nature of the customer's decision. When decisions are important and risky, the buying process is longer; customers spend more time and effort on information search and evaluating alternatives. When buying decisions are less important to customers, they spend little time in the buying process and their buying behaviour may become habitual. The buying process of consumers is influenced by their personal beliefs, attitudes, and values and by their social environment. The primary social influences are provided by the consumers' families, reference groups, and culture.

To develop cost-effective retail programs, retailers group customers into segments. Some approaches for segmenting markets are based on geography, demographics, geodemographics, lifestyles, usage situations, and benefits sought. Since each approach has its advantages and disadvantages, retailers typically define their target segment by several characteristics.

KEY TERMS

accessibility, *77*

actionability, *76*

benefit segmentation, *85*

buying situation
  segmentation, *84*

buzz, *92*

compatibility, *92*

complexity, *92*

composite segmentation, *85*

culture, *87*

demographic segmentation, *79*

fashion, *89*

geodemographic
  segmentation, *82*

geographic segmentation, *78*

hype, *92*

identifiability, *77*

knock-off, *91*

lifestyle, *83*

lifestyle segmentation, *83*

mass-market theory, *91*

observability, *93*

psychographics, *83*

reference group, *86*

retail market segment, *76*

subculture, *88*

subculture theory, *92*

trialability, *92*

trickle-down theory, *91*

Get Out & Do It!

1. **OLC EXERCISE** Access the Online Learning Centre at www.mcgrawhill.ca/olc/levy to develop a multi-attribute model describing your evaluation and decision concerning some relatively expensive product you bought recently, such as a car or consumer electronics. Open the multiattribute model exercise. List the attributes you considered in the left-hand column. List the alternatives you considered in the top row. Now fill in the importance weight for each attribute in the second column on the left (10—very important, 1—very unimportant). Now fill in your evaluation of each product on each attribute (10—excellent performance, 1—poor performance). Based on your weight and beliefs, the evaluation of each product is shown in the bottom row. Did you buy the product with the highest evaluation?

2. **INTERNET EXERCISE** Visit SRI's Web site at www.future.sri.com/VALS/presurvey. shtml. Click on the "Take the survey" button near the bottom of the page and answer the questions used to classify people into different VALS segments. When you have completed the survey and click on "submit," you should get a form that states your primary and secondary types. You can read descriptions of the types at www.

future.sri.com/VALS/ types.shtml. Type up a two-page, double-spaced report on what the survey said about you and whether you agree with it.

3. **INTERNET EXERCISE** Go to the following Internet sites offering information about the latest fashions: www.style. com (*Vogue*), www.fashioninformation. com (U.K.), www.fashion.telegraph. co.uk (U.K.), www.t-style.com (Japan), and www. infomat.com/information/trends. Write a report describing the latest apparel fashions that are being shown by designers. Which of these fashions do you think will be popular? Why?

4. **INTERNET EXERCISE** Check out www. ytvmedia.com and learn more about tweens.

5. **INTERNET EXERCISE** What are the consumer trends at www.trendwatching. com?

6. **INTERNET EXERCISE** How does West 49 connect to their tween customers?
   a) What influences purchases for tweens?
   b) Visit www.boardzone.com.

DISCUSSION QUESTIONS AND PROBLEMS

1. Does the customer buying process end when a customer buys some merchandise? Explain your answer.

2. What would get a consumer to switch from making a habitual choice decision to eat at Wendy's to making a limited or extended choice decision?

3. Reflect on your decision process in selecting a university. (Universities are nonprofit service retailers.) Was your decision-making process extensive, limited, or habitual?

4. Why is geodemographic segmentation used by retailers to locate stores?

5. Any retailer's goal is to get a customer in its store to stop searching and buy a product at its outlet. How can a sporting goods retailer ensure that the customer buys athletic equipment at its outlet?

6. A family-owned used CD store across the street from a major university campus wants to identify the various segments in its market. What approaches might the store owner use to segment its market? List two potential target market segments based on this segmentation approach. Then contrast the retail mix that would be most appropriate for two potential target segments.

7. Develop a demographic profile for two different target market segments for a hardware store. Outline the difference in the retail mixes that would be most appealing to each of these target markets.

8. How would you expect the buying decision process to differ when shopping on the Internet compared to shopping in a store?

9. Using the multiattribute attitude model, identify the probable choice of a local car dealer for a young single woman and for a retired couple with limited income (see the table that follows). What can the national retail chain do to increase the chances of the retired couple patronizing its dealership? You can use the multiattribute model template at the Online Learning Centre (www.mcgrawhill.ca/olc/levy) to analyze this information.

	IMPORTANCE WEIGHTS		PERFORMANCE BELIEFS		
Performance Attributes	Young Single Woman	Retired Couple	Local Gas Station	National Service Chain	Local Car Dealer
Price	2	10	9	10	3
Time to complete repair	8	5	5	9	7
Reliability	2	9	2	7	10
Convenience	8	3	3	6	5

retailing strategy

CHAPTER FIVE
RETAIL MARKET
STRATEGY

CHAPTER SIX
RETAIL LOCATIONS
STRATEGY—TRADE AREA
DECISIONS AND SITE
ASSESSMENT

CHAPTER SEVEN
STORE DESIGN,
LAYOUT, AND VISUAL
MERCHANDISING
STRATEGY

CHAPTER EIGHT
INTERNATIONAL
RETAILING STRATEGY

Section I described retail management decisions; the different types of retailers, including how retailers use multiple selling channels—stores, the Internet, and catalogues—to reach their customers; and factors that affect consumers' buying decisions. This broad overview of retailing provided the background information needed to develop and implement an effective retail strategy.

Section II discusses strategic decisions made by retailers.

Chapter 5 describes the development of a retail market strategy.

Chapter 6 discusses the location strategy for retail outlets including trade areas analysis and site assessment.

Chapter 7 examines the retailer's strategy for store design, layout, and visual impact to encourage sales.

Chapter 8 discusses strategies that retailers assess when considering international retail opportunities.

These decisions are strategic rather than tactical because they involve committing significant resources to developing long-term advantages over competition in a target market segment.

CHAPTER 5

retail market strategy

Executive Briefing

Robert Dutton, President and CEO, RONA Inc.

RONA was established in 1939 as a buying group for independent Quebec hardware retailers. RONA has evolved from a dealer-owned chain into a publicly traded company. Robert Dutton, president of RONA, sees the company as the market leader in hardware, and forecasts a 25 percent market share by 2007. Dutton's growth plans entail building new corporate stores, signing up franchisees, and inking affiliate deals that will make RONA their distributor.

In 2000 RONA purchased the 66-store chain Cashway Building Centres; in 2001 western-based Revelstoke and Revy and Ontario's Lansing were added to the RONA banner. Rona has also purchased the Chester Dawe Ltd. chain of stores in Newfoundland. More recently the company is benefiting from economic growth in Western Canada.

RONA is a mixed toolbox with a variety of retail formats, including big boxes, franchisee stores, and independents. The stores have been designed with a boutique approach to merchandising departments called "RONA Zones." The RONA zone concept includes easy-to-shop fully decorated departments, including a colour centre, kitchen boutique, and a seasonal zone. The store also boasts an installation service and an indoor lumberyard with drive-through shopping. RONA's customer-focused approach and knowledgeable staff create a shopping experience unique in the home improvement industry.

The battle for the home hardware man, or more often today, woman, continues across Canada with the three major competitors RONA, Home Depot, and Home Hardware all doing about $4 billion a year in Canadian sales. The home hardware retail market is extremely competitive, and RONA's aggressive expansion and rising stock prices are impressive, but are they positioned to battle the newest competitor? The entrance of the U.S. hardware giant Lowes will pressure all players in the battle for the home hardware consumer.

In 2005, RONA signed a deal as official home improvement partner for the Vancouver Organizing Committee for the 2010 Olympic and Paralympic Winter Games, an investment it hopes will pay off with a boost in brand recognition, especially in Western Canada. Included in the deal were the sponsorship rights for the Canadian Olympic team in Turin 2006 and Beijing in 2008. The deal is valued at $68 million, including a $7 million investment in youth sports initiatives.

RONA's aggressive bid to secure a spot as a leader in home improvement retailing in Canada will no doubt continue to keep the company in the headlines.

The growing intensity of retail competition due to the emergence of new competitors, formats, and technologies, as well as shifts in consumer preferences is forcing retailers to devote more attention to long-term strategic planning. This chapter on retailing strategy is the bridge between understanding the world of retailing, that is, the analysis of the retail environment, and the more tactical merchandise management decisions and store operations activities undertaken to implement the retail strategy. The retail strategy provides the direction retailers need to take to deal effectively with their environment, their customers, and competitors.[1]

Canadian retailers must be innovative and differentiate themselves from their competitors if they are to survive in a marketplace that is characterized by a blurring of retail channels, increasing competition, and changing consumer preferences.

Retailers need to examine every aspect of their business; assessing the "easy-to-navigate" factor of their store layout, merchandise offerings, efficiency of distribution systems, service attributes, loyalty programs, and their position in the retail marketplace.

> refact
>
> The word *strategy* comes from the Greek word meaning the "art of the general."[2]

what is a retail strategy?

The term *strategy* is frequently used in retailing. For example, retailers talk about their merchandise strategy, promotion strategy, location strategy, and private-brand strategy. In fact, the term is used so commonly it appears that all

exhibit 5–1
Retail Strategy

☐ **The Retail Mix**

☐ **External/Environmental Factors**

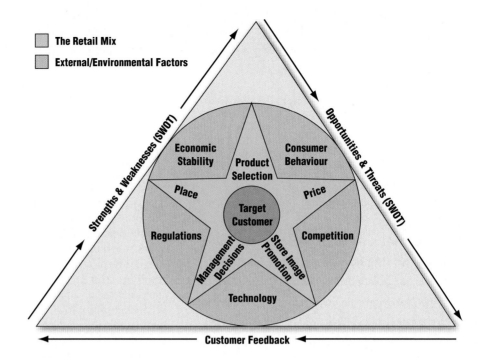

retailing decisions are now strategic decisions. But retail strategy isn't just another expression for retail management.

DEFINITION OF RETAIL MARKET STRATEGY

A retail strategy is a statement identifying the retailer's

- target market
- the format the retailer plans to use to satisfy the target market's needs
- the bases upon which the retailer plans to build a sustainable competitive
  advantage[3]

The **target market** is the market segment(s) toward which the retailer plans to
focus its resources and retail mix. A **retail format** is the retailer's mix (nature of merchandise and services offered, pricing policy, advertising and promotion program,
approach to store design and visual merchandising, and typical location). A **sustainable competitive advantage** is an advantage over competition that cannot be easily
copied and can be maintained over a long period of time. Here are two examples of a
retailing strategies.

- Curves has grown to more than 8400 franchises in all 50 states and 28 countries,
  making it by far the world's top fitness centre in terms of number of clubs. One
  in every four fitness clubs in the United States is a Curves. Other clubs go after
  the prized 18-to-34-year-old demographic segment; Curves' customers are
  aging baby boomers, typically living in small towns. This retailer's fitness centres
  don't have treadmills, saunas, locker rooms, mirrors, aerobics classes, or free
  weights. Members work out on 8 to 12 hydraulic resistance machines, stopping
  between stations to walk or jog in place. The clubs' standard routine is finished
  in 30 minutes and designed to burn 500 calories. Club members usually pay $29
  a month, far less than conventional fitness clubs. Rather than attract customers

from other clubs, Curves generates customers who haven't considered joining a fitness club before.[4]

- Starbucks operates more than 5000 stores and kiosks, selling gourmet coffee in Asia, Australia, Europe, and North America. Starbucks generates annual sales of over US$2.6 billion (2001). The cafés provide an opportunity for people to take a break from their busy lives to savour specialty coffee drinks in a relaxing atmosphere. Friendly, knowledgeable counter servers, called *baristas* (Italian for bartenders), educate customers about Starbucks' products. The company has entered into some creative partnerships to put its cafés in Barnes & Noble stores, Chapters bookstores, airports, and other nontraditional locations. It serves its coffee on United Airlines. Licensing the brand name for other food products such as ice cream and soft drinks has increased its brand awareness.[5]

Most fitness centres target the 18–34-year-old segment; Curves' retail offering appeals to aging baby boomers.

Every retail strategy involves:

- selecting a target market segment
- selecting a retail format
- developing sustainable competitive advantage that enables the retailer to reduce the level of competition it faces

Now let's examine these central concepts in a retail strategy, as shown in Exhibit 5–1.

the strategic retail planning process

The **strategic retail planning process** is the set of steps a retailer goes through to develop a strategic retail plan[6] (see Exhibit 5–2). It describes how retailers select target market segments, determine the appropriate retail format, and build sustainable competitive advantages. It is not always necessary to go through the entire process each time an evaluation is performed. For instance, a retailer could evaluate its performance and go directly to Step 2, conduct a situation audit.

The planning process can be used to formulate strategic plans at different levels within a retail business. For example, the corporate strategic plan of American Express indicates how resources are to be allocated across the corporation's various businesses such as credit cards and travel services. Each business within American Express has its own strategic plan, and then strategies are developed for products within a business such as for the American Express Gold card.

STEP 1: DEFINE THE BUSINESS MISSION

The first step in the strategic retail planning process is to define the business mission. The **mission statement** is a broad description of a retailer's objectives and the scope of activities it plans to undertake.[7] The objective of a publicly held firm is to maximize its stockholders' wealth by increasing the value of its stock and paying dividends.[8]

exhibit 5–2
Steps in the Strategic
Retail Planning Process

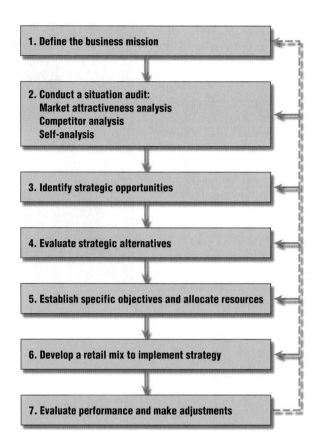

Owners of small, privately held firms frequently have other objectives, such as achieving a specific level of income and avoiding risks rather than maximizing income.

The mission statement should define the general nature of the target segments and retail formats that the firm will consider. For example, the mission statement of an office supply category specialist, "Serve the customer, build value for shareholders, and create opportunities for associates," is too broad. It does not provide a sense of strategic direction.

In developing the mission statement, managers must answer five questions:

- What business are we in?
- What should be our business in the future?
- Who are our customers?
- What are our capabilities?
- What do we want to accomplish?

STEP 2: CONDUCT A SITUATION AUDIT

After developing a mission statement and setting objectives, the next step in the strategic planning process is to do a situation audit. A **situation audit** or SWOT analysis is an analysis of the strengths and weaknesses of the retail business relative to its competitors and the opportunities and threats in the retail environment. The elements in the situation analysis are shown in Exhibit 5–3.[9]

MARKET FACTORS

Size
Growth
Seasonality
Business cycles

COMPETITIVE FACTORS

Barriers to entry
Bargaining power of vendors
Competitive rivalry

ENVIRONMENTAL FACTORS

Technological
Economic
Regulatory
Social/Cultural

ANALYSIS OF STRENGTHS AND WEAKNESSES

Management capabilities
Financial resources
Locations
Operations
Merchandise
Store management
Customer loyalty

exhibit 5–3

Elements in a Market Analysis/ SWOT (Strengths, Weaknesses, Opportunities, and Threats)

Market Factors Some critical factors related to consumers and their buying patterns are market size and growth, sales cyclicality, and seasonality. Market size, typically measured in retail sales dollars, is important because it indicates a retailer's opportunity for generating revenues to cover its investment. Large markets are attractive to large retail firms. But they are also attractive to small entrepreneurs because they offer more opportunities to focus on a market segment. Some retailers, however, prefer to concentrate on smaller markets.

Growing markets are typically more attractive than mature or declining markets. For example, retail markets for specialty stores are growing faster than those for department stores. Typically, margins and prices are higher in growing markets because competition is less intense than in mature markets. Since new customers are just beginning to patronize stores in growing markets, they may not have developed strong store loyalties and thus might be easier to attract to a new store. Some retailers, however, prefer to locate in mature markets. These locations are attractive when the customer base is stable and competition is weak.

Firms are often interested in minimizing the business cycle's impact on their sales. Thus, retail markets for merchandise affected by economic conditions (such as cars and major appliances) are less attractive than retail markets unaffected by economic conditions (such as food). In general, markets with highly seasonal sales are unattractive because a lot of resources are needed to accommodate the peak season, but then resources are underutilized the rest of the year. For example, to minimize these problems due to seasonality, ski resorts promote summer vacations to generate sales during all four seasons.

Competitive Factors The nature of the competition in retail markets is affected by barriers to entry, bargaining power of vendors, and competitive rivalry.[10] Retail markets are more attractive when competitive entry is costly. **Barriers to entry** are conditions in a retail market that make it difficult for firms to enter the market. These conditions include scale economies, customer loyalty, and availability of great locations.

Scale economies are cost advantages due to a retailer's size. Markets dominated by large competitors with scale economies are typically unattractive. For example, a small entrepreneur would avoid becoming an office supply category specialist because the market is dominated by Staples Business Depot. This firm has a considerable cost advantage over the entrepreneur because it can buy merchandise more cheaply and operate more efficiently by investing in the latest technology and spreading its overhead across more stores.

Retail markets dominated by a well-established retailer that has developed a loyal group of customers offer limited profit potential. For example, Home Depot's high customer loyalty makes it hard for a competing home improvement centre to enter the same market.

Finally, the availability of locations may impede competitive entry. A retail market with high entry barriers is very attractive to retailers presently competing in that market because those barriers limit competition. However, markets with high entry barriers are unattractive to retailers not already in the market. For example, the lack of good retail locations in Hong Kong makes this market attractive to retailers already in the region, but less attractive to retailers desiring to enter the market.

Another competitive factor is the **bargaining power of vendors.** Markets are less attractive when a few vendors control the merchandise sold in them. In these situations, vendors have an opportunity to dictate prices and other terms (such as delivery dates), reducing the retailer's profits. For example, the market for retailing fashionable cosmetics is less attractive because two suppliers, Estée Lauder (Estée Lauder, Clinique, Prescriptives, Aramis, Tommy Hilfiger, M.A.C., and Origins)[11] and L'Oréal (Maybelline, Giorgio Armani, Helena Rubinstein, Lancôme, Lanvin, and Ralph Lauren brands),[12] provide the most desired premium brands. Since department stores need these brands to support a fashionable image, these suppliers have the power to sell their products to retailers at high prices.

The final industry factor is the level of competitive rivalry in the retail market. **Competitive rivalry** is the frequency and intensity of reactions to actions undertaken by competitors. When rivalry is high, price wars erupt, advertising and promotion expenses increase, and profit potential falls. Conditions that may lead to intense rivalry include:

- a large number of competitors that are all about the same size
- slow growth
- high fixed costs
- the lack of perceived differences between competing retailers

Macro-Environment   The macro-environment factors that affect market attractiveness span technological, economic, regulatory, and social changes.[13] When a retail market is going through significant changes in technology, present competitors are vulnerable to new entrants that are skilled at using the new technology. For example, in the late 1990s, many traditional retailers were nervously scrambling to define their space in e-tailing. Thousands of pure-play e-tailers with technological sophistication flooded the Internet. Many of the bricks-and-mortar retailers invested heavily in Internet technology and were able to integrate the Internet with their other selling channels.

Some retailers may be more affected by economic conditions than others. Harry Rosen employs many well-paid salespeople to provide high-quality customer service. When unemployment is low, costs may increase significantly, as salespeople's wages rise due to the difficulty in hiring qualified people. But retailers such as Wal-Mart that provide little service and have much lower labour costs as a percentage of sales may be less affected by low unemployment.

Government regulations can reduce the attractiveness of a retail market. For example, it is difficult for large retailers to open new stores in France due to size restrictions placed on new stores. Also, many local governments within Canada have tried to stop Wal-Mart from entering their market in an attempt to protect locally owned retailers.[14]

Finally, trends in demographics, lifestyles, attitudes, and personal values affect retail markets' attractiveness. Harry Rosen, for example, has been struggling with several

In performing a self-analysis, the retailer considers the potential areas for developing a competitive advantage listed below and answers the following questions:

- What is our company good at?
- In which of these areas is our company better than our competitors?
- In which of these areas does our company's unique capabilities provide a sustainable competitive advantage or a basis for developing one?

exhibit 5–4
Strengths and Weaknesses Analysis

 MANAGEMENT CAPABILITY
Capabilities and experience of top management
Depth of management—capabilities of middle management
Management's commitment to firm

 MERCHANDISING CAPABILITIES
Knowledge and skills of buyers
Relationships with vendors
Capabilities in developing private brands
Advertising and promotion capabilities

 FINANCIAL RESOURCES
Cash flow from existing business
Ability to raise debt or equity financing

 OPERATIONS
Overhead cost structure
Quality of operating systems
Distribution capabilities
Management information systems
Loss prevention systems
Inventory control system

 STORE MANAGEMENT CAPABILITIES
Management capabilities
Quality of sales associates
Commitment of sales associates to firm

 LOCATIONS
Competition
Accessibility/traffic flow
Visual impact

 CUSTOMERS
Loyalty of customers

trends simultaneously. Known for traditional suits and dress shirts, the company had to learn how to appeal to younger customers and businesspeople who prefer to dress casually without alienating its traditional customer base.[15]

Retailers need to answer three questions about the macro-environment:

- What new developments or changes might occur, such as new technologies and regulations or different social factors and economic conditions?
- What is the likelihood that these environmental changes will occur? What key factors affect whether these changes will occur?
- How will these changes impact each retail market, the firm, and its competitors?

Strengths and Weaknesses Analysis The most critical aspect of the situation audit is for a retailer to determine its unique capabilities in terms of its strengths and weaknesses relative to the competition.[16] A **strengths and weaknesses analysis** indicates how well the business can seize opportunities and avoid harm from threats in the environment. Exhibit 5–4 outlines issues to consider in performing a self-analysis.

STEP 3: IDENTIFY STRATEGIC OPPORTUNITIES

After completing the situation audit, the next step is to identify opportunities for increasing retail sales. Some growth opportunities could involve a redefinition of the retailer's mission statement. The strategic opportunities could involve market preparation, market expansion, retail format development, or diversification.

STEP 4: EVALUATE STRATEGIC OPPORTUNITIES

The fourth step in the strategic planning progress is to evaluate opportunities that have been identified in the situation audit. The evaluation determines the retailer's

refact
In 1957, brothers Tom, Joe, and Gus Longo began Longo's, a family-owned and -run business that now employs 2000 staff and operates 14 stores in the Toronto area. Seasonal fruit and vegetables reach Longo stores within six hours of the time they were picked by local farmers.[17]

potential to establish a sustainable competitive advantage and reap long-term profits
from the opportunities under evaluation. Thus, a retailer must focus on opportunities
that utilize its strengths and its area of competitive advantage. For example, expertise
in developing private-label apparel is one of Club Monaco's sources of competitive
advantage. Thus, Club Monaco would positively evaluate opportunities that involve
development of private-label merchandise. Some of the areas retailers should consider
when evaluating new opportunities are shown in Exhibit 5–4.

Both the market attractiveness and the strengths and weaknesses of the retailer
need to be considered in evaluating strategic opportunities. The greatest investments
should be made in market opportunities where the retailer has a strong competitive
position.

STEP 5: ESTABLISH SPECIFIC OBJECTIVES AND ALLOCATE RESOURCES

After evaluating the strategic investment opportunities, the next step in the strategic
planning process is to establish a specific objective for each opportunity. The retailer's
overall objective is included in the mission statement. The specific objectives are goals
against which progress toward the overall objective can be measured. Thus, these specific objectives have three components:

- the performance sought, including a numerical index against which progress may
be measured
- a time frame within which the goal is to be achieved
- the level of investment needed to achieve the objective

Typically, the performance levels are financial criteria such as return on investment,
sales, or profits.

STEP 6: DEVELOP A RETAIL MIX TO IMPLEMENT STRATEGY

The sixth step in the planning process is to develop a retail mix for each opportunity
in which investment will be made and to control and evaluate performance.

STEP 7: EVALUATE PERFORMANCE AND MAKE ADJUSTMENTS

The final step in the planning process is evaluating the results of the strategy and implementation program. If the retailer is meeting or exceeding its objectives, changes
aren't needed. But if the retailer fails to meet its objectives, reanalysis is needed.
Typically, this reanalysis starts with reviewing the implementation programs; but it
may indicate that the strategy (or even the mission statement) needs to be reconsid-
ered. This conclusion would result in starting a new planning process, including a new
situation audit. Changes in the macro-environment can force retailers to reevaluate
their strategy. For example, the strategy could involve targeting a new market segment, and tailoring their offering to meet the needs of this new segment.

STRATEGIC PLANNING IN THE REAL WORLD

The planning process in Exhibit 5–2 indicates that strategic decisions are made in a
sequential manner. After the business mission is defined, the situation audit is performed, strategic opportunities are identified, alternatives are evaluated, objectives
are set, resources are allocated, the implementation plan is developed, and, finally,
performance is evaluated and adjustments are made. But actual planning processes
have interactions among the steps. For example, the situation audit may uncover a

logical alternative for the firm to consider, even though this alternative isn't included in the mission statement. Thus, the mission statement may need to be reformulated. Development of the implementation plan might reveal that resource allocation to the opportunity is insufficient to achieve the objective. In that case, the objective would need to be changed or the resources would need to be increased, or the retailer might consider not investing in the opportunity at all.

Remember that a SWOT analysis is an essential part of developing a sustainable retail strategy. The analysis will reveal the retailer's potential for success by analyzing both the macro-environment and the micro-environment to highlight the retailer's unique capabilities. It is a competitive business world and smart retailers are always on alert for a competitive edge. Retail is a game of survival of the fittest!

target market and retail format

The **retailing concept** is a management orientation that focuses a retailer on determining the needs of its target market and satisfying those needs more effectively and efficiently than its competitors. Successful retailers satisfy the needs of customers in their target segment better than the competition does. The selection of a target market focuses the retailer on a group of consumers whose needs it will attempt to satisfy. The selection of a retail format outlines the retail mix to be used to satisfy needs of those customers. The retail strategy determines the markets in which a retailer will compete. Traditional markets, such as a farmers' market, are places where buyers and sellers meet and make transactions—say, a consumer buys six ears of corn from a farmer. But in modern markets, potential buyers and sellers aren't necessarily located in one place. Transactions can occur without face-to-face interactions. For example, many customers contact retailers and place orders over the Internet using a computer.

A **retail market** is a group of consumers with similar needs (a market segment) and a group of retailers using a similar retail format to satisfy those consumer needs.[20] Exhibit 5–5 illustrates a set of retail markets for women's clothing, with a number of retail formats listed down the left-hand column. Each format offers a different retail mix to its customers. Customer market segments are listed in the exhibit's top row. These segments can be defined in terms of the customers' geographic location, demographics, lifestyle, buying situation, or benefits sought. In this illustration, we divide the market into three fashion-related segments: conservative, those who place little importance on fashion and are price-sensitive; traditional, those who want classic styles that are moderately priced; and fashion-forward, those who want the most fashionable merchandise. Each square of the matrix shown in Exhibit 5–5 describes a potential retail market where two or more retailers compete with each other. For example, Wal-Mart and Zellers stores in the same geographic area compete with each other using a discount store format targeting value-oriented conservative customers. Sears and The Bay compete against each other with a department store format targeting the traditional segment looking for moderately priced fashions.

The women's clothing market in Exhibit 5–5 is just one of several representations that could have been used. Retail formats could be expanded to include outlet stores and electronic retailing. Rather than being segmented by fashion orientation, the market could have been segmented using other approaches. Although Exhibit 5–5 isn't the only way to describe the women's retail clothing market, it does illustrate how retail markets are defined in terms of retail format and customer market segment. Each fashion segment—conservative, traditional, and fashion-forward—is likely to shop

exhibit 5–5   Retail Market for Women's Apparel

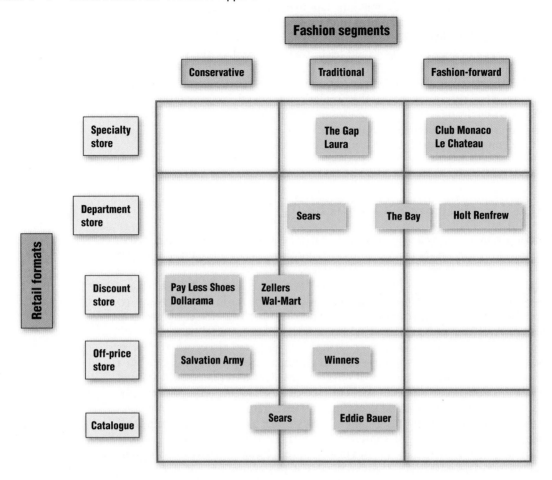

multiple retail formats. For example, a fashion-forward customer might shop Denise for casual wear, Holt Renfrew for shoes, and Winners for a sweater.

Basically, Exhibit 5–5's matrix describes the battlefield on which women's clothing retailers compete. The position in this battlefield indicates the first two elements of a retailer's strategy: its target market segment and retail format. Consider the situation confronting The Gap as it develops a retail strategy for the women's clothing market. Should The Gap compete in all 15 retail markets shown in Exhibit 5–5, or should it focus on a limited set of retail markets? If The Gap decides to focus on a limited set of markets, which should it pursue? The Gap's answers to these questions define its retail strategy and indicate how it plans to focus its resources.

building a sustainable competitive advantage

Any business that retailers engage in can be the basis for a competitive advantage, but some advantages are more sustainable over a long period of time. When developing a retail strategy, two sets of variables that will impact your retail business must be assessed:

- the micro-environment
- the macro-environment

Consider the **micro-environment** to be all of the things that are within your control and can be changed; this would include the retail product that will be sold, the price at which you will sell the product, the location of your store, the promotion including the visual image of your store and promotion activities, and the store management decisions. Remember that a retailer can change these factors as needed. But it must be understood that these decisions are never made in a vacuum.

The external environmental that the retailer cannot control is called the **macro-environment**. The macro-environment consists of five subsections: competition; economic stability of a trade area; the technology that will make retailing more efficient; the regulatory and ethical environment in which the business operates;

retailing view MAXINE CLARK, FOUNDER
AND CHIEF EXECUTIVE BEAR, BUILD-A-BEAR WORKSHOP

5.1

I had a passion for retailing even when I was a young girl. At an early age, I recognized the importance of having exciting merchandise and providing an engaging store experience for customers. But I never realized how significant these feelings would be in my life. I started my retail career, like many college graduates going into retailing, as an executive trainee at May Department Stores Company. Over the next 20 years I held a variety of store and merchandise positions of increasing responsibility. In 1992, I became President of Payless Shoe Stores, then a division of May Department Store with over 4500 stores and $2 billion plus in annual sales at the time.

In early 1997, I decided to launch a retail concept I had been thinking about—Build-A-Bear Workshop®. While most retailers are merchandise driven, Build-A-Bear Workshop® offers highly interactive experiences like a theme park. It combines the universal appeal of plush animals with an interactive assembly line that allows children of all ages to create and accessorize their own huggable companions. We opened the first Build-A-Bear Workshop in St. Louis in the fall of 1997 and have now grown to over 200 stores and in 2003, $300 million in annual sales.

The keys to our success are great merchandise, great people, and great store execution. These three factors combine to create an environment where families share quality time and form irreplaceable memories. Our passion for serving our guests is emulated by our dedicated associates, known as "Master Bear Builders," who make every effort to ensure that each visit is memorable and enjoyable. Employees are empowered to make sure that every guest feels special every time they visit their stores.

We have a company culture where great service and recognition are a daily occurrence. Ninety percent of guests rate the quality of experience in the highest two categories and 76 percent indicate that nothing could be done to improve their store experience.

We also believe strongly that we need to give back to the communities in which we have stores. For example, as part of our ongoing commitment to children's health and wellness, we introduced a series of Nikki's Bears to honor Nikki Giampolo, a young girl who lost her life to cancer. A portion of proceeds from the sale of Nikki's is donated to support programs that help children maintain normal lives while they struggle with difficult health issues including cancer, diabetes, and autism. To date, the program has raised nearly $700 000 for important children's health and wellness causes.

www.buildabear.ca

and the social trends, including consumer behaviour and demographic and lifestyle trends. A **SWOT analysis** (**s**trengths, **w**eaknesses, **o**pportunities, and **t**hreats) is designed to assess both the micro- and macro-environments and the retailer's position relative to these issues.

Developing a proactive position based on the knowledge of what is happening in your retail trade area will help establish a sustainable competitive advantage. Any business activity that a retailer engages in can be a basis for a competitive advantage, but some advantages are sustainable over a long period of time, while others can be duplicated by competitors almost immediately.[21] For example, it would be hard for Starbucks to get a long-term advantage over Tim Hortons by simply offering the same coffee specialties at lower prices. If Starbucks' lower prices were successful in attracting customers, Tim Hortons would know what Starbucks had done and would match the price reduction. Similarly, it's hard for retailers to develop a long-term advantage by offering broader or deeper merchandise assortments. If broader and deeper assortments attract a lot of customers, competitors will simply go out and buy the same merchandise for their stores.

Establishing a retailer's competitive advantage is similar to building a strong wall around its position in a retail market. If the wall is strong it will be hard for competitors outside the wall to contact customers in the retailer's target market. If the retailer has built a wall around an attractive market, competitors will attempt to break down the wall. Over time, advantages may be eroded due to these competitive forces; but by building high, thick walls, retailers can sustain their advantage, minimize competitive pressure, and boost profits for a longer time. Thus, establishing a sustainable competitive advantage is the key to positive long-term financial performance.

Seven important opportunities for retailers to develop sustainable competitive advantages are:

- customer loyalty
- location
- human resource management
- distribution and information systems
- unique merchandise
- vendor relations
- customer service

Exhibit 5–6 shows the aspects of these sources of competitive advantage that are more and less sustainable. Let's look at each of these approaches.

CUSTOMER LOYALTY

Customer loyalty means that customers are committed to shopping at a particular retailer. For instance, having dedicated employees, unique merchandise, and superior customer service all help solidify a loyal customer base. But having loyal customers is, in and of itself, an important method of sustaining an advantage over competitors.

Loyalty is more than simply preferring one retailer over another.[22] Loyalty means that customers will be reluctant to patronize competitive retailers. For example, loyal customers will continue to shop at Canadian Tire even if Home Depot opens a store nearby and provides a slightly superior assortment or slightly lower prices. Some ways that retailers build loyalty are by:

- developing clear and precise positioning strategies
- developing a strong brand for the store or store brands
- creating an emotional attachment with customers through loyalty programs[23]

exhibit 5–6
Methods for
Developing
Competitive Advantage

| Sources of Advantage | SUSTAINABILITY OF ADVANTAGE | |
	Less Sustainable	More Sustainable
Customer loyalty	Habitual repeat purchasing; repeat purchases because of limited competition in the local area	Building a brand image with an emotional connection with customers; using databases to develop and utilize a deeper understanding of customers
Location		Convenient locations
Human resource management	More employees	Committed, knowledgeable employees
Distribution and information systems	Bigger warehouses; automated warehouses	Shared systems with vendors
Unique merchandise	More merchandise; greater assortment; lower price; higher advertising budgets; more sales promotions	Exclusive merchandise
Vendor relations	Repeat purchases from vendor due to limited alternatives	Coordination of procurement efforts; ability to get scarce merchandise
Customer service	Hours of operation	Knowledgeable and helpful salespeople

Positioning   A retailer builds customer loyalty by developing a clear, distinctive image of its retail offering and consistently reinforcing that image through its merchandise and service. **Positioning** is the design and implementation of a retail mix to create an image of the retailer in the customer's mind relative to its competitors.[24]

Positioning emphasizes that the image in the customer's mind (not the retail manager's mind) is critical. Thus, the retailer needs to research what its image is and make sure that it is consistent with what customers in its target market want. A perceptual map is frequently used to represent the customer's image and preference for retailers.

Exhibit 5–7 is a hypothetical perceptual map of retailers selling women's clothing. The two dimensions in this map, fashion/style and service, represent the two primary characteristics that consumers in this example use in forming their impression of retail stores. Perceptual maps are developed so that the distance between two retailers' positions on the map indicates how similar the stores appear to consumers. For example, Sears and The Bay are very close to each other on the map because consumers in this illustration see them as offering similar service and fashion. On the other hand, Holt Renfrew and Zellers are far apart, indicating that consumers think they're quite different. Note that stores close to each other compete vigorously with each other because consumers feel they provide similar benefits.

According to this example, The Gap has an image of offering moderately priced fashionable women's clothing with good service. Winners offers more fashionable clothing with less service. Sears is viewed as a retailer offering women's clothing that's less fashionable and has relatively limited service.

The ideal points (marked by green dots on the map) indicate characteristics of an ideal retailer for consumers in different market segments. For example, consumers in Segment 3 prefer a retailer that offers high-fashion merchandise with low service, whereas consumers in Segment 1 want less expensive/more traditional apparel and aren't concerned about service. The ideal points are located so that the distance between the retailer's position (marked with a blue "x") and the ideal point indicates how consumers in the segment evaluate the retailer. Retailers that are closer to an ideal point are evaluated more favourably by the consumers in the segment than

exhibit 5–7   Hypothetical Perceptual Map of Women's Apparel Market

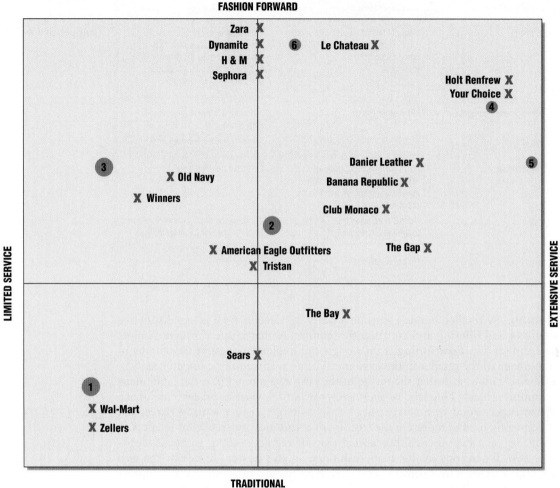

retailers located farther away. Thus, consumers in Segment 6 prefer Le Château to Holt Renfrew because their target customers do not require such high service levels.

Starting in 2000, The Gap began a streak of monthly sales declines for stores that have been open at least a year. The chief executive officer of the company at that time, Millard "Mickey" Drexler, had many explanations, including staying with outdated styles too long and then overreacting by filling the stores with too many trendy looks. Customers have since complained that they can't get the same assortment of high-quality basics—button-down shirts and khaki pants—that made The Gap famous. Probably the biggest problem is that The Gap's success spawned lower-priced imitators, including its own lower-priced chain, Old Navy, which is closer to Segment 2 than The Gap. At the same time, Target has become more fashion forward. So both Target and Old Navy are vying for customers in the huge Segment 2 in Exhibit 5–5. Additionally, The Gap is positioned too far away from Segment 5 to compete successfully with Holt Renfrew on service. In fact, its sister chain, Banana Republic, is closer to Segment 5 and is therefore also siphoning sales from The Gap.[25] Finally, The Gap has two strong competitors for Segment 2 with Tristan and American Eagle Outfitters.

Loyalty Programs   Loyalty programs are part of an overall customer relationship management (CRM) program. These programs are prevalent in retailing, from airlines and department stores to the corner pizza shop. Popular examples include Canadian Tire Money, Shoppers Optimum Card, HBC Rewards, Air Miles, and Aeroplan.

Customer loyalty programs work hand-in-hand with CRM. Members of loyalty programs are identified when they buy because they use some type of loyalty card. The purchase information is stored in a huge database known as a **data warehouse.** From this data warehouse, analysts determine what types of merchandise and services certain groups of customers are buying. Data/information gathered can be used to build store loyalty by targeting promotional activities to specific market segments, providing a more focused merchandise mix, and can produce higher profits by efficiently targeting advertising efforts.

LOCATION

The classic response to the question, "What are the three most important things in retailing?" is "Location, location, and location." Location is the critical factor in consumer selection of a store. It is also a competitive advantage that is not easily duplicated. For instance, once Shoppers Drug Mart has put a store at the best location of an intersection, other drug stores are relegated to the second-best location. Finding great locations is particularly challenging in older urban locations, where space is limited and tenant turnover is relatively low.

Starbucks has developed a national presence and a strong competitive advantage with its location strategy. It conquers one area of the city at a time and then expands in the region, saturating a major market before entering a new market. Starbucks will frequently open several stores close to one another. It has two stores on two corners of the intersection of Robson and Thurlow in Vancouver. Starbucks has such a high density of stores that it lets the storefront promote the company and does very little media advertising. In heavily trafficked downtown districts, Starbucks often operates kiosks in commercial buildings. Neighbourhood locations that attract customers in the evenings and on weekends are important because they become part of the path of people's weekly shopping experience or their route to work.

By concentrating its locations, Starbucks creates a market presence that is difficult for competition to match. In addition, multiple locations facilitate scale economies that enable frequent deliveries, thereby ensuring fresh merchandise.

In contrast to Starbucks' urban locations, Tim Hortons chooses suburban locations with easy drive-through access in smaller cities, communities, and neighbourhoods across Canada.

HUMAN RESOURCE MANAGEMENT

Retailing is a labour-intensive business. Employees play a major role in providing services for customers and building customer loyalty. Knowledgeable and skilled employees committed to the retailer's objectives are critical assets that support the success of companies such as Harry Rosen Menswear, Whole Foods, Canadian Tire, and Black's Photography.

Recruiting and retaining great employees is not easy. Retailers gain a sustainable competitive advantage by developing programs to motivate and coordinate employee efforts, by providing appropriate incentives, by fostering a strong and positive organizational culture and environment, and by managing diversity.

DISTRIBUTION AND INFORMATION SYSTEMS

All retailers strive for efficient operations, to reduce operating costs—the costs associated with running the business and making sure the merchandise customers want is available. The goal is to get their customers the merchandise they want, when they want it, in the quantities that are required, at a lower delivered cost than their competitors. By so doing, they will satisfy their customers' needs and, at the same time, either provide them with lower-priced merchandise than their competition or decide to use the additional margin to attract customers from competitors by offering even better service, merchandise assortments, and visual presentations.

Retailers can achieve these efficiencies by developing sophisticated distribution and information systems. For instance, merchandise sales information flows seamlessly from Wal-Mart to its vendors such as Procter & Gamble to facilitate quick and efficient merchandise replenishment. Wal-Mart has the largest data warehouse in the world, enabling the company to fine-tune merchandise assortments on a store-by-store, category-by-category basis. Wal-Mart's distribution and information systems have enabled the retailer to be the lowest-cost provider of merchandise in every market in which it competes.

UNIQUE MERCHANDISE

It is difficult for retailers to develop a competitive advantage through merchandise because most competitors can purchase and sell the same popular national brands. But many retailers realize a sustainable competitive advantage by developing **private-label brands** (also called *store brands*), which are products developed and marketed by a retailer and available only from that retailer. For example, if you want to buy a Kenmore washer or dryer, you have to buy it from Sears. Store brands now account for one of every five items sold and are achieving new levels of growth every year; for example, the distinctive President's Choice line of gourmet flavours created by Loblaws. The low search associated with electronic shopping increases the importance of unique merchandise as a source of competitive advantage.

Sears has a strong private label program. If you want to buy Craftsman tools or Kenmore appliances, you have to purchase them from Sears.

VENDOR RELATIONS

By developing strong relations with vendors, retailers may gain exclusive rights to:

- sell merchandise in a specific region
- obtain special terms of purchase that are not available to competitors who lack such relations
- receive popular merchandise in short supply

Relationships with vendors, like relationships with customers, are developed over a long time and may not be easily offset by a competitor.[26] For example, Ahold, the Holland-based food retailer, works very closely with Swiss food giant

Nestlé to provide products tailored to meet the local tastes of customers in specific markets.[27]

CUSTOMER SERVICE

Retailers also build a sustainable competitive advantage by offering excellent customer service.[28] Offering good service consistently is difficult because customer service is provided by retail employees—and humans are less consistent than machines. Retailers that offer good customer service instill its importance in their employees over a long period of time. Customer service must become part of the retailer's organizational culture through coaching and training.

retailing view   5.2
HARRY ROSEN, PRESIDENT, HARRY ROSEN MENSWEAR

Harry Rosen has been in the business of selling high-priced menswear for 50 years and has become a Canadian icon. The business has evolved from a tiny tailor shop in Toronto to 15 stores from Montreal to Vancouver. This retailer, with annual sales of $150 million, accounting for 30% of all sales of high-end menswear in Canada, has a celebrity clientele and a long list of honours. Not only is Rosen a dynamic retailer, he's a great corporate citizen, initiating major fundraising events in support of prostate cancer research. In 2004 Harry Rosen was named to the prestigious Order of Canada.

Harry Rosen at 72 is a psychoanalyst, social anthropologist,

Harry Rosen builds loyalty and competitive advantage by using its customer database to tailor its promotional offerings.

businessman, and brilliant marketer. His prize-winning advertisements have become recognized for innovation, such as the series, "What So and So Is Wearing Today" featuring well-known Canadians, from former NHL star Frank Mahovlich to musician Oscar Peterson. Always enthusiastic, Rosen once posed nude, except for a strategically placed necktie; all part of a very creative advertising campaign.

Each Harry Rosen salesperson has a commitment to their customers and can access the firm's data warehouse with customer information from any POS terminal in the store. The database tells what the customer has bought in the past and also provides personal information, such as preferences in style and colour. All sales associates are urged to contribute to the database. Harry Rosen believes

that men are in need of help; they are not like women who like to shop and will make an enlightened choice. Rosen thinks most men are lazy and lack the knowledge critical to choosing quality menswear. The customer database is designed to enable sales associates to advise customers on promotions and develop valuable one-to-one relationships.

Even though only three percent of Canadian men actually shop in his stores, the first name that comes to mind when most men dream of buying a special wardrobe is Harry Rosen's. Rosen attributes his success to two things: his commitment to quality clothing and his insistence that staff make sure their clients understand why quality matters.

McDonald's has great locations all over the world, including this one in Bangkok, Thailand.

It takes considerable time and effort to build a tradition and reputation for customer service, but good service is a valuable strategic asset. Once a retailer has earned a service reputation, it can sustain this advantage for a long time because it's hard for a competitor to develop a comparable reputation.

MULTIPLE SOURCES OF ADVANTAGE

To build a sustainable advantage, retailers typically don't rely on a single approach such as low cost or excellent service.[29] They need multiple approaches to build as high a wall around their position as possible. For example, the success of McDonald's is based on providing customers with a good value that meets their expectations, having good customer service, maintaining good vendor relations, and having great locations. By doing all of these things right, McDonald's has developed a huge cadre of loyal customers.

McDonald's has always positioned itself as providing fast food at a good value—customers get a lot for not much money. Its customers don't have extraordinary expectations. They don't expect a meal prepared to their specific tastes. But customers do expect and get hot, fresh food that is reasonably priced.

McDonald's customers also don't expect friendly table service with linen tablecloths and sterling silverware. Their service expectations, which are typically met, are simple. By developing a system for producing its food and using extensive training for store managers, McDonald's reduces customers' waiting time. This training also means that customers will be handled quickly and courteously.

McDonald's vendor relationships ensure that it will always have quality ingredients. Its distribution and inventory control systems enable it to make sure that the ingredients are available at each location.

Finally, McDonald's has a large number of great locations. It is important for convenience products, such as fast food, to have lots of locations. Given its market power, it has been successful in finding and opening stores in prime retail locations. In every city in which it operates around the world, McDonald's has outstanding locations.

By developing unique capabilities in a number of areas, McDonald's has maintained its position as a service retailer, using a fast-food format directed toward families with young children.

Each of the retail strategies outlined in the chapter involves multiple sources of advantage. For example, Tim Hortons has developed a strong competitive position through its excellent product line with a strong Canadian brand name, high-quality service provided by committed employees, and excellent and plentiful locations. Tim Hortons' donuts are a tradition in all communities across Canada.

growth strategies

Four types of growth opportunities that retailers may pursue (market penetration, market expansion, retail format development, and diversification) are shown in Exhibit 5–8.[30] The vertical axis indicates the synergies between the retailer's present markets and growth-opportunity markets—whether the opportunity involves markets

TARGET MARKETS

	Existing	New

exhibit 5–8
Growth Opportunities

the retailer is presently pursuing or new markets. The horizontal axis indicates the synergies between the retailer's present retail mix and the growth-opportunity retail mix—whether the opportunity exploits the retailer's present format or requires a new format.

MARKET PENETRATION

A **market penetration opportunity** involves directing efforts toward existing customers by using the present retailing format. The retailer can achieve this growth strategy either by attracting consumers in its current target market who don't shop at its outlets or by devising strategies that induce current customers to visit a store more often or to buy more merchandise on each visit.

Approaches for increasing market penetration include attracting new customers by opening more stores in the target market and keeping existing stores open for longer hours. Other approaches are displaying merchandise to increase impulse purchases and training salespeople to cross-sell. **Cross-selling** means that sales associates in one department attempt to sell complementary merchandise from other departments to their customers. For example, a sales associate who has just sold a dress to a customer will take the customer to the accessories department to sell her a handbag or scarf that will go with the dress. More cross-selling increases sales from existing customers.

For example, The Bay, Canada's popular mid-priced department store, refocused its women's wear strategy to attract middle-income women aged 35 to 55. The strategy included bringing in three new exclusive clothing lines that focused on a fresher, more fashionable image. The goal was to increase The Bay's women's wear sales, which had weakened over the years under pressure from specialty clothing stores. It is estimated that there are 10 times more women in Canada with a household income of $65 000 than there are with a household income of $100 000. The Bay's strategy was to grow this middle market. The exclusive brands were a result of a deal

refact
A 4 percent increase in weekly store visits by customers can result in a 58 percent increase in profits for a typical grocery store.[31]

with Federated Department Stores Inc., the U.S. parent of department store chains Macy's and Bloomingdale's. The style update promoted a funky new lifestyle image in TV and print media that was positioned to attract working women. The addition of the exclusive Federated brands was part of the retail strategy designed to change the customer's perception of the department store, to earn customer trust, and to build loyalty.[32]

MARKET EXPANSION

A **market expansion opportunity** employs the existing retail format in new market segments. For example, Abercrombie & Fitch (A&F) Co.'s primary target market is university students, not high-schoolers. Since university-aged people don't particularly like to hang out with teens, A&F is rolling out a new, lower-priced chain called Hollister Co. to appeal to teens. Although the merchandise and ambience are slightly different than A&F, the retail format is essentially the same.[33] When the French hypermarket chain Carrefour expanded into other European and South American countries, it was also employing a market expansion growth strategy because it was entering a new geographic market segment with essentially the same retail format.[34]

RETAIL FORMAT DEVELOPMENT

A **retail format development opportunity** involves offering a new retail format—a format with a different retail mix—to the same target market. For example, Chapters, a specialty book store-based retailer, exploited a format development opportunity when it began selling books to its present target market over the Internet (www. chapters.indigo.ca). Another example of a retail format development opportunity occurs when a retailer adds merchandise categories, such as when Amazon.com began selling DVDs and electronics in addition to books. Adjusting the type of merchandise or services offered typically involves a small investment; whereas providing an entirely different format, such as a store-based retailer going into electronic retailing, requires a much larger and riskier investment.

Another example of a retail format development opportunity is Best Buy offering professional services to install new high-tech electronic equipment for consumers. Best Buy offers a Geek Squad to customers with 24-hour computer support and service. Although this growth opportunity is directed toward the same customers who buy merchandise in the stores, it involves running a service rather than a merchandise-based retail business.

DIVERSIFICATION

A **diversification opportunity** occurs when a retailer introduces a new retail format directed toward a market segment that's not currently served, such as when La Senza opened La Senza Girl to attract the lucrative tween market. Today's tweens will be La Senza women in the future. Diversification opportunities are either related or unrelated.

Related versus Unrelated Diversification   In a **related diversification opportunity**, the present target market or retail format shares something in common with the new opportunity. This commonality might entail purchasing from the same vendors, using the same distribution or management information system, or advertising in the same newspapers to similar target markets. In contrast, an **unrelated diversification** lacks any commonality between the present business and the new business.

After several attempts at unrelated diversification, Foot Locker decided to stick to its core business, athletic shoes.

Foot Locker, the world's largest retailer of athletic footwear and apparel, became involved in several unrelated diversification endeavours in the 1990s.[35] For instance, it owned some Burger King franchises and Afterthoughts accessory stores. After realizing that athletic apparel and footwear was its core business, it dumped businesses that didn't fit the mold and streamlined and remodelled the remaining stores. Unrelated diversifications are considered to be very risky and often don't work, as was the case with Foot Locker. As a result, most retailers apply the old adage "stick to your knitting" and seek growth opportunities that are closer in nature to their current operations.

Foot Locker now operates Foot Locker stores, Lady Foot Locker, Kids Foot Locker, Champs Sports, and Foot Locker stores in Europe. Foot Locker also has highly profitable Internet and catalogue business (see www.footlocker.com).

Vertical Integration   Vertical integration is diversification by retailers into wholesaling or manufacturing.[36] Examples of vertical integration are The Limited's acquisition of Mast Industries (a trading company that contracts for private-label manufacturing) and Zale Corporation's manufacturing of jewellery. When retailers integrate by manufacturing products they are making risky investments because the skills required to make products are different from those associated with retailing. Additionally, retailers and manufacturers have different customers; the immediate customers for a manufacturer's merchandise are retailers, whereas a retailer's customers are consumers. Thus, a manufacturer's marketing activities are very different from those of a retailer. Designing private label merchandise is a related diversification because it builds on the retailer's knowledge of its customers, but actually making the merchandise is considered an unrelated diversification. Some manufacturers and designers such as Nike, Prada, and Ralph Lauren forward integrate into retailing. In this case the designer/manufacturer has control of both the manufacturing and distribution processes and makes the strategic decision to move forward and control the retailing process by opening its own stores.

STRATEGIC OPPORTUNITIES AND COMPETITIVE ADVANTAGE

Typically, retailers have the greatest competitive advantage in opportunities that are similar to their present retail strategy. Thus, retailers would be most successful engaging in market penetration opportunities that don't involve entering new, unfamiliar markets or operating new, unfamiliar retail formats.

When retailers pursue market expansion opportunities, they build on their strengths in operating a retail format and apply this competitive advantage to a new market. Those retailers that successfully expand globally are able to translate what they do best—their core competencies—to a new culture and market.

A retail format development opportunity builds on the retailer's reputation and success with present customers. Even if a retailer doesn't have experience and skills in operating the new format, it hopes to attract its loyal customers to it. For example, retailers that have successfully developed multichannel strategies by seamlessly integrating stores, the Internet, and catalogues provide extra convenience and multiple opportunities for their current customers to shop.

Retailers have the least competitive advantage when they pursue diversification opportunities. Thus, these opportunities are generally risky and often don't work, as was the case with Foot Locker/Burger King. Vertical integration, however, albeit risky, often has overwhelming benefits for those large and sophisticated retailers that can invest heavily for the long term. By making direct investments in distribution or manufacturing facilities, these retailers have total control over the entire marketing channel.

refact

Of the largest 100 retailers worldwide, over 89 percent are from France, Germany, Japan, the United Kingdom, and the United States.[37]

global growth opportunities

International expansion is a market growth opportunity that successful retailers find attractive. The most commonly targeted regions are Mexico, Latin America, Europe, China, and Japan. International expansion can be risky because retailers must deal with differences in government regulations, cultural traditions, supply chain considerations, and language. The issues connected to global expansion are discussed in Chapter 8, International Retailing Strategy.

SUMMARY

This chapter on strategic planning provides an overview of the issues involved in developing a competitive retail strategy. Successful retailers develop a proactive position including a SWOT (strengths, weaknesses, opportunities, threats) analysis based on knowledge of the macro-environment, including retail competition, economic stability, technological environment, regulatory requirements, and consumer behaviour. The micro-environment must respond to the needs of the target market operating within the goals of the strategic plan. This includes the right product mix, at the right price, in the right quantities, offered at a desirable retail location.

Dynamic innovation combined with knowledge of the retail environment is essential to remain competitive in today's challenging retail marketplace. Strategic planning is an ongoing process. Every day, retailers audit their situations, examine lifestyle trends, study new technologies, and monitor competitive activities. But the retail strategy statement isn't changed every year or every six months. The strategy statement is reviewed and altered only when major changes in the retailer's environment or capabilities occur.

When a retailer undertakes a major reexamination of its strategy, the process for developing a new strategy statement may take a year or two. Potential strategic directions are generated by people at all levels of the organization. These ideas are evaluated by senior executives and operating people to ensure that the eventual strategic direction is profitable in the long run and can be implemented.

A retailer's long-term performance is largely determined by its strategy. The strategy coordinates employees' activities and communicates the direction the retailer plans to take. Retail market strategy describes both the strategic direction and the process by which the strategy is to be developed.

The strategic planning process consists of a sequence of steps, including a detailed analysis of (1) the macro-environment in which the retailer operates and (2) the retailer's unique capabilities. Based on this analysis, the retailer can evaluate alternatives.

The retail strategy statement includes identification of a target market and the retail offering to be directed toward the target market. The statement also needs to indicate the retailer's methods to build a sustainable competitive advantage.

KEY TERMS

bargaining power of vendors, *104*
barriers to entry, *103*
competitive rivalry, *104*
cross-selling, *117*
customer loyalty, *110*
data warehouse, *113*
diversification opportunity, *118*
macro-environment, *109*
market expansion opportunity, *118*
market penetration opportunity, *117*

micro-environment, *109*
mission statement, *101*
positioning, *111*
private-label brands, *114*
related diversification opportunity, *118*
retail format, *100*
retail format development opportunity, *118*
retailing concept, *107*
retail market, *107*
scale economies, *103*
situation audit, *102*

strategic retail planning process, *101*
strengths and weaknesses analysis, *105*
sustainable competitive advantage, *100*
SWOT analysis, *110*
target market, *100*
unrelated diversification, *118*

Get Out & Do It!

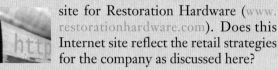

1. **INTERNET EXERCISE** Visit the website for Restoration Hardware (www. restorationhardware.com). Does this Internet site reflect the retail strategies for the company as discussed here?

2. **GO SHOPPING** Visit two stores that sell similar merchandise categories and cater to the same target segment(s). How are their retail formats similar? Dissimilar? On what bases do they have a sustainable competitive advantage?

Explain which you believe has a stronger position.

3. **GO SHOPPING** Develop a strategic plan for your favourite retailer. Go to the store. Observe and interview the store manager. Supplement your visit with information available online through Hoovers, the store's Web site (which should include its annual report), and other published sources.

DISCUSSION QUESTIONS AND PROBLEMS

1. What approaches can a retailer use to develop a competitive advantage?

2. Give an example of a market penetration, a retail format development, a market expansion, and a diversification growth strategy for Future Shop.

3. Draw and explain a positioning map such as that shown in Exhibit 5–7 for the retailers and customer segments (ideal points) for your favourite retailer.

4. View the video "Build-A-Bear Workshop" and complete a situation analysis identifying the retailer's strategy (see Exhibit 5-1). Detail the micro-environment and the macro-environment in the analysis. What are the strengths and weaknesses? Explain what threats and opportunities exist for this unique retailer.

5. Read the profile of Harry Rosen. Identify why Harry has been so successful in marketing to the high-end menswear market segment.

6. Read the RONA profile. What is RONA's sustainable competitive advantage?

7. Do a situation analysis for McDonald's. What is its mission? What are its strengths and weaknesses? What environmental threats might it face over the next 10 years? How could it prepare for these threats?

8. Assume you are interested in opening a restaurant in your town. Go through the steps in the strategic planning process shown in Exhibit 5–2. Focus on doing a situation audit of the local restaurant market, identifying alternatives, evaluating alternatives, and selecting a target market and a retail mix for the restaurant.

9. Walt Disney Co. is splitting its Disney Stores chain into two separate retail concepts. The first group, Disney Play, is aimed at kids. The second group, Disney Kids at Home, is targeted toward parents, with a greater focus on apparel and lifestyle goods such as sheets, furniture, and mirrors for kids. Do you believe this is a good strategy?

10. Identify a store or service provider that you believe has an effective loyalty program. Explain why it is effective.

CHAPTER 6

retail locations strategy— trade area decisions and site assessment

Executive Briefing

*Edward Kennedy, CEO,
North West Company Inc.*

The North West Company Inc. operates where most retailers would fear to tread, with many of its retail locations above the tree line, the majority inaccessible by road. Surviving in a territory that is cold, vast, and underserviced by the retail sector for over three hundred years has yielded The North West Company special insight into the customs and traditions of northern policies.

The Winnipeg-based company has 184 stores in remote northern communities across Canada and Alaska. The North West Company, formerly part of Hudson's Bay Company, is the oldest Canadian-owned retailer in Canada, established in 1779.

The North West Company remains one of the only sources of food and clothing for remote communities across northern Canada and Alaska. The stores service remote communities such as Arctic Bay on the upper reaches of Baffin Island and Kotzebue, Alaska, as well as communities from British Columbia in the west to Labrador in Eastern Canada. The company serves roughly 250 000 customers spread over millions of square kilometres and seven time zones. It is estimated that Nunavut, Canada's newest territory, will have a growth rate of 16.4%, three times the national average. The territory is also estimated to be the youngest in Canada, with 60% of the population under age 25 and with good earning power due to many federal

QUESTIONS
What types of locations are available to retailers?
What are the relative advantages of each location type?
Which types of locations are growing in popularity with retailers?
Why are some locations particularly well-suited to specific retail strategies?
What factors should retailers consider when determining where to locate stores?
What is a trade area? How do retailers determine the trade area for a retail store?
What factors should retailers consider when deciding on a retail site?
Where can retailers get information to evaluate potential store locations?
What issues are involved in negotiating a lease?

government initiatives in the north. So, despite difficult obstacles such as extreme cold weather and unfriendly landscape, The North West Company has become a success story, posting profits of $9.1 million.

In an attempt to offer northern communities what they want, North West has expanded its product line to include everything from fresh produce, groceries (including traditional foods such as muktuk, the outer flesh of whales), fashions to furniture, home electronics, four-wheel vehicles and banking services, gas bars, tax preparation services, and pharmacies. It is the largest dealer of Inuit art in Canada; yet, 70% of its revenue is from groceries. According to Edward Kennedy, North West CEO, "For a company like us to succeed in the retail scene, we have to be very focused on niches that give us distinct advantages over much bigger retailers."

Understanding the difficulties of distribution to remote areas, North West has forged strategic alliances with southern retailers to increase their purchasing power. The situation benefits all involved as new markets become available to retail partners and northern consumers enjoy lower prices and expanded product offerings. The North West Company has learned to adapt its location strategy in a land of bitter cold weather, endless Arctic nights, and polar bears.

For several reasons, store location is often the most important decision made by a retailer. First, location is typically the prime consideration in a customer's store choice. For instance, when choosing where you're going to have your car washed, you usually pick the location closest to your home or work. Second, location decisions have strategic importance because they can be used to develop a sustainable competitive advantage. Retailers can change their pricing, service, and merchandise assortments in a relatively short time. However, location decisions are harder to change because retailers frequently have to either make substantial investments to buy and develop real estate or commit to long-term leases with developers. It's not unusual, for instance, for a national chain store to sign a lease for seven to ten years. If that location is the best in a particular mall or central business district, the retailer then has a strategic advantage competitors can't easily copy, because they are precluded from locating there.

Location decisions have become even more important in recent years. First, there are more retailers opening new locations, making the better locations harder to obtain. This problem is made more complex by a slowdown in both population growth and new shopping centre construction. A retailer may find a suitable location, but high rent, complicated leases, and expensive fixturing and remodelling can make it very costly. Many experts believe that there is too much retail space in Canada and that the best retail locations are already taken. Retailers must consider issues of suitability or compatibility, availability, affordability, accessibility, and visability.

This chapter describes the types of locations available to retailers and the relative advantages

exhibit 6–1   Location Decisions Based on Four Levels

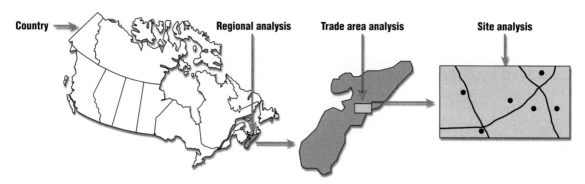

of each. We then examine factors that retailers should consider when choosing a particular location type.

Many types of locations are available for retail stores—each with its own strengths and weaknesses. Choosing a particular location type involves evaluating a series of trade-offs. These trade-offs generally concern the cost of the location versus its value to customers.

Exhibit 6–1 breaks the location decision into four levels: country, region, trade area, and specific site. The country is a decision of international expansion that will be discussed in Chapter 8. The **region** refers to the country, part of the country, a particular city, or CMA (Census Metropolitan Area). A **trade area** is the geographic area encompassing most of the customers who would patronize a specific retail site, and that accounts for the majority of the store's sales and customers. A trade area may be part of a city, or it can extend beyond the city's boundaries, depending on the type of store and the density of potential customers surrounding it. For instance, a DVD rental store's trade area may be only a few city blocks within a major metropolitan area. On the other hand, a Wal-Mart Supercentre's trade area in a rural area may encompass 1000 square kilometres.

In making store location decisions, retailers must examine all four levels simultaneously. For instance, suppose Pizza Pizza is expanding operations in the Atlantic provinces and has plans to open several stores simultaneously. Its research indicates that competition in the Halifax market is relatively weak, making it an attractive region. But maybe it can't find enough suitable sites, so it must temporarily postpone locating there.

In examining a site, we look at the factors that affect the attractiveness of a particular region and trade area. Then we examine what retailers look for in choosing a particular site. Of course, the most important factor in choosing a site is the amount of sales it can generate. Thus, we will examine several methods of predicting the amount of sales.

factors affecting the demand for a region or trade area

The best regions and trade areas are those that generate the highest demand or sales for a retailer. Although the regional analysis is distinct from the trade area analysis, the factors that make them attractive are the same. To assess overall demand in a particular region/market or trade area, the retail location analyst considers economies

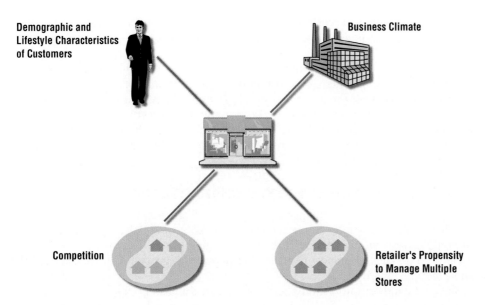

exhibit 6–2
Factors Affecting the
Demand for a Region
or Trade Area

of scale versus cannibalization (where one store eats the sales of another store in the same chain), the population's demographic and lifestyle characteristics, the business climate, competition from other retailers in the area, and the retailer's propensity to manage multiple stores (see Exhibit 6–2). Locating in a trade area outside a retailer's home country requires the analyst to examine all these factors, plus additional issues such as differences in the legal, political, and cultural environments.

ECONOMIES OF SCALE VERSUS CANNIBALIZATION

At first glance, you would expect that a retailer should choose the one best location in a given trade area. But most chains plan to go into an area with a network of stores. After all, promotion and distribution economies of scale can be achieved with multiple locations. The total cost is the same to run a newspaper ad for a retailer with 20 stores in an area as it is if the retailer has only one store. Likewise, chains such as Canadian Tire expand into areas only where they have distribution capabilites designed to support the stores.

The question is, What is the best number of stores to have in an area? The answer depends on who owns the stores. For company-owned stores, the objective is to maximize profits for the entire chain. In this case, the retailer would continue to open stores as long as the marginal revenues achieved by opening a new store are greater than the marginal costs. Home Depot subscribes to this fundamental axiom of site selection: It is better to have two stores producing $75 million each than one store producing $100 million. The company believes that a store can do too much business. The store might be overcrowded, offer poor service, have a hard time staying in stock, and actually be underperforming. Home Depot believes that the solution to an underperforming store is to build another store in the same trade area. Although this strategy may seem

Home Depot believes that if a store is underperforming, then it may be overcrowded. So the company builds another store in the same trade area.

illogical at first glance, it works for Home Depot. Best Buy and Future Shop, owned by the same company, use a similar location strategy to control the electronics retail market.

For franchise operations, however, each individual franchise owner wants to maximize his or her profits. Some **franchisors** (owners of the franchise) grant their **franchisees** (owners of the individual stores) an exclusive geographic territory so that other stores under the same franchise do not compete directly with them. In other franchise operations, the franchisees have not been afforded this protection and often have been involved in very antagonistic negotiations with the franchisors in an attempt to protect their investment.

DEMOGRAPHIC AND LIFESTYLE CHARACTERISTICS

In most cases, areas where the general population is growing are preferable to those with declining populations. Some retailers, such as Subway, often go into new strip shopping centres in anticipation that the surrounding suburban area will eventually be built up enough to support demand. Yet population growth alone doesn't tell the whole story.

Size and composition of households in an area can also be important success determinants. For instance, Laura, Laura Petites, and Laura II (a chain specializing in traditional and business apparel for women) generally locates in areas with high-income, dual-career families; household size, however, isn't a particularly critical issue.

Toys "R" Us, on the other hand, is interested in locations with heavy concentrations of families with young children.

Finally, lifestyle characteristics of the population may be relevant, depending on the target market(s) a particular retailer is pursuing. Many university students, for instance, have relatively low incomes. However, they may come from well-to-do families, and, by the fact that they are in university, they're relatively educated. Their lifestyles more closely resemble those of recent university graduates in professional jobs making a good income than they do people with similar incomes working odd jobs in a rural area. Thus, the way people spend their money is often as important as how much money people make.

Some retailers, such as Subway, often go into new strip shopping centres in anticipation that the surrounding suburban area will eventually be built up enough to support demand.

BUSINESS CLIMATE

It's important to examine a market's employment trends because a high level of employment usually means high purchasing power. Also, it's useful to determine which areas are growing quickly and why. For instance, Ottawa has become a desirable retail location because of its proximity to government and corporate headquarters. Retail location analysts must determine how long such growth will continue and how it will affect demand for their merchandise. For instance, the economies of some cities such as Oshawa experience greater peaks and valleys due to their dependence on specific industries such as automobiles (General Motors plant).

Employment growth in and of itself isn't enough to ensure a strong retail environment in the future. If growth isn't diversified in a number of industries, the area may suffer from adverse cyclical trends. For instance, many areas that have been traditionally dependent on agriculture have attempted to bring in new industries, either manufacturing or high-tech, to help diversify their economies.

COMPETITION

The level of competition in an area also affects demand for a retailer's merchandise. The level of competition can be defined as saturated, understored, or overstored. A **saturated trade area** offers customers a good selection of goods and services, while allowing competing retailers to make good profits. Since customers are drawn to these areas because of the great selections, retailers who believe they can offer customers a superior retail format in terms of merchandise, pricing, or service may find these areas attractive. Some restaurants such as Burger King seek locations where their major competition—McDonald's—has a strong presence. They believe that it's important to go head-to-head with their strongest competitors so that they can develop methods and systems that will allow them to compete successfully with them. They contend that locating in areas with weak competition allows them to become complacent. The strongest competitor will eventually enter the trade area. By then, however, it will have lost its competitive edge.[2]

Another strategy is to locate in an **understored trade area**—an area that has too few stores selling a specific good or service to satisfy the needs of the population. Wal-Mart's early success was based on a location strategy of opening stores in small towns that were relatively understored. Now these stores experience high market share in their towns and draw from surrounding communities.

In effect, these areas have gone from being understored before Wal-Mart arrived to being **overstored trade areas**—having so many stores selling a specific good or service that some stores will fail. Unable to compete head-to-head with Wal-Mart on price or breadth of selection, many family-owned retailers in those cities have had to either reposition their merchandising or service strategies or else go out of business.

SPAN OF MANAGERIAL CONTROL

Some retailers focus on certain geographic regions or trade areas. Their advantages stem from their regional orientation. They can maintain a loyal customer base by remaining a regional chain. They have excellent visibility and are well known throughout the area. Second, their merchandising, pricing, and promotional strategies specifically target the needs of a regional market rather than a national market. Finally, the management team can have greater locus of control over a regional market. Managers can easily visit the stores and assess competitive situations.

location and retail strategy

The selection of a location type must reinforce the retailer's strategy. Thus, the location type decision needs to be consistent with the shopping behaviour and size of its target market and the retailer's positioning in its target market. Each of these factors is discussed next.

SHOPPING BEHAVIOUR OF CONSUMERS IN RETAILER'S TARGET MARKET

A critical factor affecting the location consumers select to visit is the shopping situation in which they are involved. Three types of shopping situations are convenience shopping, comparison shopping, and specialty shopping.

Convenience Shopping When consumers are engaged in convenience shopping situations, they are primarily concerned with minimizing their effort to get the product or service they want. They are indifferent about which brands to buy or the retailer's image and are somewhat insensitive to price. Thus, they don't spend much time evaluating different brands or retailers; they simply want to make the purchase as quickly and easily as possible. Examples of convenience shopping situations are getting a cup of coffee during a work break or buying milk for breakfast in the morning.

Retailers targeting customers involved in convenience shopping, such as convenience stores, usually locate their stores close to where their customers are and make it easy for them to park, find what they want, and go about their other business. Thus, convenience stores should and generally do locate in neighbourhood strip centres, freestanding spots, and city and town locations. Drugstores and fast-food restaurants also cater to convenience shoppers and thus select locations with easy access, parking, and locations that enable them to offer the additional convenience of a drive-through window. Convenience also plays an important role for supermarkets and full-line discount stores. Generally, shoppers at these stores are not particularly brand or store loyal and do not find shopping in these stores enjoyable. Thus, these stores typically are also located in neighbourhood strip centres and freestanding locations.

Comparison Shopping Consumers involved in comparison shopping situations have a general idea about the type of product or service they want, but do not have a strong preference for a brand, model, or specific retailer to patronize. Similar to many convenience shopping situations, consumers are not particularly brand or store loyal. However, the purchase decisions are more important to them, so they seek information and are willing to expend considerable effort planning and making their purchase decisions. Consumers typically engage in this type of shopping behaviour when buying furniture, appliances, apparel, consumer electronics, hand tools, and cameras.

Furniture retailers, for instance, often locate next to each other to create a "furniture row." In Toronto, a number of retailers selling furniture are all located on Dundas Street West. These competing retailers locate near one another because doing so facilitates comparison shopping and thus attracts customers to the locations to compare different types of furniture and prices. The advantage of attracting a large number of shoppers to this area of Dundas Street outweighs the disadvantage of sharing these customers with other retailers.

Enclosed malls offer the same benefits to consumers interested in comparison shopping for fashionable apparel. For example, a customer who was looking for a business suit for job interviews could easily compare the suits offered at The Bay and Club Monaco with the suits at Sears by simply walking to these other stores located in the same mall. Thus, department stores and specialty apparel retailers locate in enclosed malls for the same reason that houseplant retailers locate together on 6th Avenue in New York City. By co-locating in the same mall, they attract more potential customers interested in comparison shopping for fashionable apparel. Even though the enclosed mall might be inconvenient compared with a freestanding location, comparison shopping is easier after the customers have arrived.

Category specialists offer the same benefit of comparison shopping as a collection of co-located specialty stores such as those described previously. Rather than going to a set of specialty stores when comparison shopping for consumer electronics, consumers know they can see almost all of the brands and models they would want to buy in either Best Buy or Future Shop. Thus, category specialists are **destination stores,** places where consumers will go even if it is inconvenient, just as enclosed malls are destination locations for fashionable apparel comparison shopping. Category specialists locate in power centres primarily to reduce their costs and create awareness of their location and secondarily to benefit from the multiple retailers attracting more consumers and the potential for cross-shopping. Basically, power centres are a collection of destination stores.

As a destination store, Best Buy offers many brands of merchandise to give consumers the opportunity to comparison shop for consumer electronics.

Specialty Shopping When consumers are going specialty shopping, they know what they want and will not accept a substitute. They are brand and/or retailer loyal and will pay a premium or spend extra effort, if necessary, to get exactly what they want. Examples of these shopping occasions include buying an expensive designer brand perfume, adopting a dog from the animal shelter, or buying a dress made by a specific designer. The retailer they patronize when specialty shopping also becomes a destination store. Thus, consumers are willing to travel to an inconvenient location to patronize a unique gourmet restaurant or a health food store that specializes in organic vegetables. Having a convenient location is not as important for retailers selling unique merchandise or services.

DENSITY OF TARGET MARKET

A second, but closely related factor that affects the choice of location type is the density of the retailer's target market in relation to the location. A good location has many people in the target market that are drawn to it. So, a convenience store located in a CBD can be sustained by customers living or working in fairly close proximity to the store. Similarly, a comparison shopping store located next to The Bay is a potentially good location because The Bay draws lots of customers from a very large area. It is not as important to have high customer density near a store that sells specialty merchandise because people are willing to search out this type of merchandise. A Porsche dealer, for instance, need not be near other car dealers or in close proximity to its target market because those seeking this luxury car will drive to wherever the dealer may be.

UNIQUENESS OF RETAIL OFFERING

Finally, the convenience of their locations is less important for retailers with unique, differentiated offerings than for retailers with an offering similar to other retailers. For example, Bass Pro Shops provide a unique merchandise assortment and store atmosphere. Customers will travel to wherever the store is located, and its location will become a destination.

types of locations

Retailers have three basic types of locations to choose from: a shopping centre, a city or town location, or a freestanding location. Retailers can also locate in a nontraditional location such as an airport or within another store. The following sections describe each type of location and present criteria for choosing a particular location type.

SHOPPING CENTRES

From the 1950s through the 1980s, suburban shopping centres grew as populations shifted to the suburbs. Large shopping centres provide huge assortments for consumers. Combining many stores under one roof creates a synergy that attracts more customers than if the stores had separate locations. It's not uncommon, for instance, for a store's sales to increase after a competing store enters a shopping centre.

The term *shopping centre* has been evolving since the early 1950s. A **shopping centre** is a group of retail and other commercial establishments that is planned, developed, owned, and managed as a single property. The two main configurations of shopping centres are strip centres and enclosed malls. **Strip centres** are shopping centres that usually have parking directly in front of the stores. **Malls**, on the other hand, are shopping centres where customers park in outlying areas and walk to the stores. Traditional malls are enclosed, with a climate-controlled walkway between two facing strips of stores. The main shopping centre types are defined in Exhibit 6-3.

The developer and shopping centre management carefully select a set of retailers that are complementary; this tenant mix is planned to attract a specific market segment to the shopping centre. The goal of a successful tenant mix is to provide customers with a one-stop shopping experience by providing a well-balanced assortment of product offering including retailers, services, and entertainment.

The shopping centre management maintains the common facilities (referred to as common area maintenance [CAM]), such as the parking area, and is responsible for activities such as providing security, parking lot lighting, outdoor signage for the centre, and advertising and special events to attract consumers. The stores in the centre typically pay a negotiated annual fee based on their size to cover the CAM costs. The shopping centre management can also place restrictions on the operating hours, signage, and even the type of merchandise sold in the stores.

Most shopping centres have at least one or two major retailers, referred to as **anchors**. These retailers are courted by the centre developer because they attract a significant number of consumers and consequently make the centre more appealing to other retailers. To get these anchor retailers to locate in a centre, developers frequently make special deals, such as reduced lease costs, for the anchor tenants. For example, the median rental cost is less than $35 per square metre for anchors in an enclosed mall but $350 for nonanchor retailers.[3]

In strip centres, supermarkets are typically anchors, whereas department stores traditionally anchor shopping malls. However, a lifestyle centre may not have anchors, whereas power centres are composed primarily of multiple "anchor" stores. The different types of shopping centres are discussed next.

A **traditional strip centre** is a shopping centre that is designed to provide convenient shopping for the day-to-day needs of consumers in their immediate neighbourhood. Smaller strip centres are typically anchored by a supermarket or a drugstore; the larger strips are anchored by discount stores, off-price stores, or category killers selling such items as apparel, home improvement/furnishings, toys, shoes, pet supplies, electronics, and sporting goods. These anchors are supported by

exhibit 6–3   Shopping Centre Definitions

Type	Concept	Square Metres	Number of Anchors	Types of Anchors	Trade Area*
Strip Centres					
Traditional	General merchandise; convenience	2790–32 550	One or more	Discount; supermarket; drug; home improvement; large specialty discount apparel	8–18 km²
Power	Category-dominant anchors; few small tenants	23 250–55 800	Three or more	Category specialist; home improvement; discount; warehouse club; off-price	13–26 km²
Shopping Malls					
Regional	General merchandise; fashion (typically enclosed)	37 200–74 400	Two or more	Department; discount; fashion apparel, other specialty stores	13–40 km²
Superregional	Similar to regional but has more variety and assortment	74 400+	Three or more	Department; discount; fashion apparel; other specialty stores	13–65 km²
Lifestyle	Higher-end, fashion-oriented	Variable	N/A	Higher-end specialty stores and restaurants	13–40 km²
Fashion/specialty	Higher-end, fashion-oriented	7440–23 250	N/A	Higher-end fashion and other specialty stores	13–40 km²
Outlet	Manufacturers' outlet stores	4650–37 200	N/A	Manufacturers' outlet stores	65–200 km²
Theme/festival	Leisure; tourist oriented	7440–23 250	N/A	Restaurants; entertainment; fashion and other specialty stores	N/A

*The area from which 60 to 80 percent of the centre's sales originate.

stores offering sundries, food, and a variety of personal services such as barber shops and dry cleaners.

Strip Shopping Centres The primary advantages of strip centres or community shopping centres are that they offer customers convenient locations and easy parking and they entail relatively low rents for retailers. The primary disadvantages are that there is no protection from the weather, and they offer less assortment and entertainment options for customers than malls. As a result, strip centres do not attract as many customers as larger shopping centres that rely on community participation.

The strip centres of today have a mix of mom-and-pop stores and national tenants such as A Buck or Two and Shoppers Drug Mart. National chains like these are able to compete effectively in strip centres against their rival stores in malls. They can offer lower prices, partly because of the lower rents, plus their customers can drive right up to the door. New spinoff grocery franchises such as No Frills and Price Chopper are popular with value-conscious consumers and are often located in strip centres.

Power Centres A **power centre** is a shopping centre that is dominated by several big-box retailers, including discount stores (Wal-Mart), off-price stores (Winners), warehouse clubs (Costco), or category specialists such as Home Depot,

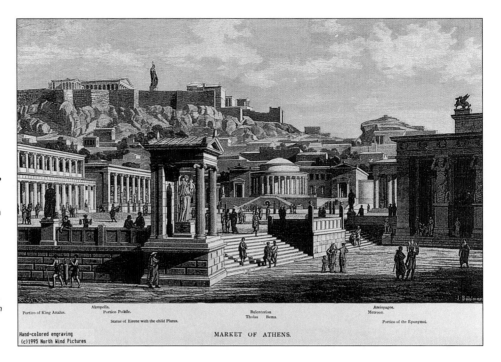

The first shopping centre, a marketplace with retail stores, was the Agora at the foot of the Parthenon in Athens in 600 B.C. It was the centre of all commerce, politics, and entertainment in ancient Greece.
Source: John Fleischman, "In Classic Athens, a Market Trading in Currency of Ideas," *Smithsonian* 24 (July 1993), pp. 38–47.

Staples Business Depot, Best Buy, and Toys "R" Us. Unlike traditional strip centres, power centres often include several freestanding (unconnected) anchors and only a minimum number of small specialty tenants. They are typically unenclosed in a strip centre configuration. Many power centres are located near an enclosed shopping mall and are becoming major competition for the shopping centres.

Power centres were virtually unknown before the 1990s, but they have steadily grown in number. Many are now larger than some regional malls and attract customers from a large trade area. Why have they become so popular? First and foremost, their tenants have experienced tremendous growth and prosperity. A power centre is a natural location for these large tenants. They don't want to pay the high rents of regional shopping malls, and they benefit from the synergy of being with other big-box stores. Also, shoppers are seeking value alternatives to the stores found in shopping malls.

SHOPPING MALLS

Shopping malls have several advantages over alternative locations. First, because of the many different types of stores, the merchandise assortments available within those stores, and the opportunity to combine shopping with entertainment, shopping malls have become the Main Street for today's shoppers. Teenagers hang out and meet friends, older citizens in Nikes get their exercise by walking the malls, and families make trips to the mall a form of entertainment. To enhance the total shopping experience, many malls incorporate food and entertainment such as movies and amusement parks.

The second major advantage of locating in a shopping mall is that the tenant mix can be planned. Shopping mall owners control the number of different types of retailers so that customers can have a one-stop shopping experience with a well-balanced assortment of merchandise. For instance, it's important to have several women's clothing stores in a major mall to draw in customers. Mall managers

refact

The first power centre featuring a general merchandise discount store, category specialists, off-price retailers, and warehouse clubs was opened in Coloma, California, in 1986.[4]

also attempt to create a complementary tenant mix. They like to have all stores that appeal to certain target markets (such as all upscale specialty clothing stores) located together. Thus, customers know what types of merchandise they can expect to find in a particular mall or location within a mall. Managers also strive for a good mix between shopping and specialty goods stores. A strong core of shopping goods stores, such as shoe stores, brings people to the mall. Specialty stores, such as computer software stores, also bring shoppers to the mall. While specialty store customers are in the mall, they'll likely be attracted to other stores.

To help keep their parents shopping, some malls provide entertainment for their kids.

The third advantage of shopping malls is that the retailers and their customers don't have to worry about their external environment. The mall's management takes care of maintenance of common areas. Mall tenants can look forward to a strong level of homogeneity with the other stores. For instance, most major malls enforce uniform hours of operation. Most malls control the external signage used for window displays and sales. Since most shopping malls are enclosed, customers are protected from the Canadian weather.

Although shopping centres are an excellent site option for many retailers, they have some disadvantages. Mall rents are higher than those of some strip centres, freestanding sites, and most central business districts. As a result, retailers that require large stores, such as home improvement centres, typically seek other options. Some tenants may not like mall managers' control of their operations. Mall managers can, for instance, dictate store hours and have strict rules regarding window displays and signage. Finally, competition within shopping centres can be intense. It may be hard for small specialty stores to compete directly with large department stores.

In addition, shopping malls are facing several challenges. First, shopping malls appeal to consumers who have the time to enjoy wandering through stores, punctuated by a leisurely lunch or an afternoon movie. The increasing number of two-income families and families with a single household head is creating more time pressures for consumers, limiting the time they can devote to shopping. Freestanding locations, strip centres, and power centres are more convenient because customers can park in front of a store, go in and buy what they want, and go about their other errands. There is increasing competition from other types of retail location alternatives, such as power and lifestyle centres, catalogues, and the Internet. Many of today's shoppers are looking for value alternatives to stores found in shopping malls. Also, the apparel business, which makes up a large percentage of mall tenants, has continued to be weak, causing some specialty store chains to close. Finally, many malls are getting old and are in need of major renovation to appeal to consumers.

What are they doing about their problems? Some mall owners are turning their centres into traditional town squares with lots of entertainment opportunities.[5] They believe if they can encourage people to spend more time in the mall, they will spend more money there. The owners are renting to nontraditional mall tenants such as dry cleaners, doctors' offices, and even chapels—everything that you would have found in a town square in the 1950s. Others are forging links to their communities by opening wellness centres, libraries, city halls, and children's play areas. In this environment, people can ride the midway, go to a movie, visit the petting zoo, or eat at a theme restaurant.

refact

At least 300 older malls, each with one or two anchor stores, have shut down since the mid-1990s in the U.S.[6]

According to the *Guiness Book of Records,* the world's largest shopping, amusement, and recreation centre is the **West Edmonton Mall in Alberta, with over 483 600 square metres of covered space.**

A more extreme approach to revitalizing a mall is known as demalling.[7] **Demalling** usually involves demolishing a mall's small shops, scrapping its common space and food courts, enlarging the sites once occupied by department stores, and adding more entrances to the parking lot.

Regional Centres   A **regional centre** is a shopping mall that provides general merchandise (a large percentage of which is apparel) and services in full depth and variety. Its main attractions are its anchors, department and discount stores, or fashion specialty stores. A typical regional centre is usually enclosed with an inward orientation of the stores connected by a common walkway, with parking surrounding the outside perimeter.

Superregional Centres   A **superregional centre** is a shopping centre that is similar to a regional centre, but because of its larger size, it has more anchors and a deeper selection of merchandise, and it draws from a larger population base. As with regional centres, the typical configuration is an enclosed mall, frequently with multilevels.

According to the *Guiness Book of Records,* the world's largest shopping, amusement, and recreation centre is the West Edmonton Mall in Alberta. It has nearly 483 600 square metres of covered space, 353 400 square metres of selling space, more than 800 stores and services, and 110 restaurants. But the mall has more than shopping to attract millions of people a year. It also sports the Galaxyland Amusement park, a three-hectare waterpark, an NHL-size ice arena, submarines, an exact replica of the Santa Maria ship, a lagoon, Fantasyland Hotel, a miniature golf course, 26 movie theatres and IMAX, and a casino. Don't worry about parking. It is also the largest capacity in the world, enough for 20 000 vehicles.

Located on an 80-hectare site just north of Toronto, Vaughan Mills will feature 15 anchor tenants (many of them big-name discount outlets from the U.S.), 200 specialty stores, theme restaurants, cinemas, and recreation activities in a 130 200 square metre complex. The mall is to be located in an area that is home to 60 percent of Ontario's population (and almost 25 percent of Canada's population), and there are 10 million people within 160 kilometres of the mall (including Buffalo and Niagara Falls, New York). Vaughan Mills is a joint venture between Ivanhoe Cambridge, Canada, and Mills Corp of the U.S., and is scheduled to open in the fall of 2004.

The design of the mall is innovative and fresh and is based on the design concept "Discover Ontario." The mall will be divided into six neighbourhoods based on the themes of lakes, nature, rural living, small towns, city, and fashion. It is estimated that Vaughan Mills and its retailers will employ more than 3500 workers on a full- or part-time basis and add approximately $12.5 million in taxes to the local economy annually.[8]

Lifestyle Centres   A **lifestyle centre** is an outdoor traditional streetscape layout with sit-down restaurants and a conglomeration of retailers such as Williams-Sonoma, Pottery Barn, and Eddie Bauer.

refact

On any given day, Mall of America near Minneapolis, Minnesota, the largest mall in the United States, has enough people in it to qualify as the third-largest city in the state. It has more than 42 million visitors each year—more than Disney World, the Grand Canyon, and Graceland combined.[9]

The centres offer shoppers convenience, safety, an optimum tenant mix, and a pleasant atmosphere. Like "Main Street" locations, shoppers go because it's an attractive, energetic place to meet their friends and have fun. Some lifestyle centres consist only of stores and restaurants; some have cinemas and entertainment; and still others mingle retail with homes and offices. Nearly all are located in high-income areas. They have gone into posh neighbourhoods where they depend on a market radius far smaller, but a lot richer, than malls.

Many of the projects are designed to look as though they've been there for decades. As a result, they are expensive to build. Park Place is a 139 500 square metre lifestyle centre planned for Barrie, Ontario, that will combine office space, retail outlets, entertainment centres, restaurants, and bars, plus four hotels and a hockey rink. High-end retailers are slated to be placed alongside big-box discount stores, and green space will allow customers to walk between stores on the outside of the centre. Park Place is designed to bring back the fun of shopping.[10]

Fashion/Specialty Centres   A **fashion/specialty centre** is a shopping centre that is composed mainly of upscale apparel shops, boutiques, and gift shops carrying selected fashions or unique merchandise of high quality and price. These centres need not be anchored, although sometimes gourmet restaurants and theatres can function as anchors. The physical design of these centres is very sophisticated, emphasizing a rich decor and high-quality landscaping.

Fashion/specialty centres are similar to lifestyle centres in terms of the clientele and the types of stores they attract. The difference is that these centres are typically enclosed and are larger than most lifestyle centres.

Fashion/specialty centres usually are found in trade areas having high income levels, in tourist areas, or in some central business districts. These centres' trade areas may be large because of the specialty nature of the tenants and their products. Customers are more likely to travel great distances to shop for specialty products sold at nationally known shops such as Holt Renfrew and Ralph Lauren/Polo than for other types of goods.

Outlet Centres   **Outlet centres** are shopping centres that consist mostly of manufacturers' outlet stores selling their own brands, supposedly at a discount.[12] These centres also sometimes include off-price retailers such as Winners or HomeSense. As a result of the shifting tenant mix in some of these centres, various industry experts now refer to outlet centres as value centres or value megamalls. Similar to power centres, a strip configuration is most common, although some are enclosed malls such as Dixie Outlet Mall, the 47-year old mall located in Mississauga, Ontario.

Outlet centre tenants view this location option as an opportunity to get rid of excess or distressed merchandise, sell more merchandise, and, to a lesser extent, test new merchandise ideas.

Consumer demand for stores in outlet centres is declining. Although customers can shop for an extensive assortment within individual brands and buy below full retail prices every day, they have to deal with broken assortments, distressed or damaged goods, and less convenient locations. Additionally, traditional retailing has become more price-competitive.

Outlet centres have progressed from no-frills warehouses to well-designed buildings with landscaping and food options that make them hard to distinguish from more traditional shopping centres. The newest outlet centres have a strong entertainment component, including movie theatres and theme restaurants, comprising about 15 to 20 percent of the leasable area.[13] Mall developers believe that these entertainment concepts help keep people on the premises longer. Outlet centre tenants

refact

The average income of lifestyle centre customers is about double that of mall shoppers: They visit 2.5 times more often, and spend 50 percent more per visit.[11]

Merchandise kiosks are found in shopping malls of all types and are a popular location alternative for retailers with small space needs.

have also upgraded their offerings by adding credit, dressing rooms, high-quality fixtures and lighting, and a merchandise return policy.

Outlet centres are often located some distance from regional shopping centres so outlet tenants don't compete directly for department and specialty store customers, although most manufacturer outlets have learned to peacefully coexist with their department and specialty store customers by editing assortments in their outlet stores to minimize overlap. Outlet centres can be located in strong tourist areas. For instance, since shopping is a favourite vacation pastime, and Niagara Falls attracts 15 million tourists per year, the 111 600 square metre Factory Outlet mega mall in Niagara Falls, New York, is a natural location for an outlet centre. Some centre developers actually organize bus tours to bring people hundreds of kilometres to their malls. As a result, the primary trade area for some outlet centres is 100 kilometres or more.

OTHER LOCATION OPPORTUNITIES

Merchandise Kiosks   Although not a type of shopping mall, merchandise kiosks are found in shopping malls of all types and are a popular location alternative for retailers with small space needs. Merchandise **kiosks** are small selling spaces offering a limited merchandise assortment. These selling spaces are typically between 3.7 and 46.5 square metres and can be in prime mall locations. They're relatively inexpensive compared to a regular store. They usually have short-term leases, shielding tenants from the liability of having to pay long-term rent in case the business fails. Some merchandise kiosks operate seasonally, for instance, selling polar fleece in winter and baseball hats in summer. Of course, vendors also can be evicted on short notice. These alternatives to regular stores are often a great way for small retailers to begin or expand.

Mall operators see these alternative selling spaces as an opportunity to generate rental income in otherwise vacant space. Some of the nation's biggest mall developers are installing merchandise kiosks in every available space. These kiosks sell everything from concert tickets to gift certificates. They also can generate excitement, leading to additional sales for the entire mall. Mall operators must be sensitive to their regular mall tenants' needs, however. These kiosks can block a store, be incompatible with its image, or actually compete with similar merchandise.

other retail location opportunities

Mixed-use developments, airports, resorts, hospitals, and stores within a store are interesting, if not unusual, location alternatives for many retailers.

Mixed-Use Developments (MXDs)   **Mixed-use developments (MXDs)** combine several different uses in one complex, including shopping centres, office towers, hotels, residential complexes, civic centres, and convention centres. MXDs are popular with retailers because they bring additional shoppers to their stores. Developers like MXDs because they use space productively. For instance, land costs the same whether a developer builds a shopping mall by itself or builds an office tower over the mall or parking structure.

Airports   One important high-pedestrian-traffic area that has become popular with national retail chains is airports. After all, what better way to spend waiting time than to have a Second Cup coffee or stop into Victoria's Secret? Sales per square metre at airport malls are often three to four times as high as at regular mall stores.[14] However, rents are at least 20 percent higher than at malls. Also, costs can be higher—hours are longer, and since the location is often inconvenient for workers, the businesses have to pay higher wages. The best airport locations tend to be ones where there are many layovers and international flights. The best-selling products are those that make good gifts, necessities, and easy-to-pack items such as books and magazines.

A smaller-format Fox Sports Sky Box sportsbar and restaurant was created for several airports and features a video control centre that resembles Fox's NFL anchor desk.

Resorts   Who needs anchor stores to bring in customers when there are mountains or a beach to attract people? Retailers view resorts as prime location opportunities for golf courses, entertainment spas, and complementary retailers. There is a captive audience of well-to-do customers with lots of time on their hands. As noted earlier, outlet malls are popular in tourist areas. Resort retailing also attracts small, unique local retailers, premium national brands such as Tim Hortons or Roots, and can support dozens of art galleries and fashion retailers. Popular resort areas such as Whistler, BC, or Big White, Kelowna, BC, have developed town centres that attract tourists worldwide.

Hospitals   Hospitals are an increasingly popular location alternative. Both patients and their guests often have time to shop. Necessities are important for patients since they can't readily leave. Gift-giving opportunities abound. Chapters has opened retail locations in large hospitals.

Store within a Store   Another nontraditional location for retailers is within other, larger stores. Retailers, particularly department stores, have traditionally leased space to other retailers such as sellers of cosmetics and fine jewellery or furs. Grocery stores have been experimenting with the store-within-a-store concept for years with service providers such as banks, film processors, and video outlets. Chapters Books has Starbucks Coffee in many of its stores. A variation on the store-within-a-store concept is the kiosk within a store that OfficeMax is partnering with Hewlett-Packard, through which customers can configure computers to order.

refact
About 25 percent of air traffic is delayed. There are 670 million U.S. air passengers per year, and the 20 busiest airports have 55 percent of all air traffic. That is a lot of potential shoppers![15]

city or town locations

Although shopping centres are also located in cities or towns, the locations that are discussed in this section are typically unplanned, have multiple owners, and have access from the street. In particular, we will examine central business districts, downtown locations (or "Main Streets"), and the redevelopment efforts being undertaken in these locations.

CENTRAL BUSINESS DISTRICTS

The **central business district (CBD)** is the traditional downtown business area in a city or town. Due to its business activity, it draws many people into the area during business hours. Also, people must go to the area for work. The CBD is also the hub for public transportation, and there is a high level of pedestrian traffic. Finally, the most successful CBDs for retail trade are those with a large number of residents living in the area.

 But many central business district locations in Canada have been declining in popularity with retailers and their customers for years. Retailers can be concerned about CBDs because high security may be required and parking is often limited. Urban decay and no control over the weather can discourage shoppers. Shopping in the evening and on weekends can be particularly slow in many CBDs. Also, unlike modern shopping centres, CBDs tend to suffer from a lack of planning. One block may contain upscale boutiques, the next may be populated with low-income housing, so consumers may not have enough interesting retailers that they can visit on a shopping trip.

DOWNTOWN LOCATIONS

A **downtown location** is the CBD located in the traditional shopping area of smaller towns, or a secondary business district in a suburb or within a larger city. Downtown locations share most of the characteristics of the primary CBD. But their occupancy costs are generally lower than that of the primary CBD. They do not draw as many people as the primary CBD because fewer people work in the area, and fewer stores generally mean a smaller overall selection. Finally, downtown locations typically don't offer the entertainment and recreational activities available in the more successful primary CBDs.

REDEVELOPMENT EFFORTS IN CITY AND TOWN LOCATIONS

Some city and town locations have become very attractive location alternatives to shopping centres. Why is this happening?

- Some of these locations have undergone a process of **gentrification,** which is the renewal and rebuilding of offices, housing, and retailers in deteriorating areas, coupled with the influx of more affluent people that often displaces earlier, usually poorer residents. Retailers are simply locating where their customers are.

- Developers aren't building as many malls as before, and it's often hard to find a good location in a successful mall.

- These same chains are finding that occupancy costs in city and town locations compare favourably to malls.

- City and town locations often offer retailers incredible expansion opportunities because of a stable and mature customer base and relatively low competition.

- Cities often provide significant incentives to locate in urban centres. Not only do these retailers bring needed goods and services to the area, but they also bring jobs. If, for instance, a major retailer hires 500 people, there would be more than 100 additional new jobs created to satisfy the retailing needs of that retailer's employees.

- Young professionals and retired empty-nesters are moving to urban centres to enjoy the convenience of shopping, restaurants, and entertainment.

Successful national chain stores such as Staples Business Depot, Mountain Equipment Co-op, and Tim Hortons need these locations to fuel their expansion. Even big-box stores such as Home Depot and Wal-Mart are opening up city and town locations. Wal-Mart solved the space problem associated with urban locations by opening a three-level store in Los Angeles.[17]

freestanding sites

Although most retailers locate in strip centres or planned shopping malls, a frequent option for large retailers is a freestanding site. A **freestanding site** is a retail location that's not connected to other retailers, although many are located adjacent to malls. Retailers with large space requirements, such as warehouse clubs and hypermarkets, are often freestanding. Category specialists such as Toys "R" Us also utilize freestanding sites. Advantages of freestanding locations are greater visibility, lower rents, ample parking, no direct competition, greater convenience for customers, fewer restrictions on signs, hours, or merchandise (which might be imposed in a shopping centre), and ease of expansion. The most serious disadvantage is the lack of synergy with other stores. A retailer in a freestanding location must be a primary destination point for customers. It must offer customers something special in merchandise, price, promotion, or services to get them into the store.

Many retailers report that freestanding stores perform better than stores in malls. Shoppers Drug Mart shifted to freestanding locations because it wanted more space for the front-end merchandise.

retail site selection

Retail site selection is a very strategic decision. Opening a store at a site often involves committing to a lease of five years or more, purchasing land and building a store, or buying an existing building, all of which requires a considerable investment. Consider the tragic results if the store's performance is below expectations: The retailer may not be able to find another business to assume the lease, damage to the business credibility can be disastrous, and the investment capital may be very difficult to recover. The difference between moving into a superior trade area and an inferior one can mean the difference between success and failure. Furthermore, even if a retailer finds the "right" neighbourhood, the wrong site can spell disaster. Consider, for instance, the location of a new doughnut shop. The retailer has the option to locate in two sites, one across the street from the other. One might think that it should simply choose the cheaper site. But one site has easier access and its signs are highly visible to motorists passing by. More important, that same site is on the way into the central business district, whereas the other is on the way to the suburbs. People who enjoy a morning doughnut know that it tastes best on the way to work with a big cup of coffee. Without careful analysis of trade areas and specific sites, multimillion dollar mistakes can be easily made. Fortunately, sophisticated statistical models are available through firms that provide geographic and demographic data and consulting services critical to evaluating specific sites, including MapInfo/Location Intelligence at www.mapinfo.com and ACNielsen Canada at www.acnielsen.ca.

The following questions will be discussed in assessing the retail site:

- What issues should be considered when determining in which region or trade area to locate a store?
- What is a trade area, and why should a retailer choose one over another?
- What factors should retailers consider when deciding on a particular site?
- How can retailers forecast sales for new store locations?

factors affecting the attractiveness of a site

Let's look at the issues that make a particular site attractive. Specifically, we'll examine the site's accessibility and locational advantages within the centre. Having decided to locate stores in an area, the retailer's next step is to evaluate and select a specific site. In making this decision, retailers condsider three factors: (1) the characteristics of the site, (2) the characteristics of the trading area for a store at the site, and (3) the estimated potential sales that can be generated by a store at the site. The first two sets of factors are tpicatlly considered in an initial screening of potential sites. The methods used to forecast store sales, the third factor, can involve a more complex analytical approach. Each of these factors is discussed in the following section.

TRAFFIC FLOW AND ACCESSIBILITY

The accessibility of a site is the ease with which a customer may get into and out of it. The accessibility analysis has two stages: a macro analysis and then a micro analysis.

Macro Analysis   The macro analysis considers the primary trade area, such as the area five to ten kilometres around the site in the case of a supermarket or drugstore. To assess a site's accessibility on a macro level, the retailer simultaneously evaluates several factors, such as road patterns, road conditions, and barriers.

In the macro analysis, the analyst should consider the **road pattern.** The primary trade area needs major arteries or highways so customers can travel easily to the site. A related factor is the **road condition,** including the age, number of lanes, number of stoplights, congestion, and general state of repair of roads in the primary trade area. For instance, a location on an old, narrow, congested secondary road in disrepair with too many stoplights wouldn't be a particularly good site for a retail store.

Natural barriers, such as rivers or mountains, and **artificial barriers,** such as railroad tracks, major highways, or parks, may also affect accessibility. These barriers' impact on a particular site primarily depends on whether the merchandise or services are available on both sides of the barrier. If, for instance, only one supermarket serves both sides of a highway, people on the opposite side must cross to shop.

Micro Analysis   The micro analysis concentrates on issues in the immediate vicinity of the site, such as visibility, traffic flow, parking, congestion, and ingress/egress.

Visibility refers to customers' ability to see the store and enter the parking lot safely. Good visibility is less important for stores with established and loyal customers and for stores with limited market areas because customers know where the store is. Nonetheless, large national retailers such as Canadian Tire insist that there be no impediments to a direct, undisturbed view of their store. In an area with a highly transient population, such as a tourist centre or large city, good visibility from the road is particularly important.

The success of a site with a good traffic flow is a question of balance. The site should have a substantial number of cars per day but not so many that congestion impedes access to the store. To assess the level of vehicular traffic, the analyst can usually obtain data from the regional planning commission, or highway department. But the data may have to be adjusted for special situations. As a result, it's sometimes easier and more accurate to do the analysis in-house. For instance, the analyst must consider that the presence of large places of employment, schools, or big trucks may lessen a site's desirability. Also, areas congested during rush hours may have a good traffic flow during the rest of the day when most shopping takes place. Finally, some retailers might wish to adjust the raw traffic counts by excluding out-of-province licence plates or counting only homeward-bound traffic.

The **amount and quality of parking facilities** are critical to a shopping centre's overall accessibility. If there aren't enough spaces or if they're too far from the stores, customers will be discouraged from entering the area. On the other hand, if there are too many open spaces, the shopping centre may be seen as a failure or as having unpopular stores. It's hard to assess how many parking spaces are enough, although location analysts use parking ratios as a starting point. A standard rule of thumb is 5.9:100 (5.9 spaces per 100 square metres of retail store space).[18] Nevertheless, there's no good substitute for observing the shopping centre at various times of the day, week, and season. The analyst must also assess the availability of employee parking, the proportion of shoppers using cars, parking by nonshoppers, and the typical length of a shopping trip.

An issue that's closely related to the amount of available parking facilities, but extends into the shopping centre itself, is the relative congestion of the area. **Congestion** can refer to the amount of crowding of either cars or people. There's some optimal range of comfortable congestion for customers. Too much congestion can make shopping slow, irritate customers, and generally discourage sales. On the other hand, a relatively high level of activity in a shopping centre creates excitement and can stimulate sales.[19]

The last factor to consider in the accessibility analysis is **ingress/egress**—the ease of entering and exiting the site's parking lot. Often, medians or one-way streets make entering or exiting difficult from one or more directions, limiting accessibility.

Adjacent Tenants   Locations with complementary, as well as competing, adjacent retailers have the potential to build traffic. Complementary retailers target the same market segment but have a different, noncompeting merchandise offering. For example, Sav-A-Lot, a limited assortment supermarket targeting price-sensitive consumers, prefers to be co-located with other retailers targeting price-sensitive consumers, such as Family Dollar or even Wal-Mart.

Have you ever noticed that competing fast-food restaurants, automobile dealerships, antique dealers, and even shoe and apparel stores in a mall are located next to one another? Consumers looking for these types of merchandise are involved in convenience or comparison shopping situations, as we described in Chapter 7. They want to be able to make their choice easily in the case of convenience shopping or to have a good assortment so the can "shop around."

This location approach is based on the principle of cumulative attraction, in which a cluster of similar and complementary retailing activities will generally have greater drawing power than isolated stores that engage in the same retailing activities.

LOCATIONAL ADVANTAGES WITHIN A CENTRE

Once the centre's accessibility is evaluated, the analyst must evaluate the locations within it. Since the better sites cost more, retailers must consider their importance. For instance, in a strip shopping centre, the more expensive locations are closest to the grocery store. A liquor store or a flower shop that may attract impulse buyers should thus be close to the grocery store. But a shoe repair store, which shouldn't expect impulse customers, could be in an inferior location because customers in need of this service will seek out the store.

The same issues apply when evaluating regional multilevel shopping centres. It's advantageous for apparel stores such as Club Monaco to be clustered in the more expensive locations near a department store in a mall. People shopping for clothing may start at the department store and naturally gravitate to stores near it. Yet a store such as SportsChek, another destination store, needn't be in the most expensive location, since many of its customers know they're in the market for this type of product before they even get to the centre.

Another consideration is to locate stores that appeal to similar target markets close together. In essence, customers want to shop where they'll find a good assortment of merchandise. This is based on the principle of **cumulative attraction** in which a cluster of similar and complementary retailing activities will generally have greater drawing power than isolated stores that engage in the same retailing activities. This is why antique shops, car dealers, and shoe and clothing stores all seem to do better if they're close to one another. Of course, an area can become overstored when it has too many competing stores to profitably satisfy demand.

The principle of cumulative attraction applies both to stores that sell complementary merchandise and those that compete directly with one another. Thus a good location is one whose tenant mix provides:

- a good selection of merchandise that competes with itself
- complementary merchandise

estimating demand for a new location

Retailers estimate the demand for a new location by defining its trade area and then estimating how much people within the trade area will spend. In this section, we will take a close look at how retailers delimit their trade areas and the factors they consider when defining trade area boundaries. Then we describe the types of information and techniques retailers use to estimate demand.

TRADE AREA

A trade area is a contiguous geographic area that accounts for the majority of a store's sales and customers. Trade areas can be divided into two or three zones. Such trade areas are called **polygons** because their boundaries conform to streets and other map features. The zones' exact definitions should be flexible to account for particular areas' nuances.

The **primary zone** is the geographic area from which the store or shopping centre derives 60 to 65 percent of its customers. The **secondary zone** is the geographic area of secondary importance in terms of customer sales, generating about 20 percent of a store's sales. The **tertiary zone** (the outermost ring) includes customers who occasionally shop at the store or shopping centre. There are several reasons for the tertiary zone. First, these customers may lack adequate retail facilities closer to home. Second, there are excellent highway systems to the store or centre so customers can get there easily. Third, customers may drive near the store or centre on the way to or from work. Finally, customers are drawn to the store or centre because it is in or near a tourist area.

Factors Defining Trade Areas   The actual boundaries of a trade area are determined by the store's accessibility, natural and physical barriers, type of shopping area, type of store, and competition. Driving time is a useful criterion for defining trade areas because the time it takes to get to a particular shopping area is more important to the potential customer than distance. For example, driving to the retailer's

A 7-Eleven convenience store's trade area is small, possibly only a kilometre or two, compared to a Sears store that may draw customers from 50 kilometres away.

location might take 5 minutes for those in the primary trade area, 10 minutes for those in the secondary trade area, and 20 minutes for those in the tertiary trade area.

Trade area size is also influenced by the type of store or shopping area. A 7-Eleven convenience store's trade area, for example, may extend less than a kilometre, whereas a category specialist such as Toys "R" Us may draw customers from 50 kilometres away. The difference is due to the nature of the merchandise sold and the total size of the assortment offered. Convenience stores succeed because customers can buy products such as milk and bread quickly and easily. If customers must drive great distances, the store is no longer convenient. Category specialists offer a large choice of shopping and specialty products for which customers are willing to put forth additional effort to shop. Thus, customers will generally drive some distance to shop at a category specialist.

Another way of looking at how the type of store influences the size of a trade area is whether it's a destination or a symbiotic store. A **destination store** is one in which the merchandise, selection, presentation, pricing, or other unique features act as a magnet for customers. A **symbiotic store** is one that does not create its own traffic and whose trade area is determined by the dominant retailer in the shopping centre or retail area. In general, destination stores have larger trade areas than symbiotic stores—people are willing to drive farther to shop there. Hakim Optical would qualify as a destination store due to the exclusive nature of its merchandise. Other examples of destination stores are: anchor stores in shopping centres, such as grocery stores or department stores; certain specialty stores such as RadioShack and Polo/Ralph Lauren; category killers such as Staples Business Depot; and some service providers such as movie theatres.

The level of competition also affects the size and shape of a trade area for a particular store. If two convenience food stores are too close together, their respective trade areas will shrink since they offer the same merchandise. On the other hand, Hakim Optical is one of several optical shops in this business district. Having similar shopping goods stores in the same vicinity generally expands the trade area boundaries; more people are drawn to the area to shop because of its expanded selection. Additionally, a retailer's trade area is limited by a large regional shopping centre that has several stores carrying similar merchandise.

This dry cleaning shop is in a strip mall. A drug store anchors the centre. Which is the symbiotic store and which is the destination store?

SOURCES OF INFORMATION

Three types of information are required to define a trade area:

* Retailers must determine how many people are in the trade area and where they live. For this, retailers use a technique known as customer spotting.

- Retailers use the demographic and GIS (geographic information systems) data to describe their potential customers in an attempt to assess how much they will buy in the proposed trade area.

- Retailers use the Internet and other published sources to assess their competition. In strongly competitive trade areas, a retailer can expect to achieve a smaller piece of the total market potential for a particular type of merchandise or store.

Customer Spotting   The purpose of the customer spotting technique is to spot, or locate, the residences of customers for a store or shopping centre.[20] Data specific to a retailer's customers are usually obtained from information from credit card or cheque purchases or from customer loyalty programs. Retailers can also collect this information manually as part of the checkout process.

Another method is to note automobile licence plates in the parking lot and trace them to the owner by purchasing the information from governments or private research companies. A word of caution, however: This method is thought to be inaccurate and is illegal in some areas. Experts believe that at least 500 plates are necessary to provide a good sample. The plates can be matched against a national vehicle registration database and summarize where the vehicles originate. This approach may, however, be the easiest way to understand the trade area of competitors.

The data collected from customer spotting can be processed in two ways: by manually plotting the location of each customer on a map, or by using a GIS system.

Once the customers are spotted, the retailer can delineate a trade area. This process involves a lot of subjectivity, so the guidelines presented earlier in this chapter are helpful.

Statistics Canada   A census is taken every five years in Canada. The population of each census tract area can range from 2500 to 8000 people, but the preferred average is 4000 people; city cores will have a higher population density. In Canada, there are 25 CMAs (Census Metropolitan Areas) across the country.

In the census, each household in the country is counted to determine the number of persons per household, household relationships, sex, race, age, and marital status. The information is detailed under the following themes: Population, Education, Earnings, Work, Income, Families, Dwellings, and Religion. Detailed census information is also available through "GeoPost Plus," which can be purchased from Canada Post. A report on each building identifies the number of housing units at the address, whether the dwelling is owned or rented, whether the dwelling is owner-occupied, the housing value, the rent, and the vacancy status. Additional information is obtained from *Financial Post Markets Canadian Demographics. FP Markets* is a valuable tool when trying to determine the profile of consumers living in a specific area. The book provides percentage increases in population over the past five years and projects population growth for the next six years. Consumer spending patterns are broadly defined, and the psychographic profiles of people living in the area are identified as well. *FP Markets* divides Canadians into 60 predefined psychographic clusters and 19 financial clusters; explanations of the clusters are included.

FP Markets features tables that identify buying indices by province, economic region, census division, urban market, metropolitan area, city, and town (see Exhibit 6–4). Retail sales estimates by class of business, economic region, and census division are identified and income projections to 2008 are included.

Demographic Data and GIS Vendors   There are hundreds of private companies specializing in providing retailers with information that will help them make better store location decisions. Some, known as demographic data vendors, such as

Claritas, specialize in repackaging and updating census-type data in a format that's easy to understand, easy and quick to obtain, and relatively inexpensive. Since the data from the census can be dated, these firms construct computer models to generate estimates of current and future population and demographic characteristics.

Other firms specialize in **geographic information systems (GIS)**, computerized systems that enable analysts to illustrate their customers' demographics, buying behaviour, and other data in a map format.[21] In many ways a GIS resembles a database program because it analyzes and relates information stored as records. Additionally, however, each record contains information used to draw a geometric shape—usually a point, a line, or a polygon—and represents a unique place on Earth to which the data corresponds. As such, GIS is a spatial database, a database that stores the location and shape of information. Using GIS, analysts can identify the boundaries of a trade area and isolate target customer groups. Data for GIS are collected at the point of sale and stored in data warehouses and combined with the type of information that is available from the demographic data vendors.

GIS firms offer a wide range of tools useful for assessing consumer demand in an area. They utilize data from consumer surveys from private marketing research companies.

Measuring Competition   Estimating the demand for a retailer's products is a critical success factor, but it tells only half the story. It's equally important to determine the level of competition in the trade area. Earlier in this chapter, we concluded that either a saturated or an understored trade area offers a potentially good location opportunity, but that retailers should avoid trade areas that are overstored. How can a retailer such as Hakim Optical determine the level of saturation of the trade area for a potential new location? In other words, what's the level of trade area competition?

One of the most powerful methods of measuring competition is over the Internet.[23] Most Web sites list not only all current locations but future sites as well. Demographic information for prospective sales in other countries might eliminate the need for an in-person visit. A more traditional method of accessing competitive information is through the Yellow Pages of the telephone book. This information is also available on CD-ROM. Other sources of competitive information are: directories published by trade associations, chambers of commerce, International Council of Shopping Centres (shopping centres), Urban Land Institute (shopping centres), local newspaper advertising departments, municipal and provincial governments, specialized trade magazines, and list brokers.

A relatively easy way to determine level of competition is to calculate the total square metres of retail space devoted to a type of store per household. For example, published sources can estimate the total square metres devoted to optical retailers in their trade area and divide it by the number of households. The higher the ratio, the higher the level of competition will be. Of course, there's no substitute for personal visits, as observation will lend valuable insight to gathering competitve intelligence.

METHODS OF ESTIMATING DEMAND

A number of complementary analytical methods are used to estimate the demand for a new store. One of the most widely used techniques, the analogue approach, was first developed by William Applebaum for the Kroger Company in the 1930s. A more formalized statistical version of the analogue approach uses regression analysis. A third approach, known as Huff's gravity model, is based on Newton's law of gravity. We discuss these location analysis methods below.

The Analogue Approach   The analogue approach could just as easily be called the *similar store approach*. Suppose European Optical wants to open a new location. Since its present location in Vancouver has been very successful, it would like to find a location whose trade area has similar characteristics. It would estimate the size and customer demographic characteristics of its current trade area and then attempt to match those characteristics to new potential locations. Thus, knowledge of customer demographics, the competition, and sales of currently operating stores can be used to predict the size and sales potential of a new location.

Using the analogue approach, European Optical would undertake the following steps:

- Complete a competitive analysis of the optional sites to estimate potential sales for the store sites.

- Define the current trade area, based on density of customers to the store, drive zones, major roads, and natural or manmade barriers.

- Determine the trade area characteristics based on demographic research and psychographic profiles.

- Match the characteristics of the current trade area with the potential new store locations to determine the best site.

Step 1: Conduct Competitive Analysis to Estimate Potential Sales   Unlike other optical stores, European Optical carries a very exclusive merchandise selection. In general, the higher the trade area potential, the lower the relative competition will be (see Exhibit 6-5).

exhibit 6–4   Vancouver Canadian Demographic 2007, *FP Markets*

VANCOUVER CMA (Census Metropolitan Area)

Population

July 1, 2007 - Estimate	2 277 996
% Cdn. Total	6.93
% Change. '01-'07	10.06
Avg. Annual Growth Rate, '01-'07. %	1.61
2009 Projected Population	2 344 311
2012 Projected Population	2 443 822
2007 Households Estimate	894 197
2009 Projected Households	930 582
2012 Projected Households	985 108

Income

% Above/Below National Average	5
2007 Total Income Estimate $	68 728 920 000
% Cdn. Total	7.27
2007 Average Hhld. Income $	76 900
2007 Per Capita $	30 200
% 2007 Hhlds., Income $100 000+	22.31
2009 Projected Income $	76 256 990 000
2012 Projected Income $	88 250 310 000

Retail Sales

% Above/Below National Average	-2
2007 Retail Sales Estimate $	27 541 630 000
% Cdn. Total	6.81
2007 per Household $	30 800
2007 per Capita $	12 100
2007 No. of Establishments	15 567
2009 Projected Retail Sales $	30 968 120 000
2012 Projected Retail Sales $	37 409 620 000

Population
2007 Estimates

Total		2 277 996
Male		1 126 997
Female		1 150 999
Age Groups	Male	Female
0-4	58 662	56 439
5-9	60 146	56 962
10-14	67 015	62 775
15-19	70 690	66 966
20-24	81 135	77 301
25-29	88 229	87 062
30-34	85 575	87 580
35-39	91 023	93 682
40-44	94 684	95 169
45-49	92,948	94 593
50-54	83 858	86 295
55-59	73 624	74 878
60-64	54 652	55 725
65-69	38 433	40 703
70+	86 323	115 869

Daytime Population
2007 Estimates

Working Population	1 113 279
At Home Population	1 014 339
Total	2 127 618

Income
2007 Estimates

Avg. Household Income $	76 862
Avg. Family Income $	85 307
Per Capita Income $	30 171

Avg. Employment Income Male $	49 433
Avg. Emloyment Income Male (Full Time) $	64 421
Avg. Employment Income Female $	32 555
Avg. Employment Income Female (Full Time) $	46 040

Disposable & Discretionary Income
2007 Estimates

Disposable Income per Hhld. $	56 021
Discretionary Income per Hhld. $	17 326

Liquid Assets
2005 Estimates

Equity Investments per Hhld. $	123 670
Interest Bearing Investments per Hhld. $	98 894
Total Liquid Assets per Hhld. $	222 565
Total Liabilities per Hhld. $	127 144

Labour Force
2007 Estimates

	Male	Female
In the Labour Force	670 217	593 440
Participation Rate	72.1	61.6
Employed	643 162	563 605
Unemployed	27 056	29 835
Unemployment Rate	4.0	5.0
Not in Labour Force	259 236	369 158

Occupations by Major Groups
2007 Estimates

	Male	Female
Management	98 763	49 380
Business, Finance & Admin.	71 015	173 409
Natural & Applied Sci. & Rel'd	71 346	16 817
Health	15 639	47 903
Social Sci., Gov't Serv's & Relig'n	19 128	34 061

Education	17 026	29 358
Arts, Culture, Recr'n & Sport	24 985	24 310
Sales & Service	141 158	169 330
Trades, Transp. & Equip. Ops. etc.	146 466	9 924
Primary Industries	15 447	6 875
Processing, Mfg. & Utilities	36 443	18 193

Level of Schooling
2007 Estimates

Population 20 years +	1 754 475
Less than Grade 9	115 041
Grades 9-13 w/o Certif.	258 451
Grades 9-13 with Certif.	210 262
Trade Certif./Dip.	185 473
Non-Univ. w/o Certif./Dip.	125 292
Non-Univ. with Certif./Dip.	294 796
Univ. w/o Degree	173 945
Univ. w/o Degree/Certif.	108 984
Univ. with Certif.	64 961
Univ. with Degree	391 215

Average Household Expenditures
2007 Estimates

Food $	8 102
Shelter $	14 444
Clothing $	2 965
Transportation $	9 451
Health & Personal Care $	2 957
Recr'n, Read'g & Education $	6 171
Taxes & Securities	19 387
Other $	9 566
Total Expenditures $	73 044

Private Households
2007 Estimates

Private Households, Total	894 187
Pop. in Private Households	2 252 985
Avg. No. per Household	2.5

Families
2007 Estimates

Families in Private Households	572 187
Husband-Wife Families	484 003
Lone-Parent Families	88 184
Avg. No. Persons per Family	3.0
Avg. No. Sons/Daughters at Home	1.2

Housing
2007 Estimates

Occupied Private Dwellings	894 189
Owned	547 700
Rented	346 028
Band Housing	459
Single-Detached House	388 285
Semi-Detached House	22 467
Row Houses	66 459
Apartment, 5+ Storeys	103 658
Owned Apartment, 5+ Storeys	36 716
Apartment, fewer than 5 Storeys	224 439
Apartment, Detached Duplex	81 055
Other Single-Attached	1 432
Movable Dwellings	6 392

Vehicles

2005 NVR ('05 YE)	108 298
03-'05 Model Yrs. VOR (July '04)	162 245
% '03-'05 Total VOR (July '04)	14.43
81-'02 Model Yrs. VOR (July '04)	961 882
% '81-'02 Total VOR (July '04)	85.57
Total VOR (July '04)	1 124 127

NVR = New Vehicle Registered.
VOR = Vehicles on the Road.

Marital Status
2007 Estimates (Age 15+)

Single (never married)	569 019
Married (legal & common law)	1 059 175
Separated (legally married)	56 740
Widowed	108 827
Divorced	123 236

PSYTE Categories
2007 Estimates

	No. of Hhlds.	% Total	Index
Canadian Elite	8 033	0.90	123
Suburban Affluence	1 874	0.21	38
Exurban Estates	6 414	0.72	178
Professional Duets	244	0.03	4
Family Comfort	11 569	1.29	76
Commuter Homesteads	14 206	1.59	162
Euro Traditionals	783	0.09	12
Primary Pursuits	778	0.09	10
Towns with Tempo.	1 175	0.13	10
Suburban Growth	11 017	1.23	87
Asian Heights	71 901	8.04	851
Urban Gentry	4 476	0.50	24
Cruising Commuters	6 735	0.75	44
Bicycles and Bookbags	10 928	1.22	91
Young Technocrats	16 526	1.85	179
Exurban Wave	6 223	0.70	38
Family Crossroads	76 796	8.59	568
Row House Streets	22 288	2.49	413
University Enclaves	43 610	4.88	218
Upbeat Blues	482	0.05	6
Town and Country	136 764	15.29	645
Satellite Suburbs	9 024	1.01	53
Urban Promise	11 432	1.28	58
South Asian Corners	18 124	2.03	596
Conservative Homebodies	408	0.05	2
Agrarian Heartland	948	0.11	6
Village Views	212	0.02	1
Workers' Landing	21 473	2.40	432
Pacific Fusion	93 639	10.47	1 462
Village Blues	216	0.02	1
Sushi and Shiraz	70 862	7.92	454
Hi-Rise Sunsets	38 306	4.28	259
New Canada Neighbours	186	0.02	4
Senior Town	2 569	0.29	59
Suburban Hi-Rise	5 756	0.64	83
Highland Havens	6 121	0.68	30
Urban Vibe	5 211	0.58	84
Middletown Mix	680	0.08	3
Cabins and Cottages	1 083	0.12	7
Blue Collar Stride	8 084	0.9	38
Elder Harbour	27 443	3.07	102
Hi-Rise Melting Pot	11 160	1.25	153
Second City Renters	11 916	1.33	71
Service Crew	76 928	8.60	351
First Peoples	25	0.00	0
Blues in Motion	16 258	1.82	71
Quebec Seniors	2 470	0.28	37
Metro Medley	831	0.09	12

Financial PSYTE
2007 Estimates

	No. of Hhlds.	% Total	Index
Platinum Domain	17 488	1.96	271
Savvy Investors	4 864	0.54	36
Blue Chip Commuters	27 572	3.08	95
Upper Middle Amenities	32 813	3.65	163
Monster Mortgage	11 147	1.25	42
Kids and Credit	265 012	29.64	756
Frugal Families	15 138	1.69	59
Cautious Consumer	131 067	14.66	406
Quiet Neighbours	59 338	6.64	26
High Rise Low Liquidity	171 934	19.23	360

Rent-to-Own	212	0.02	0
Just Checking	39 565	4.42	28
New Beginnings	118 255	13.22	98

Home Language
2007 Estimates

	% Total	
English	1 472 739	65.37
French	3 884	0.17
Arabic	1 510	0.07
Chinese	177 224	7.87
Croatian	1 343	0.06
German	1 355	0.06
Gujarati	1 701	0.08
Hindi	6 229	0.28
Italian	2 864	0.13
Japanese	5 519	0.24
Korean	17 223	0.76
Persian (Farsi)	10 590	0.47
Polish	3 080	0.14
Portuguese	1 613	0.07
Punjabi	50 117	2.22
Romanian	1 650	0.07
Russian	3 575	0.16
Serbian	2 082	0.09
Spanish	6 495	0.29
Tagalog (Pilipino)	6 631	0.29
Urdu	1 888	0.08
Vietnamese	11 917	0.53
Other languages	27 989	1.24
Multiple Responses	433 767	19.25
Total	2 525 985	100.00

Building Permits

	2005	2004	2003
Value $000	5 650 982	4 842 765	3 677 471

Housing Starts

	2005	2004	2003
No.	18 914	19 430	15 626

Community Newspaper(s)

	Total Circulation
Bowen Island, West Vancouver:	
Bowen Island Undercurrent	n.a.
Burnaby: Burnaby Now	
Wednesday	49 111
Saturday	49 113
Burnaby, New Westminster: Burnaby/New Westminster News Leader (The)	
Thursday, Saturday	61 456
Coquitlam, Port Coquitlam, Port Moody: Coquitlam Now	
Wednesday, Friday	54 271
Coquitlam, Port Coquitlam, Port Moody: Tri-City News (The)	
Wednesday	54 936
Friday	n.a.
Saturday	54 599
Delta: Delta Optimist (The)	
Wednesday, Saturday	16 825
Delta (South), Twaawwassen, Ladner: South Delta Leader (The)	15 702
Langley: Langley Advance News (The)	
Tuesday, Friday	39 856
Langley: Langley Times	
Wednesday	38 618
Friday	38 594
Sunday	38 575
Maple Ridge, Pitt Meadows: Maple Ridge News (The)	
Wednesday	29 138
Saturday	29 142

Maple Ridge, Pitt Meadows:
  Maple Ridge-Pitt Meadows Times
  Tuesday   27 900
  Friday   27 901
New Westminster: New Westminster Now/
  Royal City Record
  Wednesday, Saturday   16 201
New Westminster, Burnaby:
  New Westminster News Leader (The)
  Thursday, Saturday   61 455
North Vancouver: North Shore News
  Wednesday   64 499
  Friday   64 490
  Sunday   64 534
Richmond: Richmond News
  Tuesday   46 033
  Friday   46 041
Richmond: Richmond Review (The)
  Thursday   46 387
  Saturday   46 400
Surrey: Cloverdale Reporter News
  (The) (monthly)   20 000
Surrey: Indo-Canadian Voice (The)   18 500
Surrey, North Delta: Surrey/N. Delta Leader (The)
  Sunday   85 850
  Wednesday, Friday   85 851
Surrey, North Delta: Surrey/N. Delta Now
  Wednesday, Saturday   112 450
Vancouver: Community Digest   25 000
Vancouver: East Side Review   3 500
Vancouver: False Creek News (The)   25 000
Vancouver: Georgia Straight (The)   115 114
Vancouver: L'Express du Pacifique   1 250
Vancouver: Nouvelles Communautaires   25 000
Community Newspaper(s) (continued)
Vancouver: Source (La/The)   4 000
Vancouver: Vancouver Courier
  Downtown Edition   24 575
Vancouver: Vancouver Courier
  East Side Edition
  Wednesday   57 929
  Friday   59 967
Vancouver: Vancouver Courier
  West Side Edition
  Wednesday   49 965
  Friday   49 355
Vancouver: West Side Review   6 500
Vancouver: West Ender   54 092
White Rock: Peace Arch News (The)
  Wednesday, Saturday   30 500

BURNABY
(City)
Vancouver CMA
In Greater Vancouver Regional District

Population
July 1, 2007 Estimate   221 008
% Cdn. Total   0.67
% Change, '01-'07   9.38
Avg. Annual Growth Rate, '01-'07, %   1.51
2008 Projected Population   227 106
2012 Projected Population   236 260
2007 Households Estimate   86 152
2009 Projected Households   90 141
2012 Projected Households   96 114

Income
% Above/Below National Average   -11
2007 Total Income Estimate $ 5 658 350 000

% Cdn. Total   0.60
2007 Average Hhld. Income $ 65 700
2007 Per Capita $ 25 600
% 2007 Hhlds., Income $100 000+   16.11
2009 Projected Total Income $ 6 269 140 000
2012 Projected Total Income $ 7 243 370 000

Retail Sales
% Above/Below National Average   10
2007 Retail Sales Estimate $ 2 980 230 000
% Cdn. Total   0.74
2007 per Household $ 34 600
2007 per Capita $ 1 566
2007 No. of Establishments   1 566
2009 Projected Retail Sales $ 3 358 010 000
2012 Projected Retail Sales $ 4 066 180 000

Population
2007 Estimates
Total   221 008
Male   109 167
Female   111 841

Age Groups	Male	Female
0-4	4 997	4 700
5--9	5 405	5 082
10--14	6 321	5 859
15-19	6 894	6 493
20-24	8 315	7 726
25-29	9 050	8 714
30-34	8 637	8 698
35-39	8 975	9 176
40-44	8 903	9 070
45-49	8 645	8 977
50-54	7 758	8 150
55-59	6 896	7 194
60-64	5 320	5 523
65-69	3 831	4 119
70+	9 219	12 360

Daytime Population
2007 Estimates
Working Population   124 420
At Home Population   103 872
Total   228 292

Income
2007 Estimates
Avg. Household Income $ 65 679
Avg. Family Income $ 72 066
Per Capita Income $ 25 602
Avg. Employment Income Male $ 41 985
Avg. Employment Income Male (Full Time) $ 55 898
Avg. Employment Income Female $ 30 005
Avg. Employment Income Female (Full Time) $ 43 925

Disposable & Discretionary Income
2007 Estimates
Disposable Income per Hhld. $ 48 286
Discretionary Income per Hhld. $ 13 679

Liquid Assets
2005 Estimates
Equity Investments per Hhld. $ 89 746
Interest Bearing Investments per Hhld. $ 81 014
Total Liquid Assest per Hhld. $ 170 781
Total Liabilities per Hhld. $ 111 890

Labour Force
2007 Estimates	Male	Female
In the Labour Force	62 141	54 995
Participation Rate	68.3	58.2
Employed	58 948	51 626
Unemployed	3 193	3 369
Unemployment Rate	5.1	6.1
Not in Labour Force	28 783	39 557

Occupations by Major Group
2007 Estimates	Male	Female
Management	8 462	4 115
Business. Finance & Admin.	7 217	17 609
Natural $ Applied Sci. & Rel'd.	8 408	2 109
Health	1 322	3 745
Social Sci., Gov't Serv's & Relig'n	1 391	3 065
Education	1 571	2 696
Arts, Culture, Recr'n & Sport	1 857	1 802
Sales & Service	12 998	15 522
Trades, Transp. & Equip. Ops, etc.	13 683	947
Primary Industries	899	176
Processing, Mfg. & Utilities	2 936	1 547

Level of Schooling
2007 Estimates
Population 20 years +   172 105
Less than Grade 9   12 631
Grades 9-13 w/o Certif.   23 458
Grades 9-13 with Certif.   21 245
Trade Certif./Dip.   18 014
Non-Univ. w/o Certif./Dip.   12 321
Non-Univ. with Certif./Dip.   28 292
Univ. w/o Degree   18 157
Univ. w/o Degree/Certif.   10 773
Univ. with Certif.   7 384
Univ. with Degree   37 987

Average Household Expenditures
2007 Estimates
Food $ 7 712
Shelter $ 12 847
Clothing $ 2 550
Transportation $ 8 764
Health & Personal Care   2 762
Recr'n, Read'g $ Education $ 5 408
Taxes & Securities $ 16 099
Other $ 8 073
Total Expenditures $ 64 215

Private Households
2007 Estimates
Private Households, Total   86 152
Pop. in Private Households   217 781
Avg. No. per Household   2.5

Families
2007 Estimates
Families in Private Households   54 522
Husband-Wife Families   45 813
Lone-Parent Families   8 709
Avg. No. Persons per Family   3.0
Avg. No. Sons/ Daughters at Home   1.2

Housing
2007 Estimates
Occupied Private Dwellings   86 152
Owned   48 564
Rented   37 598
Single-Detatched House   30 908
Semi-Detached House   3 085
Row Houses   7 020
Apartment, 5+ Storeys   14 791
Owned Apartment, 5+ Storeys   7 355
Apartment, Fewer than 5 Storeys   22 718
Apartment, Detached Duplex   7 502
Other Single-Attached   105
Movable Dwellings   23

Cluster Classification	Population Count in Five-Kilometre Ring	Percentage of Population in Each Classification
Young Urban Professionals	9129	26.00%
Asian Mosaic	5175	14.90
The Affluentials	4257	12.30
Urban Gentry	4211	12.10

exhibit 6–5

Neighbourhood Lifestyle Clusters for Five-Kilometre Ring Surrounding European Optical

Step 2: Define the Current Trade Area   On the basis of customer spotting data gathered from a data warehouse of current customers, a trade area map can be generated. The trade area map can also be defined based on drive times: 5 minutes for the primary trade area, 10 minutes for the secondary trade area, and 20 minutes for the tertiary trade area. Major highways and heavily travelled roads will bring traffic to the area but can also divide a trade area, as can a river or bridge, and may limit trade area potential.

Because European Optical is in a business district, the trade area will be smaller than it would be if located in a regional shopping centre. The regional shopping centre has complementary stores that attract more people to the area to shop because of the expanded selection of retailers and restaurants.

Step 3: Determine Trade Area Characteristics   The *Financial Post Markets* charts demographic trends (see Exhibit 6-4), including data on population, on households by number of persons, race, ethnic origin, and on age by sex. An interesting characteristic of the area surrounding European Optical is that an estimated 53.1 percent of the population was of Chinese descent (2006).

As we said earlier in this chapter, it is just as important to look at consumer lifestyles or psychographics as it is to examine their demographics. We know that European Optical's trade area is generally affluent, but are the residents the kind of people who would purchase its upscale fashion eyewear?

Exhibit 6–5 summarizes the most prominent lifestyle report for the five-kilometre ring surrounding European Optical. These segments, described in Exhibit 6–6, indicate an interesting mix of potential customers. The Affluentials and Urban Gentry both represent affluent, older groups—perfect for European Optical. Young Urban Professionals and Asian Mosaic will also be drawn to European Optical's high-fashion product lines. Generally, the reports show that the area is affluent and is therefore ideal for selling exclusive and expensive eyewear.

Step 4: Match Characteristics of Current Store with Potential New Store's Location to Determine the Best Site   Now that the trade area for European Optical's existing store is defined, the information can be used to choose a new store location. The trick is to find a location whose market area is similar or analogous to its existing store.

On the basis of the factors affecting demand described earlier in the chapter, it can be concluded that the five factors that contribute most to the success of European Optical's current location are high income, predominantly white-collar occupations, relatively large percentage of older residents, upscale profile, and relatively low competition for expensive, high-fashion eyewear. Exhibit 6–7 compares European Optical's current location with four potential locations on these five factors. These locations are pictured in Exhibit 6–8.

exhibit 6–6
Descriptions of Largest Clusters Surrounding European Optical

Young Urban Professionals

These single professionals are well educated and working; their growing incomes support their affluent tastes. They join health clubs and environmental groups, go dancing at clubs, and attend the theatre or museums. They also jog, bike, and play racquet sports. They use credit cards to buy expensive clothing.

Asian Mosaic

This diverse segment has married couples with either very young or adult children. Most work; unemployment is low. Despite their relative affluence, they don't invest or save, and few take out loans. Their home values or rents are unusually high because of location; most live in urban areas. They travel overseas, make long-distance phone calls, and enjoy going to theme parks.

The Affluentials

These are the wealthiest neighbourhoods. They receive their income from salaries, interest, dividends, owning rental properties, or self-employment. Their single-family homes in older suburbs are valued at more than four times the national average. These residents are older married couples with sophisticated tastes. They purchase luxury items and enjoy visiting museums and other cultural events. They frequently order clothing via phone or mail, drive expensive cars, vacation, play racquet sports, and read newspapers.

Urban Gentry

This segment is found along the West Coast. These middle-aged, married professionals are at the peak of their earning years. They don't have young children, but many are empty-nester wannabes whose adult children still live at home. Their income sources include salaries, dividends, interest, and owning rental properties. Some receive pensions or retirement income. Their single-family homes built in the 1950s or 1960s are valued at more than twice the national average. They keep physically fit by working out at the gym, playing racquet sports and golf, and taking vitamins. When not vacationing, they purchase home furnishings and contract for home improvements.

The potential customers of Site A typically have white-collar occupations; they have relatively good incomes and are comparatively young. Asian Mosaic also tend to have young families, so expensive eyewear may not be a priority purchase. Finally, there's a medium level of competition in the area.

The older residents surrounding Site B have moderate incomes and are mostly retired. Even though competition would be low and most residents need glasses, these customers are more interested in value than in fashion.

Site C has strong potential since the twenty-something residents in the area are young and have a strong interest in fashion. Although working, they are busy furnishing their first homes and apartments and paying off university loans. Although

exhibit 6–7   Descriptions of European Optical and Four Potential Locations' Trade Areas

Store Location	Average Household Income	White-Collar Occupations	Percentage Residents Age 45 and Over	Predominant Profile	Level of Competition
European					
Optical	$ XXX	High	37%	The Affluentials	Low
Site A	60 000	High	25	Asian Mosaic	Medium
Site B	70 000	Low	80	Retirement Communities	Low
Site C	100 000	High	30	Young Urban Professional	High
Site D	120 000	High	50	Upper-Income Empty-Nesters	Medium

Average household income is taken from the year 2006 projections in Exhibit 6–5. Level of white-collar occupations is estimated from data in Exhibit 6–6. Percentage of residents 45 years old and over is estimated from Exhibit 6–5. Level of competition was subjectively determined.

they would appreciate European Optical's fashionable assortment, they won't appreciate the high prices. Also, other high-end optical stores are entrenched in the area.

Site D is the best location for European Optical. The residents are older professionals, or early retirees with high incomes. Upper-Income Empty-Nesters are sophisticated consumers of adult luxuries such as high-fashion eyewear. Importantly, this cluster is similar to The Affluentials and Urban Gentry.

exhibit 6–8

Potential Locations for a European Optical Store

Unfortunately, finding analogous situations isn't always as easy as in this example. The weaker the analogy, the more difficult the location decision will be. When a retailer has a relatively small number of outlets (say, 20 or fewer), the analogue approach is often best. Even retailers with just one outlet can use the analogue approach. As the number of stores increases, it becomes more difficult for the analyst to organize the data in a meaningful way. More analytical approaches are necessary.

estimating potential sales for a store

Three approaches for using the information about the trade area to estimate the potential sales for a store at the location are (1) the Huff gravity model, (2) regression analysis, and (3) the analogue method.

HUFF GRAVITY MODEL

The **Huff gravity model**[24] for estimating the sales of a retail store is based on the concept of gravity: Consumers are attracted to a store location just like Newton's falling apple was attracted to the Earth. In this model, the force of the attraction is based on two factors: the size of the store (larger stores have more pulling power) and the time it takes to travel to the store (stores that take more time to get to have less pulling power). The mathematical formula to predict the probability of a customer going to a specific store location is as follows:

$$P_{ij} = \frac{S_j \div T_{ij}^{\,b}}{\sum\limits_{j=1}^{n} S_j \div T_{ij}^{\,b}}$$

where

P_{ij} = probability that customer i shops at location j,

S_j = size of the store at location j, and

T_{ij} = travel time for customer i to get to location j.

The formula indicates that the larger the size (S_j) of the store compared with competing stores' sizes, the greater probability that a customer will shop at the location. A larger size is generally more attractive in consumers' eyes because it means more merchandise assortment and variety. Travel time of distance (T_{ij}) has the opposite effect

exhibit 6–9

Application of Huff Gravity Models for Estimating Store Sales

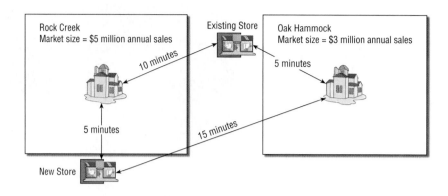

on the probability that a consumer will shop at the location. The greater the travel time or distance to the consumer, compared with that of competeting locations, the lower the probability that the consumer will shop at the location. Generally, customers would rather shop at a close store rather than a distant one.

The exponent λ reflects the aelrtive effect of travel time versus store size. When λ is equal to 1, store size and travel time have an equal but opposite effect on the probability of a consumer shopping at a store location. When λ is greater than 1, travel time has a greater effect, and when λ is less than 1, store size has a greater effect. he value of λ is affected by the nature of the shopping trips consumers generally take when visitin the specific type of store. For instance, travel time or distance is generally more important for convience goods than for shopping goods because people are less willing to travel a great distance for a liter of milk than they are for a new pair of shoes. Thus, a larger value for λ is assigned if the store being studied specializes in convenience shopping trips rather than comparison shopping trips. The value of λ is usually estimated statistically using data that describe shopping patterns at existing stores.

To illustrate the use of the Huff model, consider the situations shown in Exhibit 6–9. A small town has two communities, Rock Creek and Oak Hammock. The town currently has one 465 square metre drug store with annual sales of $8 million, $3 million of which come from Oak Hammock residents and $5 million from Rock Creek residents. A competitive chain is considering opening a 930 square metre store. As the exhibit illustrates, the driving time for the averalge Rock Creek resident to the exisiting store is ten minutes but would only be five minutes to the new store. In contrast, the driving time for the typical Oak Hammock resident to the existing drug store is five minutes and would be fifteen minutes to the new store. Based on its past experience, the drug store chain has found that λ equals 2 for its store locations. Using the Huff formula, the probability of a Rock Creek resident shopping at the new location, P_{RC}, is

$$P_{RC} = \frac{10\,000/5^2}{10\,000/5^2 + 5000/10^2} = .889.$$

The probability of Oak Hammock residents shopping at the new location, P_{OH}, is

$$P_{OH} = \frac{10\,000/15^2}{10\,000/15^2 + 5000/5^2} = .182.$$

The expected sales (probability of patronage times market size) for the new location thus would be

.889 × $3 million + .182 × $5 million = $4 910 000.

This simple application assumes that the market size for drug stores in the community will remain the same at $8 million with the addition of the new store. We also could have considered that two drug stores would increase the total size of the market. In addition, rather than do the calculations for the average customer located in the middle of each community, we could have calculated the probabilites that each customer in the two communities would go to the new location.

Even though the Huff gravity model only considers two factors affecting store sales—travel time and store size—its predictions are quite accurate because these two factors typically have the greatest effect on store choice.[25] The regression approach discussed in the next seciton provides a way to incorporate additional factors into the sales forecast for a store under consideration.

REGRESSION ANALYSIS

The **regression analysis** approach is based on the assumption that factors that affect the sales of exisiting stores in a chain will have the same impact on stores located at new sites being considered. When using this approach, the retailer employs a technique called multiple regression to estimate a statistical model that predicts sales at existing store locations. The technique can consider the effects of the wide range of factors discussed in this chapter, including site characteristics such as visibility and access and characteristics of the trade area such as demographics and lifestyle segments.

Consider the following example: A chain of sporting goods stores has analyzed the factors affecting sales in its existing stores and found that the following model is the best predictor of store sales (the weights for the factors, such as 275 for the number of households, are estimated using multiple regression):

Store sales = 275 × number of households in trade area (15-minute drive time)
+ 1 800 000 × percentage of households in trade area with children under 15 years of age
+ 2 000 000 × percentage of households in trade area in Tapestry segment "aspiring young"
+ 8 × shopping centre square metres
+ 250 000 if visible from the street
+ 300 000 if Wal-Mart in centre

The sporting goods chain is considering the following two locations:

Variable	Location A	Location B
Households within 15 minute drive time	11 000	15 000
% of households with children under 15 years old	70%	20%
% of households in aspiring young geodemographic segment	60%	10%
Sq m of shopping centre	200 000	250 000
Visible from street	yes	no
Wal-Mart in shopping centre	yes	no

Using the statistical model, the forecasted sales for location A are:

Store sales at location A = $7 635 000 = 275 × 11 000
+ 1 800 000 × .7
+ 2 000 000 × .6
+ 8 × 200 000
+ 250 000
+ 300 000

and forecasted sales for location B are:

Store sales at location B = \$6 685 000 = 275 × 15 000
$$+ 1\ 800\ 000 \times .2$$
$$+ 2\ 000\ 000 \times .1$$
$$+ 8 \times 250\ 000$$

Note that location A has greater forecasted sales, even though it has a smaller trading area population and shopping centre size, because the profile of its target market fits the profile of the trade area better.

ANALOGUE APPROACH

As discussed, to develop a regression model, a retailer needs data about the trade area and site characterists from a large number of stores. Because small chains cannot use the regression approach, they use the similar but more subjective analogue approach. When using the **analogue approach**, the retailer simply describes the site and trade area characteristics for its most successful stores and attempts to find a site with similar characteristics.

Suppose European Optical was deciding to open another location and had four potential sites as identified in Column 1. Using the analogue approach, the retailer undertakes the following steps to estimate potential sales for a store site:

First, estimate the number of eyeglasses sold per person per year in Column 2. The area population is identified in Column 3 (this includes the number of your targeted customers living in the area); these numbers can be taken from Statistics Canada or *Financial Post Markets*. Next, estimate the trade area potential by multiplying Column 2 by Column 3. This will identify the total eyeglasses potential for the area in Column 4.

Column 5 is the rough estimates of the number of eyeglasses sold in the trade areas, based on visits to the competitive stores. Column 6 represents the unit sales potential for eyeglasses in the trade areas (Column 4 minus Column 5). The trade area potential penetration is calculated by dividing Column 6 by Column 4. For instance, because the total eyeglasses potential for the current Vancouver store trade area is 17 196 pairs and an additional 9646 pairs could be sold in that trade area, 56.09 percent of the eyeglasses market in the area remains untapped.

In general, the higher the trade area potential, the lower the relative competition will be. Column 8, the relative level of competition, is subjectively estimated on the basis of Column 7. According to the information in Exhibit 6-10, the best location for the new optical store would be Site B. The trade area potential is high and the competition is low.

exhibit 6–10   Competitive Analysis of Potential Locations

Trade Area (1)	Eyeglasses/ Year/ Person (2)	Trade Area Population (3)	Total Eyeglasses Potential (4)	Estimated Eyeglasses Sold (5)	Trade Area Potential Units (6)	Trade Area Potential Percentage (7)	Relative Level of Competition (8)
South Miami	0.2	85 979	17 196	7 550	9 646	56.09%	Low
Site A	0.2	91 683	18 338	15 800	2537	13.83	Medium
Site B	0.2	101 972	20 394	12 580	7814	38.32	Low
Site C	0.2	60 200	12 040	11 300	740	6.15	High
Site D	0.2	81 390	16 278	13 300	2978	18.29	Medium

Choosing the Best Method(s)   In any decision, the more information that's available, the better the outcome is likely to be. This is true for research in general and location analysis in particular. Therefore, if a combination of the techniques is applied and the same conclusion is reached, the retailer should have more confidence in the decision.

Some methods used for analyzing trade areas are better in certain situations, however. The analogue and Huff approaches are best when the number of stores with obtainable data is small, usually fewer than 30. These approaches can also be used by small retailers. The regression approach, on the other hand, is best when there are multiple variables expected to explain sales, since it's hard to keep track of multiple predictor variables when using a manual system such as the analogue approach. Also, the Huff gravity model explicitly considers the attractiveness of competition and customers' distance or travel time to the store or shopping centre in question. Finally, since Huff's gravity model usually does not utilize demographic variables, it's particularly important to use it in conjunction with the analogue or regression methods.

There are three trends that will shape site selection research in the next few decades.[26] First, it will be easier to collect and store data on customers in data warehouses. Second, advanced statistical modelling techniques, such as CHAID (chi square automatic interaction detection) and spatial allocation models, will become more popular. Finally, geographic information systems will become more sophisticated and at the same time more accessible to users.

refact
Quebec's European influence within North America makes it an ideal place for European companies to launch new products and a logical location from which North American companies can expand into Europe.[27]

SUMMARY

Location decisions are probably the most important decisions that a retailer will make. Compensation for a poor location may mean lowering prices and spending extra money on advertising to draw customers to the store. Remember that the most important factors in store location are the traffic flow and the demographics of people living in the area. If either attribute is inappropriate for the store location, then the site should be avoided.

Decisions about where to locate a store are critical to any retailer's success. A clear, coherent strategy should specify location goals. A location decision is particularly important because of its high cost and long-term commitment. A location mistake is clearly more devastating to a retailer than a buying mistake, for instance.

Retailers have a plethora of types of sites from which to choose. Many central business districts and downtown locations have become a more viable option than in the past due to gentrification of the areas and lack of suburban mall opportunities. Retailers also have many types of shopping centres from which to choose. They can locate in a strip or power centre, or they can go into a mall. We examined the relative advantages of several types of malls, including regional and superregional centres, lifestyle, fashion/specialty centres, theme/festival centres, and outlet centres. We also examined the viability of kiosks, freestanding sites, mixed-use developments, and other nontraditional locations.

Retailers have a hard time finding a perfect site. Each site has its own set of advantages and disadvantages. In assessing the viability of a particular site, a retailer must make sure the store's target markets will patronize that location. The location analyst's job isn't finished until terms of occupancy and other legal issues are considered.

Retailers consider several issues when assessing the attractiveness of a particular region, market, or trade area. They want to know about the people living in the area. What are their lifestyles? How wealthy and large are the households? Is the area growing or declining? Does it have a favourable business climate? Importantly, what is the level of competition?

Retailers should only locate in areas with heavy competition if they believe their retailing format is superior to that of their competitors. A safer strategy is to locate in an area with little competition. Of course, in today's overbuilt retail environment, such areas are nearly impossible to find. Does a retailer have the ability to manage multiple stores in an area or in multiple areas? What is the most profitable number of stores to operate in a particular area?

In assessing the viability of a particular site, a retailer must consider the location's accessibility as well as locational advantages within the centre.

Trade areas are typically divided into primary, secondary, and tertiary zones. The boundaries of a trade area are determined by how accessible it is to customers, the natural and physical barriers that exist in the area, the type of shopping area in which the store is located, the type of store, and the level of competition.

Retailers have three types of information at their disposal to help them define a trade area. First, they use a customer spotting technique to determine how many people are in their trade area and where they live. Second, they use demographic data and GIS firms and Statistics Canada. Finally, to assess their competition they use the Internet, other sources of secondary information, and a good old-fashioned walk through the neighbourhood.

Once retailers have the data that describes their trade areas, they use several analytical techniques to estimate demand. The analogue approach—one of the easiest to use—can be particularly useful for smaller retailers. Using this method, the retailer makes predictions about the sales of a new store based on sales in stores in similar areas. Regression analysis uses the same logic as the analogue approach but is statistically based and requires more objective data. Finally, we showed how Huff's model is used to predict the probability that a customer will frequent a particular store in a trade area. It is based on the premise that customers are more likely to shop at a given store or shopping centre if it's conveniently located and offers a large selection.

KEY TERMS

amount and quality of parking facilities, *143*

analogue approach, *156*

anchors, *132*

artificial barrier, *142*

central business district (CBD), *140*

congestion, *143*

cumulative attraction, *144*

demalling, *136*

destination store, *131, 145*

downtown location, *140*

fashion/specialty centre, *137*

franchisee, *128*

franchisor, *128*

freestanding site, *141*

gentrification, *140*

geographic information system (GIS) , *147*

Huff gravity model, *153*

ingress/egress, *143*

kiosk, *138*

lifestyle centre, *136*

mall, *132*

mixed-use development (MXD), *138*

natural barrier, *142*

outlet centres, *137*

overstored trade area, *129*

polygon, *144*

power centre, *133*

primary zone, *144*

region, *126*

regional centre, *136*

regression analysis, *155*

road condition, *142*

road pattern, *142*

saturated trade area, *129*

secondary zone, *144*

shopping centre, *132*

strip centre, *132*

superregional centre, *136*

symbiotic store, *145*

tertiary zone, *144*

trade area, *126*

traditional strip centre, *132*

understored trade area, *129*

visibility, *142*

Get Out & Do It!

1. **INTERNET EXERCISE** The largest mall in the world is the West Edmonton Mall in Alberta. Go to www.westedmontonmall.com. Do you think the attractions overshadow the shopping?

2. **GO SHOPPING** Go to your favourite shopping centre and analyze the tenant mix. Do the tenants appear to complement each other? What changes would you make in the tenant mix to increase the overall health of the centre?

3. **INTERNET EXERCISE** ESRI and Claritas both provide the types of information and maps described in this section. Go to their Web sites at www.esri.com and www.claritas.com and compare their product/service offerings. Which company would you call first?

4. **INTERNET EXERCISE** Do a competitive trade area analysis for a store of your choice by going to competitors' Internet corporate Web sites and determining the probability that they will be entering a particular trade area.

5. **GO SHOPPING** Go to two stores owned by the same chain. Define and evaluate their trade area. Which store do you think is more successful?

6. **GO SHOPPING** Go to a shopping mall. Get or draw a map of the stores. Analyze whether or not the stores are clustered appropriately. For instance, are all the high-end stores together? Is there a good mix of shopping goods stores adjacent to each other?

DISCUSSION QUESTIONS AND PROBLEMS

1. Why have location decisions become more important in recent years?

2. Pick your favourite store. Explain why you believe it is (or isn't) in the best location, given its target market.

3. Read the profile of the North West Company. What are the strengths and weaknesses of their location strategy?

4. As a consultant to 7-Eleven convenience stores, American Eagle Outfitters, and BMW Car Dealerships, what would you say is the single most important factor in choosing a site for these three very different types of stores?

5. Retailers have a tradition of developing shopping centres and freestanding locations in neighbourhoods or central business districts that have suffered decay. Some people have questioned the ethical and social ramifications of this process, which is known as gentrification. What are the benefits and problems associated with gentrification?

6. Staples and Office Depot both have strong multichannel strategies. How does the Internet affect their strategies for locating stores?

7. In many malls, fast-food retailers are located together in an area known as a food court. What are this arrangement's advantages and disadvantages to the fast-food retailer?

8. Why would a Payless ShoeSource store locate in a neighbourhood shopping centre instead of a regional shopping mall?

9. Why would a company such as Coach, a manufacturer of high-quality leather goods, open outlet stores? What are the disadvantages to such a strategy?

10. What are the shape and size of the trade area zones of a shopping centre near your school?

11. When measuring trade areas, why is the analogue approach not a good choice for a retailer with several hundred outlets?

12. True Value Hardware plans to open a new store. Two sites are available, both in middle-income neighbourhood centres. One neighbourhood is 20 years old and has been well maintained. The other was recently built in a newly planned community. Which site is preferable for True Value? Why?

13. Trade areas are often described as concentric circles emanating from the store or shopping centre. Why is this practice used? Suggest an alternative method. Which would you use if you owned a store in need of a trade area analysis?

14. Under what circumstances would a retailer use the analogue approach for estimating demand for a new store? What about regression?

15. Some specialty stores prefer to locate next to or close to an anchor store. But Little Caesars, a takeout pizza retailer typically found in strip centres, wants to be at the end of the centre away from the supermarket anchor. Why?

16. Retailers have a choice of locating on a mall's main floor or second or third level. Typically, the main floor offers the best, but most expensive, locations. Why would specialty stores such as RadioShack and Foot Locker choose the second or third floor?

17. A drugstore is considering opening a new location at shopping centre A, with hopes of capturing sales from a new neighbourhood under construction. Two nearby shopping centres, C and E, will provide competition. Using the following information and Huff's probability model, determine the probability that residents of the new neighbourhood will shop at shopping centre A:

Shopping Centre	Size (sq. m.)	Distance from New Neighbourhood (kilometres)
A	325 500	4
C	139 500	5
E	27 900	3

Assume that $b = 2$.

18. Identify the location strategies for each of the following types of retailers:
- Department stores
- Specialty apparel stores
- Category killers/specialists
- Grocery stores

CHAPTER 7

store design, layout, and visual merchandising strategy

Executive Briefing

Greg Helps, Visual Presentations Manager, Harry Rosen

Greg Helps, visual presentations manager at Harry Rosen, knows that everything that he does has to achieve one goal: "to create a better shopping experience for their customer."

Responsible for the overall merchandising and display presentation of 15 Harry Rosen stores across Canada, Greg Helps stays on top of the newest trends that will support the overall look of the season. It is not just developing the ideas for the next season that is important but the ability to communicate those ideas and to collaborate with a talented visual team consisting of seven regional visual presentation managers and 31 visual presentation associates who work closely with the merchandise manager in each store. The team develops seasonal window campaigns that tie directly into the overall marketing strategies; i.e., *Harry* magazine and Mainline Advertising. Working closely with Mark Texeira, Rosen's store designer, Helps collaborates on all new projects to review fixturing and furniture for any renovation or new store opening.

According to Helps, there are two major changes he has seen over his twenty years of working in the visual presentations area within Harry Rosen: There is a much greater focus on customer lifestyle; and the increased influence of fashion designers on visual merchandising. "Today we present merchandise based on two customer profiles, *Classic* and *Modern*, and we choose backdrops, paint colours and props based on what will best represent that customer profile." When Helps first started at Harry Rosen, American designer Ralph Lauren was just opening

QUESTIONS
What are the critical issues in designing a store?
What are the advantages and disadvantages of alternative store layouts?
How is store space assigned to merchandise and departments?
What are the best techniques for merchandise presentation?
How can stores increase customer appeal and sales?
How does the retail image strategy reflect the retailer's target market?

the "mansion" in New York City and designer shops were a relatively new concept. Now, "we receive a great deal of direction from each designer brand on how they see their product presented in our stores." It can be a challenging endeavour to satisfy all involved, but ultimately it is in the best interests of Rosen's and their customers to utilize the information. Working closely with vendors, Helps uses the concepts of fashion designers (including Hugo Boss, Ermengildo Zegna, and Giorgio Armani) to plan shop-within-a-shop areas that work within the Harry Rosen environment,

Knowing your customer is crucial to success, and appealing to the sophisticated and complex male customer is no easy task. The customer influences a lot of the visual decisions at Harry Rosen; for example, the *Classic* sportswear customer shops for complete outfits, so this product is merchandised in a package that suggests colour and style combinations that work. The *Modern* customer shops more frequently and likes to shop on his own, so specific item merchandising is key; e.g., jeans departments.

Visual merchandisers are often the unsung heroes of the retail world, working behind the scenes to convey the retailer's image and enhance customer appeal. Over the years at Rosen's, Greg Helps has learned the importance of a keen eye that constantly scrutinizes every aspect of the store to determine what can be done better to keep customers loyal to "Harry." That's the difference between good and great.

Retail revenue accounts for about six percent of Canada's gross domestic product. Retail also represents nearly 50 percent of total household spending in this country. Retailers should ask: "How do I get consumers to stop, shop, and keep coming back to my store?" To solve these challenges, retailers must link store design to their strategic plan.

The store image that a retailer creates is strategically planned to attract a specific target market's demographic and psychographic profile and to enhance the appeal of merchandise to that customer.

A good store design should be like a good story.[1] Every story has a beginning, middle, and end, usually in that order. The entrance sets up the story. It creates expectations and contains promises. As for the first impression, the storefront says, "I'm cheap" or "I'm sophisticated" or "I'm cool." Too often, stores launch right into "Here's what we've got to sell. Don't you love it?" A good entrance should entice, hint, and tease. There should be mystery. The cost of making an eye-catching window display doesn't have to be great, but the price of not making the effort could be.

Inside the store comes the middle of the story. It should start off slow. Customers need a few seconds to orient themselves after the entrance. A single message has a far greater chance of sticking than do a dozen products cluttering the way.

Seventy percent of purchase decisions are made in the store. This statistic is driving in-store marketing trends. Shopping today is less about utility and more about experience. Consumers want and now usually expect more from stores than products lined up neatly on a shelf. Customers need to be led on a journey throughout the store. Using visuals, light, and motion, take customers down a path of discovery.

There should, for instance, be visual destinations at the end of a long aisle. Exciting stores should be like Paris. Sighting down the Champs-Elysées, you are enticed by the Arc de Triomphe as a powerful destination. Finally, the cash wrap or checkout counter is the story's climactic finale. It's where retailers can convey subtle messaging without hard-selling.

objectives of good store design

Retail giants such as Holt Renfrew, Mountain Equipment Co-op, and Home Depot increase store traffic by creating experiences that go beyond attractive sales prices and product samples, from store events and interactive displays to in-store emotional and memorable experiences for shoppers. A growing trend in experiential marketing known as "retailtainment" is a concept in retail marketing that engages shoppers in various interactive events such as contests, shows, giveaways, and activities. The results are sales increases and long-term customer loyalty. When designing or redesigning a store, four objectives must be met.

DESIGN SHOULD BE CONSISTENT WITH IMAGE AND STRATEGY

To meet the first objective, retail managers must define the target customer and then design a store that complements customers' needs.[2] For instance, warehouse clubs, such as Sam's or Costco, have high ceilings with metal grids and concrete floors instead of tile—all of those things are perceived to indicate low prices. Actually, they are more expensive than some alternatives, but they are used to maintain an image.[3] ACNielsen Canada, the world's leading marketing information provider, offers services to help its customers create tailored retail experiences and ultimately increase sales. Customers would find it hard to accurately judge value if the physical environment were inconsistent with the merchandise or prices. REI is a master of matching its target customer with store design (see Retailing View 7.1).

DESIGN SHOULD POSITIVELY INFLUENCE CONSUMER BEHAVIOUR

To meet the second design objective of influencing customer buying decisions, retailers concentrate on store layout and space-planning issues. Grocery stores are organized to facilitate the shopping trip and to display as much merchandise as possible to encourage impulse sales. Yet boutiques are laid out in a free-form design that allows customers to browse.

Customers' purchasing behaviour is also influenced, both positively and negatively, by the store's atmosphere.[4] Signs are designed to attract attention. On a more subtle level, Mrs. Fields stores attract customers because of the smell of cookies. This chapter explores the methods retailers use to positively influence consumers' purchase behaviour and in-store experience.

DESIGN SHOULD CONSIDER COSTS VERSUS VALUE

Consistent with any retail decision, the third design objective is to consider the costs associated with each store design element versus the value received in terms of higher sales and profits. For instance, the free-form design found in many boutiques is much more costly than rows of gondolas in a discount store. (A *gondola* is an island type of self-service counter with tiers of shelves, bins, or pegs.) Also, the best locations within a store are "worth" the most, so they're reserved for certain types of merchandise.

For instance, many grocery stores place their produce near the store's entrance because it has a higher margin than other merchandise categories and it creates a nice atmosphere. Retailers develop maps called *planograms* that prescribe the location of merchandise based on profitability and other factors. Finally, when considering atmospheric issues of store design, retailers must weigh the costs along with the strategy and customer attraction issues. For instance, certain types of lighting used to highlight expensive jewellery and crystal cost more than rows of bare fluorescent bulbs.

DESIGN SHOULD BE FLEXIBILE

As merchandise changes, so must a store's image. Thus, store planners attempt to design stores with maximum flexibility. Flexibility can take two forms: the ability to physically move store components, and the ease with which components can be modified.

For instance, a sporting goods store must be prepared to accommodate seasonal merchandise demands, expanding or contracting space to accommodate the seasonal flux inherent in the sporting goods business. Stores with built-in design flexibility can

retailing view
PEAK EXPERIENCE

7.1

Recreational Equipment Inc. (REI) has transformed a decaying 99-year-old historic landmark building in Denver into a modern retail adventure. The 8742 square metre, three-level store raises the bar on interactive retailing, taking the try-it-before-you-buy-it concept to new heights.

Among the new attractions: a large, steel-encased freezer-like fixture where shoppers can test winter parkas and sleeping bags. The temperatures inside can drop to as low as −30° F. Simulated wind chills can make it seem even colder. Mountain bikes can be tested on a rugged 97 metre trail that runs through the store's landscaped outdoor courtyard. Inside, shoppers can try out hiking boots on a footwear test track, compare bike lights and reflectors in an illuminator room, and test water purifiers in a ministream.

The centerpiece of the store is a 13.7 metre sculptured indoor rock-climbing pinnacle. It offers a variety of climbing terrains, including routes specifically geared to children. Weary shoppers can take a break at the on-premise Starbucks.

Customers at REI get to enjoy the excitement of rock climbing and trying the equipment when visiting the store. This experience cannot be duplicated with their other retail channels.

REI is in an industry where people love to get the product in their hands and test it. Letting them do so makes for a happier and better-informed customer—one who enters into the purchase with a much better feel as to how the product is supposed to perform.

Source: Marianne Wilson, "Peak Experience," *Chain Store Age*, June 2000, pp. 144–45. Copyright Lebhar-Friedman, Inc. 425 Park Avenue, New York, NY 10022. Reprinted by permission.

respond to seasonal changes and renew themselves from an image perspective without the need for large-scale renovations. For example, as much as 30 percent more retail space can be provided for in-season sports equipment or apparel through the use of flexible fixturing systems that are movable and accommodate additional tie-in units and shelves.

IT'S ALL ABOUT YOUR CUSTOMER

Who are my customers?
- What are the characteristics of my customers and how do they compare to my competitor's customers?
- How loyal are my shoppers?
- Who are my core customers?

Where do my customers shop?
- Where else do my customers shop and what are they buying?
- What store locations are they most likely to shop at?

How do my customers shop?
- What do they buy?
- What drives their buying decision?

---

store layout

Research shows that 70 percent of final retail purchase decisions are made in the store. Increasingly, retailers must understand the power of the retail environment to influence customers at that critical moment when awareness, brand loyalty, and impulse converge.

To develop a good store layout, store designers must balance many objectives—objectives that often conflict. For example, the store layout should entice customers to move around the store to purchase more merchandise than they may have originally planned. However, if the layout is too complex, customers may find it difficult to locate the merchandise they are looking for and decide not to patronize the store. A well-thought-out store layout will increase store traffic, drive sales, and build store loyalty.

The study of customer movement is a science. Research indicates that about 80 to 90 percent of consumers will turn to the right when entering a store unless they have a specific destination. According to Joseph Weisher, international store designer and president of New Vision Studios, it does not seem to matter whether you are right- or left-handed, read from left to right, drive on the left side of the road, or are male or female: Consumers are predisposed to turn right. The reason for this is that we receive and compute information from the left to the right side of our brains.

This right-entry pattern seems to be consistent as consumers enter, scan the space from left to right, and proceed right. At the same time, the head moves in a natural 45-degree turn and the right foot leads into the retail space. Having this knowledge can be an asset when designing a store and positioning high-margin merchandise. Placing fixtures at a 45-degree angle to the entrance of the store will encourage customers to move along a fixed path exposing maximum merchandise and stimulating impulse sales. The Gap places its new and high-margin merchandise at key points along a path, leading the eyes and the body to the wall.

Traffic patterns are meant to lead the customer from the entrance in and around merchandise, creating various points of interest along the way. The proper distance for visualizing a presentation is up to 8 metres from the point of entry. Larger stores (over 465 square metres) will need to map traffic patterns and place multiple merchandise presentations along the customer's path. The goal is to move the customer from the aisles to the wall, the most important fixture in the store. There is a saying in retail that, "The longer a customer stays in a store, the more he or she will buy."

Sixty percent of sales come from impulse purchases.

If customers enter to the right, then they will naturally exit on the left. Placing the cash/transaction area at the end of the shopping trip near the front left—in other words, putting it on the customers' right when they exit—will encourage impulse sales at the point of purchase.[5]

The trade-off between ease of finding merchandise and providing a varied and interesting layout is determined by the needs of the customers shopping at the store. For example, supermarket shoppers typically have specific things they want to buy, so these retailers need to place an emphasis on the ease of locating merchandise. On the other hand, department store shoppers are not as goal-oriented and are therefore more willing to explore the store for new merchandise. Thus, department store retailers can place more emphasis on browsing rather than ease of finding merchandise.

Customers can be enticed to follow what amounts to a yellow brick road, as in *The Wizard of Oz*. For instance, Toys "R" Us uses a layout that almost forces customers to move through sections of inexpensive impulse-purchase products to get to larger, more expensive goods. It takes a strong-willed parent to navigate through the balloons and party favours without making a purchase.

Another method of helping customers move through the store is to provide interesting design elements. For example, antique stores have little nooks and crannies that entice shoppers to wander around. Off-price retailers intentionally create some degree of messiness so that people will be encouraged to look through the racks for bargains. Another objective of a good layout is to provide a balance between giving customers adequate space in which to shop and productively using this space for merchandise. For example, some customers may be attracted to stores with wide aisles and fixtures whose primary purpose is to display rather than to hold the merchandise. However, this type of design reduces the amount of merchandise that can be shown to the customer, which may also reduce the customer's chances of finding what he or she is looking for. Also, a store with lots of people creates a sense of excitement and, it is hoped, increases buying. But too many racks and displays in a store can cause customers frustration. The issue of overcrowding display fixtures and merchandise is particularly important as retailers consider the special needs of the disabled.

To meet their objectives, retailers must decide which design type to use and how to generate traffic through feature areas.

TYPES OF DESIGN

Today's modern retailers use three general types of store layout design: grid, racetrack, and free-form.

Grid   The **grid layout** is best illustrated by most grocery and drugstore operations. It contains long gondolas of merchandise and aisles in a repetitive pattern (Exhibit 7–1). The grid isn't the most aesthetically pleasing arrangement, but it's very good for shopping trips in which customers need to move throughout the entire store and easily locate products they want to buy. For instance, when customers do their weekly grocery shopping, they weave in and out of the specific aisles picking up similar products every week. Since they know where everything is, they can minimize the time spent on a task that many don't especially enjoy. The grid layout is also cost-efficient.

There's less wasted space with the grid design than with others because the aisles are all the same width and are designed to be just wide enough to accommodate shoppers and their carts. Since the grid design is used with long gondolas that have multiple shelf levels, the amount of merchandise on the floor can be significantly more than with other layouts. Thus, space productivity is enhanced. (Space productivity is discussed later in this chapter.) Finally, since the fixtures are generally standardized and repetitive, the fixturing cost is reduced.

7.2   retailing view KEVIN BRAILSFORD, VICE-PRESIDENT, STORE ENVIRONMENT, BLOCKBUSTER, INC.

"Creating an appealing environment in our video stores is really a challenge. Our merchandise all looks alike—13 × 18 cm boxes with movie graphics, which are then arranged basically, in alphabetical order. We have experimented with merchandising the stores in a variety of ways. As a result, we've found we need to appeal to two basic customer types, browsers and transactors. Browsers want to spend more time in the store shopping, while transactors want to get in and out fast. Our newest store designs and philosophies break the merchandising and communications down so that transactors can find what they want quickly and browsers can shop at a leisurely pace.

"Another interesting planning challenge is that our prime real estate in the store is the back wall, which is opposite most traditional retailers. Many of our customers go directly to the new releases, which are merchandised on the back wall. One of my design objectives is to encourage traffic to move through the centre of the store as well, in order to expose our entire inventory. Our latest merchandising challenge is to increase awareness of our huge movies for sale category. By designing new fixtures and graphics, the store environment takes the lead in communicating to our consumers that we are the best place to buy as well as rent.

"I have always been attracted to retailing. I was a mall rat when I was a teenager. After college, I took a job at Diamonds department store and was intrigued with the way merchandising of a department can affect sales. The exciting part of retailing is the constant change. It seems like every day there is a new challenge.

"While retailing is exciting, there is an extra layer added by working for Blockbuster. I am not just designing our stores to increase sales and rentals, I am merchandising movie stars."

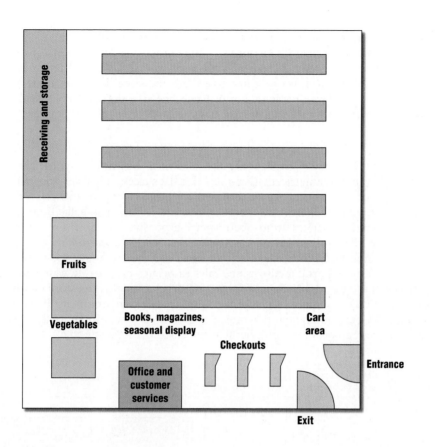

exhibit 7–1
Grid Store Layout

Many of the massive superstores opened in the past few years run aisles horizontally. The layout allows a wider central aisle for promotions and breaks up the large expanse with effective endcaps facing the main aisle. Loblaws' addition of the Joe Fresh apparel line to the traditional grocery mix breaks the repetitive grid pattern with a fashion image boutique layout.

Racetrack   One problem with the grid design is that customers aren't exposed to all of the merchandise in the store. This isn't an issue in grocery stores, where most customers have a good notion of what they're going to purchase before they enter the store. But how can design pull customers through stores to encourage them to explore and seek out new and interesting merchandise?

The racetrack layout facilitates the goal of getting customers to visit multiple departments. The **racetrack layout,** also known as a **loop,** is a type of store design that provides a major aisle to facilitate customer traffic, with access to the store's multiple entrances. This aisle loops through the store, providing access to all the departments. The racetrack design encourages impulse purchasing. As customers go around the racetrack, their eyes are forced to take different viewing angles rather than looking down one aisle as in the grid design.

Exhibit 7–2 shows the layout of a department store. Since the store has multiple entrances, the loop design tends to place all departments on the main aisle by drawing customers through the store in a series of major and minor loops. To entice customers through the various departments, the design has placed some of the more important departments, such as juniors, toward the rear of the store. The newest items are featured on the aisles to draw customers into departments and around the loop. IKEA's reactrack layout leads the cutomer in a particular direction using arrows on the floor to move customers throughout the lifestyle vignettes and merchandise groups. To direct customers through the store, the aisles must be defined by a change in surface or colour. For instance, the aisle flooring is of marble-like tile, and the departments vary in material, texture, and colour, depending on the desired ambiance.

Free-Form   A **free-form layout**, also known as **boutique layout**, arranges fixtures and aisles asymmetrically (Exhibit 7–3). It's successfully used primarily in small specialty stores or within the departments of large stores. In this relaxed environment, customers feel like they're at someone's home, which facilitates shopping and browsing. A pleasant atmosphere isn't inexpensive, however. For one thing, the fixtures are likely to be expensive custom units. Since the customers aren't naturally drawn around the store as they are in the grid and racetrack layouts, personal selling becomes more important. Also, since sales associates can't easily watch adjacent departments, theft is higher than with the grid design. Finally, the store sacrifices some storage and display space to create the more spacious environment. If the free-form layout is carefully designed, however, the increased costs can be easily offset by increased sales and profit margins because the customer feels at home.

exhibit 7–2   Racetrack Layout

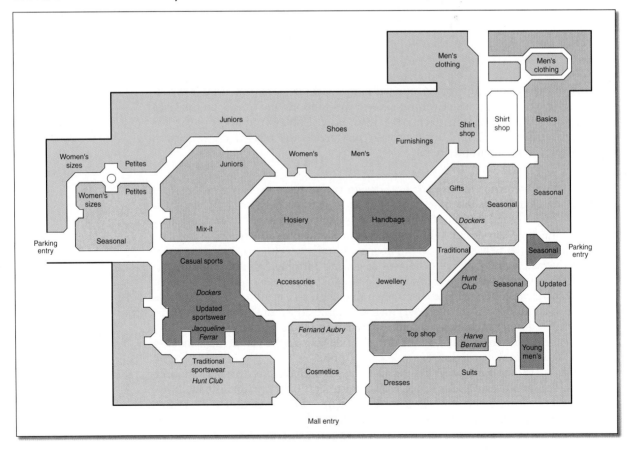

To illustrate a free-form boutique within a racetrack layout, consider the picture on page 173. The designers' objective was to create a simple, clear space that draws customers into the area. Fixtures with the latest garments are placed along the perimeter of the boutique. Yet the flooring and lighting clearly delineate the area from adjacent departments and the walkway.[6]

This racetrack layout draws customers through the store and encourages impulse purchasing.

FEATURE AREAS

Besides the area where most of the merchandise is displayed and stored, there are **feature areas**—areas within a store designed to get the customer's attention. They include end caps, promotional aisles or areas, freestanding fixtures and mannequins that introduce a soft goods department, windows, point-of-sale or cash-wrap areas, and walls.

End Caps   **End caps** are displays located at the end of an aisle. For instance, a food store's large end-cap display of Coca-Cola is designed to catch consumers' attention. The Coca-Cola is located near the rest of the soft drinks, but is on sale. It's not always necessary to use end caps for sales, however. Due to their high visibility, end caps can also be used to feature special promotional items.

Promotional Aisle or Area   A **promotional aisle or area** is an aisle or area used to display merchandise that is being promoted. Canadian Tire, for instance, uses a promotional aisle to sell seasonal merchandise, such as lawn and garden in the summer and Christmas decorations in the fall. Apparel stores, such as The Gap, often place their sale merchandise in the back of the store so customers must wander through the full-price merchandise to get to the sale merchandise.

Freestanding Fixtures and Mannequins   **Freestanding fixtures** and mannequins located on aisles are designed primarily to get customers' attention and bring them into a department. These fixtures often display and store the newest, most exciting merchandise in the department.

Windows   Although windows are clearly external to the store, they can be an important component of the store layout. Properly used, window displays can help draw customers into the store. They provide a visual message about the type of merchandise for sale in the store and the type of image the store wishes to portray. Window displays should be tied to the merchandise and other displays in the store window. For instance, if beach towels are displayed in a Bed, Bath & Beyond store, they should also be prominently displayed inside. Otherwise, the drawing power of the window display is lost. Finally, windows can be used to set the shopping mood for a season or holiday such as Christmas or Valentine's Day.

Point of Sale Areas   **Point-of-sale areas**, also known as **point-of-purchase (POP) areas**, **checkout areas**, or **cash-wrap areas**, are places in the store where customers can purchase merchandise. These areas can be the most valuable piece of real estate in the store, because the customers often wait there for the transactions to be

exhibit 7–3
Free-Form Store
Layout

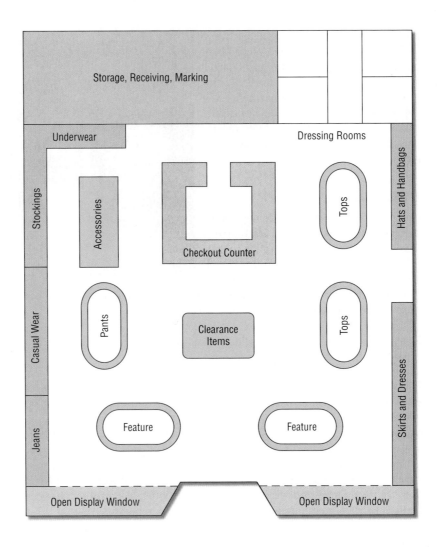

completed. While waiting in a long checkout line at a grocery store, notice how people pick up things such as batteries, candy, razors, and magazines. Did they need these items? Not really, but the wait bored them, so they spent the extra time shopping.

Several department store chains are experimenting with centralized checkout stations.[7] Discount and value-priced retailers, such as Zellers, have long used centralized checkouts at the front of their stores. But department stores have traditionally placed cash registers deep within each department. By centralizing the checkout areas, these department stores hope to reduce staff as well as customer complaints arising from slow or poor checkout service. The Bay and Sears have moved to centralized checkout stations located in the centre of the store.

Walls   Since retail space is often scarce and expensive, many retailers have successfully increased their ability to store extra stock, display merchandise, and creatively present a message by utilizing wall space. Merchandise can be stored on shelving and racks. The merchandise can be coordinated with displays, photographs, or graphics featuring the merchandise.

The goal of good store design is to get customers to approach the wall. The distance from the main aisle to the wall (or column) should be no more than 7 to 10

In this store, mannequins with the latest garments are placed in the front window to draw customers in.

metres—beyond this, a customer's visual perception diminishes. The wall is the most important fixture, according to visual merchandiser John Weishar. The wall:

- holds more merchandise
- can present coordinated face-outs with a multiple fashion story in a small space
- can facilitate a variety of fixturing methods, such as shelving and hanging
- is the focal point for seasonal merchandise
- can present a feature display to attract the customer
- effectively sells more high-margin merchandise than floor fixtures
- is visible from a distance

The power wall is usually considered to be the wall space to the right as the customer enters the store or department. Most often associated with the free-form layout, this wall space is capable of generating the highest sales. Skilled visual merchandisers will plan the wall presentation first and then group the floor fixtures. The most successful retailers are those that understand the power of the wall to sell.[8]

space planning

Allocation of store space to merchandise categories and brands, the location of the departments in the store, and where to place items to attract attention are a few of store planners' and buyers' most complicated and difficult decisions. They must answer four questions:

1. What items, brands, categories, and departments should be carried?
2. How much of each item should be carried?
3. How much space should the merchandise take?
4. Where should the merchandise be located to create maximum exposure?

Store planners in conjunction with buyers typically start by allocating space based on sales productivity. For instance, if knit shirts represent 15 percent of the total expected sales for the men's furnishings department, they will initially get 15 percent of the space. Store planners must then adjust the initial estimate on the basis of the following five factors:

- How profitable is the merchandise?
- How will the planned inventory turnover and the resulting stock-to-sales ratio affect how many SKUs will normally be carried in stock? Buyers and store planners must allocate space on the basis of seasonal fluctuations that recognize space demands during peak times, such as Christmas and Back-to-School.
- How will the merchandise be displayed?
- Will the location of certain merchandise draw the customer through the store, thus encouraging sales?
- What items does the retailer wish to emphasize?

Exhibit 7–4 shows typical floor space allocation based on sales potential. The front of the store is a much stronger selling space, with the potential to produce 48 percent of sales, whereas the back of the store generates only 16 percent of store sales. Thus, the newest merchandise should be placed at the front of the store to encourage customer response.

We've discussed in general terms how store planners and buyers plan the space requirements for a category such as knit shirts or beer. Similar decisions are made for larger groups of merchandise such as classifications, departments, and even merchandise groups. Now let's examine how retailers decide where to locate departments and where to locate merchandise within departments.

exhibit 7–4   **Floor Space Allocation Based on Sales Potential**

5%	6%	5%
10%	12%	14%
12%	18%	18%
Window	↑ Entrance	Window

**Rent Allocation by Areas
Based on consumer traffic
patterns and sales potential**

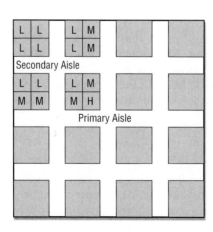

**Rent Allocation
Based on
traffic aisles**

H = High-rent area/high sales
M = Medium-rent area/medium sales
L = Low-rent area/low sales

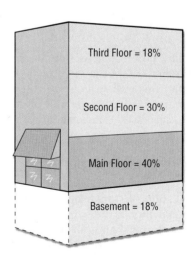

Third Floor = 18%

Second Floor = 30%

Main Floor = 40%

Basement = 18%

**Rent Allocation by Floors
Based on consumer traffic
patterns and sales potential**

LOCATION OF DEPARTMENTS

Sandy Williams recently went to The Bay for a haircut. On the way in, she stopped at the cosmetics counter to buy makeup. Then on the escalator, she spotted a red dress to examine on her way out. Before leaving the store, she stopped by the lingerie department to browse.

Did she simply take a random walk through the store? Probably not. The departments she shopped are strategically located to maximize the entire store's profits. The profit-generating abilities of various locations within a store aren't equal. The more traffic through a department, the better the location will be. Unfortunately, every department can't be situated in the best location. Retailers must consider additional demand-generating factors and the interrelations between departments when determining their locations.

Relative Location Advantages   The best locations within the store depend on the floor location, the position within a floor, and its location relative to traffic aisles, entrances, escalators, and so on. In general, in a multilevel store, a space's value decreases the farther it is from the entry-level floor. Since men aren't generally as avid shoppers for clothing as women, many large stores locate the men's department on the entry-level floor to make shopping as easy as possible.

The position within a floor is also important when assigning locations to departments. The best locations are those closest to the store's entrances, main aisles, escalators, and elevators. Multilevel stores often place escalators so customers must walk around the sales floor to get to the next level. Also, most customers turn right when entering a store or floor, so the right side will be especially desirable space. Finally, most customers won't get all the way to the centre of the store, so many stores use the racetrack design to induce people to move into the store's interior.

Impulse Products   **Impulse products** are products that are purchased without prior plans, such as fragrances and cosmetics in department stores and magazines in supermarkets. They are almost always located near the front of the store, where they're seen by everyone and may actually draw people into the store. The reality is that many large malls get a lot of traffic, but often the customer has just got off the subway system or is leaving work and is not focusing on displays. Visit www.envirosell.com, Paco Underhill, "Why We Buy."

Demand/Destination Areas   Children's, expensive specialty goods, and furniture departments as well as customer-service areas such as beauty salons, credit offices, and photography studios are usually located off the beaten path—in corners and on upper floors. Due to the exclusive nature of Steuben glass, for instance, the department is typically located in a low-traffic area of high-end stores. A purchase of one of these unique, expensive pieces requires thought and concentration. Customers would probably become distracted if the department were adjacent to a high-traffic area. Besides, customers looking for these items will find them no matter where they're located in the store. These departments are known as **demand/destination areas** because *demand* for their products or services is created before customers get to their *destination*. Thus, they don't need prime locations.

Seasonal Needs   Some departments need to be more flexible than others. For instance, it's helpful to locate winter coats near sportswear. Extra space in the coat department can be absorbed by sportswear or swimwear in the spring when most of the winter coats have been sold.

Why are cosmetics counters typically located near the front of the store?

Physical Characteristics of Merchandise   Departments that require large amounts of floor space, such as furniture, are often located in the less desirable locations. Some departments, such as curtains, need significant wall space, while others, such as shoes, require accessible storage.

Adjacent Departments   After trying on the red dress, Williams found complementary shoes nearby. Retailers often cluster complementary products together to facilitate multiple purchases.

Some stores are now combining traditionally separate departments or categories to facilitate multiple purchases using market-basket analysis. Stores are laid out according to the way customers purchase merchandise (by brand, for example, or by lifestyle image), rather than by traditional categories or departments.

The Special Case of Grocery Stores   Now consider some of the special departmental location issues in grocery stores. As a customer walks in, there is typically a barricade—checkout stands and grocery carts—that pushes the customer to the right. The items almost everyone buys—milk, eggs, butter, and bread—are in the back left-hand corner. To get to them, a shopper tending to turn right must travel half the store's perimeter and go past every aisle.

Most supermarkets steer shoppers immediately into the produce section because they can see and feel and smell the food there. The appearance of fresh fruits and vegetables gets a shopper's mouth watering, and the best grocery store customer is a hungry one.

The first produce item the customer sees is apples, and that's no accident either. Apples are by far the most popular item in produce, almost twice as popular as oranges, bananas, lettuce, and potatoes, the runners-up.

Supermarkets place private-label brands and other higher-margin items to the right of national brands. Most languages are read from left to right. So a customer will see the higher-priced national brand first and then see the lower-priced private-label item on the right.

Evaluating a Departmental Layout   Envirosell, a consulting firm in New York, has made a science out of determining the best ways to lay out a department or a store.[9] Here are just a few of the things the researchers have learned:

- *Avoid the butt-brush effect.* The researchers taped shoppers attempting to reach the tie rack while negotiating an entrance during busy times. They noticed that after being bumped once or twice, most shoppers abandoned their search for neckwear. The conclusion: Shoppers don't like to shop when their personal space is invaded.
- *Place merchandise where customers can readily access it.* This sounds easy and obvious. But until little kids and old ladies were observed having difficulty reaching treats for their pets in a supermarket, they were typically stocked near the top of the shelf.
- *Allow a transition zone.* The first product encountered in a department isn't always going to have an advantage. Sometimes, just the opposite will happen. Allowing some space between the entrance of a store and a product gives it more time in the shopper's eye as he or she approaches it. For instance, cosmetics firms don't usually want to occupy the first counter inside the entrance of a department store because they know that women want a little privacy.

LOCATION OF MERCHANDISE WITHIN DEPARTMENTS: THE USE OF PLANOGRAMS

To determine where merchandise should be located within a department, retailers of all types generate maps known as planograms. A **planogram** is a diagram created from photographs, computer output, or artists' renderings that illustrates exactly where every SKU (stock-keeping unit) should be placed. Planograms should be visually appealing, represent the manner in which a consumer shops (or the manner in which the retailer would like the consumer to shop), and embody the strategic objectives of the corporation. There is an art and a science to planogramming. The art is in ensuring that the proper visual impact and presentation are maintained; the science is in the financial analysis portion. A planogrammer must be able to balance these two elements in creating a planogram that is best for the store. Technology for computer-generated planograms can be somewhat sophisticated, lending to advanced analysis, or it can be fairly simple.[10]

Electronic planogramming requires the user to input model numbers or UPC codes, product margins, turnover, sizes of product packaging or actual pictures of the packaging, and other pertinent information into the program. The computer plots the planogram based on the retailer's priorities. For instance, if the retailer wants prime shelf space given to products that produce the highest turnovers, the computer will locate those products in the best locations. If margins are more important, the computer will determine the shelf space priority and the optimal number of SKUs to stock in that space. Adjustments to the initial planogram can be made to see how additional space or different fixtures would affect the productivity measures.

Planograms are also useful for merchandise that doesn't fit nicely on gondolas in a grocery or discount store. The Gap and Banana Republic, for instance, provide their managers with photographs and diagrams of how merchandise should be displayed.

Recent advances in computer graphics and three-dimensional modelling allow planograms to be designed, tested with consumers, and changed, all in a "virtual" shopping environment.[11] A consumer can view merchandise on a computer screen that looks like a real store. The shopper can "pick up" a package by touching its image on the monitor. She can turn the package so it can be examined from all sides.

If she wants, she can "purchase" the product. In the meantime, the computer tracks the time spent shopping for and examining a particular product and the quantity purchased. Armed with this information, the retailer can test the effectiveness of different planograms. Retailing View 7.3 describes how Marketmax's planogramming system automated Marks & Spencer's food business.

retailing view
MARKS & SPENCER AUTOMATES PLANOGRAMS

Marks & Spencer is a large retailer of clothing, home goods, and high-quality food products. Its food business, specializing in high-quality convenience fresh foods such as sandwiches and home dinners, occupies a prominent position in the U.K. food retailing sector.

The retailer is continuously updating its product range with new products developed in conjunction with leading manufacturers of short-lived food products. Until recently, this has been a labour-intensive process. For example, the adjustment of 50 displays in 50 stores requires 2500 new individual planograms, unless some stores are exactly the same, which is not likely. It would take between 80 and 100 full-time planogrammers to implement weekly changes in the 310 stores.

Seeking to turn its food supply chain from a push to a pull system, the US$4.2 billion retailer began looking for a planogramming system for its fresh-food products. Store-specific space plans were necessary to reflect each store's individual needs.

Working with Massachusetts-based Marketmax, the 310-unit retailer was able to develop an automated planogramming system that could optimize weekly fresh-food assortments to individual stores, as well as improve product layout and customer satisfaction.

The Marks & Spencer/Marketmax system calculates an optimal layout by determining how many shelf-facings are needed for each SKU in each store. At the same time, the system maintains a consistent look but considers specific fixtures and store layouts.

By implementing automated space planning, Marks & Spencer has greatly increased the productivity of its centralized space planning team and gained control over store layout and product presentation. It can now do weekly plans with 20 planogrammers—and it does a much better job. Product placement is now more efficient and uniform throughout the chain, and customers can more easily find specific products. This is of particular importance to Marks & Spencer as many of its customers shop in more than one of its stores, particularly in clusters of high density (e.g., six stores within a five-kilometre radius).

Sources: "A New Approach to Merchandise Planning, Distribution and Logistics," March 2002, www.groceryheadquarters.com; and RetailSystems Alert, www.retailsystems.com, February 1, 2002.

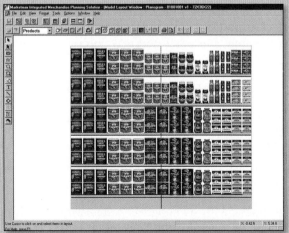

Marks & Spencer in the U.K. utilizes a sophisticated planogram system by Marketmax to help lay out and evaluate the productivity of its food business.

Most retailers measure the productivity of space using **sales per square metre,** since rent and land purchases are assessed on a per-square-metre basis. But sometimes it's more efficient to measure profitability using **sales per linear metre.** For instance, in a grocery store, most merchandise is displayed on multiple shelves on long gondolas. Since the shelves have approximately the same width, only the length, or linear dimension, is relevant. Sales per cubic metre may be most appropriate for stores such as wholesale clubs that use multiple layers of merchandise.

When allocating space to merchandise or a department, a retail manager must consider the profit impact on all departments. Remember, the objective is to maximize the profitability of the store, not just a particular department. Since the cosmetics department has a relatively high gross margin per square metre, should management give it more or less space? The answer depends on whether profitability of the entire store would increase if more space were allotted to this department. A department may be achieving its high productivity ratio because it's too small and has only a limited assortment. Conversely, a department may actually be too large—if so, almost as much profit could be generated with a smaller space. The buyer could buy smaller quantities more often, thereby making more productive use of a smaller space. If management decides to shrink the cosmetics department, more space would be available for, say, women's apparel. If the store's overall profitability would be increased by making this move, then the retailer should do it.

merchandise presentation techniques

Many methods are available to retailers for effectively presenting merchandise to the customer. To decide which is best for a particular situation, store planners must consider the following four issues:

• Merchandise should be displayed in a manner consistent with the store's image. For instance, some traditional men's stores display dress shirts by size, so all size 15 1/2–34 shirts are together. Thus, the customer can easily determine what's available in his size. This is consistent with a no-nonsense image of the store.

retailing view   **7.4**
GIVING NEW MEANING TO WINDOW SHOPPING

Optiadmedia, a Toronto-based media company has launched Window F/X, a storefront multimedia projection technology where a projection film is applied to a glass surface giving the appearance of a floating screen. This technology can be programmed to run video or still images to touchscreen features for passersby to browse merchandise. Windows F/X can also incorporate full audio and wireless capabilities. This is the new wave of "window shopping."

Other stores keep all colour/style combinations together. This presentation evokes a more fashion-forward image and is more aesthetically pleasing.

- Store planners must consider the nature of the product. Basic jeans can easily be displayed in stacks, but skirts must be hung so the customer can more easily examine the design and style.

- Packaging often dictates how the product is displayed. Discount stores sell small packages of nuts and bolts, for example, but some hardware stores still sell individual nuts and bolts. Although the per-unit cost is significantly higher for the packages, self-service operations don't have adequate personnel to weigh and bag these small items.

- Products' profit potential influences display decisions. For example, low-profit/high-turnover items such as back-to-school supplies don't require the same elaborate, expensive displays as Mont Blanc fountain pens.

In this section, we'll examine some specific presentation techniques. Then we'll describe the fixtures used in these merchandise presentations. First, however, consider how Diesel stores seem to break all the store design rules (see Retailing View 7.5).

IDEA-ORIENTED PRESENTATION

Some retailers successfully use an **idea-oriented presentation**—a method of presenting merchandise based on a specific idea or the image of the store. Women's fashions, for instance, are often displayed to present an overall image or idea. Also, furniture is combined in room settings to give customers an idea of how it would look in their homes. Individual items are grouped to show customers how the items could be used and combined. This approach encourages the customer to make multiple complementary purchases.

STYLE/ITEM PRESENTATION

Probably the most common technique of organizing stock is by style or item. Discount stores, grocery stores, hardware stores, and drugstores employ this method for nearly every category of merchandise. Also, many apparel retailers use this technique. When customers look for a particular type of merchandise, such as sweaters, they expect to find all items in the same location.

Arranging items by size is a common method of organizing many types of merchandise, from nuts and bolts to apparel. Since the customer usually knows the desired size, it's easy to locate items organized in this manner.

COLOUR PRESENTATION

A powerful merchandising technique is referred to as colour blocking. Fashion apparel and home fashion retailers realize that by grouping merchandise by colour, not only does the store look more attractive but the technique also encourages multiple sales. Women are particularly attracted to colour presentation, and most will have strong colour preferences according to personal favourites or fashion dominance. Red is the most noticeable colour and has the ability to grab the customer's attention when used in visual presentation and signage. Home Outfitters uses colour blocking to increase buyer appeal in everything from kitchenware to home fashions.

These wooden tulips are arranged by colour. This is an example of colour blocking.

PRICE LINING

Organizing merchandise in price categories, or *price lining* (when retailers offer a limited number of predetermined price points within a classification), is a strategy that helps customers easily find merchandise at the price they wish to pay. For instance, men's dress shirts may be organized into three groups selling for $30, $45, and $60. Moore's Clothing has an effective program of price lining: good–better–best.

VERTICAL MERCHANDISING

Another common way of organizing merchandise is **vertical merchandising.** Here merchandise is presented vertically using walls and high gondolas. Customers shop much as they read a newspaper—from left to right, going down each column, top to bottom. Stores can effectively organize merchandise to follow the eye's natural movement. Good vertical merchandising techniques will maximize product visibility as the customer scans from left to right. A poor presentation would be horizontal merchandising, where the customer only sees a small assortment of products for sale. See Exhibit 7–5 for a comparison of vertical and horizantal merchandising.

retailing view
DIESEL BREAKS STORE DESIGN RULES

7.5

Diesel jeans stores are so confusing that it begs a question: Are they the worst run stores in America, or is something sneaky going on? The answer: something sneaky.

Walking into a Diesel jeans store feels a lot like stumbling into a rave. Techno music pounds at a mind-rattling level. A television plays a videotape of a Japanese boxing match, inexplicably. There are no helpful signs pointing to men's or women's departments and no obvious staff members in sight.

Customers who are industrious, or simply brave enough to reach the "denim bar"—Diesel's name for the counter separating shoppers from the wall of jeans at the back of the store—find themselves confronted by 35 different types of blue jeans costing US$115 to $210 a pair. A placard intending to explain the various options looks like an organizational chart for a decent-size federal agency.

The company, which was founded in Italy in 1978 and last year had its sales climb 40 percent from 2000, reaching US$500 million, is one of the brands most successfully exploiting young men's new fashion interest—expensive denim.

Whereas large clothing retailers such as Banana Republic and The Gap have standardized and simplified the layout of their stores in an effort to put customers at ease, Diesel's approach is based on the unconventional premise that the best customer is a disoriented one. They intentionally designed an intimidating, user-unfriendly environment so that customers have to interact with the sales staff.

Diesel stores create a unique shopping environment by breaking the basic store design rules used by other retailers.

Indeed, it is at just the moment when a potential Diesel customer reaches a kind of shopping vertigo that members of the company's intimidatingly with-it staff make their move. Acting as salespeople-in-shining-armor, they rescue—or prey upon, depending on one's point of view—wayward shoppers.

Source: Warren St. John, "A Store Lures Guys Who Are Graduating from Chinos," *New York Times*, July 14, 2002, www.nytimes.com. Reprinted by permission.

exhibit 7–5
Vertical versus
Horizontal
Presentation

Retailers take advantage of this tendency in several ways. Many grocery stores put national brands at eye level and store brands on lower shelves because customers scan from eye level down. Finally, retailers often display merchandise in bold vertical bands of an item. For instance, you'll see vertical columns of towels of the same colour displayed in a department store or a vertical band of yellow-and-orange boxes of Tide detergent followed by a band of blue Cheer boxes in a supermarket.

By presenting the merchandise vertically, stores show more merchandise per square metre—making better use of floor space by increasing its selling capacity and getting a better return for their money (floor space is expensive). The customer has a category or style of merchandise right in front of her—at eye and hand level—and does not have to run back and forth along the fixture to find what the store has in a given category or style. Customer access to merchandise on the sales floor has positive implications for payroll.

TONNAGE MERCHANDISING

As the name implies, **tonnage merchandising** is a display technique in which large quantities of merchandise are displayed together. Customers have come to equate tonnage with low price, following the retail adage "stock it high and let it fly." Tonnage merchandising is therefore used to enhance and reinforce a store's price image. Using this display concept, the merchandise itself is the display. The retailer hopes customers will notice the merchandise and be drawn to it. For instance, before many holidays, grocery stores use an entire end of a gondola (i.e., an end cap) to display six-packs of pop.

FRONTAL PRESENTATION

refact
Aldo, the Canadian
shoe company, boasts
average sales of more
than $10 420 per
square metre.[13]

It is important to show as much of the merchandise as possible. The **frontal presentation** is a method of displaying merchandise in which the retailer exposes as much of the product as possible to catch the customer's eye. Book manufacturers, for instance, make great efforts to create eye-catching covers. But bookstores usually display books exposing only the spine. To create an effective display and break the monotony, book retailers often face the cover out like a billboard to catch the customer's attention. A similar frontal presentation is achieved on a rack of apparel by simply turning one item out to show the merchandise. The goal is to face the merchandise out to the customer's viewpoint whenever possible. For example, clothing on a straight rack may show only the sleeve; using the face-out technique for the garment will show its collar and unique details. Employing merchandise face-outs will encourage sales.

FIXTURES

The primary purposes of fixtures are to efficiently hold and display merchandise. At the same time, they must help define areas of a store and encourage traffic flow. Fixtures must be in concert with the other physical aspects of the store, such as floor coverings and lighting, as well as the overall image of the store. For instance, in stores designed to convey a sense of tradition or history, customers automatically expect to see lots of wood rather than plastic or metal fixtures. Wood mixed with metal, acrylic, or stone changes the traditional orientation. The rule of thumb is that the more unexpected the combination of textures, the more contemporary the image.

Fixtures come in an infinite variety of styles, colours, sizes, and textures, but only a few basic types are commonly used. For apparel, retailers utilize the straight rack, rounder, and four-way. The mainstay fixture for most other merchandise is the gondola.

The **straight rack** consists of a long pipe suspended with supports going to the floor or attached to a wall (Exhibit 7–6A). Although the straight rack can hold a lot of apparel, it's hard to feature specific styles or colours. All the customer can see is a sleeve or a pant leg. As a result, straight racks are often found in discount and off-price apparel stores.

(A) Straight rack

(B) Rounder

(C) Four-way

(D) Gondola

exhibit 7–6
Four Fixture Types

A **rounder,** also known as a **bulk fixture** or **capacity fixture,** is a round fixture that sits on a pedestal (Exhibit 7–6B). Although smaller than the straight rack, it's designed to hold a maximum amount of merchandise. Since they're easy to move and they efficiently store apparel, rounders are found in most types of apparel stores. But as with the straight rack, customers can't get a frontal view of the merchandise.

A **four-way fixture,** also known as a **feature fixture,** has two crossbars that sit perpendicular to each other on a pedestal (Exhibit 7–6C). This fixture holds a large amount of merchandise and allows the customer to view the entire garment. The four-way is harder to properly maintain than the rounder or straight rack, however. All merchandise on an arm must be of a similar style and colour, or the customer may become confused. Due to their superior display properties, four-way fixtures are commonly utilized by fashion-oriented apparel retailers.

Gondolas are extremely versatile (Exhibit 7–6D). They're used extensively, but not exclusively, in grocery and discount stores to display everything from canned foods to baseball gloves. Gondolas are also found displaying towels, sheets, and housewares in department stores. Folded apparel too can be efficiently displayed on gondolas, but because the items are folded, it's even harder for customers to view apparel on gondolas than on straight racks.

signage and graphics

VISUAL COMMUNICATIONS

Visual communications—composed of graphics, signs, and theatrical effects, both in the store and in windows—help boost sales by providing information on products, special purchases, and value propositions. Signs and graphics also help customers find a department or merchandise. Graphics, such as photo panels, can add personality, beauty, and romance to the store's image.

Retailers should consider the following seven issues when designing visual communications strategies for their stores.

Coordinate Signs and Graphics with the Store's Image   Signs and graphics should act as a bridge between the merchandise and the target markets. The colours and tone of the signs and graphics should complement the merchandise. For example, a pastel pink sign in a store selling nautical supplies would not be as appropriate as bold red, white, and blue. Also, a formally worded black-and-white rectangular sign doesn't relate to a children's display as well as a red-and-yellow circus tent design does. Colour combinations should appeal to specific target customers or highlight specific merchandise—primary colours for kids, hot vivid colours for teens, pastels for lingerie, brights for sportswear, and so forth. At Athlete's Foot, for instance, sliding graphic panels highlight the lifestyles of the target market while at the same time displaying product and concealing inventory (see photo on page 185).

Inform the Customer   Informative signs and graphics make merchandise more desirable. For instance, Athlete's Foot uses a series of freestanding prints to explain its five-step fitting process.[14] The process begins with a foot scanner, which ensures a perfect fit for each customer. Then after analyzing customers' activity levels, in-store personnel help them choose the right shoes and determine the best way to tie shoes to fit their feet.

Use Signs and Graphics as Props

Using signs or graphics that masquerade as props, or vice versa, is a great way to unify a theme and merchandise for an appealing overall presentation. For instance, a store selling educational toys uses lively graphics and props in a unifying theme that is consistent with the store's image.

Keep Signs and Graphics Fresh

Signs shouldn't be left in the store or in windows after displays are removed. Forgotten, faded, and fraught with water spots, such signs do more to disparage a store's image than sell merchandise. Also, new signs imply new merchandise.

At Banana Republic graphic panels highlight the target market's lifestyles.

Limit the Copy on Signs   As a general rule, signs with too much text won't be read. Customers must be able to quickly grasp the information on the sign as they walk through the store.

Use Appropriate Typefaces on Signs   Different typefaces impart different messages and moods. For instance, carefully done calligraphy in an Old English script provides a very different message than a hastily written price-reduction sign.

Create Theatrical Effects   To heighten store excitement and enhance store image, retailers have borrowed from the theatre. Bold graphic posters, photographs, or fabrics can be hung from ceilings and walls to decorate, provide information, or camouflage less aesthetic areas, such as the ceiling structure.

atmospherics

Atmospherics refers to the design of an environment via visual communications, colours, lighting, music, and scent to stimulate customers' perceptual and emotional responses and ultimately to affect their purchase behaviour.[15] Many retailers have discovered the subtle benefits of developing atmospherics that complement other aspects of the store design and the merchandise. Research has shown that it is important for these atmospheric elements to work together, for example, the right music with the right scent.[16] Now let's explore some basic principles of good atmospheric design and examine a few new, exciting, and somewhat controversial trends.

LIGHTING

Good lighting in a store involves more than simply illuminating space. Lighting is used to highlight merchandise, sculpt space, and capture a mood or feeling that enhances the store's image. Lighting can also be used to downplay less attractive features that can't be changed. Having the appropriate lighting has been shown to positively influence customer shopping behaviour.[17]

Galleri Orrefors Kosta Boda on Manhattan's Madison Avenue uses special lighting to make its limited and one-of-a kind glass sculptures POP.

Highlight Merchandise   A good lighting system helps create a sense of excitement in the store. At the same time, lighting must provide an accurate colour rendition of the merchandise. A green silk tie should look the same colour in the store as outside. Similarly, lighting should complement the customer. A department store's cosmetics area, for instance, requires more expensive lighting than the fluorescent lighting found in many grocery stores because it has to complement the customer and make her skin look natural.

Another key use of lighting is called **popping the merchandise**—focusing spotlights on special feature areas and items. Using lighting to focus on merchandise moves shoppers' eyes to the merchandise and draws customers strategically through the store. For example, limited and one-of-a-kind glass sculptures are highlighted with special lighting.

Capture a Mood and Maintain an Image   Traditionally, North American specialty and department stores have employed incandescent lighting sources to promote a warm and cozy ambience.[18] Overall lighting sources are reduced and accent lighting is added to call attention to merchandise and displays.

European stores have long favoured high light levels, cool colours, and little contrast or accent lighting. European lighting design has been bolder, starker, and more minimal than in North America, creating a very different mood and image than the softer incandescent lighting. Lighting can hide errors and outmoded store designs. A popular technique is to focus product lighting very high compared to the rest of the store and paint the ceiling dark to downplay unsightly concrete and ventilation ducts.

COLOUR

The creative use of colour can enhance a retailer's image and help create a mood. Research has shown that warm colours (red and yellow) produce opposite physiological and psychological effects from cool colours (blue and green), which are opposite on the colour spectrum.[19] For example, red and other warm colours have been found to increase blood pressure, respiratory rate, and other physiological responses. As we translate these findings to a retail store environment, warm colours are thought to attract customers and gain attention, yet they can be distracting and even unpleasant if too strong a hue. Fast-food restaurants often use warm colours to facilitate rapid turnover.

In contrast, research has shown that cool colours, such as blue or green, are relaxing, peaceful, calm, and pleasant. Thus, cool colours may be most effective for retailers selling anxiety-causing products, such as expensive shopping goods, or services such as those provided at a dentist's office. See Web site for colour theory details.

MUSIC

Like colour and lighting, music can either add to or detract from a retailer's total atmospheric package. Unlike other atmospheric elements, however, music can be easily changed. Although research in grocery stores indicates that music's tempo and volume don't significantly influence patrons' shopping time or purchase amount,[20] other research has shown that the presence of music positively affects customers' attitudes toward the store.[21]

Retailers can also use music to affect customers' behaviour. Music can control the pace of store traffic, create an image, and attract or direct consumers' attention. For instance, the Disney Stores pipe in soundtracks from famous Disney movies that are tied directly to the merchandise.

SCENT

Researchers say smell can affect a shopper's behaviour, but it's mainly about trying to make sure that shoppers are having a pleasant experience; for example, the smell of baby powder in an infant clothing department or the aroma of freshly baked cookies in a model home. Consider the ice cream chain that introduced the smell of waffle cones and saw sales rise by more than a third. Vancouver-based Enhance Air Technologies believes that tapping customers' noses will also open their wallets to beat slow retail sales.

Many buying decisions are based on emotions, and smell has a large impact on our emotions. "Smell, more than any other sense, is a straight line to feelings of happiness, hunger, disgust, and nostalgia—the same feelings marketers want to tap."[22] Research has shown that scent, in conjunction with music, has a positive impact on impulse buying behaviour and customer satisfaction.[23] Scents that are neutral were found to produce better perceptions of the store than no scent. The research found that customers in the scented store perceived that they had spent less time in the store than subjects in the no-scent store. This study suggests that stores using scents may improve customers' subjective shopping experience by making them feel that they are spending less time examining merchandise or waiting for sales help or to check out.

Retailers must carefully plan the scents that they use, depending on their target market. Gender of the target customer should be taken into account in deciding on the intensity of the fragrance in a store. Research has shown that women have a better ability to smell than men. Age and ethnic background are also factors. As people get older, their sense of smell decreases. Half of all people over 65 and three-quarters over 80 have almost no sense of smell at all.[24] Nevertheless, many retailers are trying to cash in on what the nose knows.

SUMMARY

This chapter explains how retailers can set up a series of stimuli through merchandise presentation that will encourage the customers to move from point to point in the store until they reach, touch, and make a purchase. Retailers have the ability to control the eye and body movements of their customers. Ultimately, store design shapes the shopping experience and has a tremendous impact on retail sales potential.

Amid the competitive marketplace, retailers are increasingly realizing that the key to success is identity. Now, more than ever, it is important to stand out from the retail crowd and be noticed. Most customers will pass by the front of a retail store in 10 seconds or less. Therefore, understanding and controlling the retail image become essential parts of the retailer's strategic plan.

This chapter examined issues facing store designers, buyers, and merchandise planners. A good store layout helps customers find and purchase merchandise. Several types of layouts are commonly used by retailers. The grid design is best for stores in which customers are expected to explore the entire store, such as grocery stores and drugstores. Racetrack designs are more common in large upscale stores such as department stores. Free-form designs are usually found in small specialty stores and within large stores' departments. Store planners also must carefully delineate different areas of the store. Feature areas, bulk of stock, and walls each have their own unique purpose but must also be coordinated to create a unifying theme.

There's more to assigning space to merchandise and departments than just determining where they'll fit. Departments' locations should be determined by the overall profitability and inventory turnover goals of the assortment, type of product, consumer buying behaviour, the relationship with merchandise in other departments, and the physical characteristics of the merchandise. Planograms, both manual and computer-generated, are used to experiment with various space allocation configurations to determine the most productive use of space. When evaluating

the productivity of retail space, retailers generally use sales per square metre.

Several tricks of the trade can help retailers present merchandise to facilitate sales. Retailers must attempt to empathize with the shopping experience and answer the following questions: How does the customer expect to find the merchandise? Is it easier to view, understand, and ultimately purchase merchandise when it's presented as a total concept or presented by manufacturer, colour, style, size, or price? Ultimately, retailers must decide on the appropriate type of fixture to use for a particular purpose.

Retailers utilize various forms of atmospherics—graphics, signs, and theatrical effects—to facilitate sales. Strategies involve lighting, colours, music, and scent.

KEY TERMS

atmospherics, *185*
boutique layout, *170*
bulk fixture, *184*
capacity fixture, *184*
cash-wrap areas, *171*
checkout area, *171*
demand/destination area, *175*
end cap, *171*
feature area, *171*
feature fixture, *184*
four-way fixture, *184*

free-form layout, *170*
freestanding fixture, *171*
frontal presentation, *182*
gondola, *184*
grid layout, *168*
idea-oriented presentation, *180*
impulse product, *175*
loop, *169*
planogram, *177*
point-of-purchase (POP) area, *171*

point-of-sale area, *171*
popping the merchandise, *186*
promotional aisle or area, *171*
racetrack layout, *169*
rounder, *184*
sales per linear metre, *179*
sales per square metre, *179*
straight rack, *183*
tonnage merchandising, *182*
vertical merchandising, *181*

Get Out & Do It!

1. **GO SHOPPING:** Go into a store of your choice and evaluate the store layout, design, and visual merchandising techniques employed. Explain your answers to the following questions:

- In general, are the store layout, design, and visual merchandising techniques used consistent with the exterior image of the store and location?
- Is the store's ambience consistent with the merchandise presented and the target customer?

- Does the store look like it needs to be redesigned? Do you think it needs a facelift, update, remodel, or renovation?
- To what extent are the store's layout, design, and merchandising techniques flexible?
- Notice the lighting. Does it do a good job in highlighting merchandise, structuring space, capturing a mood, and downplaying unwanted features?
- Is the store's layout designed to maximize sales potential?

- Are the fixtures consistent with the merchandise and the overall ambience of the store? Are they flexible?
- Evaluate the store's signage. Does it do an effective job in selling merchandise?
- Has the retailer used any theatrical effects to help sell merchandise?
- Does the store layout help draw people through the store?
- Evaluate the retailer's use of empty space.
- Has the retailer taken advantage of the opportunity to sell merchandise in feature areas?
- Does the store make creative use of wall space?
- What type of layout does the store use? Is it appropriate for the type of store? Would another type of layout be better?
- Ask the store manager how the profitability of space is evaluated; for example, profit per square metre. Is there a better approach?
- Ask the store manager how space is assigned to merchandise. Critically evaluate the answer.
- Ask the store manager if planograms are used. If so, try to determine what factors are considered when putting together a planogram.
- Has the retailer employed any techniques for achieving greater space productivity, such as using the cube, downsizing gondolas and racks, and minimizing nonselling space?
- Are departments in the most appropriate locations? Would you move any departments?
- What method(s) has the retailer used for organizing merchandise? Is this the best way? Suggest appropriate changes.

2. **INTERNET EXERCISE** Envirosell (www. envirosell.com) is a New York-based research company specializing in studying retail and service environments. Envirosell has worked in 26 countries around the world studying spaces—stores banks, restaurants, and service facilities. Visit the Web site and answer the following questions:

   a) Describe the three proprietary research tools used by Envirosell to document and analyze consumer behaviour.
   b) In their research Envirosell collects data to measure shopping behaviour in a retail environment. Identify the specific data that are collected.
   c) Read the case study on Staples and make observations regarding the research process.
   d) View the videos on the Envirosell Web site. Observe and discuss consumer behaviour.

DISCUSSION QUESTIONS AND PROBLEMS

1. Name you favourite retail store.
   a) Describe in detail the aspects of store design and merchandise that appeal to you.
   b) Describe how this image attracts the target customer.
2. Assume you have been hired as a consultant to assess a local discount store's space productivity. What analytical tools would you use to assess the situation? What suggestions would you make to improve the store's space productivity?
3. What are the different types of design that can be used in a store layout? Why are some stores more suited for a particular type of layout than others?
4. Generally speaking, departments located near entrances, on major aisles, and on the main level of multilevel stores have the best profit-generating potential. What additional factors help to determine the location of departments? Give examples of each factor.
5. A department store is building an addition. The merchandise manager for furniture is trying to convince the vice-president to allot this new space to the furniture department. The merchandise manager for men's clothing is also trying to gain the space. What points should each manager use when presenting his or her rationale?

6. Which retailers are particularly good at presenting their store as theatre? Why?

7. Lighting in a store has been said to be similar to makeup on a model. Why?

8. Why do supermarkets put candy, gum, and magazines at the front of the store, and milk and eggs at the back of the store?

9. One of the fastest-growing sectors of the population is the over-60 age group. But these customers may have limitations in their vision, hearing, and movement. How can retailers develop store designs with the older population's needs in mind?

10. Name your favourite store. Analyze the merchandise layout with reference to Exhibit 7–4 sales potential.

APPENDIX 7A | Principles of Display Design

DISPLAY ARRANGEMENTS

Knowledge of various generic display arrangements and their power to attract and direct the customer's eye may help you achieve this goal:

- Pyramid display is triangular in shape, with each ascending level becoming narrower; the top of the pyramid is usually the central point of the display arrangement.

- Step display places objects at different heights to give the effect of stairs, so the eye travels from the bottom up or top down.

- Zigzag display is a variation of step display but is more interesting visually—it follows a double reverse curve, with the middle object to one side of the highest item.

- Radiation starts from a central point, taking the viewer's gaze out to a variety of points.

- In repetition, all the items are the same shape and size, repeated, spaced equally apart, and in a direct line; it needs a break to avoid monotony.

- Alternation, varying the basic rhythm, prevents the possible boredom involved in the use of repetition.

- Progression places similar items in varying sizes next to each other, for a steplike arrangement.

BALANCE

Throughout all of these arrangements, a key standard of good balance is retained, regardless of the type of arrangement chosen. This assists in tying all items in the display together to give equal emphasis to all merchandise.

Balance is usually an essential quality of a well-designed display (although, where appropriate, imbalance or dynamic stress can provide a special kind of excitement). In a balanced (symmetrical) display, items and props are pleasingly arranged so that their weights, sizes, and colours are equalized. In formal balance, objects of similar size or weight are placed on both sides of a central point, with the most important merchandise featured in the centre. One side of the display is a mirror image of the other.

Informal balance (asymmetrical) places items of unequal size, weight, or quantity in the display; the most important unit may be off-centre and balanced by smaller, less important items. This is often a more interesting technique as it has a freer arrangement.

HARMONY

In merchandise display, harmony is very desirable. All objects in the display should be arranged in a compatible, orderly, and pleasing way, building around a unifying theme. Key components of harmony are line, texture, proportion, space, and emphasis.

- *Lines* can be vertical, horizontal, diagonal, or curved. They can make a display look taller, shorter, wider, or narrower. Vertical lines suggest height, growth, strength, and boldness; horizontal lines give the illusion of width, tranquility, and stability, and de-emphasize height; diagonal lines convey an impression of instability, action, and movement, and also depth or movement back in space; curved lines in a steady rhythm convey an impression of elegance, softness, and spontaneity, also of forms such as waves, clouds, and landscapes.

- Surface *texture* adds contrast, variety, and richness, and can suggest a certain character or mood. Whether you are using the rough texture of sandpaper, the gloss of high-tech steel, or the softness of satin, the textures should relate to the merchandise displayed.

- *Proportion* is the relationship of size and space of one object related to the display as a whole. Good proportion means the display objects and display as a whole are in proper relationship, appear to belong together, and fit properly into the space allotted. A small display in a large window will be lost; similarly, large objects in small spaces appear very crowded.

- The distance between objects reflects the character of the store; crowded spaces connote mass merchandise and a lower-price image. Merchandise displayed with a lot of empty space surrounding it will gain importance and suggest prestige pricing.

- Arrangements and design stimulate and draw the viewer's eye to a specific centre of interest, creating *emphasis* or impact, which is achieved through line, shape, colour, props, and the merchandise itself.

PLANNING A DISPLAY

When planning a merchandise display, whether window or interior, remember the acronym AIDA: your display must attract **A**ttention, stimulate **In**terest, create **D**esire, and motivate the customer to **A**ction (i.e., to make a purchase).

Sales are increased with windows that are theme-oriented. A display without a theme is like a story without a plot. The theme captivates the customers' thoughts and directs them to logical reasons for a purchase.

Before undertaking the display, consider carefully what message you want to give to your customer. A well-planned theme will give life to your merchandise and attract the customer's attention. Christmas red and green, pastel Easter eggs, or a current movie theme will add pizzazz to your display themes and be the means of relating merchandise to the consumer in graphic form he or she can understand, remember, and identify with.

Preparatory work involves drawing a layout of the composition. The sketch may be small and simple, but will enable you to analyze the arrangement, checking the focal point and customer's eye movement, and save time in setting up the actual display.

Big display budgets mean nothing, especially today when few have them. Some of the finest, most impressive displays have arisen from props that barely cost anything. So remember, when choosing props, look around you; it is often clear thinking, determination, and creativity that will be your best friends when it comes to effective display on a limited budget.

Selecting merchandise for the display is as much an art as displaying it. It should tell a story, along with the theme of the display. The merchandise may be selected first and the idea developed around it, but this is usually more difficult. The easier it is to see and understand the merchandise, the more impulse buying is heightened. So remember to keep it simple—sell only one idea.

Colour is one of the most versatile and inexpensive elements available to accomplish a desired mood, create drama, or develop impact in presenting merchandise. People prefer a sense of order and thus prefer colour harmony. Even the untrained person is capable of recognizing whether the colours in a display are attractive. Keep in mind the guidelines on colour usage; look upon colour as a tool, as a medium to stimulate action and generate sales. Effective colour usage can attract customers' attention, draw emphasis to a product, and relate to current seasonal trends.

Retailers like "special" or featured displays because they move merchandise much faster. They do not always create new store traffic, but they increase total purchases per customer. Special displays help balance inventories by cutting out surplus goods without markdowns. They strengthen advertising and can feature advertised merchandise. They can also help dispel monotony; a too-ordered store needs a change of pace.

You may find it useful to keep a record of the displays used in your store, with pictures if possible. This will ensure that your look is always fresh, and that you're not unconsciously returning to frequently used themes because they're comfortable.

DISPLAY LIGHTING

Careful consideration must be given to display lighting because what the customer sees and how he or she sees the merchandise in a display depends on the light. Planned lighting will highlight the merchandise and will maintain continuity in the display.

Light is the medium that transmits the visual ability to evaluate colour, shape, and texture. It creates a store personality that will assist in projecting the image of a high- or low-end strategy. Research has shown that a display brightly lit with fluorescent lights or floodlights will create a lack of shadow and texture, establishing a low-price image for the merchandise. As the overall illumination of the display is decreased and spotlights employed to focus on featured items, a more dramatic and higher-price image is created.

Lighting in a window should create a desired mood, enhance the character of the store, draw attention to specific display elements, coordinate parts to the total window, and promote the appearance of the merchandise. Lighting should be installed as the last step in putting the window together, after the display has been designed.

There are three types of window lighting—primary, secondary, and atmosphere. The primary represents the minimum adequate lighting for basic window illumination. Secondary is added to highlight and sell, using spotlights and floodlights. Atmosphere lighting creates dramatic effects and moods; it may play light against shadow, or use twinkling miniature lights, rotating colour wheels in front of spots, ultraviolet fluorescents, etc.

The major light source in the window should come from the top and as close to the window as possible. It should be directed in toward the merchandise, and care must be taken to ensure that it's not directed outward, toward the passerby. The light must define the space. Do not light the corners of the windows or parts of the display that are not to be seen or emphasized. Direct the lights either to expand or to reduce the visual field and depth.

A display window should be lighted with ceiling spots for highlight; then add overall backlight to illustrate contour, show the display's depth, and light the backdrop. Ceiling spots should be arranged at the window proscenium line from left to right and from front to back of the window. The ceiling spots must vary in intensity. Use the brightest lights to highlight the central product and lights of lesser intensity to illuminate support display materials and secondary products. Light from the side illustrates the texture of the product and dramatizes the vertical planes, emphasizing the separation of one plane in front of the other. The side lights emphasize solid geometric shapes. Side lights are most effective if they are placed at different levels from the floor to the ceiling.

When lighting mannequins in a window, a spotlight should be aimed at the waist to throw light above and below the garment, with another to highlight the face. If there's a special detail about the garment that justifies highlighting, a third spot could be used for that purpose.

Several small items arranged in a large window look insignificant if the window is lighted with uniform intensity. The focus is on the total window, not the specific merchandise. There is a danger that the merchandise will become lost in this environment. Reduce the light, and let it all focus on the objects, thereby diminishing the field of vision and lessening the window size.

In trying to create activity in a display, off-balance the lighting to stress tension. Add strobe lights to heighten activity. Some window displays should be more brightly lit in the day than at night to compensate for sun reflecting on the glass, producing glare.

CHAPTER 8

international retailing strategy

Executive Briefing

IKEA: Bringing Its Philosophy to a World Market

refact
The name IKEA was derived from the founder's initials plus the first letters of the farm and village where he grew up.

As it expands globally, IKEA is not just selling products, it's also selling its philosophy: This is how things are done in Sweden. The IKEA concept is based on offering unique, well-designed, functional furniture at low prices. Home furnishing solutions and products are displayed in realistic room settings. Customers are encouraged to get actively involved in the shopping experience by sitting on the sofas and opening and closing drawers. Price and product information is clearly marked on large, easy-to-read tags, making it easier for customers to serve themselves. Merchandise is purchased in unassembled flat packs. The guiding philosophy is: "You do your part. We do our part. Together, we save money."

Store openings generate tremendous excitement and large crowds. In September 2004, two men were trampled to death and 16 shoppers were injured in a rush by 20 000 people to claim vouchers at the first IKEA in Saudi Arabia. In February 2005, a riot at the opening of a new IKEA in North London forced the store to close just 30 minutes after opening. IKEA currently operates 130 stores in 29 countries.

Other global retailers such as McDonald's make changes to adapt to local preferences; IKEA is less willing to make concessions. For example, there is only one set of instructions to assemble a piece of IKEA furniture, wherever you are in the world. Every store opening begins in the same way: a Swedish breakfast and a traditional log sawing ceremony, which founder

QUESTIONS
What factors in the home marketplace would encourage a move to international retail expansion?

What is the difference between a global retailer and a multinational retailer?

Why do Canadian retailers have a low success rate in the American market?

What strategic decisions must be considered when entering the international retail marketplace?

Which Canadian retailers are best positioned to become global retailers?

Ingvar Kamprad often attends. Every store is decorated in blue and yellow, the colours of Sweden's flag, with a complex layout. One of the most frequently asked questions is how to get out of the store.

When IKEA entered North America in 1987, it discovered that consumers were not buying into its "one size fits all" philosophy, and it had to make some changes. For example, IKEA initially tried to sell its Scandinavian beds in Canada before discovering they were the wrong size for North American bed linens. Its Scandinavian-styled bookshelves were too small to hold a TV for Canadians who wanted shelving for an entertainment system. Even IKEA's European-style bath towels were too small and thin, and its glasses were deemed too small for the super-sized thirsts of North Americans. The European-style sofas were too hard for Canadian bottoms, and the IKEA dining room tables weren't big enough to fit a turkey in the centre on Thanksgiving.

IKEA's system of self-service, self-assembly, and consumer involvement in the whole retail process also was a new concept to many Canadians. However, rather than deviate from its philosophy and sell assembled merchandise, IKEA decided to improve its instructions and offer an assembly service.

Sources: Elen Lewis, "Is IKEA for Everyone?" *Brandchannel.com*, March 28, 2005; James Scully, "IKEA," *Time*, Summer 2004, pp. 16–17; http://www. IKEA.com.

international retailing: canadian issues

AMERICAN RETAILERS COME TO CANADA

Faced with an overcrowded domestic market, a growing number of American retailers looked northward to augment their brands. In 1952, the multimillion-dollar merger of two of the world's largest mail-order companies—Simpsons Ltd. of Toronto and Sears, Roebuck and Co. of Chicago—transpired to create Simpsons-Sears. The Canadian consumer became attracted to Sears and so it was that the Simpsons name was dropped in 1971 to avoid confusion. In 1994, Wal-Mart acquired 120 Canadian Woolco stores and wisely kept the former president of the Woolco chain (who had 28 years of Canadian retail experience and could provide cultural guidance). Sears and Wal-Mart account for approximately two-thirds of all department store sales in Canada. Wal-Mart continues to catch the public's attention by adding organics to the grocery mix, developing energy efficient lighting systems for their stores, and setting reduced packaging requirements for their vendors.

The Hudson's Bay Company, Canada's oldest retailer, was acquired in 2006 by American billionaire businessman, Jerry Zucker. Hudson's Bay, established in 1670, has more than 500 retail outlets across Canada, including The Bay, Zellers, Home Outfitters, and Designer Depot.

Free trade also encouraged American retailers to venture north as many retailers regarded Canada as "The Promised Land." The North American Free Trade Agreement (NAFTA, 1994) prompted a surge of big-box retailers and category killers across the border. As a result, by 1995 the Canadian retail industry was in crisis, experiencing a record number of bankruptcies and the descent into receivership of five major Canadian retailers: Eaton's, Woolco, Kmart, Woolworth Inc., and Consumer's Distributing. According to retail analyst John Winter, by the fall of 1997, 15 percent of the Canadian retail sales market was made up of warehouse outlets. The fallout also forced many Canadian retailers who had moved into the American market to withdraw, bringing the failure rate of Canadian retailers expanding into the U.S. to 90 percent, according to the Centre for Commercial Activity at Ryerson University.

Then there were the buyouts, and many popular Canadian retailers were acquired by American giants. Examples include Shoppers Drug Mart (acquired in 1999 by Manhattan-based buyout experts Kohlberg Kravis Roberts and Co.), Club Monaco Inc. (purchased in 1999 for $80 million by Polo Ralph Lauren, U.S.), Canadian icon Tim Hortons (merged with American fast-food giant Wendy's), the successful Future Shop electronics chain (purchased in 2002 by Best Buy), and Winners (now owned by TJ Max).

Success in Canada came quickly, and U.S. retail banners now control approximately 35 percent of all retail sales in Canada. San Francisco's Gap Inc. expanded quickly to include Gap stores, urban chic Banana Republic stores, and the trendy youth-oriented, big-box store, Old Navy.

What is the trouble with Canadian retailing and why is the sector becoming Americanized so quickly? Retail experts are quick to judge, pointing toward the lack of attention to customer service, lacklustre Canadian stores that need an image update, and sales staff who lack initiative and product knowledge. According to experts at the Retail Council of Canada, this is a bad rap as many Canadian retailers at all levels strive to exceed customer expectations and remain very competitive in an increasingly complex marketplace. Still, Nordstrom in the U.S. remains the gold standard globally and a tough act to follow, excelling in visual merchandising, knowledgeable staff, and unbeatable customer service.

Perhaps the reality is that Canadian retailers do not have the deep pockets of their southern neighbour. Consider this: When the 127-year-old T. Eaton Co. Ltd. was going through its bankruptcy problems in 1998 and trying desperately to attract customers, a $60 million renovation took place across its 64-store chain. In stark contrast, Marshall Fields in Chicago spent twice that amount on a single store.[1]

CANADIAN RETAILERS IN THE UNITED STATES

Retailers who have made unsuccessful ventures into the United States include Canadian Tire (twice), Future Shop, Mark's Work Wearhouse, Shoppers Drug Mart, Coles Books, Colour Your World, Second Cup, and La Senza. Cheap-chic fashion retailer Le Chateau and Danier Leather have both managed through several difficult years operating a handful of stores in New York. Canadian companies such as Jean Coutu and Alimentation Couche Tard have had better luck buying existing U.S. stores and turning them around. Canadian retailers often choose to penetrate the United States market because of the close proximity, but are poorly prepared to conquer the market. Some of the problems have been identified as:

- Inability to secure good real estate
- Underfunded advertising budgets. U.S. retailers spend about 6% of overall sales on advertising compared to 3% in Canada.
- underestimating the competitiveness of the U.S. market
- failing to do adequate research
- not devoting enough money and resources to the project

Montreal's Aldo Shoes has 100 shoe stores in several states and Roots, which has drawn on its popularity resulting from outfitting the U.S. Olympic team, operates six stores in major cities. Unfortunately, Roots' inability to secure the Canadian Olympic clothing deal has had a negative impact on the Roots image globally.

The copycat approach to retail strategy provides no strong basis for being a competitor in the American marketplace and is a formula for disaster. A more successful route for Canadian retailers has been to expand cautiously through:

- acquisition of existing U.S. retailers
- developing a unique product that people want

retailing view MICHAEL BUDMAN AND DON GREEN, CO-OWNERS, ROOTS CANADA LTD., A GLOBAL BRAND

8.1

Michael Budman and Don Green founded Roots Canada Ltd in 1973 and launched their first product, the weird looking "negative heel" shoe. The Roots dream began as two Detroit boys grew up spending their summers camping in Ontario's Algonquin Park. Today, the Canadian wilderness is a dominant part of the company's marketing image.

Roots is a company focused on lifestyle, selling everything from mouse pads to expensive leather furniture, and trendy licensed products including watches, jewellery, fragrances, and cosmetics. The company's annual revenues for 2002 exceeded $300 million. In Canada, Roots operates a retail chain of 140 Roots stores and 50 Roots Kids stores.

The energetic team of Budman and Green has been actively pursuing expansion both nationally and internationally for many years. Both admit that U.S. expansion was tough; Roots was an unknown retailer trying to succeed in the competitive American marketplace. The big break came in 1998 when Roots secured the contract to outfit the Canadian athletes for the Nagano Olympics. Roots' poorboy cap was the fashion hit of the games and assisted in expanding Roots' visible presence as a sought-after brand. After outfitting the Canadian Olympic athletes with the popular poorboy cap, next came the Sydney Games in 2000 followed by the Salt Lake City Games in 2002. The Roots mania continued, and at the Salt Lake City Games, U.S. Olympic beret sales were reported to be 25 000 hats a day. Success continues to follow the Roots team, and in 2003 Roots secured international deals to outfit Olympic teams from the United States, Britain, and Barbados.

Roots has become a highly desired global brand, and its widening global influence has prompted the opening of casual wear and leather goods boutiques worldwide. Expansion in the U.S. continues, and global growth proceeds in the Far East; there are 65 stores with plans to include future store openings.

Roots' Olympic legacy has created a global brand that continues to promote the outdoorsy Canadian image.

Riding the wave of success, Roots Olympic legacy had created a global brand, but the momentum slowed with the loss of the Canadian Olympic clothing deal. Roots will need to strengthen their franchise division and build their image to attract global growth.

Sources: Brian Hutchinson, "Merchants of Boom," *Canadian Business*, May 1997; Hollie Shaw, "Roots Ponders Massive US Expansion: Olympic Fever Catalyst," *The National Post*, February 21, 2002; and Hollie Shaw, "Roots to Open 100 Stores in Chain: It Has Managed to Create a Global Brand," *The National Post*, October 10, 2004.

The Quebec-based, 50-year-old Pharm-Escomptes Jean Coutu pharmacy practically owns the Quebec market, with 269 stores. Looking to expand further into the U.S. market, the company announced in 2004 the purchase of Eckerd drug stores in the eastern United States for $3.1 billion. This strategic move was based on Coutu's long track record of successfully operating in the U.S., extending back to 1987 and its takeover of 333 Brooks Pharmacies in seven northeastern states. Coutu's success was built on retaining the old management at Brooks and learning the business before making any major moves.

The Canadian brand Aldo has been successful internationally since 2001; it expanded globally into 15 countries, with 10 corporate stores in England and another 50 franchised stores. Aldo sells shoes in the mid-market price range ($59 to $89); the private label fashion-oriented shoes are designed by and made for the company through a well-established distribution network and licensee agreements. Aldo is one of the few Canadian retailers to succeed internationally and one of the few to build a global consumer brand.

global growth opportunities

International expansion is one form of a market expansion strategy. The most commonly targeted regions are Mexico, Latin America, Europe, China, India, and Japan. International expansion is risky because retailers using this growth strategy must deal with differences in government regulations, cultural traditions, different supply chain considerations, and language. Following changing consumer attitudes and retail trends around the world has provided a unique career for Canadians Anthony Stoken and Russell Connolly. In their book, *Naked Consumption*, they highlight ten global retail trends:

1. *It's a Wally, Wally World*—Wal-Mart will increase its retail power across all income levels.

2. *The Death of Inspiration*—Price emphasis focuses on utilitarian store environments.

3. *Experience Shopping*—Go beyond entertainment to attract niche markets.

4. *Empowered Consumers*—Consumers use the Internet to comparison shop.

5. *Kidopoly*—Kids are a big market opportunity; $25 billion in direct sales and $500 billion worth influencing parents' spending in North America.

6. *Dollar Store Euphoria*—Consumers like the value—low priced merchandise.

7. *Luxury for All*—Affordable luxury elements in product for all shoppers.

8. *E-Commerce: Action/Transaction*—Sales online will remain a minor share of overall retail sales.

9. *The Loyalty Myth*—Value in keeping and growing existing customer base.

10. *The New Brand Management*—Successful retailers will build their own brands.

Retailers engage in international ventures for many reasons. When the home marketplace is not producing desired sales and profits diminish over time, some of the problems may be attributed to:

- Saturated home marketplace with no room to grow
- Highly competitive marketplace
- Aging population that spends less and saves more
- Economic recession, which limits consumer spending

- High operating costs including staff wages, rental costs, and taxes
- Restrictive policies on retail development
- Shareholder pressure

The age factor is a dominant issue in Canada and the U.S., where aging populations have put their spending years behind them; the prediction for the future is that the North American economy will be much slower growing. North American retailers who want to maintain growth rates have no alternative but to sell their products in an international arena. The reality is that if you want 8 percent growth in sales you are forced to go to new growing economies, probably in South America, Mexico, or Chile, where a dominant young population between the ages of 15 and 25 (the desirable demographic) is entering the workplace, producing and spending.

It should be noted that countries such as Taiwan, South Korea, and Singapore are also now aging quite rapidly. Although younger than Canada, these countries over the next 10 years will experience a dramatic slowdown in consumption. China has an immense population of 1.2 billion, and even if you get a small portion of the market, success can be huge. China appears to have stronger retail market potential than India, with a population of 1 billion. China has a one-child-per-family policy, whereas Indians still have three children per family. If a population includes many children then much of its resources are used for the health care and education of its young people, inevitably putting a taxation burden on those of working age and limiting disposable income for retail purchases.

To succeed as an international retailer, the company must have a thorough understanding of the macro-environment, including cultural differences, government policies, and the economic stability in the international trade area. Other important factors include the sources of product production and the distribution capabilities within the international market. Some of the factors that would encourage a retailer to enter into the international marketplace include:[4]

- Limited competition in the international marketplace
- Rising numbers of middle-class consumers with improved standard of living
- Younger population with purchasing power
- Trade agreements, including North American Free Trade Act (NAFTA), World Trade Organization (WTO), European Union (EU)
- Relaxed regulatory framework
- Favourable operating costs, including lower wages and taxes
- Opportunity to diversify
- Opportunity to try innovative concepts

Both the micro- and macro-environments must be wisely managed for a retailer to be successful.

Italian designer Giorgio Armani made his first venture into Beijing, China, in 1998. According to Armani, "The Chinese market is growing full steam ahead. We are seeing very good results from Chinese tourists buying in our Hong Kong flagship store and the future possibilities are endless." The designer is well aware of the growing Chinese market for luxury goods; the decision to open a new flagship store in Shanghai in 2004 is part of an ambitious strategy to have 30 stores in China by 2008.[5]

THE WORLD'S LARGEST SHOPPING DISTRICT

Launched in May 2006, Bawadi, the multi-billion dollar leisure and tourism destination in Dubailand, will have the world's largest shopping experience, with 40 million

> **refact**
> The annual cost for The Gap's 1767 square metre flagship store on the Champs-Elysées in Paris is over $10 million.[3]

square metres of gross leasable area. Dubai is one of the United Arab Emirates in the eastern Arabian Peninsula, and Dubai City is the main city.

As part of Dubai's Strategic Plan 2015, the world's largest shopping area will provide support to the tourism and hospitality industry which in turn will play a major role in the diversification and development of Dubai's economy. Bawadi includes a 10 kilometre-long hotel and shopping strip, entertainment, convention centres, and residential complexes. The 31 hotels, ranging from three to five star, will focus Dubai as one of the world's premier family destinations.

The centerpiece of Bawadi will be the world's largest hotel, Asia-Asia, with 6500 rooms. The first phase of the development will be completed in 2010. See www.bawadi.ae. Also go to www.estatesdubai.com/2007/05/bawadi-to-be-biggest-retail-zone-in.html.

Dubai's fantastic, even bizarre previous developments include The Mall of the Emirates, featuring a ski slope in the desert and manmade islands shaped like palm fronds. It helped draw six million tourists in 2006 to this tiny desert land that is fast running out of oil.

WHO IS SUCCESSFUL AND WHO ISN'T

Retailers—particularly specialty store retailers with strong brand names such as The Gap and Zara, and food and discount retailers such as Wal-Mart, Carrefour, Royal Ahold, and Metro AG—may have a strong competitive advantage when competing globally.

Some retailers such as Roots and Gap have a competitive advantage in global markets because the North American culture is emulated in many countries, particularly by young people. Due to rising prosperity and rapidly increasing access to cable TV with North American programming, fashion trends are spreading to young people in emerging countries. The global MTV generation prefers Coke to tea, athletic shoes to sandals, Chicken McNuggets to rice, and credit cards to cash.[6] In the last few years, China's major cities have sprouted American stores and restaurants, including KFC, Pizza Hut, and McDonald's. Shanghai and Beijing each have more than two dozen Starbucks. Coffee was not the drink of choice until Starbucks came to town. But these Chinese urban dwellers go there to impress a friend or because it's a symbol of a new kind of lifestyle. Although Western products and stores have gained a reputation for high quality and good service in China, in some ways it is the American culture that many Chinese want.[7]

On the other hand, some large European and Japanese retailers have considerably more experience operating retail stores in non-domestic markets. For example, France's Carrefour has been operating stores in nondomestic markets for almost 30 years. It is very good at adapting its hypermarket format to local tastes. The company buys many products locally and hires and trains local managers, passing the power and authority to them quickly. Even though Wal-Mart has a more efficient distribution system, Carrefour has competed effectively against Wal-Mart in Brazil and Argentina.[8]

Category killers and hypermarket retailers may be particularly suited to succeed internationally because of the expertise they've already developed at home. First, these retailers are leaders in the use of technology to manage inventories, control global logistical systems, and tailor merchandise assortments to local needs. For instance, firms such as Home Depot provide consumers with an assortment of brand-name merchandise procured from sources around the world. This advantage is particularly valuable if brand-name merchandise is important to

Coffee was not the drink of choice until Starbucks came to China. But now Shanghai and Beijing each have more than two dozen Starbucks.

consumers. Second, retailers such as Wal-Mart and Carrefour have become the low-price provider in every market they enter because of their buying scale economies and efficient distribution systems. Third, despite idiosyncrasies in the international environment, category killers and hypermarket retailers have developed unique systems and standardized formats that facilitate control over multiple stores. These systems and procedures should work well regardless of the country of operation. Fourth, because of the category killer's narrow assortment and focused strategy, communications across national boundaries and cultures are specifically focused, which improves management coordination. Finally, at one time, people felt that consumers outside North America were used to high levels of personalized service and would not accept the self-service concept employed by category killers and hypermarket retailers. However, consumers around the globe are willing to forgo the service for lower prices.[9] Retailing View 8.2 examines Costco's strategy for success in Japan.

> **refact**
> The world's largest retailers are likely to be global players. Thirty-eight out of the top 50 global retailers operate in more than one country. The implication: Eventually one must go global to keep growing.[10]

retailing view
COSTCO, JAPANESE STYLE

8.2

Spiraling deflation, shrinking consumer spending, and white-hot competition—that's the state of play in the Japanese retail market. So why would any U.S. company want in? For one thing, Japan's retail market is the second-largest in the world, after the United States. For another, deregulation has finally leveled the playing field for foreign companies and domestic rivals. If a company can succeed in this market, it's virtually guaranteed success anywhere else. Following are some strategies Costco is using in Japan:

- *Open multiple stores.* Costco's current two-store operation in Japan is not profitable. But six or seven stores will generate the scale economies necessary to be profitable. Real estate prices have come down, so the chain can find sites that are relatively inexpensive.

- *Learn from past experience.* Costco learned a few lessons from its earlier ventures in Asia. First, it doesn't think of Asia as one big market. Each market is quite distinct. But, second, it can learn from the similarities. For instance, a lot of its start-up experiences in Taiwan and South Korea were similar to Japan: things like real estate negotiations and supplier relations. Also, Japanese and Korean commercial and labour laws are very similar.

- *Recognize different operating cost structures.* Operating costs, such as utilities, service, and maintenance expenses are high in Japan compared to the United States. Therefore, sales per store need to be higher to be profitable.

- *Adjust the assortment to meet local needs.* Japanese people are very particular about food packaging. They will buy in bulk, but not in the large packages like those purchased in the United States. So Costco is experimenting with smaller multipacks.

Costco has taken the plunge by opening two stores in Japan.

- *Buy direct.* Japan's distribution channels are fraught with multiple layers of wholesalers, which can be inefficient and keep prices unnecessarily high. To avoid this problem, Costco purchases 86 percent of its merchandise directly from manufacturers. If a manufacturer won't sell directly to the company because it wants to protect its long-standing relationships with other retailers, Costco goes elsewhere.

- *Sell "Made in the U.S.A."* U.S. imports have done very well, and demand is growing. Costco's top-selling U.S. items are nonfood: clothing, sporting goods such as basketball hoops, jewelry, and housewares.

Source: "Costco: Still Finding Its Way in Japan," *Businessweek Online*, March 25, 2002. www.businessweek.com

Global expansion is often difficult and full of pitfalls. For instance, The Gap is pulling back on some of its European store base. U.K.-based Marks & Spencer (M&S) has sold off its Canadian operations, Brooks Brothers, as part of an overall withdrawal from markets outside Britain. Its plan to close its 18 stores in France demonstrates the difficulty of operating in foreign markets. M&S found it was in violation of French labour laws when it announced the closures. The laws require prior consultation with the employees. U.K.-based J. Sainsbury, on the other hand, got caught up in a geopolitical conflict. It has abandoned expansion plans into Egypt because of a consumer boycott and heavy losses. The Egyptians believe that the company is pro-Israel, despite Sainsbury's denials.[11]

KEYS TO SUCCESS

Four characteristics of retailers that have successfully exploited international growth opportunities are:

- **globally sustainable competitive advantage**
- **adaptability**
- **global culture**
- **deep pockets**[12]

Globally Sustainable Competitive Advantage   Entry into nondomestic markets is most successful when the expansion opportunity is consistent with the retailer's core bases of competitive advantage. Some core competitive advantages for global retailers are shown below:

Core Advantage	Global Retailer
Low cost; efficient operations	Wal-Mart, Carrefour
Strong private brands	Royal Ahold, Ikea, Starbucks
Fashion reputation	The Gap, Zara, H&M (Hennes & Mauritz)
Image	Disney, Warner Brothers

Thus, Wal-Mart and Carrefour are successful in international markets where price plays an important role in consumer decision making and distribution infrastructure is available to enable these firms to exploit their logistical capabilities. On the other hand, The Gap and Zara are successful in international markets that value fashionable merchandise.

Adaptability   Successful global retailers build on their core competencies. They also recognize cultural differences and adapt their core strategy to the needs of local markets.[15] Colour preferences, the preferred cut of apparel, and sizes differ between cultures. For example, in China, white is the colour of mourning and brides wear red dresses. Food probably has the greatest diversity of tastes. Ahold operates under nearly 20 brand names around the globe, including Superdiplo in Spain, ICA in Sweden, Albert Heijn in the Netherlands, and Stop & Shop and Giant in the United States. Ahold firmly believes that, like politics, all retailing is local, as customers develop loyalty toward a store brand they've known for decades. Ahold's mantra: "Everything the customer sees, we localize. Everything they don't see, we globalize."[16]

Selling seasons also vary across countries. The Gap's major Canadian selling season is back-to-school in August; however, this is one of the slowest sales periods in Europe because most people are on vacation. Back-to-school in Japan is in April.

Store designs need to be adjusted. In some cultures, social norms dictate that men's and women's clothing cannot be displayed next to each other. In North America, the standard practice is to place low-priced, private-label merchandise on the shelf to the right of national brands, assuming that customers' natural eye movement is from left to right. This merchandising approach does not work in cultures where people read from right to left or up and down. IKEA initially tried to sell its Scandinavian beds in Canada before discovering they were the wrong size for North American bed linens.

Government regulations and cultural values also affect store operations. Some differences such as holidays, hours of operation, and regulations governing part-time employees and terminations are easy to identify. Other factors require a deeper understanding. For example, the Latin American culture is very family oriented. Thus, North American work schedules need to be adjusted so that employees can have more time with their families. Boots, a U.K. drugstore chain, has the checkout clerks in its Japanese stores standing up because it discovered that Japanese shoppers found it offensive to pay money to a seated clerk. Retailers in Germany must recycle packaging materials sold in their stores.[17] Also in Germany, seasonal sales can be held only during specific weeks and apply to only specific product categories, and discounts are limited. Unlimited guarantees are generally forbidden, which is why Lands' End may not describe such a guarantee on its goods in an ad and may only talk about it if customers ask for it first.[18]

Global Culture   To be global, one has to think globally. It is not sufficient to transplant a home-country culture and infrastructure into another country. In this regard, Carrefour is truly global. In the early years of its international expansion, it started in each country slowly, which reduced the company's ethnocentrism. Further enriching its global perspective, Carrefour has always encouraged rapid development of local management and retains few expatriates in its overseas operations. Carrefour's management ranks are truly international. One is just as likely to run across a Portuguese regional manager in Hong Kong as a French or Chinese one. Finally, Carrefour discourages the classic overseas "tour of duty" mentality often found in North American firms. International assignments are important in themselves, not just as stepping stones to ultimate career advancement back in France. The globalization of Carrefour's culture is perhaps most evident in the speed with which ideas flow throughout the organization. A global management structure of regional "committees," which meet regularly, advances the awareness and implementation of global best practices.

The proof of Carrefour's global commitment is in the numbers. It has had almost 30 years of international experience in 21 countries—both developed and developing.[19]

Deep Pockets   Expansion into international markets requires a long-term commitment and considerable upfront planning. Retailers find it very difficult to generate short-term profit when they make the transition to global retailing. Wal-Mart's US$8.2 billion cash flow and 48 percent share of the US$225 billion discount store industry in the United States provides the financial ability to maintain this type of staying power.[20] Wal-Mart is the world's largest retailer.

See Retailing View 8.3 for a discussion of how the makeup of European retailing has been affected by the advent of multinational retailers onto Main Street Europe.

ENTRY STRATEGIES

Four approaches that retailers take when entering nondomestic markets are:

- direct investment
- joint venture
- strategic alliance
- franchising[21]

Direct Investment   **Direct investment** involves a retail firm investing in and owning a division or subsidiary that builds and operates stores in a foreign country. This entry strategy requires the highest level of investment and exposes the retailer to significant risks, but it has the highest potential returns. One advantage of direct

8.3   retailing view
MAIN STREET EUROPE: THE FATE OF MOM-AND-POP STORES

During the 1990s, European retailing changed at the expense of the traditional mom-and-pop retail stores. In the past, mom-and-pop stores were the town or village meeting place. The locals would shop at these stores for convenience and service and because the owner was their neighbour.

Yet in most of Europe, the number of small and medium-size stores has fallen over the past several years. In the U.K., for example, shopping centres are growing twice as fast as retail sales as a whole. Less than a third of consumers describe the CBD (or High Street as it is known in the U.K.) as their preferred shopping location. Downtown and corner stores are threatened with extinction as suburban hypermarkets, such as French-based Carrefour, selling everything under one roof—from food and cosmetics to clothing and electronics—have become more popular. The two countries experiencing the largest expansion of superstores are Germany (in particular, what was East Germany) and the Commonwealth of Independent States (formerly the USSR).

In countries where this change has been occurring steadily over the past few years, local governments have tried to restrain superstores' growth by limiting their size, thus helping local entrepreneurs compete. For instance, in metropolitan Norwich, England, a horse trots down a dirt lane. It may sound sleepy and pastoral, but this is all happening only five kilometres from the centre of this county capital of 250 000. The nearby downtown has more than 500 shops and 200 restaurants, an open-air market, and a new mall that lures a quarter of a million shoppers into the city centre each week.

Were this an American city of similar size, the dirt lane no doubt would be replaced by a highway, the plowed field by a Wal-Mart, and the meadows by a multiplex

cinema. European cities such as Norwich like to do things differently, partly because they have less space and partly because they take great pride in their heritage. Strict planning and greenbelt laws force a sharp division between town and country. Suburbs are few. There is no place for the urban area to sprawl.

The efforts help Main Streets thrive and protect the underdeveloped countryside. The London-based Association of Town Centre Management says 80 percent of U.K. retail sales are still conducted in towns, despite a crusade by food superstores, mall developers, and other big retailers that want to locate outside downtown. In the United States, only 4 percent of the retail market is still downtown, according to the International Downtown Association in Washington, DC.

But preservation comes at a cost for Europe. The limits on out-of-town retailing reduce competition and retailing efficiency, causing higher prices. Looking for a Trivial Pursuit game? It will cost about US$55 in downtown Norwich. A short-sleeve Polo shirt from Ralph Lauren? US$90. What's more, the protection of town centres may also be a culprit behind Europe's chronic unemployment woes. A McKinsey & Co. study said policies such as strict zoning laws "represent the most obvious and easily correctable barriers to increased employment" in retail.

Sources: Sally Patten, "Pressure on High Street 'Set to Grow,'" *Financial Times*, February 26, 2001; Sarah Ellison and Christopher Rhoads, "Already Hurting, European Retailers Hold Their Breath—-Confidence and Consumption Were Already Weakening," *The Wall Street Journal*, September 24, 2001, p. 25; Jonathan Reynolds, "Who Will Dominate European E-Commerce? Threats and Opportunities for European Retailers," *International Journal of Retail & Distribution Management* 28, no. 1 (2000), p. 9; and Dana Milbank, "Guarded by Greenbelts, Europe's Town Centres Thrive," *The Wall Street Journal*, May 3, 1995, pp. B1, B9.

investment is that the retailer has complete control of the operations. For example, McDonald's chose this entry strategy for the U.K. market, building a plant to produce buns when local suppliers could not meet its specifications.

Joint Venture

A **joint venture** is formed when the entering retailer pools its resources with a local retailer to form a new company in which ownership, control, and profits are shared. Examples of successful joint ventures are Royal Ahold (the Netherlands) and Velox Holdings (Argentina); Metro AG (Germany) and Koc Group's Migros (Turkey); Carrefour and Sabanci Holding (Turkey); Metro AG (Germany) and Marubeni (Japan); and Monsoon (United Kingdom) and Charming Shoppes (United States).[22]

A joint venture reduces the entrant's risks. Besides sharing the financial burden, the local partner understands the market and has access to resources—vendors and real estate. Many foreign countries, such as China, require joint ownership, although these restrictions may loosen as a result of World Trade Organization (WTO) negotiations.[23] Problems with this entry approach can arise if the partners disagree or the government places restrictions on the repatriation of profits.

Strategic Alliance

A **strategic alliance** is a collaborative relationship between independent firms. For example, a foreign retailer might enter an international market through direct investment but develop an alliance with a local firm to perform logistical and warehousing activities.

Franchising

Franchising offers the lowest risk and requires the least investment. However, the entrant has limited control over the retail operations in the foreign country, potential profit is reduced, and the risk of assisting in the creation of a local domestic competitor is increased. U.K.-based Marks & Spencer, for example, has 136 franchised stores in 27 countries, including Cyprus (8), Greece (28), Indonesia (10), and Thailand (10).[24]

Retailing View 8-4 describes how Chinese manufacturers achieve low costs by developing economies of scale, not exploiting workers.

Costs Associated with Global Sourcing Decisions

Retailers use production facilities located in developing economies for much of their private-label merchandise because of the very low labour costs in these countries. To counterbalance the lower acquisition costs, however, there are other more subtle expenses that increase the costs of sourcing private-label merchandise from other countries. These costs include foreign currency fluctuations, tariffs, longer lead times, and increased transportation costs.

Fluctuations in currency exchange rates can increase costs. For example, if the Indian rupee increases relative to the Canadian dollar, the cost of private-label merchandise produced in India and imported for sale into Canada will increase. If this increase occurs between the time the order is placed and when it is delivered, Canadian retailers will have to pay more for the merchandise than planned. Most retailers use financial instruments such as options and futures contracts to minimize the effects of currency fluctuations.

Tariffs, also known as **duties,** are taxes placed by a government on imports that increase the cost of merchandise imported from international sources. Import tariffs have been used to shield domestic manufacturers from foreign competition. Because tariffs raise the cost of imported merchandise, retailers have a strong incentive to use their political clout to reduce them.

refact

Workers in China cost about 92 cents an hour compared with $1.20 in Thailand, $1.70 in Mexico, and about $21.80 in the United States. Only India among the major export countries, at about 70 cents an hour, is cheaper.[25]

Inventory turnover is likely to be lower when purchasing from suppliers outside the United States than from domestic suppliers, which will result in higher inventory carrying costs. Consider The Spoke bicycle store in Aspen, Colorado, which is buying Moots bicycles manufactured in Steamboat Springs, Colorado. The Spoke

8.4   retailing view
DATANG, CHINA, IS SOCK CITY

Datang, China, is called Sock City because nine billion pairs of socks, more than one set for every person in the world, are produced there each year. Its annual trade fair attracts 100 000 buyers from around the world. Southeast of Datang is Shenzhou, which is the world's necktie capital; to the west is Sweater City and Kids' Clothing City; and to the south is Underwear City.

This specialization creates the economies of scale that have made Chinese businesses the world's leading garment manufacturers. Buyers from New York to Tokyo can now place orders for 500 000 pairs of socks all at once—or 300 000 neckties, 100 000 children's jackets, or 50 000 size 36B bras—in China's giant new specialty cities.

Textile production is a prime example of how the Chinese government guides development indirectly through local planning instead of state ownership. In the late 1970s, Datang was a

As a result of government and private investment, China has become the leading manufacturer of private-label and national brand merchandise.

refact

Twelve percent of China's exports to the United States are sent to Wal-Mart. Wal-Mart's purchases account for 1 percent of China's gross domestic product.[26]

rice-farming village with 1000 people, who gathered in small groups and stitched socks together at home and then sold them in baskets along the highway. But the government designated Datang's sock makers as producers and ordered them to stop retailing socks. Now, they produce over one-third of the world's output.

Due to the policy, there are many rags-to-riches tales in Datang, such as that of Dong Ying Hong, who in the 1970s gave up a $9-a-month job as an elementary-school teacher to make socks at home. Now, she is the owner of Zhejiang Socks and a sock millionaire.

The Chinese government has also designated large areas for development, formed giant industrial parks, given tax benefits, and developed the infrastructure and transportation networks needed to move products quickly to

market. It has created networks of support businesses located near one another, such as the button capital that furnishes most of the buttons on the world's shirts, pants, and jackets. Private companies, with the support of the government, have built huge textile factory complexes, complete with dormitories and hospitals, that provide food, shelter, and health care, along with close supervision.

Huafang Group, one of China's largest textile companies, has over 100 factory buildings, 30 000 employees, and round-the-clock operations. More than 20 000 workers live free of charge in Huafang's dormitories. Conditions aren't great, but they are often better than the conditions in the inland provinces from which the workers come. Many women go there after high school, stay for a few years, and then return home to be married. As they return home, another 10 000 are bused in from the countryside.

Sources: David Barboza, "In Roaring China, Sweaters Are West of Socks City," *New York Times,* December 24, 2004, p. C2; David Francis, "Will China Clothe the World?" *Christian Science Monitor,* August 5, 2004, p. 1.

buyer knows that the lead time—the amount of time between the recognition that an order needs to be placed and the point at which the merchandise arrives in the store and is ready for sale—is usually two weeks, plus or minus three days. But if The Spoke ordered bikes from Italy, the lead time might be three months, plus or minus three weeks. Since lead times are longer, retailers using foreign sources must maintain larger inventories to ensure that merchandise is available when the customer wants it. Larger inventories mean larger inventory carrying costs.

International Human Resources Issues   The legal-political system in countries often dictates the human resource management practices that retailers can use. For example, Canada has led the world in eliminating workplace discrimination. However, in Singapore it is perfectly legal to place an employment ad specifying that candidates must be male, between the ages of 25 and 40, and ethnic Chinese. In the Netherlands, a retailer can make a substantial reduction in its workforce only if it demonstrates to the government that the cutback is absolutely necessary. In addition, a Dutch retailer must develop a plan for the cutback, which must then be approved by unions and other involved parties.

In countries with a collectivist culture such as China and Japan, employees downplay individual desires and focus on the needs of the group. Thus, group-based evaluations and incentives are more effective in those countries.

Finally, the staffing of management positions in foreign countries raises a wide set of issues. Should management be local or should expatriates be used? How should the local managers or expatriates be selected, trained, and compensated? Cole Peterson, vice-president of the People Division of Wal-Mart, says its biggest problem with international expansion is its lack of "human capital." Wal-Mart makes every effort to replace expatriates with locals, and in every overseas country except China, its operations are now led by a non-American. Yet it is expanding faster than it can train people internally and has lost high-quality local managers to rivals.[27]

global versus multinational retailers

A McDonald's in China looks the same as a McDonald's in Calgary or in Chicago: It has the same visual concept with the golden arches and the always popular Big Mac and fries. But, worldwide, there may be some differences: In Germany, the restaurant looks the same but beer is added to the menu; and in Japan, the same predictable Big Mac and fries is accompanied by an unusual blue drink. The same holds true with The Gap and The Body Shop throughout the world. These retailers use a **global strategy**, which means that they replicate their standard retail format and centralized management throughout the world in each new market. Often the global retailer will develop franchising initiatives based on its standardized form of doing business in return for a substantial franchise fee. The global retailer can expand rapidly but it is learning little from its internationalization.[28]

Retailers who change their products and image to reflect the international marketplace use a **multinational strategy**. These retailers use a decentralized format, learning about the country's culture and changing their retail concept to adapt to cultural differences and cater to local market demands. Each country they enter enhances their knowledge portfolio. The greater the cultural diversity, the more likely is the multinational retailer to enter a joint venture with a company from the host country. The Spanish retailer Zara has opened at the Eaton Centre in Toronto. The trendy fashions are ordered daily with the newest fabrics and styles to appeal to the

refact

The first Wal-Mart Discount City was opened in Rogers, Arkansas, in 1962.[31]

trend-conscious Canadian consumer. Zara's just-in-time small production facilities are able to cater to specific market demands with quick turnaround time.[29]

GLOBAL LOCATION ISSUES

Many of the issues and procedures used for making global location decisions are the same as we have discussed in the previous chapter.[30] The retailer needs to decide on a region, a trade area within that region, and a specific site. The retailer still needs to examine competition, the population characteristics, traffic patterns, and the like. What makes global location decisions more difficult and potentially interesting is that those in charge of making these decisions are typically not as familiar with the nuances of the foreign location issues as they are with the same issues in their home country. Furthermore, national chains in Canada typically have close working relationships

8.5   retailing view
ZARA DELIVERS FASHION FAST

Zara, located in La Coruna, Spain, is now the third-largest clothing retailer in the world, with profits growing at 30 percent per year. It operates over 800 stores in 55 countries. Its supply chain management process begins with the store managers, who are equipped with handheld devices linked directly to the company's design rooms in Spain. They report daily on what customers are buying and not buying and what they are asking for but not finding. For instance, when buyers found that customers were requesting a purple shirt that was similar to one they were selling in pink, they passed this information on to the designers in Spain.

Fabrics are cut and dyed by robots in the company's 23 highly automated factories in Spain. The final assembly is entrusted to a network of 300 or so small suppliers that are located near the factories in Galicia and northern Portugal.

Because Zara controls the entire production and design process, it can make products in small lots. By so doing, it can see how the first few hundred items are selling before making more. Instead of shipping new products once a season like many fashion retailers, Zara makes deliveries to each of its stores every few days. The purple shirts were in stores in two weeks—compared with the several months it would take for most department stores and other specialty apparel stores to accomplish the same feat.

Zara successfully reduces lead time by communicating electronically with the factory, using automated equipment, employing assemblers who are in close proximity to the factory, and using premium transportation such as airfreight to get merchandise to the stores. For instance, if a Zara store is running low on a medium kelly-green sweater, its supply chain management system ensures a shorter lead time than that of more traditional retailers.

Zara gains competitive advantage by carefully coordinating its production, design, and distribution process so that the most current fashions are available when they are in high demand, which increases the percentage of merchandise sold at full price.

As a result, it's less likely that the Zara store will be out of stock before the next sweater shipment arrives.

Due to the efficiency of its supply chain, Zara does not have to discount merchandise that is not selling as much as other specialty store apparel retailers do. Zara's sales are 85 percent of the initial sales prices, whereas The Gap's sales are 60–70 percent of the initial price. Zara is able to achieve these results and still design 40 000 new SKUs each year.

Sources: Susan Reda, "Retail's Great Race Getting Fashion to the Finish Line," *Stores*, March 2004, pp. 36–40; Kasra Ferdows, Michael Lewis, and Jose Machuca, "Rapid-Fire Fulfillment," *Harvard Business Review*, November 2004, pp.104–10.

with a handful of major developers. Developers work with retailers on a strategic level while the malls are still on the drawing board.

Although similar developer–retailer relationships are growing worldwide, often retailers must deal with landlords directly—and cope with a confusing world of site requirements, red tape, and restrictions. For example, a retailer may be surprised to learn that the local government requires a $1 million key payment upfront. A landlord may demand a 25-year lease. And if there's to be construction, it's likely to be a slow, politically charged process.

Real estate selection is where many grand global designs ultimately succeed or fail. A retailer may devote months to targeting a region—Latin America, for instance—before choosing a country to enter. From that point, a city must be chosen. But when it comes to picking an exact site within that city—a decision that often demands knowing local **traffic flows,** the most desirable side of a street, or urban development patterns—the decision is sometimes rushed and made without the right knowledge. As with many locations in Canada, particularly congested urban areas, if the retailer chooses the wrong side of the street, it may fail.

Costs can also be troublesome. Compared to North American locations, occupancy costs in cities such as London, Paris, or Tokyo are extremely high. Retailers have to be extremely high-volume to survive. Real estate rental costs are 30 percent more in the U.K. than they are in Germany, which are 30 percent more than they are in the United States, which are 30 percent more than they are in Canada.

Real estate restrictions also complicate international location decisions. For instance, tough European laws make it difficult for big-box retailers to open large stores that have historically required a large piece of property. Solutions occasionally demand a little ingenuity and flexibility. Costco Wholesale's solution, for example, has been to modify store formats in some overseas markets—most notably, the adoption of two-level operations in Korea and Taiwan. Some retailers prefer to open locations within a mall setting, and for some, the bigger the mall, the better. See Exhibit 8–1 for a list of the world's 10 largest shopping malls.

Although there may be a downturn in outlet centres in North America, their popularity is beginning to take off in other areas such as Japan and Europe. Japan is particularly attractive given its large population, love for American brands, and growing consumer enthusiasm for value retailing concepts. European growth is

refact

H&M opened three stores ranging from 1395 to 3255 square metres in the Toronto area, and receives merchandise daily from Europe. In 2004, the company had 40 000 employees, including 200 designers, with 950 stores in 18 countries.[32]

Name	Location	Gross Leasable Space (in square metres)
West Edmonton Mall	Edmonton, Alberta	483 600
Mall of Asia	Manila, Philippines	465 000
Mall of America	Blooomington, MN, USA	390 600
SM Prime's Megamall	Manila, Philippines	325 500
Del Amo Fashion Center	Torrance, CA, USA	279 000
South Coast Plaza	Costa Meso, CA, USA	251 100
Seacon Square	Thailand	251 100
Plaza/Crystal Court Woodfield Mall	Schaumburg, IL, USA	251 100
The Plaza and the Court at King of Prussia	King of Prussia, PA, USA	232 500
Sawgrass Mills	Sunrise, FL, USA	232 500

exhibit 8–1
The World's Largest Shopping Malls

Sources: Susan Thorn, "Megamalls Gaining Favor in Asia," *Shopping Centers Today,* April 1, 1997, p. 1; Susan Thorn, "Recovery Slow in Thailand, Malaysia, Philippines," *Shopping Centers Today,* May 2000; and "100 Largest Shopping Centers in the U.S.," ICSC Library.

more problematic, however, given Western Europe's more restrictive planning environment, strong opposition by High Street (downtown) retailers,[33] and overall lower levels of enthusiasm for American brands. Compared to American outlet centres, the existing European centres are smaller, have fewer entertainment options, and have fewer well-known manufacturer outlets of European brands due to concern about channel conflict.

THE TOP 25 GLOBAL RETAILERS

refact

John de Laurentiis, owner of Toronto fashion retailer Le Firme, jets to Italy every 15 weeks to buy fashion merchandise from rural factories.[35]

Exhibit 8–2 lists the 20 largest global retailers in 2003.[34] With worldwide retail sales estimated at US$7 trillion by *Euromonitor*, the 25 largest retailers represent a 14 percent share. Combined, the 200 largest retailers capture 30 percent of worldwide sales.

Wal-Mart remains the undisputed leader in the retail world. Its sales are three times as large as those of Carrefour, the second-largest retailer. Home Depot also has made significant sales gains over the last several years. Its fourth-place ranking in 2000 was up from 24th in 1996. Most of Home Depot's growth has come from store openings and new formats such as the popular Expo home furnishings stores.

8.6   retailing view
ONCE-PROUD JAPANESE DISCOVER OUTLET MALLS

On any given Saturday more than 20 000 people venture into an industrial district of the port city of Yokohama, Japan, and converge on a fake New England fishing village named Sawtucket.

Sawtucket has a clock tower, quaint storefronts, and windmills. But the big lure isn't ersatz Americana. It's shopping. Within the Sawtucket complex, which opened in September 1998, is Yokohama Bayside Marina Shops and Restaurants, a factory outlet mall offering famous brands—J. Crew, Eddie Bauer, Reebok, and the like—at bargain prices. Crowds of yen-pinching consumers are heeding the call.

A familiar retail format in the United States, the outlet mall is a revolutionary retailing concept in Japan. For decades, Japanese retailers had assumed, with considerable reason, that consumers wanted only the newest versions of products. And manufacturers avoided selling leftovers openly, often destroying inventory so as not to risk hurting their brand images or annoying department stores that sold at list price.

Then came national economic distress, overturning the assumptions of retailers and altering the attitudes of consumers, who increasingly patronized secondhand stores and discounters. Today, factory outlet malls can be found in or near Japan's big cities and are increasingly popular with shoppers.

In the past, Japanese tourists by the busload descended on American outlet malls armed with the floor plans of stores and Japanese translations of important English phrases such as "Buy one, get one free." The mall developers wanted to have consumers experience an American outlet mall without ever getting on an airplane. So they courted 50 outlet tenants, including U.S. outlet regulars such as Nike, Levi's, Guess, and Coach. It was much harder attracting Japanese tenants, many of whom worried about backlash from the department stores.

Some Japanese companies that agreed to open a store in the Yokohama mall are still reluctant to describe just what they're doing. Some insist that their products are ones that were on regular store shelves just a few weeks ago and aren't the season's leftovers. In many stores, big banners on the walls assure customers that the discounted products are legitimate. Products marked "second-class," one banner explains, are items that are slightly damaged and thus can't be sold in regular stores.

Sources: "Chelsea Osaka Outlet to Add 40 Stores, Become Japan's Largest," *Jiji Press English News Service,* February 6, 2002, p. 1; George Wehrfritz, "Destination Shoppers; They Come From All Over Japan To Reach This Factory Outlet," *Newsweek,* international ed., November 13, 2000, p. 44; and Yumiko Ono, "Once-Proud Japanese Discover Outlet Malls," *The Wall Street Journal,* December 30, 1998, p. B1.

Rank	Retailer	Headquarters	2003 Retail Sales ($ millions)	Number of Formats	Number of Countries	Five-Year *CAGR%
1	Wal-Mart	U.S.	229 617	5	11	14.2%
2	Carrefour	France	85 011	6	31	18.7
3	Home Depot	U.S.	58 247	2	4	19.2
4	Kroger	U.S.	51 760	5	1	14.3
5	Metro	Germany	48 349	6	26	12.4
6	Target	U.S.	42 722	3	1	9.0
7	Ahold	Netherlands	40 755	7	17	12.5
8	Tesco	U.K.	40 071	5	10	9.7
9	Costco	U.S.	37 993	1	8	9.8
10	Sears	U.S.	35 698	1	3	22.9
11	Albertsons	U.S.	35 626	3	1	19.4
12	Aldi Einkauf	Germany	33 837	2	12	15.2
13	Safeway	U.S.	32 398	1	3	7.6
14	JCPenney	U.S.	32 347	2	3	1.8
15	Intermarche	France	31 688	8	7	9.2
16	Rewe	Germany	31 404	7	12	7.4
17	Kmart	U.S.	30 762	2	1	20.9
18	Walgreens	U.S.	28 281	1	1	16.5
19	Edeka/AVA	Germany	26 514	5	6	17.2
20	Lowe's	U.S.	26 491	1	1	21.2

exhibit 8–2

20 Largest Retailers Worldwide

*Compound annual growth rate.

SOURCE: "2004 Global Powers of Retailing," *Stores*, January 2004, pp. G11–12. Courtesy of STORES Magazine/Deloitte.

Through merger and acquisition activity, many of these large retailers are diversifying their format offerings to consumers. But 47 percent of the 200 largest retailers still operate only one store type. A significant number of these large global retailers, therefore, are continuing to focus on a single business segment.

The majority of the largest global retailers remain involved in the food sector. More than half of the 200 largest retailers have supermarket, warehouse, hypermarket, or cash and carry formats, or some combination of them.

Geographically, U.S. companies dominate the 200 largest retailer list. The 78 American companies in the top 200 list represent 49 percent of the sales. Wal-Mart alone represents 9.1 percent of the top 200 sales.

Despite a decade of poor economic performance, the Japanese remain major global retailers. By country of origin, the 30 companies based in Japan are the second-largest group of the top 200.

Historically, a large consumer market and relatively abundant land have kept many Canadian retailers from seeking global expansion. But with domestic markets reaching saturation, companies are seeking opportunities abroad. Still, the North American companies have not caught up to the largest European firms, which operate in an average of seven countries.

STRUCTURE OF RETAILING AND DISTRIBUTION CHANNELS AROUND THE WORLD

The nature of retailing and distribution channels in North America is unique. Some critical differences between Canadian, U.S., European, and Japanese retailing and distribution systems are summarized in Exhibit 8–3.

exhibit 8–3   Comparison of Retailing and Distribution Channels across the World

| Characteristic | Canada | U.S. | EUROPE | | | | | | | | Japan |
| | | | NORTHWEST | | | | SOUTHERN | | CENTRAL | | |
			U.K.	Belgium	France	Germany	Spain	Italy	Hungary	Czech	
Concentration (% of retail sales in category by top three firms)	High	High	High				Low		Very low		Medium
Number of outlets per 1000 people	Medium	Medium	Medium				High		Low		High
Retail density (sq. m. of retail space per person)	High	High	Medium				Low		Low		Medium
Store size (% of retail sales made in stores over 930 sq. m.)	High	High	Medium				Low		Low		Low
Role of wholesaling (wholesale sales as a % of retail sales)	Low	Low	Medium				Medium		High		High
Distribution Inefficiency (average maintained markup–distribution costs as a % of retail price)	Low	Low	Medium				High		High		High

refact

The biggest doughnut chain in Canada, Tim Hortons (which was named after a famous Canadian hockey player of the 1960s and '70s), has been owned by the U.S. hamburger chain Wendy's since 1995.[36]

refact

India's working age population is expected to grow by 335 million by 2030, an increase equal to the working age population of the European Union and the United States combined.[37]

The U.S. distribution system has the greatest retail density and the greatest concentration of large retail firms. Some people think that North America is overstored. Many retail firms are large enough to operate their own warehouses, eliminating the need for wholesalers. The fastest-growing types of retailers sell through large stores with over 1860 square metres. The combination of large stores and large firms results in a very efficient distribution system.

In contrast, the Japanese distribution system is characterized by small stores operated by relatively small firms and a large independent wholesale industry. To make daily deliveries efficiently to these small retailers, merchandise often moves through three distributors between the manufacturer and retailer. This difference in efficiency results in a much larger percentage of the Japanese labour force being employed in distribution and retailing than in Canada.

The European distribution system falls between North American and Japanese systems on this continuum of efficiency and scale, but the northern, southern, and central parts of Europe have to be distinguished, with Northern European retailing being the most similar to the North American system. In Northern Europe, concentration levels are high—in some national markets 80 percent or more of sales in a sector such as food or home improvements are accounted for by five or fewer firms. Southern European retailing is more fragmented across all sectors. For example, traditional farmers' market retailing is still important in some sectors, operating alongside large "big-box" formats. In Central Europe the privatization of retail trade has resulted in a change from a previously highly concentrated government-controlled structure to one of extreme fragmentation characterized by many small family-owned retailers.

Some factors that have created these differences in distribution systems in the major markets are:

- Social and political objectives—A top priority of the Japanese economic policy is to reduce unemployment by protecting small businesses such as neighbourhood retailers. The Japanese Large Scale Retail Stores Law regulates the locations and openings of stores of over 465 square metres. Several European countries have also passed laws protecting small retailers. For example, in 1996, France tightened its existing laws to constrain the opening of stores of over 279 square metres. European governments have also passed strict zoning laws to preserve green spaces, protect town centres, and inhibit the development of large-scale retailing in the suburbs.

- Geography—The population density in Canada is much lower than in Europe and Japan. Thus, Europe and Japan have less low-cost real estate available for building large stores.

- Market size—The North American retail market is larger than Japan or any single European country. In Europe, distribution centres and retail chains typically operate within a single country and are therefore not able to achieve the scale economies of North American retailers serving a broader customer base. Even with the euro and other initiatives designed to make trade within European countries easier and more efficient, barriers to trade still exist that are not found in the Canadian and American marketplaces.

refact
Mountain Equipment Co-op has more than 2 million members in 192 countries.[38]

COUNTERFEITING IS A GLOBAL THREAT

A **counterfeit** is an imitation or a fake that usually is made with the intent to deceptively represent its contents or origins. Counterfeiting usually involves forged currency or documents, but can also describe clothing, software, electronic stock shares or certificates, pharmaceuticals, watches, or more recently, auto parts, cars, and motorcycles. Often this results in patent infringement and trademark infringement. Widespread use of counterfeit products undermines the North American system of standards, testing, and certification that is designed to protect consumers, retailers, manufacturers, and regulators.

The term **bootleg** is more often used when there is little or no attempt at hiding the fact that this is a counterfeit product, as in CDs, DVDs, computer software, and toys. The user is fully aware of its illegal status. By contrast, a **knockoff** item may imitate a well-known brand, may be sold for a lower price, and may be of inferior quality, but there is usually no attempt to deceive the buyer or infringe upon the original product.

The appearance of counterfeit products in North America has increased dramatically in recent years. According to Manny Gratz, manager of Anti-Counterfeiting & Intellectual Property Enforcement, the manufacture and distribution of counterfeit products have been linked to organized crime. He feels that people who deliberately choose to buy counterfeit products are not victims; instead they support the criminally deceptive practices of counterfeiters by creating a built-in market for their goods.

SUMMARY

This chapter provides an overview for understanding international retailing. Understanding the macro-environment becomes increasingly critical in making strategic decisions to expand internationally. Questions about the local economy, legal environment, technological capabilities, consumer behaviour, and the retail competition must be answered. Business laws and regulations will not only impact the ability to conduct business but will also dictate how to function operationally in a global marketplace. The macro-environment is different for each country and must be constantly monitored.

Issues of global location strategy will impact retailing success or failure on a day-to-day basis.

International retailers must be intimately aware of the cultural climate in domestic markets and respond to the market demands of the micro-environment. Understanding the importance of place, including the retail location and store environment, the product mix, the price, and management decisions is critical. Retailing is geographically tied and must therefore gain insight into the direct-to-customer link.

Global retailers will develop strength through centralized management and a standardized image, whereas multinational retailers gain success through adapting to the local environment through decentralized management and a more flexible approach to retail store design.

KEY TERMS

adaptability, *202*
bootleg, *213*
counterfeit, *213*
deep pockets, *202*
direct investment, *204*
duties, *205*
global culture, *202*

global strategy, *207*
globally sustainable
    competitive advantage, *202*
joint venture, *205*
knockoff, *213*
market attractiveness/
    competitive position
    matrix, *215*

multinational strategy, *207*
strategic alliance, *205*
tariffs, *205*
traffic flows, *209*

Get Out & Do It!

1. **INTERNET EXERCISE** Go to the websites for Wal-Mart (www.walmartstores.com), Carrefour (www.carrefour.com), Royal Ahold (www.ahold.com), and Metro AG (www.metro.de). Which chain has the most global strategy? Justify your answer.

2. **INTERNET EXERCISE** Choose your favourite national retail chain. Pick a country for it to enter. Using information 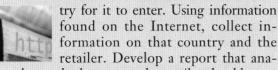 found on the Internet, collect information on that country and the retailer. Develop a report that analyzes whether or not the retailer should enter the country, and if so, how it should do so.

3. **OLC EXERCISE** Access the Online Learning Centre at **LearningCentre** www.mcgrawhill.ca/olc/levy and click on Market Position Matrix.

Exercise 1: This spreadsheet reproduces the analysis of international growth opportunities discussed in the appendix to Chapter 8. What numbers in the matrices would have to change to make China and France more attractive opportunities? To make Brazil and Mexico less attractive opportunities? Change the numbers in the matrices and see what effect it has on the overall position of the opportunity in the grid.

4. **INTERNET EXERCISE**
     a) Go to www.counterfeitchic.com. Review recent blogs.
    b) Read the report "The Economic Impact of Counterfeiting and Piracy" at www.estatesdubai.com/2007/05/bawadi-to-be-biggest-retail-zone-in.html Visit www.counterfeitlawblog.com and see the "Evils of Counterfeiting."

Explain the economic impact of counterfeiting.

DISCUSSION QUESTIONS AND PROBLEMS

1. Read "IKEA: Bringing its Philosophy to a World Market" at the beginning of the chapter and visit www.ikea.com.
   a) Explain why IKEA has had such strong appeal in the global marketplace.
   b) Why does the philosophy "one size fits all" not work in global markets? Suggest situations where this policy is problematic.

2. Explain how global culture can impact the success or failure of a global retailer such as Toys R Us.

3. What advantages does a multinational retailer such as Avon have over a global retailer?

4. Why are global companies such as McDonald's Restaurants gaining worldwide customer appeal?

5. Explain the strengths and weaknesses of global companies versus multinational retailers.

6. Why is a joint venture alliance often a favourable approach to facilitating an international retail venture?

7. Why is it important to understand the macro-environment when making decisions about an international retail venture?

8. Explain the importance of understanding the micro-environment when planning to open a retail store in an international location.

9. Complete a research study to determine what laws and regulations exist for opening a retail store in the following countries.
   - China
   - India
   - Russia
   - Mexico

10. Choose a retailer that you believe would be, but is not yet, successful in other countries. Explain why you think it would be successful.

APPENDIX 8A   Using the Market Attractiveness/Competitive Position Matrix

The following example illustrates an application of the **market attractiveness/competitive position matrix**.[39] The matrix (Exhibit 8–4) provides a method for analyzing opportunities that explicitly considers both the retailer's capabilities and the retail market's attractiveness. The matrix's underlying premise is that a market's attractiveness determines its long-term profit potential for the opportunity, and the retailer's competitive position indicates the profit potential for the opportunity. The matrix indicates that the greatest investments should be made in opportunities where the retailer has a strong competitive position.

There are six steps in using the matrix to evaluate opportunities for strategic investments:

1. Define the strategic opportunities to be evaluated. For example, a store manager could use the matrix to evaluate departments in a store; a vice-president of stores for a specialty store chain could use it to evaluate stores or potential store sites; a merchandise vice-president could

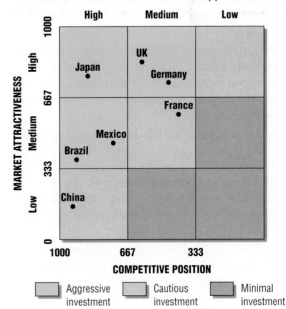

exhibit 8–4
Evaluation of International Growth Opportunities

exhibit 8–5   Data on International Markets

	U.S.	Mexico	Brazil	Germany	France	U.K.	Japan	China
Population, 2002 (millions)	287	103	176	83	60	60	127	1284
Population's projected annual growth rate (%)	0.86	1.37	0.78	0.22	0.29	0.18	0.06	0.75
GDP, 2000 (billion US$)	9963	575	624	1878	1299	1415	4753	1100
Projected GDP annual growth rate 2001–2005 (%)	2.7	4	3.7	2.2	2.5	2.3	1	7.8
Per capita GDP, 2000 (US$)	35 352	5800	3763	22 845	21 863	23 793	37 558	869
Retail sales per capita, 2000 (US$)	8135	962	533	5448	4833	5268	8578	307
% of consumer expenditures on clothing	5	6	4	7	6	6	6	8
% of wealth in top 20% of population	42	55	67	40	42	44	38	44
Population density (per sq. km)	30	51	20	235	107	246	336	134
% living in urban areas	75	74	81	86	74	90	78	36
Business climate index	2	31	37	11	15	3	26	41
Retail industry concentration	High	Avg.	Low	High	High	High	Avg.	Low
Logistical infrastructure	Very good	Good	Moderate	Very good	Very good	Very good	Good	Moderate
Local vendors	Exc.	Avg.	Avg.	Exc.	Exc.	Exc.	Avg.	Poor

Sources: 2001 World Population Data Sheet, www.prb.org//content/NavigationMenu/Other_reports/2000-2002/2001 world_ population_data_sheet.htm; Laura M. Beaudry, "Apparel: Statistical Overview," *Catalog Age* 17, no. 4 (March 15, 2000), pp. 52–56; and "2002 Global Powers of Retailing," Stores Online, January 2002, www.stores.org.

use it to evaluate merchandise categories sold by the retailer; or a retail holding company's CEO could use it to evaluate international growth opportunities.

2. Identify key factors determining market attractiveness and the retailer's competitive position. Factors that might be selected are discussed in the market attractiveness, competitor analysis, and self-analysis sections of the situation audit.

3. Assign weights to each factor used to determine market attractiveness and competitive position. The weights assigned to each factor indicate that factor's importance in determining the market attractiveness and competitive position. Typically, weights are selected so that they add up to 100.

4. Rate each strategic investment opportunity on (1) the attractiveness of its market and (2) the retailer's competitive position in that market. Typically, opportunities are rated on a 1-to-10

scale, with 10 indicating a very attractive market or very strong competitive position and 1 indicating a very unattractive market or very weak competitive position.

5. Calculate each opportunity's score for market attractiveness and competitive position. Scores are calculated by (1) multiplying the weights by each factor's rating and (2) adding across the factors.

6. Plot each opportunity on the matrix in Exhibit 8–4.

In this example, a fashion-oriented U.S. women's apparel retailer is evaluating seven countries for international expansion: Mexico, Brazil, Germany, France, the U.K., Japan, and China. Some information about the markets is shown in Exhibit 8–5.

To evaluate each country's market attractiveness, management identified five market factors, assigned a weight to each factor, rated the markets on each factor, and calculated a market attractiveness score for each alternative (Exhibit 8–6). Here

exhibit 8–6   Market Attractiveness Ratings for International Growth Opportunities

	Weight	Mexico	Brazil	Germany	France	U.K.	Japan	China
Market size	20	2	2	7	6	5	10	4
Market growth	10	10	7	3	3	3	2	6
Economic stability	15	2	2	10	9	9	5	2
Business climate	25	4	2	7	7	10	6	2
Attitude toward U.S.	30	7	5	8	3	10	10	2
Total	100	480	340	735	550	815	745	280

exhibit 8–7   Competitive Position for International Growth Opportunities

	Weight	Mexico	Brazil	Germany	France	U.K.	Japan	China
Cost	10	9	10	5	5	5	7	10
Brand image	30	8	10	4	3	7	9	6
Vendor relations	20	7	7	4	4	3	8	8
Locations	20	6	8	6	5	7	6	10
Marketing	20	8	8	6	3	6	8	10
Total	100	750	860	490	380	630	780	840

management assigned the highest weight to the attitude that consumers in the country have to the United States (30) and gave the lowest weight to economic stability (15). Ratings for market size and market growth are based on country data; the firm had to consider size of its target market—middle-class women between the ages of 25 and 50. For this reason, Brazil, Mexico, and China had low ratings on market size. These countries are also low on economic stability; however, the retailer did not think that factor was particularly important because the buying power of its target segment is relatively insensitive to the country's economy. The business climate factor includes an assessment of the degree to which the government supports business and foreign investment. The European countries and Japan are high on this dimension.

Exhibit 8–7 shows the factors, weights, and ratings used to evaluate the retailer's position in each country versus the competition. In evaluating the competitive position, management felt that brand name was the most critical aspect of competitive position because

image is particularly important in selling fashionable merchandise. Since cost was viewed as the least important factor in determining the competitive position of a high-fashion retailer, it received a weight of only 10.

In terms of the retailer's competitive position within each country, the firm felt its brand name was very well known in Japan and Brazil but not well known in France and Germany. Brazil, Mexico, and China offer the best opportunities to operate efficiently due to the low labour costs in these countries.

Evaluations of each of the countries are plotted on the business attractiveness/competitive position matrix shown in Exhibit 8–4. Based on the recommended investment level and objectives associated with each cell in the exhibit, the retailer should invest substantially in Japan, the U.K., Germany, Mexico, and Brazil and be cautious about investments in China and France.

refact

The 10 major Asian countries have over one-half of the world's population.[40]

SECTION III

financial management

Section II, Retailing Strategy, provided an over-all framework for making the tactical decisions that will be examined more closely in Section III, Financial Management. In Sections III and IV, we offer tactical solutions to strategic problems.

Section III provides an in-depth discussion of the decisions involved in the financial management of the retail business.

Chapter 9 examines the financial strategy associated with measuring and evaluating a retailer's performance.

Chapter 10 discusses how retailers develop profitable assortments and forecast sales.

Chapter 11 examines the buying systems used to make appropriate buying decisions to generate a profitable return on investment.

Chapter 12 explores branding options, sourcing, and establishing and maintaining a competitive advantage by developing loyal relationships with vendors.

Chapter 13 addresses the important question of how to set and adjust retail prices.

CHAPTER 9

financial strategy

Executive Briefing

Count Lorenzo Rossi di Montelera, Chairman of the Board, Birks&Mayors Inc.

As Canada's premier jewellery retailer, Birks has a distinguished history of family silversmiths who over the years served an elite clientele that included royalty and heads of state. It was in 1879 that Henry Birks was inspired to start his jewellery business based on a set of core values including quality, exclusivity, excellent service, and an openness to design innovation. Henry's keen business sense, combined with his skills as a jeweller led him to open the first Birks jewellery shop 123 years ago in downtown Montreal. Today, Birks has prestige destinations across Canada, acquisitions in the U.S., and a network that includes online shopping and corporate sales. www.birks.com

In 1993 Regaluxe Investment acquired Henry Birks & Sons, following a very difficult time in the mid-nineties when increased competition in the jewellery market and a trend to discounting eventually took its toll. Regaluxe, a privately owned Italian company, had ambitious plans for Birks' revitalization. The rebuilding included hiring Tom Andruskevich, former executive with Tiffany & Co., and to support its international expansion, in 2002 Birks acquired a controlling interest in Mayors Jewelers Inc, a leading force in fine jewellery retailing in the southeastern U.S. Birks embarked on the exciting adventure of becoming a world-class luxury brand and joined the two companies in 2005 to form Birks&Mayors Inc.

QUESTIONS

How is retail strategy reflected in retailers' financial objectives?

Why do retailers need to evaluate their performance?

What measures do retailers use to assess their performance?

What is the strategic profit model and how is it used?

The decision to reinvigorate the Birks' brand came out of consumer research which suggested that although people had a great deal of respect for Birks they felt that the store lacked excitement. The revitalization strategy included a sophisticated new store design and a contemporary marketing approach with an emphasis on courting those who can afford luxury and a focus on the younger consumer. Previously, Birks' typical customer had been 45 years and over and had a family income of $70 000. The new contemporary look was designed to attract a younger generation of consumers who had money to spend but were not aware of the Birks' experience.

The turnaround plan met with success, and by the end of the 2005 fiscal year annual sales were approaching $239.3 million, showing a 17% increase in net sales during the holiday season. The percentage of sales from private label products grew from 25% to 74%, taking advantage of Birks' manufacturing capabilities while producing higher profit margins. The Birks&Mayors retail empire has emerged today to include 39 Birks stores in Canada and 29 Mayors stores in the U.S.

The Birks name has come to represent luxury goods, selling exclusive brands such as Cartier and Baume & Mercier, and producing innovative private label Birks' designs. The familiar blue box has become a symbol of the company's reputation for quality and is among the most recognized retail icons in Canada.

Financial decisions are an integral component in every aspect of a retailer's strategy. In this chapter, we look at financial tools retailers use to measure and evaluate their performance.

Retail store owners need to know how well they are doing because they want to be successful and stay in business. Retailers are aware of how many customers enter their stores and count up the receipts at the end of the day to see how much has been sold. Unfortunately, these simple measures aren't enough. For instance, sometimes a retailer finds that sales are good, but still can't afford to buy new merchandise. When things are good, they often don't think about their retail strategy. But when things go bad, the retailer thinks about nothing else.

Based on strategies the retailer set, it is important to establish quantifiable performance objectives. If the retailer is achieving objectives, changes in strategy or implementation programs aren't needed. But if the performance information indicates that objectives aren't being met, the retailer needs to reanalyze plans and programs. For example, after reviewing the accountant's financial report, the retailer might conclude that she is not earning a fair return on the time and money invested in the stores. Based on this evaluation, she might consider changing the strategy by appealing to a different target market and lowering the average price point of the merchandise in order to improve the turnover rate.

*This chapter was prepared with the assistance of Andrea L. Godfrey, PhD student, University of Texas at Austin, while an MBA student at Babson College.

objectives and goals

As we discussed in Chapter 5, the first step in the strategic planning process involves articulating the retailer's strategy and the scope of activities it plans to undertake to be successful. Three types of objectives that a retailer might have are (1) financial, (2) societal, and (3) personal.[1]

FINANCIAL OBJECTIVES

When assessing financial performance, most people focus on profits: What were the retailer's profits or profit margin (profit as a percentage of sales) last year, and what will they be this year and into the future? But the appropriate financial performance measure is not profits but rather return on investment (ROI). Kelly Bradford set a financial objective of making a profit of at least $100 000 a year, but she really needs to consider how much she needs to invest to make the $100 000, the profit she desires from her investment.

Think of the decisions you might make when planning how to invest some money you might have. In making this investment, you want to determine the highest percentage return you can—the highest interest rate or greatest percentage increase in stock price—not the absolute amount of the return. You can always get a greater absolute return by investing more money. For example, Kelly Bradford would be delighted if she made $100 000 and only needed to invest $500 000 (a 20 percent ROI) in the business but disappointed if she had to invest $2 000 000 to make $100 000 profit (a 5 percent ROI). A commonly used measure of the return on investment is **return on assets (ROA),** or the profit return on all the assets possessed by the firm.

SOCIETAL OBJECTIVES

Societal objectives are related to broader issues about providing benefits to society—making the world a better place to live. For example, retailers might be concerned

This store owner/ manager develops a retail strategy and coordinates the day-to-day operations to ensure that financial objectives are being met.

about providing employment opportunities for people in a particular area or more specifically for minorities or the handicapped. Other societal objectives might include offering people unique merchandise, such as environmentally sensitive products, providing an innovative service to improve personal health, such as weight reduction programs, or sponsoring community events.

For example, McDonald's values diversity among its employees and suppliers. The company ensures diversity among its corporate employees by including it in the business planning process. "As business units and corporate departments put together their business plans, diversity is included in them. We have diversity business planning guidelines that we provide to the McDonald's leadership, so that they're incorporated in the strategic planning process," explains chief diversity officer Pat Harris. McDonald's also values diversity in its supply chain and has been recognized by *Fortune* magazine as the "top purchaser from minority suppliers, spending more than $3 billion a year, or 27 percent of its total, at minority-owned firms."[2]

Performance with respect to societal objectives is more difficult to measure than financial objectives. But explicit societal goals can be set, such as the percentage of executives or store managers that are women or minorities or the percentage of profits donated to worthy charities.

PERSONAL OBJECTIVES

Many retailers, particularly owners of small, independent businesses, have important personal objectives, including self-gratification, status, and respect. For example, the owner/operator of a book store may find it rewarding to interact with others who like reading and authors that visit the store for book-signing promotions. By operating a popular store, a retailer might be recognized as a well-respected business leader in the community.

Whereas societal and personal objectives are important to some retailers, financial objectives should be the primary focus of managers of publicly held retailers—retailers whose stocks are listed on and bought through a stock market. Investors in publicly held companies, namely, the people who buy stock in a company, are primarily interested in getting a return on their investment, and the managers of these companies must have the same objectives as the investors. Therefore, the remaining sections of this chapter focus on financial objectives and the factors affecting a retailer's ability to achieve financial goals.

overview: strategic profit model

The **strategic profit model,** illustrated in Exhibit 9–1, is a method for summarizing the factors that affect a firm's financial performance as measured by ROA. The model decomposes ROA into two components: (1) net profit margin and (2) asset turnover. The **net profit margin** is simply how much profit (after tax) a firm makes divided by its net sales. Thus, it reflects the profits generated from each dollar of sales. If a retailer's net profit margin is 5 percent, it makes $.05 for every dollar of merchandise or services it sells.

Asset turnover is the retailer's net sales divided by its assets. This financial measure assesses the productivity of a firm's investment in its assets and indicates how many sales dollars are generated by each dollar of assets. Thus, if a retailer's asset turnover is 3.0, it generates $3 in sales for each dollar invested in the firm's assets.

exhibit 9–1

Components of the
Strategic Profit Model

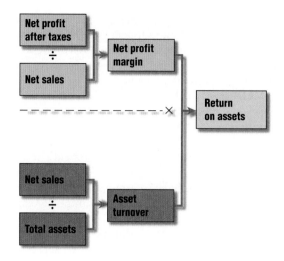

The retailer's ROA is determined by multiplying the two components together:

Net profit margin   ×   Asset turnover   =   Return on assets (ROA)

$$\frac{\text{Net profit}}{\text{Net sales}} \qquad \frac{\text{Net sales}}{\text{Total assets}} \qquad \frac{\text{Net profit}}{\text{Total assets}}$$

These two components of the strategic profit model illustrate that ROA is determined by two sets of activities, profit margin management and asset management, and that a high ROA can be achieved by various combinations of net profit margin and asset turnover.

Specifically, retailers have two paths available to achieve a high level of performance: the profit path and the turnover path. Different retailers, however, pursue different strategies, resulting in different types of financial performance. The two paths are combined into the strategic profit model to illustrate that retailers using very different strategies and financial performance characteristics can both be financially successful. As a vehicle for discussion, we'll compare the financial performance of two very different retailers: Birks (a national jewellery store chain) and Wal-Mart (the world's largest retailer).

Then we will discuss how retailers set performance objectives and how different performance measures are used throughout the organization. The chapter concludes with an appendix that describes activity-based costing and how it is used to make retailing decisions.

We begin our examination of corporate-level performance measures by looking at the strategic profit model.

		PROFIT PATH		**TURNOVER PATH**
Return on assets (ROA)	=	Net profit margin	×	Asset turnover
	=	$\dfrac{\text{Net profit}}{\text{Net sales}}$	×	$\dfrac{\text{Net sales}}{\text{Total assets}}$
	=	$\dfrac{\text{Net profit}}{\text{Total assets}}$		

retailing view
WAL-MART: THE WORLD'S LARGEST RETAILER

9.1

How big is Wal-Mart? Some 100 million people a week buy into the "we're just like you" message. The company's annual sales rival the gross domestic product of Austria, the world's twenty-second largest economy. Wal-Mart topped *Forbes* magazine's list of the top 500 companies based on revenue, stealing the top spot from long-time holders General

Motors and Exxon Mobil. Wal-Mart ranks as the largest retailer in Canada, with 284 outlets nationwide. Wal-Mart has also opened six Sam's Club warehouse stores in Ontario and employs over 70 000 Canadians. An additional 130 new stores are planned for international markets. Even as discount retailers face intense competition from category specialists, such as Best Buy, Canadian Tire, and Home Depot, and increasingly compete against grocery and pharmacy retailers, there seems to be no end to Wal-Mart's success story.

Most experts agree that Wal-Mart's amazing results can be attributed to efficiency and innovation. Wal-Mart is an industry leader in supply chain and information systems. It was the first to use a hub-and-spoke distribution system in which the company opens stores around a central distribution facility. The company pioneered the policy of providing suppliers with access to sales and in-stock information through electronic data interchange (EDI) and has developed a process known as collaborative planning, forecasting, and replenishment (CPFR), which is quickly becoming the standard product planning procedure for retailers and their suppliers. Innovation in technology has led to radio frequency identification (RFID) to track and detail merchandise.

In addition, Wal-Mart invested in most of the waves of information technology systems earlier and more aggressively than did its competitors. This allowed Wal-Mart to reduce inventory significantly, which resulted in cost savings and higher productivity. Founder Sam Walton summed up the company's attitude toward IT: "People think we got big by putting big stores in small towns. Really we got big by replacing inventory with information." These innovations have made Wal-Mart the industry leader in buying and distribution efficiency.

Wal-Mart uses its competitive advantages in computer systems and logistics to create a "productivity loop"—a cycle of lowering prices and margins but reinvesting in the business to keep prices low and squeeze out compe-

tition. Wal-Mart was the first retailer to sustain this pricing strategy. Because of its efficient operations, Wal-Mart can keep its prices low enough to offer the lowest-priced basket of merchandise in every market in which it competes.

Although much of its success can be attributed to its innovative use of technology, Wal-Mart's edge also stems from managerial innovations that have nothing to do with IT. For example, Wal-Mart's appeal with consumers is largely based on its promotion of small-town flavour. From a people greeter in every store to in-store events and contests, the company's goal of spreading that hometown flavour has been a key to its success.

This distinctive approach to discount retailing is embedded in the company's corporate culture. This culture began with Sam Walton's own charismatic personality and is fostered among the company's employees, who are referred to as "associates." The company puts an almost obsessive focus on exceeding customer expectations and continuously mines the associates for fresh ideas. In return, the company receives a cult-like loyalty from its associates, some of whom have become millionaires as a result of the company stock options.

To ensure continued growth and success, Wal-Mart continues to innovate its retail format. Wal-Mart Canada has approximately 80 000 different products in each store and plans to start offering products and services as part of its companywide program to drive environmental best practices; it hosted a "green product fair" in Montreal in 2007. Wal-Mart has become the world's largest food retailer and has developed an organic food initiative, leading one of the most significant trends in grocery retailing, making room for an increasing range of green products.

Sources: Laurent Belsie, "Wal-Mart's Ascent to No. 1 Signals Many Things," *Christian Science Monitor*, February 19, 2002; Bradford C. Johnson, "Retail: the Wal-Mart Effect," *McKinsey Quarterly*, no. 1 (2002); Michael Levy and Dhruv Grewal, "So Long Kmart Shoppers," *The Wall Street Journal*, www.wsj.com, January 28, 2002; Barbara Thau, "Sam Walton's Wal-Mart," *HFN Visionaries Supplement*, November 27, 2001; Anthony Bianco and Wendy Zellner, "Is Wal-Mart Too Powerful?" *Business Week*, McGraw-Hill, October 6, 2003; Kevin Libin, "The Last Retailer in Canada," *Canadian Business*, March 18, 2002; and "Wal-Mart Canada Makes the Grade," *Canada Newswire*, April 30, 2004.

exibit 9–2

Return on Assets
Model for a Bakery and
Jewellery Store

	Net profit margin	×	Asset turnover	=	Return on assets
La Madeline Bakery	1%		10 times		10%
Kalame Jewellery	10%		1 time		10%

To illustrate how the strategic profit model works, consider the two very different hypothetical retailers in Exhibit 9–2. La Madeline Bakery has a net profit margin of 1 percent and asset turnover of 10 times, resulting in a return on assets of 10 percent. The profit margin is low due to the competitive nature of this commodity-type business. Asset turnover is relatively high, because the firm doesn't have its own credit card system (no accounts receivable). Also, it rents its store, so fixed assets are relatively low, and it has a very fast inventory turnover—in fact, its inventory turns every day!

On the other hand, Kalame Jewellery Store has a net profit margin of 10 percent and an asset turnover of one time, again resulting in a return on assets of 10 percent. The difference is that even though the jewellery store has higher operating expenses than the bakery, its gross margin is much more—it may double the cost of jewellery to arrive at a retail price. Kalame's asset turnover is so low compared to the bakery's because Kalame has very expensive fixtures and precision jewellery-manufacturing equipment (fixed assets), offers liberal credit to customers (accounts receivable), and has very slow inventory turnover—possibly only one-half to one turn per year. In sum, these two very different types of retailers could have exactly the same return on assets.

Thus, La Madeline is achieving its 10 percent return on assets by having a relatively high asset turnover—the *turnover path*. Kalame Jewellery, on the other hand, achieves its return on assets with a relatively high net profit margin—the *profit path*.

We will examine the relationship between these ratios and retailing strategy and describe where the information can be found in traditional accounting records.

One way to define financial success is to provide the owners of the firm with a good return on their investment. Although retailers pursue similar financial goals, they employ different strategies. For instance, Birks has broad assortments of jewellery and gifts, exceptionally high levels of service, and a beautiful store image. Birks concentrates on the profit path. Wal-Mart, described in Retailing View 9.1, takes the opposite approach. It concentrates on the turnover path. Wal-Mart has narrow assortments, relatively little service, and functional decor. Based on this description, why would anyone shop at Wal-Mart? The answer is that Wal-Mart strives for and maintains everyday low prices. The strategic profit model is used to evaluate the performance of different retailers that, like Birks and Wal-Mart, may employ very different strategies.

Jewellery stores typically have a higher net profit margin than bakeries, but their asset turnover is much lower. How can return on assets of a jewellery store and a bakery be the same?

the profit path

The information used to analyze a firm's profit path comes from the income statement. The income statement summarizes a firm's financial performance over a period of time. Exhibit 9–3 shows income statements in a hypothetical situation for Wal-Mart and Birks. The profit path portion of the strategic profit model that utilizes such income statement data appears in Exhibit 9–4. Let's look at each item in the income statement.

NET SALES

The term **net sales** refers to the total number of dollars received by a retailer after all refunds have been paid to customers for returned merchandise:

$$\text{Net sales} = \frac{\text{Gross amount}}{\text{of sales}} + \frac{\text{Promotional}}{\text{allowance}} - \frac{\text{Customer}}{\text{returns}}$$

Customer returns represent the value of merchandise that customers return and for which they receive a refund of cash or a credit. **Promotional allowances** are payments made by vendors to retailers in exchange for the retailer promoting the vendor's merchandise. For example, consumer packaged good manufacturers will frequently pay supermarket chains to stock a new product (called slotting fees) or advertise a product. Retailing View 9.2 describes the impact of these promotional allowances on a retailer's reported net sales. For warehouse clubs such as Costco, membership fees are an additional source of revenue. About 4 percent of Costco's $48 billion in sales are from membership fees.

Sales are an important measure of performance because they indicate the activity level of the merchandising function. Retailers are particularly interested in sales growth due to its direct link to the firm's overall profitability.

GROSS MARGIN

$$\text{Gross margin} = \text{Net sales} - \text{Cost of goods sold}$$

Gross margin, also called **gross profit,** is an important measure in retailing. It gives the retailer a measure of how much profit it's making on merchandise sales without considering the expenses associated with operating the store.

	Wal-Mart	Birks
Net sales	219 812	1 607
Less: Cost of goods sold	171 562	663
Gross margin	48 250	944
Less: Operating expense	36 173	634
Less: Interest expense	1 326	20
Total expense	37 499	653
Net profit, pretax	10 751	291
Less: Taxes*	3 897	116
Tax rate	36.25%	39.79%
Net profit after tax	6 854	175

*Effective tax rates often differ among corporations due to different tax breaks and advantages.

exhibit 9–3
Hypothetical Income Statements for Wal-Mart Stores, Inc., and Birks, 2002 ($ in millions)

exhibit 9–4   Profit Margin Models for Wal-Mart Stores, Inc., and Birks, 2002 ($ in millions)

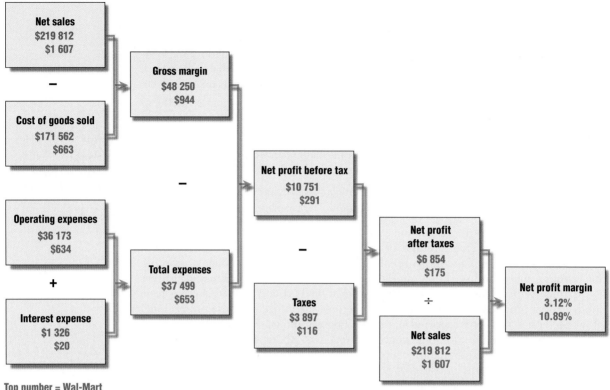

Top number = Wal-Mart
Bottom number = Birks

Gross margin, like other performance measures, is also expressed as a percentage of net sales so that retailers can compare performances of various types of merchandise and their own performance with other retailers.

$$\frac{\text{Gross margin}}{\text{Net sales}} = \text{Gross margin \%}$$

Wal-Mart: $\dfrac{\$48\,250}{\$219\,812}$ = 21.95%

Birks: $\dfrac{\$944}{\$1607}$ = 58.75%

(Throughout this chapter, dollar figures are expressed in millions.)

Superficially, Birks appears to outperform Wal-Mart on gross margin. However, further analysis will show that other factors interact with gross margin to determine overall performance. But first, let's consider the factors that contribute to differences in gross margin performance.

Discount stores such as Wal-Mart generally have lower gross margins than jewellery stores because discount stores pursue a deliberate strategy of offering merchandise at everyday low prices with minimal service to several cost-oriented market segments. Discount stores have tried to increase their average gross margin by adding specialty products and departments such as gourmet foods and jewellery. Discount stores grow profit based on volume of sales.

exhibit 9–5
Types of Retail
Operating Expenses

Selling expenses	= Sales staff salaries + Commissions + Benefits
General expenses	= Rent + Utilities + Miscellaneous expenses
Administrative expenses	= Salaries of all employees other than salespeople + Operations of buying offices + Other administrative expenses

exhibit 9–5
Types of Retail
Operating Expenses

EXPENSES

Expenses are costs incurred in the normal course of doing business to generate revenues. One expense category in Exhibit 9–5, operating expenses, is further defined in Exhibit 9–6.

Another major expense category, interest, is the cost of financing everything from inventory to the purchase of a new store location. For instance, if a bank charges Birks 10 percent interest, Birks pays $49 million in interest to borrow $490 million.

Birks has significantly higher total expenses as a percentage of net sales than Wal-Mart. Like gross margin, total expenses are also expressed as a percentage of net sales to facilitate comparisons across items and departments within firms.

$$\frac{\text{Total expenses}}{\text{Net sales}} = \text{Total expenses/Net sales ratio}$$

Wal-Mart: $\dfrac{\$37\ 499}{\$219\ 812} = 17.06\%$

Birks: $\dfrac{\$653}{\$1607} = 40.65\%$

retailing view ACCOUNTING FOR PROMOTIONAL ALLOWANCES CAN PROVIDE MISLEADING INFORMATION ABOUT RETAIL SALES

9.2

Manufacturers of branded consumer products pay promotional allowances, also called rebates, to retailers for a variety of actions, such as to get them to meet sales targets, stock new products in their stores, or place products in prime store locations (known as slotting allowances)— even to compensate for damaged goods. For example, rather than have the supermarket chain return damaged merchandise for credit, the vendor simply gives the supermarket chain an allowance of 3 percent of the merchandise bought.

These promotional allowances can have a significant impact on reported sales. A typical manufacturer may spend 20 percent of its sales with a retailer on promotional allowances; a $50 million contract for cookies or tomato sauce thus would include a $10 million promotional allowance. The payments are usually made upfront but can also take the form of volume-based bonuses. If a retailer fails to deliver the volume, the bonus is not paid or may have to be renegotiated.

The effect of these promotional allowances on a retailer's reported sales and profit has made headlines in the business press. In 2003, vendors such as Sara Lee Corp. and ConAgra Foods Inc. paid U.S. Foodservice rebates that

executives recognized as sales before the sales goals were realized. U.S. Foodservice is a division of Ahold, one of the largest global supermarket retailers, headquartered in The Netherlands. By inflating sales and earnings, the executives met their annual goals and received significant bonuses. In response to an SEC (Securities and Exchange Commission) complaint, two U.S. Foodservice executives pleaded guilty to criminal charges in the matter, while two others are fighting the charges.

In response to this scandal, an accounting task force was established by the Federal Accounting Standards Board (FASB) to define how promotional allowances should be treated in financial statements. Although Safeway Inc. discloses vendor allowances in detail—breaking them down into promotional and stocking allowances on a quarterly basis—many other companies disclose little new information and describe minimal effects on earnings because they feel the information is propriety.

Sources: Diya Gullapalli, "In the Grocery World, Rebates Remain the Mystery Meat," *The Wall Street Journal,* August 9, 2004, p. C.1; Constance L. Hays, "Reliance on Promotional Allowances Can Result in Shortfalls," *New York Times,* February 25, 2003, p. C.8.

Grocery stores attempt to increase their average gross margin by emphasizing high-margin departments like produce.

The total expenses/net sales ratio is only approximately 17 percent for Wal-Mart; at Birks, it's over 40 percent. This difference is to be expected. Discount stores have relatively low selling expenses. They're also typically located on comparatively inexpensive real estate so rent is relatively low. Finally, discount stores operate with a smaller administrative staff than a store like Birks. For instance, buying expenses are much lower for discount stores. Their buyers don't have to travel very far, and much of the purchasing consists of rebuying staple merchandise that's already in the stores. On the other hand, a jewellery store's total expenses are much higher because its large, experienced sales staff requires a modest salary plus commission and benefits. Unlike Wal-Mart stores' locations that are usually suburban or in rural areas, Birks stores are in some of the most expensive areas in the country. Birks locations therefore command high rent and incur other expenses.

NET PROFIT

Net profit is a measure of the firm's overall performance:

$$\text{Net profit} = \text{Gross margin} - \text{Expenses}$$

Net profit can be expressed either before or after taxes. Generally, it's more useful to express net profit after taxes, since this is the amount of money left over to reinvest in the business, disburse as dividends to stockholders or owners, or repay debt.

Net profit margin, like gross margin, is often expressed as a percentage of net sales:

$$\text{Net profit percentage} = \frac{\text{Net profit}}{\text{Net sales}}$$

However, net profit measures the profitability of the entire firm, whereas gross margin measures the profitability of merchandising activities. In Exhibit 9–5, the after-tax net profit margin is 3.12 percent for Wal-Mart and 10.89 percent for Birks. From a profit perspective alone, Birks, with 39 stores in Canada, is outperforming Wal-Mart. Even though Birks has a higher total expenses/net sales ratio, its gross margin percentage is so large compared to Wal-Mart's that it still surpasses the discount store's profit performance in this scenario. Check risk management at www.rmahg.org and facts from the business database at www.bizstats.com.

the turnover path

The information used to analyze a firm's turnover path primarily comes from the balance sheet. The income statement summarizes the financial performance over a period of time; the balance sheet summarizes a retailer's financial position at a given point in time, such as the last day of the year. The balance sheet shows the following relationship:

$$\text{Assets} = \text{Liabilities} + \text{Owners' equity}$$

Assets are economic resources (such as inventory or store fixtures) owned or controlled by an enterprise as a result of past transactions or events. **Liabilities** are an enterprise's obligations (such as accounts or notes payable) to pay cash or other

	Wal-Mart (as of 1/31/02)	Birks (as of 1/31/02)
ASSETS		
Current assets		
Accounts receivable	$ 2 000	$ 99
Merchandise inventory	22 614	612
Cash	2 161	174
Other current assets	1 471	71
Total current assets	28 246	955
Fixed assets		
Building, equipment, and other fixed assets, less depreciation	55 205	675
Total assets	$83 451	$1 630
LIABILITIES		
Current liabilities	$27 282	$ 341
Long-term liabilities	18 732	221
Other liabilities	2 335	30
Total liabilities	$48 349	$ 593
OWNERS' EQUITY		
Common shares	$ 1 929	$ 332
Retained earnings	33 173	705
Total owners' equity	$35 102	$1 037
Total liabilities and owners' equity	$83 451	$1 630

exhibit 9–6
Hypothetical Balance
Sheets for
Wal-Mart Stores, Inc.,
and Birks ($ in millions)

economic resources in return for past, current, or future benefits. **Owners' equity** (owners' investment in the business) is the difference between assets and liabilities. It represents the amount of assets belonging to the owners of the retail firm after all obligations (liabilities) have been met.

Continuing the scenario, Exhibit 9–6's balance sheets for Birks and Wal-Mart are examined. The turnover path portion of the strategic profit model is shown in Exhibit 9–7's asset turnover model. The remainder of this section covers elements of the balance sheet.

CURRENT ASSETS

By accounting definition, **current assets** are those that can normally be converted to cash within one year. In retailing,

$$\text{Accounts receivable} + \text{Merchandise inventory} + \text{Cash} + \text{Other current assets} = \text{Current assets}$$

ACCOUNTS RECEIVABLE

Accounts receivable are monies due to the retailer from selling merchandise on credit. This current asset is substantial for some retailers. For example, Wal-Mart's investment in accounts receivable is proportionally much smaller than Birks' due to Wal-Mart customers' high propensity to pay cash or use third-party credit cards such as Visa or MasterCard. Here are their accounts receivable:

Wal-Mart: $2000, or 0.9 percent of sales
Birks: $99, or 6.1 percent of sales

exhibit 9–7
Asset Turnover Model
for Wal-Mart Stores,
Inc., and Birks
($ in millions)

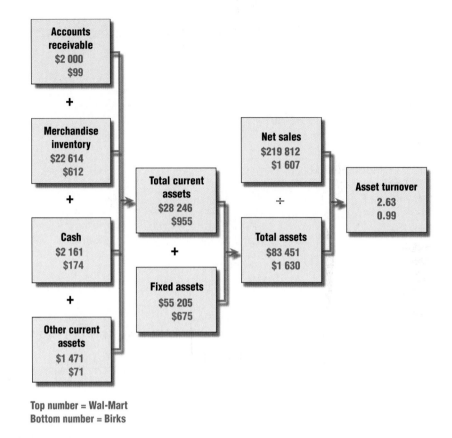

Top number = Wal-Mart
Bottom number = Birks

From a marketing perspective, the accounts receivable generated from credit sales may be the result of an important service provided to customers. The retailer's ability to provide credit, particularly at low interest rates, could make the difference between making or losing a sale. Paying cash for a sizable purchase such as a diamond engagement ring or car may be difficult for many people.

Unfortunately, having a large amount of accounts receivable is expensive for retailers, who of course would like to sell a product for cash and immediately reinvest the cash in new merchandise. When merchandise is sold on credit, proceeds of the sale are tied up as accounts receivable until collection is made. The money invested in accounts receivable costs the retailer interest expense and keeps the retailer from investing proceeds of the sale elsewhere. To ease the financial burden of carrying accounts receivable, retailers can use third-party credit cards such as Visa or MasterCard, give discounts to customers who pay with cash, discourage credit sales, and control delinquent accounts.

MERCHANDISE INVENTORY

Merchandise inventory is a retailer's lifeblood, representing approximately 27.10 percent of total assets for Wal-Mart and 37.53 percent of total assets for Birks. An exception to this generalization is service retailers such as Sears Pest Control Service, Marriott Hotels, and your local barber shop/beauty salon, which carry little or no merchandise inventory.

$$\frac{\text{Inventory}}{\text{Total assets}}$$

$$\text{Wal-Mart: } \frac{\$22\ 614}{\$83\ 451} = 27.10\%$$

$$\text{Birks: } \frac{\$612}{\$1630} = 37.53\%$$

Inventory turnover is used to evaluate how effectively managers utilize their investment in inventory. Inventory turnover is defined as follows:

$$\text{Inventory turnover} = \frac{\text{Net sales}}{\text{Average inventory}}$$

Note that average inventory is expressed at retail rather than at cost.

Think of inventory as a measure of the productivity of inventory—how many sales dollars can be generated from \$1 invested in inventory. Generally, the larger the inventory turnover, the better. Exhibit 9–8 illustrates the concept of inventory turnover. Inventory is delivered to the store, spends some time in the store, and then is sold. We can think of inventory turnover as how many times, on average, the inventory cycles through the store during a specific period of time (usually a year). Not only is it important to determine how many sales dollars can be generated from one dollar invested in inventory, but keep in mind the gross margin generated on each sales dollar.

Think of inventory as "merchandise in motion." The faster it moves through the store, the greater the inventory turnover.

Wal-Mart's inventory turnover is about seven times Birks': 7.59 compared to 1.08.[6]

$$\frac{\text{Net sales}}{\text{Average inventory}} = \text{Inventory turnover}$$

$$\text{Wal-Mart: } \frac{\$219\ 812}{\$28\ 974} = 7.59$$

$$\text{Birks: } \frac{\$1607}{\$1484} = 1.08$$

	Margin	Turnover
Birks	High	Low
Wal-Mart	Low	High

exhibit 9–8
Inventory Turnover

Wal-Mart's faster inventory turnover is expected due to the nature of discount and grocery stores. First, most items in Wal-Mart are commodities and staples such as batteries, housewares, and basic apparel items. Its new superstores carry grocery products such as baked goods, frozen meat, and produce. Birks, on the other hand, specializes in unique luxury items. Second, since Wal-Mart–type merchandise is available at other discount and grocery stores, it competes by offering lower prices, which results in rapid turnover. Third, discount stores carry a simpler stock selection than jewellery stores do. In a Wal-Mart store, for example, there may be only two brands of ketchup, each in two sizes, which represents four inventory items. Jewellery stores, on the other hand, may stock 100 distinctly different types of necklaces. Finally, due to Birks' unique positioning strategy, much of its inventory, particularly the jewellery, is made especially for it in other countries, requiring buyers to place orders several months in advance of delivery. Discount stores, on the other hand, order items daily or weekly. These factors, when taken together, explain why Wal-Mart has a faster inventory turnover than Birks.

CASH AND OTHER CURRENT ASSETS

Cash = Monies on hand

+ Demand and savings accounts in banks to which a retailer has immediate access

+ Marketable securities such as treasury bills

Other current assets = Prepaid expenses + Supplies

Wal-Mart reports cash of about 0.98 percent of sales, whereas Birks' cash percentage is 10.81 percent.

FIXED ASSETS

Fixed assets are assets that require more than a year to convert to cash. In retailing,

Fixed assets = Buildings (if store property is owned rather than leased)

+ Fixtures (such as display racks)

+ Equipment (such as computers or delivery trucks)

+ Long-term investments such as real estate or stock in other firms

Fixed assets represent 66.15 percent and 41.44 percent of total assets for Wal-Mart and Birks, respectively. Wal-Mart's fixed assets are relatively higher than Birks' because they have vast real estate holdings in stores and distribution centres, whereas Birks typically rents space in malls and has direct store delivery.

Asset cost – Depreciation = Fixed assets

Since most fixed assets have a limited useful life, those assets' value should be less over time—in other words, they're depreciated. For instance, Birks stores require refurbishing every few years due to general wear-and-tear. So, carpet and some fixtures are depreciated over 3 to 5 years, whereas a building may be depreciated over 25 years.

These trucks belonging to 7-Eleven Stores in Japan are fixed assets.

ASSET TURNOVER

Asset turnover is an overall performance measure from the asset side of the balance sheet.

$$\frac{\text{Net sales}}{\text{Total assets}} = \text{Asset turnover}$$

Although fixed assets don't turn over as quickly as inventory, asset turnover can be used to evaluate and compare how effectively managers use their assets. When a retailer redecorates a store, for example, old fixtures, carpeting, and lights are removed and replaced with new ones. Thus, like inventory, these assets cycle through the store. The difference is that the process is a lot slower. The life of a fixture in a Birks store may be five years (instead of five months, as it might be for a diamond ring in the store's inventory), yet the concept of turnover is the same. When a retailer decides to invest in a fixed asset, it should determine how many sales dollars can be generated from that asset.

Suppose that Birks needs to purchase a new fixture for displaying dinnerwear. It has a choice of buying an expensive antique display cabinet for $5000 or having a simple plywood display constructed for $500. Using the expensive antique, it forecasts sales of $50 000 in the first year, whereas the plywood display is expected to generate only $40 000. Ignoring all other assets for a moment,

$$\frac{\text{Net sales}}{\text{Total assets}} = \text{Asset turnover}$$

Antique cabinet: $\dfrac{\$50\ 000}{\$5000} = 10$

Plywood cabinet: $\dfrac{\$40\ 000}{\$500} = 80$

The antique cabinet will certainly help create an atmosphere conducive to selling expensive dinnerwear. Exclusively from a marketing perspective, the antique would thus appear appropriate. But it costs much more than the plywood shelves. From a strictly financial perspective, Birks should examine how much additional sales can be expected to be generated from the added expenditure in assets. Clearly, by considering only asset turnover, the plywood shelves are the way to go. In the end, a combination of marketing and financial factors should be considered when making the asset purchase decision.[8]

In this case, Wal-Mart's asset turnover is 2.7 times Birks'. The asset turnover is 2.63 for Wal-Mart and 0.99 for Birks. This finding is consistent with the different strategies each firm is implementing. We saw earlier that Wal-Mart has a higher inventory turnover. Its other assets are relatively lower than Birks' as well. For instance, the fixed assets involved in outfitting a store (such as fixtures, lighting, and mannequins) would be relatively lower for a discount store than a jewellery store.

The other side of the balance sheet equation from assets involves liabilities and owners' equity. Now let's look at the major liabilities and components of owners' equity.

LIABILITIES AND OWNERS' EQUITY

Current Liabilities   Like current assets, **current liabilities** are debts that are expected to be paid in less than one year. The most important current liabilities are accounts payable, notes payable, and accrued liabilities. Current liabilities as a percentage of net sales are 12.41 percent for Wal-Mart and 21.24 percent for Birks.

Accounts Payable   **Accounts payable** refers to the amount of money owed to vendors, primarily for merchandise inventory. Accounts payable is an important source of short-term financing. Retailers buy merchandise on credit from vendors. The longer the period of time they have to pay for that merchandise, the larger their accounts payable—and the less they need to borrow from financial institutions (notes payable), issue bonds or shares, or finance internally through retained earnings. Since retailers normally don't have to pay interest to vendors on their accounts payable, they have strong incentive to negotiate for a long time period before payment for merchandise is due.

Accounts payable management can play an important role in a retailer's profit strategy. This is the case for many European hypermarkets such as Carrefour. Hypermarkets are similar to Canadian-style super-centres but have some key differences. Hypermarkets are primarily food-based and emphasize fresh products to drive customer traffic, whereas super-centres are primarily nonfood retailers that focus on dry goods. Carrefour is able to negotiate extended supplier terms because, like most European food retailers, it has national scope and is able to exert significant influence over its suppliers. As a result, Carrefour manages its accounts payable as a profit centre. For example, Carrefour typically has about 42 days of inventory on hand and roughly 90 days in payables. That 48-day float generates income that contributes as much as 25 to 35 percent of Carrefour's operating profit.[9]

Notes Payable   **Notes payable** under the current liabilities section of the balance sheet are the principal and interest the retailer owes to financial institutions (banks) that are due and payable in less than a year. Retailers borrow money from financial institutions to pay for current assets, such as inventory.

Accrued Liabilities   **Accrued liabilities** include taxes, salaries, rent, utilities, and other incurred obligations that haven't yet been paid. These are called accrued liabilities because they usually accumulate daily but are only paid at the end of a time period, such as a month.

Long-Term Liabilities   **Long-term liabilities** are debts that will be paid after one year. The notes payable entry in the long-term liability section of the balance sheet is similar to the one in the current liability section except that it's due to be paid in more than one year. Other long-term liabilities include bonds and mortgages on real estate.

Owners' Equity   Owners' equity, also known as **shareholders' equity**, represents the amount of assets belonging to the owners of the retail firm after all obligations (liabilities) have been met. In accounting terms, the relationship can be expressed as

Owners' equity = Total assets – Total liabilities

Although there are several entries in the owners' equity category, two of the most common are common shares and retained earnings.

Common shares are the type of shares most frequently issued by corporations.[10] Owners of common shares usually have voting rights in the retail corporation. They also have the right to share in distributed corporate earnings. If the firm is liquidated, common share owners have the right to share in the sale of its assets. Finally, they have the right to purchase additional shares to maintain the same percentage ownership if new shares are issued.

Retained earnings refers to the portion of owners' equity that has accumulated over time through profits but hasn't been paid out in dividends to owners. The decision of how much of the retailer's earnings should be retained in the firm and how much should be returned to the owners in the form of dividends is related to the firm's growth potential. Specifically, retailers with a propensity toward and opportunities for growth will retain and reinvest their profits to fund growth opportunities. For example, a high-growth retailer such as Wal-Mart retains most of its earnings to pay for the new stores, inventory, and expenses associated with its growth.

In the case discussed, total owners' equity is over $35 102 million for Wal-Mart and over $1037 million for Birks.

examining the strategic profit model

The previous sections defined the most important balance sheet and income statement entries as well as the most useful performance ratios. Yet many of these items are interrelated, and when examined alone they can be confusing. More important, it's hard to compare the performance of retailers with different operating characteristics, such as Birks and Wal-Mart. The strategic profit model (Exhibit 9–9) combines the two performance ratios from the income statement and balance sheets: net profit margin and asset turnover. By multiplying these ratios together, you get return on assets.

exhibit 9–9   The Strategic Profit Model

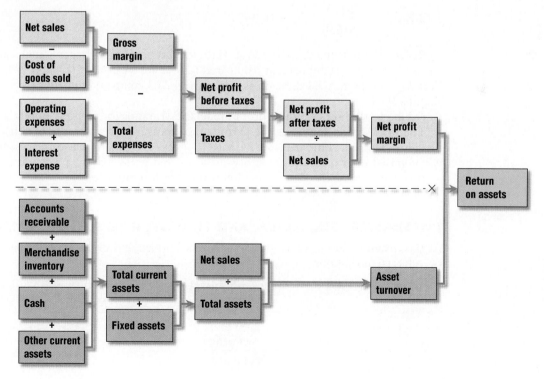

RETURN ON ASSETS

$$\text{Return on assets} = \text{Net profit margin} \times \text{Asset turnover}$$

$$= \frac{\text{Net profit}}{\text{Net sales}} \times \frac{\text{Net sales}}{\text{Total assets}}$$

$$= \frac{\text{Net profit}}{\text{Total assets}}$$

Return on assets determines how much profit can be generated from the retailer's investment in assets. (Note that when we multiply net profit margin by asset turnover, net sales drops out of the equation.)

The most important issue associated with return on assets is that the money that would be invested in retailing could also be invested in any other asset, such as a CD or Canada Savings Bond. For instance, if a retailer can achieve 9 percent return on assets by opening a new store, and 10 percent by investing in a nearly risk-free savings bond, the retailer should take the higher-yield, lower-risk investment. In fact, should the return on assets of another investment with similar risk be greater, it would be the manager's fiduciary duty to invest in the other asset. In general, return on assets is effective in evaluating the profitability of individual investments in assets because it can easily be compared with yields of other investments with similar risk. It has also been shown to be an effective predictor of business failures.[11]

$$\frac{\text{Net profit}}{\text{Total assets}} = \text{Return on assets}$$

Wal-Mart: $\dfrac{\$6854}{\$83\ 451} = 8.21\%$

Birks: $\dfrac{\$175}{\$1630} = 10.74\%$

Return on assets for Birks and Wal-Mart are very similar! Birks generated a larger net profit margin, 10.89 percent, compared to 3.12 for Wal-Mart (Exhibit 9–4). But Wal-Mart outperformed Birks on asset turnover, 2.63 compared to 0.99, respectively (Exhibit 9–7).

Exhibit 9–10 shows strategic profit model (SPM) ratios for a variety of retailers.

The next section examines the performance measure on which the merchandise plan is evaluated. This measure, GMROI (gross margin/return on investment) is composed of two ratios: inventory turnover and gross margin percentage. The section concludes with a discussion of how retailers forecast sales.

PUTTING MARGIN, SALES, AND TURNOVER TOGETHER: GMROI

At the corporate level, return on assets is used to plan and evaluate performance of overall retail operations.

$$\text{Return on assets} = \text{Net profit margin} \times \text{Asset turnover}$$

$$= \frac{\text{Net profit}}{\text{Net sales}} \times \frac{\text{Net sales}}{\text{Total assets}}$$

$$= \frac{\text{Net profit}}{\text{Total assets}}$$

exhibit 9–10
Strategic Profit Models
for Selected Retailers

	(1) Net Profit Margin (%) Net profit / Net sales	(2) Asset Turnover Net sales / Total assets	(3) Return on Assets (%) Net profit margin × Asset turnover
DISCOUNT STORES			
Costco Wholesale Corporation	1.73	3.45	5.97
Family Dollar Stores, Inc.	5.17	2.62	13.54
Best Buy Co., Inc.	2.58	3.17	8.17
GROCERY STORES			
Winn-Dixie Stores, Inc.	0.35	4.24	1.48
The Kroger Company	2.08	2.62	5.46
Safeway Inc.	3.66	1.96	7.18
DEPARTMENT STORES			
Sears	1.79	1.11	1.99
SPECIALTY STORES			
The Gap, Inc.	−0.06	1.82	−0.11
Barnes & Noble, Inc.	1.31	1.86	2.44
CATALOGUES			
Spiegel, Inc.	3.46	1.44	4.99
Lands' End, Inc.	4.26	2.62	11.16

With the strategic profit model, one can use return on assets to plan and compare the performance of executives since they are responsible for managing all of the retailer's assets and realizing a return based on these assets.

But merchandise managers have control over only the merchandise they buy and manage. Buyers generally have control over gross margin but not expenses involved with the operation of the stores and the management of the retailer's human resources, locations, and systems. As a result, the financial ratio that is useful for planning and measuring merchandising performance is a return on investment measure called gross margin return on inventory investment, or GMROI.[12] It measures how many gross margin dollars are earned on every dollar of inventory investment.

GMROI is a similar concept to return on assets, only its components are under the control of the buyer rather than other managers. Instead of combining net profit margin and asset turnover, GMROI uses gross margin percentage and the sales-to-stock ratio, which is similar to inventory turnover.

$$\text{GMROI} = \text{Gross margin percentage} \times \text{Sales-to-stock ratio}$$
$$= \frac{\text{Gross margin}}{\text{Net sales}} \times \frac{\text{Net sales}}{\text{Average inventory}}$$
$$= \frac{\text{Gross margin}}{\text{Average inventory}}$$

Average inventory in GMROI is measured at cost, because a retailer's investment in inventory is the cost of the inventory, not its retail value.

Like return on assets, GMROI combines the effects of both profits and turnover. It's important to use a measure that considers both of these factors so that departments with different margin/turnover profiles can be compared and evaluated.

exhibit 9–11
Illustration of GMROI

			Bread	Prepared Foods
	Gross margin		$2 000	$150 000
	Sales		$150 000	$300 000
	Average inventory		$1 000	$75 000

		$\dfrac{\text{Gross margin}}{\text{Net sales}}$	$\times$	$\dfrac{\text{Net sales}}{\text{Average inventory}}$	$=$	$\dfrac{\text{Gross margin}}{\text{Average inventory}}$
	GMROI =					
Bread	GMROI =	$\dfrac{\$2000}{\$150\,000}$	$\times$	$\dfrac{\$150\,000}{\$1000}$	$=$	$\dfrac{\$2000}{\$1000}$
	=	1.333%	$\times$	150 times	$=$	200%
Prepared Foods	GMROI =	$\dfrac{\$150\,000}{\$300\,000}$	$\times$	$\dfrac{\$300\,000}{\$75\,000}$	$=$	$\dfrac{\$150\,000}{\$75\,000}$
	=	50%	$\times$	4	$=$	200%

For instance, within a grocery store, some departments (such as wine) are high margin/low turnover, whereas other departments (such as dairy products) are low margin/high turnover. If the wine department's performance is compared to that of dairy products using inventory turnover alone, the contribution of wine to the grocery store's performance will be undervalued. On the other hand, if only gross margin is used, wine's contribution will be overvalued.

Consider the situation in Exhibit 9–11. Here a grocery store manager wants to evaluate performance of two classifications: bread and ready-to-eat prepared foods. If evaluated on gross margin percentage or sales alone, prepared foods is certainly the winner with a 50 percent gross margin and sales of $300 000 compared to bread's gross margin of 1.333 percent and sales of $150 000. Yet prepared foods turns (sales-to-stock ratio) only four times a year, whereas bread turns 150 times a year. Using GMROI, both classifications achieve a GMROI of 200 percent and so are equal performers from a return on investment perspective.

GMROI is used as a return on investment profitability measure to evaluate departments, merchandise classifications, vendor lines, and items. It's also useful for management in evaluating buyers' performance since it can be related to the retailer's overall return on investment. As we just demonstrated, merchandise with different margin/turnover characteristics can be compared. Exhibit 9–12 shows GMROI percentages for selected departments from discount stores. The range is from 235 (for

The **GMROI** for low margin/high turnover products such as bread can be the same as high margin/low turnover products such as prepared foods.

Category	Gross Margin (%)	Inventory Turnover	GMROI
Apparel	37	4	235
Housewares	35	3	162
Food	20	7	175
Jewellery	38	2	123
Furniture	31	2	90
Health and beauty	22	4	113
Consumer electronics	21	4	106

exhibit 9–12

Gross Margin Percentage, Inventory Turnover, and GMROI for Selected Departments in Discount Stores

apparel) to 90 (for furniture). It's no wonder that many discount stores are placing so much emphasis on apparel and that some have discontinued furniture. They continue to carry consumer electronics and health and beauty products—both with low GMROIs—because they have traditionally brought customers into the store. The retailers hope that while there, customers will purchase higher-GMROI items.

The gross margin component of GMROI is affected by pricing decisions. GMROI answers the question, For each dollar at cost, how many dollars of gross profit will I generate in one year? GMROI is traditionally calculated by using one year's gross profit against the average of 12 or 13 units of inventory at cost. A rule of thumb is that a GMROI of at least 3.2 is the break-even point for a business.

MEASURING INVENTORY TURNOVER

The notion of inventory turnover was introduced as "merchandise in motion." Jeans are delivered to the store through the loading dock in the back, spend some time in the store on the racks, and then are sold and go out the front door. The faster this process takes place, the higher the inventory turnover will be. We thus can think of inventory turnover as how many times, on average, the jeans cycle through the store during a specific period of time, usually one year. It's a measure of the productivity of inventory—that is, how many sales dollars can be generated from a dollar invested in jeans.

Inventory turnover is defined as follows:

A. $\text{Inventory turnover} = \dfrac{\text{Net sales}}{\text{Average inventory at retail}}$

or

B. $\text{Inventory turnover} = \dfrac{\text{Cost of goods sold}}{\text{Average inventory at cost}}$

Since most retailers tend to think of their inventory at retail, the first definition is preferable. Arithmetically there's no difference between these two definitions; they yield the same result.[13] Be careful, however; since both the numerator and denominator must be at retail or at cost, it is different than the sales-to-stock ratio where the inventory is always expressed at cost. To illustrate:

$\text{Sales-to-stock ratio} = \dfrac{\text{Net sales}}{\text{Average cost inventory}}$

So if

Sales = $100 000

and

Average cost inventory = $33 333

then

$$\text{Sales-to-stock ratio} = \frac{\$100\ 000}{\$33\ 333} = 3$$

Thus,

Inventory turnover = Sales-to-stock ratio $\times (100\% - \text{Gross margin }\%)$ [14]

Continuing the example, if

Gross margin = 40 percent

then

Inventory turnover = $3 \times (100\% - 40\%) = 1.8$

Retailers normally express inventory turnover rates on an annual basis rather than for parts of a year. Suppose the net sales used in an inventory turnover calculation are for a three-month season. If turnover for a quarter is calculated as 2.3 turns, then annual turnover will be four times that number (9.2). Thus, to convert an inventory turnover calculation based on part of a year to an annual figure, multiply it by the number of such time periods in the year.

Exhibit 9–12 shows inventory turnover ratios for selected departments from discount stores. The range is from 7 (for food) to 2 (jewellery and furniture). There are no real surprises in these data. One would expect food to have the highest turnover. Food is either sold quickly or it spoils. It is perishable. By the same token, being a luxury item, jewellery turns relatively slowly. Furniture achieves a low turnover because a relatively large assortment of expensive items is needed to support the sales level.

Calculating Average Inventory   Average inventory is calculated by dividing the sum of the inventory for each of several months by the number of months:

$$\text{Average inventory} = \frac{\text{Month}_1 + \text{Month}_2 + \text{Month}_3 + \ldots}{\text{Number of months}}$$

But how many months should be used? How could we determine the inventory for the month? One approach is to take the end-of-month (EOM) inventories for several months and divide by the number of months available. For example:

Month	Retail Value of Inventory
EOM January	$22 000
EOM February	$33 000
EOM March	$38 000
Total inventory	$93 000
Average inventory = $93 000 ÷ 3 = $31 000	

This approach is adequate only if the end-of-month figure doesn't differ in any appreciable or systematic way from any other day. For instance, January's end-of-month inventory is significantly lower than the other two since it represents the inventory position at the end of the winter clearance sale and before the spring buildup.

Most retailers no longer need to use physical counts to determine average inventory. Point-of-sale terminals capture daily sales and automatically subtract them from on-hand inventory. Retailers with POS systems can get accurate average inventory estimates by averaging the inventory on hand for each day in the year. Retailers do typically take occasional physical inventories, usually twice a year, to determine the amount of inventory shrinkage due to theft or paperwork/entry mistakes.

ADVANTAGES OF HIGH INVENTORY TURNOVER

Retailers want rapid inventory turnover—but not too rapid, as we'll soon see. Advantages of rapid inventory turnover include increased sales volume, less risk of obsolescence and markdowns, improved salesperson morale, more money for market opportunities, decreased operating expenses, and increased asset turnover.[15]

Increased Sales Volume   A rapid inventory turnover increases sales volume since fresh merchandise is available to customers, and fresh merchandise sells better and faster than old, shopworn merchandise. Fresh merchandise encourages customers to visit the store more frequently because they see new things. Also, notice the produce next time you're in a less-than-successful supermarket... brown bananas! Since turnover is slow, the produce is old, which makes it even harder to sell.

Quick response delivery systems are inventory management systems designed to reduce retailers' lead time for receiving merchandise. Retailers order less merchandise, more often, so merchandise supply is more closely aligned with demand. As a result, inventory turnover rises since inventory investment falls, and sales climb since the retailer is out of stock less often.

A rapid rate of inventory turnover ensures fresh merchandise. Since fresh merchandise is easier to sell, sales increase and so does employee morale.

Less Risk of Obsolescence and Markdowns   The value of fashion and other perishable merchandise is said to start declining as soon as it's placed on display. When inventory is selling quickly, merchandise isn't in the store long enough to become obsolete. As a result, markdowns are reduced and gross margins increase.

Improved Salesperson Morale   With rapid inventory turnover and the fresh merchandise that results, salesperson morale stays high. No one likes to sell yesterday's merchandise. Salespeople are excited over new merchandise, the assortment of sizes is still complete, and the merchandise isn't shopworn. When salespeople's morale is high, they try harder so sales increase—increasing inventory turnover even further.

More Money for Market Opportunities   When inventory turnover is high, money previously tied up in inventory is freed to buy more merchandise. Having money available to buy merchandise late in a fashion season can open tremendous profit opportunities. Suppose Levi Strauss overestimates demand for its seasonal products. It has two choices:

• hold the inventory until next season

• sell it to retailers at a lower-than-normal price

If retailers have money available because of rapid turnover, they can take advantage of this special price. Retailers can pocket the additional markup or choose to maintain their high-turnover strategy by offering the special merchandise at a reduced cost to the consumer. In either case, sales and gross margin increase.

Decreased Operating Expenses   An increase in turnover may mean that a lower level of inventory is supporting the same level of sales. And lower inventory means lower inventory carrying costs, which is an operating expense. For instance, if a retailer has $1 million in inventory and the cost to carry the inventory—including money borrowed from a bank, insurance, and taxes—is 20 percent a year, the inventory carrying cost is $200 000. Lowering inventory can therefore represent a significant savings.

Increased Asset Turnover   Finally, since inventory is a current asset, and if assets decrease and sales stay the same or increase, then asset turnover increases. This directly affects return on assets, the key performance measure for top management.

DISADVANTAGES OF TOO HIGH AN INVENTORY TURNOVER

Retailers should strike a balance in their rate of inventory turnover. An excessively rapid inventory turnover can hurt the firm due to a lower sales volume, an increase in the cost of goods sold, and an increase in operating expenses.

Lowered Sales Volume   One way to increase turnover is to limit the number of merchandise categories or the number of SKUs within a category. But if customers can't find the size or colour they seek—or even worse, if they can't find the product line at all—a sale is lost. Customers who are disappointed on a regular basis will shop elsewhere and will possibly urge their friends to do the same. In this case, not only is a sale lost, but so are the customers and their friends.

Increased Cost of Goods Sold To achieve rapid turnover, merchandise must be bought more often and in smaller quantities, which reduces average inventory without reducing sales. But by buying smaller quantities, the buyer can't take advantage of quantity discounts and transportation economies of scale. It may be possible, for instance, to buy a year's supply of Levi's at a quantity discount that offsets the high costs of carrying a large inventory.

Retailers who pay transportation costs must consider that the more merchandise shipped and the slower the mode of transportation, the smaller the per-unit transportation expense. For instance, to ship a 10–kilogram package of jeans from Toronto to Halifax, overnight delivery, would cost about $50 ($5 per kilogram). If the retailer could order 50 kilograms of jeans at the same time and could wait 5 to 10 days for delivery, the cost would be only about $30 (60 cents per kilogram). In this example, it costs over eight times more to ship small packages quickly.

Increased Operating Expenses Economies of scale can also be gained when a retailer purchases large quantities. A buyer spends about the same amount of time meeting with vendors and writing orders whether the order is large or small. It also takes about the same amount of time, for both large and small orders, to print invoices, receive merchandise, and pay invoices—all factors that increase merchandise's cost.

In summary, rapid inventory turnover is generally preferred to slow turnover. But the turnover rate can be pushed to the point of diminishing returns, a key concern for merchandise managers in all retail sectors.

recap of the strategic profit model

The strategic profit model is useful to retailers because it combines two decision-making areas—margin management and asset management—so managers can examine interrelationships between them. The strategic profit model uses return on assets as the primary criterion for planning and evaluating a firm's financial performance.

The strategic profit model can also be used to evaluate financial implications of new strategies before they're implemented. For instance, suppose a retailer wishes to increase sales by 10 percent. Using the strategic profit model, he/she can estimate this action's impact on other parts of the strategic profit model. For instance, to increase sales, they may choose to have a sale. Lowering prices will reduce gross margin. In addition, they would have to advertise the sale and hire additional sales help, thus increasing operating expenses. So, although they may be able to achieve the 10 percent sales increase, net profit margin might go down.

Looking at the turnover path, increasing sales without an appreciable change in inventory will increase inventory turnover. Assuming other assets aren't affected, asset turnover will also increase. When they multiply the lower net profit margin by the higher asset turnover, the resulting return on assets may remain unchanged.

setting performance objectives

Setting performance objectives is a necessary component of any firm's strategic planning process. How would a retailer know how it has performed if it doesn't have specific objectives in mind to compare actual performance against? Performance objectives should include:

- the performance sought, including a numerical index against which progress may be measured
- a time frame within which the goal is to be achieved
- the resources needed to achieve the objective

For example, "earning reasonable profits" isn't a good objective. It doesn't provide specific goals that can be used to evaluate performance. What's reasonable? When do you want to realize the profits? A better objective would be "earning $100 000 in profit during calendar year 2005 on $500 000 investment in inventory and building."

In general, since productivity measures are a ratio of outputs to inputs, they can be used to compare different business units. Suppose a retail chain's two stores are different sizes: One has 465 square metres and the other has 930 square metres. It's hard to compare stores' performances using just output or input measures. The larger store will probably generate more sales and have higher expenses. But if the larger store generates $1950 net sales per square metre and the smaller store generates $3250 per square metre, the retailer knows that the smaller store is operating more efficiently even though it's generating lower sales.

SUMMARY

Financial management involves a thorough understanding of the importance of return on investment and how this relates to the retailer's image. It must also be understood that clearly defined quantifiable performance objectives are essential to evaluating business strategies and making changes to correct problems.

This chapter explains some basic elements of retailing financial strategy and examines how retailing strategy affects the financial performance of a firm. We used the strategic profit model as a vehicle for understanding the complex interrelations between financial ratios and retailing strategy. We found that different types of retailers have different financial operating characteristics. Specifically, jewellery store chains such as Birks generally have higher profit margins and lower turnover than discount stores such as Wal-Mart. Yet, when margin and turnover are combined into return on assets, we showed that it's possible to achieve similar financial performance.

We also described some financial performance measures used to evaluate different aspects of a retailing organization. Although the return on assets ratio in the strategic profit model is appropriate for evaluating the performance of retail operating managers, other measures are more appropriate for more specific activities. For instance, gross margin return on investment (GMROI) is appropriate for buyers, whereas store managers should be concerned with sales or gross margin per square metre.

The chapter concludes with an appendix describing the use and benefits of activity-based costing. Based on contribution analysis, activity-based costing is a method of allocating the cost of all major activities a retailer performs to products, product lines, SKUs, and the like. Using activity-based costing, retailers can make more informed and profitable decisions, since they have a clear understanding of the costs associated with the different activities involved in making those decisions.

KEY TERMS

accounts payable, *236*

accounts receivable, *231*

accrued liabilities, *236*

activity-based costing (ABC), *249*

asset turnover, *223*

assets, *230*

current assets, *231*

current liabilities, *235*

Get Out & Do It!

1. **INTERNET EXERCISE** Go to www.hoovers.com and use the financial information to update the numbers in the profit margin model in Exhibit 9–4 and the asset turnover model in Exhibit 9–7. Use these two models to develop the strategic profit model in Exhibit 9–9 for Wal-Mart and Birks. Then repeat the process for Amazon and Bally Total Fitness. Have there been any significant changes in their financial performance? Why are the key financial ratios for these four retailers so different?

2. **GO SHOPPING** Go to your favourite store and interview the manager. Determine how the retailer sets its performance objectives. Evaluate its procedures relative to the procedures presented in the text.

3. **INTERNET EXERCISE/GO SHOPPING** Get balance sheet and income statement information for your favourite publicly traded retailer by going to www.hoovers.com or by visiting the store and interviewing the owner/manager. Construct a strategic profit model and evaluate its financial performance. Explain why you believe its ratios are or are not consistent with its strategy.

4. **OLC EXERCISE** Access the Online Learning Centre at www.mcgrawhill.ca/olc/levy and go to the Strategic Profit Model (SPM). The SPM tutorial was designed to provide a refresher for the basic financial ratios leading to return on assets. The tutorial walks you through it step-by-step. A "calculation page" is also included that will calculate all the ratios. You can type in the numbers from a firm's balance sheet and income statement to see the financial results that are produced with the current financial figures. You can also access an Excel spreadsheet for doing SPM calculations. The calculation page or the Excel spreadsheet can be used for the case on Holt Renfrew and Dollarama.

5. **INTERNET EXERCISE** Go to www.retailowner.com "Benchmarks for 50 Retail Segments" select
   a) Department stores
   b) Lumber and building materials
   c) Jewellery stores
   d) Motorcycle dealers and compare GMROI.

6. **INTERNET EXERCISE** Go to www.birksandmayors.com. Go to Finanical News. What do you find on this site? Click on livecast of Birks and Mayors presentation, January 11, 2007.

7. **INTERNET EXERCISE** Go to www.bizstats.com. What is shoppertrak? Why is this information important to retailers?

DISCUSSION QUESTIONS AND PROBLEMS

1. Why must a retailer use multiple performance measures to evaluate its performance?

2. Describe how a multiple-store retailer would set its annual performance objectives.

3. Buyers' performance is often measured by their gross margin. Why is this figure more appropriate than net profit or loss?

4. How does the strategic profit model (SPM) assist retailers in planning and evaluating marketing and financial strategies?

5. Holt Renfrew (a high-service department store) and Price/Costco (a chain of warehouse clubs) target different groups of customers. Which should have the higher asset turnover, net profit margin, and return on assets? Why?

6. Given the following information, construct an income statement and determine if there was a profit or loss. (Figures are in $000.)

Sales	$3 015 534
Cost of goods sold	2 020 954
Operating expenses	193 628
Interest expense	15 188
Taxes	67 807

7. Using the following information taken from Sharper Image Corporation's balance sheet, determine the asset turnover. (Figures are in U.S. $000.)

Net sales	$383 222
Total assets	162 338
Total liabilities	67 595

8. Using the following information taken from the balance sheet and income statement for Lands' End, Inc., develop a strategic profit model. (Figures are in US$000.)

Sales	$1 448 230
Cost of goods sold	758 792
Operating expenses	575 662
Interest expenses	(1 350)
Inventory	227 220
Accounts receivable	13 297
Other current assets	162 067
Accounts payable	83 363
Notes payable	0
Other current liabilities	102 201
Fixed assets	196 536
Long-term liabilities	0

9. Assume Sears is planning a special promotion for the upcoming holiday season. It has purchased 2.5 million Santa Bears, stuffed teddy bears dressed like Santa Claus, from a vendor in Taiwan. The GMROI for the bears is expected to be 144 percent (gross margin = 24 percent and sales-to-stock ratio = 6), about average for a seasonal promotion. Besides the invoice cost of the bears, Sears will incur import fees, transportation costs from Taiwan to distribution centres and then to stores, and distribution centre and store costs such as marking and handling. Since the bears arrived early in April, additional storage facilities are needed until they are shipped to the stores the first week of October. Is GMROI an adequate measure for evaluating the performance of Santa Bears? Explain your answer.

10. Increasing inventory turnover is an important goal for a retail manager. What are the consequences of turnover that is too slow?

11. The fine jewellery department in a department store has the same GMROI as the small appliances department even though characteristics of the merchandise are quite different. Explain this situation.

12. Calculate GMROI and inventory turnover given:

Annual sales	$20 000
Average inventory (at cost)	$75 000
Gross margin	45%

13. Calculate GMROI and inventory turnover given

Annual sales	$12 000
Average inventory (at cost)	$4000
Gross margin	35%

14. Using the following information taken from the 2005 balance sheet and 2005 income statement for Urban Outfitters, develop a strategic profit model. (Figures are in $000.) You can access an Excel spreadsheet for SPM calculations on the student side of the book's Web site.

Net sales	$827 750
Cost of goods sold	489 000
Operating expenses	198 384
Interest expenses	0
Inventory	98 996
Accounts receivable	8 364
Other current assets	171 508
Fixed assets	271 776

<table>
<tr><td>**APPENDIX 9A**</td><td>**Activity-Based Costing**</td></tr>
</table>

Activity-based costing (ABC) is a financial management tool that has been recently adopted by many retail companies.[16] This accounting method is superior to traditional methods in that it enables retailers to better understand costs and profitability. Retailers that adopt ABC gain an information-based means of improving financial analysis and performance.

In activity-based costing, all major activities within a cost centre are identified and the costs of performing each are calculated. The resulting costs are then charged to cost objects, such as stores, product categories, product lines, specific products, customers, and suppliers. Using ABC to plan and evaluate merchandising performance provides an alternative to the standard gross margin and inventory turnover measures. As discussed in this chapter, maximizing these traditional measures may produce less than optimal results.

Although ABC uses General Ledger data, it differs from other costing methods in that it assigns all expenses—all sales, marketing, administrative, financing, and operating costs. The process of assigning all these costs is difficult because they are typically not easily identified.

Retailers have focused on improving costing analyses for some time. For example, the direct product profit (DPP) accounting system was developed and used by food and general merchandise retailers beginning in the mid-1970s to permit the calculation of product profitability. Activity-based costing represents a more comprehensive approach because, unlike DPP, it recognizes overhead and administrative expenses as well as direct product costs.

IMPLEMENTATION OF ACTIVITY-BASED COSTING

The five-step process used to conduct activity-based costing is as follows:

1. *Summarize the resources.* Organize costs by grouping those that are related. For example, people-related costs could be grouped as wages and benefits.
2. *Define the activities.* Identify the activities performed in the key departments or cost centres that represent significant work.
3. *Define the resource drivers.* Convert General Ledger costs into activity costs by quantifying the relationship between resources and activities.
4. *Specify the cost objects.* Identify the focus of the profitability assessment. For example, the cost object could be a product category such as paper goods, health and beauty aids, or gourmet foods.
5. *Identify the activity drivers.* Measure the amount of activity performed in servicing the cost object. These drivers are aspects of the activity that are highly correlated with the activity cost.

AN ILLUSTRATION OF ABC

Consider the following hypothetical example illustrated in Exhibit 9–13. Loblaws is considering reducing the amount of shelf space dedicated to Pepperidge Farm's line of premium cookies in order to expand Loblaws' own private-label cookie line. The company is performing an ABC analysis to evaluate the profitability of the two lines. Based on past experience, Loblaws believes that, in general, private-label, (store-brand) items offer higher profits.

Suppose Loblaws' cost is $2 per unit ($24 per case of 12) for each variety of Pepperidge Farm cookies. The retail selling price is $2.60 ($31.20 per case), so the gross margin (per case) is $7.20, or 23 percent. Loblaws pays $1.50 per unit ($18 per case of 12) for its private-label cookies, which retail for $2.25 ($27 per case). The gross margin per case is $9, or 33.33 percent.

The traditional gross margin measure of profitability suggests that the private-label cookies are Loblaws' more attractive option. However, the "real" profit picture may be obscured because all relevant costs have not been applied directly to the products.

*This appendix was written by Professor Kathleen Seiders, Babson College.

exhibit 9–13

Activity-Based Costing
Profitability Statement
for Pepperidge Farm
and Private-Label
Cookies at Loblaws

	Pepperidge Farm	Private-Label Cookies
Retail price per case	$31.20	$27.00
Cost per case	24.00	18.00
Gross margin	7.20	9.00
Other relevant costs	1.50	5.00
Operating margin	5.70	4.00

The cost of handling the private-label cookies must be considered because there are no distribution costs related to the Pepperidge Farm cookies, which are delivered directly to each Loblaws store by the vendor (a direct-store-delivery [DSD] approach). Pepperidge Farm allows 30 days for payment and gives immediate credit for any damaged merchandise. The private-label cookies are shipped to a Loblaws distribution centre, stored, and then shipped to individual stores. The private-label vendor demands payment in 10 days, rather than 30, and is not responsive to damaged-goods claims. Loblaws' ABC analysis, which followed the steps outlined above, included an examination of the warehouse costs related to the company's private-label cookies.

1. *Summarize the resources.* The accounts identified for this analysis included warehouse expenses related to:
   - wages and benefits
   - equipment depreciation
   - occupancy (depreciation and utilities)

2. *Define the activities.* The key warehouse activities identified were receiving, storing, shipping, and quality control.

3. *Define the resource drivers.* Wages were assigned based on the number of workers performing the activity. Depreciation was allocated based on each activity's use of the equipment. Occupancy costs were assigned based on square metres used by the activity.

4. *Specify the cost objects.* The cost objects in this case were initially specified as Loblaws' private-label cookie line and Pepperidge Farm's cookie line.

5. *Identify the activity drivers.* Receiving was based on: number of receipt transactions; storing on number of pallet positions; shipping on number of cases shipped; and inspection on a complexity factor.

The total costs (classified as operating expenses) of receiving, inspection, storage, and shipping Loblaws' private-label cookie line were calculated to be $5 per case. The cost for Pepperidge Farm (primarily for receiving) was calculated at $1.50 per case. Operating margins are $5.70 per case (or 18.3 percent) for Pepperidge Farm and $4 per case (14.8 percent) for Loblaws' private label. The ABC analysis, unlike the traditional gross margin analysis, suggests that it would not be optimal for Loblaws to expand its private-label cookie line by reducing Pepperidge Farm's shelf space.

APPENDIX 9B — Retail Inventory Method

Like firms in most industries, retailers can value their inventory at cost—and in fact, some retailers do so. Yet many retailers find significant advantages to the retail inventory method (RIM).[17] RIM has two objectives:

1. To maintain a perpetual or book inventory in terms of retail dollar amounts
2. To maintain records that make it possible to determine the cost value of the inventory at any time without taking a physical inventory

THE PROBLEM

Retailers generally think of their inventory at retail price levels rather than at cost. They take their initial markups, markdowns, and so forth as percentages of retail. (These terms are thoroughly defined in the Glossary.) When retailers compare their prices to competitors', they compare their retail prices. The problem is that when retailers design their financial plans, evaluate performance, and prepare financial statements, they need to know the cost value of their inventory. One way to keep abreast of their inventory cost is to take physical inventories. Anyone who has worked in retailing knows that this process is time-consuming, costly, and not much fun. So retailers usually only take physical inventories once or twice a year. By the time management receives the results of these physical inventories, it's often too late to make any changes.

Many retailers use POS terminals that easily keep track of every item sold, its original cost, and its final selling price. The rest of the retail world faces the problem of not knowing the cost value of its inventory at any one time. RIM can be used by retailers with either computerized or manual systems.

ADVANTAGES OF RIM

RIM has five advantages over a system of evaluating inventory at cost.

- The retailer doesn't have to "cost" each time. For retailers with many SKUs, keeping track of each

item at cost is expensive and time-consuming, and it increases the cost of errors. It's easier to determine the value of inventory with the retail prices marked on the merchandise than with unmarked or coded cost prices.

- RIM follows the accepted accounting practice of valuing assets at cost or market, whichever is lower. The system lowers the value of inventory when markdowns are taken but doesn't allow inventory's value to increase with additional markups.

- As a by-product of RIM, the amounts and percentages of initial markups, additional markups, markdowns, and shrinkage can be identified. This information can then be compared with historical records or industry norms.

- RIM is useful for determining shrinkage. The difference between the book inventory and the physical inventory can be attributed to shrinkage.

- The book inventory determined by RIM can be used in an insurance claim in case of a loss (e.g., due to fire).

DISADVANTAGES OF RIM

RIM is a system that uses average markup. When markup percentages change substantially during a period, or when the inventory on hand at a particular time isn't representative of the total goods handled in terms of markup, the resulting cost figure may be distorted. As with inventory turnover, merchandise budget planning, and open-to-buy, RIM should be applied on a category basis to avoid this problem.

The record-keeping process involved in RIM is burdensome. Buyers must take care so that changes made to the cost and retail inventories are properly recorded.

STEPS IN RIM

Exhibit 9–14 is an example of RIM in action. The following discussion, which outlines the steps in RIM, is based on this exhibit.

exhibit 9–14

Retail Inventory
Method Example

Total Goods Handled	Cost		Retail	
Beginning Inventory		$ 60 000		$ 84 000
Purchases	$50 000		$70 000	
– Return to vendor	(11 000)		(15 400)	
Net purchases		39 000		54 600
Additional markups			4 000	
– Markup cancellations			(2 000)	
Net markups				2 000
Additional transportation		1 000		
Transfers in	1 428		2 000	
– Transfers out	(714)		(1 000)	
Net transfers		714		1 000
Total goods handled		$100 714		$141 600

Reductions	Retail	
Gross sales		$ 82 000
– Customer returns and allowances		(4 000)
Net sales		$ 78 000
Markdowns		6 000
– Markdown cancellations		(3 000)
Net markdowns		3 000
Employee discounts		3 000
Discounts to customers		500
Estimated shrinkage		1 500
Total reductions		$86 000

Calculate Total Goods Handled at Cost and Retail To determine the total goods handled at cost and retail:

1. *Record beginning inventory at cost ($60 000) and at retail ($84 000).* The initial markup is reflected in the retail inventory.

2. *Calculate net purchases ($39 000 at cost and $54 600 at retail)* by recording gross purchases ($50 000 at cost and $70 000 at retail) and adjusting for merchandise returned to vendor ($11 000 at cost and $15 400 at retail).

3. *Calculate net additional markups ($2000)* by adjusting gross additional markups ($4000) by any additional markup cancellations ($2000). *Note:* These are recorded only at retail because markups affect only the retail value of inventory.

4. *Record transportation expenses ($1000).* Here transportation is recorded at cost because it affects only the cost of the inventory.

5. *Calculate net transfers ($714 at cost and $1000 at retail)* by recording the amount of transfers in

and out. A transfer can be from one department to another or from store to store. Transfers are generally made to help adjust inventory to fit demand. For instance, a sweater may be selling well at one store but not at another. A transfer is, in effect, just like a purchase (transfer in) or a return (transfer out). Thus, it's recorded at both cost and retail.

6. *The sum is the total goods handled ($100 714 at cost and $141 600 at retail).*

Calculate Retail Reductions Reductions are the transactions that reduce the value of inventory at retail (except additional markup cancellations, which were included as part of the total goods handled). Reductions are calculated as follows:

1. *Record net sales.* The largest reduction in inventory is sales. Gross sales ($82 000) are reduced to net sales ($78 000) by deducting customer returns and allowances ($4000).

2. *Calculate markdowns.* Net markdowns ($3000) are derived by subtracting any markdown cancelations ($3000) from gross markdowns ($6000).

3. *Record discounts to employees* ($3000) *and customers* ($500).

4. *Record estimated shrinkage* ($1500). Estimated shrinkage is used to determine the ending book inventory if the buyer is preparing an interim financial statement. The estimate is based on historical records and is presented as a percentage of sales. Estimated shrinkage wouldn't be included, however, if a physical inventory were taken at the time the statement was being prepared. In this case, the difference between physical inventory and book inventory would be the amount of shrinkage due to loss, shoplifting, and so forth.

5. *The sum is the total reductions* ($86 000).

Calculate the Cumulative Markup and Cost Multiplier   The cumulative markup is the average percentage markup for the period. It's calculated the same way the markup for an item is calculated:

$$\text{Cumulative markup} = \frac{\text{Total retail} - \text{Total cost}}{\text{Total retail}}$$

$$28.87\% = \frac{\$141\ 600 - \$100\ 714}{\$141\ 600}$$

The cumulative markup can be used as a comparison against the planned initial markup. If the cumulative markup is higher than the planned initial markup, then the category is doing better than planned.

The cost multiplier is similar to the cost complement.

$$\text{Cost multiplier} = (\$100\% - \text{Cumulative markup \%})$$
$$71.13\% = 100\% - 28.87\%$$

or

$$\frac{\text{Total cost}}{\text{Total retail}} = \frac{\$100\ 714}{\$141\ 600} = 71.13\%$$

The cost multiplier is used in the next step to determine the ending book inventory at retail.

Determine Ending Book Inventory at Cost and Retail

$$\text{Ending book inventory at retail} = \text{Total goods handled at retail} - \text{Total reductions}$$
$$\$55\ 600 = \$141\ 600 - \$86\ 000$$

The ending book inventory at cost is determined in the same way that retail has been changed to cost in other situations—multiply the retail times (100% − gross margin percentage). In this case,

$$\text{Ending book inventory at cost} = \text{Ending book inventory at retail} \times \text{Cost multiplier}$$
$$\$39\ 548 = \$55\ 600 \times 71.13\%$$

exhibit 9–15
Sample Profit and Loss
Statement

**Profit and Loss Statement
for the Period Ending (*date*)**

Revenue
 Gross Sales $ _____
 Cash Discounts   _____
Net Sales $ _____ (A)

Less: Cost of goods sold
 Beginning inventory $ _____
 Plus: net purchases   _____
 Total   _____
 Less: ending inventory   _____
Cost of Goods Sold   _____ (B)

Gross Margin (or Profit) (C = A – B) $ _____ (C)

Less: Operating Expenses
 Owner's Salary $ _____
 Employees' Wages and Salaries   _____
 Employee Benefits   _____
 Rent   _____
 Utilities (heat, light, water, power)   _____
 Telephone   _____
 Supplies and Postage   _____
 Repairs and Maintenance   _____
 Advertising and Promotion   _____
 Delivery Expense   _____
 Taxes and Licences   _____
 Depreciation   _____
 Bad Debt Allowance   _____
 Interest   _____
 Travel   _____
 Insurance   _____
 Legal and Accounting Fees   _____
Total Operating Expenses   _____ (D)

Net Operating Profit (Loss) (E = C – D)   _____ (E)
Income Tax (estimated)   _____ (F)
Net Profit (Loss) after Income Tax (G = E – F)   _____ (G)

exhibit 9–16
Sample Balance Sheet

Balance Sheet for (*Name of Company*) as of (*date*)		

Assets

Current Assets
  Cash $ _____
  Accounts Receivable _____
  Inventory _____
  Other Current Assets _____
  Total Current Assets $ _____ (A)

Fixed Assets
  Buildings $ _____
  Furniture and Fixtures _____
  Equipment _____
  Trucks and Automobiles _____
  Other Fixed Assets _____
  Total Fixed Assets $ _____ (B)

Total Assets (C = A + B) $ _____ (C)

Liabilities

Current Liabilities (debt due within 12 months)
  Accounts Payable $ _____
  Bank Loans/Other Loans _____
  Taxes Owed _____
  Total Current Liabilities $ _____ (D)

Long-Term Liabilities
  Notes Payable (due after 1 year) _____
  Total Long-Term Liabilities $ _____ (E)

Total Liabilities (F = D + E) $ _____ (F)

Net Worth (Capital)

Total Net Worth (G = C – F) $ _____ (G)

Total Liabilities and Net Worth (H = F + G) $ _____ (H)

planning merchandise assortments

Executive Briefing

Mark Foote, Executive Vice-president, General Merchandise, Loblaw Cos. Ltd.

Loblaw Cos. Ltd., Canada's largest food retailer, is building for its future success in an unexpected direction—clothing. Although the core strength of the retailer is being the best food retailer in Canada, it is expected that the Joe Fresh brand of apparel launched in 2006 will grow to $1 billion in two years. The clothing line is fun, stylish, and inexpensive, and is both popular with customers and profitable for Loblaws. The concept is that shopping for clothes can be compatible with buying weekly groceries for the family, provided the price is right.

Loblaw operates 1000 stores across Canada under various names, including Loblaws, No Frills, Fortinos, and Maxi. Galen Weston Jr., Loblaw CEO, admitted that the company has been organizationally too complex and ineffective, and was slow to respond to the customer and the competitive environment. Plans to make Loblaw more competitive include a company that is committed to cutting prices, boosting customer service, and investing in product innovation. Loblaw needs to be well-positioned to defend itself against Wal-Mart—the world's number one general merchandiser which has been moving aggressively into the grocery sector.

As a major step toward innovation Loblaw adopted the in-house brand Joe Fresh, a line of casual clothing created exclusively for Loblaw by Toronto designer Joe Mimran. The clothing offers "integrity of design and a good price-value ratio." Mimran was the founder of the popular Club Monaco concept which was bought out by Ralph Lauren. Initially the Joe Fresh

QUESTIONS
How is the buying process organized?

How do retailers determine the profitability of their merchandising decisions?

How do retailers forecast sales for merchandise classifications?

What trade-offs must retailers make to ensure that stores carry the appropriate type and amount of merchandise?

How do retailers plan their assortments?

line included 350 different products, aimed at men and women eighteen and up, with an average price of $14 per item, but the Joe Fresh label has since been expanded to include kids' clothes and accessories.

The company is making a major commitment to Joe Fresh, devoting up to 558 square metres selling space to apparel in stores ranging from 11 160 to 18 000 square metres. The Joe Fresh clothing area will also have dedicated sale associates and separate cash registers. In the larger format stores general merchandise accounts for 55 percent of the floor space. With the guidance of Mark Foote, executive vice-president, General Merchandise, Loblaw stores will be strategically positioned to offer the customer one-stop shopping, with pharmacies, electronics, seasonal household goods, items for the kitchen, bedroom, and bathroom, and now clothing along with groceries. Additionally, Foote sees an alliance with Esso to sell some 300 President's Choice products at Esso's On-the-Run convenience stores as a way to grow the PC brand.

In the fast changing, fiercely competitive market, it is critical for Loblaw to build market share to defend its position as Canada's supermarketer of choice.

The company announced it would stop building superstores until the economics of these new formats is proven. The action plan includes making immediate improvements in all stores, including designating some stores as "learning centres" where new staff receive training, and ensuring goods get moved from the back door to the shelves on time.

The primary goal of most retailers is to sell merchandise and services. Nothing is more central to the strategic thrust of the retailing firm.

Merchandise management is the process by which a retailer attempts to offer the *right quantity of the right merchandise in the right place at the right time while meeting the company's financial goals.*

Small and large retailers are required to make decisions about thousands of individual items from hundreds of vendors. If the buying process is not organized in a systematic, orderly way, chaos will result.

As in any business, a retailer's ultimate objective is to achieve an adequate return on the investment. In this chapter, we show how financial objectives trickle down the merchandising organization, and how these objectives are used to make buying decisions.

Once the financial objectives are set, the retailer starts the task of determining what to buy. Retailers are limited by the amount of money available for merchandise and the space in the store. They must decide whether to carry a large variety of different types of clothing (categories)—for example, dresses, blouses, and jeans—or carry fewer categories but a larger assortment of more styles and colours within each category. To complicate the situation, they need to decide how much backup stock to carry for each item. The more backup stock, the less likely they are to run out of a particular item. On the other hand, if they decide to carry a lot of backup stock, they will have less money available to invest in a deeper assortment or in more categories.

This chapter examines strategic and planning issues that lay the foundation for the merchandise management process shown in the top portion of Exhibit 10–1. The issues examined in this chapter are used as input into the buying systems, as shown in the green portion of Exhibit 10–1.

exhibit 10–1
Merchandise
Management Issues

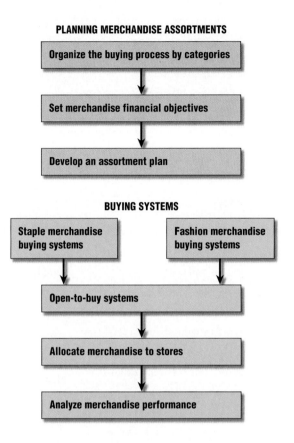

It is acknowledged that when approaching the study of merchandise assortments, building the merchandise financial plan (introduced in Chapter 11) is often preferred as the first step in the learning process. The financial budgets including merchandise plans are the starting point to beginning a season because the merchandise cannot be purchased without the financial commitment, although the product research and assortment development is a parallel activity. This chapter on Planning Merchandise Assortments therefore is presented first to provide background knowledge.

An **assortment plan** is a list of merchandise that indicates in general terms what the retailer wants to carry in a particular merchandise category. For instance, an assortment plan for girls' jeans would include the average number and percentage of each style/fabric/colour/size combination that the retailer would have in inventory.

organizing the buying process by categories

THE BUYING ORGANIZATION

Merchandise Group   The **merchandise group** is managed by the senior vice-presidents of merchandise, also called general merchandise managers, or GMMs (Exhibit 10–2). These merchandise managers are responsible for several departments. For instance, the second senior vice-president on the chart in the exhibit is responsible for men's, children's, and intimate apparel.

exhibit 10–2   Standard Merchandise Classification Scheme and Organizational Chart

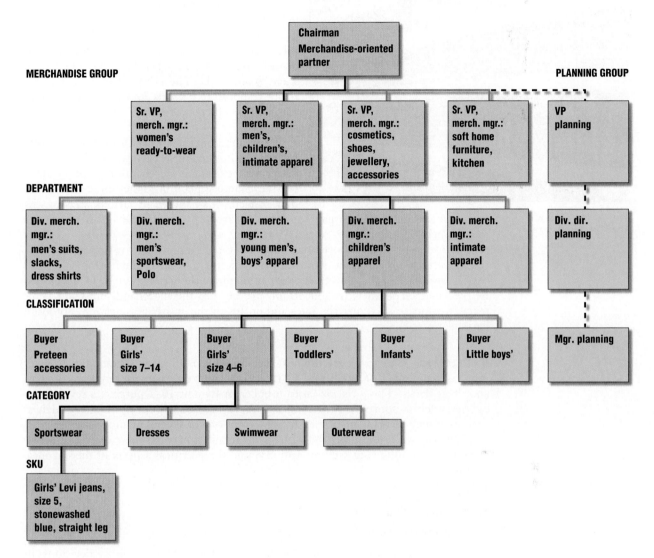

Department   The second division in the exhibit is the **department**. These departments are managed by divisional merchandise managers who report to the vice-presidents. For example, the vice-president of merchandising for men's, children's, and intimate apparel has responsibility for five divisional merchandise managers. Each divisional merchandise manager is responsible for a department. For example, the divisional merchandise manager highlighted in Exhibit 10–2 is responsible for children's apparel.

Classification   The classification is the third level in the exhibit's classification scheme. Each divisional merchandise manager is responsible for a number of buyers or category managers. The children's apparel divisional merchandise manager here is responsible for six buyers. Each buyer purchases a **classification**—a group of items or SKUs for the same type of merchandise (such as men's pants as opposed to men's

How many SKUs are there in this picture?

jackets or suits) supplied by different vendors. A stock keeping unit (SKU) is the smallest unit available for keeping inventory control. In soft goods merchandise, for instance, a SKU usually means size, colour, and style. For example, a pair of girls' size 5, stonewashed blue, straight-legged Levis is one SKU. The exhibit highlights the one buyer responsible for girls' apparel sizes 4 to 6. In some cases, a buyer is responsible for several classifications.

Many retail organizations divide responsibility for buying merchandise between a buyer or category manager and a merchandise planner. Since the merchandise planning function is a relatively new concept, it's handled in various ways by different retailers. In some organizations, the category manager or buyer supervises the planners; in others, they're equal partners.

The planners' role is more analytical. They are responsible for buying the correct quantities of each item, allocating those items to stores, monitoring sales, and suggesting markdowns. In effect, they implement the assortment plan developed by the buyer. Together, the buyer and planner are the merchandising team. This team attempts to maximize the sales and profits of the entire classification, not just a particular category or brand.

Categories   Categories are the next level in the classification scheme. Each buyer purchases a number of categories. So the men's pants buyer might buy jeans, khakis, and dress slacks. The girls' size 4 to 6 buyer in Exhibit 10–2 purchases several categories, such as sportswear, dresses, swimwear, and outerwear. A category such as swimwear may be made up of merchandise from one or several manufacturers.

Now that we've examined how and why retailers manage their merchandise by categories, the following sections will examine three critical aspects of merchandise planning:

- the objectives of the plan
- sales forecasting
- the assortment plan

The category is the basic unit of analysis for making merchandising decisions. In this section, we define the category, look at category life cycles, and develop a sales forecast, examine the process of category management, explain the role of a category captain, and describe where the category fits into the buying organization.

THE CATEGORY—THE PLANNING UNIT

It would be virtually impossible to keep the buying process straight without grouping items into categories. In general, a **category** is an assortment of items that the customer sees as reasonable substitutes for each other. Girls' apparel, boys' apparel, and infants' apparel are categories. Each of these categories has similar characteristics. For instance, girls' jeans are purchased from a set of vendors that are similar to each other. Also, the merchandise is priced and promoted to appeal to a similar target market. The price promotions are timed to occur at the same times of the year, such as back-to-school in August.

Retailers and their vendors might begin with different definitions of a category. A vendor might assign shampoos and conditioners, for example, to different categories, on the basis of significant differences in product attributes. The category manager for a grocery store, however, might put them and other combination shampoo–conditioner products into a single category on the basis of common consumers and buying behaviour. Paper towels could be assigned to a "paper products" category or combined with detergent, paper tissues, and napkins in a "cleaning products" category.

Some retailers such as department stores may define categories in terms of brands. For example, Tommy Hilfiger might be one category and Estée Lauder and Polo/Ralph Lauren another. Why? Because a "Tommy" customer buys Tommy and not Ralph. Also, it is easier for the buyer to purchase merchandise and plan distribution and promotions if the entire line is coordinated. No matter how the category is defined, supply chain members must agree on the category definition, and it must be based on what is logical to the consumer.

CATEGORY MANAGEMENT

Category management is the process of managing a retail business with the objective of maximizing the sales and profits of a category.

The category management approach to managing breakfast cereals would be to have one buyer or category manager who oversees every aspect of the merchandising function.[1] Although a category manager is more than a buyer in the traditional sense, we will interchange the terms. For instance, the buyer is responsible for developing the assortment plan for the entire category, working with vendors, selecting merchandise, pricing merchandise, and coordinating promotions with the advertising department and stores.

Two reasons for adopting category management are as follows:

• The category manager is ultimately responsible for the success or failure of a category. It's harder to identify the source of a problem and solve it without category management. Suppose, for instance, an ad is placed in a newspaper for a Valentine's Day sale, but the store doesn't receive the merchandise. Who caused the problem? Was it because the buyer didn't order the merchandise in time? Did the advertising manager fail to inform the buyer or the logistics manager that the ad was going to run? Did the distribution centre fail to get the merchandise to the stores? Importantly, without the emphasis on category management, the buyer doesn't have the power to solve the problem. By using category management, all of the activities and responsibilities just mentioned come under the control of the buyer's staff.

• It is easier to manage to maximize profits using category management. For example, the breakfast cereal category manager has a choice of purchasing corn flakes from Kellogg, General Mills, General Foods, a private-label vendor, and a popular locally produced brand. The category manager cannot purchase every size box from each of these vendors or there wouldn't be any room for any other cereal type in the cereal section. By the same token, the category manager needs some representation for each brand. An analysis indicates that there is relatively little demand for the giant-size box of corn flakes, when aggregated across all brands. It also indicates that although the locally produced brand is not a top seller, it has a strong following. If the store drops the local brand, it may lose some very good customers. Managing by category can help assure that the store's assortment is represented by the "best" combination of sizes and vendors, that is, the one that will get the most profit from the allocated space.

THE CATEGORY CAPTAIN

The importance of establishing strategic relationships with vendors has been emphasized. Since retailers and their vendors share the same goals—to sell merchandise and make profits—it's only natural for them to share the information that will help them achieve those goals. Since vendors can develop systems for collecting information for all of the areas that they service, they can provide buyers with valuable information. Later in Chapter 11 we discuss CPFR (collaboration, planning, forecasting, and replenishment), a system some retailers use with their vendors to share sales data to better manage inventories.

Some retailers turn to one favoured vendor to help them manage a particular category. Known as the **category captain,** this supplier forms an alliance with a retailer to help gain consumer insight, satisfy consumer needs, and improve the performance and profit potential across the entire category.

Kraft acts as a category captain by working with key retailers to help balance assortments.[2] Since it spends US$850 million a year on promotion and advertising, Kraft has a lot of influence in the grocery industry. As category captain, grocery chains give Kraft access to all market and store information, including costs and sales of its competitors. In return, the captain works with the category manager/buyer to make decisions about product placement on shelves, promotions, and pricing for all of the brands in the category. Before category management, these decisions were often made by whichever vendor was able to make the best argument to the store manager. Shelf space allocation, for instance, could change daily, depending on which vendor's salesperson was in the store that day.

A potential problem with establishing a category captain, however, is that vendors could take advantage of their position. It is somewhat like letting the fox into the henhouse. Suppose, for example, that Kraft chose to maximize its own sales at the expense of its competition. There are also serious competition regulations to consider.[3] The captain could collude with the retailers to fix prices. It could also block other brands, particularly smaller brands, from access to shelf space.

Appointing a category captain can be enticing for a retailer. It makes the category manager's job easier and brings the promise of higher profits. But retailers should not turn over important decisions to their vendors. Working with their vendors and carefully evaluating their suggestions is a much more prudent approach.

sales forecasting

CATEGORY LIFE CYCLES

When developing a sales forecast, a retailer must be able to predict how well product categories will sell over time. Product categories typically follow a predictable sales pattern—sales start off low, increase, plateau, and then ultimately decline. Yet the shape of that pattern varies considerably from category to category and will help buyers forecast sales. This section describes the most fundamental form of sales pattern, the category life cycle. Using the category life cycle as a basis, we'll examine some commonly found variations on it: fad, fashion, staple, and seasonal.

In the retail industry "forecast" is the term used for forecasting short-term sales and other financial factors based on current business conditions. For example, a six-month merchandise plan is created six to nine months prior to the beginning of the season. As the season begins and business starts to occur, planners will forecast sales, markdowns, etc. for the current month and perhaps the following two months as well. This process measures the actual results against the original plan and helps the

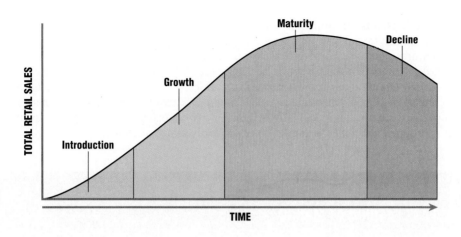

exhibit 10–3
The Category Product
Life Cycle

merchandise teams manage and assess their original plan objectives. In summary, the term often used is "plan" or "budget."

The **category life cycle** describes a merchandise category's sales pattern over time. The category life cycle (Exhibit 10–3) is divided into four stages: introduction, growth, maturity, and decline. Knowing where a category, or specific item within a category, is in its life cycle is important in developing a sales forecast and merchandising strategy.

When personal digital assistants (PDAs) were first introduced in 1996, the target market was businesspeople who were high-tech aficionados, people who wanted to be first in adopting an innovation and were willing to pay for the convenience of having a very small computer.[4] PDAs were very expensive compared to paper address and appointment books, and they weren't available at all stores that normally sell office supplies or computers. PDAs were next marketed to doctors, stockbrokers, and business executives, who use them for access to medical databases, stock markets, and e-mail. As categories reach the growth and maturity stages, they usually appeal to broader, mass-market customers who patronize discount stores and category specialists.

Knowing where a category is in its life cycle is useful for predicting sales. However, the shape of the life cycle can be affected by the activities undertaken by retailers and vendors. For instance, a vendor might set a low introductory price for a new product to increase the adoption rate of the product, or set a high price to increase profits even though sales might not grow as fast. Care must be taken, however, that use of the category life cycle as a predictive tool does not adversely affect sales. If a product is classified as being in decline, it's likely that retailers will stock less variety and limit promotions. Naturally, sales will go down. Thus, the decline classification may actually become a self-fulfilling prophecy. Many products have been successfully maintained at the maturity stage because their buyers have maintained innovative strategies that are consistent with a mature product. For instance, Kellogg's Corn Flakes has been the best-selling ready-to-eat cereal over many decades because it has innovative advertising and competitive pricing.

Variations on the Category Life Cycle   Most categories follow the basic form of the category life cycle: sales increase, peak, and then decline. Variations on the category life cycle—fad, fashion, staple, and seasonal—are shown in Exhibit 10–4. The distinguishing characteristics between them are whether the category lasts for many seasons, whether a specific style sells for many seasons, and whether sales vary dramatically from one season to the next.

Life cycle trends can impact many different categories. For example, consider the popular colours for kitchen appliances, cars, and paint for home items such as bathroom fixtures that have now become jewellery for the home.

A **fad** is a merchandise category that generates a lot of sales for a relatively short time—often less than a season. Examples are Pogs, Furbys, Pokémon, butterfly hair clips, and some licensed characters such as Star Wars action figures. More mainstream examples are certain computer games, new electronic equipment, and some apparel, such as cropped and flared jeans. Fads are primarily aimed at children and teens.

10.1 retailing view
FAST FASHION AT MANGO

With the opening of *The Matrix: Reloaded*, designers at the European specialty store retailer Mango planned a series of women's styles inspired by the third film in the *Matrix* trilogy. The designs were heavy on black, with lots of leather and high necklines. But the film was not the anticipated blockbuster; softer, more feminine clothes appeared on European runways; and the sci-fi look was doomed. So the company dropped the entire line.

"We know how to improvise," says David Egea, Mango's merchandising director and a top executive. "To react and have what people want, we have to break some rules." Mango/MNG Holding SL, with over 700 stores in 72 countries, typifies the new retail trend of "fast fashion," pioneered by Spain's Zara and Sweden's H&M. These chains fill their racks with a steady stream of new, gotta-have-it merchandise. Their retail strategy combines stylistic and technological resources built on flexibility and speed from design sketch to the store shelf.

Mango is famous for an eclectic mix of body-hugging styles; a black pinstriped jacket sells for $60 and a tight black minidress for $40. It maintains tight controls over the design and manufacturing of its private-label merchandise. Last minute changes, such as substituting a fabric or dropping a hemline, are a built-in part of the creative process. So long as the company has fabric in stock, it can move a design from sketchpad to store in four weeks.

Mango's merchandise planning cycle begins every three months when designers meet to discuss important new trends for each of its main collections, which contain five or six mini-collections. So shops receive a near-constant stream of merchandise, ranging from clingy short dresses to work wear and sparkly evening gowns. New items are sent to its stores once a week, roughly six times as often as the typical American clothing chain.

Mango stocks high-fashion, trendy merchandise to attract its target shoppers.

To get ideas for each collection, designers attend the traditional fashion shows and trade fairs. But they also stay close to the customer. They take photos of stylish young women and note what people are wearing on the streets and in nightclubs. "To see what everyone's going to do for next season is very easy," says Egea. "But that doesn't mean this is the thing that is going to catch on." Hoping to stay au courant, design teams meet each week to adjust to ever-changing trends.

When collection designs are set, Mango's product management and distribution team assigns them personality traits, denoting SKUs as trendy, dressy, or suitable for hot weather. Depending on an item's personality, it heads to one of Mango's 731 stores, which also has its own set of traits, such as the climate, where the shop is located, and whether large or small sizes sell best. A proprietary computer program then matches compatible shops and styles.

Orders get programmed into a large distribution machine, surrounded by a rotating ring of cardboard boxes on hooks. Clothes are scanned and dropped into one of 466 store-specific slots. Then they're boxed and shipped to shops, where managers can adjust store layouts daily on the basis of input from regional supervisors and headquarters.

Mango stores only display a limited merchandise assortment. On each rack, only one size per item is hung. This policy encourages a sense of urgency by playing on customers' worst fear: Maybe your size is going to run out.

Sources: Erin White, "For Retailer Mango, Frenzied 'Fast Fashion' Proves Sweet," *The Wall Street Journal*, May 28, 2004, p. B1; and Leonie Barrie, "Making a Mark: Some of the Issues to Watch in 2004: Fast Fashion Continues to Speed Up," *Just—Style*, January 2004, pp. 17–20.

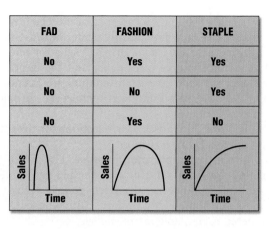

Variations in Category
Life Cycles

	FAD	FASHION	STAPLE
Sales over many seasons	No	Yes	Yes
Sales of a specific style over many seasons	No	No	Yes
Sales vary dramatically from one season to the next	No	Yes	No
Illustration (Sales against Time)			

Fads are often illogical and unpredictable. The art of managing a fad comes in recognizing the fad in its earliest stages and immediately locking up distribution rights for merchandise to stores nationwide before the competition does. Marketing fads is one of the riskiest ventures in retailing because even if the company properly identifies a fad, it must still have the sixth sense to recognize the peak so it can bail out before it's stuck with a warehouse full of merchandise.

retailing view   10.2
IS IT FAD OR A FASHION?

To determine whether an item will be a fad or a more en-during fashion, retailers must ask the following questions:

- *Is it compatible with a change in consumer lifestyles?* Innovations that are consistent with lifestyles will endure. For example, denim jeans are an enduring fashion because they are comfortable to wear and can be worn on multiple occasions. Leather pants, on the other hand, can be hot, heavy, and are typically worn in the evening. They are a fad.

- *Does the innovation provide real benefits?* The switch to poultry and fish from beef is not a fad because it provides real benefits to a health-conscious society.

- *Is the innovation compatible with other changes in the marketplace?* For example, shorter skirts resulted in a greater emphasis on women's hosiery. Now the sales of hosiery are declining due to the growing emphasis on casual apparel.

- *Who adopted the trend?* If it is not adopted by large, growing segments such as working mothers, baby boomers, Generation Y, or the elderly, it is not likely to endure.

Source: Martin Letscher, "How to Tell Fads from Trends," *American Demographics*, December 1994, pp. 38–45. Reprinted by permission.

These Japanese teenagers have the latest fashions. Or are they fads? Is Harry Potter a fashion or a fad?

Unlike a fad, a fashion is a category of merchandise that typically lasts several seasons, and sales can vary dramatically from one season to the next. A fashion is similar to a fad in that a specific style or SKU sells for one season or less. A fashion's life span depends on the type of category and the target market. For instance, double-breasted suits for men or certain colours are fashions whose life may last several years. On the other hand, fashions such as see-through track shoes may last only a season or two.

Retailing View 10.2 poses four questions for determining whether a new item or category will be a fad or a fashion.

Items within the **staple merchandise**, also called **basic merchandise**, category are in continuous demand over an extended period of time. Even certain brands of basic merchandise, however, ultimately go into decline. Most merchandise in grocery stores, as well as housewares, hosiery, basic blue jeans, and women's intimate apparel are considered to be staple merchandise.

Seasonal merchandise is inventory whose sales fluctuate dramatically according to the time of the year. Both fashion and staple merchandise usually have seasonal influences. For instance, wool sweaters sell in fall and winter, whereas staples such as lawn mowers and garden tools are popular in spring and summer. Retailers carefully plan their purchases and deliveries to coincide with seasonal demand.

On the other hand, forecasting staple merchandise is fairly straightforward. Sales of staple merchandise categories are relatively constant from year to year, therefore there's a sales history for each SKU. SKU-based inventory management systems are readily available and will facilitate forecasting future sales using information from the past.

Armed with information about where an item or a category is in its life cycle, retailers develop their sales forecast.

DEVELOPING A SALES FORECAST

A simple way to develop a sales forecast for a merchandise category is to adjust the past sales to make projections into the future. This type of sales forecasting technique is done at the category, rather than SKU, level and is used primarily for fashion merchandise. Forecasting sales of staple merchandise is typically done at the SKU level.

Sources of Information for Category-Level Forecasts   Buyers utilize a variety of sources in making these decisions. Discussed in the following sections, these include examining previous sales volume, reading published sources, analyzing customer information, shopping at the competition, and utilizing vendors and buying offices.

Previous Sales Volume   Exhibit 10–5 shows Levi's sales by season over a 10-year period. Sales have been increasing by about 25 percent per season for several years. The exhibit illustrates a strong seasonality pattern. Typically, 40 percent of the annual sales occur in fall, 30 percent in winter, and 15 percent each in spring and summer. In the eighth year, the fall season was unusually strong due to early cold weather, whereas spring sales were particularly weak because of a temporary turndown in the local economy.

Seasonal merchandise, such as Christmas tree ornaments, is prominently displayed before the holiday to help shoppers find decorations for their homes and gifts for their friends and family members.

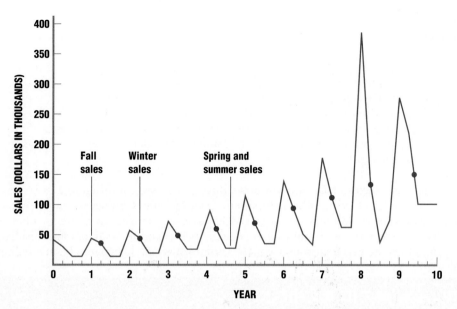

exhibit 10–5
Sales for Levi's Jeans
at Trendsetters
Department Store

Note: The peaks show the falls sales, typically 40 percent of annual sales; the horizontal lines typify 15 percent of annual sales each in spring and summer; and the dots (the winter sales) are typically 30 percent of annual sales. These data are for illustrative purposes only. They do, however, represent typical growth patterns for a category such as jeans.

For fashion merchandise, where styles change from year to year, sales figures older than three years probably aren't very useful. When forecasting sales, retailers must identify real trends (either up or down) and try to isolate a real change in demand from random occurrences. Thus, the unusually high and low sales in the eighth year should be ignored when trying to forecast sales for the current season.

More Information 10.1 shows a simple method of forecasting sales, using the data from Exhibit 10–5.

Published Sources   Adjustments to sales trends are based on economic trends in the geographic area for which the forecast is developed. For example, a buyer for The Gap would consider national economic indicators such as the gross national product (GNP), interest rates, and employment rates, whereas an independent local clothing store would primarily consider local conditions. Even if national unemployment rates are low, they may be significantly higher where a particular retailer has a store. If so, people may spend less money on fashion in this region than in other areas.

Data on a monthly basis are obtainable from Statistics Canada. This information source covers general trends, but it may not be particularly helpful for a buyer forecasting sales for a particular merchandise category.

Retailers and their vendors can also buy data from private firms. Market research companies buy information from individual supermarkets on price and promotion activity that has been scanned through their POS terminals and aggregates the data by region, chain, or market area. Information on customer demographics and psychographics as well as competitive information is available. Finally, general retail trade publications such as *Canadian Retailer*, published by the Retail Council of Canada, analyze general retail trends.

Customer Information   Customer information can be obtained either by measuring customer reactions to merchandise through sales, by asking customers about the merchandise, or by observing customers and trendsetters. Knowing what customers want today is very helpful in predicting what should be purchased in the future.

Shop the Competition   Buyers need to observe their competition, shop retail stores, Web sites, and catalogues. They need to remain humble and keep in mind that, no matter how good they are, their competition and similar stores in other markets may be even better. Shopping at local competition helps buyers gauge the immediate competitive situation. For instance, a Bay buyer shopping at a Sears store may determine that The Bay's prices on a particular line of handbags are too high.

With the popularity of the Internet, the local competition may not be the most important competition to shop. Retailers must therefore be constantly aware of all of their competitive venues. Pretend to be a customer and open your eyes to things that are new and different.

Vendors and Resident Buying Offices   Buyers may seek information from vendors and resident buying offices. **Resident buying offices** either are independent organizations or are directly associated with particular retailers that offer a number of services associated with the procurement of merchandise. Vendors and resident buying offices are excellent sources of market information. They know what's selling

10.1   more information about...
FORECASTING SALES FOR LEVI'S JEANS

The procedure for forecasting sales by season is accomplished in two steps. First, the retailer determines a sales forecast for the entire year. Then it considers seasonal sales patterns for each season.

The accompanying exhibit summarizes sales by season for Levi's jeans for years 6 through 9 from Exhibit 10–5. For instance, during the fall season of year 6, the store sold $152 587 in jeans, which represents 41.9 percent of the total sales for year 6 ($152 587 ÷ $364 247 = 41.9 percent). The last column indicates the percentages of the increases for the previous three years: 30.1, 48.5, and 5 percent. The 30.1 percent increase from year 6 to year 7 was calculated as follows: ($364 247 – $476 835) ÷ $364 247. Unfortunately, the data don't show a consistent pattern due to unusually high sales in year 8. The buyer should probably discount the impact of year 8 sales on the forecast and examine sales increases from earlier years

as well as more qualitative factors. The average sales increase over the previous nine years has been 25 percent, general economic indicators in the area are strong, and top management sees an opportunity to grow this classification, so the buyer estimates the sales increase for year 10 to be 30 percent. Thus, the sales forecast for year 10 is [($745 056 × 0.3) + $745 056] or $968 573.

The second step is to apply the seasonal sales pattern to the annual sales forecast to determine sales for each season. The percentage of annual sales occurring in each season has been fairly stable except in year 8. Thus, the buyer decides to apply the same percentages as those in years 7 and 9. To forecast sales for each season, the buyer multiplies the annual sales by each of the seasonal sales percentages. For instance, fall sales for year 10 should equal ($968 573 × 0.4) or $387 429.

Year	SEASON				Total	Percentage Increase
	Fall	Winter	Spring	Summer		
6	$ 152 587	$114 440	$ 57 220	$ 40 000	$ 364 247	
	41.9%	31.4%	15.7%	11.0%	100%	
7	190 734	143 051	71 525	71 525	476 835	30.1%
	40.0%	30.0%	15.0%	15.0%	100%	
8	400 000	178 813	40 000	89 406	708 219	48.5%
	56.5%	25.3%	5.6%	12.6%	100%	
9	298 023	223 517	111 758	111 758	745 056	5.0%
	40.5%	30.0%	15.0%	15.0%	100%	
6–9 (total)	1 041 344	659 821	280 503	312 689	2 294 357	
	45.4%	28.2%	12.2%	13.6%	100%	
10 (forecast)	387 429	290 572	145 286	145 286	968 573	

in markets around the world. Buyers, vendors, and buying offices must share such information if all are to succeed. Shopping markets in buying centres such as New York, Milan, London, and Paris provides information on trends.

Market Research   Information on how customers will react to new merchandise can be obtained by asking customers about the merchandise and measuring customer reactions to merchandise through sales tests. For example, a cashier at a restaurant may ask how a customer liked a new item on the menu. But retailers need to have a systematic way to collect this information and relay it to the appropriate buyers. Some retailers have their salespeople maintain **want books** in which out-of-stock and requested merchandise is recorded. This information is then collected by buyers for making forecasts and purchasing decisions.

Customer information also can be collected through traditional forms of marketing research such as depth interviews and focus groups. The **depth interview** is an unstructured personal interview in which the interviewer uses extensive probing to get individual respondents to talk in detail about a subject. For example, one grocery store chain goes through the personal checques received each day and selects all customers with large purchases of groceries and several with small purchases. Representatives from the chain call these customers and interview them to find out what they like and don't like about the store.

A more informal method of interviewing customers is to require buyers to spend some time on the selling floor waiting on customers. In most national retail chains, buyers are physically isolated from their customers. For example, buying offices for Target and The Gap are in northern California and Minnesota, respectively, yet their stores are throughout America. It has become increasingly hard for buyers in large chains to be attuned to local customer demand. Frequent store visits help the situation. Some retailers require their buyers to spend a specified period of time, such as one day a week, in a store.

A **focus group** is a small group of respondents interviewed by a moderator using a loosely structured format. Participants are encouraged to express their views and comment on the views of others in the group. To keep abreast of the teen market, for instance, some stores have teen boards comprised of opinion leaders who meet to discuss merchandising and other store issues.[5]

Finally, many retailers have a program of conducting merchandise experiments. For example, Claire's, an international specialty accessory retail chain targeting teens, continually runs tests to determine whether new merchandise concepts will produce adequate sales. It introduces the new merchandise into a representative group of stores and sees what sales are generated for the items. Multichannel retailers often run similar tests by offering new items on their Web sites before making a decision to stock them in their stores.

STORE-LEVEL FORECASTING[6]

As retailers respond to increased competition, oversaturated markets, and shoppers who want more of everything for less, it is becoming increasingly important for retailers to become more efficient and quickly tailor merchandise offerings to meet the needs and desires of smaller and smaller market segments. To do this requires the merchandise planner to predict sales at the store SKU (stock keeping unit) level (colours, sizes, etc.) The forecasting method described in the previous sections was performed by buyers at more aggregate levels, such as a region or a distribution centre servicing many stores, and it was done by category, not by SKU. The problem with forecasting at more aggregate levels is that store-level variability gets averaged or summed out of the data. This, for example, happens when one store sells more single-serving-sized food products and a different store sells more family-sized products. Combining results from the two stores results in demand data that report evenly distributed sales.

Although sophisticated systems infrastructure and computational power enable the move to store-level forecasting, traditional approaches are not designed to address the complexity and operational issues related to store-level data in a timely manner. To predict store-level demand, forecasting systems need to be able to measure simultaneously the impacts of many factors on unit sales. These factors include promotion, price, placement of merchandise in the store, substitution, competition, location, and others. These factors are described in Exhibit 10–6.

Observing the impact of, say, adding another SKU to a supermarket shelf or of making a 2 percent price increase when weekly sales are fluctuating by 30 percent presents a daunting task, especially since most routine merchandising changes are made in response to manufacturer price increases or other incentives or seasonal trends and therefore affect competition as well. When multiple changes occur simultaneously, it is difficult to determine how much of the change should be attributed to each independent change. Traditional forecasting techniques such as exponential smoothing that are found in spreadsheets or standard statistical packages cannot pick up the subtle differences at the store level.

Today, most large retailers have implemented sophisticated systems that can track and archive weekly sales at the store and SKU level. With the advent of low-cost data storage and computing, it is now economically feasible to implement sales forecasting solutions that require massive computational power, such as advanced planning systems that are commercially available to retailers.

exhibit 10–6   Factors Impacting Sales Forecasts, Merchandise Plans, Budgets

Price   The amount of unit sales of an item obviously depends on the price at which it is offered. Generally, with a few exceptions, raising the price causes unit sales to decrease, and vice versa. The question is, by how much? The answer can be found by determining the item's elasticity—the percentage change in unit sales resulting from a given percentage change in price. Thus, items that have a high elasticity are price-sensitive, and items with a low elasticity are insensitive to price.

Promotion   The degree and type of promotion are also critical in determining the unit sales of an item. Promotional techniques include weekly circulars, store signage, end-caps and other special product displays, and manufacturer coupons and rebates.

Store Location   There can be large variations in demand depending on store location. Snow shovels obviously have a much higher demand in Northern Ontario than in Vancouver. Even in the same metropolitan area, the same item could have a different demand depending on whether the store is in a downtown location or a suburban or rural location. Customer demographics also plays a role. For example, the buying patterns in a store adjacent to a retirement community will be different from those in a store located in a residential neighbourhood with many young families.

Product Placement   The amount of shelf space afforded an item, as well as its location on the shelf, can have a large impact on sales. A diagram that shows how and where specific products should be placed on the shelves, called a planogram, is created to help maximize sales.

Seasonality   Some categories, most notably apparel, are highly seasonal in nature. In the extreme case, all of the sales of a particular merchandise category will occur during a single season. Seasonality also refers to increased sales associated with Christmas, Thanksgiving, Mother's Day, and others.

Other Factors   There are many other factors that impact sales, usually to a lesser degree, but sometimes significantly. Among these are:

- *Product life cycle*—knowledge of whether product demand is growing, stable, or in decline, is important.
- *Product availability*—the degree to which the merchandise is, or is not, on the shelves ready for sale impacts sales.
- *Competitor price and promotional activity*—these also affect a retailer's sales.
- *Business cycles*—sales may be higher at the beginning of the month due to payroll cycles; also, sales are higher on weekends than on weekdays.
- *Weather*—late or early arrival of hot or cold weather can have a significant impact on sales of seasonal items.
- *Unusual events*—a new highway, an unexpected or severe storm, and other natural disasters can have a large local impact.
- *Cannibalization*—for example, decreasing the price of Apple Jacks would increase sales, but perhaps to the detriment of the sales of Froot Loops.
- *Complementary products*—putting hot dogs on sale will also cause an increase in sales of hot dog buns.

SOURCE: Adapted from KhiMetrics.

setting objectives for the merchandise plan

Retailers cannot hope to be financially successful unless they preplan the financial implications of their merchandising activities. Financial plans start at the top of the retail organization and are broken down into categories, while buyers and merchandise planners develop their own plans and negotiate up the organization. Top management looks at the overall merchandising strategy. They set the merchandising direction for the company by:

- defining the target market
- establishing performance goals
- deciding, on the basis of general trends in the marketplace, which merchandise classifications deserve more or less emphasis

Buyers and merchandise planners, on the other hand, take a more micro approach. They study their categories' past performance, look at trends in the market, and try to project the assortments for their merchandise categories for the coming seasons.

The planning process is similar for smaller retailers. Although there aren't as many layers of management involved in planning and negotiations, they still start with the firm's overall financial goals and break them down into categories.

The resulting **merchandise plan** is a financial buying blueprint for each category. It considers the firm's financial objectives along with sales projections and merchandise flows. The merchandise plan tells the buyer and planner how much money to spend on a particular category of merchandise in each month so that the sales forecast and other financial objectives are met. Once the merchandise plan is set, the buyers and planners develop the assortment plan. The buyers work with vendors choosing merchandise, negotiating prices, and developing promotions. The merchandise planners break down the overall financial plan into how many of each item to purchase and how they should be allocated to stores.

As you can imagine, there's a great deal of negotiating at each step. Merchandise managers and buyers compete with each other over the size of their merchandise budgets.

the assortment planning process

All retailers face the fundamental strategic question of what type of retail format to maintain to achieve a sustainable competitive advantage. A critical component of this decision is determining what merchandise assortment will be carried. Merchandise decisions are constrained by the amount of money available to invest in inventory and the amount of space available in the store. Based on the financial objectives that have been set at the top and have trickled through the retail organization, decisions regarding variety, assortment, and product availability must be made.

VARIETY

Variety is the number of different merchandising categories within a store or department. Stores with a large variety are said to have good **breadth**—the terms *variety* and *breadth* are often used interchangeably. Some stores, such as Banana Republic, carry a large variety of categories of sportswear to meet all the needs of their target customers.

refact

Who has the best product assortment in the U.S.? Wal-Mart was rated best for discount clothing, shoe, and accessory; Publix for grocery; Macy's for department stores; CVS for drug; Best Buy for electronics; Barnes & Noble for specialty; and Wal-Mart overall.[7]

Banana Republic carries updated slacks, sweaters, shirts, outerwear, and other categories for both men and women. Levi Strauss & Co. stores, on the other hand, carry a much more limited number of categories (variety): jeans and related apparel.

Assortment planning involves decisions concerning the amount of merchandise choice that is available to the customer. Overstocking merchandise results in lower turnover and reduced profits; understocking may mean lost sales and unhappy customers who will take their business elsewhere. The ideal situation is the right merchandise, in the right quantity, at the right price, and at the right time.

Breadth of stock refers to the number of SKUs, which could be the variety of brands, sizes, or colours available to the customer.

- Broad assortment will include numerous choices.

- Narrow assortment will provide the customer with only a few choices.

Depth of merchandise, or the amount of a particular item that a retailer will stock, includes the attributes of brand, size, or colour; for example, how many styles of a specific brand of bicycle.

- Deep assortment refers to a large quantity of a single item.

- Shallow assortment consists of only a few of a single item.

Examples:

Broad and shallow assortment planning is typical of the fashion retailer Club Monaco, which will stock a broad assortment of styles to satisfy the style-conscious consumer but does not carry depth in any particular item. The fashion customer is more selective about style, size, and colour, and will change with the newest trends.

Narrow and deep assortment planning is an assortment strategy typical of the mass merchandisers, such as Wal-Mart and Zellers. The assortment mix has only a few choices in a particular category, but it is stocked in considerable depth so as to be seldom out of stock within that product group. There may be, for example, three brands.

retailing view
COSTCO GOES FOR VARIETY, OR DOES IT?

10.3

The Costco experience is often described as a treasure hunt. Products can include everything from blue jeans, air conditioners, and computer games one day to books, children's toys, and diamond rings the next, plus a huge selection of food products. Costco keeps customers on their toes by offering a wide variety of merchandise that changes from day to day. This is the place where individual and business customers pay $45 to $100 per year for a membership to buy 24 rolls of toilet paper or none at all. This is where laundry detergent and Italian olive oil come in extra-large sizes and where a 1000-piece lot of Ralph Lauren golf jackets, selling at 75 percent below retail, will vanish in an afternoon. In Costco's 1.5-hectare stores you can also visit the meat counter with its onsite butchers, order a cake from the bakery, or pick up a prescription and talk to the resident pharmacist to receive health advice.

All of these disparate categories provide an illusion of expansive variety. A Wal-Mart Supercentre carries as many as 125 000 items; a grocery store will stock approximately 40 000. Not so at Costco, where you will find just 3800 to 4000 carefully chosen products. This makes it easier for the company to manage inventory and to monitor prices obsessively. Three-quarters of the merchandise is basic stock, such as canned tuna and paper towels; the other items are discretionary, often with high-end brands such as Godiva chocolates and Waterford crystal. The stores' periphery offers a variety of services, including film development, an optical centre, a pharmacy, and a tire shop.

Costco's successful strategy is planned so that a pallet of product must bring in a specific amount of cash or it is out; it is about volume per item, operating with a margin of about 8 percent, and how to increase the volume per item. Traditional category management does not apply to Costco; for example, because Costco sells computer printers does not mean that it will sell printer paper. Unusual product jux-tapositions, such as face creams next to crackers, are all part of a selling formula that homes in on the middle-class tastes for cross-shopping and impulse purchases.

The typical Costco customer is 35 to 55 years old and earns on average $100 000 in family income, about double the income of most Canadians. Costco's Canadian customers number about 3.5 million households, with up to 35 percent of its business in grocery. There are 60 Canadian Costco stores, whose average size is 15 248 sq. metres, with sales figures averaging about $118 million per store.

Growth continues internationally with 504 stores worldwide that have outpaced the sales of Sam's Club (which has 579 stores). Internationally, Costco has extremely low operating expenses, pegged at 8.74 percent of sales, and an enviable shrink that is almost nonexistent. It is extreme attention to detail that has made Costco a retail success story.

Sources: Julia Drake, "Welcome to the Big Time: Big Stores, Big Products, Big Savings, Big Profits: They're All Part of the Costco Experience," *Canadian Grocer*, May 2001; Ann Zimmerman, "Costco goes for Variety, or Does It?" *Retailing*. McGraw-Hill Ryerson.

Square assortment planning is a moderate assortment strategy that is adopted by traditional department stores. In order to provide customers with a greater product selection than the mass merchandisers, The Bay and Sears will adapt a square assortment plan. This assortment strategy is planned to have limited depth within the categories to avoid having an overstock situation that could result in markdowns and a loss of revenue at the end of the season.

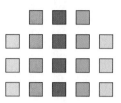

PRODUCT AVAILABILITY

The backup stock in the model stock plan determines product availability. **Product availability** defines the percentage of demand for a particular SKU that is satisfied. For instance, if 100 people go into a Levi Strauss & Co. store to purchase a pair of tan jeans in size 33–34, and it sells only 90 pairs before it runs out of stock, its product availability is 90 percent. Product availability is also referred to as the **level of support** or **service level.**

ASSORTMENT PLANNING FOR SERVICE RETAILERS

The Chippery in Vancouver rates high on assortment and low on variety. It is THE place to get fresh potato (or beet, or yam) chips, a selection of gourmet dips and fruit smoothies. That is it!

Consider health clubs. Some offer a large variety of activities and equipment from exercise machines to swimming, wellness programs, and New Age lectures. Others, such as Gold's Gym, don't offer much variety but have an excellent assortment of bodybuilding equipment and programs. Some hospitals, such as big municipal hospitals found in most urban areas, offer a large variety of medical services. Smaller private hospitals often specialize in physical rehabilitation or psychiatry. For service retailers, the level of product availability is a sales forecasting issue.

TRADE-OFFS BETWEEN VARIETY, ASSORTMENT, AND PRODUCT AVAILABILITY

How do retailers make the trade-off between variety, assortment, and product availability? It depends on their particular marketing strategy. A retail strategy identifies:

- the target market toward which a retailer plans to commit its resources
- the nature of the retail offering that the retailer plans to use to satisfy the target market's needs
- the bases upon which the retailer will attempt to build a sustainable competitive advantage

As a specialty store, Banana Republic tries to be the one-stop shopping alternative for its target markets. It carries a large variety of merchandise categories for both men and women. As a result, it can't physically or financially carry either gigantic assortments within each category or sufficiently high backup stock so as never to be out of stock. Alternatively, Levi Strauss & Co. stores have developed a marketing strategy around a target market of

Banana Republic (left) tries to be the one-stop shop for its target market. It carries a large variety of merchandise categories. Levi Strauss & Co (right) stores don't have a large variety, but the assortment of jeans and related items is fantastic!

people who are particularly interested in buying jeans. As a result, they provide a large assortment of a limited number of categories. At Levi stores, product availability is high; they don't want to miss a sale because they don't have the right size. If any of these three elements—variety, assortment, or product availability—aren't what the customer expects or needs, a retailer will likely lose the sale and possibly the customer.

The trade-offs between variety, assortment, and product availability are strategic issues. Of the three issues, variety is the most strategic. Variety is most important in defining the retailer in the customer's eyes. For instance, is the retailer perceived to be a category specialist like Toys "R" Us or a generalist like a department store? Variety also defines the retailer's vendor structure. Does it purchase from many different types of manufacturers or just a few? Finally, decisions regarding variety are typically made less often and at higher levels in the organization than decisions regarding assortment or product availability. Top managers, for instance, make decisions about whether to delete categories or even departments from the store. Since these decisions have important ramifications, they're made only after serious consideration.

DETERMINING VARIETY AND ASSORTMENT

In attempting to determine the variety and assortment for a category such as jeans, the buyer would consider the following factors:

- profitability of the merchandise mix
- the corporate philosophy toward the assortment
- physical characteristics of the store, layout of the Internet site
- balance between too much versus too little assortment
- complementary merchandise

Profitability of Merchandise Mix   Since retailers are constrained by the amount of money they have to invest in merchandise and space to put the merchandise in, they're always trying to find the most profitable mix of products. Thus, for a chain of stores such as Levi Strauss & Co. to add a category like shoes to the assortment,

refact

Macy's has roughly 250 000 SKUs on its Internet site. A typical Macy's store has 2 million to 3 million SKUs.[9]

a reduction must be made elsewhere. It would attempt to take the inventory invest-ment that it's been making in a less profitable merchandise category (flannel shirts in which it's invested $1 million to generate $2 million in sales) and shift it to shoes, which it hopes will generate $2.5 million.

Corporate Philosophy toward the Assortment   The corporate strategy toward the assortment helps the buyer determine the number of styles and colours to purchase. To illustrate, let's again consider the hypothetically different philosophies of Levi Strauss stores and Banana Republic. Both chains have a merchandise budget of $150 000 to spend on jeans that retail for $50. Thus, both stores can purchase 3000 pairs. The Levi Strauss stores purchase 30 different style/colour combinations (100 units per com-bination); Banana Republic purchases 10 (300 per combination). The Levi Strauss stores with 30 styles and colours are more diversified than Banana Republic.

With Levi Strauss stores, since there are so many style/colour combinations, on average the category will perform adequately even if a few don't sell. But by spread-ing the 3000 pairs across so many style/colour combinations, the buyer runs the additional risk of **breaking sizes,** which means running out of stock on particular sizes. Typically, retailers take markdowns on assortments with broken sizes since they become harder to sell. Additionally, a large assortment of styles and colours won't enable the buyer to maximize profits by investing a large portion of the budget on the big winners.

Another issue is whether top management wants to grow or shrink a particular merchandise category. Some department stores, for instance, have dropped furniture and major appliances altogether because of low turnover, low profit margins, or lack of space.

Physical Characteristics of the Store and Layout of the Internet Site   Retailers must consider how much space to devote to the category—in terms of both physical space and space on their Internet site. If many styles and colours are in the assortment, much space will be required to properly display and store the merchandise. The display area's physical characteristics are also important in the case of bricks-and-mortar retailers. A rack, for instance, may hold 300 pairs of jeans. It wouldn't be aesthetically pleasing to display only 100 units on the rack or to mix the jeans with another merchandise category.

By the same token, Web sites must be designed so that the customer can easily navigate through them. If there are too many choices, if the merchandise is orga-nized in a less than obvious fashion, if the customer perceives the site to be cluttered, or if the checkout process is difficult, customers click and are off to another site.

Balance between Too Much versus Too Little Assortment   Both tradi-tional retailers and multichannel retailers must contend with the balance between having too much versus too little assortment. In general, retailers must offer enough assortment to satisfy the customers' needs and expectations, but not too much so as to confuse them and turn them off.

Complementary Merchandise   When retailers plan to add to their assortment, they must consider whether the merchandise under consideration complements other merchandise in the department. For instance, Dockers may stimulate the sale of shirts and belts. After the customer selects a book, Amazon.com suggests books that have been purchased by other customers who purchased that book.

DETERMINING PRODUCT AVAILABILITY

Another dimension of the assortment planning process is product availability. Recall that product availability defines the percentage of demand for a particular SKU that is satisfied. The higher the product availability, the higher the amount of backup stock necessary to ensure that the retailer won't be out of stock on a particular SKU when the customer demands it. Choosing an appropriate amount of backup stock is critical to successful assortment planning because if the level of backup stock is too low, the retailer will lose sales, and possibly customers too, due to stockouts. If the level is too high, scarce financial resources will be wasted in needless inventory that could be more profitably invested.

Exhibit 10–7 shows the trade-off between inventory investment and product availability. Although the actual inventory investment varies in different situations, the general relationship is that a very high level of service results in a prohibitively high inventory investment. This relationship can be explained by the relationship between cycle stock and backup stock.

Cycle stock, also known as **base stock,** is inventory that results from the replenishment process and is required to meet predicted demand. Replenishment times (lead times) are depicted in orange in Exhibit 10–8. In this case, 96 units of SKU are ordered. During the next two weeks, much of the inventory is sold. But before the store is out of stock, the next order arrives. The cycle then repeats in this typical zigzag fashion.

Retailers carry **backup stock,** also known as **safety stock** or **buffer stock,** as a cushion for the cycle stock so they won't run out before the next order arrives. Backup stock is depicted in yellow in Exhibit 10–8.

Several issues determine the level of required backup stock:

- First, inventory management systems should calculate safety stock requirements for each SKU. That way, SKUs with smooth demand won't be overstocked, and the retailer won't constantly be out of stock on SKUs with erratic demand.

- Second, determine the product availability the retailer wishes to provide. If, for instance, a Levi Strauss store wants to satisfy almost all its customers who wish to purchase a pair of Levi's 501 jeans in size 31–32, it must carry a great deal of backup stock compared to what it needs if it decides to satisfy only 75 percent of the demand for the SKU.

exhibit 10–7

Relationship between Inventory Investment and Product Availability

exhibit 10–8

Cycle and Backup Stock

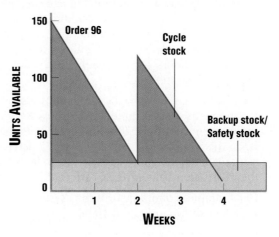

exhibit 10–9
EOQ-Based Computer
Ordering System

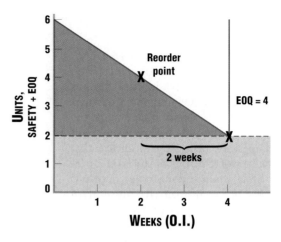

EOQ = 4
OF (order frequency) = 12 X
OI (order interval) = 4 weeks
Re-order level = 4 units
Backup/safety stock = 2 units
Lead time = 2 weeks

- Third, the higher the fluctuations in demand, the greater the need for backup stock. In some weeks, sales are greater or less than the average. When sales are less than average, the retailer ends up carrying a little more merchandise than it needs. But if sales are more than average, there must be some backup stock to ensure that the retailer doesn't go out of stock. Note in Exhibit 10–8 that during week 4, sales were greater than average so the retailer had to dip into backup stock to avoid a stockout.

- Fourth, the amount of backup stock also depends on lead time from the vendor. **Lead time** is the amount of time between recognition that an order needs to be placed and the point at which the merchandise arrives in the store and is ready for sale. If it took two months to receive a shipment of jeans, the possibility of running out of stock would be greater than if lead time were only two weeks because the Levi Strauss stores would have to forecast for a longer period. The shorter lead times inherent in quick response inventory systems result in a lower level of backup stock required to maintain the same level of product availability.

- Fifth, fluctuations in lead time also affect the amount of backup stock. If Levi Strauss & Co. knows that lead time for jeans is always two weeks, plus or minus one day, it can more accurately plan its inventory levels. But if lead time is plus or minus one day on one shipment and then plus or minus five days on the next shipment, the stores must carry additional backup stock to cover the uncertainty in lead time. Many retailers using quick response inventory systems are forcing their vendors to deliver merchandise within a very narrow window—sometimes two or three hours—to reduce the fluctuations in lead time and thus the amount of required backup stock.

- Finally, the vendor's product availability also affects the retailer's backup stock requirements. For example, Levi Strauss & Co. can more easily plan its inventory requirements if it normally ships every item that the Levi Strauss stores order. If, on the other hand, Levi only ships 75 percent of the ordered items, the stores must maintain a higher backup stock to be certain that the jeans' availability to their customers isn't adversely affected.

For example, computer-ordering systems are based on EOQ (economic order quantity), as shown in Exhibit 10–9.

The EOQ model is suitable for staple merchandise with a consistent demand and rate of sale. It permits a systematic way to automate reorders based on a set reorder point calculation. The reorder point can be established as a stock level point at which an order for the economic order quantity can be placed at an appropriate time in order to allow for the delivery time required and the maintenance of a basic stock level.

EOQ also takes into account the holding costs associated with maintaining inventory over time and the ordering costs associated with placing orders. This system prevents stock outages since it builds in a safety stock level and the reorder can happen automatically when inventory drops to the reorder point.

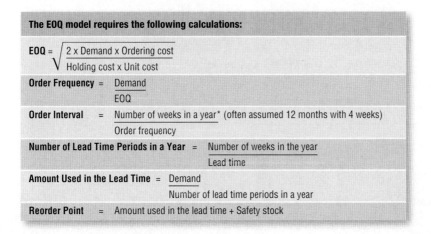

The EOQ model requires the following calculations:

$$EOQ = \sqrt{\frac{2 \times Demand \times Ordering\ cost}{Holding\ cost \times Unit\ cost}}$$

$$Order\ Frequency = \frac{Demand}{EOQ}$$

$$Order\ Interval = \frac{Number\ of\ weeks\ in\ a\ year^* \text{ (often assumed 12 months with 4 weeks)}}{Order\ frequency}$$

$$Number\ of\ Lead\ Time\ Periods\ in\ a\ Year = \frac{Number\ of\ weeks\ in\ the\ year}{Lead\ time}$$

$$Amount\ Used\ in\ the\ Lead\ Time = \frac{Demand}{Number\ of\ lead\ time\ periods\ in\ a\ year}$$

$$Reorder\ Point = Amount\ used\ in\ the\ lead\ time + Safety\ stock$$

the assortment plan

After setting financial goals and determining the relative importance of variety, assortment, and product availability, the retailer is ready to determine what merchandise to stock using an assortment plan. An assortment plan describes in general terms what should be carried in a particular merchandise category. The assortment plan for fashion merchandise doesn't identify specific SKUs since fashions change from year to year. The more fashion-oriented the category, the less detail will be found in the assortment plan because the merchandise planner requires more flexibility to adjust to fashion changes.

Historical precedent is the starting point for developing the assortment plan for the current season. The merchandise planner uses the sales, GMROI, and turnover forecast along with the assortment plan from the previous season to develop the plan for the current season. Adjustments are then made based on the merchandise planner's expectations for what items or fashions will be important in the coming season. For instance, if a particular style, such as boot-cut jeans, is expected to be especially popular in the coming season, the merchandise planner will use more of the merchandise budget for that style and cut back on traditional jeans.

Exhibit 10–10 shows an abbreviated assortment plan for girls' jeans. This assortment plan identifies general styles (traditional five-pocket, straight-leg jeans, and boot-cut jeans), general price levels ($20, $35, and $45 for traditional jeans; $25 and $40 for boot-cut jeans), composition of fabric (regular denim and stonewashed), and colours (light blue, indigo, and black).

exhibit 10–10   Assortment Plan for Girl's Jeans

Styles	Traditional	Traditional	Traditional	Traditional	Traditional	Traditional
Price levels	$20	$20	$35	$35	$45	$45
Fabric composition	Regular denim	Stonewashed	Regular denim	Stonewashed	Regular denim	Stonewashed
Colours	Light blue	Light blue	Light blue	Light blue	Light blue	Light blue
	Indigo	Indigo	Indigo	Indigo	Indigo	Indigo
	Black	Black	Black	Black	Black	Black

Styles	Boot-Cut	Boot-Cut	Boot-Cut	Boot-Cut
Price levels	$25	$25	$40	$40
Fabric composition	Regular denim	Stonewashed	Regular denim	Stonewashed
Colours	Light blue	Light blue	Light blue	Light blue
	Indigo	Indigo	Indigo	Indigo
	Black	Black	Black	Black

exhibit 10–11

Size Distribution for Traditional Denim Jeans—Model Stock Plan

					SIZE						
LENGTH	1	2	4	5	6	8	10	12	14		
Short	2	4	7	6	8	5	7	4	2	%	
Short	9	17	30	26	34	21	30	17	9	units	
Medium	2	4	7	6	8	5	7	4	2	%	
Medium	9	17	30	26	34	21	30	17	9	units	
Long	0	2	2	2	3	2	2	1	0	%	
Long	0	9	9	9	12	9	9	4	0	units	
								Total		100%	
										429 units	

Assortment plans for apparel and shoes also typically include a size distribution. To illustrate, Exhibit 10–11 breaks down size and length for the 429 units for girls' traditional $20 denim jeans. Thus, the store wants to have nine units of size 1–short, which represent 2 percent of the 429 total. Note that the size distribution approximates a normal distribution or bell-shaped curve. The buyer buys less of the small and large sizes, and more of the middle sizes. The process of applying the size distribution is repeated for each style/colour combination for each store.

The development of an assortment plan can be complicated. In an actual multistore chain, the process is even more complex than in our example. A good assortment plan requires a good forecast for sales, GMROI, and inventory turnover along with a mix of subjective and experienced judgment. A good inventory management system that combines these elements is also critical to successful merchandise management.

SUMMARY

Planning merchandise assortments involves a range of activities including organizing the category, setting financial objectives, and developing the assortment mix. Successful merchandise management will involve the planning of what to buy and how much to buy—the merchandise mix—and allocating the appropriate merchandise budget. The goal is to offer the right quantity of the right merchandise in the right place at the right time while meeting the company's financial objectives.

This chapter was the first of five on merchandise management. As such, it examined basic strategic issues and planning tools for managing merchandise. First, merchandise must be broken down into categories for planning purposes. Buyers and their partners, merchandise planners, control these categories, often with the help of their major vendors.

Tools to develop a merchandising plan include GMROI, inventory turnover, and sales forecasting. GMROI is used to plan and evaluate merchandise performance. The GMROI planned for a particular merchandise category is derived from the firm's overall financial goals broken down to the category level. Gross margin percentage and inventory turnover work together to form this useful merchandise management tool.

Calculating inventory turnover and determining inventory turnover goals are important. Retailers strive for a balanced inventory turnover. Rapid inventory turnover is imperative for the firm's financial success. But if the retailer attempts to push inventory turnover to its limit, severe stockouts and increased costs may result.

When developing a sales forecast, retailers must know what stage of the life cycle a particular category is in and whether the product is a fad, fashion, or staple so they can plan their merchandising activities accordingly. Creating a sales forecast involves such sources of information as previous sales volume, published sources, customer information, and shopping at the competition as well as utilizing vendors and buying offices.

The trade-off between variety, assortment, and product availability is a crucial issue in determining merchandising strategy. Examining this trade-off helps retailers answer the important question of what type of store to be: a specialist or generalist.

The culmination of planning the GMROI, inventory turnover, sales forecast, and assortment planning process is the assortment plan. The assortment plan supplies the merchandise planner with a general outline of what should be carried in a particular merchandise category.

KEY TERMS

assortment plan, *258*
backup stock, *277*
base stock, *277*
basic merchandise, *266*
breadth, *271*
breaking sizes, *276*
buffer stock, *277*
category, *260*
category captain, *262*
category life cycle, *263*
category management, *261*

classification, *259*
cycle stock, *277*
department, *259*
depth, *272*
depth interview, *269*
fad, *264*
focus group, *269*
lead time, *278*
level of support, *274*
merchandise group, *258*

merchandise management, *257*
merchandise plan, *271*
product availability, *274*
resident buying office, *268*
safety stock, *277*
seasonal merchandise, *266*
service level, *274*
staple merchandise, *266*
variety, *271*
want books, *269*

Get Out & Do It!

1. **GO SHOPPING** Go to your favourite apparel specialty store and your favourite department store. Do an audit of the variety and assortment at the specialty store. (Tabulate how many merchandise categories it carries and how many SKUs within each category.) Compare the variety and assortment for the same type of merchandise in the department store.

2. **GO SHOPPING** Go to a retailer that has both bricks and clicks formats. Describe the differences in merchandise variety and assortment available.

DISCUSSION QUESTIONS AND PROBLEMS

1. What are the differences between a fashion, fad, and staple? How should a merchandise planner manage these types of merchandise differently?

2. How and why would you expect variety and assortment to differ between a traditional bricks-and-mortar store and its Internet counterpart?

3. Assume you are the grocery buyer for canned fruits and vegetables at a five-store supermarket chain. Del Monte has told you and your boss that it would be responsible for making all inventory decisions for those merchandise categories. It would determine how much to order and when shipments should be made. It promises a 10 percent increase in gross margin dollars in the coming year. Would you take Del Monte up on its offer? Justify your answer.

4. An assortment plan indicates that a buyer can purchase 1000 units of fashion wristwatches. The buyer must choose between buying 20 styles of 50 units each or 5 styles of 200 units each. In terms of the store's philosophy toward risk and space utilization, how does the buyer make this decision?

5. A buyer has had a number of customer complaints that he has been out of stock on a certain category of merchandise. The buyer subsequently decides to increase this category's product availability from 80 percent to 90 percent. What will be the impact on backup stock and inventory turnover? Will your answer be the same if the buyer is implementing a quick response inventory system?

6. Variety, assortment, and product availability are the cornerstones of the assortment planning process. Provide examples of retailers that have done an outstanding job of positioning their stores on the basis of one or more of these issues.

7. Given the following information, calculate:
   (a) EOQ
   (b) Order frequency
   (c) Order interval
   (d) Reorder point

   When:
   - Demand is 156
   - Unit cost is $1.00
   - Ordering cost is $0.34
   - Holding cost is 65 percent
   - Lead time is two weeks
   - Safety stock is three units

   Graph your results, showing the EOQ points [(a) to (d)].

8. How does Canadian Tire change its merchandise inventory on a seasonal basis? How has this retailer used its merchandise offerings to attract more female customers?

9. Give examples of products that you have purchased that are fad, fashion, and staple items according to the category life cycle. How does each item fit the definitions given in Exhibit 10-4?

10. Refer to Exhibit 10.6, Factors Impacting Sales Forecasts/Merchandise Plans/Budgets. Discuss how the seasonal weather had an impact on the sale of specific merchandise carried by retailers in your area.

CHAPTER 11

merchandise planning systems

Executive Briefing
Glen Murphy, CEO, Gap Inc.

Gap Inc. is the largest specialty clothing chain in North America and, as the leading apparel retailer, its goal must be to bring great style and value to customers year round. Glen Murphy, who was named CEO of Gap Inc. in 2007, faces tough challenges in turning around the fortunes of the struggling Gap which has more than 3000 stores worldwide. Gap Inc. is a great brand with well-recognized labels including Gap, Banana Republic, and Old Navy, but has been losing consumer appeal as the king of khaki.

Retail competition is fierce, with fast-fashion retailers such as H&M, Zara, and Mexx. These retailers have cut the clothing cycle down from six months to six weeks, replenishing their stores constantly with fresh styles. Gap, on the other hand, with its huge operations and slower reaction times, has been forced into the riskier business of guessing up front how a season's trends will sell. Gap's goal of providing the right merchandise, to the right store, at the right time, and at the right price is increasingly difficult as consumers now expect higher quality at a bargain price.

Glen Murphy sees that the immediate goals are to simplify the business process, give merchandisers more leeway to make quick decisions, improve the look of the stores, and reduce costs to improve productivity. Gap makes all of its own products exclusively for its own stores and must deliver new styles and new products throughout the year; Murphy feels that it is important to ensure that product developers are not controlled by corporate bureaucracy and research.

QUESTIONS

- What are a merchandise budget plan and open-to-buy systems, and how are they prepared?
- How does a staple merchandise buying system operate?
- How do multistore retailers allocate merchandise to stores?
- How do retailers evaluate their buying performance?
- How does merchandise and information flow from vendor to retailer to consumer and back?
- What advanced information technology developments are facilitating vendor/retailer communications?
- What is the importance of quick response delivery systems to retailer profits?

In its restructuring, Gap is directing efforts to refocus on its core market of 24 to 34-year-olds, and is directing a return to the basics of casual weekend and work wear. One of the company's many challenges is to plan and forecast accurately. The merchandise planning process is very complex, requiring technology to support supply chain management that includes hundreds of factories producing significant volumes of merchandise for the more than 3000 stores worldwide.

Upgraded information technology systems with sophisticated planning and forecasting software provide information needed at the top management level (for example, profits across the retail chain), while at the same time providing information that is needed at the store level (such as the date of merchandise arrival and coordinating merchandise lines). The key to this software is that it can predict the impacts of decisions and point out any necessary action for success. Gap Inc.'s merchandise planners now more easily integrate all their assortment strategies onto one computer application. The company has a more consistent, streamlined, and efficient planning process, and, with integrated forecasting, optimization capabilities, and the ability to change and improve plans quickly and efficiently. Gap Inc. can make better, faster, and more accurate decisions for forecasting sales and making price and markdown optimization decisions. The result is expanded communication of vital information needed for planning.

Providing great style and value to its customers has always been a guiding philosophy of Gap Inc.

Forecasting sales and developing assortment plans indicate in very general terms what product and how much should be carried in a particular merchandise category. This chapter examines the merchandise management process in more depth by showing how retailers utilize various tools in formal buying systems. Although the assortment plan provides a general outline of what types of merchandise should be carried, it doesn't tell you how much to buy.

Selling generates revenue, but buying right generates profit.

Specifically, these systems and tools help buyers and merchandise planners determine how much to buy. Retailers use two distinct types of buying systems:

- a staple merchandise buying system for basics
- a merchandise budget for fashion merchandise

Forecasting demand is much more straightforward for staples than for fashion merchandise. Since there's an established sales history for each staple SKU, standard statistical techniques are used to forecast sales. Since there is no sales history for specific fashion SKUs, buyers forecast sales at the category level. Buyers must determine the quantity of specific SKUs to purchase on the basis of many factors, such as current trends and customer preferences.

The open-to-buy system keeps track of the merchandise flows while they are occurring so buyers don't spend too much or too little. Once the merchandise is purchased, it is allocated to stores. In the end, the merchandise and the buyer's performance are evaluated.

exhibit 11–1
Merchandise
Management Issues

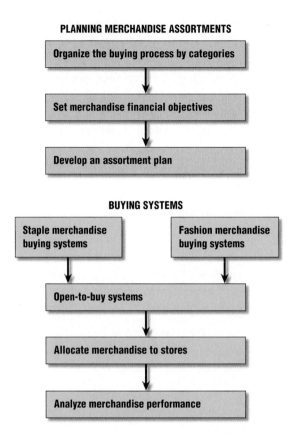

PLANNING MERCHANDISE ASSORTMENTS

Organize the buying process by categories

Set merchandise financial objectives

Develop an assortment plan

BUYING SYSTEMS

Staple merchandise buying systems

Fashion merchandise buying systems

Open-to-buy systems

Allocate merchandise to stores

Analyze merchandise performance

Exhibit 11–1 provides an overview of this chapter, which begins with a look at buying systems for staple merchandise. Buying systems for fashion merchandise are examined next, followed by a look at open-to-buy systems. The chapter then discusses how multistore retailers allocate merchandise among stores and how buying performance is evaluated. At the end of this chapter, Appendix 11A describes the retail inventory method (RIM).

staple merchandise buying systems

Staple merchandise buying systems are used for merchandise that follows a predictable order–receipt–order cycle. Most merchandise follows this pattern. These systems don't work well with fashion merchandise, however, because they use past history to predict sales for the future—and fashion merchandise has no history from previous seasons on specific SKUs. These systems are used for buying most of the merchandise found in food and discount stores in addition to some categories in specialty and department stores such as underwear, socks, and housewares.

Exhibit 11–2 illustrates the function of a staple merchandise management system. In the left panel of the figure, the inventory of an SKU in a retailer's distribution centre or store is depicted as a container. Orders received from the vendor fill up the container and increase the inventory level, whereas sales of the SKU to customers decrease the level of inventory in the container. The level of inventory in the container is shown in the right panel of the exhibit.

At the beginning of week 1, the retailer had 150 units of the SKU in inventory. At that time, the buyer placed an order for 96 units. During the next two weeks, customers purchased the SKU, and the inventory level decreased to 20 units. At the end of week 2, the 96-unit order from the vendor arrived, and the inventory level jumped up to 116 units. The buyer places another order with the vendor that will arrive two weeks later, before customer sales decrease the inventory level to 0 and the retailer stocks out.

Inventory that goes up and down due to the replenishment process is called **cycle stock**, or **base stock**. The retailer would like to reduce the base stock inventory to keep its inventory investment low. One approach to reducing the base stock is to reorder and receive merchandise from the vendor more often instead of once every other week. But more frequent ordering and shipments would increase administrative and transportation costs.

Because sales of the SKU and receipts of orders from the vendor cannot be predicted with perfect accuracy, the retailer has to carry **backup stock**, also known as **safety stock** or **buffer stock**, as a cushion so it doesn't stock out before the next order arrives. Backup stock is shown in yellow in Exhibit 11–2.

Several factors determine the level of required backup stock. First, it depends on the product availability the retailer wishes to provide. If Lowe's wants to rarely stock out of white paint, it needs to have a higher level of backup stock. However, if it is willing to accept a 75 percent product availability for melon-coloured paint, a lower level of buffer stock is needed for that SKU.

Second, the greater the fluctuation in demand, the more backup stock is needed. Suppose a Canadian Tire store sells an average of 135 liters of purple paint in two weeks. Yet, in some weeks, sales are 225 litres, and some weeks they are only 45 liters. When sales are less than average, the store ends up carrying a little more merchandise than it needs. But when sales are much more than average, there must be more backup stock to ensure that the store does not stock out. Note in Exhibit 11–2 that during week 4, sales were greater than average so the retailer had to dip into its backup stock to avoid a stockout.

Third, the amount of backup stock needed is affected by the lead time from the vendor. **Lead time** is the amount of time between the recognition that an order needs to be placed and the point at which the merchandise arrives in the store and is ready for sale. If it took two months to receive a shipment of purple paint, the possibility of

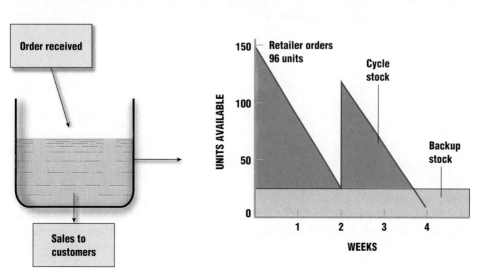

exhibit 11–2
Inventory Levels for
Staple Merchandise

running out of stock would be greater than if lead time were only two weeks, because the Canadian Tire store would have to forecast for a longer period. The shorter lead times inherent in collaborative supply chain management systems result in a lower level of backup stock required to maintain the same level of product availability.

Fourth, fluctuations in lead time also affect the amount of backup stock. If Canadian Tire knows that lead time for purple paint is always two weeks, it can more accurately plan its inventory levels. Many retailers using collaborative supply chain management systems require their vendors to deliver merchandise within a very narrow window—sometimes two or three hours—to reduce the fluctuations in lead time and thus the amount of required backup stock.

When planning the amount of inventory to order for a staple merchandise category, such as paint, Canadian Tire's buyers must consider current inventory, customer demand, lead time for replenishment, and backup stock needed to avoid stockouts in the department.

Fifth, the vendor's product availability also affects the retailer's backup stock requirements. For example, Canadian Tire can more easily plan its inventory requirements if the vendor normally ships every item that is ordered. If, however, the vendor only ships 75 percent of the ordered items, Canadian Tire must maintain more backup stock to be certain that the paint availability for their customers isn't adversely affected. The percentage of complete orders received from a vendor is called the **fill rate**.

WHAT THE STAPLE MERCHANDISE BUYING SYSTEM DOES

Staple merchandise buying systems contain a number of program modules that show how much to order and when. These systems assist buyers by performing three functions:

- Monitoring and measuring average current demand for items at the SKU level
- Forecasting future SKU demand with allowances made for seasonal variations and changes in trend
- Developing ordering decision rules for optimum restocking

The inventory management report, discussed in the next section, provides the information for performing these functions.

THE INVENTORY MANAGEMENT REPORT

The inventory management report provides information about the current sales rate or sales velocity, inventory availability, the amount on order, sales forecast, and most important, the quantity to order for each SKU.

The retailer will have a prespecified schedule for each vendor. The schedule is determined by weighing the cost of carrying inventory versus the cost of buying and handling the inventory. The more the retailer purchases at one time, the higher the carrying costs, but the lower the buying and handling costs.

Basic Stock–List   Rubbermaid is a manufacturer of household plastic products. The first four columns of Exhibit 11–3 represent what many retailers call the basic stock list. The **basic stock list** describes each SKU and summarizes the inventory position. Specifically, it contains the stock number and description of the item, how many items are on hand and on order, and sales for the past 12 and 4 weeks.

The basic stock list differs from the assortment plan used in fashion-based systems in that it defines each SKU in precise rather than general terms. Examine the first item: stock number 4050, a Rubbermaid bath mat in avocado green. There are 6 on hand and 120 on order. Thus, the quantity available is 126. (Quantity on hand + Quantity on order = Quantity available.) Sales for the past 12 and 4 weeks were 215 and 72 units, respectively.

The basic stock list is a necessary component of any inventory management system, yet many retailers go beyond the basic record-keeping function. The last eight columns of Exhibit 11–3 are needed too. Using this information, the inventory management part of the system manipulates the numbers in the basic stock list to arrive at sales forecasts and suggested order quantities. Now let's talk about the remaining entries in Exhibit 11–3 and how they fit into the system.

Most merchandise at home improvement centres such as Canadian Tire is staples.

Inventory Turnover   The planned inventory turnover is based on overall financial goals and drives the inventory management system. The buyer achieves an actual inventory turnover of 9 for the avocado bath mat, but the planned turnover was 12.

Product Availability   In the avocado bath mat example, on average, out of every 100 customers wanting the item, 96 found it in stock. The appropriate planned level of product availability for staple merchandise is relatively easy to determine based on past orders. Staple merchandise consists of items that are in constant demand by the customer and therefore have a predictable reorder pattern.

Backup Stock   Backup stock, also known as safety stock or buffer stock, is inventory used to guard against being out of stock when customer demand exceeds forecasts or when merchandise is delayed. Backup stock for the avocado bath mat is 20 units.

exhibit 11–3   Inventory Management Report for Rubbermaid SKUs

Marketmax - Performance Analysis - Worksheet: Inventory Management Report : Admin (Business View: 'Inventory Management Report : Admin')

Worksheet   Performance Analysis

Plan   Edit   View   Tools   Help

Skip To

Loc - 01 / Time - Spring 2002	Quantity On Hand	Quantity On Order	Sales Last 12 Wks	Sales Last 4 Wks	Turnover Actual	Turnover Plan	Product Availability	Backup Stock	Forecast Current 4 Wks	Forecast Next 8 Wks	Order Point	Order Quantity
RMBath - RM Bath												
4050 - RM Bath Mat avocado	6	120	215	72	9	12	96	20	94	117	167	42
4051 - RM Bath Mat Blue	0	96	139	56	5	9	100	17	58	113	110	96
4052 - RM Bath Mat Gold	1	60	234	117	9	12	95	27	42	196	200	144
4053 - TM Bath Mat Pink	2		41	31	5	9	95	10	41	131	58	60

Forecast   Sales forecasts for staple items are fairly straightforward and mechanical. Forecasting sales of staple items entails extending sales trends from the past into the future.

Order Point   The **order point** is the amount of inventory below which the quantity available shouldn't go or the item will be out of stock before the next order arrives. The order point in the periodic system is defined as

$$\text{Order point} = [(\text{Sales/Day}) \times (\text{Lead time} + \text{Review time})] + (\text{Backup stock})$$

The lead time is the amount of time between recognition that an order needs to be placed and when it arrives in the store and is ready for sale. Assume demand per day is 1 and lead time is zero days. (This may be the case in a pharmacy receiving shipments from its wholesaler more than once a day.) Here the order point would be zero. The buyer would wait until stock ran out and then order and replenish the merchandise almost instantaneously.

With lead time of two weeks, there's some point below which the buyer shouldn't deplete the inventory without ordering, or the retailer would start selling the backup stock before the next order arrived. Further, the buyer only reviews the line once a week, and 20 units of backup stock are necessary to maintain a high service level. In this case, if demand is 7 units per day, then

$$\text{Order point} = [(7 \text{ units}) \times (14 + 7 \text{ days})] + (20 \text{ units}) = 167 \text{ units}$$

Here the buyer orders if quantity available falls to 167 units or fewer.

Order Quantity   The question remains, How much should the buyer order when the quantity available is less than the order point? He or she should order enough so the cycle stock isn't depleted and sales dip into backup stock before the next order arrives—this is the difference between the quantity available and the order point. Using the avocado bath mats in Exhibit 11–3, since quantity available is 126, the buyer orders 41 units, because the order point is 167 (i.e., 167 − 126 = 41). The actual suggested order quantity is 42 since the bath mats are packed 6 to a carton, and the computer rounds up to the next whole carton.

Now that we've seen how inventory management systems work for staple merchandise, let's look at a system designed for fashion merchandise.

$$\text{Order point} - \text{Quantity on hand} = \text{Order quantity}$$
$$167 \quad - \quad 126 \quad = \quad 41$$

merchandise budget plan for fashion merchandise

The system for managing fashion merchandise categories is typically called a merchandise budget plan. The merchandise budget plan specifies the planned inventory investment in dollars in fashion merchandise category over time. The plan just specifies how much money should be spent each month to support sales and achieve desired inventory turnover and GMROI objectives.

Exhibit 11–4 shows a sample six-month merchandise plan for menswear.

Sales for month = Planned sales for season × Sales percentage allocation per month

BOM = Planned sales for month × Stock to sales ratio

Markdown = Planned sales for month × Reduction allocation percentage per month

exhibit 11–4   Sample Six-Month Merchandise Plan for a Menswear Retailer

SIX-MONTH MERCHANDISE PLAN		Spring / Fall	Feb. / Aug.	Mar. / Sept.	Apr. / Oct.	May / Nov.	June / Dec.	July / Jan.	Total
DEPARTMENT Men's Furnishings **DEPARTMENT NO.** 327 **FROM** August 1 20____ **TO** January 31 20____	Sales	Last Year	$26 000	$39 000	$39 000	$65 000	$52 000	$39 000	$260 000
		Plan							
		Actual							
Department Control Data	Retail EOM	Last Year	103 000	103 000	129 000	116 000	103 000	104 000	
		Plan							
		Actual							
LY. T.Y. % Initial Markup 41.3 % Reductions 9.0 11.0 % Maintained Markup 36.0 % Alteration Expense 3.0 3.0 % Cash Discount 1.0 1.0 % Gross Margin 34.0 % Operating Expense 31.0 32.0 % Net Profit 3.0 3.0 Season Turnover 2.5 2.5 Control Period 4.5 4.5	Reductions	Last Year	3 510	3 510	2 340	2 340	3 510	8 190	23 400
		Plan							
		Actual							
Planning and Authorization	Retail BOM	Last Year	90 000	103 000	103 000	129 000	116 000	103 000	
		Plan							
Buyer J.J. Tranell		Actual							
Merchandise Controller A.P. Edwards	Retail Purchases	Last Year	42 510	42 510	67 340	54 340	42 510	46 190	295 400
		Plan							
		Actual							
Date Prepared 6/15	Cost Purchases	Last Year	24 953	24 953	39 529	31 888	24 953	27 114	173 390
		Plan							
Date Authorized 6/30		Actual							

Purchases = Sales + EOM (next month's BOM) + Markdown – BOM

Retail purchases = Retail BOM – Reductions + Retail EOM + Sales

Data that can assist in making inventory decisions are available at www.bizstats.com in the form of industry benchmarks and at www.statscan.ca, retail and wholesale statistics. Exhibit 11–5 shows a six-month merchandise budget plan for men's tailored suits at a national specialty store chain. For a category like this, the buyer is probably doing the plan in the summer for the following spring. The buyer needs to plan how much merchandise should be delivered in each month to achieve the financial goals for the period.

Actual sales might differ from the sales forecasted in the merchandise budget plan. Even with this uncertainty, the plan is used to coordinate the supply and demand for merchandise and to ensure that the financial goals are realized. In addition, the plan coordinates the activities of buyers for different merchandise categories, so that there is not too much merchandise in some categories and not enough in others. From a

exhibit 11–5   Marketmax Six-Month Merchandise Budget Plan for Men's Tailored Suits

Marketmax - Financial Planning - Worksheet: Merchandise Budget Plan - Mens (Business View: 'Financial Planning : Admin')

Worksheet   Financial Planning

Plan Edit View Tools Help

Skip To Month

Loc - 01 / Merch - Mens	Spring 2002	April 2002	May 2002	June 2002	July 2002	August 2002	September 2002
1. Sales % Distribution to Season	100.00%	21.00%	12.00%	12.00%	19.00%	21.00%	15.00%
2. Monthly Sales	$130 000	$27 300	$15 600	$15 600	$24 700	$27 300	$19 500
3. Reduc.% Distribution to Season	100.00%	40.00%	14.00%	16.00%	12.00%	10.00%	8.00%
4. Monthly Reductions	$16 500	$6 600	$2 310	$2 640	$1 980	$1 650	$1 320
5. BOM Stock to Sales Ratio	4.00	3.60	4.40	4.40	4.00	3.60	4.00
6. BOM Inventory	$98 280	$98 280	$68 640	$68 640	$98 800	$98 280	$78 000
7. EOM Inventory	$65 600	$68 640	$68 640	$275 080	$98 280	$78 000	$65 600
8. Monthly Additions to Stock	$113 820	$4 260	$17 910	$48 400	$26 160	$8 670	$8 420

Spring: April 2002, May 2002, June 2002 — Summer: July 2002, August 2002, September 2002

global perspective, the merchandise variety could become unbalanced and be less appealing to customers.

Take a close look at line 8, "Monthly Additions to Stock," in Exhibit 11–5. In the next few pages, we will systematically work through Exhibit 11–5 on our way to this last line. "Monthly Additions to Stock" tells the buyer how much money to spend in each month, given the category's sales forecast, GMROI, inventory turnover, and monthly fluctuations in sales. As such, the merchandise budget plan coordinates purchases to coincide with the category's financial goals.

Even relatively small stores now use advanced computer technologies like this one to plan merchandise budgets. Following are some equations that we will use in our examination of the merchandise budget plan. Note that BOM stands for "beginning of month" and EOM stands for "end of month."

In the remaining portion of this section, we will examine each line in the merchandise budget plan. The merchandise planning system illustrated here was developed by Marketmax.

MONTHLY SALES PERCENTAGE DISTRIBUTION TO SEASON (LINE 1)

Line 1 of the plan projects what percentage of the total sales is expected to be sold in each month. Thus, in Exhibit 11–5, 21 percent of the six-month sales are expected to occur in April.

The starting point for determining the percentage distribution of sales by month is historical records. The percentage of total sales that occurs in a particular month doesn't vary appreciably from year to year. Even so, it's helpful to examine each month's percentage over a few years to check for any significant changes. For instance, the buyer realizes that the autumn selling season for men's tailored suits continues to be pushed further back into summer. Over time, this general shift toward earlier purchasing will affect the percentage distribution of sales by month. The distribution may also vary due to changes made by the buyer or the competitors' marketing strategies. The buyer must include special sales that did not occur in the past, for instance, in the percentage distribution of sales by month in the same way that they're built into the overall sales forecast.

| | Six-month data | Spring | | | Summer | | |
		April	May	June	July	August	September
1. Sales % Distribution to Season	100.00%	21.00%	12.00%	12.00%	19.00%	21.00%	15.00%

MONTHLY SALES (LINE 2)

Monthly sales equal the forecast total sales for the six-month period (first column = \$130 000) multiplied by each sales percentage by month (line 1). In Exhibit 11–5, monthly sales for April = \$130 000 × 21% = \$27 300.

Sales % Distrubution	Six-month data	Spring			Summer		
		April	May	June	July	August	September
2. Monthly Sales	\$130 000	\$27 300	\$15 600	\$15 600	\$24 700	\$27 300	\$19 500

MONTHLY REDUCTIONS PERCENTAGE DISTRIBUTION TO SEASON (LINE 3)

To have enough merchandise every month to support the monthly sales forecast, the buyer must consider factors that reduce the inventory level. Although sales are the primary reduction, the value of the inventory is also reduced by markdowns, shrinkage, and discounts to employees. The merchandise budget planning process builds these additional reductions into the planned purchases. Otherwise, the retailer would always be understocked. Note that in Exhibit 11–5, 40 percent of the season's total reductions occur in April as a result of end-of-season sales.

Reduction	Six-month data	Spring			Summer		
		April	May	June	July	August	September
3. % Distribution to Season	100.00%	40.00%	14.00%	16.00%	12.00%	10.00%	8.00%

Markdowns can be forecast fairly accurately from historical records. Of course, changes in markdown strategies—or changes in the environment, such as competition or general economic activity—must be taken into consideration when forecasting markdowns.

In the seven days before Christmas, retailers have marked peaks in their sales that can amount to as much as 40 percent of their December sales figures.

Discounts to employees are like markdowns, except that they're given to employees rather than to customers. Cost of the employee discount is tied fairly closely to the sales level and number of employees. Thus, its percentage of sales and dollar amount can be forecast fairly accurately from historical records.

Shrinkage is an inventory reduction that is caused by shoplifting by employees or customers, by merchandise being misplaced or damaged, or by poor bookkeeping. The buyer measures shrinkage by taking the difference between:

- the inventory's recorded value based on merchandise bought and received
- the physical inventory in stores and distribution centres

(Physical inventories are typically taken semiannually.) Shrinkage varies by department and season. Typically, shrinkage also varies directly with sales. So if sales of men's tailored suits rise 10 percent, then the buyer can expect a 10 percent increase in shrinkage.

MONTHLY REDUCTIONS (LINE 4)

The buyer calculates the monthly reductions in the same way as the monthly sales. The total reductions are multiplied by each percentage in line 3. In Exhibit 11–5,

$$\text{April reductions} = \$16\ 500 \times 40\% = \$6600$$

		Spring			Summer		
	Six-month data	April	May	June	July	August	September
3. Reduc. % Distribution to Season	100.00%	40.00%	14.00%	16.00%	12.00%	10.00%	8.00%
4. Monthly Reductions	$16 500	$6600	$2310	$2640	$1980	$1650	$1320

BOM (BEGINNING-OF-MONTH) STOCK-TO-SALES RATIO (LINE 5)

The **stock-to-sales ratio** specifies the amount of inventory that should be on hand at the beginning of the month to support the sales forecast and maintain the inventory turnover objectives. Thus, a stock-to-sales ratio of 2 means that we plan to have twice as much inventory on hand at the beginning of the month as we plan to sell for that month.

$$\text{Stock-to-sales} = \frac{\text{BOM}}{\text{Sales}}$$

		Spring			Summer		
	Six-month data	April	May	June	July	August	September
5. BOM Stock to Sales Ratio	4.00	3.60	4.40	4.40	4.00	3.60	4.00

The stock-to-sales ratio is equivalent to the amount of **inventory** on hand at the beginning of the month to support sales forecast and maintain the inventory objective for the category. A stock-to-sales ratio of 2 means we have two months of inventory, or approximately 60 days, on hand at the beginning of the month. A stock-to-sales ratio of 1/2 represents a half month's supply of merchandise, or approximately 15 days. Many retailers express this relationship as weeks of inventory. **Weeks of inventory** is the months of supply times four weeks. So a stock-to-sales ratio and months of supply of 2 is equivalent to eight weeks of supply.

As you will see in the next few paragraphs, there is a direct relationship between GMROI, the sales-to-stock ratio, inventory turnover, and the stock-to-sales ratio. Importantly, if inventory turnover is six times per year, on average you have a two-month supply of inventory, or an eight-week supply, and a BOM stock-to-sales ratio of 2. Likewise, a 24 inventory turn represents only a half month's supply (2 weeks), or 15-day supply, that is, a BOM stock-to-sales ratio of 1/2.

The stock-to-sales ratios are calculated in four steps.

Step 1: Calculate Sales-to-Stock Ratio GMROI is equal to the gross margin percentage times the sales-to-stock ratio. The sales-to-stock ratio is conceptually similar to inventory turnover except the denominator in the sales-to-stock ratio is expressed in retail sales dollars, whereas the denominator in inventory turnover is the cost of goods sold (sales at cost). The buyer's target GMROI for the category is 123 percent, and the buyer feels the category will produce a gross margin of 45 percent. Thus,

To reduce losses from internal theft, this sophisticated security device enables security personnel to monitor checkout lanes and sales transactions simultaneously.

GMROI = Gross margin % × Sales-to-stock ratio

Sales-to-stock ratio = GMROI × Gross margin percent × 123 / 45 = 2.73

Because this illustration of a merchandise budget plan is for a six-month period rather than a year, the sales-to-stock ratio is based on six months rather than annual sales. So for this six-month period, sales must be 2.73 times the inventory at cost to meet the targeted GMROI.

Step 2: Convert the Sales-to-Stock Ratio to Inventory Turnover Inventory turnover is

Inventory turnover = Sales-to-stock ratio × (1.00　Gross margin %　100)

= 2.73　　　　　× (1.00　45 100)

1.50　　　= 2.73　　　　　×　.55

This adjustment is necessary because the sales-to-stock ratio defines sales at retail and inventory at cost, whereas inventory turnover defines both sales and inventory at cost. Like the sales-to-stock ratio, this inventory turnover is based on a six-month period.

Step 3: Calculate Average Stock-to-Sales Ratio The average stock-to-sales ratio is

Average stock-to-sales ratio = 6 months / Inventory turnover

= 6 / 1.5

= 4

If preparing a 12-month plan, the buyer divides 12 by the annual inventory turnover. Since the merchandise budget plan in Exhibit 11–5 is based on retail dollars, it's easiest to think of the numerator as BOM retail inventory and the denominator as sales for that month. Thus, to achieve a six-month inventory turnover of 1.5, on average, the buyer must plan to have a BOM inventory that equals four times the amount of sales for a given month, which is equivalent to four months, or 16 weeks, of supply.

One needs to be careful when thinking about the average *stock-to-sales ratio*, which can be easily confused with the *sales-to-stock ratio*. These ratios are not the inverse of each other. Sales are the same in both ratios, but stock in the sales-to-stock ratio is the average inventory at cost over all days in the period, whereas stock in the stock-to-sales ratio is the average BOM inventory at retail. Also, the BOM stock-to-sales ratio is an average for all months. Adjustments are made to this average in line 5 to account for seasonal variation in sales.

Step 4: Calculate Monthly Stock-to-Sales Ratios The monthly stock-to-sales ratios in line 5 must average the stock-to-sales ratio calculated previously to achieve the planned inventory turnover. Generally, monthly stock-to-sales ratios vary in the opposite direction of sales. That is, in months when sales are larger, stock-to-sales ratios are smaller, and vice versa.

To make this adjustment, the buyer needs to consider the seasonal pattern for men's casual slacks in determining the monthly stock-to-sales ratios. In the idea situation, men's casual slacks would arrive in the store the same day and in the same quantity that customers demand them. Unfortunately, the real-life retailing world isn't this simple. Note in Exhibit 11–5 (line 8) that men's casual slacks for the spring season start arriving slowly in April ($4260 for the month), yet demand lags behind these arrivals until the weather starts getting warmer. Monthly sales then jump from 12 percent of annual sales in May and June to 19 percent in July (line 1). But the stock-to-sales ratio (line 5) decreased from 4.4 in May and June to 4.0 in July. Thus, in months when sales increase (e.g., July), the BOM inventory also increases (line 6) but at a slower rate, which causes the stock-to-sales ratios to decrease. Likewise, in months when sales decrease dramatically, such as in May (line 1), inventory also decreases (line 6), again at a slower rate, causing the stock-to-sales ratios to increase (line 5).

When creating a merchandise budget plan for a category such as men's casual slacks with a sales history, the buyer also examines previous years' stock-to-sales ratios. To judge how adequate these past ratios were, the buyer determines if inventory levels were exceedingly high or low in any months. Then the buyer makes minor corrections to adjust for a previous imbalance in inventory levels, as well as for changes in the current environment. For instance, assume the buyer is planning a promotion for Memorial Day. Since this promotion has never been done before, the stock-to-sales ratio for that May should be adjusted downward to allow for the expected increase in sales. Note that monthly stock-to-sales ratios don't change by the same percentage as the percentage distribution of sales by month is changing. In months when sales increase, stock-to-sales ratios decrease but at a slower rate. Because there is no exact method of making these adjustments, the buyer must make some subjective judgments.

BOM STOCK (LINE 6)

The amount of inventory planned for the beginning of the month (BOM) equals

BOM inventory = Monthly sales (line 2) × BOM stock-to-sales ratio (line 5)

When doing this multiplication, sales drops out of the equation, leaving BOM stock. In Exhibit 11–5,

$$\text{BOM stock for April} = (\$27\ 300) \times \left(\begin{array}{c}\text{BOM stock-to-sales}\\ \text{ratio } 3.6\end{array}\right) = \begin{array}{c}\text{BOM inventory}\\ \$98\ 280\end{array}$$

		Spring			Summer		
	Six-month data	April	May	June	July	August	September
6. BOM Inventory	$98 280	$98 280	$68 640	$68 640	$98 800	$98 280	$78 000

EOM (END-OF-MONTH) STOCK (LINE 7)

The BOM stock from the current month is the same as the EOM (end-of-month) stock in the previous month. So to derive line 7, the buyer simply moves the BOM stock in line 6 down one box and to the left.

In Exhibit 11–5, the EOM stock for April is the same as the BOM stock for May, $68 640. We must forecast ending inventory for the last month in the plan.

		Spring			Summer		
	Six-month data	April	May	June	July	August	September
7. EOM Inventory	$65 600	$68 640	$68 640	$98 800	$98 280	$78 000	$65 600

MONTHLY ADDITIONS TO STOCK (LINE 8)

The monthly additions to stock is the amount to be ordered for delivery in each month, given turnover and sales objectives.

Additions to stock = Sales (line 2) + Reductions (line 4) + EOM inventory (line 7) − BOM inventory (line 6)

In Exhibit 11–5,

Additions to stock for April = $27 300 + 6600 + 68 640 − 98 280 = $4260

		Spring			Summer		
	Six-month data	April	May	June	July	August	September
8. Monthly Additions to Stock	$113 820	$4260	$17 910	$48,400	$26 160	$8670	$8420

This formula isn't particularly enlightening, so consider the following explanation. At the beginning of the month, the inventory level equals BOM stock. During the month, merchandise is sold and various reductions, such as markdowns, occur. So BOM stock minus monthly sales minus reductions equals EOM stock if nothing is purchased. But something must be purchased to get back up to the forecast EOM stock. The difference between EOM stock if nothing is purchased (BOM stock − Sales − Reductions) and the forecast EOM stock is the additions to stock.

EVALUATING THE MERCHANDISE BUDGET PLAN

GMROI, inventory turnover, and the sales forecast are used for both planning and control. The previous sections have described how they all fit together in planning the merchandise budget. A buyer negotiates a GMROI, inventory turnover, and sales forecast goal based on the top-down/bottom-up planning process. Well in advance of the season, the buyer purchases the amount of merchandise found in the last line of the merchandise budget plan to be delivered in those specific months—the monthly additions to stock.

After the selling season, the buyer must determine how the category actually performed compared to the plan for control purposes. If the actual GMROI, turnover, and forecast are greater than those in the plan, then performance is better than expected. No performance evaluation should be based on any one of these measures; several additional questions must be answered to evaluate the buyer's performance: Why did the performance exceed or fall short of the plan? Was the deviation from the plan due to something under the buyer's control? (For instance, was too much merchandise purchased? Did the buyer react quickly to changes in demand by either purchasing more or having a sale? Was the deviation due to some external factor, such as a change in competitive level or economic activity?) Every attempt should be made to discover answers to these questions.

open-to-buy

The open-to-buy system starts after the merchandise is purchased using the merchandise budget plan or staple merchandise system. That is, these systems provide the buyer with a plan for purchasing merchandise. The **open-to-buy** system is one that keeps track of merchandise flows while they're occurring. Specifically, open-to-buy systems record how much is spent each month, and therefore how much is left to spend.

Even if everything in the buyer's merchandise budget goes according to plan, without careful attention to the recordkeeping performed in the open-to-buy system, the buyer might buy too much or too little. In order for the merchandise budget plan to be successful (i.e., meet the sales, inventory turnover, and GMROI goals for a category), the buyer attempts to buy merchandise in quantities and with delivery dates such that the actual EOM stock for a month will be the same as the projected or forecasted EOM stock. For example, at the end of September, which is the end of the spring/summer season, the buyer would like to be completely out of spring/summer men's tailored suits so there will be room for the fall collection. Thus, the buyer would want both the projected EOM stock and the actual EOM stock to equal zero.

CALCULATING OPEN-TO-BUY FOR THE CURRENT PERIOD

Buyers develop plans indicating how much inventory for the merchandise category will be available at the end of the month. However, these plans might be inaccurate. Shipments might not arrive on time, sales might be greater than expected, and/or reductions (price discounts due to sales) might be less than expected. The open-to-buy is the difference between the projected EOM inventory and the planned EOM inventory. Thus, open-to-buy for a month is:

exhibit 11–6   Six-Month Open-to-Buy

Loc - 10		Spring			Summer	
Merch - Aged Soft ...	April	May	June	July	August	September
EOM Stock Plan	$68,640	$68 640	$98 800	$98 280	$78 000	$65 600
EOM Actuals	$59 500					
BOM Stock Plan	$98 280	$68 640	$68 640	$98 800	$98 280	$78 000
BOM Stock Actual	$95 000	$59 500				
Monthly Additions Plan	$4 260	$17 910	$48 400	$26 160	$8 670	$8 420
Monthly Additions Actuals	$3 500	$7 000				
OnOrder	$45 000	$18 000	$48 400			
Sales Plan	$27 300	$15 600	$15 600	$24 700	$27 300	$19 500
Sales Actuals	$26 900					
Monthly Reductions Plan	$6 600	$2 310	$2 640	$1 980	$1 650	$1 320
Monthly Reductions Actuals	$1 650					
Projected EOM Stock Plan	$59 500	$66 590	$96 750	$70 070	$41 120	$20 300
Projected BOM Stock Plan	$24 570	$59 500	$66 500	$96 750	$70 070	$41 120
OTB	$0.00	$2 050	$2 050	$28 210	$36 880	$45 300

Open-to-buy = Actual EOM planned inventory – Projected EOM inventory

The EOM planned inventory is taken from the merchandise budget plan, and the EOM projected inventory is calculated as follows:

Projected EOM inventory = Actual BOM inventory
+ Monthly additions actual
   (received new merchandise)
+ On order (merchandise to be delivered)
– Sales plan (merchandise sold)
– Monthly reductions plan

Thus, the projected EOM inventory will be less than the planned EOM inventory if sales or reductions are greater than the merchandise budget plan or less merchandise is delivered than planned.

Exhibit 11–6 presents the six-month open-to-buy for the same category of men's casual slacks discussed in the fashion merchandise planning section of this chapter. Consider May as the current month. The BOM stock (inventory) actual level is $59 500, but there is no EOM actual inventory yet because the month hasn't finished. When calculating the open-to-buy for the current month, the projected EOM stock plan comes into play. Think of the projected EOM stock plan as a new and improved estimate of the planned EOM stock from the merchandise budget plan. This new and improved version takes information into account that wasn't available when the merchandise budget plan was made. The formula for projected EOM inventory for the category is

Projected EOM inventory = Actual BOM inventory $59 500
                          + Monthly additions actual   ⟶   + 7 000
                          + On order   ⟶   + 18 000
                          – Sales plan   ⟶   – 15 600
                          – Monthly reductions plan   ⟶   – 2 310
                          =   ⟶ $66 590

The open-to-buy for the current month is:

Open-to-buy plan = EOM inventory planned – Projected EOM inventory
$2050   = $68 640   – $66 590

Therefore, the buyer has $2050 left to spend in May to reach the planned EOM stock of $68 640. This is a relatively small amount, so we can conclude that the buyer's plan is right on target. But if the open-to-buy for May were $20 000, the buyer could then go back into the market and look for some great buys. If one of the vendors had too much stock of men's casual slacks, the buyer might be able to use the $20 000 to pick up some bargains that could be passed on to customers.

If, however, the open-to-buy was a negative $20 000, the buyer would have overspent the budget. Therefore, the buyer would have to cut back on spending in future months so the total purchases would be within the merchandise budget. Alternatively, if the buyer believed that the overspending was justified because of changes in the marketplace, a negotiation could take place between the buyer and the DMM, GMM, merchandise manager or planning director, etc. to negotiate open-to-buy (OTB).

allocating merchandise to stores

After developing a plan for managing merchandise inventory in a category, the next step in the merchandise management process is to allocate the merchandise purchased and received to the retailer's stores. Research has found that these allocation decisions have a much bigger impact on profitability than does the decision about the quantity of merchandise to purchase.[2] In other words, buying too little or too much merchandise has less impact on category profit than making mistakes in allocating the right amount and type of merchandise to stores. Thus, many retailers have created positions called either "allocators" or "planners" to specialize in making store allocation decisions. Allocating merchandise to stores involves three decisions: (1) how much merchandise to allocate to each store, (2) what type of merchandise to allocate, and (3) when to allocate the merchandise to different stores.

Exhibit 11–7 illustrates a traditional percentage contribution method through which a planner allocates additions to stock of $150 000 among 15 stores of girls' $35 denim jeans.

Chain stores traditionally classify their stores as *A*, *B*, or *C* stores based on their potential sales volume (column 1). This chain has four *A* stores, each of which is expected to sell 10 percent of the total, equaling $15 000 per store; three *B* stores, each expected to sell 6.7 percent, equaling $10 000 per store; and eight *C* stores, each expected to sell 5 percent, equaling $7500 per store (columns 2, 3, and 4). The percentage breakdown (column 3) is based on historical records for similar merchandise for that chain.

Every chain's allocation of merchandise to stores is different. A **core assortment** is a relatively large proportion of the total assortment that is carried by each store in the chain, regardless of size. The core assortment is necessary to maintain the image of the chain. If the chain were to cut back the assortment too far in smaller stores, customers would perceive the smaller stores as having an inferior assortment. Hence, smaller stores require a higher-than-average stock-to-sales ratio. The opposite is true for stores with larger-than-average sales.

If a store generates 4 percent of the sales of a classification for the chain, it should also receive 4 percent of the inventory. Note that stores with sales below 4 percent require proportionally more inventory. For instance, the smallest store, which generates only 1 percent of sales, requires 1.5 percent of the total inventory—inventory equals 1.5 times the level of sales.

Even though this store has low sales, it still needs to stock an adequate assortment and backup stock. Customers must not feel that just because the store is small or has relatively low sales that it isn't well stocked.

exhibit 11–7
Allocation Based
on Sales Volume
Breakdown by Store
of Traditional $35
Denim Jeans

(1) Type of Store	(2) Number of Stores	(3) Percentage of Total Sales, Each Store	(4) Sales per Store (total sales × col. 3)	(5) Sales per Store Type (col. 2 × col. 4)	(6) Unit Sales per Store (col. 4/$35)
A	4	10.0%	$15 000	$60 000	429
B	3	6.7	10 000	30 000	286
C	8	5.0	7 500	60 000	214
Total sales $150 000					

TYPES OF MERCHANDISE ALLOCATED TO STORES

The process of allocating merchandise to stores that was just described is useful for fashion merchandise and new staple items. As merchandise sells, it must be replenished, either by the vendor or through distribution centres. Retailers use either a pull or a push distribution strategy to replenish merchandise. With a **pull distribution strategy**, orders for merchandise are generated at the store level on the basis of demand data captured by point-of-sale terminals. With a **push distribution strategy**, merchandise is allocated to the stores on the basis of historical demand, the inventory position at the distribution centre, and the needs of the stores. A pull strategy is used by more sophisticated retailers because it's more responsive to customer demand.

The assortment offered in a ready-to-eat cereal aisle should match the demands of the demographics of shoppers in the local area.

In addition to classifying stores on the basis of their size and sales volume, retailers classify stores according to the characteristics of the stores' trading area. The profiles of trading areas are used in making store location decisions. Store trade area geodemographics are also used to develop merchandise assortments for specific stores. Consider the allocation decision of a national supermarket for its ready-to-eat cereal assortment. Some stores are located in areas dominated by segments called "Rustbelt Retirees," and other areas are dominated by the "Laptops and Lattes segment."

The ready-to-eat breakfast cereal buyer would certainly want to offer different assortments for stores in these two areas. Stores with a high proportion of older retirees in their trading areas would have better results with an assortment of lower priced, well-known brands and less expensive private-label cereals. Stores in areas dominated by the Laptops and Lattes geodemographic segment would do better with an assortment with higher priced brands that are low in sugar, organic, and whole wheat. President's Choice private-label brands would be favoured by an upwardly mobile market segment.

Even the sales of different apparel sizes can vary dramatically from store to store in the same chain. Some stores sell significantly more large sizes and fewer small sizes than is average for the chain. If the buyer allocated the same size distribution of merchandise to all stores in the chain, Store X would stock out of large sizes, have an oversupply of small sizes, or be out of some sizes sooner than other stores in the chain.

analyzing merchandise performance

As part of the ongoing merchandise planning process, retailers should continually ask when to add or delete SKUs, vendors, classifications, or departments. Here we examine three procedures for analyzing merchandise performance.

* The first, known as *ABC analysis*, is a method of rank-ordering merchandise to make inventory stocking decisions.
* The second procedure, *a sell-through analysis*, compares actual and planned sales to determine whether early markdowns are required or whether more merchandise is needed to satisfy demand.

- The third approach is a method for evaluating vendors using the *multiattribute model.*

ABC ANALYSIS—EVALUATING THE ASSORTMENT PLAN AND VENDORS

An **ABC analysis** identifies the performance of individual SKUs in the assortment plan. It is used to determine what SKUs should be in the plan and how much backup stock and resulting product availability is provided for each SKU in the plan. In an ABC analysis, the SKUs in a merchandise category are rank ordered by several performance measures, such as sales, gross margin, inventory turnover, and GMROI. Typically, this rank order reveals the general 80–20 principle; namely, approximately 80 percent of a retailer's sales or profits come from 20 percent of the products. This principle suggests that retailers should concentrate on products that provide the biggest returns.

- *A items* are those that account for 5 percent of items and represent 70 percent of sales. These items should never be out of stock. *A* items can be expensive to carry because they generally require high levels of backup stock to buffer against variations in demand and lead times. They include most sizes of long- and short-sleeve white and blue dress shirts.

- *B items* represent 10 percent of the SKUs and an additional 20 percent of sales. The store should pay close attention to the *B* items, which include some of the other better-selling colours and patterned shirts. Occasionally, however, it will run out of some SKUs in the *B* category because it's not carrying the same amount of backup stock as for *A* items.

- *C items* account for 65 percent of SKUs but contribute only 10 percent of sales. The planner may plan to carry *C* items only in certain odd sizes (very small or very large), with special orders used to solve out-of-stock conditions.

- Although the analysis is called *ABC*, there are also *D* items. *D items*, the remaining 20 percent of SKUs, had no sales whatsoever during the past season, having become out of date or shopworn. Not only is excess merchandise an unproductive investment, but it also distracts from the rest of the inventory and clutters the store. Most retailers with excess merchandise should have a simple decision strategy: Mark it down or give it away, but get rid of it.

The first step in the *ABC analysis* is to rank-order SKUs using one or more criteria. The most important performance measure for this type of analysis is contribution margin:

Contribution margin = Net sales – Cost of goods sold – Other variable expenses

An example of an "other variable expense" in retailing is sales commissions. It's important to do *ABC* analyses using multiple performance measures since different measures give the planner different information. Other measures commonly used in *ABC* analysis are:

- sales dollars
- sales in units
- gross margin
- GMROI

For instance, offering batteries supports the retailer's brand strategy. Although batteries may be sold at a low price, they are important in supporting the sale of items such as cameras and flashlights. Selling batteries minimizes the likelihood of customers visiting other stores where they could develop post-purchase anxiety if they were to observe other items at lower prices. Retailers want to build tall fences around their customers, and an in-stock position of supplementary items contributes to building retail loyalty.

Sales or gross margin per square metre measures are also useful in *ABC* analyses. For instance, a line of sunglasses may not appear particularly profitable in comparison to other items on the basis of contribution margin, sales, or units. But the display also takes relatively little space. Thus, performance of the merchandise on a square-metre basis may be very high. Check www.bizstats.com for "sales per foot and sales per store."

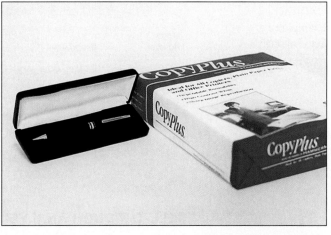

At Staples Office Depot, copier paper is an "A" item, whereas a Mont Blanc pen is a "B" item. What could be a "C" item at Staples Office Depot?

The next step is to determine how items with different levels of profit or volume should be treated differently. Consider the dress shirts for a chain of men's stores in Exhibit 11–8. Even though the exact distribution varies across products, the general shape of the curve is the same for most types of products due to the *80–20 principle*. Here the planner has defined the *A, B, C,* and *D* SKUs by rank-ordering each SKU by sales volume and examining the distribution of those sales.

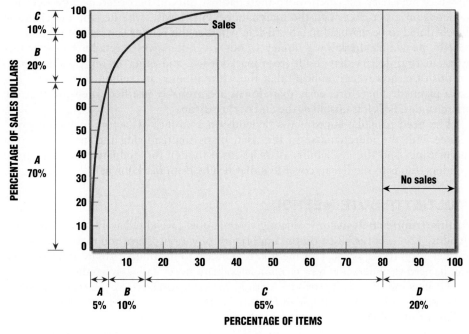

exhibit 11–8
ABC Analysis for Dress Shirts

exhibit 11–9

Example of a
Sell-Through
Analysis for Blouses

Stock Number		Description	WEEK 1			WEEK 2		
				Actual-to-Plan			Actual-to-Plan	
			Plan	Actual	Percentage	Plan	Actual	Percentage
1011	Small	White silk V-neck	20	15	–25%	20	10	–50%
1011	Medium	White silk V-neck	30	25	–16.6	30	20	–33
1011	Large	White silk V-neck	20	16	–20	20	16	–20
1012	Small	Blue silk V-neck	25	26	4	25	27	8
1012	Medium	Blue silk V-neck	35	45	29	35	40	14
1012	Large	Blue silk V-neck	25	25	0	25	30	20

SELL-THROUGH ANALYSIS EVALUATING MERCHANDISE PLAN

A **sell-through analysis** compares actual and planned sales to determine whether early markdowns are required or whether more merchandise is needed to satisfy demand. Exhibit 11–9 shows a sell-through analysis for blouses for the first two weeks of the season. Because the blouses are high fashion items, the buyer believes that, if necessary, corrective action should be made to the buying plan after only two weeks. In reality, this corrective action is likely too soon after only two weeks of exposure, but should be based on early season traffic.

Examine the week 1 columns for the first SKU, the small white blouse. Planned sales were 20 units. The actual sales were 15 units. Therefore, the actual-to-plan percentage was –25 percent [(15 – 20) ÷ 20 = –25 percent]. This means that actual sales were 25 percent less than the planned sales. In fact, the actual-to-plan percentage is negative for all of the white blouses and positive for all of the blue blouses.

What should the buyer do? There's no exact rule for determining when a markdown is necessary or when more merchandise should be ordered. The decision depends on experience with the merchandise in the past, whether the merchandise is scheduled to be featured in advertising, whether the vendor can reduce the buyer's risk by providing markdown money (funds a vendor gives a retailer to cover lost gross margin dollars that result from markdowns), and other merchandising issues. In this case, however, it appears that the white blouses are selling significantly less than planned. Therefore, early markdowns are probably justified to ensure that the merchandise isn't left unsold at the end of the season.

The need to make adjustments depends on a variety of factors including experience with the merchandise in the past, plans for featuring the merchandise in advertising, and the availability of markdown money for evaluating vendors from vendors (funds to retailer to cover loss that results from markdowns).

MULTIATTRIBUTE METHOD

Multiattribute analysis for evaluating vendors uses a weighted average score for each vendor. This score is based on the importance of various issues and the vendor's performance on those issues. This method is identical to the multiattribute approach that can be used to understand how customers evaluate stores and merchandise.

To illustrate the multiattribute method for evaluating vendors, either current or proposed, consider the example in Exhibit 11–10 for a vendor of men's tailored suits. A buyer can evaluate vendors by using the following five steps:

1. *Develop a list of issues to consider in the decision* (column 1).[3] The list should be balanced to access several issues of vendor performance.

Issues (1)	Importance Evaluation of Issues (I) (2)	Brand A (P_a) (3)	Brand B (P_b) (4)	Brand C (P_c) (5)	Brand D (P_d) (6)
PERFORMANCE EVALUATIONS OF INDIVIDUAL BRAND ACROSS ISSUES					
Vendor reputation	9	5	9	4	8
Service	8	6	6	4	6
Meets delivery dates	6	5	7	4	4
Merchandise quality	5	5	4	6	5
Markup opportunity	5	5	4	4	5
Country of origin	6	5	3	3	8
Product fashionability	7	6	6	3	8
Selling history	3	5	5	5	5
Promotional assistance	4	5	3	4	7
Overall evaluation $\sum_{i=1}^{n} I_j * P_{ij}$		290	298	212	341

exhibit 11–10

Evaluating a Vendor: A Weighted Average Approach

$\sum_{i=1}^{n}$ = Sum of the expression

I_j = Importance weight assigned to the i/th dimension

P_{ij} = Performance evaluation for j/th brand alternative on the i/th issue

1 = Not important

10 = Very important

2. *Include a ranking* for each issue in column 1. This importance ranking should be determined by the buyer/planner in conjunction with the merchandise manager (column 2). Here we used a scale of 1 to 10, where 1 equals not important and 10 equals very important. In developing these importance scores, be sure that all issues don't receive high (or low) ratings. For instance, the buyer and the merchandise manager might believe that vendor reputation should receive a 9 since it's very important. Merchandise quality could receive a 5 since it's moderately important. Finally, a vendor's selling history is less important, so it could be rated 3.

3. *Make judgments* about each individual brand's performance on each issue (the remaining columns). This procedure should also be a joint decision between the category and merchandise managers. Note that some brands have high ratings on some issues but not on others.

4. *Evaluate the overall performance* score of each vendor by combining the importance ranking and performance scores of the vendor. We do this by multiplying the importance for each issue by the rating given to the vendor for performance. For instance, vendor reputation importance (9) multiplied by the vendor performance rating (5) for brand *A* is 45. Vendor promotional assistance importance ranking (4) multiplied by the vendor performance rating (7) for vendor *D* is 28. This type of analysis illustrates an important point: It doesn't pay to perform well on issues that customers don't believe are very important. Although vendor *D* performed well on promotional assistance, the buyer didn't rate this issue highly on importance so the resulting score was still low.

5. *Determine a vendor's overall rating*, add the products for each brand for all of the issues. In Exhibit 11–10, brand *D* has the highest overall rating (341), so *D* is the preferred vendor.

information systems and supply chain management

Retailers continue to embrace the "science of merchandising," making intelligent use of retail data. Using transaction data and analytics to generate added value in areas such as markdown optimization and inventory management, business intelligence solutions are helping retailers to better understand how their suppliers are working, how they are servicing their customers, and the profitability of their different product groups.

When you walk into a Bay store to buy a Black & Decker toaster, your transaction triggers a series of information flows that result in merchandise replenishment. Your toaster is scanned at the point of sale (POS). The information on the black-and-white bar code (UPC, or universal product code) goes directly to a computer at The Bay's regional distribution centre and, importantly, to Black & Decker's computer as well.

When a specified number of toasters are sold, a replenishment order is automatically generated from the POS data and sent electronically to The Bay's distribution centre. There is a loading dock assigned at a specified time waiting for the truck from Black & Decker to arrive. The Black & Decker merchandise is unloaded, combined with merchandise from other vendors, and immediately loaded onto a Bay truck going to the store that is running out of toasters. As a result of this immediate access to information, both The Bay and Black & Decker know exactly what, where, and when something is being sold. Additionally, Bay stores collect information on customers to be used to plan promotions and to merchandise their stores. By sharing this information, The Bay and Black & Decker have become partners in this supply chain. Everyone benefits. Black & Decker can plan its production and distribution activities, and The Bay has better merchandise availability because it works together with Black & Decker to get merchandise to stores.

We now describe how retailers can gain a strategic advantage through supply chain management. We then examine supply chain information flows, with an emphasis on how retailers communicate with their vendors over the Internet. This is followed by a discussion of merchandise flows from the point of sale at the store, to distribution centres, and on to vendors.

strategic advantages gained through supply chain management

Supply chain management is the integration of business processes from end user through original suppliers that provides products, services, and information that add value for customers.[4]

Retailers may be the most important link in the marketing supply chain. It is the retailers' responsibility to gauge customers' wants and needs and work with the other members of the supply chain—wholesalers, manufacturers, transportation companies—to make sure the merchandise customers want is available when they want it. A simplified supply chain is illustrated in Exhibit 11–11. Manufacturers ship merchandise either to a distribution centre operated by a retailer (as is the case for manufacturers M_1 and M_3), or they ship directly to stores (as is the case for manufacturer M_2). The relative advantages of shipping directly to stores versus to distribution centres will cut out a number of costs.

Retailers have increasingly taken a leadership position in their respective supply chains. Over the past 30 years, chains such as Wal-Mart, Carrefour (France), 7-Eleven (Japan), Home Depot, and Zara (Spain) have grown to dominate and control their

exhibit 11–11   A Simplified Supply Chain

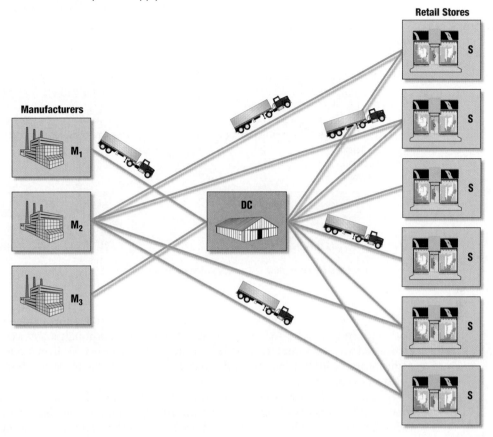

supply chains. Not only does size generate power, but knowledge of their customers plays a vital role as well. As a result of their position in the supply chain, retailers are in a unique position to collect information about their customers' transactions, and provide details of product preferences. This knowledge can help suppliers to plan production, promotions, deliveries, assortments, and inventory levels.

IMPROVED PRODUCT AVAILABILITY

An efficient supply chain has two benefits for customers:

- fewer stockouts
- assortments of merchandise that customers want, when and where they want them.

These benefits translate into greater sales, higher inventory turns, and lower markdowns for retailers.

To meet the specific needs of a wide variety of customers, retailers are carrying more stock keeping units (SKUs). For instance, only a few years ago a bath department in a discount store consisted of three sizes of towels in five colours. Now there are twice as many SKUs in towels, plus rugs, shower curtains, wastebaskets, toothbrush holders, and other accessories—all in matching colours and patterns. This SKU explosion means that the retailer must carry additional inventory that needs to be carefully managed and distributed.

exhibit 11–12
Information and
Merchandise Flows

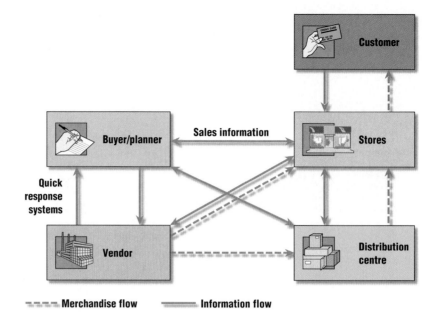

Merchandise flow   **Information flow**

The challenge is national, and even international, in scope for many chain stores. Bath and Body Works, for instance, has 1600 stores.[5] Although many items are carried at all stores, some are tailored to meet the needs of local markets. Without sophisticated supply chain and information systems, it would be impossible for the chain to stay in stock.

Exhibit 11–12 shows the complexities of the merchandise and information flows in a typical multistore chain. Although information and merchandise flows are intertwined, in the following sections we describe how information on customer demand is captured at the store and then triggers a series of responses from the buyer, distribution centre, and vendor that are designed to ensure that merchandise is available at the store when the customer wants it.

the flow of information

The flow of information is complex in a retail environment. A purchase will trigger a series of information messages throughout the system (depicted in Exhibit 11–13). We'll use the purchase of a pair of jeans as an example:

1. The sales associate scans the UPC tag on the jeans. A sales receipt is created.

2. The purchase information is recorded in the POS terminal and sent to the buyer/planner. The buyer/planner uses this information to plan additional purchases and make markdown decisions.

3. The purchase information is typically aggregated by the retailer, and an order is created and sent to the vendor using a system called electronic data interchange (EDI)—the computer-to-computer exchange of business documents from retailer to vendor, and back. Issues surrounding EDI are also discussed later in this section. In situations where the merchandise is reordered frequently, the ordering process can be automatic and virtually bypass the buyer. In other cases, such as for newer or more fashion-oriented items, the buyer's input is required prior to sending the order.

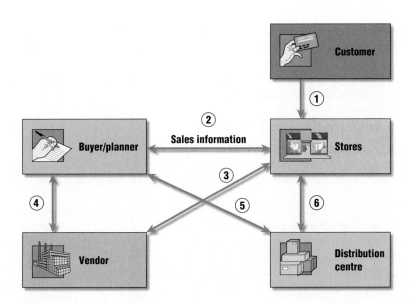

exhibit 11–13
Information Flows

4. The buyer/planner communicates with the vendor regarding the purchase order for the merchandise. At this point they often negotiate shipping dates and terms of purchase.

5. The buyer/planner communicates with the distribution centre to coordinate deliveries from the vendor and to the stores, check inventory status, and so on.

6. Store managers also communicate with the distribution centre to coordinate deliveries and check inventory status.

In the next sections of this chapter, we will explore how retailers store information in data warehouses and how the information is transmitted to vendors through EDI.

DATA WAREHOUSING

Purchase data collected at the point of sale goes into a huge database known as a data warehouse. (See flow number 2 in Exhibit 11–13.) A data warehouse is the coordinated and periodic copying of data from various sources, both inside and outside the enterprise, into an environment ready for analytical and informational processing.[6] The information stored in the data warehouse is accessible on several dimensions and levels, depicted in the data cube in Exhibit 11–14. As shown on the horizontal axis, data can be accessed by level of merchandise aggregation—SKU (item), vendor, category (dresses), department (women's apparel), or all merchandise. Along the vertical axis, data can be accessed by level of the company—store, division, or the total company. Finally, along the third dimension, data can be accessed by point in time—day, season, or year. Thus, a CEO interested in how the corporation is generally doing could look at the data by all merchandise, by division or total corporation, and by year. A buyer may be more interested in a particular vendor in a certain store, on a particular day.

Analysts from various levels of the retail operation extract information from the data warehouse for making a plethora of marketing decisions about developing and replenishing merchandise assortments. Data warehouses also contain detailed information about customers, which is used to target promotions and group products together in stores. On January 1, 2004, new privacy rules took effect in Canada that change the way companies do business and how marketers collect, use, and disclose customer information. The new legislation may impact the way data warehouses store and share customer information with their suppliers.

Now let's take a look at how information flows back and forth from retailer to vendor (flow numbers 3 and 4 in Exhibit 11–13).

ELECTRONIC DATA INTERCHANGE

Electronic data interchange (EDI) is the computer-to-computer exchange of business documents from retailer to vendor, and back. In addition to sales data, purchase orders, invoices, and data about returned merchandise are transmitted from retailer to vendor.

Many retailers now require vendors to provide notification of deliveries before they take place. An **advanced shipping notice (ASN)** is an electronic document received by the retailer's computer from a supplier in advance of a shipment. It tells the retailer exactly what to expect in the shipment. If accurate, the retailer can dispense with opening cartons and checking in merchandise. Information about on-hand inventory status, vendor promotions, and cost changes can be transmitted from vendor to retailer too, or in the case of vendor-affixed price tickets from retailer to vendor as well. It's also possible to exchange information about purchase order changes, order status, retail prices, and transportation routings by EDI.

There are a variety of ways in which EDI data can be transmitted: proprietary systems and web-based systems, which include intranets and extranets.

exhibit 11–14   Retail Data Warehouse

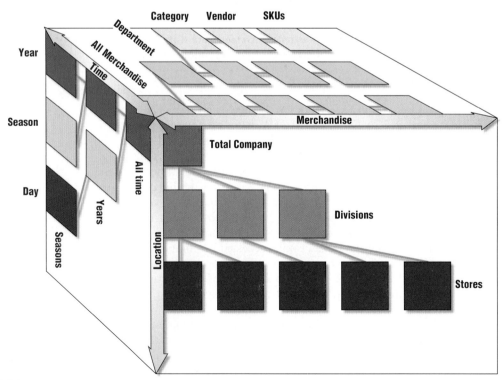

SOURCE: Marketmax.

Intranets Also available over the Internet are **intranets**, which are secure communication systems that take place within one company. For instance, in Exhibit 11–13, communications from store to buyer (flow 2), buyer to distribution centre (flow 5), and distribution centre to store (flow 6) could all be accomplished through intranets. Using intranets, buyers can communicate and coordinate with store and distribution centre personnel.

Extranets Increasingly, EDI data are transmitted over the Internet through extranets. An **extranet** is a collaborative network that uses Internet technology to link businesses with their suppliers, customers, or other businesses. Extranets are typically private and secure in that they can be accessed only by certain parties. An extranet is generally an extension of a company's intranet, modified to allow access by specified external users. Although the largest retailers and their vendors have embraced EDI through proprietary networks for some time, the Internet empowers smaller concerns—particularly international vendors—that could not afford to implement their own systems to participate in a secure system and take advantage of EDI.

Radio Frequency Identification Technology **Radio Frequency Identification (RFID) Technology** is rapidly evolving technology that enables the consumer-driven supply chain by providing improved business insight. RFID-based inventory visibility and management systems help make merchandising more efficient, facilitate shelf-level management, and streamline the replenishment process. RFID technologies provide real-time data collection and detection of product via automated messages received by an RFID antenna which reads radio frequency tags on product facilitated by an RFID reader which disseminates data. The benefits include a positive shopping experience for the customer, simplified merchandise processing for sales associates, and cost reduction for the retailer.

- Reduced over-ordering and over-production on the part of the supplier
- Reduced inventory in stores
- Increased inventory turns
- Increased efficiency for employees in finding and handling inventory facilitating inventory replenishment
- Reduced loss on date-coded items
- Reduced shrinkage

From the customer's point of view, RFID facilitates merchandise selection in the store. Customer self-selection is facilitated by an RFID display that indicates how many garments are on the shelf and in which sizes, helping to reduce disorder and customer frustration. A fitting room RFID scanner will identify merchandise when it goes in and keeps track of it until it goes back on the shelf or out to the cash register.

RFID technology will allow businesses to follow inventory from manufacturing, by tracking shipments and distribution, to stores, and onto the retail floor, taking into account the consumer who demands the widest possible selection of product at the lowest price. RFID is expected to be one of the most important technologies for business success.

refact
According to supply chain specialists, US\$200 billion to US\$300 billion in excess inventory and missed sales in the United States could be eliminated through closer collaboration between retailers and their suppliers.[8]

Product tracking
Technologies, such as RFID, to provide realtime data collection and detection of product in the pipeline. Sends automated messages to the event engine.

RFID

Tag

Antenna

Reader

Popular in the grocery and drug industries, **collaboration, planning, forecasting, and replenishment (CPFR)** is an inventory management system using EDI in which a retailer will send information to a manufacturer and the manufacturer will use the data to construct a computer-generated replenishment forecast that will be shared with the retailer before it's executed. Using CPFR, the manufacturer and retailer jointly decide on replenishment issues.

SECURITY

To help control this changing information environment, retailers need to develop a corporate security policy. A **security policy** is a set of rules that apply to activities in the computer and communications resources that belong to an organization. Although security policies cover theft and the security of individuals and property, we will limit our discussion here to network security. It is not enough, however, to have a security policy; retailers must train employees and add the necessary software and hardware to enforce the rules.

The security policy should meet the following objectives:

- *Authentication.* The system should be able to ensure or verify that the person or computer at the other end of the session really is what it claims to be.

- *Authorization.* The system should be able to ensure that the person or computer at the other end of the session has permission to carry out the request.

- *Integrity.* The system should be able to ensure that the arriving information is the same as that sent. This means that the data are protected from unauthorized changes or tampering (data integrity).

the physical flow of merchandise—logistics

refact

Corporations have become obsessed with driving down logistics-related costs, including transportation and warehousing. Logistics accounts for about 10 percent of the U.S. gross domestic product.[11]

Logistics is that part of the supply chain process that plans, implements, and controls the efficient, effective flow and storage of goods, services, and related information from the point of origin to the point of consumption in order to meet customers' requirements.[9] Supply chain management includes logistics, but it is a more comprehensive and strategic concept that includes customer relationship management, inventory management, and vendor relations.[10] For instance, supply chain management would be involved in new-product development because logistics considerations may affect the profitability of a new product. When Ford Motor Company's engineers design a new component for its cars, for example, they attempt to get all divisions, including Jaguar and Mazda, involved. The entire supply chain would be more efficient if newly designed parts could be manufactured at one or several strategically located plants and then shipped globally. In this section, however, we will concentrate on issues limited to the physical flow of merchandise.

Exhibit 11–15 illustrates the different merchandise flows.

- Merchandise flows from vendor to distribution centre.

- Merchandise then goes from distribution centre to stores.

- Alternatively, merchandise can also go from vendor directly to stores.

Sometimes merchandise is temporarily stored at the distribution centre; other times it's immediately prepared to be shipped to individual stores. This preparation may include breaking shipping cartons into smaller quantities that can be more readily utilized by the individual stores (breaking bulk), as well as tagging merchandise

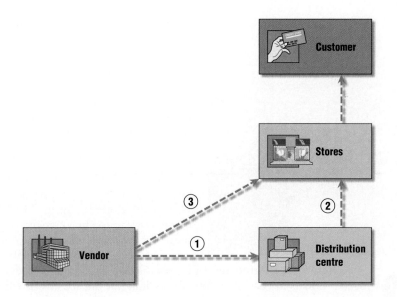

exhibit 11–15
Merchandise Flows

with price tags or stickers, UPC codes, and the store's label. A **UPC code** is the black-and-white bar code printed on the package of most products—UPC stands for universal product code.

Logistics has presented new challenges and opportunities for multichannel retailers.

QUICK RESPONSE DELIVERY SYSTEMS

There are only two groups of retail businesses today: the quick and the dead.[12]

Quick response (QR) delivery systems are inventory management systems designed to reduce the retailer's lead time for receiving merchandise, thereby lowering inventory investment, improving customer service levels, and reducing logistics expenses. QR is the integrating link between the information and the merchandise flows depicted in Exhibit 11–12.

Many of the concepts that comprise QR systems have been previously discussed in this chapter. In this section, however, we describe how they all work together. The origins of the present QR systems were derived from just-in-time (JIT) initiatives undertaken by manufacturers and adapted for retailing. QR is part of the efficient consumer response (ECR) initiatives undertaken by packaged goods manufacturers and food and drugstore retailers.[13] EDI facilitates the exchange of data between retailer and vendors.

Originally, quick response delivery systems seemed better suited to basic items—such as underwear, paper towels, or toothpaste—than to high fashion. By its nature, however, fashion dictates being able to adjust quickly to the changing seasons as well as to new colours and styles. Thus, quick response is as important in managing fashion inventories as in managing basic-item inventories. Fashion retailers need to determine what's selling (so it can be reordered quickly) and what isn't selling (so it can be marked down).

To illustrate a QR system, consider how the system works at Zara.[14] Zara, located in Galicia, Spain, is now the third-largest clothing retailer in the world, with profits growing at 30 percent per year. It operates over 500 stores in 31 countries, including nine Candian stores—in Toronto, Montreal, Quebec City, Calgary, and Vancouver.

refact

Almost all food items are marked with a UPC bar code. In fact, Wal-Mart's buying office has a sign reading, IF YOUR PRODUCT DOESN'T HAVE A BAR CODE, DON'T BOTHER TO TAKE A CHAIR IN OUR WAITING ROOM.

refact

Who returns merchandise? Women and affluent customers are more likely to return items than men and university students.[15]

Instead of shipping new products once a season like many fashion retailers, Zara makes deliveries to each of its stores every few days. Small shipments more often are the key to QR systems.

The process starts with the store managers, who are equipped with handheld devices linked directly to the company's design rooms in Spain. They report daily on what customers are buying, scorning, and asking for but not finding. For instance, when buyers found that customers were requesting a purple shirt that was similar to one they were selling in pink, they passed this information on to the designers in Spain. Fabrics are cut and dyed by robots in the company's 23 highly automated factories in Spain. The final assembly is entrusted to a network of 300 or so small shops that are located near the factories in Galicia and Northern Portugal.

Because Zara controls the entire production and design process, it can make products in very small lots. By so doing, it can see how the first few hundred items are selling before making more. Instead of shipping new products once a season like many fashion retailers, Zara makes deliveries to each of its stores every few days. The purple shirts were in stores in two weeks—compared to the several months it would take for most department stores and other specialty apparel stores to accomplish the same feat. Small shipments more often are the key to QR systems.

Benefits of a QR System   The benefits of a QR system are reduced lead time, increased product availability, lower inventory investment, and reduced logistics expenses.

Reduces Lead Time   By eliminating the need for paper transactions using the mail, overnight deliveries, or even fax, EDI in the QR system reduces lead time. Lead time is the amount of time between the recognition that an order needs to be placed and its arrival in the store, ready for sale. Since the vendor's computer acquires the data electronically, no manual data entry is required on the recipient's end. As a result, lead time is reduced even more, and vendor recording errors are eliminated. Thus, use of EDI in the QR system can cut lead time by a week or more. Shorter lead times further reduce the need for inventory because the shorter the lead time, the easier it is to forecast demand; therefore, the retailer needs less inventory.

Zara successfully reduces lead time by communicating electronically with the factory, by using automated equipment, by using assemblers who are in close proximity to the factory, and by using premium transportation such as air freight to get merchandise to the stores.

Increases Product Availability and Lowers Inventory Investment   In general, as a retailer's ability to satisfy customer demand by being in stock increases, so does its inventory investment. Yet with QR, the ability to satisfy demand can actually increase while inventory decreases! Since the retailer can make purchase commitments or produce merchandise closer to the time of sale, its inventory investment is reduced. Stores need less inventory because they're getting less merchandise on each order, but they receive shipments more often. Inventory is further reduced because the retailer isn't forecasting sales so far into the future. For instance, fashion retailers that don't use QR make purchase commitments as much as six months in advance and receive merchandise far in advance of actual sales. QR systems align deliveries more closely with sales.

The ability to satisfy customer demand by being in stock also increases in QR systems as a result of the more frequent shipments. For instance, if a Zara store is running low on a medium kelly-green sweater, its QR system will ensure a shorter lead time than that of more traditional retailers. As a result, it's less likely that the Zara store will be out of stock before the next sweater shipment arrives.

Reduces Logistics Expenses   QR systems also have the potential to significantly reduce logistics expenses. Many retailers receive merchandise in their distribution centres, store it, consolidate shipments from multiple vendors, attach price labels and theft prevention devices, and then reship the merchandise to stores. Retailers have two options for reducing these logistics expenses using QR systems. They can either use a crossdocking warehouse system or they can negotiate a direct store delivery system. Crossdocking eliminates storage and some handling costs. Direct store delivery eliminates all distribution centre costs and transportation costs from the distibution centre to stores. If the merchandise is floor-ready, there's no need to devote expensive retail space to receiving and processing merchandise in the store, and sales associates can devote all of their attention to their customers.

Costs of a QR System   Although retailers achieve great benefits from a QR system, it's not without costs. The logistics function has become much more complicated with more frequent deliveries. With greater order frequency come smaller orders, which are more expensive to transport. The greater order frequency also makes deliveries and transportation more difficult to coordinate.

retailing view   11.1
AMAZON.COM SHIPS 200 000 ITEMS A DAY

Ever since it built five vast warehouses, Amazon.com has boasted of the wonders of the machinery inside them—16 kilometres of conveyer belts and myriad other gadgets. Amazon is focused on filling orders accurately.

One big goal had been to reduce errors that occur in keeping track of the several million items continually being placed onto and pulled off of hundreds of thousands of bins on metal shelves. To reduce errors, Amazon wrote new software to take better advantage of the gizmo that each warehouse worker was already carrying—a shoe-horn-size device that combines a bar-code scanner, a display screen, and a two-way data transmitter. The new software checks their work by forcing them to scan each item every time they put it on or take it off a shelf.

Amazon also built a special sorting machine. The machine reads the bar code on each item and routes it into one of 2100 chutes, each chute representing an order for a single customer. When all the items in an order are in the chute, a light flashes, and a worker rushes to put them in a box. They are then sent on other conveyers to machines that print packing slips, seal the boxes, and send them off to shippers' trucks.

Source: Saul Hansell, "Amazon Ships to Sorting Machine Beat," *New York Times,* NYTimes.com January 21, 2002. Reprinted by permission.

At Amazon.com, an Internet order is filled using sophisticated material handling equipment.

QR systems also require a strong commitment by the retailer and its vendors to cooperate, share data, and develop systems such as EDI and CPFR. Successful QR systems not only require financial support from top management but also a psychological commitment to become partners with their vendors. Large retailers often apply their power to get their vendors to absorb many of these expensive logistics costs.

THE LOGISTICS OF ELECTRONIC RETAILING

Fulfilling Internet orders from customers is very different from distributing merchandise to stores. Retailers with stores are concerned with moving a large amount of merchandise from distribution centres to individual stores. These distribution centres typically have automated material-handling equipment and warehouse-management software linked to store POS terminals. Internet retailers, on the other hand, have outbound shipments averaging 1.8 items per order that are shipped to addresses all over the world.[16]

How do traditional retailers with a successful Web presence handle these two disparate distribution tasks? Some, like Staples Business Depot, have a fully integrated information system, whereby distribution to stores and to customers ordering through a Web site or catalogue is handled by the same information system. Yet they use different distribution centres to service stores and Internet and catalogue customers. Staples Business Depot makes deliveries by trucks or UPS. Sharper Image, which started as a catalogue merchant, now operates almost 100 stores in the United States and has a fast-growing Web site. One distribution centre serves all three retail formats. Catalogue and Web orders are treated identically but are separated from the store-based distribution system. Toys "R" Us is partnering with Internet retailers such as Amazon.com to assist it in online fulfillment needs.

SUMMARY

This chapter examines buying systems and tools that help buyers determine how much to buy. Retailers use two distinct buying systems: *staple merchandise* for basics and *merchandise budget* for fashion merchandise. Buying systems for staple merchandise are very different than for fashion merchandise. Since information is available on past sales for each SKU, it is relatively straightforward to forecast future merchandise needs.

The sales forecast and inventory turnover work together to drive the merchandise budget plan for fashion merchandise. The sales forecast is broken down by month, based on historical seasonality patterns. It's necessary to purchase more in months when sales are forecast to be higher than average. Planned inventory turnover is converted to stock-to-sales ratios and used in the merchandise budget plan to determine the inventory level necessary to support sales. Monthly stock-to-sales ratios are then adjusted to reflect seasonal sales patterns. The end product of the merchandise budget planning process is the dollar amount of merchandise a buyer should purchase each month for a category if the sales forecast and inventory turnover goals are to be met.

The open-to-buy system begins where the merchandise budget plan and staple goods inventory management systems leave off. It tracks how much merchandise is purchased for delivery in each month. Using an open-to-buy system, buyers know exactly how much money they've spent compared to how much they plan to spend.

Once the merchandise is purchased, merchandise buyers in multistore chains must allocate the merchandise to stores. Not only must the buyers look at the differences in sales potential among stores, but they also must consider the differences in the characteristics of the customer base.

In the end, the performance of buyers, vendors, and individual SKUs must be determined. We examined three different approaches to evaluating merchandise performance. In *ABC* analysis, merchandise is rank-ordered from highest to lowest. The merchandising team uses this information to set inventory management policy. For example, the most productive SKUs should carry sufficient backup stock so as to never be out of stock. The second evaluation technique, sell-through analysis, is more useful for examining the performance of individual

SKUs. The buyer compares actual-to-planned sales to determine whether more merchandise needs to be ordered or whether the merchandise should be put on sale. Finally, the multiattribute method is most useful for evaluating vendors' performance. The chapter concludes with Appendix 11A, in which we examine the retail inventory method.

Supply chain management and information systems have become important tools for achieving a sustainable competitive advantage. Customers are demanding better product availability and broader assortments than in the past. Developing more efficient methods of distributing merchandise creates an opportunity to reduce expenses and improve customer service levels.

The systems used to control the flow of information to buyers and on to vendors have become quite sophisticated. Retailers have developed data warehouses that provide them with intimate knowledge of who their customers are and what they like to buy. These data warehouses are being used to strengthen the relationship with their customers and improve the productivity of their marketing and inventory management efforts. Data warehouses must comply with Canadian privacy legislation as implemented in 2004. Electronic data interchange enables retailers to communicate electronically with their vendors. The Internet has accelerated the adoption of EDI, especially among smaller, less sophisticated vendors. Information security has become such an important issue in the world of multichannel retailing that retailers are advised to adopt a stringent security policy.

Quick response delivery systems represent the nexus of information systems and logistics management. QR systems reduce lead time, increase product availability, lower inventory investment, and reduce overall logistics expenses. Retailers are forcing their vendors to supply them with floor-ready merchandise and adhere to strict delivery schedules as part of their quick response delivery system. Other retailers are having vendors deliver merchandise directly to their stores and are using pull logistics strategies that base inventory policy on consumer demand. Retailers are outsourcing many of these logistics functions to third-party logistics companies. RFID is expected to become one of the most important technologies for major retailers by improving the customer experience, employee efficiency, and the retailer's profit.

KEY TERMS

ABC analysis, *302*

advanced shipping notice (ASN), *310*

backup stock, *287*

base stock, *287*

basic stock list, *288*

buffer stock, *287*

collaboration, planning, forecasting, and replenishment (CPFR), *312*

core assortment, *300*

cycle stock, *287*

electronic data interchange (EDI), *310*

extranet, *311*

fill rate, *288*

intranet, *311*

inventory, *294*

lead time, *287*

logistics, *312*

multiattribute analysis, *304*

open-to-buy, *298*

order point, *290*

pull distribution strategy, *301*

push distribution strategy, *301*

quick response (QR) delivery system, *313*

Radio Frequency Identification (RFID) Technology, *311*

safety stock, *287*

security policy, *312*

sell-through analysis, *304*

shrinkage, *294*

stock-to-sales ratio, *294*

supply chain management, *306*

UPC code, *313*

weeks of inventory, *294*

Get Out & Do It!

1. **OLC EXERCISE** *Learning*Centre The merchandise budget plan determines how much merchandise should be purchased in each month of a fashion buying season (in dollars), given the sales and reduction forecast, inventory turnover goals, and the seasonal monthly fluctuations in sales.

Access the Online Learning Centre at www. mcgrawhill.ca/olc/levy and click on Merchandise Budget Plan. The merchandise budget plan generally covers one fashion season for one merchandise category. This application presents both a one-month and a six-month example. In addition, practice calculations are presented for the one-month example. So have your calculator ready. Finally, in the calculation section you have access to an Excel-based six-month merchandise budget plan that can be used for doing Case number 20 in the text.

2. **OLC EXERCISE** The Vendor Evaluation Model utilizes the multiattribute method for evaluating vendors described in the chapter.

Access the Online Learning Centre at www. mcgrawhill.ca/olc/levy and click on Vendor Evaluation Model. There are two spreadsheets. Open the first spreadsheet, vendor evaluation 1.xls. This spreadsheet is the same as Exhibit 11–10. If you were selling Brand A to the retailer, which numbers would change? Change the numbers in the matrix and see the effect of the numbers you might change on the overall evaluation.

Go to the second spreadsheet, labelled evaluation 2.xls. This spreadsheet can be used to evaluate brands or merchandise you might stock in your store. Assume you own a bicycle shop. List the brands you might consider stocking and the issues you would consider in selecting brands to stock. Fill in the importance of the issues (10 = very important, 1 = not very important) and the evaluation of each brand on each characteristic (10 = excellent, 1 = poor). Determine which is the best brand for your store.

3. **INTERNET EXERCISE** Oracle Corporation is the world's second-largest independent software company and the information management company of choice for 70 percent of the *Fortune* 500 and 64 percent of the *Fortune* 100. Oracle uses Internet technology to help businesses manage information so that it is reliable, secure, and accessible to the right people, at the right time. Go to www.oracle.com and see how it can help manage retailers' information flow.

4. **INTERNET EXERCISE** SAP, a German firm, specializes in integrated software solutions. Go to www.sap.com/products/industries/retail/index.aspx and see what it's doing to help retailers.

5. **INTERNET EXERCISE** The Council of Logistics Management is the premier industry organization in the logistics area. Go to its Web site (www.clm1.org) and find out about new trends in logistics.

6. **INTERNET EXERCISE** According to The Bay's home page, available at http://www.hbc.com/, the company has a Merchandise Focus with an emphasis on basic merchandise—staple, everyday items that consumers use and need most. Combined with an aggressive fashion strategy, this foundation in basics enables The Bay to compete as a life-style trend merchandiser in all merchandise categories, from apparel to personal care, and home decor. How does this retailer manage a buying system to ensure that both staple and fashion merchandise are properly stocked to meet customer demand?

DISCUSSION QUESTIONS AND PROBLEMS

1. Inventory shrinkage can be a problem for many retailers. How does the merchandise budget planning process account for inventory shrinkage?

2. Using the following information, calculate additions to stock:

Sales	$24 000
EOM stock	$90 000
BOM stock	$80 000

3. Using the following information, calculate the average beginning-of-month stock-to-sales ratio for a six-month merchandise budget plan:

GMROI   150%
Gross margin   40%

4. Today is July 19. The buyer is attempting to assess his current open-to-buy given the following information:

Actual BOM stock	$50 000
Monthly additions actual	25 000
Merchandise on order to be delivered	10 000
Planned monthly sales	30 000
Planned reductions	5 000
Planned EOM stock	65 000

What is the open-to-buy on July 19? What does this number mean to you?

5. Now it is July 31 and we need to calculate the open-to-buy for August given the following information:

Planned monthly sales	$20 000
Monthly additions actual	40 000
Planned markdowns	5 000
Projected BOM stock	50 000
Projected EOM stock	30 000

Calculate open-to-buy and explain what the number means to you.

6. Typically, August school supplies sales are relatively low. In September, sales increase tremendously. How does the September stock-to-sales ratio differ from the August ratio?

7. Using the 80–20 principle, how can a retailer make certain that there's enough inventory of fast-selling merchandise and a minimal amount of slow-selling merchandise?

8. What's the order point and how many units should be reordered if a food retailer has an item with a 7-day lead time, 10-day review time, and daily demand of 8 units? Say 65 units are on hand and the retailer must maintain a backup stock of 20 units to maintain a 95 percent service level.

9. A buyer at a sporting goods store in Vancouver receives a shipment of 400 ski parkas on October 1 and expects to sell out by January 31. On November 1, the buyer still has 375 parkas left. What issues should the buyer consider in evaluating the selling season's progress?

10. If you have a stock-to-sales ratio of 2, how many months of supply do you have? How many weeks of supply?

11. Retail system acronyms include QR, EDI, POS, and UPC. How are these terms related to each other?

12. Explain how QR systems can increase a retailer's level of product availability and decrease its inventory investment.

13. This chapter has presented trends in logistics and information systems that benefit retailers. How do vendors benefit from these trends?

14. What would you include in the ideal retailing data warehouse? Why would you include it?

15. Why haven't more fashion retailers adopted a quick response system similar to Zara's?

16. Why is global logistics much more complicated than domestic logistics?

17. A buyer is trying to decide from which vendor to buy a certain item. The item can be purchased as either a manufacturer brand or private-label brand. Using the following information, determine which vendor the buyer should use.

Data for Question 17

	PERFORMANCE EVALUATIONS OF BRANDS		
Issues	Importance Weight	Manufacturer Brand	Private-Label Brand
Vendor reputation	8	5	5
Service	7	6	7
Meets delivery dates	9	7	5
Perceived merchandise quality	7	8	4
Markup opportunity	6	4	8
Demand-generating ability	5	7	5
Promotional assistance	3	6	8

CHAPTER 12

buying strategies

Executive Briefing

David Russell, Co-owner and President, Sporting Life

Sporting Life is a 24-year-old success story in the competitive Canadian sportswear marketplace. The privately owned company operates four stores in Toronto and Collingwood, Ontario, with estimated annual sales of $100 million. The company's distinctive strategy has an unusual merchandise mix of high-end fashions with sporting goods, selling snowboards alongside designer labels such as DKNY and Hugo Boss. A master at good timing, Sporting Life is riding the wave of popular athletic-inspired fashions.

Sporting Life has become an industry leader with its distinctive strategy of following the hottest trends in both fashion and sport, stocking over 200 brand names. But the basics are also always available for customers who want mainstream products such as Nike and Lacosta. The core sporting goods of skis, snowboards, racquets, and running equipment remain the mainstays of the merchandise mix. Productivity levels are excellent, averaging $5375 per square metre (by comparison, Wal-Mart estimates sales at $4730 a square metre).

Sporting Life's original three owners are active in the day-to-day operations of the business, with each having a personal special area of responsibility. Brian McGrath is responsible for footwear, Patti Russell deals with fashion, and David Russell looks after hard goods such as sports equipment

QUESTIONS   What branding options are available to retailers?

What issues should retailers consider when sourcing internationally?

How do retailers prepare for and conduct negotiations with their vendors?

Why are retailers building strategic relationships with their vendors?

and advertising. This designation of responsibilities recognizes the importance of experience and knowledge needed to develop Sporting Life's high performance strategy. The store has grown from the early days of having a staff of 15 to now having close to 700 associates.

According to David Russell, the company's spokesperson, it is important to understand the extremely competitive nature of Canadian retailing. Shoppers today are value hunters, and as upscale as the retailer is, Sporting Life recognizes that consumers are looking for a deal. The promotion strategy includes full-page newspaper ads emphasizing discounts, a newly conceived loyalty program that rewards its top 20 000 customers with gift coupons worth up to $50, four times a year, and a fully integrated digital marketing and communications strategy that includes instore digital and an interactive network.

Sources: Marina Strauss, "Sporting Life Puts Game Plan to Test." *Globe and Mail*, August 22, 2003; and Larry Till, "Rag-Trade Troubles." *The Metropolitan Business Journal*, Toronto: September 1990.

The process that buyers go through to determine what and how much merchandise to buy is not all analytical. There are lots of subjective issues that buyers and their merchandise managers must deal with strategically and on a day-to-day basis.

Specifically, retailers must determine their branding strategy. Should they buy well-known national brands, or should they develop private brands under their own name? The issue of branding goes hand in hand with international sourcing decisions, particularly for those retailers purchasing private-label merchandise. How should retailers determine whether they should buy merchandise made in other countries or from their home country?

Retailers also must determine how and where they will meet and communicate with their vendors. Will it be face to face or over the Internet? Negotiations occur when communicating with vendors on purchasing. There are many issues, such as price and delivery times, that need to be negotiated. Retailers need to plan ahead for these negotiations and leave as little as possible to chance.

Many retailers have developed strategic partnerships with some of their vendors. There is a trend toward developing long-term strategic relationships with key suppliers. These partnerships enable the collaboration needed to develop efficient supply chains as well as joint merchandise and marketing programs. In this chapter, we examine why these relationships can be important and what it takes to solidify a strategic partnership.

branding strategies

Buyers have lots of branding choices. They can buy manufacturer brands such as Levi's, Kellogg's, or Black & Decker. Or they can develop their own private labels such as Gap jeans, President's Choice cookies from Loblaws, or Craftsman tools from Sears. Some use a mix of the two. In this section, we examine the relative advantages of these branding decisions, which are summarized in Exhibit 12–1.

MANUFACTURER BRANDS

Manufacturer brands, also known as **national brands,** are products designed, produced, and marketed by a vendor and sold to many different retailers. The manufacturer is responsible for developing the merchandise and establishing an image for the brand. In some cases, the manufacturer will use an umbrella or family-branding strategy in which its name appears as part of the brand name for a specific product, such as Kellogg's Corn Flakes. However, some manufacturers, such as Philip Morris—owner of Kraft Foods, Miller Brewing Company, as well as Philip Morris (tobacco products)—don't associate their name with the brand.

Some retailers organize some of their categories around their most important national brands. For instance, buyers in department stores are responsible for brands, such as Clinique or Estée Lauder, rather than for products, such as lipstick and fragrances. Clothing is also often organized by manufacturer brand (e.g., Polo/Ralph Lauren, Levi's, Liz Claiborne, or DKNY). These brands often have their own boutique within stores. Managing a category by national brand, rather than a more traditional classification scheme, is useful so that merchandise can be purchased in a coordinated manner around a central theme.

Buying from vendors of manufacturer brands can help store image, traffic flow, and selling/promotional expenses. Retailers buy from vendors of manufacturer brands because they have a customer following—people go into the store and ask for them by name. Loyal customers of manufacturer brands generally know what to expect from the products and feel comfortable with them; for example, Samsonite luggage.

Manufacturers devote considerable resources to creating demand for their products. As a result, relatively less money is required by the retailer for selling and promotional expenses for manufacturer brands. For instance, Guess? Inc., manufacturer of jeans and other casual clothing, attempts to communicate a constant and focused message to the consumer by coordinating advertising with in-store promotions and displays.

exhibit 12–1

Relative Advantages of Manufacturer versus Private Brands

Impact on Store	TYPE OF VENDOR	
	Manufacturer Brands	Private-Label Brands
Store loyalty	?	+
Store image	+	+
Traffic flow	+	+
Selling and promotional expenses	+	−
Restrictions	−	+
Differential advantages	−	+
Margins	?	?

+ advantage to the retailer, − disadvantage to the retailer, ? depends on circumstances.

Manufacturer brands typically have lower realized gross margins than private-label brands. These lower gross margins are due to the manufacturer assuming the cost of promoting the brand and increased competition among retailers selling these brands. Typically, many retailers offer the same manufacturer brands in a market so customers compare prices for these brands across stores. Retailers often offer significant discounts on some manufacturer brands to attract customers to their stores.

Liz Claiborne (cotton top), Nike (Pegasus running shoes), and Levi's jeans are among the most recognized national brands in the U.S.

Stocking national brands may increase or decrease store loyalty. If the manufacturer brand is available through a limited number of retail outlets (e.g., Lancôme cosmetics or Diesel jeans), customers loyal to the manufacturer brand will also become loyal to the stores selling the brand. If, on the other hand, manufacturer brands are readily available from many retailers in a market, customer loyalty may decrease because the retailer can't differentiate itself from the competition.

Another problem with manufacturer brands is that they can limit a retailer's flexibility. Vendors of strong brands can dictate how their products are displayed, advertised, and priced. Jockey, for instance, tells retailers exactly when and how its products (such as underwear) should be advertised.

Licensed Brands A special type of manufacturer brand is a **licensed brand**, in which the owner of a well-known brand name (licensor) enters a contract with a licensee to develop, produce, and sell the branded merchandise. The licensee may be either the retailer that contracts with a manufacturer to produce the licensed product or a third party that contracts to have the merchandise produced and then sells it to the retailer. Fashion designers often license their name to sunglass and perfume companies.

Licensed brands' market share has grown increasingly large in recent years. Owners of trade names not typically associated with manufacturing have also gotten into the licensing business. For instance, the manufacturer of the sweatshirt or baseball cap emblazoned with your university or college's logo pays your school a licensing fee. If it didn't, it would be infringing on the university or college's logo (a trademark) and therefore would be involved in counterfeiting.

PRIVATE-LABEL BRANDS

Private-label brands, also called **store brands,** are products developed by a retailer and available for sale only from that retailer. Victoria's Secret and The Gap are in the top 20 private-label brands. Exhibit 12–2 gives examples of more private-label brands. Retailers typically develop specifications for the merchandise and then contract with manufacturers who are often located in countries with developing economies to produce the products. But the retailer, not the manufacturer, is responsible for promoting the brand.

The size of retail firms has increased through consolidation, and private labels have assumed a new level of significance by establishing distinctive identities among retailers. Some retailers, such as The Gap and Club Monaco, sell their own labels exclusively as an integral element of their distinctiveness. Other retailers, such as The Bay and Sears, successfully mix manufacturer brands with their own retailer brands to project their unique image statement.

> **refact**
> Macy's was among the first department stores to pioneer the concept of private brands for fashion goods. In the 1890s, its "Macy's" and "Red Star" brands were the rage in New York.[2]

exhibit 12–2

Examples of Private-Label Brands

Industry	Store	Brand
Grocery stores	A&P	Master Choice
	Loblaws	President's Choice
	Sobey's	Our Compliments, Smartchoice
Mass merchandisers	Wal-Mart	Sam's Choice, B.U.M.
	Zellers	Truly
Department stores	The Bay	Baycrest, House and Home
	Sears	Kenmore, Craftsman, Martha Stewart
Specialty stores	Canadian Tire	Mastercraft
	Holt Renfrew	Holts, Miss Renfrew
	Home Depot	Husky

refact

Private labels are big business in Europe: Aldi's private brands account for 95 percent of its sales; Lidl, 80 percent; Sainsburys, 60 percent; Tesco's, 40 percent; Wal-Mart in Europe, 40 percent; and Carrefour, 33 percent.[5]

Private-branded products now account for an average of 25 percent of the purchases in North America and roughly 45 percent in Europe.[3] Private-label dollar volume in supermarkets, drug chains, and mass merchandisers is increasing twice as fast as national brands.

Private labels have always added value to retailers, and The Bay, Sears, and Zellers are clearly leading the way. The Bay claims 60% of its apparel assortment is private brand, and this trend is expected to grow. Holt Renfrew, a retailer that earns most of its profit from carrying powerful, high-fashion brand names, has 25% of their apparel inventory in private brands with desirable price points.

Consumer attitudes are driving the trend. Consumers are replacing more expensive brands with private brands from retailers. The trend seems to be about price rather than designer label: Eighty percent of the jeans sold in Canada are under $39.00.

Offering private labels provides a number of benefits to retailers, as Exhibit 12–1 shows.

- The exclusivity of strong private labels boosts store loyalty. For instance, the MotoMaster line of auto parts and accessories in Canadian Tire won't be found at other stores.

- Private labels enhance store image if the brands are of high quality and fashionable.

- Successful private-label brands can draw customers to the store. They can be a good deal—10 to 18 percent less expensive than national brands in Canada and as much as 25 percent cheaper in Europe.[4]

- Retailers that purchase private-label brands don't have the same restrictions on display, promotion, or price that often encumber their strategy with manufacturer brands. Retailers purchasing private brands also have more control over manufacturing, quality control, and distribution of the merchandise.

- Gross margin opportunities may be greater with private-label brands.

But there are drawbacks to using private-label brands. Although gross margins may be higher for private-label brands than for manufacturer brands, there are other expenses that aren't readily apparent. Retailers must make significant investments to design merchandise, create customer awareness, and develop a favourable image for their private-label brands. When private-label manufacturers are located outside

Canada, the complications become even more significant. Sales associates may need additional training to help them sell private-label brands against better-known brands. If the private-label merchandise doesn't sell, the retailer can't return the merchandise to the manufacturer. These problems are most severe for high-fashion merchandise.

Private-Label Options[6]   Retail branding strategies have run the gamut from closely imitating manufacturer-brand packaging and products to distinct brand images, from low product quality and prices to premium positioning, and from non-existent promotion and merchandising to intense activity. We group private brands into four broad categories: generic, premium, copycat, and parallel.

Generic branding targets a price-sensitive segment by offering a no-frills product at a discount price. Known as **generic** or **house brands,** such unbranded, unadvertised merchandise is found mainly in drug, grocery, and discount stores. The generic brand, frequently referred to as the house brand, generally is perceived by the consumer to be of lower quality, and its packaging identifies it as a brand of the retailer.

In the context of differentiating the retailer, generic branding is primarily defensive. Its value comes from neutralizing competitors who may gain an advantage from discount pricing and by serving a secondary market segment whose patronage potentially leads to collateral sales.

Premium branding offers the consumer a private label at a comparable manufacturer-brand quality, usually with modest price savings. A&P's Master Choice brand in grocery products is an example. The premium brand attempts to match or exceed the product quality standard of the prototypical manufacturer brand in its category. There is no intention to duplicate the packaging or to trade off the brand equity of a particular manufacturer brand. However, consumers frequently perceive the retailer premium labels as competing manufacturer brands.

Retailer premium brands, with the appearance of comparability, compete directly with manufacturer national brands. To succeed, the retailer must commit the resources in market research, product development, quality control, and promotion in its market area commensurate with its manufacturer-brand competitors. Consequently, development of a premium branding program precludes many retailers that have few resources from diverting to this strategy.

Copycat branding imitates the manufacturer brand in appearance and packaging, generally is perceived to be of lower quality, and is offered at a lower price. For example, copycat brands abound in the fragrance market. By not drawing attention to the brand's origin, the copycat can confuse the consumer about the source of the product. Copycat branding is a risky private-branding alternative because close copies can violate packaging and patent laws. Poor copies are ineffective.

Parallel branding represents private labels that closely imitate the packaging and product attributes of leading manufacturer brands but with a clearly articulated "invitation to compare" in its merchandising approach and on its product label. This invitation to compare on the product label was the basis for a recent legal action. Like copycat branding, parallel branding seeks to benefit from the brand equity of the manufacturer brand by closely imitating the national brand's packaging and product qualities. However, the invitation to compare leaves little doubt that different manufacturers produce the two products. Consequently, the imitative packaging does not constitute a trademark infringement. Nevertheless, patent considerations can be an issue if appropriate discretion is not used.

Parallel branding is a leveraging strategy used to bolster a retailer's private-brand sales. The closer two products are in form, logo, labelling, and packaging, the more they are perceived as substitutes. Parallel brands attempt to produce a product and packaging so similar to the manufacturer brand that the only noticeable difference between the two is price. This promotes the view that the parallel brand provides better value for the consumer. Manufacturer brands produce store traffic, and the parallel brand leverages this traffic into parallel brand sales through similar packaging and aggressive store signage, displays, and shelf location.

A BRAND OR A STORE?

The distinction between a store and a brand has become blurred in recent years. Some large retailers have developed strong private-label merchandise. Other retailers, such as Roots, have such a strong brand name that the average consumer cannot make a distinction between store and brand. Roots, the Canadian casual clothing retailer, has capitalized on its strong name recognition by widening the variety of merchandise offered at its stores. It now sells a range of products, including home decorating items. Manufacturers are trying to emulate the success of retailers such as Zara, whose name has become a brand in its own right.

A natural extension of the retailer's brand strategy is to exploit strong retail name recognition by selling its products through channels other than its own stores. For instance, Roots sells its products to The Bay and runs Olympic retail promotions. Starbucks made one of the most aggressive moves by a retailer to broaden its customer base. The coffee shop retailer that brought North America the "decaf latte" has teamed up with PepsiCo to market Frappuccino, a coffee-and-milk blend sold through traditional grocery channels. Starbucks is also engaged in a joint venture with Dreyer's Grand Ice Cream to distribute Starbucks coffee-flavoured ice cream and has entered into a long-term licensing agreement with Kraft Foods, Inc., to accelerate the growth of the Starbucks brand in the grocery channel.

On the other side of the distribution spectrum, several firms that have traditionally been exclusively manufacturers have become retailers. Examples are Guess?, Calvin Klein, Ralph Lauren, Levi's, Harley-Davidson, Sony, and Nike. Why have these manufacturers chosen to become retailers?

- First, by becoming retailers they have total control over the way their merchandise is presented to the public. They can price, promote, and merchandise their line with a unified strategy. They don't have to worry about retailers cherry-picking certain items or discounting the price, for instance.

- Second, they can use these stores to test new merchandise and merchandising concepts. Based on these tests' results, they can better advise other retailers what to buy and how to merchandise their stores.

- Third, these manufacturers/retailers use their stores to showcase their merchandise to the public as well.

- Finally, although these stores often compete with stores that carry the same merchandise, some would argue that having a stronger retail presence creates a name recognition and synergy between the manufacturer and retailer that benefits both parties.

international sourcing decisions

A decision that's closely associated with branding decisions is to determine where the merchandise is made. Retailers involved in private branding are faced with many challenges related to international sourcing decisions. Retailers buying manufacturer brands usually aren't responsible for determining where the merchandise is made, but a product's country of origin is often used as a signal of quality. Certain items are strongly associated with specific countries, and products from those countries, such as gold jewellery from Italy or cars from Japan, often benefit from those linkages.

In this section, we'll first examine the cost implications of international sourcing decisions. Initially, it often looks like retailers can get merchandise from foreign suppliers more cheaply than from domestic sources. Unfortunately, there are lots of hidden costs, including managerial issues, associated with sourcing globally that make this decision more complicated. We then examine the trend toward sourcing closer to home or actually reversing the trend toward international sourcing by buying "made in Canada." This section concludes by exploring ethical issues associated with retailers who buy from vendors engaged in human rights and child-labour violations.

COSTS ASSOCIATED WITH GLOBAL SOURCING DECISIONS

A direct reason for sourcing globally rather than domestically is to save money. Retailers must examine several cost issues when making these decisions. The cost issues discussed in this chapter are country-of-origin effects, foreign currency fluctuations, tariffs, free trade zones, inventory carrying costs, and transportation costs.

Country-of-Origin Effects   The next time you're buying a shirt made in Western Europe (e.g., Italy, France, or Germany), notice that it's probably more expensive than a comparable shirt made in a developing country such as Hungary, Ecuador, or Cambodia. These Western European countries have a reputation for high fashion and quality. Unfortunately for the Canadian consumer, however, the amount of goods and services that can be purchased from those countries is significantly less than the amount of merchandise that can be purchased from developing countries for the same amount of money. When making international sourcing decisions, therefore, retailers must weigh the savings associated with buying from developing countries with the image associated with buying merchandise from a country that has a reputation for fashion and quality.

Other countries might have a technological advantage in the production of certain types of merchandise and can therefore provide their products to the world market at a relatively low price. For example, Japan has always been a leader in the development of consumer electronics. Although these products often enter the market at a high price, the price soon drops as Japanese manufacturers learn to produce the merchandise more efficiently.

Foreign Currency Fluctuations   An important consideration when making global sourcing decisions is fluctuations in the currency of the exporting firm. Unless currencies are closely linked, for example, between Canada and the United States, changes in the exchange rate will increase or reduce the cost of the merchandise.

Suppose, for instance, that The Bay were purchasing watches from Swatch in Switzerland for $100 000, which would be equivalent to 150 000 Swiss francs (SFr) if the exchange rate were 1.5 SFr for each dollar. If the dollar

When making global sourcing decisions, retailers must consider country-of-origin effects. Switzerland is known for its quality watches; Japan for high-quality, reliable automobiles.

Maquiladoras are manufacturing plants in Mexico that make goods and parts or process food for export. They are very popular because their costs are lower than those of their Canadian and U.S. counterparts.

fell to, say, 1.1 SFr before the firm had to pay for the watches, it would end up paying $136 364 (or 150,000 SFr ÷ 1.1). The euro has all but eliminated this problem among the participating European countries.

Tariffs A **tariff**, also known as a **duty**, is a tax placed by a government on imports.[9] Import tariffs have been used to shield domestic manufacturers from foreign competition and to raise money for the government. In general, since tariffs raise the cost of imported merchandise, retailers have always had a strong incentive to reduce them. The General Agreement on Tariffs and Trade (GATT), the North American Free Trade Agreement (NAFTA), and foreign trade zones all reduce tariffs.

World Trade Organization The World Trade Organization (WTO) replaced GATT in 1996. With 144 member-countries, the WTO has become the global watchdog for free trade. As a result of the WTO and its predecessor GATT, worldwide tariffs have been reduced from 40 percent in 1947 to an estimated 4 percent in 2000.[10] The WTO will continue to push for tariff reductions on manufactured goods as well as liberalization of trade in agriculture and services.

North American Free Trade Agreement The ratification of NAFTA on January 1, 1994, created a tariff-free market with 364 million consumers. NAFTA members are currently Canada, the United States, and Mexico. NAFTA is expected to strengthen North America's position when negotiating with the European Union.

Canadian retailers gain from NAFTA for two reasons. First, Mexican labour is relatively low-cost and abundant. Thus, retailers can either search for low-cost suppliers in Mexico or begin manufacturing merchandise there themselves. **Maquiladoras**—plants in Mexico that make goods and parts or process food for export—are plentiful, have lower costs than their Canadian counterparts, and are located throughout Mexico, particularly in border towns such as Nogales and Tijuana. Second, with the growing importance of quick response inventory systems, the time it takes to get merchandise into stores becomes ever more critical. Transit times are shorter and managerial control problems are reduced when sourcing from Mexico, compared to the Far East or Europe.

refact

In 2001, the WTO welcomed more than a quarter of the world's population into its membership, including China, Chinese Taipei, Lithuania, and Moldova.[11]

Free Trade Zones Retailers involved in foreign sourcing of merchandise can lower import tariffs by using free trade zones. A **free trade zone** is a special area within a country that can be used for warehousing, packaging, inspection, labelling, exhibition, assembly, fabrication, or transshipment of imports without being subject to that country's tariffs.

To illustrate how a free trade zone can benefit retailers, consider how German cars are imported to a foreign trade zone in Guatemala for distribution throughout Central America. The duty for passenger vehicles is 100 percent of the landed cost of the vehicle. The duty for commercial vehicles, however, is only 10 percent. The German manufacturer imported commercial vans with no seats or carpeting, and with panels instead of windows. After paying the 10 percent import duty, it converted the vans to passenger station wagons in the free trade zone in Guatemala and sold them throughout Latin America.

Inventory Carrying Cost   The cost of carrying inventory is likely to be higher when purchasing from suppliers outside Canada than from domestic suppliers.

$$\text{Cost of carrying inventory} = \text{Average inventory value (at cost)} \times \frac{\text{Opportunity cost of capital}}{}$$

The **opportunity cost of capital** is the rate available on the next best use of the capital invested in the project at hand. It would include the cost of borrowing money for a similar investment, plus insurance and taxes.

refact

Together, America's NAFTA partners, Canada and Mexico, purchase 27 percent of U.S. agricultural exports.[12]

Transportation Costs   In general, the farther merchandise has to travel, the higher the transportation cost will be for any particular mode of transportation. For instance, the cost of shipping a container of merchandise by ship from China to Vancouver is significantly higher than the cost from Panama to Vancouver. Quick delivery via air express will increase end costs significantly.

MANAGERIAL ISSUES ASSOCIATED WITH GLOBAL SOURCING DECISIONS

In the previous section, we examined the specific costs associated with global sourcing decisions. In most cases, retailers can obtain hard cost information that will help them make their global sourcing decisions. The managerial issues discussed in this section—quality control and developing strategic partnerships—are not as easily evaluated.

Quality Control   When sourcing globally, it's harder to maintain and measure quality standards than when sourcing domestically. Typically, these problems are more pronounced in countries that are far away and underdeveloped. For instance, it's easier to address a quality problem if it occurs on a shipment of dresses from Costa Rica to Canada than if the dresses were shipped from Jakarta because Costa Rica is much closer than Indonesia.

Why are many Canadian retailers buying more merchandise made in North America?

• It may be less expensive.

• It is consistent with quick response inventory systems.

• Their customers prefer it.

• There are concerns about abuses of human rights and child labour in factories in other countries.

There are both direct and indirect ramifications for retailers if merchandise is delayed because it has to be remade due to poor quality. Suppose The Bay is having pants made in Haiti. Before the pants leave the factory, The Bay representatives find that the workmanship is so poor that the pants need to be remade. This delay reverberates throughout the system. The Bay could have extra backup stock to carry it through until the pants can be remade, but more likely, however, it won't have advance warning of the problem, so the stores will be out of stock.

A more serious problem occurs if the pants are delivered to the stores without the problem having been detected. This could happen if the defect is subtle, such as inaccurate sizing. Customers can become irritated and question merchandise quality. Also, markdowns ensue because inventories become unbalanced and shopworn.

Building Strategic Partnerships   The importance of building strategic partnerships is examined later in this chapter. It is typically harder to build these alliances when sourcing globally, particularly when the suppliers are far away and in underdeveloped countries. Communications are more difficult. There is often a language barrier, and there are almost always cultural differences. Business practices—everything from terms of payment to the issues of trade practices such as commercial bribery—are different in a global setting. The most important element in building a strategic alliance—maintaining the supplier's trust—is more arduous in an international environment.

SOURCE CLOSE TO HOME OR BUY "MADE IN CANADA"?

Some retailers are shifting suppliers from Asia and Europe to nearby Central American and Caribbean countries, or they're seeking products made in Canada. There are four reasons for this shift:

- First, it may be more profitable for the reasons detailed above.

- Second, quick response delivery systems and sourcing globally are inherently incompatible. Yet both are important and growing trends in retailing. Quick response systems are based on short and consistent lead times. Vendors provide frequent deliveries with smaller quantities. There's no room for defective merchandise. For a quick response system to work properly, there needs to be a strong alliance between vendor and retailer that is based on trust and a sharing of information through electronic data interchange (EDI) or radio frequency identification data (RFID) and collaborative planning, forecasting, and replenishment (CPFR). In the preceding section we argued that each of these activities is more difficult to perform globally than domestically. Further, the level of difficulty increases with distance and the vendor's sophistication. Catalogue and Internet retailer Coldwater Creek (www.coldwatercreek.com), for instance, sources about 75 percent of its merchandise from North America so it can purchase relatively small orders and receive quick delivery.[13]

- Third, some of their customers prefer products that are made in Canada. Retailers are simply reacting to their customers' quality perceptions.

refact

American territories overseas are an attractive site for garment factories producing for consumers in the United States. Minimum wage is lower than on the mainland— U.S. $3.05 an hour in Saipan—and products can come in without import quotas or tariffs and bear a Made in America label. In Saipan, 30 factories make clothes for dozens of American brands such as The Gap, Dayton Hudson, and The Limited.[14]

In response to the anti-sweatshop movement, high-profile companies like Reebok, Nike, and Liz Claiborne Inc. are publishing reports about audits undertaken in their factories.

• Fourth, it's easier to police potential violations of human rights and child labour. The Bay, Ralph Lauren, The Gap, Nordstrom, J. Crew, The Limited, and others have had to publicly deflect allegations about human rights, child labour, or other abuses involving factories and countries where their goods are made.[15]

Long the target of anti-globalization movements, Gap Inc released a report in the spring of 2004 outlining its monitoring and enforcement of labour standards among its global suppliers. The report details by region the compliance efforts at the hundreds of factories in its supply chain. The Hudson's Bay Co., which operates The Bay and Zellers, included an update of its global compliance effort in its annual report. The Bay, motivated by their stockholders, hosted senior executives from international department store chains and established labour standards for a factory monitoring system in the developing world. See www.hbc.com media centre.[16]

Canadian consumers must understand that they are going to have to balance their desire for low prices with their concern for social responsibility before Third World sweatshop conditions improve dramatically. Unfortunately, there has been very little effort from the majority of Canadian retailers to improve Third World labour conditions.[17]

connecting with vendors

Now that we've examined the different branding decisions available to retailers and the issues surrounding global sourcing, we will concentrate on how and where retailers connect with their vendors. Retailers "go to market" to see the variety of available merchandise and to buy. A **market,** from the retail buyer's perspective, is a concentration of vendors within a specific geographic location, perhaps even under one roof or over the Internet. These markets may be Internet exchanges, permanent wholesale market centres, or temporary trade fairs. Retailers may also buy on their own turf, either in stores or at corporate headquarters. Finally, buyers can use resident buying offices that prearrange opportunities for buyers to visit vendors in major market centres in North America and abroad. Buyers of fashion apparel and accessory categories typically make major buying decisions five or six times a year, six months before the beginning of a season. Buyers of staple merchandise replenish the merchandise on a continuous basis. A listing of over 3000 trade shows and market weeks for the fashion industry can be viewed at infomat (www.infomat.com).

WHOLESALE MARKET CENTRES

For many types of merchandise, retailers can do much of their buying in established market centres. Wholesale market centres have permanent vendor sales offices retailers can visit throughout the year. Probably the world's most significant wholesale market centre for many merchandise categories is in New York City. The Fashion Centre, also known as the Garment District, is located from Fifth to Ninth Avenues and from 35th to 41st Streets. An estimated 22 000 apparel buyers visit every year for five market weeks and 65 annual related trade shows. The Garment District has 5100 showrooms and 4500 factories.[18] The Garment District in Toronto is located in the Spadina Avenue and Queen Street West area.

The United States also has a number of regional wholesale market centres. The Dallas Market Centre, the world's largest, is a 641 700 square metre complex of six buildings.[19] Over 26 000 manufacturers and importers display their international products in its 2200 permanent showrooms and 42 780 square metres of temporary spaces. Some regional centres have developed into national markets for specific merchandise categories (for example, the Miami Merchandise Mart for swimwear).

refact

An estimated US$7.5 billion of wholesale transactions are conducted within the Dallas Market Centre complex annually.[20]

TRADE SHOWS

Many wholesale market centres host **trade shows,** also known as **merchandise shows** or **market weeks.** Permanent tenants of the wholesale market centres and vendors leasing temporary space participate. Here retailers place orders and get a concentrated view of what's available in the marketplace.

Although the high profile prêt-à-porter (ready to wear) is most obvious in New York, London, Milan, and Paris, Toronto is also quickly becoming an established fashion centre. One of the most anticipated events on Toronto's fashion calendar, the New Labels show, gives new designers the chance to showcase their innovations during the annual Fashion Week events.[21]

Another annual Toronto event is The Canadian Gift and Tableware Association's CGTA Gift Show. It offers attendees a unique, one-stop-shop experience featuring an expansive selection of quality gift products with over 1000 exhibitors displayed in the 93 000 square metres of space.[22]

support services for the buying process

Two services available to buyers that can help them more effectively acquire merchandise are resident buying offices and Internet exchanges.

RESIDENT BUYING OFFICES

Resident buying offices are organizations located in major buying centres that provide services to help retailers buy merchandise.

To illustrate how buying offices operate, consider how David Smith, owner of a Canadian prestige menswear store, utilizes his resident buying offices when he goes to market in Milan. Smith meets with market representative Alain Bordat of the Doneger Group, a buying office. Bordat, an English-speaking Italian, knows Smith's store and his upscale customers, so in advance of Smith's visit he sets up appointments with Italian vendors he believes would fit the Canadian store's image.

When Smith is in Italy, Bordat accompanies him to the appointments and acts as translator, negotiator, and accountant. Bordat informs Smith of the cost of importing the merchandise into Canada, taking into account duty, freight, insurance, processing costs, and so forth.

Once the orders are placed, Bordat writes the contracts and follows up on delivery and quality control. The Doneger Group also acts as a home base for buyers like Smith, providing office space and services, travel advisers, and emergency aid. Bordat and his association continue to keep Smith abreast of what's happening on the Italian fashion scene through reports and constant communication. Without the help of a resident buying office, it would be difficult, if not impossible, for Smith to penetrate the Italian wholesale market.

INTERNET EXCHANGES

Retail exchanges are providers of Internet-based solutions and services for retailers. The software and services offered by exchanges help retailers, manufacturers, and their trading partners reduce costs and improve efficiency by streamlining and automating sourcing and supply chain processes. They provide an opportunity for vendors and retailers to interact electronically rather than meeting face-to-face in a physical market. Retail exchanges can increase the efficiency of the buying process by offering software to support several of the systems discussed in previous chapters, such as reverse auctions; supply chain management; and collaborative planning, forecasting, and replenishment.

Two major retail exchanges, WorldWide Retail Exchange (WWRE) (www. wwre. org) and GlobalNetXchange (GNX) (www.gnx.com), were launched in 2000 as nonprofit organizations owned and supported by groups of large retailers. The objective of these exchanges was to promote collaboration between retailers and vendors. They planned to provide a single, central hub that connected trading partners. Retailers would have unlimited access to their vendors' production data, and vendors would have instant access to retailers' sales projections.

The original vision of GNX and WWRE had a number of flaws. First, the exchanges underestimated the technological complexity of building such an exchange. Although some companies such as Wal-Mart and Liz Claibourne had built effective private exchanges, they were designed to connect one trading partner to many, not many to many, as GNX and WWRE envisioned. Second, the cost of the software to provide some services, such as reverse auctions, dropped in price to the point that individual retailers could afford to administer their own reverse auctions. Third, the retail industry is extremely competitive, and retailers are reluctant to share information, preferring instead to keep their data and plans secret.[23]

In 2005, the two exchanges merged. The combined entity includes about 50 food, drug, and apparel retailers, including Carrefour SA, Sears Holdings Corp., Walgreen Co., Kroger Co., and Federated Department Stores Inc. Executives of the newly merged exchanges continue to hope that by creating a bigger and more sophisticated marketplace, retailers will be better equipped to face off against Wal-Mart. The combined exchange will facilitate transactions for a retail group with about $1 trillion in combined annual sales.[24]

USING INTERNET EXCHANGES TO FACILITATE BUYING

Retailers are exploring many strategies that provide consumers with the tools they need to purchase merchandise and services from them. Retailers also use the Internet for doing research for buying merchandise or services.

One of the most innovative and potentially useful developments stemming from retailers' growing level of sophistication with the Internet is retail exchanges. **Retail exchanges** are electronic marketplaces operated by organizations that facilitate the buying and selling of merchandise using the Internet. They provide an opportunity for vendors and retailers to interact electronically rather than meet face to face in a physical market. Retail exchanges can increase the efficiency of the buying process by integrating systems such as EDI with the ability to view merchandise and negotiate prices online. Although exchanges will never replace going to markets and interacting with vendors, they now make it possible for buyers to access any type of merchandise information with a mouse click.

Functions of Exchanges   Retail exchanges are still evolving. As such, we still do not know which functions or activities will become the most valuable to retailers. Some of the more prominent exchange functions are directory, selection, pricing, collaboration, and content.

Directory   No longer do buyers have to wander trade shows or showrooms. Retail exchanges enable them to search for merchandise by vendor or type of product electronically.

Selection   Buyers can then narrow the search to a particular vendor. Much of what used to be accomplished in the vendor's showroom can now be done online. Buyers can view individual SKUs. With technology improving all the time, they can be increasingly confident in the online catalogue's picture quality and colour. To help determine order quantities, buyers can obtain sales history from prior seasons for specific SKUs or for complementary products. Rather than travelling to Paris or Milan, buyers can replay runway fashion shows and obtain 360-degree views of merchandise from the comfort of their offices.

Pricing   Retail exchanges utilize several pricing methods. In fact, the same exchange may use more than one pricing method depending on the situation. Merchandise can be offered at a fixed price where everyone pays the same amount. Or, the price of merchandise can be negotiated; in this case, the exchange acts as a broker between vendors and retailers. Finally, merchandise can be auctioned.

In traditional auctions like those conducted by eBay, there is one seller and many buyers. Auctions conducted by retailer buyers are called **reverse auctions** because there is one buyer and many potential sellers. In reverse auctions, retail buyers provide a specification for what they want to a group of potential vendors. The competing vendors then bid down the price at which they are willing to sell until the buyer accepts a bid.[25] However, the retailer is not required to place an order with the lowest bidder. The retailer can choose to place the order at the price of the vendor who the retailer feels will provide the merchandise in a timely manner at the specified quality.

Reverse auctions have not been very popular with vendors. Few want to be anonymous contestants in bidding wars where price alone, not service or quality, is the sole basis for winning the business. Strategic relationships are also difficult to nurture when the primary interactions with vendors are through electronic auctions.[26]

The most common application for reverse auctions is to buy products and services used in retail operations rather than merchandise for resale. For example, a number of retailers worked together to develop a specification for POS terminal paper tape and then pooled their buying power to run a reverse auction and find a low-cost supplier that would meet all of their needs. Other operating materials that are frequently bought on reverse auctions are store carpeting, fixtures, and supplies. Reverse auctions can also be used by retailers to procure private-label merchandise, commodities, and seasonal merchandise such as lawn furniture.

Collaboration   Collaboration with vendors on every phase of the production and distribution process may become the most important benefit of retail exchanges. EDI, quick response inventory systems, and CPFR are integral components of retail exchanges.

The fashion world, where a short time period from idea conception to store shelf is a key success factor, stands to benefit significantly from retail exchanges. Although retailers have always provided design input to their vendors, it is the speed and clarity with which collaboration is facilitated with exchanges that is important. Suppose a buyer spots a potentially hot item on the street or in a movie. She snaps a digital picture and sends it simultaneously to a designer in Hong Kong and a fabric supplier in Thailand. The designer works out the specifications for the item, while the supplier sends both parties electronic versions of the fabric. All three parties collaborate on fine-tuning the design and product specifications. Not only does this collaborative effort shorten the lead time to market, but it minimizes the potential for errors.

Collaboration with other retailers for sourcing merchandise also has potential, but it may be difficult to achieve. Competing retailers aren't used to talking to each other. In fact, antitrust legislation may prohibit them from so doing.

refact

Human rights advocates estimate that as many as one in 10 diamonds sold today is a "conflict" stone, meaning it came from a country—say, Sierra Leone, Angola, or the Congo—where the diamond trade uses slave labour and funds warlords who routinely kill innocent civilians.[27]

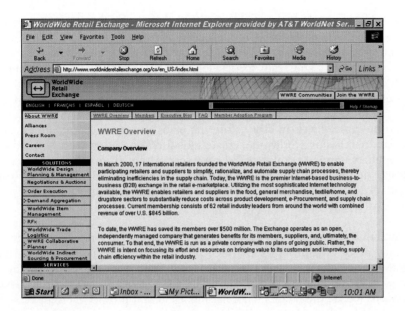

WorldWide Retail Exchange is a consortium exchange owned by retailers and used to facilitate the purchase of goods and services.

Content   Exchanges can even be an excellent source of general information. Many provide the latest industry news, trends, and fashions.

Types of Exchanges   There are three basic types of exchanges: consortium, private, and independent. These types of exchanges are defined in terms of who owns and operates the exchange.

Consortium Exchanges   A **consortium exchange** is a retail exchange that is owned by several firms within one industry. A firm must be a member of the consortium to participate in the exchange. The three consortium exchanges are Transora, the WorldWide Retail Exchange, and GlobalNetXchange.

- Transora is a consortium of 50 leading food, beverage, and consumer products companies, including Heinz, Gillette, Coca-Cola, Kraft Foods, Procter & Gamble, Sara Lee, Unilever, NV, and the Grocery Manufacturers of America (the leading trade organization in the grocery industry).

- The WorldWide Retail Exchange is a consortium composed of 61 retailers (not manufacturers), including Ahold (the Netherlands), Albertson's, Best Buy, The Boots Company (U.K.), CVS, The Gap, JCPenney, Target, and Safeway.

- GlobalNetXchange is also a consortium composed of retailers. They include Carrefour (France), Kroger, Metro AG (Germany), J. Sainsbury Plc (U.K), Coles Myer (Australia), Pinault-Printemps-Redoute SA (Europe), and Sears.

The potential advantage of these exchanges is that retailers can pool their buying power to get better prices and the fixed cost of developing the software and administering the exchange is shared across member-firms. However, coordinating the activities of different firms, and in some cases competing firms, has been difficult. There are often conflicting agendas among the founding members. Although not all members are in competition with one another, some are, making communication and goal setting complicated.[28] Also, since these exchanges are in competition with one another, companies are hesitant to back one for fear that it might be the wrong one. Finally, several major players have opted out of these consortia: Wal-Mart, Costco, Home Depot, Aldi, Office Depot, and Staples, just to name a few.

Private Exchanges **Private exchanges** are exchanges that are operated for the exclusive use of a single firm. Although currently relatively small in number, they represent large players such as Wal-Mart and Dell Computer. These larger companies have the size and scale to develop and operate their own exchanges. For example, Wal-Mart moved its existing information system, Retail Link, to the Internet.[29] Retail Link was built during the 1990s at an estimated cost of US$1 billion. Wal-Mart's private network enables its 10 000 suppliers to get information about sales and inventory levels in every store. Its plans are to use its private exchange to consolidate purchasing worldwide, create global collaboration with its vendors, and bring suppliers online to compete for contracts. Although this and other exchanges are clearly designed to benefit the operator/owner, the vendors benefit from the strategic relationship and immediate access to sales and inventory data for planning purposes, such as CPFR.

Independent Exchanges An **independent exchange** is a retail exchange owned by a third party that provides the electronic platform to perform the exchange functions. For example, a retailer is interested in running a reverse auction for an air-conditioning system. It contacts an independent exchange such as FreeMarkets. In the previous weeks, the retailer's purchasing agent and prospective suppliers prepare for the auction with the help of FreeMarkets. Now, the purchasing agent and the 12 suppliers log on to a FreeMarkets secure private network, and the bidding begins. Within minutes, the purchasing agent has saved thousands of dollars from its historic spending level. New bids come in every couple of minutes, driving the unit price lower and lower. In the ensuing hours, more than 250 interactive bids are received, saving the retailer more than US$400 000—a 16 percent savings below its historic spending level of US$2.5 million.[30]

negotiating with vendors

Negotiations are as basic to human nature as eating or sleeping. A negotiation takes place any time two parties confer with each other to settle some matter. Negotiations take place between parents and their children about issues such as allowances. People negotiate with their friends about what to do on the weekend.

Business negotiations occur daily. People negotiate for higher salaries, better offices, and bigger budgets. Negotiations are crucial in buyers' discussions with vendors.

No one should go into a negotiation without intensive planning. We first provide guidelines for planning negotiations with vendors. Then we discuss some tips for conducting the negotiation face to face.

GUIDELINES FOR PLANNING NEGOTIATIONS WITH VENDORS

As a vehicle for describing how a buyer should prepare for and conduct a negotiation with a vendor, consider the hypothetical situation in which a men's designer shirt buyer at Sears is preparing to meet with the salesman from Tommy Hilfiger in the office in New York. The Sears buyer is ready to buy Tommy Hilfiger's spring line, but has some merchandising problems yet to be resolved from last season. Let's go over seven general guidelines for planning a negotiation session and for conducting a face-to-face negotiation session.

KNOWLEDGE IS POWER! The more the buyer knows about the vendor, the better his/her negotiating strategy will be.

Consider History   Buyers need a sense of what has occurred between the retailer and vendor in the past. Sears and Tommy Hilfiger Inc have had a long, profitable relationship; a sense of trust and mutual respect has been established. An established vendor may be more likely to take care of old problems and accept new demands if a long-term, profitable relationship already exists.

Assess Where Things Are Today   Although Tommy Hilfiger shirts have been profitable for Sears in the past, three patterns sold poorly last season. Some vendors believe that once they've sold merchandise to the retailer, their responsibility ends. This is a short-term perspective, however. If the merchandise doesn't sell, a good vendor, like Tommy Hilfiger, will arrange to share the risk of loss. The Sears buyer will ask to return some merchandise or provide markdown money—funds a vendor gives a retailer to cover lost gross margin dollars due to markdowns and other merchandising issues—usually in the form of a credit to the Sears account.

Set Goals   Besides taking care of last season's leftover merchandise, the Sears buyer has set goals in six areas for the upcoming meeting: additional markup opportunities, terms of purchase, transportation, delivery and exclusivity, communications, and advertising allowances.

Additional Markup Opportunities   Vendors may have excess stock (manufacturers' overruns) due to order cancellations, returned merchandise from retailers, or simply an overly optimistic sales forecast. To move this merchandise, vendors offer it to retailers at lower-than-normal prices. Retailers can then make a higher-than-normal gross margin or pass the savings on to the customer. Since Sears is noted as a popular menswear store, it probably isn't interested in any excess inventory that Tommy Hilfiger has to offer. Off-price retailers such as Winners or Internet retailer Bluefly.com specialize in purchasing manufacturers' overruns. Another opportunity for additional markups is with private-label merchandise as previously discussed.

Terms of Purchase   It's advantageous for buyers to negotiate for a long time period in which to pay for merchandise. Long terms of payment improve the firm's cash flow position, lower its liabilities (accounts payable), and can cut its interest expense if it's borrowing money from financial institutions to pay for its inventory. According to the *Competition Act*, however, a vendor can't offer different terms of purchase or prices to different retailers unless the difference can be cost-justified. But buyers would be remiss if they didn't ask for the best terms of purchase available.

Transportation   Transportation costs can be substantial, though this doesn't pose a big problem with the Tommy Hilfiger shirts due to their high unit cost and small size. Nonetheless, the question of who pays for shipping merchandise from vendor to retailer can be a significant negotiating point.

Delivery and Exclusivity   In retailing in general, and in fashion in particular, timely delivery is essential. Being the only retailer in a market to carry certain products helps a retailer hold a fashion lead and achieve a differential advantage. The buyer for Sears wants to be certain that shipment of the new spring line arrives as early in the season as possible, and that some shirt patterns won't be sold to competing retailers.

Communications   Vendors and their representatives are excellent sources of market information. They generally know what is and isn't selling. Providing good, timely information about the market is an indispensable and inexpensive marketing research tool, so the Sears buyer plans to spend at least part of the meeting talking about market trends to the Hilfiger sales representative.

Advertising Allowances   Retailers have the choice of advertising any product in the store. They can sometimes share the cost of advertising through a cooperative arrangement with vendors known as co-op advertising—a program undertaken by a vendor in which the vendor agrees to pay all or part of a pricing promotion. By giving retailers advertising money based on a percentage of purchases, vendors can better represent their product to consumers. Under the *Competition Act*, vendors are allowed to give advertising allowances on an equal basis—the same percentage to everyone—usually based on a percentage of the invoice cost. As a fashion retailer, Sears advertises heavily and would like Tommy Hilfiger to support a number of catalogues with a generous ad allowance.

Know the Vendor's Goals and Constraints   Negotiation can't succeed in the long run unless both parties believe they've won. By understanding what's important to Tommy Hilfiger, the Sears buyer can plan for a successful negotiating session. Generally, vendors are interested in providing a continuous relationship, testing new items, facilitating good communications, and providing a showcase to feature their merchandise.

A Continuous Relationship   Vendors want to make a long-term investment in their retailers. For seasonal merchandise such as men's designer shirts, they have to plan their production in advance, so it's important to Tommy Hilfiger Inc that certain key retailers such as Sears continue their support. The buyer plans to spend some time at the beginning of the meeting reviewing their mutually profitable past and assuring the Tommy Hilfiger sales rep that Sears hopes to continue their relationship.

Testing New Items   There's no better way to test how well a new product will sell than to put it in a store. Retailers are often cautious with new items due to the risk of markdowns and the opportunity cost of not purchasing other, more successful merchandise. Yet vendors need their retailers to provide sales feedback for new items. Sears has always been receptive to some of Tommy Hilfiger's more avant-garde styles. If these styles do well in certain Sears stores, they'll likely succeed in similar stores around the country.

Communication   Just as Tommy Hilfiger can provide market information, Sears can share sales information. Also, the Sears buyer travels the world market and on one buying trip to England, found an attractive scarf, bought the scarf, and gave it to Tommy Hilfiger, who had it copied for a shirt. It was a big success!

Showcase   In certain urban centres—notably Toronto, New York, London, Milan, and Paris—vendors use large stores to showcase their merchandise. For instance, many North American buyers go to market in New York. Most stop at the major retailers to see what's new, what's selling, and how it's displayed.

A good understanding of the legal, managerial, and financial issues that constrain a vendor will facilitate a productive negotiating session. For instance, the Sears buyer should recognize from past experience that Tommy Hilfiger normally doesn't allow merchandise to be returned, but does provide markdown money. If the Hilfiger rep initially says that giving markdown money is against company policy, the Sears buyer will have strong objective ammunition for her position.

Plan to Have at Least as Many Negotiators as the Vendor There's power in numbers. Even if the vendor is more powerful, aggressive, or important in the marketplace, the retailer will have a psychological advantage at the negotiating table if the vendor is outnumbered. At the very least, the negotiating teams should be of equal number. The Sears buyer plans to invite a merchandise manager into the discussion if the Tommy Hilfiger rep comes with a sales manager.

Choose a Good Place to Negotiate The Sears buyer may have an advantage in the upcoming meeting since it will be in the Sears office. The buyer will have everything at her fingertips, such as information plus secretarial and supervisory assistance. From a psychological perspective, people generally feel more comfortable and confident in familiar surroundings. On the other hand, if the negotiation were to be in Hilfiger's office, Sears would be able to learn a lot about the Hilfiger Inc company. In the end, the preferable location for a negotiation is a personal choice.

Be Aware of Real Deadlines To illustrate the importance of deadlines, consider when labour strikes are settled. An agreement is often reached one minute before everyone walks out. There's always pressure to settle a negotiation at the last minute. The Sears buyer recognizes that the Tommy Hilfiger sales rep must go back to the office with an order in hand since there is a quota to meet by the end of the month. The Sears buyer must get markdown money or permission to return the unsold shirts by the end of the week or there will not be sufficient open-to-buy to cover the orders the buyer wishes to place. Recognizing these deadlines will help Sears come to a decisive closure in the upcoming negotiation.

establishing and maintaining strategic relationships with vendors

Maintaining strong vendor relationships is an important method of developing a sustainable competitive advantage. In previous chapters we discussed some of the ways partnering relations can improve information, exchange, planning, and the management of supply chains. For example, electronic data interchange could not be accomplished without the vendor and retailer making a commitment to work together and have a trusting relationship. In the same way, category management using category captains and CPFR (collaborative planning, forecasting, and replenishment) would be impossible without partnering relationships. In this section, we examine how retailers can develop strategic relationships and the characteristics of a successful long-term relationship.

DEFINING STRATEGIC RELATIONSHIPS

Relationships between retailers and vendors are often based on arguing over splitting up a profit pie.[31] This is basically a win–lose relationship because when one party gets a larger portion of the pie, the other party gets a smaller portion. Both parties are interested exclusively in their own profits and are unconcerned about the other party's welfare. These relationships are common when the products are commodities and have no major impact on the retailers' performance. Thus, there is no benefit to the retailer to entering into a strategic relationship.

A **strategic relationship,** also called a **partnering relationship,** exists when a retailer and vendor are committed to maintaining the relationship over the long term and investing in opportunities that are mutually beneficial to the parties. In these relationships, it's important for the partners to put their money where their mouth is. They've taken risks to expand the pie—to give the relationship a strategic advantage over other companies.

Thus, a strategic relationship is a win–win relationship. Both parties benefit because the size of the pie has increased—both the retailer and vendor increase their sales and profits. Strategic relationships are created explicitly to uncover and exploit joint opportunities. Members in strategic relationships depend on and trust each other heavily; they share goals and agree on how to accomplish those goals; and they're willing to take risks, share confidential information, and make significant investments for the sake of the relationship.

 A strategic relationship is like a marriage. When businesses enter strategic relationships, they're wedded to their partners for better or worse. For example, the U.K.'s Marks & Spencer had jointly developed a kitchen product with a vendor.[32] Four months after the product's introduction, the manufacturer realized that it had miscalculated the product's cost and, as a result, had underpriced the product and was losing money on the deal. It was a big hit at Marks & Spencer because it was underpriced. Marks & Spencer decided not to raise the price because the product was already listed in its catalogue. Instead, it helped the vendor reengineer the product at a lower cost, cut its own gross margin, and gave that money to the manufacturer. It took a profit hit to maintain the relationship.

MAINTAINING STRATEGIC RELATIONSHIPS

The four foundations of successful strategic relationships are mutual trust, open communication, common goals, and credible commitments.

Mutual Trust The glue in strategic relationships is trust. **Trust** is a belief that a partner is honest (reliable, stands by its word, sincere, fulfills obligations) and is benevolent (concerned about the other party's welfare).[34] When vendors and buyers trust each other, they're more willing to share relevant ideas, clarify goals and problems, and communicate efficiently. Information shared between the parties becomes increasingly comprehensive, accurate, and timely. There's less need for the vendor and buyer to constantly monitor and check up on each other's actions because each believes the other won't take advantage, given the opportunity.[35]

Strategic relationships and trust are often developed initially between the leaders of organizations. For example, when Wal-Mart started to work with Procter & Gamble to coordinate its buying activities, Sam Walton got together with P&G's vice-president of sales on a canoeing trip. They discussed the mutual benefits of cooperating and the potential risks associated with altering their normal business practices. In the end, they must have concluded that the potential long-term gains were worth the additional risks and short-term setbacks that would probably occur as they developed the new systems.

Open Communication In order to share information, develop sales forecasts together, and coordinate deliveries, Wal-Mart and P&G have to have open and honest communication. This may sound easy in principle, but most businesses don't like to share information with their business partners. They believe it is none of the other's concern. But open, honest communication is a key to developing successful relationships. Buyers and vendors in a relationship need to understand what's driving each other's business, their roles in the relationship, each firm's strategies, and any problems that arise over the course of the relationship.

Common Goals   Vendors and buyers must have common goals for a successful relationship to develop. Shared goals give both members of the relationship incentive to pool their strengths and abilities and to exploit potential opportunities between them. There's also assurance that the other partner won't do anything to hinder goal achievement within the relationship.

For example, Wal-Mart and P&G recognized that it was in their common interest to remain business partners—they needed each other—and to do so, both had to be allowed to make profitable transactions. Wal-Mart can't demand prices so low that P&G can't make money, and P&G must be flexible enough to accommodate the needs of its biggest customer. With a common goal, both firms have incentive to cooperate because they know that by doing so, each can boost sales.

Common goals also help to sustain the relationship when expected benefit flows aren't realized. If one P&G shipment fails to reach a Wal-Mart store on time due to an unfortunate event such as misrouting by a trucking firm, Wal-Mart won't suddenly call off the whole arrangement. Instead, Wal-Mart is likely to view the incident as a simple mistake and will remain in the relationship; this is because Wal-Mart and P&G are committed to the same goals in the long run.

Credible Commitments   Successful relationships develop because both parties make credible commitments to the relationship. Credible commitments are tangible investments in the relationship. They go beyond just making the hollow statement "I want to be a partner." Credible commitments involve spending money to improve the supplier's products or services provided to the customer.[36] For example, one of the strengths of the Wal-Mart/P&G partnership is the obvious and significant investments both parties have made in EDI systems, CPFR forecasting systems, and material handling equipment.

BUILDING PARTNERING RELATIONSHIPS

Although not all retailer–vendor relationships should or do become strategic partnerships, the development of strategic partnerships tends to go through a series of phases characterized by increasing levels of commitment:

- *Awareness:* No transactions have taken place. This phase might begin with the buyer seeing some interesting merchandise at a retail market or in an ad in a trade magazine. Reputation and image of the vendor can play an important role in determining if the buyer moves to the next stage.

- *Exploration:* The buyer and vendor begin to explore the potential benefits and costs. At this point, the buyer may make a small purchase and try to test the demand for the merchandise in several stores. In addition, the buyer will get information about how easy it is to work with the vendor.

- *Expansion:* The buyer has collected enough information about the vendor to consider developing a longer-term relationship. The buyer and the vendor determine that there is a potential for a win–win relationship. They begin to work on joint promotional programs, and the amount of merchandise sold increases.

- *Commitment:* Both parties continue to find the relationship mutually beneficial, and it moves to the commitment stage and becomes a strategic relationship. The buyer and vendor make significant investments in the relationship and develop a long-term perspective toward it.

refact

In 2003, Mountain Equipment Co-op sales totalled $168.6 million.[37]

refact

Executives at Sears Canada said sales of Martha Stewart's brands spiked after her March 2004 conviction on conspiracy charges; it appears that people were voting sympathetically by buying lots of her products.[38]

It is difficult for retailer–vendor relationships to be as committed as some supplier–manufacturer relationships. Manufacturers can enter into monogamous (sole source) relationships with other manufacturers. However, an important function of retailers is to provide an assortment of merchandise for their customers. Thus, they must always deal with multiple, sometimes competing suppliers.

SUMMARY

Retail buying involves various issues, including determining a retailer's branding strategy, sourcing objectives, and vendor relationship strategies. The reality is that the bigger the retailer the more buying clout it wields in dealing with suppliers. Long-term vendor relationships are created to establish a win–win situation that will develop a sustainable competitive advantage for both parties involved. To survive, retailers must be able to count on a predictable supply of merchandise at competitive prices and with sufficient promotional support.

Retailers can purchase either manufacturers' brands or private-label brands. Each type has its own relative advantages. Choosing brands and a branding strategy is an integral component of a firm's merchandise and assortment planning process.

A large percentage of the merchandise we buy is manufactured outside of Canada. The decision to buy from domestic manufacturers or source internationally is a complicated one. The cost, managerial, and ethical issues surrounding global sourcing decisions were discussed. Buyers and their merchandise managers have several opportunities to meet with vendors, view new merchandise, and place orders. They can utilize Internet exchanges or visit their vendors at wholesale market centres such as Toronto, New York, Paris, or Milan. Virtually every merchandise category has at least one annual trade show at which retailers and vendors meet. Buyers often meet with vendors on their own turf—in the retail store or corporate offices. Finally, meetings with vendors are facilitated by resident buying offices. Market representatives of these resident buying offices facilitate merchandising purchases in foreign markets.

Retailers should prepare for and conduct negotiations with vendors. Successful vendor relationships depend on planning for and being adept at negotiations.

Retailers that can successfully team up with their vendors can achieve a sustainable competitive advantage. There needs to be more than just a promise to buy and sell on a regular basis. Strategic relationships require trust, shared goals, strong communications, and a financial commitment.

With thousands of annual transactions taking place between retailers and their vendors, there's plenty of room for ethical and legal problems. The issues of charging vendors for shelf space or taking bribes are discussed in Appendix 12A. There are also problems associated with counterfeit and grey-market merchandise and issues that vendors face when selling to retailers, such as exclusive territories and tying contracts. Care should be taken when making restrictions on which retailers they will sell to, what merchandise, how much, and at what price.

Retailers face a plethora of discount/payment date combinations. A working knowledge of these terms of purchase is essential for any person involved in merchandising. More important, the most advantageous application of the terms can make a significant impact on corporate profits.

KEY TERMS

alternative dispute resolution, 344
arbitration, 344
buyback, 345
chargeback, 344
commercial bribery, 344
consortium exchange, 335
copycat branding, 325
copyright, 346
counterfeit merchandise, 346
diverted merchandise, 347
duty, 328
exclusive dealing agreements, 348
exclusive geographic territory, 348
free trade zone, 328
generic brand, 325

grey-market good, *347*
house brand, *325*
independent exchanges, *336*
intellectual property, *346*
licensed brand, *323*
lift-out, *345*
manufacturer brands, *322*
maquiladoras, *328*
market, *331*
market weeks, *332*
med-arb, *344*

mediation, *344*
merchandise shows, *332*
national brands, *322*
opportunity cost of capital, *329*
parallel branding, *325*
partnering relationship, *340*
premium branding, *325*
private exchanges, *336*
private-label brands, *323*
retail exchanges, *332*
reverse auctions, *334*

slotting allowance, *345*
slotting fee, *345*
stocklift, *345*
store brands, *323*
strategic relationship, *340*
tariff, *328*
trademark, *346*
trade show, *332*
trust, *340*
tying contract, *348*

Get Out & Do It!

1. **GO SHOPPING** Go to your favourite department or discount store. Perform an audit of national and private brands. Interview a manager to determine whether the percentage of private brands has increased or decreased over the last five years. Ask the manager to comment on the store's philosophy toward national versus private brands. On the basis of what you see and hear, assess its branding strategy.

2. **INTERNET EXERCISE** Go to the WorldWide Retail Exchange (www.wwre.org) and GlobalNetXchange.com (www.gnx.com). Compare their offerings. Write a recommendation to a retailer of your choice regarding which of these exchanges it should join. You can also recommend that it doesn't join either exchange.

3. **GO SHOPPING** See if you can find some counterfeit, grey-market or diverted merchandise. Compare it with the real thing. (Refer to Appendix 12A.)

DISCUSSION QUESTIONS AND PROBLEMS

1. Do retailers take advantage of their power positions by charging slotting fees, buybacks, and chargebacks (see Appendix 12A)?

2. Assume you have been hired to consult with The Gap on sourcing decisions for sportswear. What issues would you consider when deciding whether you should buy from Mexico or China, or find a source in Canada?

3. How would the decision to source outside Canada affect a retailer's need to carry backup stock?

4. Does your favourite clothing store have a strong private-brand strategy? Should it?

5. When setting goals for a negotiation session with a vendor, what issues should a buyer consider?

6. A $500 invoice is dated October 1, the merchandise arrives October 15, and the terms are 3/30, n/60 ROG (see Appendix 12A).
   a. How many days does the retailer have to take advantage of the discount?
   b What is the percentage of discount?
   c. How much is due November 10?
   d. What's the final date the retailer can pay the invoice without being considered late?

7. What do you think will be the future of retail exchanges?

8. What factors should a buyer consider when deciding with which vendors to develop a close relationship?

APPENDIX 12A   Purchasing Merchandise

ETHICAL AND LEGAL ISSUES IN PURCHASING MERCHANDISE*

As you can imagine, given the thousands of relationships and millions of transactions between retailers and their vendors, unethical or illegal situations may arise. In this section, we'll view ethical and legal issues from both retailers' and vendors' perspectives. The most fundamental question is whether a retailer and vendor have a binding contract for a particular transaction. If they do, the next question is how to resolve disputes under that contract. In addition, retailers should not take advantage of their position of power in the marketing channel. In this regard, we'll examine chargebacks, commercial bribery, slotting allowances, buybacks, and category management.

To protect their customers' interests and their own reputation, retailers must be cognizant of whether the merchandise is counterfeit or from the diverted market (the grey market). Vendors aren't likely to become legally entangled with their retailers so long as they sell to whoever wants to buy, sell whatever they want, and sell at the same price to all. But since most vendors don't want to be this free with their merchandise, we'll look at exclusive territories, exclusive dealing agreements, tying contracts, and refusals to deal.

Contract Disputes

Contract formation in the retail context is usually straightforward. The retailer places an order with a vendor that in most cases the vendor accepts. This creates a binding mutual obligation for the vendor to deliver the promised goods in exchange for the retailer agreeing to pay the specified price. Disputes arise when one party does not perform or when the parties disagree about details of the transaction such as the precise specifications of the goods.

Most retailers and vendors are more interested in continuing sales relationships than expensive litigation over legal rights. For this reason, many

*This section was developed with the assistance of Professor Ross Petty, Babson College.

disputes are simply settled by negotiation and agreement between the two parties. It is common to include **alternative dispute resolution** provisions in contracts. Such provisions can include methods of settling the dispute that the parties agree upon, such as mediation, arbitration, or med-arb. **Mediation** involves selecting a neutral mediator to assist the parties in reaching a mutually agreeable settlement. **Arbitration** involves the appointment of an arbitrator who considers the arguments of both sides and then makes a decision that is usually agreed upon in advance as binding. **Med-arb** involves an initial attempt at mediation followed by binding arbitration if the mediation is unsuccessful. Overworked courts routinely enforce alternative dispute resolution contract provisions in the United States.

Chargebacks

A **chargeback** is a practice used by retailers in which they deduct money from the amount they owe a vendor. There are two reasons for a chargeback. The first occurs when the retailer deducts money from an invoice because merchandise isn't selling. The second reason is vendor mistakes such as shoddy labelling, lost billings, wrong-size boxes or hangers, missing items, and late shipments. Although often legitimate contract disputes, chargebacks are frequently viewed as being unjustified by vendors. Retailers can use chargebacks as a profit centre. For instance, one senior executive at a large department store chain was told to collect US$50 million in chargebacks.[39] What makes chargebacks especially difficult for vendors is that once the money is deducted from an invoice, and the invoiced is "paid," it is difficult to get the missing amount back, and negotiations or threats of litigation often appear to fall on deaf ears.

Commercial Bribery

Commercial bribery occurs in retailing when a vendor or its agent offers to privately give or pay a retail buyer "something of value" to influence purchasing decisions. Say a sweater manufacturer takes a department store buyer to lunch at a fancy private club and then proposes a ski weekend in Banff. The buyer enjoys the lunch but graciously turns down the ski trip. These gifts could be construed as bribes or kickbacks, which are illegal unless the buyer's manager is informed of them (and is also not receiving private payments or gifts). In fact, the goernment doesn't allow money paid for bribes to be deducted as a business expense. From an ethical perspective, there's a fine line between the social courtesy of a free lunch and an elaborate free vacation.

To avoid these problems, many companies forbid employees to accept any gifts from vendors. They want their buyers to decide on purchases based solely on what is best for the retailer. One major U.S. discount store chain specifically forbids the taking of "bribes, commissions, kickbacks, payments, loans, gratuities, or other solicitations, including any item of value from suppliers to the company." But many companies have no policy against receiving gifts, and some unethical employees accept and even solicit gifts, even if their company has a policy against it. A good rule of thumb is to accept only limited entertainment or token gifts, such as flowers or a bottle of wine, for Christmas, birthdays, or other occasions. When the gift or favour is perceived to be large enough to influence a buyer's purchasing behaviour, it's considered to be commercial bribery and therefore is illegal.

Slotting Allowances

Slotting allowances, also called **slotting fees** when viewed from the vendor's perspective, are fees paid by a vendor for space in a retail store.[40] They differ from commercial bribes in that they are made to the retailer itself rather than to an individual buyer. This is considered to be a legal form of competition among vendors for shelf space in Canada.

Here's an example. When Kraft or any other consumer package goods manufacturer wants to introduce a new product, it often pays a slotting allowance to grocery and discount store chains for the space (slot) on the shelf. The fee varies depending on the nature of the product and the relative power of the retailer. Products whose brand names command relatively low customer loyalty pay the highest slotting allowances. Likewise, large grocery chains can demand higher

slotting allowances than small, independent stores. Industry reports estimate the total amount spent on slotting fees in the United States to be around US$16 billion per year.[41] The per-item store costs are estimated to be $3000 to $40 000.[42] At that rate, it may cost US$1 million or more to get national distribution of a new product!

Slotting fees are not only present in the food industry. They are becoming prevalent in other retail venues, such as those that sell over-the-counter drugs, apparel, magazines, and computer software. In the music industry, for instance, retailers regularly charge vendors for the right to display and sell their merchandise.

Some retailers argue that slotting allowances are a reasonable method for ensuring that their valuable space is used efficiently. Such fees cover their costs of adding a new SKU to their computerized system of inventory, knowing that most new products fail and the SKU must later also be removed.

As part of a program to develop strategic relationships, some manufacturers avoid slotting allowances by working closely with retail store s and sharing the financial risk of new products. For instance, Wal-Mart reportedly refuses to charge slotting allowances, preferring instead to have vendors participate in its centralized purchasing system.[43]

Concerns with slotting allowances arise when a dominant firm uses them to exclude rivals. If a dominant vendor pays large slotting fees that rivals cannot match, then the fees may have the effect of limiting competition among vendors. This may be particularly true when the vendor pays to obtain the best retail display space or to limit the space available to rivals.[44] Similarly, retail competition may be injured when large retailers extract much larger slotting allowances than those available to smaller retailers, giving the large firms a cost advantage.[45]

Buybacks

Similar to slotting allowances, the **buyback,** also known as a **stocklift** or **lift-out,** is a strategy vendors and retailers use to get products into retail stores. Specifically, a buyback can occur under two scenarios. The first and most ethically troubling is when a retailer allows a vendor to create space for its goods by "buying back" a competitor's inventory and removing it from a retailer's system. In the second case, the retailer forces a vendor to buy back slow-moving merchandise.

Consider the following buyback scenario. At a national home improvement store chain, thousands of garden gloves manufactured by the store's main source of supply vanished almost overnight. The empty shelves were restocked with gloves made by another glove manufacturer. The second manufacturer purchased all of the original gloves in stock so it could fill the shelves with its own product. The purchased gloves were probably dumped into a sprawling underground pipeline for resale by faraway, perhaps foreign, retailers. There are about a half-dozen companies that provide buyback-type liquidation services.

Are buybacks illegal? Technically, a company with market power may violate laws if it stocklifts from a competitor so often as to shut it out of a market. But such cases brought under the *Competition Act* are difficult to prove.

Counterfeit Merchandise

Counterfeit merchandise includes goods made and sold without the permission of the owner of a trademark, a copyright, or a patented invention that is legally protected in the country where it is marketed. Trademarks, copyrights, and patents are all under the general umbrella of intellectual property. **Intellectual property** is intangible and is created by intellectual (mental) effort as opposed to physical effort. A **trademark** is any mark, word, picture, device, or nonfunctional design associated with certain merchandise (for instance, the crown on a Rolex watch and the GE on General Electric products). A **copyright** protects original work of authors, painters, sculptors, musicians, and others who produce works of artistic or intellectual merit. The copyright protects only the physical expression of the effort, not the idea. This book is copyrighted, so these sentences cannot be used by anyone without the consent of the copyright owners. However, anyone can take the ideas in this book and express them in different words. The owner of a patent controls the right

to make, sell, and use a product for a period of 20 years or a design for 14 years.

The nature of counterfeiting has changed over the past decade. Although manufacturers of high-visibility, strong–brand-name consumer goods are still tormented by counterfeiters, there's now a thriving business in counterfeit high-tech products such as software, CDs, and CD-ROMs. For instance, some experts believe that the software publishing and distribution industries lose almost US$12 billion a year.[47] Why is this type of merchandise so attractive to counterfeiters? It has a high unit value, is relatively easy to duplicate and transport, and has high consumer demand. For instance, suppose *Retailing Management* were available on a CD-ROM. It could be easily duplicated as a CD or reprinted as a book for a few dollars in a foreign country. Neither the publishers nor the authors would receive any money. In fact, it's likely that they wouldn't even know about the copyright infringement.

Retailers and their vendors have four avenues to pursue to protect themselves against the ravages of counterfeiting and intellectual property rights violations: product registration, legislative action, bilateral and multilateral negotiations, and measures taken by companies.[48]

First, the product must be trademarked, copyrighted, or patented in the countries in which it's sold. Unfortunately, registration in Canada provides no protection in another country, although treaties and other international agreements allow for prompt and easy registration in other countries based on initial registration in Canada.

The second method of protection is through legislative action. Several laws protect businesses against counterfeiting. Counterfeiting is a criminal rather than a civil offence.

Third, the Canadian government is engaged in bilateral and multilateral negotiations and education to limit counterfeiting. For instance, the WTO has rules on intellectual property protection.

Finally, companies are aggressively taking steps to protect themselves. The International Anti-Counterfeiting Coalition is a group of 375 firms that lobbies for strong legal sanctions worldwide. Individual companies are also taking an aggressive stance against counterfeiting.

refact

Retailers estimate that sales of counterfeit goods jumped 25 percent to US$2 billion per year in 2000.[46]

Grey-Market and Diverted Merchandise

A **grey-market good** is merchandise that possesses a valid North American registered trademark and is made by a foreign manufacturer but is imported into North America without permission of the trademark owner. Grey-market merchandise is not counterfeit. This merchandise often is the same quality and may actually be identical to merchandise brought into the country through normal channels.

Selling grey-market merchandise may be legal in the United States. Recently, the Supreme Court ruled that American manufacturers cannot stop discount stores from buying North American products overseas and selling them domestically at reduced prices if the foreign manufacturer and domestic trademark owner fall under a common corporate umbrella.[49] Interestingly, the European Court of Justice decided to allow grey-market imports only from one member-state to another but not from outside the European Union.[50]

Without realizing it, we see grey-market goods in the marketplace all the time. Some manufacturers of cars, jewellery, perfume, liquor, watches, cameras, crystal ware, ski equipment, tractors, baby powder, and batteries are all involved in grey marketing in the United States.

Here's an example of how the grey market for watches might work in the United States. To help create a prestigious image, to offset an unfavourable exchange rate, and to pad profit margins, Swiss watch manufacturers often charge a higher wholesale price in the United States than in Europe and other countries. A Swiss watchmaker such as Patek Philippe may sell 1000 watches to a retailer in Italy, whose price is about 30 percent less than an authorized retailer in the United States. The Italian retailer sells several of the more expensive watches that are slow sellers to a grey-market (unauthorized) retailer in the United States. Both the Italian and U.S. retailers can make a profit, and the watches can still be sold to a U.S. customer significantly below the manufacturer's suggested retail price (MSRP).

Diverted merchandise is similar to grey-market merchandise except there need not be distribution across international boundaries. Suppose, for instance, fragrance manufacturer Givenchy grants an exclusive territory to all Bay stores. A discount store in Toronto purchases Givenchy products from a wholesale distributor in Las Vegas and sells it for 20 percent below the suggested retail price. The merchandise is diverted from its legitimate channel of distribution, and the wholesaler in this case would be referred to as a diverter.

Some discount store operators argue that customers benefit from the lack of restriction on grey-market and diverted goods because it lowers prices. Competition with retailers selling grey-market and diverted merchandise forces authorized dealers to cut their prices.

Traditional retailers, on the other hand, claim grey-market and diverted merchandise has a negative impact on the public. They believe that important after-sale service will be unavailable through retailers of grey-market or diverted goods, because they do not have adequate training or access to appropriate replacement parts. They also think that a less expensive grey-market or diverted product may hurt the trademark's image. Importantly, the grey-market product may be an out-of-date model or not work properly in a different country. For example, Philip Morris makes cartons of Marlboro cigarettes in the United States earmarked for foreign markets where prices are lower. These cigarettes often carry warning labels that are different from the federally required surgeon general's message. Further, the packages and formulation may be different as well.[52]

Vendors wishing to avoid the grey-market problem have several remedies. First, they can require all of their retail and wholesale customers to sign a contract stipulating that they will not engage in grey marketing. If a retailer is found in violation of the agreement, the vendor will refuse to deal with it in the future. Another strategy is to produce different versions of products for different markets. For instance, a camera manufacturer could sell the same camera in the United States and the European Union but with different names and warranties. This strategy would not prevent the European product from being sold in the United States. But distinctive packaging, design, instructions, and other features may discourage its sale.

> **refact**
>
> Grey markets are significant as they now exceed $10 billion per year in North America and affect almost every major trademarked product. Grey markets are growing at more than 22 percent annually.[51]

Exclusive Territories

As noted in the diverted goods example above, vendors often grant **exclusive geographic territories** to retailers so no other retailer in the territory can sell a particular brand. These territorial arrangements can benefit vendors by assuring them that "quality" retailers represent their products. In cases of limited supply, providing an exclusive territory to one retailer helps ensure that enough inventory can be carried to make a good presentation and offer the customer an adequate selection. For instance, by granting exclusive territories, the luxury Ferrari Automobile Company gives its dealers a monopoly for its products—a strong incentive to push Ferrari products. The dealers know there will be no competing retailers to cut prices, so their profit margins are protected. The retailer with an exclusive territory has the incentive to carry more inventory; use extra advertising, personal selling, and sales promotions; provide special displays and display areas; and develop special services for customers. The courts have tended to hold exclusive territories legal unless they restrict competition. Competition is restricted when other retailers have no access to similar products. For example, having exclusive Ferrari dealers wouldn't be a restraint of trade since other luxury cars are readily available to the public. On the other hand, if De Beers, the South African diamond cartel, granted exclusive territories to certain jewellery retailers, this would probably be seen as a restraint of trade because diamonds wouldn't be readily available through other sources and the De Beers dealers would not compete directly against each other because of their exclusive territories.

Exclusive Dealing Agreements

Exclusive dealing agreements occur when a manufacturer or wholesaler restricts a retailer to carrying only its products and nothing from competing vendors. Again, the effect on competition determines these contracts' legality. For instance, suppose a retailer signs an agreement with Lee to sell only its jeans. There's no real harm done to competition because other manufacturers have many alternative retail outlets, and Lee's market share isn't large enough to approach monopolistic levels.

Tying Contracts

A **tying contract** exists when a vendor and a retailer enter into an agreement that requires the retailer to take a product it doesn't necessarily desire (the *tied product*) to ensure that it can buy a product it does desire (the *tying product*). Tying contracts are illegal if they may substantially lessen competition or tend to create a monopoly, but the complaining party has the burden of proof. For example, a postcard jobber sued a postcard manufacturer for requiring that it purchase as many "local view" postcards as it did licensed Disney character postcards. The postcard manufacturer was the sole source for licensed Disney character postcards. The court dismissed the tying case because the jobber failed to prove a substantial lessening of competition.[53]

Refusal to Deal

The practice of refusing to deal (buy from or sell to) can be viewed from both suppliers' and retailers' perspectives. Generally, both suppliers and retailers have the right to deal or refuse to deal with anyone they choose. But there are exceptions to this general rule when there's evidence of anticompetitive conduct by one or more firms wielding market power.

A manufacturer may refuse to sell to a particular retailer, but it can't do so for the sole purpose of benefiting a competing retailer. For example, Mattel decided not to offer certain popular Barbie packages to wholesale clubs. This action in itself would have been legal. However, it was determined that Mattel agreed to do so as part of a conspiracy among 10 toy manufacturers orchestrated by Toys "R" Us to prevent wholesale clubs from underselling the same toy packages that Toys "R" Us sells. The refusal to deal then became an illegal group boycott. After the U.S. Federal Trade Commission enjoined this conspiracy, the 10 toy manufacturers agreed to settle private antitrust lawsuits by distributing money to states for children's charities and distributing toys directly to children's charities such as Toys for Tots.[54]

In summary, any time two parties interact, there's a potential for ethical and legal problems. Buyers face issues such as how much to charge a vendor for shelf space in their stores or whether they should accept a gift or favour from a vendor with no strings attached. An eye toward fairness and the desire to maintain a strong relationship should dictate behaviour in these areas. Retailers must also be concerned with the origin of their merchandise. Specifically, is it counterfeit or grey-market merchandise? Vendors encounter a different set of issues. In general, vendors need not worry about legal problems when selling to retailers so long as they sell whatever the retailers want, to whoever wants to buy, at the same price to all. But when vendors start making restrictions and exceptions, there may be legal violations.

TERMS OF PURCHASE

Now that we have chosen our merchandise, developed relationships with our suppliers, and considered the legal ramifications of our actions, we must negotiate the terms of purchase. There are two sides to the pricing equation. Later, we'll examine the price at which merchandise is sold. In this section, we look at the price at which merchandise is purchased. When determining price, vendors must examine the different types of discounts they may offer. These discounts—referred to as the terms of purchase—include trade or functional discounts, chain discounts, quantity discounts, seasonal discounts, cash discounts, anticipation discounts, and shipping terms and conditions.

Quantity Discounts

Quantity discounts are of two types: cumulative and noncumulative. Retailers earn cumulative quantity disounts by purchasing certain quantities over a specified period of time. For instance, a vendor may grant an additional discount to a retailer that purchases $100 000 worth of merchandise in one year. These discounts have the same effect as a year-end rebate. Vendors grant cumulative quantity discounts as an incentive to buy more merchandise and to encourage retailer loyalty. Under the *Competition Act*, however, it's hard for a vendor to justify lower costs for higher quantities on a cumulative basis.[55] To justify cumulative quantity discounts, a vendor could show that having retailers commit to certain levels of purchases in advance allows the vendor to plan production more efficiently and thus cut costs. Cumulative quantity discounts could be easily justified in the garment industry, for instance, since garment manufacturers must commit to their cloth suppliers months in advance.

Noncumulative quantity discounts are offered to retailers as an incentive to purchase more merchandise on a single order. Larger, less frequent orders may save vendors order processing, sales, and transportation expenses. These expenses are often found in retailing and are more easily cost-justified than cumulative quantity discounts.[56]

Exhibit 12–3 presents a sample price list that combines trade/functional, chain, and noncumulative quantity discounts for an appliance manufacturer. The headings "Price to Wholesaler" and "Price to Retailer" illustrate trade/functional discounts. The "40–5%," "50–10," and "50–10–5" under the "Price to Wholesaler, Discount" represent different chain discounts. Finally, the first column, "Quantity per Order," illustrates noncumulative quantity discounts.

Examine the columns under "Price to Retailer." At which price should the retailer buy? At first glance, the lowest price appears to be $54. But the lowest price isn't always the most profitable. If the dealer purchases 26 or more TV sets all at once, it may have more than a year's supply. Inventory turnover and the cost of carrying the inventory would be unsatisfactory. The merchandise may become shopworn, and the large quantity might even require more space than is available.[57]

| Quantity per Order | PRICE TO WHOLESALER | | PRICE TO RETAILER | | |
	Discount	Price	Discount	Price	
1–10	40–5%	$57*	30%	$70	
11–25	50–10	45	40	60	
26+	50–10–5	42.75	40–10	54	

exhibit 12–3
A Sample Price List

*Based on a $100 suggested retail price.

Seasonal Discounts

A seasonal discount is an additional discount offered as an incentive to retailers to order merchandise in advance of the normal buying season. For instance, Black & Decker garden tools may be offered to retailers at a special price in January. Black & Decker can more easily plan its production schedules and lower its finished goods inventory if it can ship early in the season. Retailers, on the other hand, must consider the benefits of a larger gross margin from the discount versus the additional cost of carrying the inventory for a longer period of time.

Cash Discounts

A cash discount is a reduction in the invoice cost for paying the invoice prior to the end of the discount period. It's applied after the functional/trade, chain, quantity, and seasonal discounts. An example is 1/30, n/60 (spoken as "one, thirty, net sixty"). This means the retailer can take a 1 percent discount if it pays on or before the 30th day after the date of invoice. Or the full invoice amount is due 60 days after the date of invoice.

Thus there are three components of a cash discount: the percentage of the discount, the number of days in which the discount can be taken, and the net credit period (when the full amount of the invoice is due). For example, a typical cash discount is 1/30, n/60. This means that if the invoice is dated on November 1, the retailer has 30 days (until December 1) to take the 1 percent discount. The full amount is due 60 days after the invoice date, on January 1. (If retailers really counted days, the full amount would be due on December 31 since there are 31 days in December. But retailers usually don't pay that much attention to the number of days in a month for the purpose of taking cash discounts.)

1/30, n/60		
Nov. 1	Dec. 1	Jan. 1
Date of invoice	30 days 1% discount	60 days Full amount due

There are a number of variations on the basic cash discount format known as dating. The term *dating* refers to the dates on which discounts can be taken and full amounts are due in a cash discount pricing policy. Here are four examples of common forms of dating.

Receipt of Goods (ROG) Dating

Using ROG dating, the cash discount period starts on the day the merchandise is received. If the merchandise is shipped and invoiced on November 1, but doesn't arrive until November 15, using dating of 1/30, n/60, ROG, the cash discount can be taken until December 15, and the full amount is due January 15.

ROG DATING			
Nov. 1	Nov. 15	Dec. 15	Jan. 15
Date of invoice	Merchandise arrives	30 days ROG 1% discount	60 days ROG Full amount due

End-of-Month (EOM) Dating

In EOM dating, the discount period starts at the end of the month in which the invoice is dated (except when the invoice is dated the 25th or later—as we'll discuss shortly). As in the previous example, if merchandise is invoiced on November 1, using dating of 1/30, n/60, EOM, the cash discount can be taken until January 1, and the full amount is due February 1. The retailer can pay 30 days later than the same terms without the EOM designation.

EOM DATING			
Nov. 1	Dec. 1	Jan. 1	Feb. 1
Date of invoice	30-day discount period begins	30 days EOM 1% discount	60 days EOM Full amount due

EOM Dating, Grace Period

A grace period is often given when an invoice with EOM dating is dated after the 25th of the month. The vendor starts counting on the first of the next month. If the merchandise is invoiced on October 25, using the same dating of 1/30, n/60, EOM, the cash discount can still be taken until January 1, and the full amount is due February

1. This time the retailer gets 36 days longer to pay than without the EOM designation. So if the retailer wanted to maximize the length of time to pay for the merchandise and still take the cash discount, the merchandise would be ordered so that it would be invoiced as close to the 25th of the month as possible.

EOM DATING, GRACE PERIOD				
Oct. 25	Nov. 1	Dec. 1	Jan. 1	Feb. 1
Date of invoice		30-day discount period begins	30 days EOM 1% discount	60 days EOM Full amount due

Extra Dating

With extra dating, the retailer receives an extra amount of time to pay the invoice and still take the cash discount. Assume again that the merchandise is invoiced on November 1. Using dating of 1/30, n/60, EOM, 60 days extra (also written 60X or 60 ex.), the cash discount could be taken until March 1, with the net amount due April 1. That is, the discount period starts December 1, due to the EOM designation. The buyer gets 30 days for the regular discount period, plus an additional 60 days.

The rationale for offering extra dating is similar to that for the seasonal discount. The vendor may need to give the retailer an additional incentive to purchase risky or seasonal merchandise. Instead of giving the retailer a lower price (as is the case with the seasonal discount), the vendor grants the retailer a longer time in which to pay.

EXTRA DATING					
Nov. 1	Dec. 1	Jan. 1	Feb. 1	Mar. 1	Aug. 1
Date of invoice	30-day discount period begins	60-day extra discount period begins		60-day extra 1% discount	Full amount due

Anticipation Discounts

Under the previously discussed dating policies, a retailer has no incentive to pay earlier than the last day of the discount period. An anticipation

discount provides this incentive. It's a discount offered in addition to the cash discount or dating if an invoice is paid before the end of the cash discount period. Let's say the dating is 1/30, n/60, EOM, with anticipation of 18 percent per year, and the invoice is dated November 1, the 30-day discount period ends at the end of December, but the retailer pays on December 1, 30 days earlier. Let's calculate the net cost on a $100 item.

Cash discount = $100 × 0.01 = $1

Invoice less discount = $100 − $1 = $99

Since the anticipation is 18 percent a year, but the retailer is paying 30 days early, we calculate the anticipation as

Anticipation = $99 × 0.18 × (30 days early ÷ 360 days per year) = $1.49

Net amount = $99.00 − $1.49 = $97.51

The retailer can earn an extra $2.49 (or $100 − $97.51) by paying early, taking the cash discount, and taking the anticipation.

Shipping Terms and Conditions

The last question in any terms of purchase policy is who (the retailer or the vendor) has responsibility for the different aspects of shipping the merchandise. Two basic issues must be agreed upon when designating the shipping terms and conditions: Who pays the freight charges, and who owns the merchandise while it's in transit?

Transportation costs for shipping merchandise from vendor to retailer can be substantial. If the retailer incurs this expense, it increases the cost of the merchandise.

The party owning the merchandise in transit is responsible for filing a claim with the transportation company in case of lost or damaged merchandise. This is a time-consuming, potentially expensive process. The party filing the claim may have to wait months before it's reimbursed for the loss or damage. Also, the party owning the merchandise while in transit may be responsible for paying insurance that might be needed above the liability of the transportation company to cover merchandise lost or damaged in transit.

Many forms of shipping terms and conditions are used. Exhibit 12–4 outlines the most common ones. The designation *freight prepaid* means freight is paid by the vendor; *freight collect* means

exhibit 12–4
Alternative Shipping
Terms and Conditions

	Pays Freight Charges	Owns Merchandise in Transit and Files Claims (If Any)
FOB origin, freight collect	Retailer	Retailer
FOB origin, freight prepaid	Supplier	Retailer
FOB destination, freight collect	Retailer	Supplier
FOB destination, freight prepaid	Supplier	Supplier

the retailer pays the freight. The term *FOB (free on board) origin* means ownership of the merchandise changes hands at the location where the shipment originates. When the ownership changes hands, so does responsibility for filing claims and insurance in case of lost or damaged merchandise. Thus FOB origin is beneficial to the vendor. The term *origin* is often substituted for plant or factory. *FOB destination* means ownership of the merchandise changes hands at the store. So the term *destination* is often substituted for *store* or *retailer*.

CHAPTER 13

retail pricing

Executive Briefing

Aldo Bensadoun, President, The Aldo Group

Aldo is a household name in Canada that is synonymous with trendy shoes. The company had humble beginnings in 1972 in Montreal as a concession within the Le Chateau clothing stores. By 1980 Aldo Bensadoun, encouraged by his entrepreneurial spirit, expanded the company to include 30 stores and began to diversify under new banners. Today the Aldo Group has seven banners in Canada, each catering to a distinct market segment: Aldo (the flagship brand), Pegabo, Simard/Calderone, Transit, Stoneridge, Globo, and Feet First focus on the mid-market price range.

Bensadoun, the son of a retailer who operated a small chain of shoe stores in France and Morocco and the grandson of a cobbler, completed his university studies at McGill University in Montreal. A degree in economics led him to a marketing research position, which found Bensadoun doing a project for a regional shoe chain. Eventually the combination of past family history in the shoe business, knowledge of Canadian population trends, and smart business sense led him to open his own company.

In Canada, Aldo stores currently number 175, plus seven additional banners. The second largest banner is Transit, with 125 stores in Canada. Aldo

QUESTIONS

What factors do retailers consider when pricing merchandise?

Why do some retailers have frequent sales while others attempt to maintain an everyday low price strategy?

How do retailers set retail prices?

What pricing strategies can retailers use to influence consumer purchases?

How is the Internet changing the way retailers price their merchandise?

Under what circumstances can retailers' pricing practices get them into legal difficulties?

What are the legal restrictions on retail pricing?

Shoes has opened 50 stores a year in United States for the past two years, and now operates 180 outlets there. Global expansion includes 10 corporate stores in England and another 50 franchised stores in Europe and Asia, with planned expansion in Australia. The company boasts average sales per square metre of more that $7527, and the chain is growing at approximately 25 to 30 stores a year. Mattel toys even approached Bensadoun to design Aldo shoes as part of a Barbie doll designer set!

Aldo sells only private label fashion-oriented shoes designed and made for the company. Analyzing population groups provides design inspiration; in fact, trends are often influenced by the environment, politics, and economics. The design team researches clothing designs and magazines to interpret the trends in footwear.

Truly a success story, today Aldo Bensadoun is one of Canada's richest retailers. Learning how to adopt his approach to different cultures has always kept Aldo on the cutting edge of footwear fashion. Bensadoun continues to grow his mid-price shoe empire with quality and cutting edge trends at affordable prices season after season, in Canada and around the world.

The importance of pricing decisions is growing because today's customers demand good value. **Value** is the relationship between what the customer gets (goods/services) and what he or she has to pay for it. To some customers, good value means always getting a low price. Increasingly, Canadian consumers have become price-sensitive. Others are willing to pay extra as long as they believe they're getting their money's worth in terms of product quality or service.

Retailers have responded to their customers' needs with retail formats that emphasize low prices as a means of creating a differential advantage. National discount store chains that offer everyday low prices, such as Wal-Mart, dominate many markets in many product categories. A close competitor in the price-oriented market is the membership-only warehouse club, such as Sam's Warehouse Club and Costco. Another retail format is the off-price retailer (e.g., Winners), which purchases closeout and end-of-season merchandise at lower-than-normal prices and passes the savings on to the customer.

Some of the more mature retailing institutions, such as department stores and supermarkets, have come to grips with these forms of price competition by adopting a more aggressive pricing strategy, with a significant amount of their merchandise being sold below the manufacturer's suggested price through a strong promotion orientation. Finally, many retailers such as Harry Rosen have successfully maintained their market appeal by providing good value by offering customers high-quality merchandise and service without attempting to offer the lowest prices.

In the middle of this price competition among national giants are the smaller retailers. Typically unable to purchase in large quantities to receive lower prices like their larger competitors, mom-and-pop retailers have either learned to use other strategies to compete (such as extending opening hours) or have gone out of business. For instance, to compete with Wal-Mart's low prices, small retailers have developed niche strategies by providing a broader assortment of merchandise within a given product category and better service.

Pricing decisions are also being affected by the development of electronic channels. Consumers can easily compare the prices for branded products sold by different retailers. The Internet also makes it easier for consumers to compare product attributes in addition to price.

The Internet has facilitated the use of an auction pricing mechanism. People have used auctions to facilitate trade for centuries. As eBay has demonstrated, no longer do auction participants have to be located at the same place.

Getting the right product onto store shelves at the right time and at the right price is the basic formula for success in retailing. Increased competition has made it more important than ever to get that formula right.

Cost cutting issues might include:

- Buying merchandise offshore to maintain higher profit potential due to higher Canadian dollar

- Cutting packaging costs by including three languages—English, French, Spanish—to serve all North American markets

- Retailers and suppliers partnering to maintain competitive prices

- Using price optimization software technology to sell as much inventory as possible at the highest possible price

Although technology can help move products off store shelves quickly, the art of retailing lies in predicting demand patterns.

pricing strategies

In today's retail market, two opposing pricing strategies prevail: everyday low pricing and high/low pricing.[2] We will describe these two strategies and the conditions under which each is used.

EVERYDAY LOW PRICING

Many retailers have adopted an **everyday low pricing (EDLP)** strategy. This strategy emphasizes continuity of retail prices at a level somewhere between the regular nonsale price and the deep-discount sale price of the retailer's competitors. The term *everyday low pricing* is therefore somewhat of a misnomer. Low doesn't necessarily mean lowest. Although retailers using EDLP strive for low prices, they aren't always the lowest price in the market. At any given time, a sale price at a competing store or a special purchase at a wholesale club store may be the lowest price. A more accurate description of this strategy is therefore everyday *same* prices because the prices don't have significant fluctuations.

Several of the biggest Canadian retailers—Canadian Tire, Wal-Mart, and Staples Business Depot—have adopted EDLP. In supermarket retailing, Loblaws, including Fortino's and Zehrs, is positioned as an EDLP store.[3] Although these retailers embrace EDLP as their strategy, they do occasionally have sales. They are just not as frequent as their high/low competitors.

Since it is difficult to always have the lowest prices, some retailers have adopted a **low price guarantee policy** in which they guarantee that they will have the lowest possible price for a product or a group of products. The guarantee usually promises to match or better any lower price found in the local market. The promise normally includes a provision to refund the difference between the seller's offer price and the lower price.

HIGH/LOW PRICING

In a **high/low pricing** strategy, retailers offer prices that are sometimes above their competition's EDLP, but they use advertising to promote frequent sales. The

Wal-Mart's Everyday Low Pricing (EDLP) strategy has helped make it the market leader in every market it enters, and the largest retailer in the world.

sales undertaken by retailers using high/low strategies have become more intense in recent years. In the past, fashion retailers would mark down merchandise at the end of a season; grocery and drugstores would have sales only when their vendors offered them special prices or when they were overstocked. Today, many retailers respond to increased competition and a more price-conscious customer by promoting more frequent sales.

DECIDING WHICH STRATEGY IS BEST

EDLP approach advantages:

- *Reduced price wars.* Many customers are skeptical about initial retail prices. They have become conditioned to buying only on sale—the main characteristic of a high/low pricing strategy. A successful EDLP strategy enables retailers to withdraw from highly competitive price wars with competitors. Once customers realize that prices are fair, they'll buy more each time and buy more frequently.

- *Reduced advertising.* The stable prices caused by EDLP limit the need for weekly sale advertising used in the high/low strategy. Instead, retailers can focus on more image-oriented messages. In addition, EDLP retailers do not have to incur the labour costs of changing price tags and signs and putting up sales signs.

- *Reduced stockouts and improved inventory management.* An EDLP reduces the large variations in demand caused by frequent sales with large markdowns. As a result, retailers can manage their inventory with more certainty. Fewer stockouts mean more satisfied customers, higher sales, and fewer rain checks. (**Rain checks** are given to customers when merchandise is out of stock; they're written promises to sell customers merchandise at the sale price when the merchandise arrives.) In addition, a more predictable customer demand pattern enables the retailer to improve inventory turnover by reducing the average inventory needed for special promotions and backup stock.

Retailers using a high/low pricing strategy start with a high price and use advertising to promote frequent sales.

High/low pricing strategy advantages:

- *Increase profit through price discrimination.* A high/low strategy allows retailers to charge higher prices to customers who are not price-sensitive and lower prices to price-sensitive customers. When fashion

merchandise first hits the store, it's offered at its highest price. Fashion leaders, those who are less sensitive to price, and hard-to-fit customers often buy as soon as the merchandise is available. As the season progresses and markdowns are taken, more price-sensitive customers enter the market and pay a lower price for the same merchandise. Finally, hard-core bargain hunters enter the market for the end-of-season deep-discount sales at the end of each season—25 percent off merchandise that has already been marked down 33 to 50 percent.

- *Sales create excitement.* A "get them while they last" atmosphere often occurs during a sale. Sales draw crowds, and crowds create excitement. Some retailers augment low prices and advertising with special in-store activities such as product demonstrations, giveaways, and celebrity appearances.

- *Sales move merchandise.* All merchandise will eventually sell—the question is, at what price? Frequent sales enable retailers to move the merchandise, even though profits erode. The reasons retailers put certain merchandise on sale are discussed later in this chapter.

- *Emphasis is on quality.* A high initial price sends a signal to customers that the merchandise is high quality. When merchandise goes on sale, customers still use the original, or reference, price to gauge quality.

approaches for setting prices

After selecting an overall pricing strategy, retailers still need to set the price for each item. Retailers want to set prices to maximize long-term profits. To do this, they need to consider the following:

- Cost, of the merchandise and services
- Demand, the price sensitivity of consumers
- Competition, because customers shop around and compare prices
- Legal considerations

The following sections examine three approaches for setting retail prices—cost-oriented, demand-oriented, and competition-oriented—and describe how retailers determine how much they need to sell to break even.

Under the **cost-oriented method,** the retail price is determined by adding a fixed percentage to the cost of the merchandise. For instance, a family-owned women's specialty store might use the **keystone method** of setting prices, in which it simply doubles the cost of the merchandise to obtain the original retail selling price. If a dress costs $50, the original selling price is $100. With the **demand-oriented method,** prices are based on what customers expect or are willing to pay. In this case, the retailer may have found a particularly good value at $50 but believes that the profit-maximizing price is $115. The retailer is aware of the price sensitivity of the consumers. With the **competition-oriented method,** prices are based on competitors' prices.

Which method is best? The answer is, all three! The cost-oriented method's strength is that it is quick, mechanical, and relatively simple to use. Retailers use it because they are making thousands of pricing decisions each week and cannot take the time to thoroughly analyze and determine the best price for each product.

As indicated by economic theory, the demand-oriented method's strength is that it allows retailers to determine which price will give them the greatest profit. But demand-oriented pricing is hard to implement, especially in a retailing environment with thousands of SKUs that require individual pricing decisions.

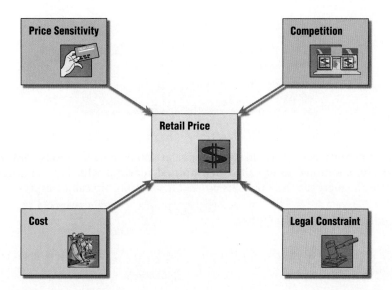

exhibit 13–1
Considerations in
Setting Retail Prices

The competition-oriented method should be considered because it is always important to keep in mind what competition is doing—after all, the customer does. The degree to which a retailer sets the market price or follows the market leader is, however, a complicated issue.

Retailers need to consider costs, demand, and competition in setting prices. The cost-oriented method would be the starting point for setting a price. The competition-oriented method provides an outside check on the marketplace. The demand-oriented method is then used for fine-tuning the strategy. Retailers would start with a price based on costs and their profit goals, consider competition, and then perform tests to determine if it's the most profitable price.

Service retailers face challenges that aren't as important to merchandise retailers.

THE COST-ORIENTED METHOD OF SETTING RETAIL PRICES

This section explains how retail prices are set on the basis of merchandise cost. Unfortunately, the process isn't always as simple as doubling the cost, which we described earlier. For instance, the retail price at which the product is originally sold may not be the same as the final retail selling price due to markdowns. So retailers have devised methods of keeping track of changes in the retail price so they can achieve their overall financial goals.

Recall that the retailer's financial goals are set by top management in terms of a target return on assets. In the strategic profit model, return on assets is calculated as net profit margin multiplied by asset turnover. Pricing goals are determined primarily from net profit margin.

For pricing decisions, the key component of net profit margin is gross profit margin percentage (Gross margin ÷ Net sales). Retailers set initial prices high enough so that after markdowns and other adjustments (known as reductions) are made, they'll end up with a gross margin consistent with their overall profit goals. We'll now describe how retailers determine their initial selling price based on their gross margin goal.

Determining the Initial Markup from Maintained Markup and Gross Margin   The performance measure usually used to evaluate pricing decisions is gross margin. Exhibit 13–2 summarizes its components. We used the traditional

exhibit 13–2
Sample Income
Statement Showing
Gross Margin

Net Sales	$120 000
–Cost of goods sold	58 000
= Maintained markup	62 000
–Alteration costs + Cash discounts	3 000
= Gross margin	$ 59 000

accounting definition of gross margin: net sales minus cost of goods sold. But retailers use an additional term called **maintained markup** which is the actual sales realized for the merchandise minus its costs. The relationship can be expressed as:

$$\text{Maintained markup percentage} = \frac{\text{Net sales} - \text{Costs of goods sold}}{\text{Net sales}}$$

$$\text{Gross margin percentage} = \frac{\text{Maintained markup} - \text{Workroom costs} + \text{Cash discounts}}{\text{Net sales}}$$

Thus, the only difference between the two terms is the workroom costs (such as alterations to a suit or the cost of putting a table together) and cash discounts (given to the store by the vendor for paying invoices early). Why do retailers make this distinction between maintained markup and gross margin? In many retail organizations, these workroom costs aren't controlled by the person who makes the pricing decision. For instance, the furniture buyer doesn't have control over costs associated with assembling a dining room table. In the same way, a buyer typically has no control over whether the accounting department takes the cash discounts offered to the company from its vendors for paying invoices early. But remember that, conceptually, maintained markup and gross margin are similar. Moores Clothiers has done an excellent job by collecting fees for alterations, a cost recovery.

Remember that gross margin is a financial term that expresses the difference between net sales (the price that the customer pays for merchandise) and the cost of the merchandise (the cost that the retailer paid for the merchandise). The gross margin return on investment (GMROI) is the financial ratio of gross margin dollars divided by the average cost of stock on hand.

The term *maintained markup* is very descriptive. It's the amount of profit (markup) a retailer plans to maintain on a particular category of merchandise. For example, in Exhibit 13–2, planned maintained markup is $62 000 on sales of $120 000, or 51.67 percent ($62 000 ÷ $120 000). In other words, to meet its profit goals, this retailer must obtain a 51.67 percent maintained markup.

A retailer's life would be relatively simple if the amount of markup it wanted to maintain (maintained markup) were the same as the initial markup.

Initial markup = Retail selling price initially placed on the merchandise minus cost of goods sold (COGS)

whereas,

Maintained markup = The actual sales that you get for the merchandise minus cost of goods sold (COGS)

Why is there a difference? A number of reductions to the value of retail inventory occur between the time the merchandise is originally priced (initial markup) and the time it's sold (maintained markup). **Reductions** include markdowns, discounts to employees and customers, and inventory shrinkage (due to shoplifting, breakage, or loss). Initial markup must be high enough so that after reductions are taken out, the maintained markup is left.

A few retail customers might feel slightly guilty when buying a product that has been drastically marked down. They shouldn't, however. Retailers that successfully plan their sales and markdowns also build the markdown into the initial price. Even though a customer may receive a very good price on a particular purchase, other people paid the premarkdown price. So, on average, the markup was maintained.

Retailers expect shrinkage and include this loss in the price customers pay. To illustrate, consider a TV campaign that ran a few years ago showing someone shoplifting. The message was "When you shoplift, you are ripping off your neighbour." If two retailers plan to achieve the same maintained markup, but one has a high percentage of shrinkage due to shoplifting, that store needs a higher initial markup if all other factors are held constant.

The relationship between initial markup and maintained markup is

$$\text{Initial markup} = \frac{\text{Maintained markup} + \text{Reductions}}{\text{Net sales} + \text{Reductions}}$$

or

$$\text{Initial markup} = \frac{\substack{\text{Maintained markup (as a \% of net sales)} \\ + \text{Reductions (as a \% of net sales)}}}{100\% + \text{Reductions (as a \% of net sales)}}$$

Using the information in Exhibit 13–2 and assuming that reductions of \$14 400 here equal 12 percent of net sales,

$$\text{Initial markup} = \frac{\$62\ 000 + \$14\ 400}{\$120\ 000 + \$14\ 400} = 56.85\%$$

or

$$\text{Initial markup} = \frac{51.67\% + 12\%}{100\% + 12\%} = 56.85\%$$

Note that the same answer is obtained using both formulas. Also, initial markup is always greater than maintained markup so long as there are any reductions. Finally, initial markup is expressed either in dollars or as a percentage of retail price. This is because retailers using the retail inventory method (RIM) of inventory accounting think of their inventory in "retail" rather than "cost" terms. Also, expressing initial markup as a percentage of retail price closely resembles the other accounting conventions of expressing net profit, gross margin, and maintained markup as percentages of net sales, which are, of course, at retail.

Thus, if the buyer setting the price for the item shown in Exhibit 13–3 planned on reductions of 10 percent of actual sales and wanted a maintained markup of 33 percent, the initial markup should be

$$\text{Initial markup percentage} = \frac{33\% + (\$0.10/\$0.90 = 11.111\%)}{100\% + 11.111\%} = 40\%$$

and the initial retail price should be

$$\text{Initial retail price} = \frac{\text{Cost}}{1 - \text{Initial markup percentage}} = \frac{\$0.60}{1 - 0.40} = \$1.00$$

exhibit 13–3

Difference between
Initial Markup and
Maintained Markup

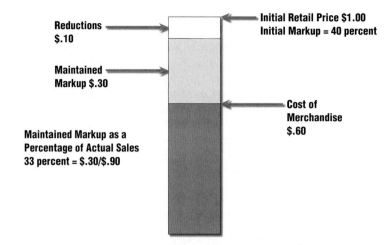

Reductions
$.10

Maintained
Markup $.30

**Initial Retail Price $1.00
Initial Markup = 40 percent**

Cost of
Merchandise
$.60

Maintained Markup as a
Percentage of Actual Sales
33 percent = $.30/$.90

Determining the Initial Retail Price under Cost-Oriented Pricing

Continuing the preceding example, with the initial markup of 56.85 percent, assume that the suggested retail price of a certain item is $100. What is the dollar markup and the merchandise cost?

Retail = Cost	+	Markup
$100 = Cost	+	(56.85% × Retail)
$100 = Cost	+	$56.85
$100 = $43.15	+	$56.85

The dollar markup is $56.85 and the merchandise cost is $43.15.

Here's another example. A salesperson comes into a buyer's office with a great new product that will cost $100. What will be the retail price if the initial markup is still 56.85 percent?

There are three ways to solve this problem. First, the buyer can convert the initial markup as a percentage of retail to initial markup as a percentage of cost using the formula[5]

$$\text{Initial markup as a \% of cost} = \frac{\text{Initial markup as a \% of retail}}{100\% - \text{Initial markup as a \% of retail}}$$

$$131.75\% = \frac{56.85\%}{100\% - 56.85\%}$$

Then the problem can be set up as before:

Retail = Cost + Markup	
Retail = $100 + (131.75% × Cost)	
$231.75 = $100 + $131.75	

The second way to solve this problem uses algebra. Let's say that R stands for the retail price.

Retail = Cost + Markup	
Retail = $100 + (56.85% × Retail)	
R = $100 + 0.5685 × R	

By subtracting $0.5685 \times R$ from both sides of the equation, the resulting initial retail price can be figured as follows:

$$0.4315 \times R = \$100$$
$$R = \$231.75$$

The third way to solve this problem uses the formula

$$\text{Retail} = \frac{\text{Cost}}{1 - \text{Markup}}$$

$$\$231.75 = \frac{\$100}{1 - 0.5685}$$

THE DEMAND-ORIENTED METHOD OF SETTING RETAIL PRICES

Demand-oriented pricing should be used in conjunction with the cost-oriented method to determine retail prices. Using this method, retailers not only consider their profit structure but also pay close attention to the effect that price changes have on sales. For instance, if customers are extremely price-sensitive, then a price cut can increase demand so much that profits actually increase. Alternatively, if customers are insensitive to price, raising the price also can boost profits, since sales likely won't decrease. Demand-oriented pricing seeks to determine the price that customers are willing to pay and that will maximize profits.

To illustrate how an initial retail price is set using the demand-oriented method, we will use a hypothetical situation of Aritzia's new ribbed sleeveless T-shirt for women. Assume that the fixed cost of developing the product is $300 000 and the variable cost is $5 each. One benefit of private-label merchandise is the flexibility of being able to set any retail price. Aritzia decides to test the T-shirt in four markets at different prices. Exhibit 13–4 shows the pricing test's results. It's clear (from column 5) that a unit price of $10 is by far the most profitable ($450 000).

Although determining the optimal price based on a demand analysis is simple for one product, most retailers carry so many products that these tests become a very expensive proposition. Also, a retailer must have multiple outlets to be able to manipulate prices in this manner.

A more sophisticated method of determining the most profitable price is a *pricing experiment*. In a pricing experiment, a retailer actually changes the price in a systematic manner to observe changes in purchases or purchase intentions. Exhibit 13–5 shows an example of a simple experiment—a classic before/after experiment with control group design. Two stores are similar in size and customer characteristics. Their weekly sales for a compact microwave oven are almost identical (10 and 12 units per week), and the ovens are selling at the same price, $100. The price at the first store

Market	(1) Unit Price	(2) Market Demand at Price (in units)	(3) Total Revenue (col. 1 × col. 2)	(4) Total Cost of Units Sold ($300 000 fixed cost + $5 variable cost)	(5) Total Profits (col. 3 – col.4)
1	$ 8	200 000	$1 600 000	$1 300 000	$300 000
2	10	150 000	1 500 000	1 050 000	450 000
3	12	100 000	1 200 000	800 000	400 000
4	14	50 000	700 000	550 000	150 000

exhibit 13–4
Results of Pricing Test

exhibit 13–5
A Pricing Experiment

	Before	After
Store 1	10 units @ $100 Gross margin = $500	21 units @ $80 Gross margin = $630
Store 2 (Control)	12 units @ $100 Gross margin = $600	13 units @ $100 Gross margin = $650

is changed to $80, but the second store's price is left at $100. Thus, the second store is used as a control to make sure that any change in sales is due to the price change rather than to some outside force such as competition or weather. Now sales at the first store jump to 21 units per week, while sales at the control store hit 13 units. Barring any circumstances unknown to the retailer, the change in sales is due to the price cut. And, by the way, the $100 price is more profitable than the $80 price in the second store! Since product cost is $50, the $100 retail price provides a $650 gross margin [($100 − $50) × 13 units], whereas the $80 price provides a $630 gross margin [($80 − $50) × 21 units].

In the past, these pricing experiments weren't regularly applied because of the time and expense of administering them. But now any retailer with point-of-sale terminals can run large-scale experiments. Retailers can utilize the data warehouses derived from their loyalty programs in conjunction with sales and price data to run experiments. These records cover what customers have purchased, prices paid, and conditions of sale (such as coupon usage and price specials). Demographic information on customers makes it possible to correlate price sensitivity with customer profiles.

Retailers and their vendors can also buy from private firms. For one of its many products, InfoScan, the company purchases information from individual supermarket chains on price and promotion activity that has been scanned through their POS terminals; it then aggregates data by region, chain, or market area.

THE COMPETITION-ORIENTED METHOD OF SETTING RETAIL PRICES

As the name implies, when retailers use competition-oriented pricing, they set their prices on the basis of their competition rather than cost or demand considerations. Retailers can price either above, below, or at parity with the competition. The chosen strategy must be consistent with the retailer's overall strategy and its relative market position. Consider, for instance, Wal-Mart and Birks as we did previously. Wal-Mart's overall strategy is to be the low-cost retailer for the merchandise it sells. It tries to price products it sells below competition. Birks, on the other hand, offers significant benefits to its customers including high quality, unique merchandise, impeccable service, and elegant locations. Those little blue boxes stamped with the Birks logo symbolize quality service and jewellery. Due to the unique nature of Birks' offering, it is able to set prices higher than its competitors'.

Market leaders cannot, however, ignore their small competitors. Suppose that a sporting goods store in North Bay, Ontario, consistently underprices Wal-Mart on fishing gear. Wal-Mart will adjust its prices to meet or even beat the competitor in that market.

What should small competitors do to compete with market leaders? A jewellery store could price at parity or below Birks. Additionally, it could strive for competitive advantages in assortment or service. A more difficult question is how a casual wear store can compete against Wal-Mart's prices. It cannot compete head to head with Wal-Mart on every item. To do so would probably put it out of business because it cannot achieve the buying quantities of scale of Wal-Mart. Instead, it should pick items that are very visible to customers and generate margin on items that customers cannot readily compare. If Wal-Mart is advertising jeans at $19.99, then the casual wear store should either carry other brands of jeans or bite the bullet and price with or below Wal-Mart.

Collecting and Using Competitive Price Data[6]   Retailers work to provide a consistent shopping experience, and part of that requires consistency between a retailer's market strategy and its pricing position within a market. Most large retailers routinely collect competitive price data from competitors to see if they need to adjust their prices to remain competitive.

Competitive price data are typically collected using store personnel, third-party providers, and vendor representatives (whose interests often bias the data). Costing between $0.15 and $2.00 per price point to collect, competitive price comparisons are typically still performed using pen and paper and sometimes without the consent of the competitor. Because the costs associated with collecting and then managing the data are significant, retailers need to be very strategic when structuring competitive price projects.

How Retailers Reduce Price Competition   Retailers have two fundamental strategies available to them for reducing price competition:

- First, they can adopt an EDLP strategy. Conditioning customers to expect a fair and relatively low price on a typical market basket of merchandise enables a retailer to charge slightly higher prices on some individual items.

- Second, they can utilize some of the branding strategies described previously. For instance, they can develop lines of premium private-label merchandise. Since the competition doesn't have such merchandise, it is difficult for the customer to comparison shop.

PROFIT IMPACT OF SETTING A RETAIL PRICE: THE USE OF BREAK-EVEN ANALYSIS

Now that we've examined how retailers set prices on the bases of the cost-, demand-, and competition-oriented methods, let's look at how retailers determine the volume of sales necessary for them to make a profit. A useful analytical tool is **break-even analysis,** which analyzes the relationship between total revenue and total cost to determine how much merchandise needs to be sold to achieve a break-even (zero) profit. For example, a retailer might want to know:

- Break-even volume and dollars for a new product, product line, or department
- Break-even sales change needed to cover a price change
- Break-even sales to cover a target profit
- Change in profit based on change in sales volume

Let's look more closely at the first two: the break-even volume of a new private-label product and the break-even sales change needed to cover a price change.

Calculating Break-Even for a New Product   Suppose PETsMART is considering the introduction of a new private-label, dry dog food targeting owners of older dogs. The cost of developing this dog food is $700 000, including salaries for the design team and testing the product. Because these costs don't change with the quantity of product that is produced and sold, they're known as **fixed costs.** PETsMART plans to sell the dog food for $12 a bag—the unit price. The **variable cost** is the retailer's expenses that vary directly with the quantity of product produced and sold. Variable costs often include direct labour and materials used in producing the product. PETsMART will be purchasing the product from a private-label manufacturer. Thus, the only variable cost is the dog food's cost, $5, from the private-label supplier. The **break-even point (BEP)** quantity is the quantity at which total revenue equals total cost, and then profit occurs for additional sales.

$$\text{Break-even quantity} = \frac{\text{Fixed cost}}{\text{Actual unit sales price} - \text{Unit variable cost}}$$

$$= \frac{\$700\ 000}{\$12 - \$5} = 100\ 000 \text{ bags}$$

Thus, PETsMART needs to sell 100,000 bags of dog food to break even, or make zero profit, and for every additional bag sold, it will make $7 profit.

Now assume that PETsMART wants to make $100,000 profit from the new product line. The break-even quantity now becomes:

$$\text{Break-even quantity} = \frac{\text{Fixed cost}}{\text{Actual unit sales price} - \text{Unit variable cost}}$$

$$= \frac{\$700\ 000 + \$100\ 000}{\$12 - \$5} = 114\ 286 \text{ bags}$$

Calculating Break-Even Sales   A closely related issue to the calculation of a break-even point is determining how much unit sales would have to increase to make a profit from a price cut or how much sales would have to decline to make a price increase unprofitable. Continuing with the PETsMART example, assume the break-even quantity is 114 286 units based on the $700 000 fixed cost, the $100 000 profit, a selling price of $12, and a cost of $5. Now PETsMART is considering lowering the price of a bag of dog food to $10. How many units must it sell to break even if it lowers its selling price by 16.67 percent to $10? Using the formula,

$$\text{Break-even quantity} = \frac{\text{Fixed cost}}{\text{Actual unit sales price} - \text{Unit variable cost}}$$

$$= \frac{\$700\ 000 + \$100\ 000}{\$12 - \$5} = 160\ 000 \text{ bags}$$

So if PETsMART decreases its price by 16.67 percent from $12 to $10, unit sales must increase by 40 percent: (160 000 − 114 286)/111 286.

Calculating Break-Even Sales   A closely related issue to the calculation of a break-even point is determining how much sales would have to increase to profit from a price cut, or how much sales would have to decline to make a price increase unprofitable.[7] Using the example of T-shirts from Aritzia, assume the break-even quantity is 57 143 units (based on the $300 000 fixed cost, the $100 000 profit, a selling price of

$12, and a cost of $5). How many T-shirts must Aritzia sell to break even if it lowers its selling price by 16.6 percent to $10? Using the formula:

$$\% \text{ break-even sales change} = \frac{-\% \text{ price change}}{\%CM + \% \text{ price change}} \times 100$$

where %CM stands for percentage contribution margin. **Contribution margin** is gross margin less any expense that can be directly assigned to the merchandise. In this example, since there are no variable costs besides the cost of the shirt, the contribution margin is the same as the gross margin. Also, don't forget the minus sign in the formula's numerator.

Contribution margin (CM) = Selling price – Variable costs
CM   = $12 – $5 = $7
%CM = (CM ÷ Selling price) × 100
%CM = ($7 ÷ $12) × 100 = 58.33%

Substituting the %CM into the formula, we can calculate the break-even sales change:

$$\% \text{ break-even sales change} = \frac{-(-16.6)}{58.33 + (-16.6)} \times 100 = 39.78\%$$

Unit break-even sales change = 39.78% × 57 143 units = 22 731 units

Thus, if Aritzia reduces its price to $10, it must sell an additional 22 731 units to break even. It should come as no surprise that when we add the break-even quantity at $12 to the break-even sales change to $10, we get 79 874 units (57 143 + 22 731)—almost the same break-even point of 80 000 units that we obtained using the first formula. (The difference is due to rounding.) The same formula can be used to determine the sales change necessary to break even with a price increase.

price adjustments

In Canada, retailers are relatively free to promote adjustments to the initial retail price with the hope of generating sales. In this section we will examine markdowns, coupons, rebates, price bundling, multiple-unit pricing, variable pricing, and some special Internet pricing issues.

MARKDOWNS

Markdowns are price reductions from the initial retail price. Markdowns are initiated because the lower price induces price-sensitive customers to buy more merchandise.

Reasons for Taking Markdowns Retailers' decision to take markdowns can be classified as either clearance (to dispose of merchandise) or promotional (to generate sales).

Clearance Markdowns When merchandise is slow-moving, obsolete, at the end of its selling season, or priced higher than competitors' goods, it generally gets marked down for clearance purposes. This merchandise can become an eyesore and impair the store's image. Further, even if the merchandise can be sold in the following season, it may become shopworn or out of style. Also, the cost of carrying

refact

Marked-down goods, which accounted for just 8 percent of department-store sales three decades ago, have climbed to around 20 percent, according to the National Retail Federation.[8]

inventory is significant. If a buyer has to carry $10 000 of unwanted inventory at cost for a year with an annual inventory carrying cost of 35 percent, the cost would be $3500 (or $10 000 × 0.35)—not a trivial amount!

Fashion retailers tend to order more merchandise than they forecast selling because they are more concerned about selling out of a popular item before the end of the season than about over-ordering and having to mark down excess merchandise. Stocking out of popular merchandise can have a detrimental effect on a fashion retailer's image, whereas discounting merchandise at the end of the season merely reduces maintained markup.

Markdowns are part of the cost of doing business, and thus retailers plan for markdowns. They set an initial markup high enough so that after markdowns and other reductions are considered, the planned maintained markup will be achieved. Thus, a retailer's objective shouldn't necessarily be to minimize markdowns. If markdowns are too low, the retailer is probably pricing the merchandise too low, not purchasing enough merchandise, or not taking enough risks with the merchandise being purchased.

Promotional Markdowns   Using a high/low pricing strategy described earlier in this chapter, retailers employ markdowns to promote merchandise to increase sales. A buyer may decide to mark down some merchandise to make room for something new. An additional benefit is that the markdown sale generates cash flow to pay for new merchandise. Markdowns are also taken to increase customers' traffic flow. Retailers plan promotions in which they take markdowns for holidays, for special events, and as part of their overall promotional program. In fact, small portable appliances (such as toasters) are called *traffic appliances* because they're often in a *leader pricing* program and sold at reduced prices to generate in-store traffic. Retailers hope that customers will purchase other products at regular prices while they're in the store. Another opportunity created by markdowns is to increase the sale of complementary products. For example, a supermarket's markdown on hot dog buns may be offset by increased demand for hot dogs, mustard, and relish—all sold at regular prices.

Optimizing Markdown Decisions   Retailers have traditionally created a set of arbitrary rules for taking markdowns.[9] One retailer, for instance, flags markdown candidates when their weekly sell-through percentages fall below a certain value. Another retailer cuts prices on the basis of how long the merchandise has been in the store—marking products down by 20 percent after eight weeks, then by 30 percent after 12 weeks, and finally by 50 percent after 16 weeks.

Such a rules-based approach, however, is limited in several ways:

• First, it assumes that all the items within a category exhibit the same, consistent behaviour. So it treats a cashmere sweater the same way it treats a wool sweater.

• Second, a rules-based approach follows a fixed schedule; it's not sophisticated enough to determine how shifts in sales trends or other factors such as promotions or holidays will affect demand.

• Third, this approach fails to take gross margin into consideration; its only goal is to clear inventory.

Instead of relying on rules developed from averages, a retailer can benefit significantly from **merchandising optimization software,** a set of algorithms that monitors merchandise sales, promotions, competitors' actions, and other factors to determine the optimal (most profitable) price and timing for merchandising activities, especially markdowns. This software is currently being used by a growing number of major retailers and is commercially available from a number of specialty firms such as SAP.

The optimization software works by constantly refining its pricing forecasts on the basis of actual sales throughout the season. For example, the software recognizes that in early November, a winter item's sales are better than expected, so it delays taking a markdown that had been planned. Each week, as fresh sales data become available, it readjusts the forecasts to include the latest information. It computes literally thousands of scenarios for each item—a process that is too complicated and time-consuming for retailers to do on their own. It then evaluates the outcomes based on expected profits and other factors and selects the action that produces the best results.

Making good markdown decisions isn't all about relying on sophisticated computer software. Retailers must also work closely with their vendor partners to coordinate deliveries and help share the financial burden of taking markdowns.

Reducing the Amount of Markdowns by Working with Vendors Retailers can reduce the amount of markdowns by working closely with their vendors to time deliveries with demand. Merchandise that arrives before it is needed takes up valuable selling space and can get shopworn or damaged. On the other hand, when merchandise arrives too late, retailers may have trouble selling it without extensive markdowns. Quick response inventory systems reduce the lead time for receiving merchandise so that retailers can more closely monitor changes in trends and customer demand, thus reducing markdowns.

Vendors have a vested interest in retailers' success. Vendors that are knowledgeable about the market and competition can help with stock selections. Of course, a retailer must also trust its own taste and intuition; otherwise, its store will have the same merchandise as all other stores. Retail buyers can often obtain **markdown money**—funds a vendor gives the retailer to cover lost gross margin dollars that result from markdowns and other merchandising issues. For instance, assume a retailer has $1000 worth of ties at retail that are given a 25 percent markdown. Thus, when the ties are sold, the retailer receives only $750. But if the vendor provides $250 in markdown money, the maintained markup is unaffected. In this way, the vendor helps share the risk. According to the *Competition Act*, markdown money should be provided to all retailers on a proportionally equal basis, typically as a percentage of purchases. (Markdown money falls under the umbrella of potentially illegal price discrimination discussed in this chapter's appendix.)

Liquidating Markdown Merchandise No matter what markdown strategy a retailer uses, some merchandise may still remain unsold. A retailer can use one of five strategies to liquidate this merchandise:

- "Job-out," sell the remaining merchandise to another retailer
- Consolidate the unsold merchandise
- Place the remaining merchandise on an Internet auction site such as eBay, or have a special clearance location on the retailer's Web site
- Give the merchandise to charity
- Carry the merchandise over to the next season

Selling the remaining marked-down merchandise to another retailer has been very popular among retailers. For instance, Winners purchases end-of-season merchandise from other retailers and sells it at deep discounts. This strategy enables the retailer to have a relatively short markdown period, provides space for new merchandise, and at the same time eliminates the often unappealing sale atmosphere.

Holt Renfrew's Last Call Clearance Centre is the last stop for merchandise that hasn't sold at sale prices at regular Holt Renfrew stores.

The problem with this strategy is that the retailer can only recoup a small percentage of the merchandise's cost—often a mere 10 percent.

Marked-down merchandise can be consolidated in a number of ways. First, the consolidation can be made into one or a few of the retailer's regular locations. Second, marked-down merchandise can be consolidated into another retail chain or an outlet store under the same ownership. Holt Renfrew (Last Call) uses this strategy. Finally, marked-down merchandise can be shipped to a distribution centre or a rented space such as a convention centre for final sale. This practice encourages a successful yet relatively short markdown period. Consolidation sales can be complex and expensive due to the extra transportation and recordkeeping involved.

The Internet is expected to be increasingly useful for liquidating marked-down merchandise. For example, an electronics store is partnering with eBay to sell goods it has received from trade-ins.

Giving clearance merchandise to charities is an increasingly popular practice. Charitable giving is always a good corporate practice. It is a way of giving back to the community and has strong public relations benefits. Also, the cost value of the merchandise can be deducted from income.

The final liquidation strategy—to carry merchandise over to the next season—is used with high-priced nonfashion merchandise, such as furniture. Generally, however, it's not worth carrying over merchandise because of excessive inventory carrying costs. Retailers need to be well aware of consumers' propensity to check out "value" on the Internet; for example, www.selloffvacations.com, and www.autotrader.com.

Markdowns and Price Discrimination   Ideally, retailers would like to have the opportunity to charge customers as much as they would be willing to pay. This practice is called **first-degree price discrimination**. For instance, if a wealthy customer wants to buy something, the retailer charges more. If a price-sensitive customer comes in, the retailer charges less. Although this practice is legal and is widely used in some retail sectors, such as by automobile and antique dealers (see this chapter's appendix), it is impractical in a retail store with 20 000 SKUs and prices that are displayed for everyone to see. Recently, however, customers are initiating first-degree price discrimination by haggling.

Consider price discrimination versus market segmentation. For example, service retailers (kitchen companies, painting contractors, landscape companies) often spend time "sizing up" or qualifying the prospect and determining the scope of work, including expanding the request, before submitting a proposal.

Markdowns and the other widely used retail adjustment practices described in the next section are known as **second-degree price discrimination**—charging different prices to different people on the basis of their willingness to do something. For example, early-bird specials at a restaurant offer lower-priced meals before 6 p.m.

COUPONS

Coupons offer a discount on the price of specific items when they're purchased. Coupons are considered to be a second-degree price discrimination because they provide an incentive for price-sensitive customers to purchase more merchandise. Coupons are issued by manufacturers and retailers in newspapers, on products, on the shelf, at the cash register, over the Internet, and through the mail. Coupons are used because they are thought to induce customers to try products for the first time, convert those first-time users to regular users, encourage large purchases, increase usage, and protect market share against competition.

The evidence on couponing's overall profitability is mixed, depending on the product category. Since coupons have the seemingly positive effect of encouraging larger purchases than without coupons, the coupon promotion may be stealing sales from a future period without any net increase in sales. For instance, if a grocery store runs a coupon promotion on sugar, households may buy a large quantity of sugar and stockpile it for future use. Thus, unless the coupon is used mostly by new buyers, the net impact on sales will be negligible, and there will be a negative impact on profits because of the amount of the redeemed coupons and the cost of coupon redemption procedures. Unfortunately, it's very hard to isolate a market for new users without allowing current users to take advantage of the coupon promotion. If, on the other hand, the coupon is for a DVD or other product whose demand is not controlled by the degree of everyday usage, it might increase overall consumption.

REBATES

A **rebate** is a portion of the purchase price returned to the buyer. Generally, the customer sends a proof of purchase to the manufacturer or a rebate clearinghouse that processes rebates for the manufacturer, and the customer is sent a rebate cheque. Rebates are most useful when the dollar amount is relatively large. Otherwise, it's not worth the customer's time and postage to redeem the rebate. For instance, rebates are often offered on cars, major and portable appliances, computers, and electronic products.

From the retailer's perspective, rebates are more advantageous than coupons since they increase demand in the same way coupons do, but the retailer has no handling costs.

Manufacturers like rebates because many consumers never bother to redeem them, allowing manufacturers to offer, in effect, phantom discounts.[10] Many advertisements prominently proclaim low prices, noting the requirement to send in for rebates in microscopic letters. Consumers are drawn to the store and purchase the product, but only 5 to 10 percent claim the rebate. As a result, consumer advocates hate rebates.

Manufacturers also like rebates because they let them offer price cuts to consumers directly. With a traditional price cut, retailers can keep the price on the shelf the same and pocket the difference. Rebates can also be rolled out and shut off quickly. That allows manufacturers to fine-tune inventories or respond quickly to competitors without actually cutting prices. Finally, because buyers are required to fill out forms with names, addresses, and other data, rebates become a great way to build a customer data warehouse. Retailers must comply with the new Canadian privacy laws as of January 2004 when collecting customer information.

PRICE BUNDLING

Price bundling is the practice of offering two or more different products or services for sale at one price. For instance, McDonalds bundles a "free" hot fudge sundae into the price of certain meals. Another form of second-degree price discrimination, price bundling is used to increase both unit and dollar sales by bringing traffic into the store. The practice allowed McDonalds to increase the average purchase, increasing overall sales. The strategy can also be used to move less desirable merchandise.

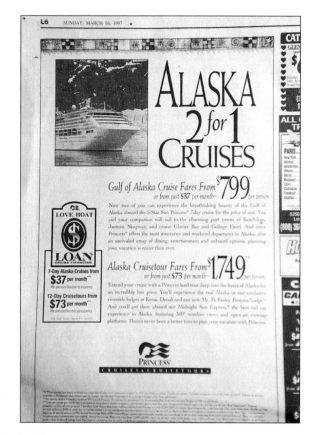

Which ad is using price bundling and which is using multiple-unit pricing?

MULTIPLE-UNIT PRICING

Multiple-unit pricing (or quality discounts) is similar to price bundling in that the lower total merchandise price increases sales, but the products or services are similar rather than different.[11] For example, a grocery store may sell three liters of fruit drink for $2.39 when the price per unit is 99 cents—a savings of 58 cents. Like price bundling, this strategy is used to increase sales volume. Depending on the type of product, however, customers may stockpile for use at a later time.

VARIABLE PRICING[12]

Variable pricing (or **zone pricing**) means charging different prices in different stores to different demographic segments, a practice referred to as third-degree price discrimination. For example, movie theatres have lower ticket prices for seniors and students. Both groups are price-sensitive. Barnes & Noble.com discounted prices on the Internet compared to its bricks-and-mortar stores in order to compete with Amazon.com. Although this may be necessary in the short run because of these highly competitive, commodity-type products, it could cause ill will among customers who become accustomed to shopping in multiple channels.

Zone pricing refers to the practice of charging different prices in different stores, markets, or regions to address different competitive situations. For instance, food retailers may have up to four or five pricing zones in a single city. They'll have one zone if they're next to a Wal-Mart and another zone if they're next to a less price-competitive regional chain. Prices can vary as much as 10 percent depending on the competition and the economic health of the neighbourhood.[14]

Variable pricing is easier in the food and drug retail sectors than for other stores because many do not **item price**—put a price tag on each item. It is easy to have different prices in various stores because it is so easy to change them—just scan the bar code on the shelf tag, change the price in the store's price database, and replace the shelf tag with a new label.

Variable pricing also doesn't conflict with their promotional strategy because many newspapers print different editions or can use different freestanding inserts (FSI), which are ads printed at the retailer's expense and distributed as an insert in the newspaper. Even if the newspaper doesn't use zones, a store might carry 40 000 SKUs, advertise 1000, and still have 39 000 left for variable pricing.

There are problems associated with variable pricing in traditional stores. First, as for multichannel retailers, if customers shop in more than one price zone, they will tend to be confused and annoyed. Also, third-degree price discrimination based on income and age is considered to be an unethical practice by many.

using price to stimulate retail sales

The price adjustments described in the previous section have the effect of increasing sales. In this section, we examine three strategies designed to increase sales without using price discrimination. Each of these strategies—leader pricing, price lining, and odd pricing—makes the processing of price information easier for consumers and therefore facilitates sales.

LEADER PRICING

In **leader pricing,** certain items are priced lower than normal to increase customers' traffic flow or to boost sales of complementary products. Reasons for using leader pricing are similar to those for coupons. The difference is that with leader pricing, merchandise has a low price to begin with, so customers, retailers, and vendors don't have to handle coupons.

Some retailers call these products *loss leaders.* In a strict sense, loss leaders are sold below cost. But a product doesn't have to be sold below cost for the retailer to be using a leader-pricing strategy. The best items for leader pricing are frequently purchased products such as white bread, milk, and eggs, or well-known brand names such as Coke used as loss leaders. Customers take note of ads for these products because they're purchased weekly. The retailer hopes consumers will also purchase their weekly groceries while buying loss leaders. Toys "R" Us has successfully used a leader-pricing strategy for disposable diapers. New parents get in the habit of shopping at Toys "R" Us when their children are infants and become loyal customers throughout their parenting.

PRICE LINING

In **price lining,** retailers offer a limited number of predetermined price points within a classification. For instance, a tire store may offer tires only at $49.99, $69.99, and

$89.99. Both customers and retailers can benefit from such a strategy for several reasons:

- Confusion that often arises from multiple price choices is essentially eliminated. The customer can choose the tire with either the low, medium, or high price. (There need not be three price lines; the strategy can use more or fewer than three.)

- From the retailer's perspective, the merchandising task is simplified. That is, all products within a certain price line are merchandised together. Further, the firm's buyers can select their purchases within the predetermined price lines.

- Price lining can also give buyers greater flexibility. If a strict formula is used to establish the initial retail price (initial markup), there could be numerous price points. But with a price-lining strategy, some merchandise may be bought below or above the expected cost for a price line. Of course, price lining can also limit retail buyers' flexibility. They may be forced to pass up potentially profitable merchandise because it doesn't fit into a price line.

- Although many manufacturers and retailers are simplifying their product offerings to save distribution and inventory costs and to make the choice simpler for consumers, price lining can be used to get customers to "trade up" to a more expensive model. Research indicates a tendency for people to choose the product in the middle of a price line. So, for example, if a camera store starts carrying a "super deluxe" model, customers will be more likely to purchase the model that was previously the most expensive. Retailers must decide whether it's more profitable to sell more expensive merchandise or save money by paring down their stock selection.[15]

ODD PRICING

Odd pricing refers to the practice of using a price that ends in an odd number, typically a nine.[16] Odd pricing has a long history in retailing. In the nineteenth and early twentieth centuries, odd pricing was used to reduce losses due to employee theft. Because merchandise had an odd price, salespeople typically had to go to the cash register to give the customer change and record the sale. This reduced salespeople's chances to take money for an item from a customer, keep the money, and never record the sale. Odd pricing was also used to keep track of how many times an item had been marked down. After an initial price of $20, the first markdown would be $17.99, the second markdown $15.98, and so on.

Although results of empirical studies in this area are mixed,[17] many retailers believe that odd pricing can increase profits. Assume that shoppers in a grocery store don't notice the last digit of a price, so the retailer is free to round a price up to the nearest nine. So, if the price would normally be $2.90, the retailers would round up to $2.99. This tactic would increase sales by three percent, more than most grocery stores' entire profit margin, with no increase in costs (increase in sales: $2.99 − $2.90 = $0.090 or $0.090 ÷ $2.99 = 3% of sales).

For products that are believed to be sensitive to price, many retailers will round the price down to the nearest nine to create a positive price image. If, for example, the price would normally be $3.09, many retailers will lower the price to $2.99. This practice is so prevalent that when planning new-product introductions, many manufacturers plan their cost to retailers such that the retail price will be rounded to a nine or a ninety-nine. Some of the more sophisticated price optimization systems (discussed earlier in this chapter) are capable of taking these factors into account, using ending numbers to optimize profits and price image.

the internet and price competition

Retailers are concerned that the growth of electronic retailing will intensify price competition. Traditionally, price competition between store-based retailers offering the same merchandise was reduced by geography because consumers typically shop at the stores and malls closest to where they live and work. However, using the Internet, consumers can search for merchandise across the globe at a low cost. The number of stores that a consumer can visit to compare prices is no longer limited by physical distance.[18]

Searching for the lowest prices is facilitated by shopping bots. **Shopping bots** or **search engines** are computer programs that search for and provide a list of all Internet sites selling a product category or price of specific brands offered. To limit price comparisons, electronic retailers initially made it hard for customers to go from one Internet site to another. The electronic retailers used different interfaces so customers needed to learn how to search through the offerings at each new site they visited. In addition, some Internet retailers electronically prevented shopping bots from accessing their sites, collecting information about the products sold at the site, or using these collected data to compare the prices offered at different electronic retailing sites.[19] Although these strategies made it more difficult to compare prices, they also made it more difficult to attract customers to Web sites.

Using shopping bots such as Bottomdollar.com, consumers can easily collect and compare prices for branded merchandise sold through an electronic retail channel.

Although consumers shopping electronically can collect price information with little effort, they can get a lot of other information about the quality and performance of products at a low cost.

Retailers using an electronic channel can reduce the emphasis on price by providing better services and information. Because of these services, customers might be willing to pay higher prices for the merchandise. For example, Amazon.com provides a customer with the table of contents and synopsis of a book, as well as reviews and comments by the author, or authors, and people who have read the book. The classic response to the question, What are the three most important things in retailing? used to be "location, location, location." In the world of electronic retailing, the answer is "information, information, information."[20]

SUMMARY

Canadian consumers are becoming increasingly price-sensitive; they put pressure on retailers to offer pricing strategies such as everyday low prices. Retailers must remember that value is the relationship between what the customer gets and what he or she has to pay. Price competition among retailers is a growing trend, often resulting in escalating lower prices ending in a price war in which there are few winners. Successful retailers will make pricing decisions to match their retail strategy objectives, and acknowledge store image, merchandise mix, and customer service offerings. Using the Internet, consumers can now search for merchandise across the globe. The number of stores that a consumer can visit to compare prices is no longer limited by physical distance.

In this chapter, we've answered several questions. First, What fundamental pricing strategies are retailers adopting? Retailers lie on a continuum from using pure everyday low pricing to pure high/low strategies, where prices start high but decrease with frequent sales. However, most EDLP retailers must resort to occasional sales, and most high/low pricers are attempting to create an image of providing customers good value.

Second, How do retailers set retail prices? There are three primary approaches for establishing prices: the cost-, demand-, and competition-oriented methods. Each method has its merits, but a mix of methods is best. In making pricing decisions, retailers also use break-even analyses to determine the volume of sales necessary for them to make a profit.

Third, Since the initial retail price isn't necessarily the price at which the merchandise is finally sold, how do retailers adjust the initial retail price and how do these adjustments affect profits? Retailers have several tactics available, including markdowns, coupons, rebates, bundling, multiple-unit pricing, variable pricing, and special Internet pricing.

Finally, How do retailers use price to stimulate sales without resorting to price discrimination? Three strategies are prevalent: price lining, leader pricing, and odd pricing.

Legal issues that impact pricing decisions come from two sides. Those that affect the buying of merchandise include price discrimination and vertical price-fixing. The legal pricing issues that affect consumers are horizontal price-fixing, predatory pricing, comparative price advertising, bait-and-switch, and scanned versus posted prices. These issues are considered in Appendix 13A.

KEY TERMS

bait-and-switch, *381*
break-even analysis, *365*
break-even point (BEP), *366*
comparative price
  advertising, *381*

competition-oriented
  method, *358*
contribution margin, *367*
cost-oriented method, *358*
coupons, *370*

demand-oriented method, *358*
everyday low pricing
  (EDLP), *356*
fair trade laws, *380*

Get Out & Do It!

1. **INTERNET EXERCISE** Price bundling is very common in the travel and vacation industry. Go to the Web site for Sandals (www.sandals.com) and see what you can get—all for one price.

2. **GO SHOPPING** Go to a retailer who retails through bricks and clicks and examine the cost of items in the store and on the Web site. Do you find the same merchandise for sale in the store and online? Describe any differences observed.

3. **GO SHOPPING** Go to two different types of stores and try to bargain your way down from the tagged price. Explain your experience. Was there any difference in your success rate as a result of type of store or type of merchandise? Did you have better luck when you spoke to a manager?

4. **GO SHOPPING** Go to five different types of stores and ask the manager of each how he or she determines when to take markdowns and how much the markdown should be. What rule-based approaches are they using? Are any using merchandising optimization software?

DISCUSSION QUESTIONS AND PROBLEMS

1. How does merchandising optimization software help buyers make better markdown decisions?

2. Simple examination of markdowns could lead us to believe that they should be taken only when a retailer wants to get rid of merchandise that's not selling. What other reasons could a retailer have to take markdowns?

3. Do you know any retailers that have violated any of the legal issues discussed in the appendix to this chapter? Explain your answer.

4. Which of the pricing strategies discussed in this chapter are used by your favourite retailer? Do you think they're used effectively? Can you suggest a more effective strategy?

5. What is the difference in the pricing strategies of ebay.com, priceline.com, and staples.com? Which firm do you think will be the strongest in 10 years? Why?

To answer Questions 6–10, use the Online Learning Centre (www.mcgrawhill.ca/olc/levy).

6. A department's maintained markup is 38 percent, reductions are $560, and net sales are $28 000. What's the initial markup percentage?

7. Maintained markup is 39 percent, net sales are $52 000, alterations are $1700, shrinkage is $500, markdowns are $5000, employee discounts are $2000, and cash discounts are 2 percent. What are gross margin in dollars and initial markup as a percentage? Explain why initial markup is greater than maintained markup.

8. Cost of a product is $150, markup is 50 percent, and markdown is 30 percent. What's the final selling price?

9. Manny Perez bought a tie for $9 and priced it to sell for $15. What was his markup on the tie?

10. Answer the following:

(a) The Gap is planning a new line of leather jean jackets for fall. It plans to retail the jackets for $100. It is having the jackets produced in the Dominican Republic. Although The Gap does not own the factory, its product development and design costs are $400 000. The total cost of the jacket, including transportation to the stores, is $45. For this line to be successful, The Gap needs to make $900 000 profit. What is its break-even point in units and dollars?

(b) The buyer has just found out that Club Monaco, one of The Gap's major competitors, is bringing out a similar jacket that will retail for $90. If The Gap wishes to match Club Monaco's price, how many units will it have to sell?

11. The manager of a sporting goods department planned to purchase $8400 worth of merchandise at cost. This merchandise was to retail at $14 000. At Supplier A he purchased $4340 at cost, with a retail value of $7000. At Supplier B he purchased $3720 at cost, with a retail value of $6300. What markup percentage must the buyer take on purchases from a third supplier, C, to meet the overall markup objective?

APPENDIX 13A   Legal Issues in Retail Pricing*

The legal environment surrounding retail pricing is complex. Let's examine legal issues surrounding the buying of merchandise (price discrimination and vertical price fixing) and legal issues affecting the customer (horizontal price-fixing, predatory pricing, comparative price advertising, bait-and-switch tactics, and scanned versus posted prices).

PRICE DISCRIMINATION

Price discrimination occurs when a vendor sells identical products to two or more customers at different prices. The Supreme Court has held that price discrimination can occur between a national brand and an identical private-label product, and the Fifth Circuit Court of Appeals has ruled that the normal price difference between these two types of products does not lessen competition, so the price discrimination is not illegal.[21] Price discrimination can occur between vendors and retailers, or between retailers and their customers, although the legal ramifications are different in the two situations. We will first examine price discrimination between vendors and retailers and then between retailers and their customers.

Although price discrimination between vendors and their retailers is generally illegal if it lessens competition (i.e., if the favoured and disfavoured retailers compete with each other), there are three situations where it's acceptable. First, different retailers can be charged different prices when justified by differences in the cost of manufacture, sale, or delivery resulting from the differing methods or quantities in which such commodities are sold or delivered. Under what conditions may these differences exist?

It's often less expensive per unit to manufacture, sell, or deliver large quantities than small quantities. Manufacturers can achieve economies of scale through the longer production runs achieved with large quantities. Cost of selling to a

*This appendix was prepared with the assistance of Professor Ross Petty, Babson College.

customer also decreases as the quantity of goods ordered increases because it costs almost the same for a salesperson to write a small order as a large order. Finally, delivery or transportation expenses decrease on a per unit basis as quantities of goods ordered increase. These exceptions give rise to **quantity discounts,** the practice of lowering prices to retailers that buy in high quantities.

The differences in methods of sale that allow for differing prices refer specifically to the practice of granting **functional discounts,** also known as **trade discounts.** Functional discounts are different prices, or percentages off suggested retail prices, granted to customers in different lines of trade (e.g., wholesalers and retailers). Wholesalers often receive a lower price than retailers for the same quantity purchased. This is legal as long as wholesalers perform more functions in the distribution process than do retailers. For instance, wholesalers store and transport merchandise, and they use salespeople for writing orders and taking care of problems in the stores. Essentially, manufacturers "pay" wholesalers for servicing retailers by giving the wholesalers a lower price.

With the growth of large chain retailers such as Home Depot and Wal-Mart, functional discounts become more difficult to justify. Wal-Mart performs virtually all the functions an independent wholesaler provides. Therefore, Wal-Mart demands and should receive the same low prices as wholesalers. These lower prices make it hard for smaller retailers to compete.

The second exception to the no-price-discrimination rule occurs when the price differential is in response to changing conditions affecting the market for or the marketability of the goods concerned, such as selling last year's fashions at a lower price today than last month when they were still this year's fashions.

The third exception occurs when the differing price is made in good faith to meet a competitor's equally low price. Suppose, for example, that Ben & Jerry's ice cream is experiencing severe price competition with a locally produced ice cream in Wisconsin. Ben & Jerry's is allowed to lower its price in this market below its price in other markets to meet the low price of local competition. In this case, market conditions have changed and Ben & Jerry's has reacted by meeting the competition's price.

Large retailers often benefit from subtle forms of price discrimination. For instance, 25 bookstores across the United States have filed an antitrust lawsuit against their large competitors, Barnes & Noble and Borders Group, Inc. They charge that the nation's largest book retailers are in violation of the *Robinson-Patman Act* because they illegally use their buying clout with publishers to get special discounts and benefits not available to smaller rivals.[22]

Unless a particular situation comes within one of the exceptions just discussed, retailers should never ask a vendor for or accept a net price (after all discounts, allowances, returns, and promotional allowances) that they know, or experience tells them, won't be offered to their competitors on a proportional basis for similar merchandise to be purchased at about the same time.

Price discrimination between retailers and their customers is not illegal under U.S. federal law. Different customers typically receive different prices after negotiating for such items as cars, jewellery, or collectibles. Price discrimination becomes illegal in some states when different groups of people, such as men and women, systematically receive different prices.

Predatory Pricing

Predatory pricing is a particular form of price discrimination where a market-dominating firm charges below-cost prices for some goods or in some areas in order to drive out or discipline one or more rival firms. Eventually, the predator hopes to raise prices and earn back enough profits to compensate for the losses during the period of predation. The firm challenging prices as being predatory bears the burden of proving three things: (1) the predator has significant market power; (2) the predator prices some goods at least below its total costs, including an allocation for overhead costs for a significant period (some courts require prices to be below variable costs, which for retailers would probably be the cost of merchandise

refact

A California survey found that gender-based price discrimination adds up to as much as US$1351 annually for each woman in the state for a total of nearly US$15 billion a year more than men's expenditures for similar volumes of similar items.[23]

without any allocation of overhead); and (3) there is a reasonable likelihood that the predator will be able to recoup its predatory losses.

Some states have old statutes that declare it illegal to sell merchandise at unreasonably low prices, usually below their cost. However, a retailer generally may sell merchandise at any price so long as the motive isn't to destroy competition. For instance, independent retailers in small towns have long accused Wal-Mart of selling goods below cost to drive them out of business and then boosting prices after seizing control of the local market. Wal-Mart maintains that it hasn't violated the law because it didn't intend to hurt competitors. But it admits it has sold some products below cost, as do other retailers. These loss-leader products are intended to attract customers into the store where it is hoped they will then buy other products that are priced to be profitable. Wal-Mart claims its loss leaders are part of its everyday low price strategy. More competition leads to lower prices; less competition leads to higher prices. Wal-Mart's so-called predatory pricing strategy has been tested in the courts. After an early conviction in a lower court, the Arkansas Supreme Court ruled that the chain had no intent to destroy competition through its practice of selling a revolving selection of prescription and nonprescription drugs at less than cost.[24] In essence, the Arkansas Supreme Court distinguished loss-leader pricing, even by a firm with market power, as a legitimate competitive tactic from predatory pricing.

VERTICAL PRICE-FIXING

Vertical price-fixing involves agreements to fix prices between parties at different levels of the same marketing channel (e.g., retailers and vendors). The agreements are usually to set prices at the manufacturer's suggested retail price (MSRP). So pricing either above or below MSRP is often a source of conflict.

Resale price maintenance laws, or **fair trade laws,** were enacted in the early 1900s to curb vertical price-fixing and have had a mixed history ever since. Initially, resale price maintenance laws were primarily designed to help protect small retailers by prohibiting retailers from selling below MSRP. Congress believed that these small, often family-owned, stores couldn't compete with large chain stores such as Sears or Woolworth, which could buy in larger quantities and sell at discount prices. By requiring retailers to maintain manufacturers' suggested retail prices, however, prices to the consumer may have been higher than they would have been in a freely competitive environment.

Due to strong consumer activism, the *Consumer Goods Pricing Act* (1975) repealed all resale price maintenance laws and enabled retailers to sell products below suggested retail prices. Congress's attitude was to protect customers' right to buy at the lowest possible free market price—even though some small retailers wouldn't be able to compete. For instance, in a 2000 settlement, Nine West, the women's shoe marketer, agreed with the Federal Trade Commission (FTC) not to fix the price at which dealers may "advertise, promote, offer of sale or sell any product." The firm also agreed to pay US$34 million to state attorneys general. The money is being used to fund women's health, educational, vocational, and safety programs.[25]

Unfortunately, some vendors coerce retailers into maintaining the MSRP by delaying or cancelling shipments.[26] A less risky tactic from a legal perspective is for a vendor to simply announce it will only sell to full-price retailers. If any of its retailers violate that policy, the vendor can terminate the discounters without discussion or negotiation. In this way, the vendor exercises its right to choose with whom it will deal but avoids forming an illegal agreement with its dealers to vertically fix prices.

Some retailers, on the other hand, want to be able to price above MSRP. For instance, Harley-Davidson motorcycles are so popular that some dealers have sold them over the manufacturer's suggested retail price. Large manufacturers and franchise companies are generally against pricing above MSRP. They argue that their brand's image can be damaged if retailers price above MSRP. Retailers like the extra profit potential and argue that competitive conditions may vary by locality. The Supreme Court ruled in 1997 that price ceilings would not necessarily violate federal antitrust laws. This was the first time the Court had carved an exception to the general ban on vertical price-fixing. From now on, each case will be judged on whether it restricts competition.[27]

Retail Pricing   CHAPTER 13   381

HORIZONTAL-PRICE FIXING

Horizontal price-fixing involves agreements between retailers that are in direct competition with each other to have the same prices. As a general rule of thumb, retailers should refrain from discussing prices or terms or conditions of sale with competitors. Terms or conditions of sale may include charges for alterations, delivery, or gift wrapping, or the store's exchange policies. If a buyer or store manager needs to know a competitor's price on a particular item, he or she can check advertisements or the Internet or send an assistant to the store to check the price. But the buyer or manager shouldn't call the competitor to get the information or personally visit the store for fear that this information would be used against him or her in a price-fixing case. Further, retailers shouldn't respond to any competitor's request to verify those prices. The only exception to the general rule occurs when a geographically oriented merchants association, such as a downtown area or a shopping centre, is planning a special coordinated event. In this situation, a retailer may announce to other merchants that merchandise will be specially priced during the event, but the specific merchandise and prices shouldn't be identified except in advertising or through in-store labelling and promotion.

COMPARATIVE PRICE ADVERTISING

A department store in Denver was selling two cutlery sets on "sale," reduced from "original" or "regular" prices of $40 and $50. The true regular prices were $19.99 and $29.99. The store sold few at the "original" price for two years. This common retailing practice, known as **comparative price advertising,** compares the price of merchandise offered for sale with a higher "regular" price or a manufacturer's list price. Consumers use the higher price, known as the *reference price,* as a benchmark for what they believe the "real" price of the merchandise should be.

This practice may be a good strategy, since it gives customers a price comparison point and makes the merchandise appear to be a good deal. Retailers, like the one in Denver, may use comparative price advertising to deceive the consumer, however. To avoid legal problems, particularly with state governments that have been actively prosecuting violators, retailers should check for local rules and guidelines.

Generally,

- The retailer should have the reference price in effect at least one-third of the time the merchandise is on sale.
- The retailer should disclose both how sale prices are set and how long they will be offered and how the reference price was determined.
- The retailer should be careful when using a manufacturer's suggested list price. Don't use it as the reference price unless it is the store's regular price, or is clearly identified only as the manufacturer's suggested price.
- If the retailer advertises that it has the lowest prices in town or that it will meet or beat any competitor's price, it should have proof that its prices are, in fact, the lowest in town before the ad is placed.
- If the retailer advertises that it will meet or beat any competitor's prices, it must have a company policy that enables it to adjust prices to preserve the accuracy of its advertising claims.[28]

BAIT-AND-SWITCH TACTICS

Bait-and-switch is an unlawful, deceptive practice that lures customers into a store by advertising a product at a lower-than-usual price (the bait) and then induces the customer to switch to a higher-priced model (the switch). Bait-and-switch can occur in two ways. Suppose customer Smith is in the market for a new refrigerator. Smith checks the ads in the newspaper and finds a particularly attractively priced unit. At the store, however, Smith finds that the retailer has significantly underestimated demand for the advertised product and no longer has any available for sale. The person begins pushing a higher-priced model that's heavily stocked.

In the second bait-and-switch method, the retailer has the advertised model in stock but disparages its quality while highlighting the advantages of a higher-priced model. In both cases, the retailer has intentionally misled the customer.

To avoid disappointing customers and risking legal problems, the retailer should have sufficient quantities of advertised items. If it runs out of stock on these items, it should offer customers a rain check. Finally, it should caution salespeople that although trying to "trade up" customers to a higher-priced model is legal, they must sell the low-priced item if that is what the customer wants.

SCANNED VERSUS POSTED PRICES

Advertising one price but charging another is obviously illegal. Studies of the accuracy of price scanning versus posted or advertised prices have generally found a high level of accuracy, but mistakes are made in about one out of 30 scans.[29] In many cases, retailers lose money because the scanned price is below the recommended price.

Experts recommend that retailers adopt specific practices to ensure accurate pricing. Most basic is the adoption of written procedures for all forms of pricing activity in the store. Adopting procedures for immediate correction of pricing errors is important to reduce exposure to possible law enforcement action and to ensure customer satisfaction. On-going training of employees, with an emphasis on the store's commitment to pricing accuracy, ensures that the procedures are properly implemented. Designating one person as the pricing coordinator, with overall responsibility for pricing accuracy, also is important. An essential component of good pricing practices is periodic price audits. Price audits of a random sample, perhaps 50 items, can be done on a daily basis. Regular price audits of the entire store can be done several times a year. Procedures for regularly checking and replacing damaged or missing shelf tags and signs help ensure that consumers get the correct price.

In summary, retailers, wholesalers, and manufacturers should be aware that whenever they decide to sell the same merchandise for different prices at different locations, or to sell merchandise at extraordinarily low prices to attract customers, they may be susceptible to federal and state prosecution and to lawsuits from competitors. But as a practical matter, the length of time and the expense of acquiring sufficient data and legal assistance to prove injury by a competitor may be so great that the injured party may still lose its business.

managing and promoting the store

Section IV focuses on issues associated with store management and promotion, including managing and training retail employees, developing a promotion strategy, and providing customer service that will exceed customer expectations.

Developing a strategic advantage through financial management alone is becoming more and more difficult. Competing stores often have similar assortments of branded merchandise.

Chapter 14 looks at the human resource management issues that have become a critical basis for developing strategic advantage, since customers can find the same assortments in a number of conveniently located retail outlets and through the Internet.

Chapter 15 talks about how, in order to gain customer loyalty, retailers are increasing their emphasis on value-added incentives to differentiate themselves from the competition—the service they get from store employees and quality of the shopping experience.

Chapter 16 looks at the relative advantages of various promotional vehicles available to retailers. In addition, it considers how promotion affects the consumer decision-making process. The chapter also describes how to develop a promotional program and how to set a budget.

CHAPTER 14

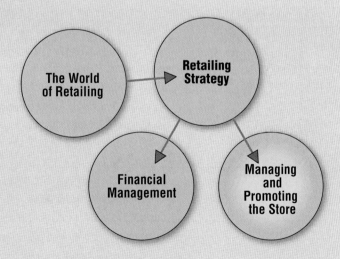

human resource management and staff training issues

Executive Briefing

PETsMART's HR Strategy Supports Re-Branding Initatives

The $1.8 billion Canadian pet supply and services market changed in 1996 when the American pet superstore giant PETsMART entered the Canadian marketplace. The company name PetsMart for the past 20 years emphasized the chain's warehouse retail style and low prices. The re-branded name spelled PETsMART, emphasizes the retailer's service offerings. This change reflects the way people think about their pets as a valued member of the family. Thus, PETsMART undertook a strategy to reposition its brand from a category killer to a caring and trusted source of products and services for pets. Canadian PETsMART companies are changing to reflect the new branding strategy that includes hiring caring staff, adding updated signage, and remodelling their interiors. The company also directed its marketing communications to be less price-orientated and more service-driven, with all messages highlighting the fact that pets are welcome in the store.

Although the number of pets per household in Canada remains roughly the same (about 8 million dogs and cats, not including birds, rodents, and reptiles), consumers are spending more on the pets they have. The trends emerging point to consumers who are looking for good quality pet food at the best prices, while at the same time pampering their pets and buying expensive treats.

PETsMART provides products and services for pets in Canada. Along with the perceived price advantage on more than 16 000 SKUs, the one-stop pet superstore implemented an array of services for pets, including grooming, obedience training, adoption services, and pet photography. The company's PetsHotel provides boarding for dogs and cats, supervision by caregivers, an on-call veterinarian, temperature-

QUESTIONS
How do retailers build a sustainable competitive advantage by developing and managing their human resources?

What activities do retail employees undertake, and how are they typically organized?

How does a retailer coordinate employees' activities and motivate them to work toward the retailer's goals?

How should store managers recruit, select, motivate, train, and evaluate their employees?

How should store managers compensate their salespeople?

What legal and ethical issues must store managers consider in managing their employees?

How can store managers reduce inventory losses due to employee theft customer, and store visitor theft?

controlled rooms, and daily special treats and play time, as well as a doggie day camp. Veterinary clinics are located close to the retailer but are facilities owned privately by local veterinarians.

The new PETsMART strategy recognized that its employees would play a crucial role in the development of the new brand image. Its front line employees in the stores had to understand and accept the brand's values and the promises that the brand was making to its customers. To develop these values in its employees, PETsMART changed the criteria it used for selecting sales associates. It was essential to hire caring people who had a deep concern for dogs or cats or tropical fish. Employees would be the front line ambassadors of the new strategy and the immediate contact with the customer and his or her pet. To develop its employees, PETsMART provided extensive training so that the retail associates would have expanded knowledge of pets and pet care products.

Canadian pet owners want to be good pet parents and deal with a company that is concerned about their pets' health and well-being. The disastrous, tainted pet food recall in 2007 affected dog and cat food sales for multiple brands and was a challenging situation for the retailer. PETsMART management dealt with the crisis in an ethical manner, taking all suspect products off the shelf, accepting all merchandise brought back to the store regardless of where the customer had made the purchase, and suppling the consumer with credit for the full price on future purchases. The response to a difficult situation gained loyalty and secured consumer trust.

This chapter focuses on the organization and management of employees—the retailer's human resources. Howard Schultz, chairman and chief global strategist of Starbucks, emphasizes that "the relationship that we have with our people and the culture of our company is our most sustainable competitive advantage."[1]

Store managers, due to their daily contact with customers, have the best knowledge of customer needs and competitive activity. From this unique vantage point, store managers play an important role in formulating and executing retail strategies.

Retailers achieve their financial objectives by effectively managing their five critical assets:

- employees
- their locations
- merchandise inventory
- stores
- customers

Human resource management is particularly important in retailing because employees play a major role in performing critical business functions. Retailing and other service businesses remain labour-intensive. Retailers rely on people to perform the basic retailing activities such as buying, displaying merchandise, and providing service to customers.

The activities undertaken to implement the retailer's human resource strategy, including recruiting, selecting, training, supervising, evaluating, and compensating sales associates, are typically undertaken by store management.

exhibit 14–1   Steps in the Process of Managing Store Employees

| 1. Recruit and select employees | 2. Socialize and train new employees | 3. Motivate and manage employees to achieve store performance goals | 4. Evaluate employee performance and provide feedback | 5. Compensate and reward employees |

store management responsibilities

It is important to clarify the term management as opposed to leadership or coaching. **Management** refers to the strategic approach of an organization to achieve its objectives by developing policies and plans and allocating resources. Human resource management then links the people with the strategic goals of the company. The term **leadership** refers to the ability of an individual to influence, motivate, and enable others to contribute toward the effectiveness and success of the organization. A good leader will act as a guide and lead by positive example. **Coaching** is the activity of supporting people so that they can achieve their goals, with goal setting, training, advising, encouraging, and rewarding their successes. See the Running Room profile with John Stanton as he coaches both staff and customers to achieve their fitness and personal goals.

Exhibit 14–1 outlines the steps in the employee management process that affect store employees' productivity: (1) recruiting and selecting effective people, (2) improving their skills through socialization and training, (3) motivating them to perform at higher levels, (4) evaluating them, and finally, (5) compensating and rewarding them.[2] Store managers also need to develop employees who can assume more responsibility and be promoted to higher-level management positions. By developing subordinates, managers help both their firms and themselves. The firm benefits from having more effective managers, and the manager benefits because the firm has a qualified replacement when the manager is promoted.

gaining competitive advantage through human resource management

Human resource management can be the basis of a sustainable competitive advantage for three reasons:

• First, labour costs account for a significant percentage of a retailer's total expenses. Thus, the effective management of employees can produce a cost advantage.

• Second, the experience that most customers have with a retailer is determined by the activities of employees who select merchandise, provide information and assistance, and stock displays and shelves.

• Third, these potential advantages, such as exceptional service, are difficult for competitors to duplicate.

OBJECTIVES OF HUMAN RESOURCE MANAGEMENT

The strategic objective of human resource management is to align the capabilities and behaviours of employees with the short-term and long-term goals of the retail firm.[4] One human resource management performance measure is **employee productivity**—the retailer's sales or profit divided by the number of employees. Employee productivity can be improved by increasing the sales generated by employees or reducing the number of employees, or both.

While employee productivity is directly related to the retailer's short-term profits, employee attitudes such as job satisfaction and commitment have important effects on customer satisfaction and subsequent long-term performance of the retailer. In addition to employee survey measures of these attitudes, a behavioural measure of these attitudes is employee turnover. **Employee turnover** is:

$$\frac{100 \times \text{Number of people in a set of positions during a year}}{\text{Number of positions}} - 100$$

refact

A study of Sears' employees found that a 5 percent increase in employee satisfaction resulted in a 1.3 percent increase in customer satisfaction, which led to 0.5 percent growth in sales.[5]

retailing view

RETAIL STORES ARE GOING HIGH TECH

14.1

Many supermarket retailers are installing self-checkout lanes. This technology offers benefits to both retailers and their customers. Ninety percent of the cost of maintaining a checkout line is the cashier. Thus, eliminating the cashier can reduce costs and/or enable the store to open more checkout lanes. To limit potential theft in the self-checkout lanes, retailers are using various techniques. Some of these deterrents are psychological, such as displaying customers on a video screen as they scan their merchandise. In addition, an electronic scale beneath the shopping bags knows what's just been scanned and how much it's supposed to weigh. So if a shopper scans a candy bar while slipping a rib roast in the shopping bag, the system beeps and asks that the item be entered again.

Airlines also are getting a high return on their investment by using kiosks for self-check-ins. A typical airline kiosk costs about $10 000, compared with a salary for a customer service agent of $20 000–$40 000, plus benefits. Self-check-in systems pay for their $80 000 price tags after about 15 months. Many travelers prefer self-check-in systems because they are quicker than waiting for an agent. Additionally, Air Canada now allows check in through their Web site 24 hours prior to departure on many North American flights.

Self-service kiosks never call in sick or go on vacations. Thus, the workforce schedule also is simplified for managers.

Sources: Doug Desjardins, "Shoppers Tapping into High Tech," *DSN Retailing Today*, January 10, 2005, pp. 16–17; Amy Harmon, "More Consumers Reach Out to Touch the Screen," *New York*

Retailers increase labour productivity when they install self-checkout systems.

Times, November 17, 2003, p. A7; Suzanne Smalley, "Next Frontiers," *Newsweek*, April 29, 2002, p. 40.

exhibit 14–2
Responsibilities of
Store Managers

MANAGING STORE EMPLOYEES
Recruiting and selecting
Socializing and training
Motivating
Evaluating and providing constructive feedback
Rewarding and compensating

CONTROLLING COSTS
Increasing labour productivity
Reducing maintenance and energy costs
Reducing inventory losses

MANAGING MERCHANDISE
Displaying merchandise and maintaining visual standards
Working with buyers
    Suggesting new merchandise
    Buying merchandise
    Planning and managing special events
    Marking down merchandise

PROVIDING CUSTOMER SERVICE

A failure to consider both long- and short-term objectives can result in mismanagement of human resources and a downward performance spiral as shown in Exhibit 14–3. Often, when retailers' sales and profits decline due to increased competition, they respond by decreasing labour costs. They reduce the number of sales associates in stores, hire more part-timers, and spend less on training. Although these actions may increase short-term productivity and profits, they have an adverse effect on long-term performance because employee morale and customer service decrease.[6]

Managing both employee and customer expectations is not an easy task, but is necessary for success. Researchers have been able to demonstrate that happy, satisfied employees, working in the best interests of the company, have a positive influence on a retailer's overall performance.

exhibit 14–3
Downward
Performance Spiral

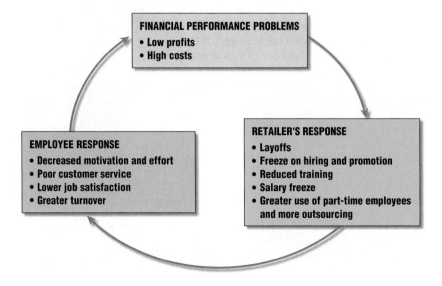

THE HUMAN RESOURCE TRIAD

Retailers such as Canadian Tire Corp. believe that human resources are too important to be left solely to the HR department.[7] The full potential of a retailer's human resources is realized when three elements of the human resource triad work together—HR professionals, store managers, and employees.

HR professionals, typically working out of the corporate office, have specialized knowledge of HR practices and labour laws. They are responsible for establishing HR policies that reinforce the retailer's strategy and provide the tools and training used by line managers and employees to implement the policies. The line managers, who primarily work in the stores, are responsible for bringing the policies to life through their daily management of employees working for them. The employees also share in the management of human resources. They can play an active role in providing feedback on the policies, managing their own careers, defining their job function, and evaluating the performance of their managers and co-workers. These three elements of the HR triad are illustrated in Exhibit 14–4.

SPECIAL HR CONDITIONS FACING RETAILERS

Human resource management in retailing is very challenging due to:

* the need to use part-time employees
* the emphasis on expense control
* the changing demographics of the workforce
* often poorly trained manager

Retailers operating in international markets face additional challenges.

Part-Time Employees   Most retailers are open long hours and weekends to respond to the needs of family shoppers and working people. In addition, peak shopping periods occur during lunch hours, at night, and during sales promotions. To deal with these peak periods and long hours, retailers have to complement their one or two shifts of full-time (40-hours-per-week) store employees with part-time workers. Part-time workers can be more difficult to manage than full-time employees. They often are less committed to the company and their jobs, and they're more likely to quit than full-time employees.

Expense Control   Retailers often operate on thin margins and must control expenses. Thus, they are cautious about paying high wages to hourly employees who perform low-skill jobs. To control costs, retailers often hire people with little or no experience to work as sales associates, bank tellers, and waiters. High turnover,

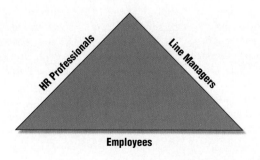

exhibit 14–4
Human Resource Triad

absenteeism, and poor performance often result from the use of inexperienced, low-wage employees.

Overtime banked hours in Canada are 1.5 hours for each hour worked. This has become an issue in the contractor field where the government is auditing various companies and determining that too many employees are only putting one hour in the bank for each hour of overtime worked. This has led to large payouts by employers when this practice has been going on for many years. This practice can become a financial liability for businesses. See www.hrsdc.gc.ca for reference.

The lack of experience and motivation among many retail employees is particularly troublesome because these employees are often in direct contact with customers. Unlike manufacturing workers on an assembly line, the lowest-paid retail employees work in areas that are highly visible to customers. Poor appearance, manners, and attitudes can have a negative effect on sales and customer loyalty.

refact

Since 1995, the Asian workforce has grown by 240 million while Europe's has only grown by 6 million.[10]

Employee Demographics   The changing demographic pattern will result in a chronic shortage of qualified sales associates, as is the experience in Calgary, Alberta, where the high employment rate has created a manpower shortage in the retail sector. Tim Hortons is paying $14 per hour in Calgary.

To satisfy their human resource needs, retailers are increasing the diversity of their workforces, employing more minorities, handicapped people, and the elderly. The work values of young employees are quite different from those of their baby boomer supervisors. Many older managers feel that younger employees have poor work ethics. Younger employees respond by saying "Get a life," as they strive to balance their personal and professional lives. Managing this growing diversity and changing values in the retail workforce creates opportunities and problems for human resource managers.[11] See Retailing View 14.2 for a discussion of generational tension in the labour force.

14.2 retailing view
GENERATIONAL TENSION

Some of the problems of dissatisfied employees and high turnover in retail are due to the generation gap between boomer store managers and Generation Xers who entered the workforce a few years ago. "A lot has been made of Generation Xers not having a strong work ethic," retail consultant Terri Kabachnick notes. "I don't agree; it's just that it is a lot different. Boomers feel they have to work a lot of hours, whereas GenXers ask, 'Why? Who are you trying to impress?'" Boomers emphasize that you need to work long and hard to get ahead, paying your dues before you get more responsibility and higher pay. The younger employee responds with "Get a life. I don't mind working hard, but what about my family, my happiness?"

Rather than getting regular performance reviews, Generation Xers want a pat on the back and recognition when they have accomplished something. They want flexibility in their work schedules and time for themselves, their interests, and their priorities.

"They don't want time off to be sick; they want time off to be well," says Kabachnick. To address this need for flexibility, retailers are experimenting with sabbaticals—weeks or months off to think about how to do your job better—and time banks, where sick days, overtime, or vacation time can be deposited for use at some time in the future with no questions asked.

Retailers also should consider personal needs by having pet and child care centres, on-site fitness centres, personnel to run personal errands such as dropping off and picking up laundry, and "relaxation rooms" where employees can go to sit, think, or nap. One company even provides back rubs at desks and workstations.

Sources: Pamela Paul, "Meet the Parents," *American Demographics*, January 2002, pp. 25–30; and David Schulz, "Generational Tensions Add to 'Quiet Rebellion' in Retail Workforce," *Stores*, March 11, 1999, pp. 61–62.

International Human Resource Issues The management of employees working for an international retailer is especially challenging because differences in work values, economic systems, and labour laws mean that human resource practices effective in one country might not be effective in another.

designing the organization structure for a retail firm

The **organization structure** identifies the activities to be performed by specific employees and determines the lines of authority and responsibility in the firm. The first step in developing an organization structure is to determine the tasks that must be performed. Exhibit 14–5 shows tasks typically performed in a retail firm. These tasks are divided into four major categories:

- strategic management
- administrative management (operations)
- merchandise management
- store management

To illustrate the connection between the tasks performed and the organization structure, the tasks are colour-coded. Orange is used to represent the strategic tasks, gold for the merchandise management, green for the store management, and blue for the administrative management tasks.

The strategic market and finance decisions are undertaken primarily by senior management: the CEO, COO, vice-presidents, and the board of directors representing shareholders in publicly held firms. Administrative tasks are performed by corporate staff employees who have specialized skills in human resource management, finance, accounting, real estate, distribution, and management information systems. People in these administrative functions develop plans, procedures, and information to assist operating managers in implementing the retailer's strategy.

In retail firms, the primary operating or line managers are involved in merchandise management and store management. These operating managers implement the strategic plans with the assistance of administrative personnel. They make the day-to-day decisions that directly affect the retailer's performance.

ORGANIZATION DESIGN CONSIDERATIONS

Once the tasks have been identified, the retailer groups them into jobs to be assigned to specific individuals and determines the reporting relationships.[13]

Specialization Rather than performing all the tasks shown in Exhibit 14–5, individual employees are typically responsible for only one or two tasks. **Specialization**, focusing employees on a limited set of activities, enables employees to develop expertise and increase productivity. For example, a real estate manager can concentrate on becoming expert at selecting retail sites, while a benefit manager can focus on becoming expert in developing creative and cost-effective employee benefits. Through specialization, employees work only on tasks for which they were trained and have unique skills.

But employees may become bored if they're assigned a narrow set of tasks, such as putting price tags on merchandise all day long, every day. Also, extreme specialization may increase labour costs. For example, salespeople often don't have many customers when the store first opens, mid-afternoon, or at closing. Rather than

refact

Seventy-three percent of consumers attribute their best customer service to store employees. Conversely, 81 percent of consumers attribute their worst customer service experience to employees.[12]

exhibit 14–5　Tasks Performed in a Retail Firm

STRATEGIC MANAGEMENT	MERCHANDISE MANAGEMENT	STORE MANAGEMENT	ADMINISTRATIVE MANAGEMENT (OPERATIONS)
• Develop a retail strategy • Identify the target market • Determine the retail format • Design organizational structure • Select locations • Scan the retail enivronment • Strategize brand development and repositioning • Plan for succession (a major priority for senior management)	• Buy merchandise 　Locate vendors 　Evaluate vendors 　Negotiate with vendors 　Place orders • Control merchandise inventory 　Develop merchandise budget plans 　Allocate merchandise to stores 　Review open-to-buy and stock position • Price merchandise 　Set initial prices 　Adjust prices	• Recruit, hire, train store personnel • Plan work schedules • Evaluate performance of store personnel • Maintain store facilities • Locate and display merchandise • Sell merchandise to customers • Repair and alter merchandise • Provide services such as gift wrapping and delivery • Handle customer complaints • Take physical inventory • Prevent inventory shrinkage	• Promote the firm, its merchandise, and services 　Plan communication programs 　Develop communication budget 　Select media 　Plan special promotions 　Design special displays 　Manage public relations • Manage human resources 　Develop policies for managing store personnel 　Recruit, hire, train managers 　Plan career paths 　Keep employee records • Distribute merchandise 　Locate warehouses 　Receive merchandise 　Mark and label merchandise 　Store merchandise 　Ship merchandise to stores 　Return merchandise to vendors • Establish financial control 　Provide timely information on financial performance 　Forecast sales, cash flow, profits 　Raise capital from investors 　Bill customers 　Provide credit

hiring a specialist for stocking shelves and arranging merchandise, many retailers have salespeople perform these tasks during slow selling periods.

Responsibility and Authority　Productivity increases when employees have the proper amount of authority to effectively undertake the responsibilities assigned to them. For example, buyers who are responsible for the profitability of a merchandise category need to have the authority to make decisions that will enable them to fulfill this responsibility. They should have the authority to select and price merchandise for their category and determine how the merchandise is displayed and promoted.

Sometimes the benefits of matching responsibility and authority conflict with benefits of specialization. For example, buyers rarely have authority over how their merchandise is sold in the stores or through the Internet. Other employees, such as store managers who specialize in management of salespeople or designers who specialize in constructing Web sites, have this authority.

Reporting Relationships   After assigning tasks to employees, the final step in designing the organization structure is determining the reporting relationships. Productivity can decrease when too many or too few employees report to a supervisor. The effectiveness of supervisors decreases when they have too many employees reporting to them. On the other hand, if managers are supervising very few employees, the number of managers increases and costs go up. The appropriate number of subordinates ranges from 4 to 12, depending on the nature of their tasks, skills, and location.

Strategic decisions are undertaken primarily by senior management in a retail firm.

Matching Organization Structure to Retail Strategy   The design of the organization structure needs to match the firm's retail strategy. For example, category specialists and warehouse clubs such as Future Shop and Costco target price-sensitive customers and thus are very concerned about building a competitive advantage based on low cost. They minimize the number of employees by having decisions made by a few people at corporate headquarters. These centralized organization structures are very effective when there are limited regional or local differences in customer needs.

On the other hand, high-fashion clothing customers often aren't very price-sensitive, but can be extremely demanding, and consumer preferences vary across the country. Retailers targeting these segments tend to have more managers and decision making at the local store level. By having more decisions made at the local store level, human resource costs are higher, but sales also increase since merchandise and services are tailored to meet the needs of local markets.

refact

The median number of stores in Canada per district manager is 11.[14]

retail organization structures

Retail organization structures differ according to the type of retailer and the size of the firm. For example, a retailer with a single store will have an organization structure quite different from a national chain.

ORGANIZATION OF A SINGLE-STORE RETAILER

Owner–managers of a single store may be the entire organization. As sales grow, the owner–manager hires employees. Coordinating and controlling employee activities is easier in a small store than in a large chain of stores. The owner–manager simply assigns tasks to each employee and watches to see that these tasks are performed properly. Since the number of employees is limited, single-store retailers have little specialization. Each employee must perform a wide range of activities, and the owner–manager is responsible for all management tasks.

As sales increase, specialization in management may occur when the owner–manager hires additional management employees. Exhibit 14–6 illustrates the common division of management responsibilities into merchandise and store management. The owner–manager continues to perform strategic management

refact

Mellerio dits Meller, the French jeweller founded in 1591, is one of the oldest family-owned retail chains still operating.[15]

exhibit 14–6   Organization of a Small Retailer

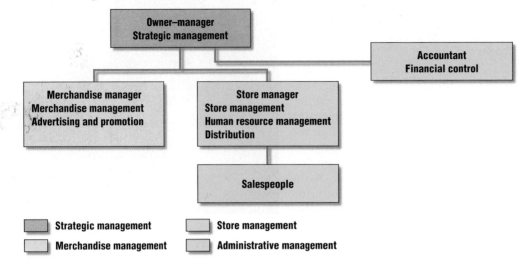

tasks. The store manager may be responsible for administrative tasks associated with receiving and shipping merchandising and managing the employees. The merchandise manager or buyer may handle the advertising and promotion tasks as well as the merchandise tasks. Often the owner–manager contracts with an accounting firm to perform financial control tasks for a fee.

retail organization design issues

Two important issues in the design of a retail organization are:

- the degree to which decision making is centralized or decentralized

- approaches used to coordinate merchandise and store management

In the context of a department store chain, the first issue translates into whether the decisions concerning activities such as merchandise management, information and distributions systems, and human resource management are made by the regional department stores or the corporate headquarters. The second issue arises because retailers divide the merchandise and store management activities into different organizations within the firm. Thus, they need to develop ways for coordinating these interdependent activities.

CENTRALIZATION VERSUS DECENTRALIZATION

Centralization occurs when authority for retailing decisions is delegated to corporate managers rather than to geographically dispersed regional, district, and store managers; **decentralization** occurs when authority for retail decisions is assigned to lower levels in the organization.

Retailers reduce costs when decision making is centralized in corporate management:

- First, overhead falls because fewer managers are required to make the merchandise, human resource, marketing, and financial decisions. Centralized retail organizations can similarly reduce personnel in administrative functions such as marketing and human resources.

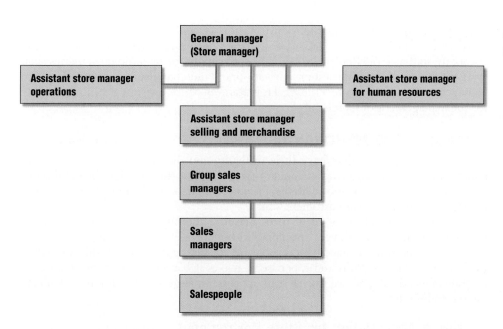

exhibit 14–7
Store Organizations

- Second, by coordinating buying across geographically dispersed stores, the company achieves lower prices from suppliers. The retailer can negotiate better purchasing terms by placing one large order rather than a number of smaller orders.

- Third, centralization provides an opportunity to have the best people make decisions for the entire corporation. For example, in a centralized organization, people with the greatest expertise in areas such as MIS, buying, store design, and visual merchandise can have all stores benefit from their skills.

- Finally, centralization increases efficiency. Standard operating policies are used for store and personnel management; these policies limit the decisions made by store managers. For example, corporate merchandisers do considerable research to determine the best method for presenting merchandise. They provide detailed guides for displaying merchandise to each store manager so that all stores look the same throughout the country. Because they offer the same core merchandise in all stores, centralized retailers can achieve economies of scale by advertising through national media rather than more costly local media.[16]

Strengths of Decentralization:

- Although centralization has advantages in reducing costs, the disadvantage of centralization is that it makes it more difficult for a retailer to adapt to local market conditions.

- In addition to problems with tailoring merchandise to local needs, the centralized retailer also may have difficulty responding to local competition and labour markets. Since pricing is established centrally, individual stores may not be able to respond quickly to competition in their market. Finally, centralized personnel policies can make it hard for local managers to pay competitive wages in their area or to hire appropriate types of salespeople.

However, centralized retailers are relying more on their information systems to react to local market conditions. By looking at buying patterns across a large number of stores, the centralized buyer might uncover opportunities that local managers would not see.

Large retailers are using their information systems to make more and more merchandise and operations decisions at corporate headquarters. For example, the corporate staff at Holt Renfrew is taking responsibility for operational activities such as distribution, information systems, private-brand merchandise, and human resource management policies. However, each Holt Renfrew store division is still responsible for the management of merchandise.

COORDINATING MERCHANDISE AND STORE MANAGEMENT

Small independent retailers have little difficulty coordinating their stores' buying and selling activities. Owner–managers typically buy the merchandise and work with their salespeople to sell it. Being in close contact with customers, the owner–managers know what their customers want.

On the other hand, large retail firms organize the buying and selling functions into separate divisions. Buyers specialize in buying merchandise and have limited contact with the store management responsible for selling it. Although this specialization increases buyers' skills and expertise, it makes it harder for them to understand customers' needs. Below, we discuss four approaches large retailers use to coordinate buying and selling.

Improving Appreciation for Store Environment   Fashion-oriented retailers use several methods to increase buyers' contact with customers and to improve informal communication between buyers and store personnel who sell the merchandise they buy. Management trainees, who eventually become buyers, are required by most retailers to work in the stores before they enter the buying office. During this six-to-ten-month training period, prospective buyers gain appreciation for the activities performed in the stores, the problems salespeople and department managers encounter, and the needs of customers.

Making Store Visits   Another approach to increasing customer contact and communication is to have buyers visit the stores and work with the departments they buy for. At Wal-Mart, all managers (not just the buyers) are required to visit stores frequently and practise the company philosophy of CBWA (coaching by wandering around). This face-to-face communication provides managers with a richer view of store and customer needs than they can get from impersonal sales reports from the company's management information system. Spending time in the stores improves buyers' understanding of customer needs, but this system is costly because it reduces the time the buyer has to review sales patterns, plan promotions, manage inventory, and locate new sources of merchandise.

Assigning Employees to Coordinating Roles   Some retailers have people in the merchandise division (the planners who work with buyers) and the stores (the managers of sales and merchandise who work for the store managers) who are responsible for coordinating buying and selling activities. Many national retail chains have regional and even district staff personnel to coordinate buying and selling activities.

Involving Store Management in Buying Decisions   Another way to improve coordination between buying and selling activities is to increase store employees' involvement in the buying process. This process would be more typical of smaller retail chains in which a decentralized buying process would assist the retailer in offering the newest trend for a specific target market. In some cases, the involvement of staff will not only provide a retail opportunity but also has the potential to build staff loyalty.

Besides developing an organization structure, human resource management undertakes a number of activities to improve employee performance, build commitment in employees, and reduce turnover. In the following two sections of this chapter, we examine these human resource management activities.

compensating and motivating retail employees

A critical task of human resource management is to motivate employees to work toward achieving the firm's goals and implementing its strategy. The task is often difficult because employees' goals may differ from those of the firm. For example, a sales associate might find it more personally rewarding to creatively arrange a display than to help a customer. Retailers generally use three methods to motivate their employees' activities: policies and supervision, incentives, and organizational culture.

Store employees receive two types of rewards from their work: extrinsic and intrinsic. **Extrinsic rewards** are rewards provided by either the employee's manager or the firm, such as compensation, promotion, and recognition. **Intrinsic rewards** are rewards employees get personally from doing their job well. For example, salespeople often like to sell because they think it's challenging and fun. Of course, they want to be paid, but they also find it rewarding to help customers and make sales.[17]

Public recognition programs make employees feel they are appreciated and motivate them to improve their performance. Marshalls stores that deliver exceptional customer service are recognized by the "All-Star Award," which includes a plaque to hang in the store.

POLICIES AND SUPERVISION

Perhaps the most fundamental method of coordination is to:

- prepare written policies that indicate what tasks employees are responsible for
- have supervisors/managers enforce these policies

For example, retailers may set policies on when and how merchandise can be returned by customers. If employees use the written policies to make these decisions, their actions will be consistent with the retailer's strategy.

But strict reliance on written policies can reduce employee motivation. Employees might have little opportunity to use their own initiative to improve performance of their areas of responsibility. As a result, they eventually might find their jobs uninteresting.

Relying on rules as a method of coordination leads to a lot of red tape. Situations will arise that aren't covered by a rule. Then employees will need to talk to a supervisor before they can deal with the situation.

INCENTIVES

The second method of motivating and coordinating employees uses incentives to motivate them to perform activities consistent with the retailer's objectives. For example, buyers will be motivated to focus on the firm's profits if they receive a bonus based on the profitability of the merchandise they buy.

Some of the criteria that managers and employees could be measured on include: customer satisfaction, average order dollar amount, market share, sales growth, top-

refact

Purdy Chocolates Ltd. of Vancouver was named among the 50 Best Employers in Canada 2003, by *Report on Business* magazine. Purdy's philosophy: "We're more than just about great chocolates —we're about great people too." [18]

of-mind awareness in a market, promotion from within, employee development, ideas and suggestions from staff that are implemented, and revenue per square metre. It should be remembered that there can be a negative impact with a straight commission program with respect to the credibility of a manager or sales associate's worth to the company. For example, the financial industry will now need to disclose how much they are going to be paid by a fund if the customer purchases that fund, see Certified Financial Planner at www.cfp-ca.org.

Types of Incentive Compensation   Two types of incentives are commissions and bonuses:

- A **commission** is compensation based on a fixed formula such as 2 percent of sales. For example, many retail salespeople's compensation is based on a fixed percentage of the merchandise they sell.

- A **bonus** is additional compensation awarded periodically based on an evaluation of the employee's performance. For example, store managers often receive bonuses at the end of the year based on their store's performance relative to its budgeted sales and profits.

Besides incentives based on individual performance, retail managers often receive additional income based on their firm's performance. These *profit-sharing* arrangements can be offered as a cash bonus based on the firm's profits or as a grant of stock options that link additional income to performance of the firm's stock.

A number of retailers such as Wal-Mart and Home Depot use *stock incentives* to motivate and reward all employees, including sales associates. Employees are encouraged to buy shares in their companies at discounted prices through payroll deduction plans. These stock incentives align employees' interests with those of the company and can be very rewarding when the company does well. However, if growth in the company's stock price declines, employee morale declines too, corporate culture is threatened, and demands for higher wages and more benefits develop.[19]

Incentive compensation plans reward employees on the basis of their productivity. Many retailers now use incentives to motivate greater sales productivity by their employees. With some incentive plans, a salesperson's income is based entirely on commission—called a **straight commission.** For example, a salesperson might be paid a commission based on a percentage of sales made minus the merchandise returned.

Incentive plans may include a fixed salary plus a commission on total sales or a commission on sales over quota. For example, a salesperson might receive a salary of $200 per week plus a commission of 2 percent on all sales over a quota of $50 per hour.

Incentive compensation plans are a powerful motivator for salespeople to sell merchandise, but they have a number of disadvantages. For example, it's hard to get salespeople who are compensated totally by commission to perform nonselling activities. Also, salespeople will concentrate on the more expensive, fast-moving merchandise and neglect other merchandise. Sales incentives can also discourage salespeople from providing services to customers. Finally, salespeople compensated primarily by incentives don't develop loyalty to their employer. The employer doesn't guarantee them an income, so they feel no obligation to the firm.

Under a straight commission plan, salespeople's incomes can fluctuate from week to week, depending on their sales. Because retail sales are seasonal, salespeople might earn most of their income during the Christmas season but much less during the summer months. To provide a steadier income for salespeople who are paid by high-incentive plans, some retailers offer a **drawing account.** With a drawing account, salespeople receive a weekly cheque based on their estimated annual income, and commissions earned are credited against the weekly payments. If the draw exceeds the earned commissions, the salespeople return the excess money they've been paid, and their weekly draw is reduced. If the commissions earned exceed the draw, salespeople are paid the difference.

Quotas are often used with compensation plans. A **quota** is a target level used to motivate and evaluate performance. Examples include sales per hour for salespeople or maintained margin and inventory turnover for buyers. For department store salespeople, selling quotas vary across departments due to differences in sales productivity levels.

A **quota–bonus plan** provides sales associates with a bonus when their performance exceeds their quota. A quota–bonus plan's effectiveness depends on setting reasonable, fair quotas, which can be difficult. Usually, quotas are set at the same level for everyone in a department, but salespeople in the same department may have different abilities or face different selling environments. Newly hired salespeople might have a harder time achieving a quota than more experienced salespeople. Thus, a quota based on average productivity may be too high to motivate the new salesperson and too low to effectively motivate the experienced salesperson. Quotas should be developed for each salesperson on the basis of his or her experience and the nature of the store area in which he or she works.[22]

Group Incentives   To encourage employees in a department or store to work together, some retailers provide additional incentives based on the performance of the department or store as a whole. For example, salespeople might be paid a commission based on their individual sales and then receive additional compensation according to the amount of sales over plan, or quota, generated by all salespeople in the store. The group incentive encourages salespeople to work together in their nonselling activities and handling customers so the department sales target will be achieved.[23]

Setting the Commission Percentage   Assume that a specialty store manager wants to hire experienced salespeople. To get the type of person she wants, she feels she must pay $12 per hour. Her selling costs are budgeted at 8 percent of sales. With compensation of $12 per hour, salespeople need to sell $150 worth of merchandise per hour ($12 divided by 8 percent) for the store to keep within its sales cost budget. The manager believes the best compensation would be one-third salary and two-thirds commission, so she decides to offer a compensation plan of $4 per hour salary (33 percent of $12) and a 5.33 percent commission on sales. If salespeople sell $150 worth of merchandise per hour, they'll earn $12 per hour ($4 per hour in salary plus $150 multiplied by 5.33 percent, which equals $8 per hour in commission).

In addition to competitive salary, vacation, and tuition reimbursement as a retailer's key retention strategies, keeping your best requires attention to each employee as an individual. Retailers will need to be creative to keep their best employees eager to advance to become future company leaders.

ORGANIZATION CULTURE

The final method for motivating and coordinating employees is to develop a strong organization culture. An **organization culture** is the set of values, traditions, and customs in a firm that guides employee behaviour. These

Ed Mirvish of Honest Ed's is giving out turkeys during the holidays.

guidelines aren't written in a set of policies and procedures; they are traditions passed along by experienced employees to new employees.[25]

Many retail firms have strong organization cultures that give employees a sense of what they ought to do on their jobs and how they should behave to be consistent with the firm's strategy. For example, Harry Rosen's strong organization culture emphasizes customer service, while Wal-Mart's organization culture focuses on reducing costs so the firm can provide low prices to its customers.

An organization culture often has a much stronger effect on employees' actions than rewards offered in compensation plans, directions provided by supervisors, or written company policies.

Harry Rosen emphasizes the strength of organization culture in the policy manual given to new employees. The manual has one rule: Use your best judgment to do anything you can to provide service to our customers. Lack of written rules doesn't mean that Harry Rosen employees have no guidelines or restrictions on their behaviour. Its organization culture guides employees' behaviour. New salespeople learn from other employees that they should always wear clothes sold at Harry Rosen, that they should park their cars at the outskirts of the parking lot so customers can park in more convenient locations, and that they should offer to meet busy executives at their offices with new menswear trend items.

Developing and Maintaining a Culture　Organization cultures are developed and maintained through stories and symbols.[26]

Disney strengthens its organization culture through the labels it uses for its employees and by steeping employees in the culture during the selection process. Management and employees view themselves as part of a team whose job is to produce a very large show. Applicants are trying out for a role in the cast rather than being hired for a job. For hourly jobs, the casting director (the person in charge of recruiting) interviews applicants to determine if they can adapt to the company's strong organizational culture. Do they understand and accept the fact that Disney has strict grooming requirements (no facial hair for men, little makeup for women)? Is the applicant willing to work on holidays? After the initial screening, the remaining applicants are judged on how well they might fit in with the show. Current employees participate in the entire process—they assess the applicant's behaviours and attitudes while also providing firsthand information on their role in the "production."

JOB ANALYSIS

The **job analysis** identifies essential activities and is used to determine the qualifications of potential employees. For example, retail salespeople's responsibilities vary from company to company and from department to department within a store.

Managers can obtain the information needed for a job analysis by observing employees presently doing the job and by determining the characteristics of exceptional performers. Exhibit 14–8 lists some questions that managers should consider in a job analysis for sales associates. Information collected in the job analysis is then used to prepare a job description.

JOB DESCRIPTION

A **job description** includes *activities the employee needs to perform* and *the performance expectations expressed in quantitative terms*. The job description is a guideline for recruiting, selecting, training, and eventually evaluating employees.

- How many salespeople will be working in the department at the same time?
- Do the salespeople have to work together in dealing with customers?
- How many customers will the salesperson have to work with at one time?
- Will the salesperson be selling on an open floor or working behind the counter?
- How much and what type of product knowledge does the salesperson need?
- Does the salesperson need to sell the merchandise or just ring up the orders and provide information?
- Is the salesperson required to make appointments with customers and develop a loyal customer base?
- Does the salesperson have the authority to negotiate price or terms of the sale?
- Does the salesperson need to demonstrate the merchandise?
- Will the salesperson be expected to make add-on sales?
- Is the salesperson's appearance important? How should an effective salesperson look?
- Will the salesperson be required to perform merchandising activities such as stocking shelves and setting up displays?
- To whom will the salesperson report?
- Under what compensation plan will the salesperson be working?

exhibit 14–8
Questions for Undertaking a Job Analysis

LOCATING PROSPECTIVE EMPLOYEES

Staffing stores is becoming a critical problem because changing demographics are reducing the size of the labour pool.[27] Here are some suggestions for recruiting employees in this tight labour market:

- Look beyond the retail industry.
- Use your employees as talent scouts.
- Provide incentives for employee referrals.
- Recruit from minority communities, immigrants, and seniors.
- Use the Internet to locate prospective employees. Today you cannot survive in business without computer skills. Employees comfortable with basic computer applications such as Word, Excel, and PowerPoint are not going to be challenged by point-of-purchase sales systems.

SCREENING APPLICANTS TO INTERVIEW

The screening process matches applicants' qualifications with the job description. Many retailers use automated prescreening programs as a low-cost method of identifying qualified candidates. Applicants either interact with a Web-enabled store kiosk or call a toll-free telephone number, and a computer program asks some basic questions that the applicants answer using the keyboard or telephone buttons.

The questions are tailored to the retailer's specific needs and environment. For example, a mall-based chain selling music-themed merchandise, asks, "Would you work in an environment where loud alternative music is played?" The response time for answering the questions is monitored and follow-up questions are asked when the answers are unusually slow. When applicants pass this automated prescreen, additional information is collected using application forms, reference checks, and tests.[28]

Application Forms **Job application forms** contain information about the applicant's employment history, previous compensation, reasons for leaving previous employment, education and training, and references. This information enables the manager to determine whether the applicant meets the minimum qualifications and also provides information for interviewing the applicant.[29]

refact
Wal-Mart receives over 4 million applications a year, many of them from customers.[30]

Internet sites such as workopolis.com can be useful recruiting tools, and ensure that job applicants are computer-literate.

References   A good way to verify the information given on an application form is to contact the applicant's references. Contacting references is also helpful for collecting additional information from people who've worked with the applicant. In addition, store managers should check with former supervisors not listed as references. Due to potential legal problems, however, many companies have a policy of not commenting on past employees.[31]

Store managers generally expect to hear favourable comments from an applicant's references or even from previous supervisors who may not have thought highly of the applicant. One approach for reducing the positive bias is to ask the reference to rank the applicant relative to others in the same position. For example, the manager might ask, "How would you rate Pat's customer service skill in relation to other retail sales associates you have worked with?" Another approach is to use a positively toned scale ranging from "somewhat effective" to "extremely effective."

Testing   Intelligence, ability, personality, and interest tests can provide insights about potential employees. For example, intelligence tests yield data about the applicant's innate abilities and can be used to match applicants with job openings and to develop training programs. However, tests must be scientifically and legally valid. They can only be used when the scores have been shown to be related to job performance. It is illegal to use tests assessing factors that are not job-related or that discriminate against specific groups.

Some retailers use tests to assess applicants' honesty and ethics. Paper-and-pencil honesty tests include questions to find out if an applicant has ever thought about stealing and if he believes other people steal ("What percentage of people take more than $1 from their employer?").[32] The use of lie detectors in testing employees is prohibited.

Realistic Job Preview   Turnover is reduced when the applicants understand both the attractive and unattractive aspects of the job. For example, PETsMART, a pet supply category specialist, has each applicant view a 10-minute video that begins with the advantages of being a company employee and then shows scenes of employees dealing with irate customers and cleaning up animal droppings. This type of job preview typically screens out 15 percent of the applicants who would most likely quit within three months if they were hired.[33]

SELECTING APPLICANTS

After screening applications, the selection process typically involves a personal inter-view. Since the interview is usually the critical factor in the hiring decision, the store manager needs to be well prepared and to have complete control over the interview.

Preparation for the Interview   The objective of the interview is to gather relevant information, not simply to ask a lot of questions. The most widely used in-terview technique, called the *behavioural interview*, asks candidates how they handled actual situations they have encountered in the past, situations requiring skills outlined in the job description. For example, applicants applying for a job requiring them to handle customer complaints would be asked to describe a situation in which they were confronted by someone who was angry with something they had done. Candidates are asked to describe the situation, what they did, and what were the outcomes of their ac-tions. These situations also can be used to interview references for the applicants.[37]

An effective approach to interviewing involves some planning by the manag-ers but also allows some flexibility in selecting questions. Managers should develop objectives for what they want to learn about the candidate. Each topic area covered in the interview starts with a broad question, such as "Tell me about your last job," designed to elicit a lengthy response. The broad opening question is followed by a sequence of more specific questions, such as "What did you learn from that job?" or "How many subordinates did you have?" Finally, managers must be careful to avoid asking questions that are discriminatory.[38]

Managing the Interview   Exhibit 14–9 shows questions the manager might ask. Here are some suggestions for questioning the applicant during the interview:

- Encourage long responses by asking questions such as "What do you know about our company?" rather than "How familiar are you with our company?"
- Avoid asking questions that have multiple parts.
- Avoid asking leading questions such as "Are you prepared to provide good customer service?"
- Be an active listener. Evaluate the information that is being presented and sort out the important comments from the unimportant ones. Some techniques for active listening are repeating or rephrasing information, summarizing the conversation, and tolerating silences.[39]
- Observe the applicant's behaviour in the interview—attitude, appropriate dress, eagerness to learn

Some managers interview candidates while giving them a tour through the store. When the manager sees a display that's out of order, he might say, "While we're talking, would you help me straighten this out?" Some candidates will stand back; others will jump right in and help out. (*Hint:* You want to hire candidates from the second group.)

LEGAL CONSIDERATIONS IN SELECTING AND HIRING STORE EMPLOYEES

Heightened social awareness and government regulations emphasize the need to avoid discrimination in hiring. Discrimination is specifically prohibited in the following human resource decisions: recruitment, hiring, discharge, layoff, discipline, promo-tion, compensation, and access to training.

exhibit 14-9   Interviewing Questions

EDUCATION

What were your most favourite and least favourite subjects in university? Why?

What types of extracurricular activities did you participate in? Why did you select those activities?

If you had the opportunity to attend school all over again what, if anything, would you do differently? Why?

How did you spend the summers during university?

Did you have any part-time jobs? Which of your part-time jobs did you find most interesting? What did you find most difficult about working and attending college or university at the same time? What advice would you give to someone who wanted to work and attend university at the same time?

What accomplishments were you most proud of?

PREVIOUS EXPERIENCE

What's your description of the ideal manager? Subordinate? Co-worker?

What did you like most/least about your last job?

What kind of people do you find it difficult/easy to work with? Why?

What has been your greatest accomplishment during your career to date?

Describe a situation at your last job involving pressure. How did you handle it?

What were some duties on your last job that you found difficult?

Of all the jobs you've had, which did you find the most/least rewarding?

What is the most frustrating situation you've encountered in your career?

Why do you want to leave your present job?

What would you do if . . . ?

How would you handle . . . ?

What would you like to avoid in future jobs?

What do you consider your greatest strength/weakness?

What are your responsibilities in your present job?

Tell me about the people you hired on your last job. How did they work out? What about the people you fired?

What risks did you take in your last job and what were the results of those risks?

Where do you see yourself in three years?

What kind of reference will your previous employer give?

What do you do when you have trouble solving a problem?

QUESTIONS THAT ARE DISCRIMINATORY AND CANNOT BE ASKED

Do you have plans for having children/a family? What are your marriage plans? What does your husband/wife do? What happens if your husband/wife gets transferred or needs to relocate? Who will take care of your children while you're at work? (Asked of men) How would you feel about working for a woman?

How old are you? What is your date of birth? How would you feel working for a person younger than you? Where were you born? Where were your parents born?

Do you have any handicaps? As a handicapped person, what help are you going to need to do your work? How severe is your handicap?

What's your religion? What church do you attend? Do you hold religious beliefs that would prevent you from working on certain days of the week?

Do you feel that your race/colour will be a problem in your performing the job? Are you of _____ heritage/race?

Discrimination arises when a member of a protected class (women, minorities, etc.) is treated differently from nonmembers of that class **(disparate treatment)** or when an apparently neutral rule has an unjustified discriminatory effect **(disparate impact).** An example of disparate treatment occurs when a qualified woman does not receive a promotion given to a less qualified man. Disparate impact occurs when a retailer requires high school graduation for all its employees, thereby excluding a larger proportion of disadvantaged minorities, when at least some of the jobs (e.g., custodian) could be performed just as well by people who did not graduate from high school. In such cases, the retailer is required to prove the imposed qualification is actually needed to be able to perform the job.

Finally, legislation opens up job opportunities for the disabled by requiring employees to provide accommodating work environments. A **disability** is defined as any physical or mental impairment that substantially limits one or more of an individual's major life activities or any condition that is regarded as being such an impairment. Although merely being HIV positive does not limit any life activities, it may be perceived as doing so and is therefore protected as a disability. Similarly, extreme obesity may be either actually limiting or perceived as such and also is protected as long as the obese person can perform the duties of the job.

building employee commitment

An important challenge in retailing is to reduce turnover.[40] High turnover reduces sales and increases costs. Sales are lost because inexperienced employees lack the skills and knowledge about company policies and merchandise to interact effectively with customers. Costs increase due to the need to continually recruit and train new employees.

To reduce turnover, retailers need to build an atmosphere of mutual commitment in their firms. When a retailer demonstrates its commitment, employees respond by developing loyalty to the company. Employees improve their skills and work hard for the company when they feel the company is committed to them over the long run, through thick and thin. Some approaches that retailers take to build mutual commitment are:

- developing employee skills through selection and training
- empowering employees
- creating a partnering relationship with employees.[41]

Research indicates that engaging in these human resource management practices increases the firm's financial performance.[42]

DEVELOPING SKILLS

Two activities that retailers undertake to develop knowledge, skills, and abilities in their human resources are selection and training. Retailers that build a competitive advantage through their human resources are very selective in hiring people and make significant investment in training.

Selective Hiring The first step in building a committed workforce is recruiting the right people. Singapore Airlines, one of Asia's most admired companies, is consistently ranked among the top airlines in terms of service quality. Since its flight attendants are the critical point of contact with its customers, senior management is personally involved in their selection. Only 10 percent of the applicants make the initial screen; only 2 percent are hired.[44]

The job requirements and firm strategy dictate the type of people hired. Simply seeking the best and the brightest often is not the best approach. For example, at a category killer in outdoor gear, the motto is "You live what you sell." Outdoor enthusiasts are hired as sales associates so they can help customers and serve as a resource for the buying staff. Chapters wants avid readers in its workforce.[45]

Socialization and Training After hiring employees, the next step in developing effective employees is introducing them to the firm and its policies. Retailers want the people they hire to become involved, committed contributors to the firm's successful performance. On the other hand, newly hired employees want to learn about their job responsibilities and the company they've decided to join. **Socialization** is the set of steps taken to transform new employees into effective, committed members of the firm. Socialization goes beyond simply orienting new employees to the firm. A principal objective of socialization is to develop a long-term relationship with new employees to increase productivity and reduce turnover costs.[46]

A key factor in socializing new employees is to create a training and work environment that articulates the retailer's culture and strategy. Training is particularly important in retailing because more than 60 percent of retail employees have direct contact with customers. They are responsible for helping customers satisfy their needs and resolve their problems. Two keys to success for a retailer are how it treats its employees and its emphasis on training.

Investing in developing employee skills tells employees that the firm considers them important. In response to the difficulty in finding qualified service workers,

11.3 retailing view
E-TRAINING IN VIRTUAL CLASSROOMS

Training store employees is costly and challenging for retailers due to the high turnover rate. Every month some employees leave, new ones are hired, and the training process needs to start all over again. To increase training effectiveness, many retailers are using the Internet to train their store employees in customer service and product knowledge.

Some of the benefits of e-training are greater consistency compared with on-the-job training by different supervisors, lower costs due to interactive self-training and reduced travel costs, and the ability to organize and launch major marketing and service programs nationwide and respond rapidly to market opportunities. In addition, e-training has contributed to strengthening vendor relationships.

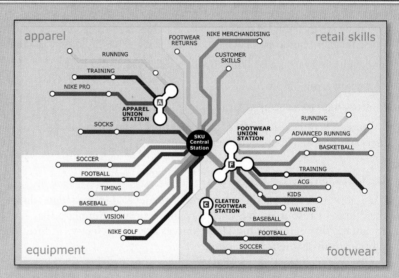

This diagram outlines the product knowledge and company policies that store employees can acquire using Nike's e-learning training solution, called Sports Knowledge Underground.

For example, many vendors provide briefings on new products to Circuit City so that store associates can learn about new product features and benefits.

Nike's training system for its store employees and those of retailers selling its merchandise is called Sports Knowledge Underground. The layout for Sports Knowledge Underground resembles a subway map, with different stations representing different training themes. As an example, Apparel Union Station branches off into the apparel technologies line, the running products line, and the Nike Pro products line. The Cleated Footwear Station offers paths to football, whereas the Central Station offers such broad lines as customer skills. Each segment is three to seven minutes long and gives the associate the basic knowledge he or she needs about various products. As new products are introduced each season, the training is updated, and Nike customizes the program for each retailer if requested. When stores implement Sports Knowledge Underground, they see a 4–5 percent increase in sales.

Sources: Jessica Marquez, "Faced with High Turnover, Retailers Boot Up E-Learning Programs for Quick Training," *Workforce Management,* August 2005, pp. 74–75; Matthew Haeberle, "Virtual Classrooms," *Chain Store Age,* March 2003, pp. 68–69.

Marriott has made a considerable investment in recruiting and training entry-level workers. The training goes beyond the basics of doing the job to include grooming habits and basic business etiquette such as calling when you can't come to work.

Starbucks creates strong commitment in its employees through an organizational culture based on standards for coffee preparation and a supportive, empowering attitude toward employees.

Orientation Programs   Orientation programs are critical in overcoming entry shock and socializing new employees.[47] Orientation programs can last from a few hours to several weeks. The orientation and training program for new salespeople might be limited to several hours, during which the new salesperson learns the retailer's policies and procedures and how to use the POS terminal. On the other hand, the orientation program for management trainees might take several weeks.

Effective orientation programs need to avoid information overload and one-way communication. When new hires are confronted with a stack of forms and company policies, they get the impression the company is very bureaucratic. Large quantities of information are hard to absorb in a short period of time. New employees learn information best when it's parcelled out in small doses.

Store managers need to foster two-way communication when orienting new employees. Rather than just presenting information about their firm, managers need to give newly hired employees a chance to have their questions and concerns addressed.

The orientation program is just one element in the overall training program. It needs to be accompanied by a systematic follow-up to ensure that any problems and concerns arising after the initial period are considered.

Structured Program   During the structured program, new employees are taught the basic skills and knowledge they'll need to do their job. For example, salespeople learn what the company policies are, how to use the point-of-sale terminal, and how to perform basic selling skills; stockroom employees learn procedures for receiving merchandise. This initial training might include lectures, audiovisual presentations, manuals, and correspondence distributed to the new employees.

The initial structured program should be relatively short so new employees don't feel they are simply back in school. Effective training programs bring new recruits up to speed as quickly as possible and then get them involved in doing the job for which they've been hired.

On-the-Job Training   The next training phase emphasizes on-the-job training. New employees are assigned a job, given responsibilities, and coached by their supervisor. The best way to learn is to practise what is being taught. New employees learn by doing activities, making mistakes, and then learning how not to make those mistakes again. Information learned through classroom lectures tends to be forgotten quickly unless it's used soon after the lecture.[48]

Employee Evaluation   Most retailers evaluate employees annually or semiannually. Feedback from evaluations is the most effective method for improving employee skills. Thus, evaluations should be done more frequently when managers are developing inexperienced employees' skills. Managers should supplement these formal evaluations with frequent informal ones. Evaluations are only meaningful if employees know what they're required to do, what level of performance is expected, and how they'll be evaluated. Exhibit 14–10 shows The Gap's criteria for evaluating sales associates.

exhibit 14–10   Factors Used to Evaluate Associates at The Gap

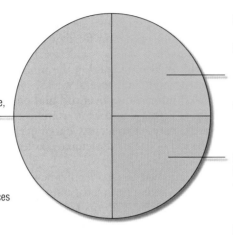

50%
SALES/CUSTOMER RELATIONS

1. Greeting. Approaches customers within 1 to 2 minutes with a smile and friendly manner. Uses open-ended questions.

2. Product knowledge. Demonstrates knowledge of product, fit, shrinkage, and price and can relay this information to the customer.

3. Suggests additional merchandise. Approaches customers at fitting room and cash/wrap areas.

4. Asks customers to buy and reinforces decisions. Lets customers know they've made a wise choice and thanks them.

25%
OPERATIONS

1. Store appearance. Demonstrates an eye for detail (colour and finesse) in the areas of display, coordination of merchandise on tables, floor fixtures, and wall faceouts. Takes initiative in maintaining store presentation standards.

2. Loss prevention. Actively follows all loss prevention procedures.

3. Merchandise control and handling. Consistently achieves established requirements in price change activity, shipment processing, and inventory control.

4. Cash/wrap procedures. Accurately and efficiently follows all register policies and cash/wrap procedures.

25%
COMPLIANCE

1. Dress code and appearance. Complies with dress code. Appears neat and well groomed. Projects current fashionable Gap image.

2. Flexibility. Able to switch from one assignment to another, open to schedule adjustments. Shows initiative, awareness of store priorities and needs.

3. Working relations. Cooperates with other employees, willingly accepts direction and guidance from management. Communicates to management.

The Gap employee's overall evaluation is based on subjective evaluations made by the store manager and assistant managers. It places equal weight on individual sales/customer relations activities and activities associated with overall store performance. By emphasizing overall store operations and performance, The Gap's assessment criteria motivate sales associates to work together as a team.

Analyzing Successes and Failures   Every new employee makes mistakes. Store managers should provide an atmosphere in which salespeople try out different approaches to providing customer service and selling merchandise. Store managers must recognize that some of these new approaches are going to fail, and when they do, managers shouldn't criticize the individual salesperson. Instead, they should talk about the situation, analyze why the approach didn't work, and discuss how the salesperson could avoid the problem in the future.

EMPOWERING EMPLOYEES

Empowerment is the process of managers sharing power and decision-making authority with employees. When employees have the authority to make decisions, they are more confident in their abilities, have greater opportunity to provide service to customers, and are more committed to the firm's success.

The first step in empowering employees is to review employee activities that require a manager's approval.

Each store in the Whole Foods chain is a profit centre, with the store employees organized in 10 self-managed teams. The teams are responsible and accountable for the store's performance. For example, the store manager recommends new hires. It takes a two-thirds vote of the team to actually hire the candidate. The team members pool their ideas and come up with creative solutions to problems. Empowerment of retail employees transfers authority and responsibility for making decisions to lower levels in the organization. These employees are close to the retailer's customers and in a good position to know what it takes to satisfy customers. For empowerment to work, managers must have an attitude of respect and trust, not control and distrust.[49]

EMPLOYEE FEEDBACK SURVEY

One of the primary benefits of an employee survey is to provide an opportunity for employees to give feedback to the retail organization. A well-designed employee survey can provide significant benefits in improving retention and organizational communication. In addition, if employees think that their personal needs and ideas are valued, this can build trust and commitment between managers and associates.

Employee feedback enables the retailer to identify gaps between organizational goals and actual policies. It helps align the retailer's goals and employee satisfaction by making employees participants in the process of business improvement and success.

All questionnaires must be anonymous and take no more than thirty minutes to complete. For larger retailers electronic or Web-based questionnaires are the most efficient and cost-effective format. When designing a questionnaire, maintain consistency of question format, and use unbiased check boxes as an effective way to control responses. Open-ended responses allow employees to share their thoughts on issues. Retailers must act on the collected results of any survey. Never let data go unused. The value of employee feedback cannot be overstated.

DEVELOPING PARTNERING RELATIONSHIPS WITH EMPLOYEES

Four human resource management activities that build commitment through developing partnering relationships with employees are:

- reducing status differences
- promoting from within
- enabling employees to balance their careers and families.
- enabling employees to pursue outside interests such as athletics and community activities

Retailers such as The Royal Bank Financial Group and Home Depot not only support Canada's Olympic athletes through financial contributions, but provide them with employment that recognizes their demanding training schedules.

Reducing Status Differences Many retailers attempt to reduce status differences between employees. With limited status differences, employees feel that they play an important role in the firm's achieving its goals and that their contributions are valued.

Status differences can be reduced symbolically through the use of language and cut substantively by lowering wage differentials and increasing communications between

Lisa Shaw, body care buyer at Whole Foods Market, is committed to the company and "feels that what I am doing is good in some larger sense."

managers at different levels in the company. For example, hourly workers at Wal-Mart are referred to as associates and managers are called partners, a practice that Sam Walton adopted when he started Wal-Mart.

Whole Foods has a policy of limiting executive compensation to less than eight times the compensation of the average full-time salaried employee.

All Home Depot senior executives spend time in the stores, wearing the orange apron, talking with customers and employees. This "management by walking around" makes employees feel that their inputs are valued by the company and reinforces the customer service culture.

Promotion from Within   **Promotion from within** is a staffing policy that involves hiring new employees only for positions at the lowest level in the job hierarchy and then promoting employees for openings at higher levels in the hierarchy. Home Depot, and Wal-Mart have had promotion-from-within policies.

Promotion-from-within policies establish a sense of fairness. When employees do an outstanding job and then outsiders are brought in over them, employees feel that the company doesn't care about them. Promotion-from-within policies also commit the retailer to developing its employees.[50]

Balancing Careers and Families   The increasing number of two-income and single-parent families makes it difficult for employees to effectively do their jobs and manage their households. Retailers build employee commitment by offering services such as job sharing, child care, and employee assistance programs to help their employees manage these problems.

Flextime is a job scheduling system that enables employees to choose the times they work. With **job sharing,** two employees voluntarily are responsible for a job that was previously held by one person. Both programs let employees accommodate their work schedules to other demands in their life such as being home when children return from school.[51]

Many retailers offer child care assistance. Sears' corporate headquarters has a 1860 square metre day care centre. At Eddie Bauer, a catalogue retailer in Seattle, the corporate headquarters cafeteria stays open late and prepares takeout meals for time-pressed employees. Some companies will even arrange for a person to be at an employee's home waiting for the cable guy to come or to pick up and drop off dry cleaning.[52]

trends in retail human resource management

In this final section we discuss three trends in human resource management:

- the increasing importance of having a diverse workforce
- the growth in legal restrictions on HR practices
- use of technology to increase employee productivity

MANAGING DIVERSITY

Managing diversity is a human resource management activity designed to realize the benefits of a diverse workforce. Today, diversity means more than differences in skin colour, nationality, and gender.

Minority groups now embrace their differences and want employers to accept them for who they are. The appropriate metaphor is a salad bowl. Each ingredient in the salad is distinctive, preserving its own identity, but the mixture of ingredients improves the combined taste of the individual elements.[53] Diversity and equity in the workplace always make good business sense. Consider the Canadian population, comprising more than 200 ethnic groups with multiple ties around the world. Businesses that embrace diversity are well positioned to be more competitive in world markets.[54]

Some legal restrictions promote diversity in the workplace by preventing retailers from practising discrimination based on non–performance-related employee characteristics. But retailers now recognize that promoting employee diversity can improve financial performance. By encouraging diversity in their workforce, retailers can better understand and respond to the needs of their customers and deal with the shrinking labour market.

Retail customers' racial and ethnic backgrounds are increasingly diverse. To compete in this changing marketplace, retailers need management staffs that match the diversity of their target markets. For example, 85 percent of the men's clothing sold in department stores is bought by women, and over 50 percent of Home Depot's sales are made to women. To better understand customer needs, department store and home improvement retailers feel that they must have women in senior management positions—people who really understand their female customers' needs.

The fundamental principle of managing diversity is the recognition that employees have different needs and require different approaches to accommodating those needs. Managing diversity goes beyond meeting equal employment opportunity laws. It means accepting and valuing differences. Some programs that retailers use to manage diversity involve offering diversity training, providing support groups and mentoring, and managing career development and promotions.[55]

Diversity Training Diversity training typically consists of two components: developing cultural awareness and building competencies. The cultural awareness component teaches people about how their own culture differs from the culture of other employees and how stereotypes they hold influence the way they treat people, often in subtle ways they might not realize. Then role-playing is used to help employees develop better interpersonal skills, including showing respect and treating people as equals.

Support Groups and Mentoring **Mentoring programs** assign higher-level managers to help lower-level managers learn the firm's values and meet other senior executives.[56]

Career Development and Promotions Although laws provide entry-level opportunities for women and minority groups, these employees often encounter a glass ceiling as they move through the corporation. A **glass ceiling** is an invisible barrier that makes it difficult for minorities and women to be promoted beyond a certain level.

Similarly, women in the supermarket business have traditionally been assigned to peripheral departments such as bakery and deli, while men were assigned to the critical departments in the store: meat and grocery. Even in the supermarket chain corporate office, women traditionally have been in staff-support areas such as human resource management, finance, and accounting, while men are more involved in store operations and buying. To make sure that more women have an opportunity to break

Retailers are increasing the diversity of their workforce to match the diversity of their customers.

through the glass ceiling in the supermarket industry, firms are placing them in positions critical to the firm's success.[60]

LEGAL AND REGULATORY ISSUES IN HUMAN RESOURCE MANAGEMENT

In Canada all employers and all employees must comply with the *Employment Standards Act*, which identifies standards based on provincial legislation. Historically, collective agreements helped shape employment standards that today apply to about two-thirds of Canadian workers who are not involved in a unionized work environment. Each of Canada's ten provinces and three territories developed its own employment standards legislation, all based on a common set of issues. The *Employment Standards Act* is a law that establishes minimum entitlements pertaining to such issues as: wages; paid holidays and vacations; leave for maternity, parental care, and adoption; bereavement leave; termination notice; overtime pay; and limits on the maximum number of hours of work permitted per day or week.[61] Managing in this complex regulatory environment requires expertise in labour laws and skills in helping other managers comply with these laws. The major legal and regulatory issues involving the management of retail employees are:

* equal employment opportunity
* compensation
* labour relations
* sexual harassment
* employee privacy

Equal Employment Opportunity Canadian employment equity legislation is not about favouring anybody—women, persons with disabilities, Aboriginal persons, or visible minorities. The law is about identifying and eliminating employment barriers. It is also about instituting positive policies and practices and making reasonable accommodations to ensure that persons in the designated groups achieve a degree of workforce representation that reflects their representation in Canadian society.[62] **Illegal discrimination** is the actions of a company or its managers that result in members of a protected class being treated unfairly and differently than others. A protected class is all of the individuals who share a common characteristic defined by the law. Companies cannot treat employees differently simply based on their race, colour, religion, sex, national origin, age, or disability status. There is a very limited set of circumstances under which employees can be treated differently. For example, it is illegal for a restaurant to hire only young, attractive servers because that is what its customers prefer. Such discrimination must be absolutely necessary, not simply preferred.

In addition, it is illegal to engage in a practice that disproportionately excludes a protected group even though it might seem to be nondiscriminatory. For example, suppose that a retailer uses scores on a test to make hiring decisions. If a protected group systematically performs worse on the test, the retailer is illegally discriminating even if there was no intention to discriminate.

Compensation   Laws relating to compensation define the 40-hour workweek, the pay rate for working overtime, and the minimum wage, and they protect employee investments in their pensions. In addition, they require that firms provide the same pay for men and women who are doing equal work of equal value.

Labour Relations   Labour relations laws describe the process by which unions can be formed and the ways in which companies must deal with the unions. They precisely indicate how negotiations with unions must take place and what the parties can and cannot do.

Employee Safety and Health   The basic premise of these laws is that the employer is obligated to provide each employee with an environment that is free from hazards that are likely to cause death or serious injury.

Sexual Harassment   Sexual harassment includes unwelcome sexual advances, requests for sexual favours, and other verbal and physical conduct. Harassment isn't confined to requests for sexual favours in exchange for job considerations such as a raise or promotion. Simply creating a hostile work environment can be considered sexual harassment. For example, actions that are considered sexual harassment include lewd comments, joking, and graffiti, as well as showing obscene photographs, staring at a co-worker in a sexual manner, alleging that an employee got rewards by engaging in sexual acts, and commenting on an employee's moral reputation.

Customers can engage in sexual harassment as well as supervisors and co-workers. For example, female pharmacists find that some male customers demand lengthy discussions when they buy condoms. Pharmacists have difficulty dealing with these situations because they want to keep the person as a customer and also protect themselves from abuse.

Employee Privacy   Employees' privacy protection is very limited. For example, employers can monitor e-mail and telephone communications, and search an employee's work space and handbag. However, employers cannot discriminate among employees when undertaking these activities unless they have a strong suspicion that employees are acting inappropriately.

Developing Policies   The human resource department is responsible for developing programs and policies to make sure that managers and employees are aware of these restrictions and know how to deal with potential violations. These legal and regulatory requirements are basically designed to treat people fairly. Employees want to be treated fairly and companies want to be perceived as treating their employees fairly. The perception of fairness encourages people to join a company and leads to trust and commitment of employees to a firm. When employees believe they are not being treated fairly, they can either complain, stay and accept the situation, stay but engage in negative behaviour, quit, or complain to an external authority and even sue the employer.

Perceptions of fairness are based on two factors—the perceptions of:

- **Distributive justice**, which arises when outcomes received are viewed as fair with respect to outcomes received by others. However, the perception of distributive justice can differ across cultures. For example, in the individualistic culture of Canada, merit-based pay is perceived as fair, whereas in collectivist cultures such as China and Japan, equal pay is viewed as fair.

> **refact**
> It costs a retailer $20 to $30 to process a paper HR form, but processing the form over an intranet only costs $0.05 to $0.10.[63]

- **Procedural justice**, which is based on fairness of the process used to determine the outcome. Canadian workers consider formal processes as fair whereas group decisions are considered fairer in collectivist cultures.[65]

store security management

With identity theft and payment fraud on the rise due to bogus purchases appearing on credit card statements or missing funds from bank accounts via credit card fraud, retailers increasingly see chargebacks at the point-of-sale as a necessity of doing business. The generous returns policy instituted by many retailers has attracted criminals seeking a low-risk, high-reward way to make money.

On January 1, 2004, the Personal Information and Protection of Electronic Documents Act (PIPEDA), took effect in Canada. This privacy legislation outlined the responsibilities of Canadian businesses to the customers they serve.

The top three risks that companies face related to privacy damage are:

- damage to reputation of the business
- loss of customers
- litigation costs

Canadian retailers need to launch employee training programs and develop privacy statements for display in the store and on their Web site. Transparency is critical to the success of retail privacy policy guidelines.

For additional information visit the office of the Privacy Commissioner of Canada at www.privcom.gc.ca.

14.4 retailing view
HOLT RENFREW USES FINGER PRINT BIOMETRICS

Biometrics such as finger print recognition can be used for controlled access to POS systems, for manager approvals, and for transaction overrides. Holt Renfrew employees sign in with their finger tips, using biometrics scanning. Holt Renfrew is currently one of the only Canadian retailers using biometrics to track employee activities as part of their workforce management strategy. The concept eliminates problems of misplaced pass cards, shared passwords, and payroll discrepancies because finger print recognition is tied into the store's time and attendance system.

Biometrics such as fingerprint recognition can be used for controlled access to POS systems, for manager approvals, and for transaction overrides. This could also pave the way for consumer applications such as biometric payment at the POS.

DON'T ASSUME THAT ALL SHOPLIFTERS ARE POORLY DRESSED

To avoid detection, professional shoplifters dress in the same manner as customers patronizing the store. Over 90 percent of all amateur shoplifters arrested have either the cash, cheques, or credit to purchase the merchandise they stole.

SPOT LOITERERS

Amateur shoplifters frequently loiter in areas as they build up the nerve to steal something. Professionals also spend time waiting for the right opportunity, but less conspicuously than amateurs.

LOOK FOR GROUPS

Teenagers planning to shoplift often travel in groups. Some members of the group divert employees' attention while others take the merchandise. Professional shoplifters often work in pairs. One person takes the merchandise and passes it to a partner in the store's restroom, phone booths, or restaurant.

LOOK FOR PEOPLE WITH LOOSE CLOTHING

Shoplifters frequently hide stolen merchandise under loose-fitting clothing or in large shopping bags. People wearing a winter coat in the summer or a raincoat on a sunny day may be potential shoplifters.

WATCH THE EYES, HANDS, AND BODY

Professional shoplifters avoid looking at merchandise and concentrate on searching for store employees who might observe their activities. Shoplifters' movements might be unusual as they try to conceal merchandise.

exhibit 14–11
Spotting Shoplifters

Security Measures   Store employees can be the retailer's most effective tool against shoplifting. They should be trained to be aware, visible, and alert to potential shoplifting situations. Exhibit 14–11 outlines rules for spotting shoplifters. Perhaps the best deterrent to shoplifting is an alert employee who is very visible. Location and type of display can also be effective tools against shoplifting. Exhibit 14–12 describes retailers' use of security measures. Department stores often chain expensive merchandise to fixtures. Another approach to deterring shoplifting is to embed dye capsules in the merchandise. If the capsules aren't removed properly by a store employee, they break and damage the merchandise.

By placing convex mirrors at key locations, employees can observe a wide area of the store. Closed-circuit TV cameras can be monitored from a central location, but purchasing the equipment and hiring people to monitor the system can be expensive. Some retailers install nonoperating equipment that looks like a TV camera to provide a psychological deterrent to shoplifters.

Although these security measures reduce shoplifting, they can also make the shopping experience more unpleasant for honest customers. The atmosphere of a fashionable department store is diminished when guards, mirrors, and TV cameras are highly visible. Customers may find it hard to try on clothing secured with a lock-and-chain or an electronic tag. They can also be uncomfortable trying on clothing if they think they're secretly being watched via a surveillance monitor. Thus, when evaluating security measures, retailers need to balance the benefits of reducing shoplifting with the potential losses in sales.

Electronic article surveillance is a promising approach to reducing shrinkage with little effect on shopping behaviour. In **electronic article surveillance (EAS) systems**, special tags are placed on merchandise. When the merchandise is purchased, the tags are deactivated by the POS scanner. If a shoplifter tries to steal the merchandise, the active tags are sensed when the shoplifter passes a detection device at the store exit and an alarm is triggered.[66]

exhibit 14–12

Use of Security
Measures by Retailers

Live closed-circuit TV	74%
Cheque approval screening systems	68
Cables, locks, and chains	46
EAS tags	43
Mystery and honesty shoppers	42
Observation mirrors	41
Secured displays	46
Uniformed guards	37
Simulated closed-circuit TV	31
Plainclothes detectives	29
Ink/dye tags	28
Fitting room attendants	13
Observation booths	11

Source: Richard Hollinger and Jason Davis, *2001 National Retail Security Survey* (Gainesville, FL: University of Florida, 2001), p. 11, web.soc.ufl.edu/SRP/NRSS_2001.pdf. Reprinted by permission.

EAS tags do not affect shopping behaviour because customers do not realize they're on the merchandise. Due to the effectiveness of tags in reducing shoplifting, retailers can increase sales by displaying theft-prone, expensive merchandise openly rather than behind a counter or in a locked enclosure.

Some large national retailers insist that vendors install EAS tags during the manufacturing process because the vendors can install the tags at a lower cost than the retailers. In addition, retail-installed tags can be removed more easily by shoplifters. Vendors are reluctant to get involved with installing EAS tags because industry standards have not been adopted. Without these standards, a vendor would have to develop unique tags and merchandise for each retailer.[67]

refact
A dishonest employee typically takes over $1000 worth of goods and cash, whereas the average customer shoplifter takes $128 in merchandise.[68]

Prosecution Many retailers have a policy of prosecuting all shoplifters. They feel a strictly enforced prosecution policy deters shoplifters. Some retailers also sue shoplifters in civil proceedings for restitution of the stolen merchandise and the time spent in the prosecution.

Reducing Employee Theft The most effective approach to reducing employee theft and shoplifting is to create a trusting, supportive work environment. When employees feel they're respected members of a team, they identify their goals with the retailer's goals. Stealing from their employer becomes equivalent to stealing from themselves or their family, and they go out of their way to prevent others from stealing from the "family." Thus, retailers with a highly committed workforce and low turnover typically have low inventory shrinkage. Additional approaches to reducing employee theft are carefully screening employees, creating an atmosphere that encourages honesty and integrity, using security personnel, and establishing security policies and control systems.

Screening Prospective Employees As mentioned previously, many retailers use paper-and-pencil honesty tests and make extensive reference checks to screen out potential employee theft problems.

Retailers use EAS tags to reduce shoplifting. The tags (left and right) contain a device that is part of the price tag. If the tags are not deactivated when the merchandise is purchased, the stolen merchandise will be detected when the shopper passes through the sensor gates (centre) at the store exit.

Using Security Personnel In addition to uniformed guards, retailers use undercover shoppers to discourage and detect employee theft. These undercover security people pose as shoppers. They make sure salespeople ring up transactions accurately.

Establishing Security Policies and Control Systems To control employee theft, retailers need to adopt policies relating to certain activities that may facilitate theft. Some of the most prevalent policies are:

- Randomly search containers such as trash bins where stolen merchandise can be stored
- Require store employees to enter and leave the store through designated entrances
- Assign salespeople to specific POS terminals and require all transactions to be handled through those terminals
- Restrict employee purchases to working hours
- Provide customer receipts for all transactions
- Have all refunds, returns, and discounts cosigned by a department or store manager
- Change locks periodically and issue keys to authorized personnel only
- Have a locker room where all employee handbags, purses, packages, and coats must be checked

SUMMARY

Human resource management plays a vital role in supporting a retailing strategy. The organization structure defines supervisory relationships and employees' responsibilities. The four primary groups of tasks performed by retailers are strategic decisions by the corporate officers, administrative tasks by the corporate staff, merchandise management by the buying organization, and store management.

In developing an organization structure, retailers must make trade-offs between the cost savings gained through centralized decision making and the benefits of tailoring the merchandise offering to local markets—benefits that arise when decisions are made in a decentralized manner.

Two critical human resource management issues are the development of a committed workforce and the effective management of a diverse workforce. Building a committed workforce is critical in retailing because high turnover has a major impact on profitability. A key factor in reducing turnover is developing an atmosphere of mutual commitment.

Effective store management can have a significant impact on a retail firm's financial performance. Store managers increase profits by increasing labour productivity, decreasing costs through labour deployment decisions, and reducing inventory loss by developing a dedicated workforce.

A well-crafted, well-executed employee feedback survey can provide significant benefits to improve employee satisfaction and retention, as well as organizational communications that ultimately improve the retailer's success.

Increasing store employees' productivity is challenging because of the difficulties in recruiting, selecting, and motivating store employees. Employees typically have a range of skills and seek a spectrum of rewards. Effective store managers need to motivate their employees to work hard and to develop skills so they improve their productivity. Store managers must establish realistic goals for employees that are consistent with the store's goals.

Store managers also must control inventory losses due to employee theft, shoplifting, and clerical errors. Managers use a wide variety of methods in developing loss prevention programs, including security devices, employee screening during the selection process, and building employee loyalty to increase attention to shoplifting.

The human resource department is also responsible for making sure that its firm complies with the laws and regulations that prevent discriminatory practices against employees and ensure that they have a safe work environment.

KEY TERMS

bonus, *400*

buyer, *423*

category manager, *423*

centralization, *396*

coaching, *388*

commission, *400*

decentralization, *396*

disability, *407*

discrimination, *406*

disparate impact, *406*

disparate treatment, *406*

distributive justice, *415*

drawing account, *400*

electronic article surveillance
  (EAS) system, *417*

employee productivity, *389*

employee turnover, *389*

empowerment, *410*

extrinsic rewards, *399*

flextime, *412*

glass ceiling, *413*

illegal discrimination, *414*

incentive compensation
  plans, *400*

intrinsic rewards, *399*

job analysis, *402*

job application form, *403*

job description, *402*

job sharing, *412*

leadership, *388*

management, *388*

managing diversity, *412*

mentoring program, *413*

merchandising planner, *423*

organization culture, *401*

organization structure, *393*

procedural justice, *416*

promotion from within, *412*

quota, *401*

quota-bonus plan, *401*

socialization, *408*

specialization, *393*

straight commission, *400*

Get Out & Do It!

1. **GO SHOPPING** Go to a store and meet with the person responsible for personnel scheduling. Report on the following:

- Who is responsible for employee scheduling?
- How far in advance is the schedule made?
- How are breaks and lunch periods planned?
- How are overtime hours determined?
- What is the total number of budgeted employee hours for each department based on?
- How is flexibility introduced into the schedule?
- How are special requests for days off handled?
- How are peak periods (hourly, days, or seasons) planned for?
- What happens when an employee calls in sick at the last minute?

2. **GO SHOPPING** Go to a store and talk to the person responsible for human resource management to find out how salespeople are compensated and evaluated for job performance.

- What are the criteria for evaluation?
- How often are they evaluated?
- How much importance does the store attach to a buyer's or manager's merchandising skill versus his or her ability to work with people?
- For an associate, what action is taken if the person does not meet sales goals? Can goals be adjusted? Can associates be moved to another area or type of function?
- Do salespeople have quotas? If they do, how are they set?
- Can sales associates make a commission? If yes, how does the commission system work? What are the advantages of a comission system? What are the disadvantages?

- If there is no commission system, are any incentive programs offered? Give an example of a specific program or project used by the store to boost employee morale and productivity.

3. **GO SHOPPING** Go to a store, observe the security measures in the store, and talk with the manager about the store's loss prevention program.

- Are there surveillance cameras? Where are they located?
- What is the store's policy against shoplifters?
- What are the procedures for approaching a suspected shoplifter?
- How are shoplifters handled?
- How are sales associates and executives involved in the security programs?
- Is employee theft a problem? Elaborate.
- How is employee theft prevented in the store?
- How is shrinkage prevented in the store?
- How is customer service related to loss prevention in the store?

4. **INTERNET EXERCISE** Go to the Society of Human Resource Management's home page, www.shrm.org. SHRM is an organization of human resource professionals. It publishes *HR Magazine* with articles available online at www.workforceonline.com. Find and summarize the conclusions of articles addressing the HR challenges that retailers are facing, such as the management of a diverse workforce, international expansion, and the use of technology to increase productivity.

5. **INTERNET EXERCISE** Go to a favourite retailer's Web site (a national chain retailer) and assess their employment application form for sales associate.

- experience
- education
- references

6. **INTERNET EXERCISE** Go to Conference Board of Canada at www. conferenceboard.ca.

   a. Download the PDF file "Employability Skills 2000+."

   b. Write 10 questions that an employer could ask an applicant in an interview based on the employability skills identified.

DISCUSSION QUESTIONS AND PROBLEMS

1. Describe the similarities and differences in the organization of small and large retail companies. Why do these similarities and differences exist?

2. How can national retailers such as Best Buy and LaSenza, which both use a centralized buying system, make sure that their buyers are aware of the local differences in consumer needs?

3. What are the positive and negative aspects of employee turnover? How can a retailer reduce the turnover in its sales associates?

4. To motivate employees, several major department stores are experimenting with incentive compensation plans. Frequently, compensation plans with a lot of incentives don't promote good customer service. How can retailers motivate employees to sell merchandise aggressively and at the same time not jeopardize customer service?

5. Three approaches to motivating and coordinating employee activities are policies and supervision, incentives, and organization culture. What are the advantages and disadvantages of each?

6. Why should retailers be concerned about the needs of their employees? What can retailers do to satisfy the needs of employees?

7. How do on-the-job training and classroom training differ? What are the benefits and limitations of each approach?

8. Give examples of a situation in which a manager of a McDonald's fast-food restaurant must utilize different leadership styles.

9. Job descriptions should be in writing so employees clearly understand what's expected of them. But what are the dangers of relying too heavily on written job descriptions?

10. What's the difference between extrinsic rewards and intrinsic rewards? What are the effects of these rewards on the behaviour of retail employees? Under what conditions would you recommend that a retailer emphasize intrinsic rewards over extrinsic rewards?

11. Many large department stores are changing their salespeople's reward system from a traditional salary to a commission-based system. What problems can incentive compensation systems cause? How can department managers avoid these problems?

12. When evaluating retail employees, some stores use a quantitative approach that relies on checklists and numerical scores. Other stores use a more qualitative approach in which less time is spent checking and adding and more time is devoted to discussing strengths and weaknesses in written form. Which is the better evaluation approach? Why?

13. What are the different methods for compensating employees? Discuss which methods you think would be best for compensating a sales associate, store manager, and buyer.

14. In addition to competitve salary, vacation, and tuition reimbursement as a retailer's key retention strategies, in what other ways can a retailer optimize employee satisfaction?

15. Discuss how retailers can reduce shrinkage from shoplifting and employee theft.

APPENDIX 14A   Organization of a Regional Department Store

In contrast to the management of a single store, retail chain store management is complex. Managers must supervise stores that are geographically distant from each other.

Traditionally, department stores were family-owned and -managed. Organization of these firms was governed by family circumstances. Executive positions were designed to accommodate family members involved in the business. Then, in 1927, Paul Mazur proposed a functional organization plan that has been adopted by most retailers.[69] The organization structures of many retail chains continue to reflect principles of the Mazur plan, such as separating buying and store management tasks into separate divisions.

Exhibit 14–13 shows a functional organization plan. Most retail chains such as The Gap, Canadian Tire, and Winners have similar organization structures. Vice-presidents responsible for administrative tasks (blue), specific merchandise categories (gold), and stores (green) report to the chairperson and president.

In most retail firms, the two senior executives, typically called the CEO and COO, work closely together in managing the firm. They are frequently referred to as principals or partners. One member of the partnership is primarily responsible for the merchandising activities of the firm—the merchandise and marketing divisions. The other partner is primarily responsible for the operating divisions—stores, human resources, distribution, information systems, and finance divisions.

MERCHANDISE DIVISION

The merchandise division is responsible for procuring the merchandise sold in the stores and ensuring that the quality, fashionability, assortment, and pricing of merchandise are consistent with the firm's strategy.

Buyers

Buyers are responsible for procuring merchandise, setting prices and markdowns, and managing inventories for specific merchandise categories. They attend trade and fashion shows and negotiate with vendors on prices, quantities, assortments, delivery dates, and payment terms. In addition, they might specify private-label merchandise or request modifications to tailor the merchandise to the retailer's target market and differentiate it from the competition.

Although buyers are given considerable autonomy to "run their own business," they must adhere to an inventory budget that will vary from season to season. The budget is the result of a negotiation between the buyers and their superiors, divisional merchandise managers.

Planners

Traditionally, buyers or **category managers** were also responsible for determining the assortment stocked in each store, allocating merchandise to the stores, monitoring sales, and placing reorders. Giving this responsibility to buyers meant that the merchandise strategy within a store might not be coordinated. For example, some buyers might allocate more expensive merchandise to a store in high-income areas, but others wouldn't make this adjustment.

To address these problems, most retail chains created merchandise planners, with a senior VP of planning and distribution, who are at the same level as the merchandise managers in the buying organization. Each **merchandising planner** is responsible for allocating merchandise and tailoring the assortment in several categories for specific stores in a geographic area. For example, the planner at The Bay would alter the basic assortment of sweaters for the different climates in south Vancouver and St. John's.

Stores Division

The stores division shown in green is responsible for the group of activities undertaken in stores. Each vice-president is in charge of a set of stores. A store manager, often called a general manager, is responsible for activities performed in each store.

refact

Rich's/Lazarus/Goldsmith's employs 17 200 people in 76 stores located in nine midwestern and southeastern states; it has annual sales of US$2.2 billion.[70]

exhibit 14–13   Functional Organization Plan

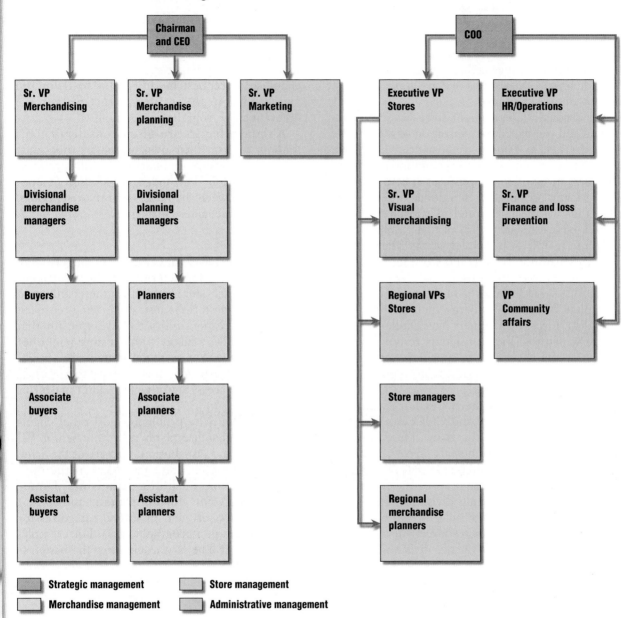

Exhibit 14–13 shows a store organization chart. General managers in large stores have three assistant store managers reporting to them. The assistant store manager for sales and merchandising manages the sales associates and presentation of the merchandise in the store. The assistant manager for human resources is responsible for selecting, training, and evaluating employees. The assistant store manager for operations is responsible for: store maintenance; store security; some

exhibit 14–13   Functional Organization Plan

CONTINUED

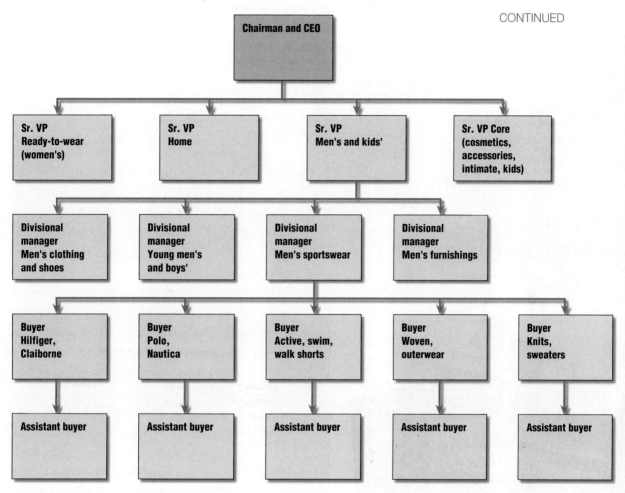

customer service activities, such as returns, complaints, and gift wrapping; the receiving, shipping, and storage areas of the store; and leased areas, including the restaurant and hair-styling salon. In smaller stores, the general manager may perform the tasks done by an assistant store manager for merchandise.

Group sales managers, sales managers, and the salespeople work with customers in specific areas of the store. For example, a sales manager might be responsible for the entire area in which kitchen appliances, gifts, china, silver, and tableware are sold, while a group sales manager might be responsible for an entire floor of the store.

CHAPTER 15 building customer loyalty: customer relationship management and service strategies

Executive Briefing

Loyalty Cards: Big Information Business

In the past, Canadians based their purchasing decisions on value, price, and convenience. Now that winning strategy includes reward points. The cornerstone of loyalty programs in Canada for the past 15 years has been points in exchange for airline tickets.

Air Miles are offered by retailers to induce you to shop there. Of course you only get something for nothing if the retailer does not raise his prices to cover the cost of giving Air Miles.

The transactional part of a loyalty program, make a purchase, pick up points—is not what loyalty is about. Retailers want loyalty from their customers, but a lot of businesses have confused loyalty programs with points-based initiatives. Points are not important, but understanding the customer is. The retailer gives the reward points in exchange for information. For example, it is the ability of the business to learn their customers' needs and wants and to tailor not just their merchandise to them but also the retail experience.

Sophisticated databases compile information to assist retailers to refine their merchandising mix and marketing strategy to gain bigger market share. Information is power, and thanks to the data amassed from loyalty cards, inquiring marketers

QUESTIONS   What is customer relationship management?

How do retailers determine who their best customers are?

How can retailers build customer loyalty and increase their share of wallet?

What is Canada's privacy legislation, and what does it mean to retailers?

What services do retailers offer customers?

How can customer service build a competitive advantage?

What activities does a retailer have to undertake to provide high-quality customer service?

How can retailers recover from a service failure?

know what music we listen to, what restaurants we prefer, and what brand names gain our loyalty. This valuable information allows the retailer to tailor its marketing programs to specific customer segments and to concentrate on profitable customers who will generate the most revenue. Retaining a current customer is far less costly than finding a new one. It is estimated it costs 10 times more for a company to attract a new customer.

Youthography, a Toronto-based marketing research firm, determined that in the 19- to 24-year-old age group, 83% own a loyalty card, and 91% of 25- to 29-year-olds own at least one loyalty card. The top loyalty programs are Air Miles, Shoppers Drug Mart, and The Bay. (It's interesting to note that none focuses their marketing efforts on youth.) On the other hand, customers using the Shoppers Optimum card see the value right away, because customers with enough points can receive money off their purchases at point of sale.

The challenge for all loyalty cards is that people want to simplify their lives, to discard things that aren't absolutely essential. If a loyalty card does not have value and becomes only an extra card in the wallet, it will fall out of shoppers' wallets very quickly.

Business press and companies are talking a lot about the importance of managing customer relationships. Companies are spending billions of dollars on computer systems to help them collect and analyze data about their customers. Putting customers at the centre of the business equation pays off in retail profits. Companies around the world are focusing on new and innovative ways to serve their customers.

Customer service is the activities and programs developed by retailers to make the shopping experience for their customers special. Customers base their evaluations of store service on their perceptions. Although these perceptions are affected by the actual service provided, service (due to its intangibility) is often hard to evaluate accurately. Five customer service characteristics that customers use to evaluate service quality are reliability, assurance, tangibility, empathy, and responsiveness.[1] Some cues that customers use to assess these service characteristics are:

- Reliability: Accuracy of billing, meeting promised delivery dates
- Assurance (trust): Guarantees and warranties, return policy
- Tangibility: Appearance of store, salespeople
- Empathy: Personalized service, receipts of notes and e-mails, recognition by name
- Responsiveness: Returning calls and e-mails, giving prompt service.

Employees can play an important role in customer perceptions of service quality.[2] Customer evaluations of service quality are often based on the manner in which store employees provide the service, not just the outcome. Consider the following situation: A customer goes to a store to return an electric toothbrush that isn't working properly. In one case, company policy requires the employee to ask the customer for a receipt, check to see if the receipt shows the toothbrush was bought at the store, examine the toothbrush to see if it really doesn't work properly, ask a manager if a refund can be provided, complete some paperwork, and finally give the customer the amount paid for the toothbrush in cash. In a second case, the store employee simply asks the customer how much he paid and gives him a cash refund. The two cases have the same outcome: The customer gets a cash refund. But the customer might be dissatisfied in the first case because the employee appeared not to trust the customer and took so much time providing the refund. In most situations, employees have a great effect on the process of providing services and, thus, on the customer's eventual satisfaction with the services.

Customer relationship management (CRM) is a business philosophy and set of strategies, programs, and systems that focus on identifying and building loyalty with a retailer's most valued customers. CRM is based on the philosophy that retailers can increase their profitability by building relationships with their better customers. By effectively managing merchandise inventory and adding services, stores provide extra value that supports the objective of building customer loyalty to increase their share of wallet. The goal of CRM is to develop a base of loyal customers who patronize the retailer frequently. In the following sections of this chapter, we discuss in more depth the objective of CRM programs and the elements in the CRM process.

the CRM process

Traditionally, retailers have focused their attention on encouraging customers to visit their stores, look through their catalogues, and visit their Web sites. To accomplish this objective, they have traditionally used mass media advertising and price promotions, treating all their customers the same. Now retailers are beginning to concentrate on providing more value to their best customers, using targeted promotions and services to increase their **share of wallet**—the percentage of the customers' purchases made from the retailer—with these customers. This change in perspective is supported by research indicating that it costs over six times more to sell products and services to new customers than to existing customers and that small increases in customer retention can lead to dramatic increases in profits.[3]

WHAT IS LOYALTY?

Customer loyalty, the objective of CRM, is more than having customers make repeat visits to a retailer and being satisfied with their experiences and the merchandise they purchased. Customer loyalty to a retailer means that customers are committed to purchasing merchandise and services from the retailer and will resist the activities of competitors attempting to attract their patronage. They have a bond with the retailer, and the bond is based on more than a positive feeling about the retailer.[4]

Loyal customers have an emotional connection with the retailer. Their reasons for continuing to patronize a retailer go beyond the convenience of the retailer's store or the low prices and specific brands offered by the retailer. They feel such goodwill toward the retailer that they will encourage their friends and family to buy from it.

Programs that encourage repeat buying by simply offering price discounts can be easily copied by competitors. In addition, these types of price promotion programs encourage customers to be always looking for the best deal rather than developing a relationship with one retailer. However, when a retailer develops an emotional connection with a customer, it is difficult for a competitor to attract the customer.[5]

Emotional connections develop when customers receive personal attention. For example, many small, independent restaurants build loyalty by functioning as neighbourhood cafés, where waiters and waitresses recognize customers by name and know their preferences.

By providing good value, Wal-Mart increases its share of its customers' wallets.

Unusual positive experiences also build emotional connections. For example, Harry Rosen sales associates will take new menswear collections to the offices of their busy loyal customers and provide personalized services for their styling and tailoring needs. Providing such memorable experiences is an important avenue for building customer loyalty.[6]

OVERVIEW OF THE CRM PROCESS

Exhibit 15–1 illustrates that CRM is an iterative process that turns customer data into customer loyalty through four activities:

- collecting customer data
- analyzing the customer data and identifying target customers
- developing CRM programs
- implementing CRM programs

exhibit 15–1
The CRM Process Cycle

The process begins with the collection and analysis of data about a retailer's customers and the identification of target customers. The analysis translates the customer information into activities that offer value to the targeted customers. Then these activities are executed through communication programs undertaken by the marketing department and customer service programs implemented by customer contact employees, typically sales associates. Each of the four activities in the CRM process is discussed in the following sections.

collecting customer data

The first step in the CRM process is constructing a **customer database.** This database, referred to as a **customer data warehouse,** contains all of the data the firm have collected about its customers and is the foundation for subsequent CRM activities.

CUSTOMER DATABASE

Ideally, the database should contain the following information:

- *Transactions*—a complete history of the purchases made by the customer, including the purchase date, the price paid, the SKUs purchased, and whether or not the merchandise was purchased in response to a special promotion or marketing activity.

- *Customer contacts*—a record of the interactions that the customer has had with the retailer, including visits to the retailer's Web site, inquiries made through in-store kiosks, and telephone calls made to the retailer's call centre, plus information about contacts initiated by the retailer, such as catalogues and direct mail sent to the customer.

- *Customer preferences*—what the customer likes, such as favourite colours, brands, fabrics, and flavours as well as apparel sizes.

- *Descriptive information*—demographic and psychographic data describing the customer that can be used in developing market segments.

- *Responses to marketing activities*—the analysis of the transaction and contact data provides information about the customer's responsiveness to marketing activities

Different members of a household might have interactions with a retailer. Thus, to get a complete view of the customer, retailers need to be able to combine the individual customer data from each member of a household. For example, without these household-level data, a supermarket retailer might underestimate the importance of a household with several people who shop at the store.

The analysis of the customer database can provide important insights for planning merchandise assortment. For example, a supermarket chain sells over 300 types of cheese. Feta cheese ranked 295th in sales, which suggested it should not have a favourable position in the cheese department and might even be a candidate for elimination from the assortment. However, further analysis uncovered that feta cheese ranked 25th in sales for the supermarket's best customers.[7]

With today's technology, even small, independent retailers can create and use a customer database. For example, Gary Mead, a 34-year-old entrepreneur, uses his customer database to take on the giants: Domino's, Little Caesar's, and Pizza Hut. With a $2500 computer system, he keeps track of the purchase history of customers patronizing his restaurant. If customers don't order for 60 days, the system spits out a postcard with a discount to lure them back. Other promotions encourage customers to try all of the dishes offered by suggesting pasta dishes to pizza lovers. The

refact

Only 50 percent of the executives attending the National Retail Federation convention indicated their companies have a customer data warehouse, but all said they intended to invest in CRM activities during the coming year.[8]

database has 8500 customers in a town of 11 000; business has been increasing 25 to 30 percent each year.[9]

IDENTIFYING INFORMATION

Constructing this database is relatively easy for catalogue and Internet shoppers and customers who use the retailer's credit card when buying merchandise in stores. Customers buying merchandise through nonstore channels must provide their contact information (their name and address) so that the purchases can be sent to them. Since some retailers issue their own credit cards, they can collect the contact information for billing when customers apply for the card. In these cases, the identification of the customer is linked to the transaction.

However, identifying most customers who are making in-store transactions is more difficult because they often pay for the merchandise with a cheque, cash, or a third-party credit card such as Visa and MasterCard. Three approaches that store-based retailers use to overcome this problem are:

- asking customers for the identifying information
- offering frequent shopper cards
- linking chequing account numbers and third-party credit cards to customer names

Asking for Identifying Information   Some retailers such as The Source, Nine West, and the Container Store have their sales associates ask customers for identifying information such as their phone number or name and address when they ring up a sale.[10] This information is then used to create the transaction database for the customer. However, this approach has two limitations. First, some customers may be reluctant to provide the information and feel that the sales associates are violating their privacy. Second, sales associates might forget to ask for the information or decide not to spend the time getting and recording it during a busy period.

Offering a Frequent Shopper Card   **Frequent shopper programs**, also called **loyalty programs**, are programs that identify and provide rewards for customers who patronize a retailer. When customers enroll in one of these programs, they provide some descriptive information about themselves or their household and are issued a card with an identifying number. The customers then are offered an incentive to show the card when they make purchases from the retailer. For example, a supermarket might offer frequent shoppers a point for every dollar spent in the store. The points can be redeemed for items in a gift catalogue. From the retailer's perspective, frequent shopper programs offer two benefits:

- customers provide demographic and other information when they sign up for the program and then are motivated to identify themselves at each transaction
- customers are motivated by the rewards offered to increase the number of visits to the retailer and the amount purchased on each visit

The major problems with using frequent shopper cards for identification are that the card is often squeezed out of the customer's wallet by other cards, the customer might forget to bring it to the store when shopping, or the customer might decide not to show it if he or she is in a hurry.

> **refact**
> Customers enrolled in a frequent shopper program only use the card for 67 percent of their purchases.[11]

Frequent shopper cards are becoming so common that consumers cannot carry the cards they have easily. Key tags are an easy alternative.

Air Miles, Canada's premier coalition loyalty program, induces consumers to shop and collect air miles as a reward for loyalty to the retailer. The Air Miles' databases compile information about customers and their shopping habits to assist retailers in tailoring merchandise and marketing strategies.

PRIVACY AND CRM PROGRAMS

Although detailed information about individual customers helps retailers provide more benefits to their better customers, consumers are concerned about retailers violating their privacy when they collect this information.

Privacy Concerns   The degree to which consumers feel their privacy has been violated depends on:

- Their control over their personal information when engaging in marketplace transactions. Do they feel they can decide on the amount and type of information collected by the retailer?

- Their knowledge of the collection and use of personal information. Do they know what information is being collected and how the retailer will be using it? Will the retailer be sharing the information with other parties?[12]

These concerns are particularly acute for customers using an electronic channel because many of them do not realize the extensive amount of information that can be collected without their knowledge. In addition to collecting transaction data, electronic retailers can collect information by placing cookies on visitor's hard drives. **Cookies** are text files that identify visitors when they return to a Web site. Due to the data in the cookies, customers do not have to identify themselves and use passwords every time they visit a site. However, the cookies also collect information about other sites the person has visited and what pages they have downloaded.[13]

Protecting Customer Privacy   Canada's privacy law went into effect on January 1, 2004. The new federal privacy legislation changes the way companies do business and how marketers collect, use, or disclose customer information in the course of a commercial activity within Canada. In order to be compliant with the legislation, organizations must appoint a privacy officer and implement detailed procedures to protect personal information. The *Privacy Act* is all about relationships with customers and employees and is based on 10 principles for the protection of personal information. The Canadian Marketing Association outlines the basic principles:

1. *Accountability*—An organization will be responsible for ensuring that personal information in its possession, including information that has been transferred to a third party for processing, is secure and that the third party is compliant with the law.

2. *Identifying Purposes*—How you plan to use customer data must be identified at the time of, or prior to, collection of the individual's information. If you want to use information already collected for a new purpose, you will have to identify the new purpose to your customer and obtain new consent.

3. *Consent*—You must have consent for the collection, use, or disclosure of personal data.

4. *Limiting Collection*—If you make marketing lists available to third parties, you will have an obligation to ensure that you have obtained consent from consumers prior to passing their personal information on to third parties. You will also need to keep records of having received that consent.

5. *Limiting Use, Disclosure, and Retention*—If you are using customer data as part of your marketing activities, you can retain this information as long as the individual is an active customer, or for the length of the marketing campaign.

6. *Accuracy*—Marketers are obligated to keep personal information on consumers as accurate and up-to-date as possible.

7. *Safeguard Security*—All those who are involved in the transfer, rental, sale, or exchange of mailing lists are responsible for protecting the data and taking appropriate measures to ensure against unauthorized access.

8. *Openness*—Organizations should undertake to develop privacy policies, train staff on the company's privacy practices, and make information available to the public concerning their privacy policy.

9. *Individual Access*—Marketers will need to make customers' personal information available upon their request.

10. *Challenging Compliance*—Marketers will be required to establish formal inquiry and complaint-handling procedures and make this known to consumers who enquire.

The Canadian Standards Association has developed an electronic resource, "The Privacy Code: A Matter of Privacy—Understanding and Applying the New Canadian Privacy Law," for any organization that needs assistance in making a smooth transition towards privacy law compliance.[14]

In summary, there is growing consensus that personal information must be fairly collected, the collection must be purposeful, and the data should be relevant, maintained as accurate, essential to the business, subject to the rights of the owning individual, kept reasonably secure, and transferred only with the permission of the consumer. To address these concerns, many retailers that collect customer information have privacy policies. They must clearly state what information is collected from

Sears provides a detailed description of its privacy policy on its Web site.

each visitor and how it will be used, give consumers a choice as to whether they give information, and allow them to view and correct any personal information held by an online retail site. Retailers using an electronic channel must also ensure that consumer information is held securely and is not passed on to other companies without the permission of the customer.[15]

analyzing customer data and identifying target customers

The next step in the CRM process is analyzing the customer database and converting the data into information that will help retailers develop programs for building customer loyalty. Data mining is one approach commonly used to develop this information. **Data mining** is a technique used to identify patterns in data, typically patterns that the analyst is unaware of prior to searching through the data. For example, an electronic retailer discovered that customers who had bought portable DVD players typically commuted to work by train. Using this information, the retailer experienced a 43 percent increase in portable DVD player sales when it redirected most of its communication budget from daytime television commercials to newspapers and billboards along the train tracks.[16]

Market basket analysis is a specific type of data analysis that focuses on the composition of the basket, or bundle, of products purchased during a single shopping occasion. This analysis is often useful for management in suggesting where to place merchandise in a store. For example, based on market basket analyses, Fortino's changed the traditional location of several items:

- Since bananas are the most common item in grocery carts, Fortino's Supercentres sell bananas next to the corn flakes as well as in the produce section.

- Kleenex tissues are in the paper-goods aisle and also mixed in with cold medicine.

- Measuring spoons are in housewares and also hanging next to Crisco shortening.

- Flashlights are in the hardware aisle and also with the Halloween costumes.

IDENTIFYING MARKET SEGMENTS

Traditionally, customer data analysis has focused on identifying market segments—groups of customers who have similar needs, purchase similar merchandise, and respond in a similar manner to marketing activities. For example, when Eddie Bauer analyzed its customer database, it discovered two types of shoppers. One group it calls "professional shoppers"—people who love fashion and value good customer service. The other group it calls "too busy to shop people"—people who want the shopping experience over as quickly as possible. The professional shoppers tended to use the alteration service, call the customer service desk, and seek out the same salesperson when they made purchases in the stores. On the other hand, the people too busy to shop typically shop from the catalogue and Web site. Eddie Bauer uses this information to develop unique advertising programs targeting each of these segments.

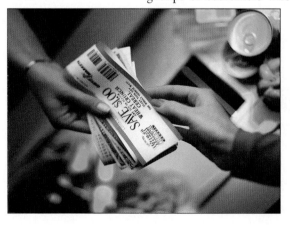

Using market basket analysis and their customer databases, supermarkets generate personalized coupons to encourage customers to patronize the store for additional merchandise categories.

Eddie Bauer also discovered that morning shoppers are more price-sensitive and like to buy products on sale more than evening shoppers. Evening shoppers tended to be in the professional shopper segment. Using this information, Eddie Bauer installed electronic window posters in some test stores that allowed different images to be displayed at different times of the day. In the morning, the displays featured lower-priced merchandise and items on sale; in the evening, the more expensive and fashionable merchandise was displayed.[18]

IDENTIFYING BEST CUSTOMERS

Using information in the customer database, retailers can develop a score or number indicating how valuable the customers are to the firm. This score can then be used to determine which customers to target.

Lifetime Value   A commonly used measure to score each customer is called lifetime customer value. **Lifetime customer value (LTV)** is the expected contribution from the customer to the retailer's profits over his or her entire relationship with the retailer.

LTV is estimated by using past behaviours to forecast future purchases, gross margin from these purchases, and costs associated with servicing the customers. Some of the costs associated with a customer are the cost of advertising and promotions used to acquire the customer and the cost of processing merchandise that the customer has returned. Thus, a customer who purchases $200 on groceries from a supermarket every other month would have a lower LTV for the supermarket than a customer who buys $30 on each visit and shops at the store three times a week. Similarly, a customer who buys apparel only when it's on sale in a department store would have a lower LTV than a customer who typically pays full price and buys the same amount of merchandise.

These assessments of LTV are based on the assumption that the customer's future purchase behaviours will be the same as they have been in the past. Sophisticated statistical methods are typically used to estimate the future contributions from past purchases. For example, these methods might consider how recently purchases have been made. The expected LTV of a customer who purchased $600 on one visit six months ago is less than the LTV of a customer who has been purchasing $100 of merchandise every month for the last six months.

Customer Pyramid   Most retailers realize that their customers differ in terms of their profitability or LTV. In particular, they know that a relatively small number of customers account for the majority of their profits. This realization is often called the **80–20 rule**—*80 percent of the sales or profits come from 20 percent of the customers.* Thus, retailers could group their customers into two groups based on the LTV scores. One group would be the 20 percent of the customers with the highest LTV scores, and the other group would be the rest. However, this two-segment scheme, "best" and "rest," does not consider important differences among the 80 percent of the customers in the "rest" segment.[19]

A commonly used segmentation scheme divides customers into four segments, illustrated in Exhibit 15–2. This scheme allows retailers to develop more appropriate strategies for each of the segments. Each of the four segments is described below.

- *Platinum segment*—This segment is composed of the retailer's customers with the top 25 percent of LTVs. Typically, these are the most loyal customers who are not overly concerned about merchandise price and place more value on customer service.

exhibit 15–2
The Customer Pyramid

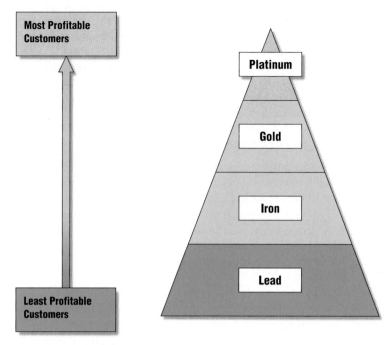

SOURCE: Valerie Zeithaml, Roland Rust, and Katherine Lemon, "The Customer Pyramid: Creating and Serving Profitable Customers," *California Management Review* 43 (Summer 2001), p. 125. Reprinted by permission.

- *Gold segment*—The next 25 percent of the customers in terms of their LTV make up the gold segment. These customers have a lower LTV than platinum customers because they are more price-sensitive. Even though they buy a significant amount of merchandise from the retailer, they are not as loyal as platinum customers and probably patronize some of the retailer's competitors.

- *Iron segment*—Customer in this third tier probably do not deserve much special attention from the retailer due to their modest LTV.

- *Lead segment*—Customers in the lowest segment can cost the company money. They often demand a lot of attention but do not buy much from the retailer. For example, real estate agents often encounter people who want to spend their weekends looking at houses but are really not interested in buying one.

The segmentation scheme described above differs from the segments of passengers in airline frequent flyer programs because it is based on LTV rather than miles flown. Thus, it recognizes that some customers who fly a lot of miles might be taking low-cost flights, whereas other customers, although flying the same number of miles, might be much more profitable because they fly first class and don't seek discount fares.

Another common segment scheme, called **decile analysis,** breaks customers into 10 deciles according to their LTV rather than the quartiles illustrated above. When using decile analysis, the 10 percent of the customers with the highest LTV would be in the top.

RFM Analysis   **RFM** (recency, frequency, monetary) **analysis,** often used by catalogue retailers and direct marketers, is a scheme for segmenting customers

exhibit 15–3
RFM Analysis for a
Catalogue Retailer

Frequency	Monetary	RECENCY			
		0–2 months	3–4 months	5–6 months	Over 6 months
1–2	<$50	0.050*	0.035	0.010	0.001
1–2	Over $50	0.050	0.036	0.011	0.001
3–4	<$50	0.080	0.050	0.015	0.006
3–4	Over $150	0.090	0.050	0.017	0.008
5–6	<$300	0.100	0.060	0.025	0.010
5–6	Over $300	0.120	0.080	0.027	0.012
Over 6	<$450	0.150	0.100	0.035	0.180
Over 6	Over $450	0.160	0.110	0.040	0.020

*Percentage of customers in the cell who made a purchase from the last catalogue mailed to them.

according to how recently they have made a purchase, how frequently they make purchases, and how much they have bought. Exhibit 15–3 is an example of an RFM analysis done by a catalogue apparel retailer that mails a catalogue each month to its customers.

The catalogue retailer divides its customers into 32 groups or segments based on how many orders the customer has placed during the last year, how much merchandise the customer has purchased and the last time the customer placed an order. Each segment is represented by one cell in Exhibit 15–3. For example, the customers in the upper-left cell have made one or two purchases in the last year, made a purchase within the last two months, and purchased less than $50 of merchandise.

Catalogue retailers often use this type of analysis to determine which customer groups should be sent catalogues. For each of the RFM groups, they will determine the percentage of customers in the group who made a purchase from the last catalogue sent to them. For example, 5 percent of the customers in the upper-left corner of Exhibit 15–3 placed an order from the last catalogue sent to them. With information about the response rate of each cell and the average gross margin from orders placed by customers in the cell, the catalogue retailer can calculate the expected profit from sending catalogues to the customers in each cell. For example, if the average gross margin from orders placed by customers in the upper-left cell is $20 and the cost of sending a catalogue to customers in the cell is $0.75, the company would make $0.25 per customer from each catalogue mailed to the customers in the cell.

$20.00 contribution × 0.05 response
= $1.00 expected contribution – $0.75 cost
= $0.25 per customer

RFM analysis is basically a method of estimating the LTV of a customer using recency, frequency, and monetary value of past purchases. Exhibit 15–4 illustrates how RFM can be used for developing customer target strategies.

Customers who have made infrequent, small purchases recently are considered to be first-time customers. The objective of CRM programs directed toward this segment of customers is to convert them into early repeat customers and eventually high-value customers. CRM programs directed toward customers in the high-value segment (high frequency, recency, and monetary value) attempt to maintain loyalty, increase retention, and gain a greater share of wallet by selling more merchandise to them. On the other hand, customers who have not purchased recently either have low lifetime value and are not worth pursuing or are committed to another retailer

exhibit 15–4
RFM Target Strategies

		RECENCY			
Frequency	Monetary	0–2 months	3–4 months	5–6 months	Over 6 months
1–2	<$50	First-time customers		Low-value customers	
1–2	Over $50				
3–4	<$150	Early repeat customers		Defectors	
3–4	Over $150				
5–6	<$300	High-value customers		Core defectors	
5–6	Over $300				
Over 6	<$450				
Over 6	Over $450				

SOURCE: Reprinted by permission of Harvard Business School Press. Adapted from Robert Blattberg, Gary Getz, and Jacquelyn Thomas, *Customer Equity: Building and Managing Relationships as Valuable Assets* (Boston: Harvard Business School Press, 2001), p. 18. Copyright © 2001 by the Harvard Business School Publishing Corporation; all rights reserved.

and may be difficult to recapture. CRM programs designed to realize these objectives are discussed in the following section.

developing CRM programs

Having segmented customers according to their future profit potential, the next step in the CRM process (see Exhibit 15–1) is to develop programs for the different customer segments. In the following sections, we discuss programs retailers use for:

- retaining their best customers
- converting good customers into high-LTV customers
- getting rid of unprofitable customers

CUSTOMER RETENTION

Four approaches that retailers use to retain their best customers are:

- frequent shopper programs
- special customer services
- personalization
- community

Frequent Shopper Programs   As mentioned previously, frequent shopper programs are used both to build a customer database by identifying customers with transactions and to encourage repeat purchase behaviour and retailer loyalty.[21] Retailers provide incentives to encourage customers to enroll in the program and use the card. These incentives are either discounts on purchases made from the retailer or points for every dollar of merchandise purchased. The points are then redeemable for special rewards. Some recommendations concerning the nature of the rewards offered are outlined in Exhibit 15–5.

Canadian Tire money is Canada's oldest and most successful loyalty program. The customer receives a cash bonus coupon equivalent to 2 1/2 percent of purchases over $2.00 made at Canadian Tire using cash, debit, or their equivalents.

Four factors limit the effectiveness of frequent shopping programs:

- First, they can be expensive. For example, a 1 percent price discount can cost large retailers over $100 million a year. In addition, for a large retailer, the launch and maintenance investment (store training, marketing, fulfillment support, and information technology and systems costs) can be as high as $30 million. Annual maintenance costs can reach $5 million to $10 million when marketing, program support, offer fulfillment, customer service, and IT infrastructure costs are figured in. Then there are the marketing support costs needed to maintain awareness of the program.[23]

Cash bonus coupons are redeemable in merchandise only at Canadian Tire stores and only in association with consumer purchases of merchandise or services.

- Second, it is difficult to make corrections in programs when problems arise. Programs become part of the customer's shopping experience. Customers must be informed about even the smallest changes in programs. They react negatively to any perceived "take away" once a program is in place, even if they are not actively involved in it. The more successful the program, the greater the customer reaction to changes made by the retailer, and these negative reactions reduce customer trust and loyalty to the retailer.

- Third, it is not clear that these programs increase customer spending behaviour and loyalty toward the retailer.[24] For example, 48 percent of the customers enrolled in frequent shopper programs with supermarkets indicated they had spent more with the retailer than they would have if the program were not offered, but only 18 percent of customers enrolled in programs with apparel retailers indicated that the program increased spending.[25]

---

exhibit 15–5
Recommendations for Frequent Shopper Reward Programs

Tiered   Rewards should be tiered according to the volume of purchase to motivate customers to increase the level of their purchases. These tiers can be based on individual transactions or cumulative transactions. For example, HBC Points Card and Shoppers Optimum Program reward customers with cumulative points based on dollars spent. Customers generally accept the idea that people who spend more should receive greater rewards.

 Offer Choices   Not all customers value the same rewards. Thus, the most effective frequent shopper programs offer customers choices. For example, Coles Myer, a leading Australian retailer, originally offered customers air miles but shifted to a menu of rewards when it discovered that many customers did not value air miles. Tesco, a U.K. supermarket chain, lets customers cash in points for special discounts on entertainment, vacation packages, or sporting events. Sainsbury, a competitor, allows customers to use their points for vouchers that can be used to make purchases at a variety of retail partners such as Blockbuster and British Gas.

Nonmonetary incentives are very attractive to some customers. For example, Holt Renfrew offers loyal customers the opportunity to attend by invitation only special shopping events, a Sotheby auction, or an underwater expedition to see the Titanic.

Some retailers link their frequent shopper programs to charitable causes. For example, Target donates 1 percent of all purchases charged to Target's Guest Card to a program that benefits local schools. Although these altruistic rewards can be an effective part of a frequent shopper program, such incentives probably should not be the focal point of the program. Research indicates that the most effective incentives benefit the recipient directly, not indirectly, as is the case with charitable contributions.

Reward All Transactions   To ensure the collection of all customer transaction data and encourage repeat purchases, programs need to reward all purchases, not just purchases of selected merchandise.

Transparency and Simplicity   Customers need to be able to quickly and easily understand when they will receive rewards, what the rewards are, how much they have earned, and how they can redeem the points they have accumulated. The ground rules need to be clearly stated. There should be no surprises or confusion.

Sources: Frank Badillo, *Customer Relationship Management* (Columbus, OH: Retail Forward, 2001); and Stephan Butscher, *Customer Clubs and Loyalty Programmes.* (Aldershot, Hampshire: Ashgate Publishing, Limited, 2002).

- Finally, and perhaps most important, is the difficulty of gaining a competitive advantage based on frequent shopper programs. Since the programs are so visible, they can be easily duplicated by competitors. For example, Tesco and Safeway, two large supermarketchains in the U.K., got into a loyalty card war. They played a game of "can you top this," which benefited their customers but reduced their profits until Safeway closed down its program.[26]

To avoid this problem, retailers are offering benefits to their best customers that are more personalized, based on their unique knowledge of the customer, and thus less visible to competitors.

Special Customer Services   Retailers provide unusually high quality customer service to build and maintain the loyalty of platinum customers. For example, the top-tier customers get calls from service reps several times a year for "a friendly chat" and get an annual call to wish them happy holidays. Due to these special services, the retention rates for top customers have increased 50 percent.

Sometimes these special services are very subtle. For example, at the retailer's Web site, only top-tier customers get the option to click on an icon that connects them to a live service agent for a phone conversation. Other customers never see this icon. When service reps bring up a customer's account, coloured squares flash on their computer screens. Green means the caller is a profitable customer and should be granted waivers and other special treatment. Reds are unprofitable customers who get no special treatment.[27]

Personalization   An important limitation of CRM strategies developed for market segments, such as a platinum segment in the customer pyramid (Exhibit 15–2) or early repeat customers in the RFM analysis (Exhibit 15–3), is that each segment is composed of a large number of customers who are not identical. Thus, any strategy will be most appealing to only the typical customer in the segment, and not as appealing to the majority of customers in the segment. For example, customers in the platinum segment with the highest LTVs might include a 25-year-old single woman who has quite different needs than the 49-year-old working mother with two children.

With the availability of customer-level data and analysis tools, retailers can now economically offer unique benefits and target messages to individual customers. They now have the ability to develop programs for small groups of customers and even specific individuals. For example, a Harry Rosen salesperson can search the company's customer database, identify customers who have bought Hugo Boss suits in the past, and send them an e-mail informing them of the shipment of new suits that just arrived in the store. Developing retail programs for small groups or individual customers is referred to as **1-to-1 retailing.**

Many small, local retailers have always practised 1-to-1 retailing. They know each of their customers, greet them by name when they walk in the store, and then recommend merchandise they know the customers will like. These local store-owners do not need customer databases and data mining tools. They have the information in their heads. But most large retail chains and their employees do not have this intimate knowledge of their customers. Thus, the CRM process enables larger retailers to efficiently develop relationships similar to those that many small local retailers have.

The Internet channel provides an opportunity for retailers to automate the practice of 1-to-1 retailing. When registered customers log on to Amazon.com, the first page they see is personalized for them. Their name is displayed in a greeting, and

Amazon.com provides personalized recommendations based on past purchases.

products are displayed based on an analysis of their past purchase behaviour. For example, if a customer has bought mystery novels from Amazon.com in the past, the latest books from mystery book authors they have bought are presented.

These personalized rewards or benefits that customers receive are based on unique information possessed by the retailer and its sales associates. This information in the retailer's customer database cannot be accessed or used by competitors. Thus, it provides an opportunity to develop a sustainable competitive advantage.

The effective use of this information creates the positive feedback cycle in the CRM process. Increasing repeat purchases with a retailer increases the amount of data collected from the customer, which enables the retailer to provide more personalized benefits that in turn increase the customer's purchases from the retailer.

Community   A fourth approach to building customer retention and loyalty is to develop a sense of community among customers. The Internet channel offers an opportunity for customers to exchange information using bulletin boards and to develop more personal relationships with each other and the retailer. By participating in such a community, customers become reluctant to leave the "family" of other people patronizing the retailer.

For example, in addition to offering merchandise for sale, a sporting goods retailer could provide an opportunity for organizers of local sporting events to post information about these events on its Web site. The volunteers organizing youth soccer and baseball leagues and tennis and golf tournaments could provide information about meetings and game dates, times, and places. Then the retailer could collect information about the participants in local leagues and offer discounts to encourage the teams to buy their uniforms and equipment and facilitate their transactions.

CONVERTING GOOD CUSTOMERS INTO BEST CUSTOMERS

In the context of the customer pyramid (Exhibit 15–2), increasing the sales made to good customers is referred to as *customer alchemy*—converting iron and gold customers into platinum customers.[29] Customer alchemy involves offering and selling more products and services to existing customers and increasing the retailer's share of wallet with these customers. For example, Tesco, the U.K. supermarket chain, added a second tier to its frequent shopper program to increase share of wallet.

Amazon uses its customer database to cross-sell complementary books.

The first tier has a traditional design to gather customer data. The second tier, targeted at its better customers, is more innovative. Customers earn a "key" when they spend US$38 or more in a single transaction. Fifty keys make the customer a "keyholder," 100 keys a "premium keyholder." When customers achieve these higher levels, they get discounts on popular entertainment events, theatre tickets, sporting events, and hotel vacations. The key program seeks to convert iron and gold customers into platinum customers. In the four years since starting the key program, Tesco has raised its market share from 13 percent to more than 17 percent.

The retailer's customer database reveals opportunities for cross-selling and add-on selling. **Cross-selling** is selling a complementary product or service in a specific transaction, such as selling a customer a printer when he or she has decided to buy a computer. For example, a supermarket chain has a frequent shopper program, called the Gold Card program, for its best customers. When Gold Card member Debra Onsager enters the store, she "swipes" her card at a kiosk, and a high-speed printer provides a personalized shopping list with up to 25 deals. The deals offered are based on Debra's purchase history. If Debra's history shows she frequently purchases corn chips but does not buy dip, she'll get a deal on bean dip printed on her shopping list to encourage her to try a new product. If she passes up the deal this time in the market, the next time the value of the bean dip coupon will be automatically increased.

Add-on selling is selling additional new products and services to existing customers, such as a supermarket chain that explored the opportunity to offer dry cleaning services in its supermarkets. To determine the stores and customers that would find this new service appealing, it looked through its customer database for households with two-income professionals, 25 to 35 years old, who sought one-stop shopping, as indicated by purchases of cosmetics, hosiery, and prepared meals.[30] Oprah Winfrey builds add-on sales for her offerings through a strong emotional bond with her target market.

DEALING WITH UNPROFITABLE CUSTOMERS

In many cases, the bottom tier of customers actually have negative LTV. Retailers actually lose money on every sale they make to these customers. For example, catalogue retailers have customers who repeatedly buy three or four items and return all but one of them. The cost of processing two or three returned items is much greater than the profits coming from the one item that the customer kept. The process of no longer selling to these unprofitable customers can be referred to as "getting the lead out," in terms of the customer pyramid.[31]

Two approaches for getting the lead out are offering less costly approaches for satisfying the needs of lead customers, and charging the customers for the services they are abusing.

implementing CRM programs

Increasing sales and profits from the CRM programs is a challenge. For example, according to a study, 52 percent of the retailers surveyed indicated that they were engaged in some type of data mining, but 76 percent of those retailers undertaking data mining indicated that the activity had made no contribution to the bottom line.[32]

This experience of retailers emphasizes that effective CRM requires more than appointing a manager of CRM, installing a computer system to manage and analyze a customer database, and making speeches about the importance of customers. The effective implementation of CRM programs requires the close coordination of activities by different functions in a retailer's organization. The MIS department needs to collect, analyze, and make the relevant information readily accessible to employees implementing the programs—the front-line service providers and sales associates and the marketers responsible for communicating with customers through impersonal channels (mass advertising, direct mail, and e-mail). Store operations and human resource management need to hire, train, and motivate the employees who will be using the information to deliver personalized services.

Most retailers are product-centric, not customer-centric. Typically, there is no area of a retail firm organized by customer type—responsible for delivering products and services to types of customers. Perhaps in the future, retailers will have market managers to perform this coordinating function.

customer service

Customer service is the set of activities and programs undertaken by retailers to make the shopping experience more rewarding for their customers. These activities increase the value customers receive from the merchandise and services they purchase. All employees of a retail firm and all elements of the retailing mix provide services that increase the value of merchandise. For example, employees in the distribution centre contribute to customer service by making sure that the merchandise is in stock. The employees responsible for store design contribute by increasing the customer's convenience in getting to the store and finding merchandise and making shopping an enjoyable experience.

Exhibit 15–6 lists some of the services provided by retailers and/or shopping centres. Most of these services encourage customers to choose a specific retailer to buy products and services. Services, such as alterations and the assembly of merchandise, actually change merchandise to fit the needs of a specific customer. Some of these services are derived from the retailer's store design or Web site or from policies established by the retailer. However, this part of the chapter focuses on some of the most important personalized services provided by sales associates interacting directly with customers.

In the next section, we discuss retailers' opportunities to develop strategic advantage through customer service. Then we examine how retailers can take advantage of this opportunity by providing high-quality service.

exhibit 15–6
Services Offered by
Retailers

Acceptance of credit cards	Parking
Alterations of merchandise	Personal assistance in selecting
Assembly of merchandise	merchandise
ATM terminals	Personal shoppers
Bridal registry	Play areas for children
Cheque cashing	Presentations on how to use
Child care facilities	merchandise
Credit	Provisions for customers with
Delivery to home or work	special needs (wheelchairs,
Demonstrations of merchandise	translators)
Display of merchandise	Repair services
Dressing rooms	Rest rooms
Extended store hours	Return privileges
Signage to locate and identify merchandise	Rooms for checking coats and
Facilities for shoppers with special needs	packages
(physically handicapped)	Shopping carts
Layaway plans	Special orders
Gift wrapping	Warranties

15.1   retailing view

SYBIL JACKSON, PET DIRECTOR FOR PETsHOTEL^{SM}

I worked in the hospitality industry as a hotel operations manager before joining PETsMART. As manager for the grooming salon and pet hotel services we offer at our store, I strive to provide the level of customer service offered at five star hotels—service that is above and beyond the expectation of our pet parents.

PETsMART is the nation's leading retail supplier of products, services, and solutions for the lifetime needs of pets. We are a multi-channel retailer operating more than 700 pet superstores in the United States and Canada, a large pet supply catalog business, and the Internet's leading pet product Web site. While our stores offer the industry's broadest assortment of products, we are now focusing on providing services for pet parents. Nearly all of our stores have pet styling salons that offer safe, quality pet grooming services, from full-service styling to baths, toenail trimming and teeth cleaning. Many of our locations have veterinary hospitals inside the store. We also offer affordable education for puppies or adult dogs and are testing PETsHOTEL^{SM}, an innovative, high-quality pet boarding and day camp concept.

I have 40 people on my team. Some of them work behind the scenes providing grooming service, keeping the hotel rooms clean, and playing with the animals during

their stay. Others, customer service representatives, interact with pet parents when they check their animals in. Providing outstanding customer service starts with hiring the right people. First and foremost, the people I hire must love animals and care about their well being. Then, for the customer representative positions, I look for people who are energetic and outgoing. When I hire for the behind-the-scenes jobs, I want them to have a realistic idea about what the job entails—the good and bad. While there are a lot of enjoyable parts of the job, they need to do unpleasant things like cleaning up after an animal messes up.

After hiring the right people, I motivate the employees on my team to provide outstanding service. I give them kudos when I see them doing something special. For example, this morning a customer came in to pick up her dog at 9:00 a.m. and decided, at the last minute, she wanted her dog to have a bath before she took her home. However, we did not have any bathers available. So the customer service representative, who is a trained and licensed groomer, rolled up her sleeves and gave the dog a bath herself. Her initiative showed me that she is a team player and cares about pleasing our customers, so I gave her a kudo on the spot—a $5 gift certificate at Starbucks.

strategic advantage through customer service

Good service keeps customers returning to a retailer and generates positive word-of-mouth communication, which attracts new customers.[33]

Providing high-quality service is difficult for retailers. Automated manufacturing makes the quality of most merchandise consistent from item to item. But the quality of retail service can vary dramatically from store to store and from salesperson to salesperson within a store. It's hard for retailers to control the performance of employees who provide the service. A sales associate may provide good service to one customer and poor service to the next customer.

In addition, most services provided by retailers are intangible—customers can't see or touch them. Clothing can be held and examined, but the assistance provided by a sales associate or an electronic agent can't. Intangibility makes it hard to provide and maintain high-quality service because retailers can't count, measure, or check service before it's delivered to customers.

The challenge of providing consistent high-quality service provides an opportunity for a retailer to develop a sustainable competitive advantage. For example, Holt Renfrew devotes much time and effort to developing an organizational culture that stimulates and supports excellent customer service. Competing department stores would like to offer the same level of service but find it hard to match Holt Renfrew's performance.[34]

> **refact**
> The word *service* is from the Latin term *servus*, meaning "slave."[35]

> **refact**
> Nearly one out of four shoppers who have a bad service experience will tell their friends about their experience and urge them not to shop there and/or will stop shopping at the store.[36]

CUSTOMER SERVICE STRATEGIES

Customization and standardization are two approaches retailers use to develop a sustainable customer service advantage. Successful implementation of the customized approach relies on the performance of sales associates or the degree to which customer interactions can be customized using an electronic channel. The standardization approach relies more on policy, procedures, and store and Web site design and layout.[37]

Customization Approach   The customization approach encourages service providers to tailor the service to meet each customer's personal needs.[38] For example, sales associates in specialty stores help individual customers locate appropriate apparel and accessories.

The office supply category killer on the left uses its signage as part of a standardization approach for providing customer service, while Wal-Mart's sales associate (right) uses a customized approach tailoring service to match the needs of individual customers.

Harry Rosen does customer service with a stylus

Harry Rosen Does Customer Service with a Stylus   Harry Rosen Inc. decided it was time to put the power of customer service technology in the hands of their sales associates. Building on existing wireless technology, the retailer equipped the 450 sales associates with PDAs that would serve as advanced "mini CRM" systems to better serve their customers. The system lets sales personnel review client files for purchase history, sizes, favourite colours, and preferences, check merchandise availability through an inventory database of all stores, and even connect to the tailor to let the customer know when alterations are completed. The new CRM system proves again that Harry does it best.

The customized approach typically results in most customers' receiving superior service. But the service might be inconsistent because service delivery depends on the judgment and capabilities of the service providers. Some service providers are better than others, and even the best service providers can have a bad day. In addition, providing the customized service is costly since it requires more well-trained service providers or complex computer software.

Standardization Approach   The **standardization approach** is based on establishing a set of rules and procedures and being sure that they are implemented consistently. By strict enforcement of these procedures, inconsistencies in the service are minimized. Through standardization, customers receive the same food and service at McDonald's restaurants across the globe. The food may not be exactly what customers want, but it's consistent and served in a timely manner at a low cost.

Store or Web site design and layout also play an important role in the standardization approach. In many situations, customers don't need the services employees provide. They know what they want to buy, and their objective is to find it in the store and buy it quickly. In these situations, retailers offer good service by providing a layout and signs that enable customers to locate merchandise easily, by having relevant information in displays, and by minimizing the time required to make a purchase.[39]

Retailing View 15.2 shows how Ikea uses a standardized, self-service approach with some unique elements.

Cost of Customer Service   As indicated previously, providing high-quality service, particularly customized service, can be very costly. For over 100 years, the Savoy Hotel in London maintained a special place in the hearts of the world's elite. Maids switched off vacuum cleaners when greeting guests entering the hallway in the morning. Each floor had it own waiter on duty from 7 a.m. to 3 p.m. Guests could get cotton sheets instead of the standard Irish linen sheets if they wished. Preferred fruits were added to the complimentary fruit bowl in each room. Rooms were personally furnished for customers who regularly had extended stays at the hotel. At times, the hotel staff moved the customers' furniture, including personal pictures, from storage into their rooms when they arrived.

But this high level of personal attention is very costly to provide. The Savoy employed about three people for each of its 200 rooms, about double the average for a hotel. These services resulted in annual losses, and the hotel was eventually sold to a corporation that eliminated some of the services.

In many cases, however, good customer service can actually reduce costs and increase profits. A study by Andersen Consulting estimates that it costs 5 to 15 times more to acquire a new customer than to generate repeat business from present customers, and a 5 percent increase in customer retention can increase profits by 25 to 40 percent.[41] Thus, it costs a business much less to keep its existing customers satisfied and sell more merchandise to them than it does to sell to people who aren't buying from the business now.

RETURNS RETHINK

Some people are admittedly shopaholics, which, when mixed with an indecisive nature, is disastrous for many retailers. These are the people who buy something one week, often wearing or using it, and expect to return it the next. These shoppers believe that anything is—and should be—returnable. Some customers may take advantage of a liberal return policy believing that the retailer wants the customer to be happy at any cost.

retailing view
CUSTOMER SERVICE AT IKEA
15.2

IKEA is a global furniture retailer based in Sweden. Its concept of service differs from that of the traditional furniture store. The typical furniture store has a showroom displaying some of the merchandise sold in the store. Complementing the inventory are books of fabric swatches, veneers, and alternative styles customers can order. Salespeople assist customers in going through the books. When the customer makes a selection, an order is placed with the factory, and the furniture is delivered to the customer's home in six to eight weeks. This system maximizes customization, but the costs are high.

In contrast, IKEA uses a self-service model based on extensive in-store displays. At information desks in the store, shoppers can pick up a map of the store, plus a pencil, order form, clipboard, and tape measure. After studying the catalogue and displays, customers proceed to a self-service storage area and locate their selections using codes copied from the sales tags. Every product available is displayed in over 70 room-like settings throughout the 1800 square metre warehouse store. Thus, customers don't need a decorator to help them picture how the furniture will go together. Adjacent to the display room is a warehouse with ready-to-assemble furniture in boxes that customers can pick up when they leave the store.

Although IKEA uses a "customers do it themselves" approach, it does offer some services that traditional furniture stores do not, such as in-store child-care centers and information about the quality of the furniture.

IKEA effectively uses a self-service method to provide customer service through signage and information in displays and on the merchandise.

Toddlers can be left in a supervised ballroom filled with 50 000 brightly coloured plastic balls. There are changing rooms in each store, complete with bottle warmers and disposable diaper dispensers. Displays cover the quality of products in terms of design features and materials, with demonstrations of testing procedures.

Sources: John Kelly, "A Good Place by Design," *Washington Post*, December 23, 2004, p. C.13; Mike Duff, "Late-Blooming IKEA U.S. Wears 20 Well," *DSN Retailing Today*, September 6, 2004, pp. 6–9.

Harry Rosen Menswear has always upheld a policy of unconditional satisfaction for customers. They will even take back a well-worn, two-year-old suit if the customer becomes unhappy with it. The rationale: It's a way to bond with the customer and reinforce the relationship in a positive way. But many stores are taking a harder stance toward returns. *The Gap* now gives customers with a receipt two weeks to claim a full cash refund or exchange. New technology enabling customers to buy and burn their own copies caused *HMV Canada* to terminate its "no questions asked" policy, which used to include cash back for open CDs. The Retail Council of Canada concludes that a tougher position on returns can improve a retailer's profit by as much as 2 percent. [42]

Retailers need to consider the costs and benefits of service policies. For example, many retailers are reconsidering their "no questions asked" return policy. *Home Depot's* policy was to take back all merchandise and give cash back. Now, if customers don't have a receipt, they can only get store credit. If they have a receipt, they can get cash back. Some consumer electronics products customers must pay a 15 percent re-stocking charge for returned merchandise. Retailers are seeing too many big-screen TVs coming back the day after the Super Bowl and too many prom dresses coming back the day after prom night. [43]

The easy return policy is an important selling feature for the department stores. Customers will put up with a lack of other services, but the return policy is an established expectation and changing this liberal policy is difficult. *The Bay* allows a 30-day period for a cash refund with a receipt, after which a store credit is considered. The eagerness to please is also apparent at *Sleep Country Canada*, which offers a "comfort guarantee" that allows customers to have mattresses returned within 60 days. Despite many problems with returned merchandise, retailers strive to ensure many happy returns—for both sides of a sale. Remember that it is more cost-effective to keep a customer than to find a new one.

refact

About 6 percent of all merchandise purchased in stores is returned. [44]

customer evaluation of service quality

When customers evaluate retail service, they compare their perceptions of the service they receive with their expectations. Customers are satisfied when the perceived service meets or exceeds their expectations. They're dissatisfied when they feel the service falls below their expectations. [45]

ROLE OF EXPECTATIONS

Customer expectations are based on a customer's knowledge and experiences. [46] For example, customers do not expect to get an immediate response to a letter or even a telephone call, but they expect to get a response to an e-mail the next time they turn on their computer.

Technology is dramatically changing the ways in which customers and firms interact. Customers now can interact with companies through automated voice response systems and place orders and check on delivery through the Internet. But customers still expect dependable outcomes, easy access, responsive systems, flexibility, apologies, and compensation when things go wrong. In other words, they still want good service. Now they just expect this level of service even when people are not involved. [47]

Expectations vary depending on the type of store. Customers expect a supermarket to provide convenient parking, to be open from early morning to late evening, to have a wide variety of fresh and packaged food that can be located easily, to display products, and to offer fast checkout. They don't expect the supermarket to have store employees stationed in the aisle to offer information about groceries or how to prepare meals.

refact

Among the retailers surveyed, only 30 percent responded to online customer service requests within 6 hours; 18 percent took 6 to 24 hours; 18 percent responded in one to three days; and 34 percent took longer than three days or did not answer the inquiry. [48]

On the other hand, when these same customers shop in a specialty store, they do expect the store to have knowledgeable salespeople who can provide information and assistance.

Since expectations aren't the same for all types of retailers, a customer may be satisfied with low levels of actual service in one store and dissatisfied with high service levels in another store. For example, customers have low service expectations for self-service retailers such as discount stores and supermarkets. Wal-Mart provides an unusual service for a discount store: An employee stands at the entrance to each store, greeting customers and answering questions. Because this service is unexpected in a discount store, customers evaluate Wal-Mart's service positively, even though the actual level of service is far below that provided by a typical specialty store.

This salesperson at the Kelo Department Store is providing the excellent personalized service that Japanese customers expect. The computer system scans the customer's feet and suggests shoes that will provide a good fit.

Department stores have many more salespeople available to answer questions and provide information than Wal-Mart does. But customer service expectations are also higher for department stores. If department store customers can't locate a salesperson quickly when they have questions or want to make a purchase, they're dissatisfied.

When retailers provide unexpected services, they build a high level of customer satisfaction, referred to as *customer delight*.[49] Some examples of unexpected positive service experiences are:

- A restaurant that sends customers who have had too much alcohol to drink home in a taxi and then delivers their cars in the morning.
- A men's store that sews numbered tags on each garment so the customer will know what goes together.
- A gift store that keeps track of important customer dates and suggests appropriate gifts.

 Customer service expectations vary around the world. Although Germany's manufacturing capability is world renowned, its poor customer service is also well known. People wait years to have telephone service installed. Many restaurants do not accept credit cards, and customers who walk into stores near closing time often receive rude stares. Customers typically have to bag merchandise they buy themselves. Because Germans are unaccustomed to good service, they don't demand it. But as retailing becomes global and new foreign competitors enter, German retailers are becoming more concerned.

On the other hand, the Japanese expect excellent customer service. In Canada, it's said that "the customer is always right." In Japan the equivalent expression is *okyakusama ha kamisama desu*, "the customer is God." When a customer comes back to a store to return merchandise, he or she is dealt with even more cordially than when the original purchase was made. Customer satisfaction isn't negotiable. The customer is never wrong! Even if the customer misused the product, retailers feel they were responsible for not telling the customer how to use it properly. The first person in the store who hears about the problem must take full responsibility for dealing with the customer, even if the problem involved another department.

the gaps model for improving retail service quaility

The Gaps Model (Exhibit 15–7) indicates what retailers need to do to provide high-quality customer service.[50] When customers' expectations are greater than their perceptions of the delivered service, customers are dissatisfied and feel the quality of the retailer's service is poor. Thus, retailers need to reduce the **service gap** (the difference between customers' expectations and perceptions of customer service) to improve customers' satisfaction with their service.

Four factors affect the service gap:

1. **Knowledge gap:** The difference between customer expectations and the retailer's perception of customer expectations.

2. **Standards gap:** The difference between the retailer's perceptions of customers' expectations and the customer service standards it sets.

3. **Delivery gap:** The difference between the retailer's service standards and the actual service provided to customers.

4. **Communication gap:** The difference between the actual service provided to customers and the service promised in the retailer's promotion program.

exhibit 15–7   Gaps Model for Improving Retail Service Quality

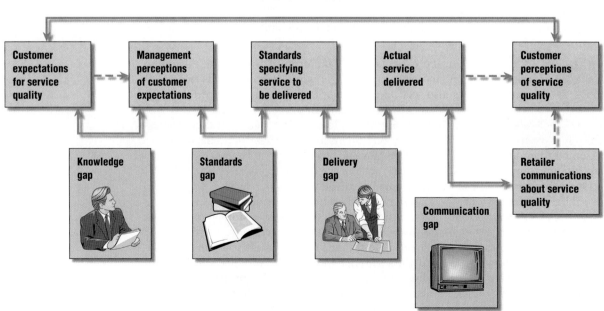

These four gaps add up to the service gap. The retailer's objective is to reduce the service gap by reducing each of the four gaps. Thus, the key to improving service quality is to:

- understand the level of service customers expect
- set standards for providing customer service
- implement programs for delivering service that meets the standards
- undertake communication programs to accurately inform customers about the service offered by the retailer

The following sections describe these gaps and methods for reducing them.

knowing what customers want: the knowledge gap

The most critical step in providing good service is to know what the customer wants. Retailers often lack accurate information about what customers need and expect. This lack of information can result in poor decisions. For example, a supermarket might hire extra people to make sure the shelves are stocked so customers will always find what they want, but it may fail to realize that customers are most concerned about waiting at the checkout line. From the customer's perspective, the supermarket's service would improve if the extra employees were used to open more checkout lines rather than to stock shelves.

Retailers can reduce the knowledge gap and develop a better understanding of customer expectations by undertaking customer research, increasing interactions between retail managers and customers, and improving communication between managers and employees who provide customer service.

> **refact**
> Eighty percent of North Americans are willing to share personal information with companies if it means getting more personal service while shopping.[51]

RESEARCHING CUSTOMER EXPECTATIONS AND PERCEPTIONS

Market research can be used to better understand customers' expectations and the quality of service provided by a retailer. Methods for obtaining this information range from comprehensive surveys to simply asking some customers about the store's service.

Comprehensive Studies   Some retailers have established programs for assessing customers' expectations and service perceptions. For example, every year JCPenney sales associates pass out questionnaires to shoppers in each store and its mall. Shoppers are asked about the service and merchandise offered by Penney and by competing department stores in the mall. Over 50 000 completed questionnaires are collected and analyzed. Since the same questionnaire is used each year, Penney can track service performance, determine whether it's improving or declining, and identify opportunities for improving service quality. The annual customer service profile is so important to Penney that it is used as part of store managers' performance evaluation.

Gauging Satisfaction with Individual Transactions   Another method for doing customer research is to survey customers immediately after a retail transaction has occurred. For example, Sears employees who deliver and assemble furniture in homes ask customers to complete a short survey describing how helpful, friendly, and professional the employees were. Airlines periodically ask passengers during a flight to evaluate the ticket-buying process, flight attendants, in-flight service, and gate agents.

The first step in providing good customer service is understanding customer expectations. This sales associate is conducting a survey to assess customer expectations.

Customer research on individual transactions provides up-to-date information about customers' expectations and perceptions. The research also indicates the retailer's interest in providing good service. Since the responses can be linked to a specific encounter, the research provides a method for rewarding employees who provide good service and correcting those who exhibit poor performance.

Focus Groups Rather than surveying many customers, retailers can use focus groups of 8 to 12 customers to gain insights into expectations and perceptions. For example, store managers might meet three times a year for one and a half to two hours with a select group of customers who are asked to provide information in a focus group about their experiences in the stores and to offer suggestions for improving service. The participants are rewarded with food and merchandise or money for their time and effort.

To reduce the knowledge gap, some managers may select customers who've made large and small purchases; they call these customers and ask them what they liked and didn't like about the store. With small purchasers, they probe to find out why the customers didn't buy more. Could they find everything they wanted? Did they get the assistance they expected from store employees?

Some retailers have consumer advisory boards composed of a cross section of their preferred customers. Members of the board complete questionnaires three to four times a year on subjects such as holiday shopping problems, in-store signage, and service quality. In exchange for their input, members receive gift certificates. Restaurants and retailers often ask for comments regarding service.

Interacting with Customers Owner–managers of small retail firms typically have daily contact with their customers and thus have accurate firsthand information about them. In large retail firms, managers often learn about customers through reports so they miss the rich information provided by direct contact with customers.

Stanley Marcus, founder of Neiman Marcus department stores, felt managers can become addicted to numbers and neglect the merchandise and customers. He used suspenders as an example of how buyers can make poor decisions by only looking at the numbers. Originally, suspenders came in two sizes: short and long. By analyzing the numbers, buyers realized they could increase turnover by stocking one-size-only suspenders. The numbers looked good, but the store had a lot of dissatisfied customers. With only one size, short men's pants fell down, and the fit was uncomfortable for tall men. "It comes back to the fact that the day is still only 24 hours long, and if you're a retailer, you've still got to spend some of those 24 hours with your customers and your products. You can't allow the computer to crowd them out as crucial sources of information."[52]

Customer Complaints Complaints allow retailers to interact with their customers and acquire detailed information about their service and merchandise. Handling complaints is an inexpensive means of isolating and correcting service problems.[53]

refact

Only 39 percent of consumers surveyed say they would complain to the store manager if they received poor service.[54]

Although customer complaints can provide useful information, retailers can't rely solely on this source of market information. Typically, dissatisfied customers don't complain. To provide better information on customer service, retailers need to encourage complaints and make it easy for customers to provide feedback about their problems. For example, some retailers set up a complaint desk in a convenient location where customers can get their problems heard and solved quickly.

Feedback from Store Employees   Salespeople and other employees in regular contact with customers often have a good understanding of customer service expectations and problems. This information will improve service quality only if the employees are encouraged to communicate their experiences to high-level managers who can act on it.

Some retailers regularly survey their employees, asking questions such as:

- What is the biggest problem you face in delivering high-quality service to your customers?

- If you could make one change in the company to improve customer service, what would it be?

USING CUSTOMER RESEARCH

Collecting information about customer expectations and perceptions isn't enough. The service gap is reduced only when retailers use this information to improve service. For example, store managers should review the suggestions and comments made by customers daily, summarize the information, and distribute it to store employees and managers.

Feedback on service performance needs to be provided to employees in a timely manner. Reporting the July service performance in December makes it hard for employees to reflect on the reason for the reported performance.

Finally, feedback must be prominently presented so service providers are aware of their performance.

setting service standards: the standards gap

After retailers gather information about customer service expectations and perceptions, the next step is to use this information to set standards and develop systems for delivering high-quality service. Service standards should be based on customers' perceptions rather than internal operations. For example, a supermarket chain might set an operations standard of a warehouse delivery every day to each store. But frequent warehouse deliveries may not result in more merchandise on the shelves or improve customers' impressions of shopping convenience.

To close the standards gap, retailers need to:

- commit their firms to providing high-quality service
- develop innovative solutions to service problems
- define the role of service providers
- set service goals
- measure service performance

COMMITMENT TO SERVICE QUALITY

Service excellence occurs only when top management provides leadership and demonstrates commitment. Top management must be willing to accept the temporary difficulties and even the increased costs associated with improving service quality. This commitment needs to be demonstrated to the employees charged with providing the service. For example, a Lands' End poster prominently displays the following inscription for employees who process customer orders:

> *What is a Customer? A Customer is the most important person in this office . . . in person or by mail. A Customer is not dependent on us . . . we are dependent on her. A customer is not an interruption in our work . . . she is the purpose of it. We are not doing her a favour by serving her . . . she is doing us a favour by giving us an opportunity to do so. A Customer is not someone to argue or match wits with.[55]*

Top management's commitment sets service quality standards, but store managers are the key to achieving those standards. Store managers must see that their efforts to provide service quality are noticed and rewarded. Providing incentives based on service quality makes service an important personal goal. Rather than basing bonuses only on store sales and profit, part of store managers' bonuses should be determined by the level of service provided. For example, some retailers use results of customer satisfaction studies to determine bonuses.

DEVELOPING SOLUTIONS TO SERVICE PROBLEMS

Frequently, retailers don't set high service standards because they feel service improvements are either too costly or not achievable with available employees. This reflects an unwillingness to think creatively and to explore new approaches for improving service.

Innovative Approaches   Finding ways to overcome service problems can improve customer satisfaction and, in some cases, reduce costs. For example, when customers complained about the long wait to check out, many hotels felt they couldn't do anything about the problem. Marriott, however, thought of a creative approach to address this service problem. It invented Express Checkout, a system in which a bill is left under the customer's door the morning before checkout and, if the bill is accurate, the customer can check out by simply using the TV remote or calling the front desk to have the bill charged automatically to his or her credit card.

Using Technology   Many retailers are installing kiosks with broadband Internet access in the stores. In addition to offering customers the opportunity to order merchandise not available in the store, kiosks can provide routine customer service, freeing employees to deal with more demanding customer requests and problems. For example, customers can use kiosks to locate merchandise in the store and to indicate whether specific products, brands, and sizes are available in the store. Kiosks can also be used to automate existing store services such

Lands' End emphasizes its commitment to high-quality service by providing an unconditional guarantee and setting high standards for employees.

as gift registry management, rain checks, film drop-off, and credit applications, and preorder service for bakeries and delicatessens.

Customers can use a kiosk to find out more information about products and how they are used. For example, a Home Depot customer can go to a kiosk to find out how to install a garbage disposal and to get a list of all of the tools and parts that are needed for the installation. A Best Buy customer can use a kiosk to provide side-by-side comparisons of two VCRs and to find more detailed information than is available from the shelf tag or from a sales associate. The customer can also access evaluations of the models as reported by *Consumer Reports*. The information provided by the kiosk could be tailored to specific customers by accessing the retailer's customer database. For example, a customer who is considering a new set of speakers might not remember the preamplifier purchased previously from Best Buy. This customer might not know whether the speakers are compatible with the preamplifier or what cables are needed to connect the new speakers. These concerns could be addressed by accessing the retailer's customer database through the kiosk.

Kiosks can also be used to provide customized solutions. For example, a customer, perhaps with the assistance of a salesperson, wants to design a home entertainment system. A kiosk could allow the customer to see what the system would look like after setup. Music store customers could use a kiosk to review and select tracks and make a custom compact disc. Finally, customers could use a kiosk to see how different colours of cosmetics would look on them without having to apply the cosmetics. These types of applications could complement the efforts of salespeople and improve the service they can offer to customers.[56]

DEFINING THE ROLE OF SERVICE PROVIDERS

Managers can tell service providers that they need to provide excellent service, but not clearly indicate what excellent service means. Without a clear definition of the retailer's expectations, service providers are directionless.

The Ritz-Carlton Hotel Company has its "Gold Standards" printed on a wallet-size card carried by all employees. The card contains the hotel's motto ("We Are Ladies and Gentlemen Serving Ladies and Gentlemen"), the three steps for high-quality service (warm and sincere greeting, anticipation and compliance with guests' needs, and fond farewell), and 20 basic rules for Ritz-Carlton employees, including:

- Any employee who receives a complaint "owns" the complaint.
- Instant guest gratification will be ensured by all. React quickly to correct problems immediately.
- "Smile. We are on stage." Always maintain positive eye contact.
- Escort guests rather than giving directions to another area of the hotel.[57]

SETTING SERVICE GOALS

To deliver consistent, high-quality service, retailers need to establish goals or standards to guide employees. Retailers often develop service goals based on their beliefs about the proper operation of the business rather than the customers' needs and expectations. For example, a retailer might set a goal that all monthly bills are to be mailed five days before the end of the month. This goal reduces the retailer's accounts receivable but offers no benefit to customers. Research undertaken by American Express showed customer evaluations of its service were based on perceptions of timeliness, accuracy, and responsiveness. Management then established goals (such as responding to all questions about bills within 24 hours) related to these customer-based criteria.

Employees are motivated to achieve service goals when the goals are specific, measurable, and participatory in the sense that they participated in setting them. Vague goals—such as "Approach customers when they enter the selling area" or "Respond to e-mails as soon as possible"—don't fully specify what employees should do, nor do such goals offer an opportunity to assess employee performance. Better goals would be "All customers should be approached by a salesperson within 30 seconds after entering a selling area" or "All e-mails should be responded to within three hours." These goals are both specific and measurable.

Employee participation in setting service standards leads to better understanding and greater acceptance of the goals. Store employees resent and resist goals arbitrarily imposed on them by management.

MEASURING SERVICE PERFORMANCE

Retailers need to continuously assess service quality to ensure that goals will be achieved.[58] Many retailers do periodic customer surveys to assess service quality. Retailers also use mystery shoppers to assess their service quality. **Mystery shoppers** are professional shoppers who "shop" a store to assess the service provided by store employees and the presentation of merchandise in the store. Some retailers use their own employees as mystery shoppers, but most contract with a firm to provide the assessment. Information typically reported by the mystery shoppers includes:

- How long before a sales associate greeted you?
- Did the sales associate act as if he or she wanted your business?
- Was the sales associate knowledgeable about the merchandise?

Retailers typically inform salespeople that they have "been shopped" and provide feedback from the mystery shopper's report. Some retailers offer rewards to sales associates who receive high marks and schedule follow-up visits to sales associates who get low evaluations.[59]

meeting and exceeding services standards: the delivery gap

To reduce the delivery gap and provide service that exceeds standards, retailers must give service providers the necessary knowledge and skills, provide instrumental and emotional support, improve internal communications and reduce conflicts, and empower employees to act in the customers' and firm's best interests.[60] Chat rooms offered through an electronic channel enable customers to help the retailer to provide services to others.

GIVING INFORMATION AND TRAINING

Store employees need to know about the merchandise they offer as well as their customers' needs. With this information, employees can answer customers' questions and suggest products. This also instills confidence and a sense of competence, which are needed to overcome service problems.

In addition, store employees need training in interpersonal skills. Dealing with customers is hard—particularly when they're upset or angry. All store employees, even those who work for retailers that provide excellent service, will encounter dissatisfied customers. Through training, employees can learn to provide better service and to cope with the stress caused by disgruntled customers.

Specific retail employees (salespeople and customer service representatives) are typically designated to interact with and provide service to customers. However, all retail employees should be prepared to deal with customers. For example, *Walt Disney World* provides four days of training for its maintenance workers, even though people can learn how to pick up trash and sweep streets in much less time. Disney has found that its customers are more likely to direct questions to maintenance people than to the clean-cut assistants wearing ASK ME, I'M IN GUEST RELATIONS buttons. Thus, Disney trains maintenance people to confidently handle the myriad of questions they'll be asked rather than responding, "Sorry, I don't know. Ask her."[61]

Toys "R" Us assesses customer satisfaction with checkout service by counting the number of abandoned shopping carts with merchandise left in the store because customers became impatient with the time required to make a purchase. After the firm noticed an alarming increase in abandoned carts, it developed a unique program to reduce customers' time in line waiting to pay. Cashiers' motions while ringing up and bagging merchandise were studied. Based on this research, a training program was developed to show cashiers how to use their right hand to record purchases on the POS terminal and their left hand to push merchandise along the counter. Counters were redesigned to have a slot lined with shopping bags in the middle of the counter. As the cashier pushes the merchandise along the counter, it drops into a bag. After the customer pays for the merchandise, the cashier simply lifts the bag from the slot and hands it to the customer, and a new bag pops into place.

> **refact**
> Two-thirds of the customers who put merchandise into an electronic shopping cart at a Web site do not complete the transaction.[63]

PROVIDING INSTRUMENTAL AND EMOTIONAL SUPPORT

Service providers need to have the **instrumental support** (the appropriate systems and equipment) to deliver the service desired by customers. For example, a hotel chain installed a computer system to speed up the checkout process. A study of the new system's effectiveness revealed that checkout time was not reduced because clerks had to wait to use the one stapler available to staple the customer's credit card and hotel bill receipts.

In addition to instrumental support, service providers need emotional support from their co-workers and supervisors. **Emotional support** involves demonstrating a concern for the well-being of others. Dealing with customer problems and maintaining a smile in difficult situations are psychologically demanding. Service providers need to be in a supportive, understanding atmosphere to deal with these demands effectively.[62]

IMPROVING INTERNAL COMMUNICATIONS AND PROVIDING SUPPORT

When providing customer service, store employees must often manage the conflict between customers' needs and the retail firms' needs.[64] For example, many retailers have a no-questions-asked return policy. Under such a policy, the retailer will provide a refund at the customer's request even if the merchandise wasn't purchased at the store or was clearly used improperly. When *JCPenney Department Stores* inaugurated this policy, some employees refused to provide refunds on merchandise that had been worn or damaged by the customer. They were loyal Penney employees and didn't want customers to take advantage of their firm.

Retailers can reduce such conflicts by having clear guidelines and policies concerning service and by explaining the rationale for these policies. Once Penney employees recognized that the goodwill created by the no-questions-asked policy generated more sales than the losses due to customers' abusing the policy, they implemented the policy enthusiastically.

Conflicts can also arise when retailers set goals inconsistent with the other behaviours expected from store employees. For example, if salespeople are expected to provide customer service, they should be evaluated on the service they provide, not just on the sales they make.

Finally, conflicts can also arise between different areas of the firm. An auto dealer with an excellent customer service reputation devotes considerable effort to reducing conflict by improving communication among its employees. The dealership holds a town hall meeting in which employees feel free to bring up service problems. For example, the receptionist discussed her frustration when she couldn't locate a sales rep for whom a customer had called. The customer finally said, "Well, I'll just take my business elsewhere." She used this example to emphasize that sales reps should tell her when they slip out to run an errand. Now no one forgets that the front desk is the nerve centre of the dealership.

EMPOWERING STORE EMPLOYEES

Empowerment means allowing employees at the firm's lowest level to make important decisions concerning how service is provided to customers. When the employees responsible for providing service are authorized to make important decisions, service quality improves.[65]

Nordstrom Department Stores provides an overall objective—satisfy customer needs—and then encourages employees to do whatever's necessary to carry out the objective. For example, a Nordstrom department manager bought 12 dozen pairs of hosiery from a competitor in the mall when her stock was depleted because the new shipment was delayed. Even though Nordstrom lost money on this hosiery, management applauded her actions to make sure customers found hosiery when they came to the store looking for it. Empowering service providers with only a rule such as "Use your best judgment" can cause chaos. At Nordstrom, department managers avoid abuses by coaching and training salespeople. They help salespeople understand what "Use your best judgment" means.

However, empowering service providers can be difficult. Some employees prefer to have the appropriate behaviours clearly defined for them. They don't want to spend the time learning how to make decisions or to assume the risks of making mistakes.

In some cases, the benefits of empowering service providers may not justify the costs. For example, if a retailer uses a standardized service delivery approach like *McDonald's*, the cost of hiring, training, and supporting empowerment may not lead to consistent and superior service delivery. Also, studies have found that empowerment is not embraced by employees in different cultures. For example, employees in Latin America expect their managers to possess all the information needed to make good business decisions. The role of employees is not to make business decisions; their job is to carry out the decisions of managers.[66]

PROVIDING INCENTIVES

As we discussed, many retailers use incentives, such as paying commissions on sales, to motivate employees. But retailers have found that commissions on sales can decrease customer service and job satisfaction. Incentives can motivate high-pressure selling, which leads to customer dissatisfaction. However, incentives can also be used effectively to improve customer service. For example, in one retail chain, managers distributed notes to store employees when they solved a customer's problem. The notes could be converted into a cash bonus. This program was particularly effective because the reward was provided at about the same time the appropriate behaviour occurred.

communicating the service promise: the communications gap

A fourth factor leading to a customer service gap is a difference between the service promised by the retailer and the service actually delivered. Overstating the service offered raises customer expectations. Then if the retailer doesn't follow through, expectations exceed perceived service, and customers are dissatisfied. For example, if a store advertises that a customer will always be greeted by a friendly, smiling sales associate, customers may be disappointed if this doesn't occur. Raising expectations too high might bring in more customers initially, but it can also create dissatisfaction and reduce repeat business. The communication gap can be reduced by making realistic commitments and by managing customer expectations.

REALISTIC COMMITMENTS

Advertising programs are typically developed by the marketing department, while the store operations division delivers the service. Poor communication between these areas can result in a mismatch between an ad campaign's promises and the service the store can actually offer. This problem is illustrated by Holiday Inn's "No Surprises" ad campaign. Market research indicated hotel customers wanted greater reliability in lodging, so Holiday Inn's agency developed a campaign promising no unpleasant surprises. Even though hotel managers didn't feel they could meet the claims promised in the ads, top management accepted the campaign. The campaign raised customer expectations to an unrealistic level and gave customers who did confront an unpleasant surprise an additional reason to be angry. The campaign was discontinued soon after it started.

MANAGING CUSTOMER EXPECTATIONS

How can a retailer communicate realistic service expectations without losing business to a competitor that makes inflated service claims? American Airlines' "Why Does It Seem Every Airline Flight Is Late?" ad campaign is an example of a communication program that addresses this issue. In print ads, American recognized its customers' frustration and explained some uncontrollable factors causing the problem: overcrowded airports, scheduling problems, and intense price competition. Then the ads described how American was improving the situation.

Information presented at the point of sale can be used to manage expectations. For example, theme parks and restaurants indicate the waiting time for an attraction or a table. Electronic retailers tell their customers if merchandise is in stock and when they can expect to receive it. Providing accurate information can increase customer satisfaction even when customers must wait longer than desired.[68]

Sometimes service problems are caused by customers. Customers may use an invalid credit card to pay for merchandise, may not take time to try on a suit and have it altered properly, or may use a product incorrectly because they failed to read the instructions. Communication programs can inform customers about their role and responsibility in getting good service and can give tips on how to get better service, such as the best times of the day to shop and the retailer's policies and procedures for handling problems.

service recovery

As we said, delivery of customer service is inherently inconsistent, so service failures are bound to arise. Rather than dwelling on negative aspects of customer problems, retailers should focus on the positive opportunities they generate. Service problems and complaints are an excellent source of information about the retailer's offering (its merchandise and service). Armed with this information, retailers can make changes to increase customer satisfaction.

Service problems also enable a retailer to demonstrate its commitment to providing high-quality customer service. By encouraging complaints and handling problems, a retailer has an opportunity to strengthen its relationship with its customers. Effective service recovery efforts significantly increase customer satisfaction, purchase intentions, and positive word of mouth. However, postrecovery satisfaction is less than that satisfaction prior to the service failure.[69]

Most retailers have standard policies for handling problems. If a correctable problem is identified, such as defective merchandise, many retailers will make restitution on the spot and apologize for inconveniencing the customer. The retailer will offer either replacement merchandise, a credit toward future purchases, or a cash refund.

In many cases, the cause of the problem may be hard to identify (did the salesperson really insult the customer?), uncorrectable (the store had to close due to bad weather), or a result of the customer's unusual expectations (the customer didn't like his haircut). In this case, service recovery might be more difficult. The steps in effective service recovery are:

- listen to the customer
- provide a fair solution
- resolve the problem quickly[70]

LISTENING TO CUSTOMERS

Customers can become very emotional over their real or imaginary problems with a retailer. Often this emotional reaction can be reduced by simply giving customers a chance to get their complaints off their chests.

Store employees should allow customers to air their complaints without interruption. Interruptions can further irritate customers who may already be emotionally upset. It's very hard to reason with or satisfy an angry customer.

Customers want a sympathetic response to their complaints. Thus, store employees need to make it clear they're happy that the problem has been brought to their attention. Satisfactory solutions rarely arise when store employees have an antagonistic attitude or assume that the customer is trying to cheat the store.

In 2004, *The Bay* launched an online survey for customers at its 99 Bay stores as well as its 300 *Zellers* and 45 *Home Outfitters* stores. The customer's receipt invites the shopper to go online and fill out a questionnaire, thus earning a chance to win 1 million HBC reward points (equivalent to $100). Feedback from the customer can pinpoint problems in specific departments, not enough sale items, or unfriendly service.

For many years, retailers have used mystery shoppers to provide feedback on customer services, but times have changed and customers are eager to log on and discuss their shopping experience. The advantage is that these are real customers who are in the store shopping and are not on the store's payroll. Customer service scores for the stores have improved since online feedback was initiated. [71]

PROVIDING A FAIR SOLUTION

When confronted with a complaint, store employees need to focus on how they can get the customer back, not simply how they can solve the problem. Favourable impressions arise when customers feel they've been dealt with fairly. When evaluating the resolution of their problems, customers compare how they were treated in relation to others with similar problems or how they were treated in similar situations by other retail service providers. This comparison is based on observation of other customers with problems or on information about complaint handling learned from reading books and talking with others. Customers' evaluations of complaints' resolutions are based on distributive fairness and procedural fairness.[72]

Distributive Fairness   **Distributive fairness** is a customer's perception of the benefits received compared to their costs (inconvenience or loss). Customers want to get what they paid for. The customer's needs can affect the perceived correspondence between benefits and costs. For example, one customer might be satisfied with a rain check for a food processor that was advertised at a discounted price but was sold out. This customer feels the low price for the food processor offsets the inconvenience of returning to the store. But another customer may need the food processor immediately. A rain check won't be adequate compensation for him. To satisfy this customer, the salesperson must locate a store that has the food processor and have it delivered to the customer's house.

Customers typically prefer tangible rather than intangible resolutions to their complaints. Customers may want to let off steam, but they also want to feel the retailer was responsive to their complaint. A low-cost reward, a free soft drink, or a discount communicates more concern to the customer than a verbal apology.

If providing tangible restitution isn't possible, the next best alternative is to let customers see that their complaints will have an effect in the future. This can be done by making a note, in front of the customer, to a manager about the problem or writing to the customer about actions taken to prevent similar problems in the future.

Procedural Fairness   **Procedural fairness** is the perceived fairness of the process used to resolve complaints. Customers consider three questions when evaluating procedural fairness:

- Did the employee collect information about the situation?
- Was this information used to resolve the complaint?
- Did the customer have some influence over the outcome?

This customer service representative is empowered to resolve the problems the customer has with a windbreaker purchased at the store.

RESOLVING PROBLEMS QUICKLY

Customers are more satisfied when the first person they contact can resolve a problem. When customers are referred to several different employees, they waste a lot of time repeating their story. Also, the chance of conflicting responses by store employees increases.

Customers should be told clearly and precisely what they need to do to resolve a problem. When American Express cardholders ask to have an unused airline ticket removed from their bill, they're told immediately that they must return the ticket to the airline or travel agency before a credit can be issued. Fast service often depends on providing clear instructions.

SUMMARY

Customer relationship management is a business philosophy and set of strategies, programs, and systems that focus on identifying and building loyalty with a retailer's most valued customers. Loyal customers are committed to patronizing a retailer and are not prone to switching to a competitor. In addition to building loyalty, CRM programs are also designed to increase the share of wallet from the retailer's best customers.

CRM is an iterative process that turns customer data into customer loyalty through four activities:

- collecting customer data
- analyzing the customer data and identifying target customers
- developing CRM programs
- implementing CRM programs

The first step of the process is to collect and store data about customers. One of the challenges in collecting customer data is identifying the customer with each transaction and contact. Retailers use a variety of approaches to overcome this challenge.

The second step is analyzing the data to identify the most profitable customers. Two approaches used to rank customers according to their profitability are calculating the customer's lifetime value and categorizing customers on the basis of characteristics of their buying behaviour—recency, frequency, and monetary value.

Using this information about customers, retailers can develop programs to build loyalty in their best customers, increase their share of wallet with better customers (converting gold customers into platinum customers), and deal with unprofitable customers (getting the lead out).

Four approaches that retailers use to build loyalty and retain their best customers are:

- launching frequent shopper programs
- offering special customer service
- personalizing the services they provide
- building a sense of community

Retailers increase share of wallet through cross-selling and add-on selling. Unprofitable customers are dealt with by developing lower-cost approaches for servicing these customers. Effectively implementing CRM programs is difficult because it requires coordinating a number of different areas in a retailer's organization.

Due to the inherent intangibility and inconsistency of service, providing high-quality customer service is challenging. However, customer service also provides an opportunity for retailers to develop a strategic advantage. Retailers use two basic approaches to providing customer service: customization and standardization approaches. The customized approach relies primarily on sales associates. The standardized approach places more emphasis on developing appropriate rules and procedures and the store design.

Customers evaluate customer service by comparing their perceptions of the service delivered with their expectations. Thus, to improve service, retailers need to close the gaps between the service delivered and the customer's expectations. These gaps are reduced by knowing what customers expect, setting standards to provide the expected service, providing support so store employees can meet the standards, and realistically communicating the service they offer to customers. Knowledge of service gaps can be determined by conducting focus groups.

Due to inherent inconsistency, service failures are bound to arise. These lapses in service provide an opportunity for retailers to build even stronger relationships with their customers.

KEY TERMS

add-on selling, *442*

communication gap, *450*

cookies, *432*

cross-selling, *442*

customer database, *430*

customer data warehouse *430*

customer relationship
   management (CRM), *428*

customer service, *443*

data mining, *434*

decile analysis, *436*

delivery gap, *450*

distributive fairness, *461*

80–20 rule, *435*

emotional support, *457*

frequent shopper program, *431*

instrumental support, *457*

knowledge gap, *450*

lifetime customer value
   (LTV), *435*

loyalty program, *431*

market basket analysis, *434*

mystery shoppers, *456*

1-to-1 retailing, *440*

procedural fairness, *461*

RFM analysis, *436*

service gap, *450*

share of wallet, *428*

standardization approach, *446*

standards gap, *450*

Get Out & Do It!

1. **GO SHOPPING** Look in your wallet: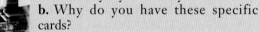
   a. What loyalty cards do you have?
   b. Why do you have these specific cards?
   c. Rate each card on a scale: 1 (poor) to 10 (fantastic).

2. **INTERNET EXERCISE** Contact the Canadian Marketing Association (CMA) a leading authority on privacy issues at www.the-cma.org. What are the major issues confronting retailers? What seminars are being offered to assist retailers in understanding Canada's new privacy legislation?

3. **INTERNET EXERCISE** Go to some of the retail sites that you frequent and compare their privacy policies. Which policies make you less concerned about violations of your privacy? Why? Which policies, or lack thereof, raise your concern? Why?

4. **SHOPPING** Are you a participant in a frequent shopper program? Why are you a member? Look at the Shoppers Optimum card program.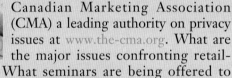
   a. How does a membership benefit the consumer?
   b Would this membership card be of value to you personally? Explain why or why not.

5. **INTERNET EXERCISE** Visit www.your shops.ca—the Air Miles virtual shopping mall. What are the shopping options and special promotions for Air Miles collectors? How does the Web site encourage you to participate and sign up for Air Miles? What information does it request from you?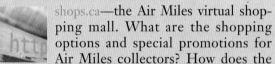

6. **GO SHOPPING** Go to a local store and be a customer: Ask for assistance and suggestions regarding a potential purchase. Write a report describing your shopping experience, and make suggestions for improving the store's customer service.

7. **GO SHOPPING** Go to a discount store such as Wal-Mart, a department store, and a specialty store to buy a pair of jeans. Compare and contrast the customer service you receive in the stores. Which store made it easiest to find the pair of jeans you would be interested in buying? Why?

DISCUSSION QUESTIONS AND PROBLEMS

1. What is CRM?

2. Why do retailers want to determine the lifetime value of their customers?

3. Why do customers have privacy concerns about frequent shopper programs that supermarkets have, and what can supermarkets do to minimize these concerns?

4. What are examples of opportunities for add-on selling that might be pursued by (a) travel agents, (b) jewellery stores, and (c) dry cleaners?

5. How would you suggest that a dry cleaner build greater loyalty and retention with its best customers?

6. Which of the following types of retailers do you think would benefit most from instituting CRM: (a) supermarkets, (b) banks, (c) automobile dealers, or (d) consumer electronic retailers? Why?

7. Develop a CRM program for a local store that sells apparel with your college or university's logo. What type of information would you collect about your customers, and how would you use this information to increase the sales and profits of the store?

8. How can a real estate agent deal with people who are just looking and not ready to buy? What are the agent's potential benefits and risks in undertaking these actions?

9. What are the different approaches retailers can use to identify customers with their transactions? What are the advantages and disadvantages of each approach?

10. A CRM program focuses on building relationships with a retailer's better customers. Some customers who do not receive the same benefits as the retailer's best customers may be upset because they are treated differently. What can retailers do to minimize this negative reaction?

11. For each of these services, give an example of a retailer for which providing the service is critical to its success. Then give an example of a retailer for which providing the service is not critical: (a) personal shoppers, (b) home delivery, (c) money-back guarantees, (d) credit.

12. Holt Renfrew and McDonald's are noted for their high-quality customer service. But their approaches to providing this quality service are different. Describe this difference. Why have the retailers elected to use these different approaches?

13. Is customer service more important for store-based retailers or electronic retailers? Explain.

14. Providing customer service can be very expensive for retailers. When are the costs of providing high-quality services justified? What types of retailers find it financially advantageous to provide high-quality customer service? What retailers can't justify providing high-quality service?

15. Gaps analysis provides a systematic method of examining a customer service program's effectiveness. Top management has told an information systems manager that customers are complaining about the long wait to pay for merchandise at the checkout station. How can the systems manager use gaps analysis to analyze this problem and suggest approaches to reducing this time?

16. How could an effective customer service strategy cut a retailer's costs?

17. Employees play a critical role in customer perceptions of quality service. If you were hiring salespeople, what characteristics would you look for to assess their ability to provide good customer service?

18. a) What is a focus group?
    b) Design 10 open-ended questions to use in a customer focus group to determine a retailer's customer service gaps and make improvements.

CHAPTER 16

appealing to the customer: retail communication mix

Executive Briefing

Tom Gauld, President,
Canadian Tire Corporation

Canadian Tire is a respected Canadian institution where you can shop for just about anything. The first Canadian Tire store opened in 1925, and the popular "Canadian Tire Money" was conceived in 1958 as a reward for purchases. Today, Canadian Tire has 465 locations in communities across the country, and research indicates that there is a Canadian Tire store within 15 minutes of 92 percent of the population and that 40 percent of adult Canadians will be in a Canadian Tire store once a week.

The strength of this respected company is its unique branding position in the Canadian retail marketplace, and its successful organizational structure based on associate dealers. Although Canadian Tire Retail is the core business, the company has diversified to include Canadian Tire Financial Services (including banking services), 253 Canadian Tire gas bars, 58 Canadian Tire car washes, 5400 car service bays, and 241 convenience stores.

The acquisition of Mark's Work Wearhouse in 2002 was part of the concept renewal plan for Canadian Tire. Many industry watchers suggested that the strategy was counterproductive. Why would Canadian Tire, a very successful hard goods company, purchase a clothing retailer? The rationale: Mark's is a well-known Canadian retailer that happens to share the same target customer and business culture as Canadian Tire. The addition of more casual apparel to its base of workwear as well as women's clothing and health care employees' uniforms, including nurse's uniforms, has increased Mark's popularity. The design of its work clothes is in direct response to customer feedback

QUESTIONS

How can retailers build brand equity for their stores and their private-label merchandise?

What are the strengths and weaknesses of the different methods for communicating with customers?

Why do retailers need to have an integrated marketing communication program?

What steps are involved in developing a communication program?

How do retailers establish a communication budget?

How can retailers use the different elements in a communication mix to alter customers' decision-making processes?

on styling and sizing—ensuring that its offerings match consumer demand. The result is that Mark's Work Wearhouse has proved to be a surprisingly strong contributor to Canadian Tire's success. Cross promotions at Canadian Tire have increased awareness of Mark's Work Wearhouse expanded product lines, and encourage customers to cross-shop the two banners. As well, retail expansion includes combination Canadian Tire-Mark's stores.

The "Celebration Station," Canadian Tire's online wedding and gift registry, launched in 2004 with approximately 42 000 products. A survey conducted by Ispos-Reid of 1294 Canadians determined that today's modern married couples prefer a kayak or a power tool with their fine china. Couples can register at a kiosk available at stores across the country or online at www.canadiantire.ca.

Always focused on customer values, Canadian Tire is getting into the power-generation business. The retailer has launched a Web site dedicated to selling solar and wind systems to homeowners, hoping that the trend toward energy self-sufficiency will translate into Canadian Tire revenues. The site, www.canadiantirepower.ca sells solar panels, wind turbines, power electronics, and battery storage—all the necessary components of a renewable energy system. It also provides system design tips, a solar calculator, and price estimates.

There is no doubt that continued innovation will keep the distinctive Canadian Tire brand a symbol of value, trust, and product reliability in the minds of Canadian consumers.

A critical step in the retail management decision-making process is developing and implementing a communication program to:

- build appealing brand images
- attract customers to stores and Internet sites
- encourage customers to buy merchandise

The communication program informs customers about the retailer as well as the merchandise and services it offers and plays a role in developing repeat visits and customer loyalty.

Communication programs can have both long-term and short-term effects on a retailer's business. From a *long-term perspective*, communications programs can be used to create and maintain a strong, differentiated image of the retailer and its store brands. This image develops customer loyalty and creates a strategic advantage. Thus, brand-image–building communication programs complement the objective of a retailer's CRM (customer relationship management) program.

On the other hand, retailers frequently use communication programs to realize the *short-term objective* of increasing sales during a specified time period. For example, retailers often have sales during which some or all merchandise is priced at a discount for a short time, for example, at the end of a season. Grocery stores usually place weekly ads with coupons that can be used to save money on purchases made during the week.

Retail advertising can be used to achieve long-term objectives such as building a brand image or short-term sales. The Payless ShoeSource ad (right) generates short-term sales through a special promotion.

using communication programs to develop brands and build customer loyalty

A **brand** is the symbolic embodiment of all the information connected to the product and/or retailer and serves to create associations and expectations around it. A brand often includes a logo, fonts, colour schemes, symbols, and sound, which may be developed to represent implicit values, ideas, and even personality. In a retailing context, the name of the retailer is a brand that indicates to consumers the type of merchandise and services offered by the retailer. Some retailers develop **private-label brands** or store brands that are exclusively sold through their channels. In some cases this private-label merchandise bears the retailer's name, such as Shoppers Drug Mart aspirins. In other cases, special brand names are used, such as Bay's Baycrest and Canadian Tire's Mastercraft. A retailer develops a brand by associating an image with the product and services that is branded into the consciousness of consumers. A brand is therefore one of the most valuable elements in a retailer's advertising strategy. One goal in brand recognition is the identification of a brand without the name of the company present. It is therefore important that a brand be protected legally by patent or copyright. The well-known brand of Apple is recognized for innovation in technology and has created immense success in the branding of iPod and iTunes.

Brand energy is the concept that links the idea that the brand creates value through meaningful experiences rather than a focus on merely generating profits. The energy that flows throughout the business develops a consistent way of thinking, feeling, and behaving toward the retailer and its products and services in all employees; an example is Mountain Equipment Coop, where customers become members for a nominal fee and embrace their environmental philosophy.

Attitude branding is the choice to represent a feeling which is not necessarily connected with the product or retailer; for example, Nike: "Just Do It"; The Body Shop: "Trade Not Aid"; Dove: "Real Beauty." A great brand adds a sense of purpose to the experience.

VALUE OF BRAND IMAGE

Brands provide value to both customers and retailers. Brands convey information to consumers about the nature of the shopping experience—the retailer's mix—they will encounter when patronizing a retailer. They also affect the customers' confidence in decisions made to buy merchandise from a retailer. Finally, brands can enhance the customers' satisfaction with the merchandise and services they buy. Consumers feel different when wearing jewellery bought from Birks than from La Claire or lingerie from La Senza than from Zellers.

The value that brand image offers retailers is referred to as **brand equity.** Strong brand names can affect the customer's decision-making process, motivate repeat visits and purchases, and build loyalty. In addition, strong brand names enable retailers to charge higher prices and lower their marketing costs.

Customer loyalty to brands arises from heightened awareness of the brand and the emotional ties toward it. For example, some brands such as Canadian Tire are so well known by consumers that they are typically in a consumer's consideration set. In addition, customers identify and have strong emotional relationships with some brands. For example, Winners has an image of offering fashionable merchandise at bargain prices. Going to Winners is a cool experience, and everybody now considers it cool to save money. On the other hand, is it cool to save at Wal-Mart? I don't think so. You walk into Wal-Mart, and there are these big boxes of corn flakes. How ugly! How totally uncool. High brand awareness and strong emotional connnections reduce the incentive of customers to switch to competing retailers.

A strong brand image enables retailers to increase their margins. When retailers have high customer loyalty, they can engage in premium pricing and reduce their reliance on price promotions to attract customers. Brands with weaker images are forced to offer low prices and frequent sales to maintain their market share.

Finally, retailers with strong brand names can leverage their brand to successfully introduce new retail concepts with only a limited amount of marketing effort. For example, The Gap has efficiently extended its brand to GapKids and BabyGap and Roots extended its brand name to Roots Kids. Toys "R" Us extended its brand name to Kids "R" Us and Babies "R" Us.

A strong brand name creates a strategic advantage that is very difficult for competitors to duplicate. Many of the most brilliant marketers can be found in Canada, and many others around the world look to Canadian companies for best practices. For example, Canadian Tire has always stayed true to its core customers but, recognizing changing times, took an innovative approach to meeting the demands of the modern bride and groom. The launch of electronic "Celebration Stations" at 345 locations across Canada created an online bridal and gift registry that has a selection of 42 000 products from barbecues to kayaks.[3]

BUILDING BRAND EQUITY

The activities that a retailer needs to undertake to build brand equity for its firm or its private-label merchandise are:

- create a high level of brand awareness
- develop favourable associations with the brand name
- consistently reinforce the image of the brand

Winners uses advertising to build its image of offering fashionable merchandise at low prices.

By using these symbols, KFC and Taco Bell build awareness for their offerings and make it easier for customers to recall their names and images.

Brand Awareness   **Brand awareness** is the ability of a potential customer to recognize or recall that the brand name is a type of retailer or product/service. Thus, brand awareness is the strength of the link between the brand name and type of merchandise or service in the minds of customers. There is a range of awareness from aided recall to top-of-mind awareness. **Aided recall** occurs when consumers indicate they know the brand when the name is presented to them. **Top-of-mind awareness**, the highest level of awareness, arises when consumers mention a brand name first when they are asked about the type of retailer, a merchandise category, or a type of service. For example, Best Buy has top-of-mind awareness if a consumer responds "Best Buy" when asked about retailers that sell consumer electronics. High top-of-mind awareness means that a retailer typically will be in the consideration set when customers decide to shop for a type of product or service.

Retailers build top-of-mind awareness by having memorable names; by repeatedly exposing their name to customers through advertising, locations, and sponsorships; and by using memorable symbols. Some brand names are easy to remember. For example, the name Home Depot, because "Home" is in its brand name, is memorable and closely associated with home improvements, as is Canadian Tire with the automotive reference and the fact that this is a Canadian company.

Tim Hortons does very little advertising but has high awareness because of the large number of stores it has. Customers walk and drive by the stores all the time. The sheer number of stores provides substantial exposure to its brand. Most Canadians are well aware of the popular "roll up the rim to win" promotion.

Symbols involve visual images that typically are more easily recalled than words or phrases and thus are useful for building brand awareness. For example, the images of Colonel Sanders and the golden arches enhance the ability of customers to recall the names KFC and McDonald's.

Many Canadian retailers are finding that sponsorships are a cost-effective means of increasing their exposure as well as helping the communities that they serve. Take a Hike—an outdoor sporting goods store in Thunder Bay, Ontario—is passionate about sponsorships and participates in local festivals and outdoor activity workshops for the community. Its Socks for Shelter House program donates one pair of socks (retail value, $16) for every four pairs sold; suppliers also get involved and contribute to the worthy cause.[4]

Associations   Building awareness is the first step in developing brand equity, but the value of the brand is largely based on the associations that customers make with the brand name. **Brand associations** are anything linked to or connected with the brand name in a consumer's memory. For example, some of the associations that consumers might have with McDonald's are golden arches, fast food, clean stores, hamburgers, French fries, Big Mac, and Ronald McDonald. In the case of McDonald's, these links are so strong that when a consumer thinks of fast food, hamburgers, or French fries, they also think of McDonald's. These strong associations influence consumer buying behaviour. For example, when consumers think about camping, Mountain Equipment Co-op might immediately come to mind, stimulating a visit to a Mountain Equipment Co-op store or its Web site.

Some common associations that retailers develop with their brand name are:

- *Merchandise category.* The most common association is to link the retailer to a category of merchandise. For example, Staples Business Depot would like to have consumers associate its name with office supplies. Then, when a need for office supplies arises, consumers immediately think of Staples Business Depot.

- *Price/quality.* Some retailers, such as Holt Renfrew, want to be associated with offering high prices and unique, high fashion merchandise. Other retailers, such as Wal-Mart, want associations with offering low prices and good value.
- *Specific attribute or benefit.* A retailer can link its stores to attributes such as convenience (7-Eleven) or service (Harry Rosen).
- *Lifestyle or activity.* Some retailers associate their name with a specific lifestyle or activity. For example, The Nature Company, a retailer offering books and equipment to study nature, is linked to a lifestyle of interacting with the environment. Future Shop is associated with computers, software, and small office equipment.

The **brand image** is a set of associations that are usually organized around some meaningful themes. Thus, the associations that a consumer might have with McDonald's might be organized into groups such as kids, service, and type of food. Mountain Equipment Co-op nurtures its brand image of selling high-quality, functional products and providing helpful service for outdoor activity.

Consistent Reinforcement   The retailer's brand image is developed and maintained through the retailer's communication program as well as other elements of the communication mix, such as merchandise assortment and pricing, the design of its stores and Web site, and the customer service it offers. To develop a strong set of associations and a clearly defined brand image, retailers need to be consistent, presenting the same message to customers over time and across all of the elements of the retail mix.

Rather than creating unique communication programs for sales associates, retailers need to develop an **integrated marketing communication program**—a program that integrates all of the communication elements to deliver a comprehensive, consistent message. Without this coordination, the communication methods might work at cross-purposes. For example, the retailer's TV advertising campaign might attempt to build an image of exceptional customer service, but the firm's sales promotions might all emphasize low prices. If communication methods aren't used consistently, customers may become confused about the retailer's image and therefore not patronize the store.

A unique example is Abercrombie & Fitch (A&F) which uses an integrated marketing communication program to reinforce its brand image associated with fun-loving, independent, and uninhibited teenagers and young adults. To stay on top of its target market's taste and find ideas for new merchandise, A&F sends employees to college and university campuses each month to chat with students about what they play, wear, listen to, and read.

The stores have comfortable armchairs, designed to be gathering places for its customers. They are staffed by high-energy "brand reps"; selling skills not required. The brand reps just need to fit the company's brand image, wear its apparel, and have fun inside the store.

A&F's main promotional tool has been its controversial "magalogue," a quarterly magazine–catalogue crammed with product information,

Abercrombie & Fitch uses webcasts as part of an integrated marketing communication program to reinforce its image associated with fun-loving, independent teenagers and young adults.

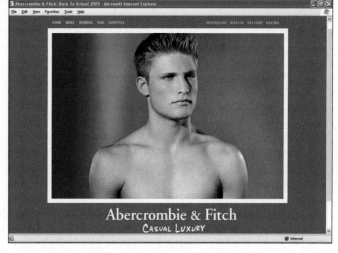

sexual imagery, and provocative articles. A **magalogue** is a combination magazine and catalogue. Large blowups of enticing photographs from the magalogue appear in store displays.[6]

Toys "R" Us is using a similar approach to target teenagers. It has created RZone boutiques within its stores, which offer video games. The visual merchandising in the boutiques is designed to appeal to teenagers. To build its image of the RZone brand with teenagers, Toys "R" Us launched *RZone Magazine*. The glossy magazine has cutting-edge graphics and content desired by teen pop-culture junkies who listen to hybrid rap and rock music and watch MTV's "Total Request." It reinforces the image and visual merchandising in the boutiques that associate the RZone brand with what is hot in the worlds of entertainment, sports, and gaming.[7]

EXTENDING THE BRAND NAME

Retailers can leverage their brand names to support their growth strategies. For example, *IKEA* used its strong brand image to successfully enter the Canadian home furnishing retail market; *Laura* introduced a *Laura II* collection for women wearing plus-sizes and *Laura Petites* for small sizes; and the *Pottery Barn* launched its *Pottery Barn Kids* catalogue to target children. In other cases, retailers have pursued growth opportunities using a new and unrelated brand name. For example, *The Gap* used the brand name *Old Navy* for its value concept, and *The Bay* named its new home store concept *Home Outfitters*.

There are pluses and minuses to extending a brand name to a new concept. An important benefit of extending the brand name is that minimal communication expenses are needed to create awareness and a brand image for the new concept. Customers will quickly transfer the original brand's awareness and associations to the new concept. However, in some cases, the retailer might not want to have the original brand's associations connected with the new concept. For example, *Suzy Shier* decided to invest in building a new and different brand image for *La Senza* rather than branding the new concept with a name like *Suzy Lingerie*.

These issues also arise as a retailer expands internationally. Associations with the retailer's brands that are valued in one country may not be valued in another. For example, French consumers prefer to shop at supermarkets that offer good service and high-quality grocery products, whereas German shoppers prefer supermarkets that offer low prices and good value. Thus, a French supermarket retailer with a brand image of quality and service might not be able to leverage its image if it decides to enter the German market.[8]

Retailers communicate with customers through five vehicles:

- advertising
- sales promotion
- publicity
- store atmosphere
- visual merchandising
- personal selling

In large retail firms, these elements of the communication mix are managed by the firm's marketing or advertising department and the buying organization. The other elements, store atmosphere and salespeople, are managed by store personnel and head office.

planning the retail communication process

Almost every retail business needs to promote itself in some way, reaching out to customers and potential customers. For businesses with large numbers of target customers in well-defined market segments, advertising is often a cost-effective way of communicating with them. Advertising attempts to inform, persuade, and remind the consumer.

Exhibit 16–1 illustrates the four steps in developing and implementing a retail communication program: setting objectives, determining a budget, allocating the budget, and implementing and evaluating the mix.

SETTING OBJECTIVES

Retailers establish objectives for communication programs to provide:

* direction for people implementing the program
* a basis for evaluating its effectiveness

Some communication programs have a long-term objective, such as creating or altering a retailer's brand image. Other communication programs focus on improving short-term performance, such as increasing store traffic on weekends.

Communication Objectives   While retailers' overall objective is to generate long- and short-term sales and profits, they often use communication objectives rather than sales objectives to plan and evaluate their communication programs. **Communication objectives** are specific goals related to the retail communication mix's effect on the customer's decision-making process.

Exhibit 16–2 shows hypothetical information about customers in the target market for a Zehrs grocery store. This information illustrates goals related to stages in the consumer decision-making process. Note that 95 percent of the customers are aware of the store (the first stage in the decision-making process) and 85 percent know the type of merchandise it sells. But only 45 percent of the customers in the target market have a favourable attitude toward the store; 32 percent intend to visit the store during the next few weeks; 25 percent actually visit the store during the next two weeks; and 18 percent regularly shop at the store.

* Set promotional objectives and decide whether to advertise. Do you want to promote awareness of a retail business and its products and services, stimulate sales directly and attract competitors' customers, or establish or modify the retail image? www.endnotes.com
* Determine your promotional budget based on percentage of sales past or future, or market share.
* Begin by developing a **positioning statement** that will explain how the retailer's product or service is different from the key competitors'. www.adcracker.com
* Determine the target audience and those that influence product purchases.
* Consider product concept, for example, What emotions does the consumer connect to the product/retailer: masculinity or femininity, sex, humour, romance, science, or fun?
* Decide where and when to advertise. Which communication media: print, audio, Internet-based, television, etc.
* Develop the advertising message. Consider the unique features of the retail business or products, think about what is likely to persuade customers to purchase the product, and assess the strengths and weaknesses of competitors' advertising. When writing the copy, be sure it is easy to read, direct, and positive. Remember an ad must catch the reader's attention quickly. www.trendwatching.com
* Measure the effectiveness of your advertising campaign using a direct response method; for example, how many coupons are redeemed or a survey with a questionnaire to determine effectiveness. www.gdsourcing.ca and http://dsp-psd.pwgsc.gc.ca/Collection-R/Statcan/63-224-XIB/63-224-XIB-e.html

exhibit 16–1
Steps in Implementing an Advertising Communications Strategy

exhibit 16–2
Communication
Objectives and
Stages in Consumers'
Decision-Making
Process at the
Supermarket

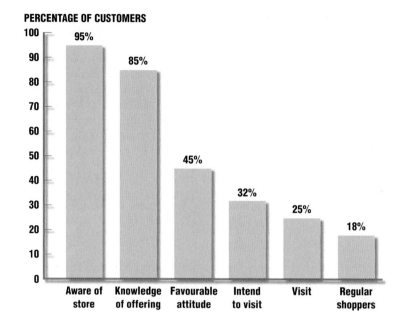

PERCENTAGE OF CUSTOMERS

In this hypothetical example, most people know about the store and its offering. The major problem confronting the supermarket is the big drop between knowledge and favourable attitude. Thus, the store should develop a communication program with the objective of increasing the percentage of customers with a favourable attitude toward it.

To effectively implement and evaluate a communication program, objectives must be clearly stated in quantitative terms. The target audience for the communication mix needs to be defined along with the degree of change expected and the time period over which the change will be realized.

For example, a communication objective for the grocery store's program might be to increase—from 45 percent to 55 percent within three months—the percentage of customers within a 10 kilometre radius of the store who have a favourable attitude toward the store. This objective is clear and measurable. It indicates the task the program should address. The people who implement the program know what they're supposed to accomplish.

The communication objectives and approaches used by vendors and retailers differ, and these differences can lead to conflicts. Some of these points of conflict are:

- *Long-term versus short-term goals*—Most communication done by vendors (manufacturers) is directed toward building a long-term image of their products. On the other hand, most retailer communication is typically used to announce promotions and special sales that generate short-term revenues.

- *Product versus location*—When vendors advertise their branded products, they don't care where the customer buys them. On the other hand, retailers don't care what brands customers buy as long as they buy them in their store.

- *Geographic coverage*—Since people tend to shop at stores near their homes or workplaces, most retailers use local newspapers, TV, and radio to target their communication. On the other hand, most vendors sell their brands nationally and thus tend to use national TV and magazines.

- *Breadth of merchandise offered*—Typically, vendors have a relatively small number of products to advertise. They can devote a lot of attention to developing consistent communication programs for each brand they make. Retailers offer a much broader set of products and often focus on building short-term sales.

Even though vendors and retailers have different goals, they frequently work together to develop mutually beneficial outcomes. An example is a coordinated program between Shoppers Drug Mart and Coppertone. The program offered a two-dollar-off coupon to the customer with the purchase of Coppertone sun care products. The addition of shelf talker signs on shelves creates awareness by providing information about the promotion and encouraging customer participation. The co-marketing promotion benefits both Shoppers Drug Mart and Coppertone by building sun care customers' loyalty.

Consumer Rights   In designing any consumer communication package, one of the objectives is to acknowledge and comply with consumer rights requirements. No retailer wants bad publicity as a result of consumer advocacy groups' negative press. Advances in consumerism have come in the form of federal and provincial legislation designed to protect the consumer and establish standards for manufacturers and retailers. The Consumers' Association of Canada (www.consumer.ca) seeks to uphold the following consumer rights:

- *The right to choice*—consumers must have a choice of products offered by a variety of manufacturers and retailers. In fact, competition usually provides the benefit of lower prices to the consumer. (*Competition Act*)

- *The right to be informed*—consumers must have access to complete information about a product before buying it. For example, consider the importance of fabric content and care labelling, food ingredients and nutritional content (which are of extreme importance to people with food allergies), and information that will describe the potential dangers of using a product. Detailed information can be an asset in the case of lawsuits. (*Packaging and Labelling Act, Textile Labelling Act, Weights and Measures Act*)

- *The right to safety*—the product must be safe for its intended use. This means that the product must be accompanied by instructions for its proper use and carry a guarantee of product quality and reliability as tested by the manufacturer. Federal agencies will take action to force businesses to recall defective products and issue public warnings. (*Food and Drug Act, Hazardous Products Act*)

- *The right to be heard*—someone will listen to consumers' complaints and take appropriate action to solve the problems. Many retailers have added customer service centres in the store to address customer concerns, and maintain a toll free telephone number and/or a Web site so customers can contact a service representative for immediate assistance.[9]

methods of communicating with customers

Exhibit 16–3 classifies communication methods used by retailers. The classification is based on whether the methods are impersonal or personal and paid or unpaid.

PAID IMPERSONAL COMMUNICATIONS

Advertising, sales promotions, store atmosphere, and Web sites are examples of paid impersonal communications.

exhibit 16–3
Communication
Methods

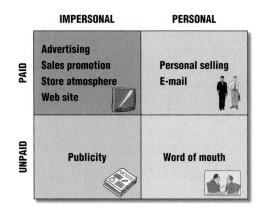

Advertising   **Advertising** is a form of paid communication to customers using impersonal mass media such as newspapers, TV, radio, direct mail, and the Internet.

Sales Promotions   **Sales promotions** offer extra value and incentives to customers to visit a store or purchase merchandise during a specific period of time. For example, a jewellery retailer has a "repair promotion" twice a year. It sends out mailers to its customers offering free jewellery checkups and special discounts on repairs. Once people are in the store they see things they haven't seen before or that complement something they have; they come in for a repair and walk out with a diamond bracelet. The most common sales promotion is a sale. Other sales promotions involve special events, in-store demonstrations, coupons, and contests.

Some retailers use in-store demonstrations and offer free samples of merchandise to build excitement in the store and stimulate purchases. In department stores, fashion shows and cooking demonstrations draw customers to the store and encourage impulse purchases.[10]

Contests are promotional games of chance. They differ from price-off sales in that only a few customers receive rewards and winners are determined by luck. For example, Tim Hortons "roll up the rim to win" promotion offers a reward to the lucky.

Coupons offer a discount on the price of specific items when they're purchased at a store. Coupons are the most common promotional tool used by grocery stores. Retailers distribute the coupons in newspaper ads and in direct-mail programs.

Manufacturers also distribute coupons for their products that can be used at retailers that stock the products. To attract customers, some grocery stores accept coupons distributed by competing retailers. Another technique is for a retailer to offer double or triple the value of coupons distributed by manufacturers.

Although sales promotions are effective at generating short-term interest among customers, they aren't very useful for building long-term loyalty. Customers who participate in the promotion might learn more about a store and return to it, but typically customers attracted by sales promotions are interested in the promoted merchandise, not the retailer. Unfortunately, when a specific promotion is effective for a retailer, competing retailers learn about it quickly and offer the same promotion, which prevents the innovating retailer from gaining any long-term advantage.

refact

The first coupons were handwritten notes given by Asa Chandler, an Atlanta druggist, offering customers a free glass of his new soft drink, Coca-Cola, in 1895.[11]

Wal-Mart, in addition to its well-advertised low prices, holds special promotions in its stores to increase store traffic.

Store Atmosphere   The retail store itself provides paid, impersonal communications to its customers. **Store atmosphere** is the combination of the store's physical characteristics, such as architecture, layout, signs and displays, colours, lighting, temperature, sounds, and smells, which together create an image in the customer's mind. The atmosphere communicates information about the store's service, its pricing, and the fashionability of its merchandise.[12]

Web Site   Finally, retailers are increasing their emphasis on communicating with customers through their Web sites. Retailers use their Web sites to build brand image; inform customers of store locations, special events, and the availability of merchandise in local stores; and sell merchandise and services.

PAID PERSONAL COMMUNICATIONS

Retail salespeople are the primary vehicle for providing paid personal communications to customers. **Personal selling** is a communication process in which salespeople assist customers in satisfying their needs through face-to-face exchanges of information.

E-mail is another paid personal communication vehicle that involves sending messages over the Internet. Retailers use e-mail to inform customers of new merchandise, confirm the receipt of an order, and indicate when an order has been shipped. Some retailers send the same message to all of their customers; but retailers can also send a personalized message to each of their customers by using the targeting capabilities of the Internet.

UNPAID IMPERSONAL COMMUNICATIONS

The primary method for generating unpaid impersonal communication is publicity. **Publicity** is communication through significant unpaid presentations about the retailer, usually a news story, in impersonal media. Examples of publicity are the newspaper and TV coverage of Home Depot's support of the Olympic Job Opportunities Program that provides part-time jobs for athletes while they train for the Olympics. Roots Olympic wear receives a lot of attention through press coverage of Olympic athletes wearing Roots designs.

Most communications are directed toward potential customers. Publicity, however, is often used to communicate with employees and investors. Favourable news stories generated by publicity can build employee morale and help improve employee performance. News about the retailer published in newspapers or broadcast over TV and radio can have a great impact on employees' positive impression of the company. Just like customers, employees place more credibility on information provided by news media than on information generated by the retailer. Similarly, shareholders, the financial community, vendors, and government agencies are influenced by publicity generated by retailers.

UNPAID PERSONAL COMMUNICATIONS

Finally, retailers communicate with their customers at no cost through **word of mouth,** communication between people about a retailer.[16] For example, retailers attempt to encourage favourable word-of-mouth communication by establishing teen boards composed of high school student leaders. Board members are encouraged to tell their friends about the retailer and its merchandise. On the other hand, unfavourable word-of-mouth communication can seriously affect store performance.

refact
Annually, consumer packaged goods manufacturers distribute over 225 billion coupons in North America, but less than 2.0 percent of the coupons are redeemed.[13]

refact
Over 400 billion e-mails are delivered annually in the United States, more than twice the number of mail pieces delivered by the Postal Service.[14]

refact
People who have an unsatisfactory experience with retail service on average tell nine other people about their experience.[15]

exhibit 16–4   Suggestions for Developing Local Ads

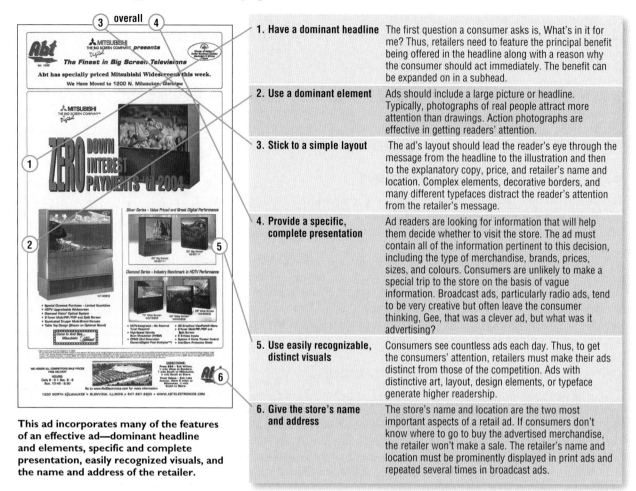

1. Have a dominant headline The first question a consumer asks is, What's in it for me? Thus, retailers need to feature the principal benefit being offered in the headline along with a reason why the consumer should act immediately. The benefit can be expanded on in a subhead.

2. Use a dominant element Ads should include a large picture or headline. Typically, photographs of real people attract more attention than drawings. Action photographs are effective in getting readers' attention.

3. Stick to a simple layout The ad's layout should lead the reader's eye through the message from the headline to the illustration and then to the explanatory copy, price, and retailer's name and location. Complex elements, decorative borders, and many different typefaces distract the reader's attention from the retailer's message.

4. Provide a specific, complete presentation Ad readers are looking for information that will help them decide whether to visit the store. The ad must contain all of the information pertinent to this decision, including the type of merchandise, brands, prices, sizes, and colours. Consumers are unlikely to make a special trip to the store on the basis of vague information. Broadcast ads, particularly radio ads, tend to be very creative but often leave the consumer thinking, Gee, that was a clever ad, but what was it advertising?

5. Use easily recognizable, distinct visuals Consumers see countless ads each day. Thus, to get the consumers' attention, retailers must make their ads distinct from those of the competition. Ads with distinctive art, layout, design elements, or typeface generate higher readership.

6. Give the store's name and address The store's name and location are the two most important aspects of a retail ad. If consumers don't know where to go to buy the advertised merchandise, the retailer won't make a sale. The retailer's name and location must be prominently displayed in print ads and repeated several times in broadcast ads.

This ad incorporates many of the features of an effective ad—dominant headline and elements, specific and complete presentation, easily recognized visuals, and the name and address of the retailer.

Retailers have very little control over the content or timing of publicity and word-of-mouth communications. Because unpaid communications are designed and delivered by people not employed by the retailer, they can communicate unfavourable as well as favourable information. For example, news coverage of a food poisoning incident at a restaurant would be devastating to retail sales.

DEVELOPING THE ADVERTISING MESSAGE

Most retail advertising messages have a short life and are designed to have an immediate impact. This immediacy calls for a copywriting style that grabs the reader's attention. Exhibit 16–4 outlines specific suggestions for developing local newspaper ads.[17]

Factors in Selecting Media   To convey their message with the most impact to the most consumers in the target market at the lowest cost, retailers need to evaluate media in terms of coverage, reach, cost, and impact of the advertising messages delivered through the medium. See Appendix 16A, "Choosing the Most Effective Media," Exhibit 16–11, on page 494.

Coverage   **Coverage** refers to the number of potential customers in the retailer's target market that could be exposed to an ad in a given medium. For example, assume that the size of the target market is 100 000 customers. The local newspaper is distributed to 60 percent of the customers in the target market, 90 percent of the potential customers have a TV set that picks up the local station's signal, and 5 percent of the potential customers drive past a billboard. Thus, the coverage for newspaper advertising would be 60 000; for TV advertising, 90 000; and for the specific billboard, 5000.

Reach   In contrast to coverage, **reach** is the actual number of customers in the target market exposed to an advertising medium. If, on any given day, 60 percent of the potential customers who receive the newspaper actually read it, then the newspaper's reach would be 36 000 (or 60 percent of 60 000). Retailers often run an ad several times, in which case they calculate the **cumulative reach** for the sequence of ads. For example, if 60 percent of the potential customers receiving a newspaper read it each day, 93.6 percent (or 1 minus the probability of not reading the paper three times in a row [$0.40 \times 0.40 \times 0.40$]) of the potential customers will read the newspaper at least one day over the three-day period in which the ad appears in the paper. Thus, the cumulative reach for running a newspaper ad for three days is 56 160 (or 93.6 percent $\times$ 60 000), which almost equals the newspaper's coverage.

When evaluating Internet advertising opportunities, the measure used to assess reach is the number of unique visitors—the number of different people who access the Web page on which the ad is located.

Cost   The **cost per thousand (CPM)** measure is often used to compare media. Typically, CPM is calculated by dividing an ad's cost by its reach. Another approach for determining CPM is to divide the cost of several ads in a campaign by their cumulative reach. If, for instance, in the previous example, one newspaper ad costs $500 and three ads cost $1300, the CPM using simple reach is $13.89, or $500/(36 000/1000). Using cumulative reach, the CPM is $23.15, or $1300/(56 160/1000). Note that the CPM might be higher using cumulative reach rather than simple reach, but the overall reach is also higher, and many potential customers will see the ad two or three times.

CPM is a good method for comparing similar-size ads in similar media, such as full-page ads in the *National Post* and the *Barrie Examiner*. But CPM can be misleading when comparing the cost-effectiveness of ads in different types of media, such as newspaper and TV. A TV ad may have a lower CPM than a newspaper ad, but the newspaper ad may be much more effective at achieving the ad's communication objectives, such as giving information about a sale.

Impact   **Impact** is an ad's effect on the audience. Due to their unique characteristics, different media are particularly effective at accomplishing different communication tasks. Exhibit 16–5 shows the effectiveness of various media for different communication tasks. TV is particularly effective at getting an audience's attention, demonstrating merchandise, changing attitudes, and announcing events. Magazines are particularly appropriate for emphasizing the quality and prestige of a store and its offering and for providing detailed information to support quality claims. Newspapers are useful for providing price information and announcing events. Web sites are particularly effective for demonstrating merchandise and providing information. Outdoor advertising is most effective at promoting a retailer's name and location.

exhibit 16–5   Effectiveness of Media by Communication Objective

Communication Task	Newspapers	Magazine	Direct Mail	TV	Radio	Web Sites	E-Mail	Outdoor
Getting attention	Low	Medium	Medium	Medium	Low	Low	High	Medium
Identifying name	Medium	High	Low	Low	Low	Low	Medium	High
Announcing events	High	Low	High	High	Medium	Low	High	Low
Demonstrating merchandise	Low	Medium	High	High	Low	Highest	Low	Low
Providing information	Low	High	High	Low	Low	Highest	Medium	Lowest
Changing attitudes	High	Medium	High	High	Medium	High	Low	Low
Building brand image	Low	Medium	High	High	Low	High	Low	Low

DETERMINING AD FREQUENCY AND TIMING

The frequency and timing of ads determine how often and when customers will see the retailer's message.

Frequency **Frequency** is how many times the potential customer is exposed to an ad. Frequency for Internet advertising is typically assessed by measuring the number of times a Web page with the ad is downloaded during a visit to the site.

The appropriate frequency depends on the ad's objective. Typically, several exposures to an ad are required to influence a customer's buying behaviour. Thus, campaigns directed toward changing purchase behaviour rather than creating awareness emphasize frequency over reach. Ads announcing a sale are often seen and remembered after one exposure. Thus, sale ad campaigns emphasize reach over frequency.

Timing Typically, an ad should appear on, or slightly precede, the days consumers are most likely to purchase merchandise. For example, if most consumers buy groceries Thursday through Sunday, then supermarkets should advertise on Thursday and Friday. Similarly, consumers often go shopping after they receive their paycheques at the middle and the end of the month. Thus, advertising should be concentrated at these times.

STRENGTHS AND WEAKNESSES OF COMMUNICATION METHODS

Communication methods differ in terms of control, flexibility, credibility, and cost.

Control Retailers have more control when using paid versus unpaid methods. When using advertising, sales promotions, Web sites, e-mail, and store atmosphere, retailers determine the message's content, and for advertising, e-mail, and sales promotions, they control the time of its delivery. Since each salesperson can deliver different messages, retailers have less control over personal selling than other paid communication methods. Retailers have very little control over the content or timing of publicity and word-of-mouth communications. Since unpaid communications are designed and delivered by people not employed by the retailer, they can communicate unfavourable as well as favourable information. For example, news coverage of food poisoning at a restaurant or discrimination at a hotel can result in significant declines in sales.

Flexibility Personal selling is the most flexible communication method, because salespeople can talk with each customer, discover their specific needs, and develop

Lowes's sponsorship for a **NASCAR** racing team generates publicity and builds brand awareness. However, this publicity could be unfavourable if its **NASCAR** team engaged in unsanctioned activities.

unique presentations for them. E-mails are also very flexible because they can be personalized to specific customer interests. Other communication methods are less flexible. For example, ads deliver the same message to all customers. However, Web sites can be tailored to individual visitors.

Credibility   Because publicity and word of mouth are communicated by independent sources, their information is usually more credible than the information in paid communication sources. For example, customers see their friends and family as highly credible sources of information. Customers tend to doubt claims made by salespeople and in ads since they know retailers are trying to promote their merchandise.

Cost   Publicity and word of mouth are classified as unpaid communication methods, but retailers do incur costs to stimulate them. For example, Staples spends US$5 million a year to name the Staples Center in Los Angeles, home of the NBA's Los Angeles Lakers. However, the local and national exposure offered by this sponsorship helped Staples successfully enter the California market and become a national office supply retailer.[20]

E-mail communications are very cost effective in targeting messages to specific customers.

Paid impersonal communications often are economical. For example, a full-page ad in the *Toronto Star* costs about two cents per person to deliver the message in the ad. In contrast, personal selling, because of its flexibility, is more effective than advertising; but it is more costly. A 10-minute presentation by a retail salesperson paid $12 per hour costs the retailer $2—100 times more than exposing a customer to a newspaper, radio, or TV ad. Although maintaining a Web site on a server is relatively inexpensive, it is costly to design, continuously update the site, and promote the site to attract visitors; however, e-mails can be sent to customers at low cost.

Due to the differences just described, communication methods differ in their effectiveness in performing communication tasks and their effectiveness in different stages of the customer's decision-making process. Typically, mass media advertising is most effective at building awareness. Web sites, direct mail, and newspaper advertising are effective for conveying information about a retailer's offerings and prices. Personal selling and sales promotion are most effective at persuading customers to purchase merchandise. Mass media and magazine advertising, publicity, Web sites, and store atmosphere are most cost-effective at building the retailer's brand image and encouraging repeat purchases and store loyalty.

SETTING THE COMMUNICATION BUDGET

The second step in developing a retail communication program is determining a budget (see Exhibit 16–1). The economically correct method for setting the communication budget is marginal analysis. Even though retailers usually don't have enough information to perform a complete marginal analysis, the method shows how managers should approach budget-setting programs.

The marginal analysis method for setting a communication budget is the approach retailers should use when making all of their resource allocation decisions, including the number of locations in a geographic area, the staffing of stores, and the floor and shelf space devoted to merchandise categories.

Marginal Analysis Method   **Marginal analysis** is based on the economic principle that firms should increase communication expenditures so long as each additional dollar spent generates more than a dollar of additional contribution. The marginal analysis method is used to determine how much should be spent on the retailer's communication program.[21]

In Exhibit 16–5, column 1 indicates 21 different communication expense levels. The retailer estimates store sales (column 2), gross margin (column 3), and other expenses (columns 4 and 5). Then the retailer calculates the contribution excluding expenses on communications (column 6) and the profit when the communication expenses are considered (column 7). To estimate the sales generated by different levels of communications, the retailer can rely on judgment and experience, or might analyze past data to determine the relationship between communication expenses and sales. Historical data also provide information about the gross margin and other expenses as a percentage of sales.

Notice that at low levels of communication expenses, an additional $5000 in communication expenses generates more than a $5000 incremental contribution. For example, increasing the communication expense from $15 000 to $20 000 increases contribution by $10 800 (or $48 400 – $37 600). When the communication expense reaches $65 000, further increases of $5000 generate less than $5000 in additional contributions. For example, increasing the budget from $65 000 to $70 000 generates only an additional $4050 in contribution ($125 350 – $121 300).

In this example, the retailer determines that the maximum profit would be generated with a communication expense budget of $65 000. But he/she notices that expense levels between $55 000 and $70 000 all result in about the same level of profit. Thus, the retailer makes a conservative decision and establishes a $55 000 budget for communication expenses.

In most cases, it's very hard to do a marginal analysis because often retail managers don't know the relationship between communication expenses and sales. Note that the numbers in Exhibit 16–6 are simply the retailer's estimates; they may not be accurate.

Sometimes retailers do experiments to get a better idea of the relationship between communication expenses and sales. Say, for example, a catalogue retailer selects several geographic areas in Canada with the same sales potential. The retailer then distributes 100 000 catalogues in the first area, 200 000 in the second area,

exhibit 16–6   Marginal Analysis for Setting a Retailer's Communication Budget

Level	Communication Expenses (1)	Sales (2)	Gross Margin Realized (3)	Rental Expense (4)	Personnel Expense (5)	Contribution Before Communication Expenses (6) = (3)–(4)–(5)	Profit After Communication Expenses (7) = (6) – (1)	
1	$0	$240 000	$96 000	$44 000	$52 200	$ (200)	$ (200)	
2	5 000	280 000	112 000	48 000	53 400	10 600	5 600	
3	10 000	330 000	132 000	53 000	54 900	24 100	14 100	
4	15 000	380 000	152 000	58 000	56 400	37 600	22 600	
5	20 000	420 000	168 000	62 000	57 600	48 400	28 400	
6	25 000	460 000	184 000	66 000	58 800	59 200	34 200	
7	30 000	500 000	200 000	70 000	60 000	70 000	40 000	Last year
8	35 000	540 000	216 000	74 000	61 200	80 800	45 800	
9	40 000	570 000	228 000	77 000	62 100	88 900	48 900	
10	45 000	600 000	240 000	80 000	63 000	97 000	52 000	
11	50 000	625 000	250 000	82 500	63 750	103 750	53 750	
12	55 000	650 000	260 000	85 000	64 500	110 500	55 500	
13	60 000	670 000	268 000	87 000	65 100	115 900	55 900	
14	65 000	690 000	276 000	89 000	65 700	121 300	56 300	Best profit
15	70 000	705 000	282 000	90 500	66 150	125 350	55 350	
16	75 000	715 000	286 000	91 500	66 450	128 050	53 050	
17	80 000	725 000	290 000	92 500	66 750	130 750	50 750	
18	85 000	735 000	294 000	93 500	67 050	133 450	48 450	
19	90 000	745 000	298 000	94 500	67 350	136 150	46 150	
20	95 000	750 000	300 000	95 000	67 500	137 500	42 500	
21	100 000	750 000	300 000	95 000	67 500	137 500	37 500	

and 300 000 in the third area. Using the sales and costs for each distribution level, it could go through an analysis like the one in Exhibit 16–6 to determine the most profitable distribution level.

Other methods that retailers use to set communication budgets are the objective-and-task method and rules of thumb, such as the affordable, percentage-of-sales, and competitive parity methods. These methods are less sophisticated than marginal analysis but easier to use.

Objective-and-Task Method   The **objective-and-task method** determines the budget required to undertake specific tasks for accomplishing communication objectives. To use this method, the retailer first establishes a set of communication objectives. Then the necessary tasks and their costs are determined. The sum total of all costs incurred to undertake the tasks is the communication budget.

Exhibit 16–7 illustrates how the retailer uses the objective-and-task method to complement the marginal analysis. The retailer establishes three objectives:

- to increase the awareness of the store
- to create a greater preference for his/her store among customers in the target market
- to promote the sale of merchandise remaining at the end of each season

exhibit 16–7
Illustration of
Objective-and-Task
Method for Setting a
Communication Budget

Objective: Increase from 25 percent to 50 percent over the next 12 months the percentage of target market living or working within 10 kilometres of our store who know of our store's location and product.	
Task: 480, 30–second radio spots during peak commuting hours (7:00 to 8:00 A.M. and 5:00 to 6:00 P.M.).	$12 300
Task: Sign with store name near entrance to mall.	4 500
Task: Display ad in the Yellow Pages.	500
Objective: Increase from 5 percent to 15 percent in 12 months the percentage of target market who indicate that our store is their preferred store to shop in.	
Task: Develop TV campaign to improve image and run 50, 30–second commercials.	$24 000
Task: Hold four information seminars followed by a wine-and-cheese social.	8 000
Objective: Selling merchandise remaining at end of season.	
Task: Special event.	$6 000
Total budget	$55 300

The total communication budget the retailer requires to achieve these objectives is $55 300.

Besides defining the objectives and tasks, the retailer must also recheck the financial implications of the communication mix by projecting the income statement for next year using the communication budget (see Exhibit 16–8). This income statement includes an increase of $25 300 in communication expenses over last year. Upon examination, the retailer feels that this increase in the communication budget will boost annual sales from $500 000 to $650 000. Based on the retailer's projections, the increase in communication expenses will raise store profits. The results of the marginal analysis and the objective-and-task methods suggest a communication budget between $55 000 and $65 000.

Rule-of-Thumb Methods   In the previous two methods, the communication budget is set by estimating communication activities' effects on the firm's future sales or communication objectives. The **rule-of-thumb methods** discussed in this section use an alternative logic.

Affordable Method   When using the **affordable budgeting method**, retailers first forecast their sales and expenses excluding communication expenses during the budgeting period. The difference between the forecast sales and expenses plus desired profit is then budgeted for the communication mix expenses. In other words, the affordable method sets the communication budget by determining what money is available after operating costs and profits are budgeted.

The major problem with the affordable method is that it assumes that the communication expenses don't stimulate sales and profit. Communication expenses are just a cost of business, like the cost of merchandise. When retailers use the affordable

exhibit 16–8
Financial Implications
of Increasing the
Communication Budget

	Last Year	Next Year
Sales	$500 000	$650 000
Gross margin (realized)	200 000	260 000
Rental, maintenance, etc.	70 000	85 000
Personnel	60 000	64 500
Communications	30 000	55 300
Profit	$ 40 000	$ 55 200

method, they typically cut "unnecessary" communication expenses if sales fall below the forecast rather than increase communication expenses to increase sales.

Percentage-of-Sales Method   The **percentage-of-sales method** sets the communication budget as a fixed percentage of forecast sales. Retailers use this method to determine the communication budget by forecasting sales during the budget period and using a predetermined percentage to set the budget. The percentage may be the retailer's historical percentage or the average percentage used by similar retailers.

The problem with the percentage-of-sales method is that it assumes the same percentage used in the past, or by competitors, is still appropriate for the retailer. Consider a retailer that hasn't opened new stores in the past but plans to open many new stores in the current year. It must create customer awareness for these new stores, so the communication budget should be much larger in the current year than in the past.

Using the same percentage as competitors also may be inappropriate. For example, a retailer might have better locations than its competitors. Due to these locations, customers may already have a high awareness of the retailer's stores. Thus, the retailer may not need to spend as much on communications as competitors with poorer locations spend.

One advantage of both the percentage-of-sales method and the affordable method for determining a communication budget is that the retailer won't spend beyond its means. Since the level of spending is determined by sales, the budget will only go up when sales go up and the retailer generates more sales to pay for the additional communication expenses. When times are good, these methods work well because they allow the retailer to communicate more aggressively with customers. But when sales fall, communication expenses are cut, which may accelerate the sales decline.

Competitive Parity Method   Under the **competitive parity method**, the communication budget is set so that the retailer's share of communication expenses equals its share of the market. For example, consider a sporting goods store in a small town. To use the competitive parity method, the owner–manager would first estimate the total amount spent on communications by all of the sporting goods retailers in town. Then the owner–manager would estimate his or her store's market share for sporting goods and multiply that market share percentage by the sporting goods stores' total advertising expenses to set its budget. Assume that the owner–manager's estimate of advertising for sporting goods by all stores was $5000 and the estimate of his or her store's market share was 45 percent. On the basis of these estimates, the owner–manager would set the store's communication budget at $2250 to maintain competitive parity.

Like the other rule-of-thumb methods, the competitive parity method doesn't allow retailers to exploit the unique opportunities or problems they confront in a market. If all competitors used this method to set communication budgets, their market shares would stay about the same over time (assuming that the retailers developed equally effective campaigns).

ALLOCATION OF THE PROMOTIONAL BUDGET

After determining the size of the communication budget, the third step in the communication planning process is allocating the budget (see Exhibit 16–1). In this step, the retailer decides how much of its budget to allocate to specific communication elements, merchandise categories, geographic regions, or long- and short-term objectives. For example, a department store must decide how much of its communication budget to spend in each area where it has stores. Sears decides how much to allocate to appliances, hardware, and apparel. The sporting goods

refact

Supermarkets spend 1.1 percent of annual sales revenue on advertising, department store retailers spend 3.7 percent of sales, and women's apparel specialty retailers spend 4.7 percent of sales.[22]

store owner–manager must decide how much of the store's $2250 communication budget to spend on promoting the store's image versus generating sales during the year and how much to spend on advertising and special promotions.

Research indicates that allocation decisions are more important than the decision on the amount spent on communications.[23] In other words, retailers often can realize the same objectives by reducing the size of the communication budget but allocating the budget more effectively.

An easy way to make such allocation decisions is just to spend about the same in each geographic region or for each merchandise category. But this allocation rule probably won't maximize profits because it ignores the possibility that communication programs might be more effective for some merchandise categories or for some regions than for others. Another approach is to use rules of thumb such as basing allocations on the sales level or contribution for the merchandise category.

Allocation decisions, like budget-setting decisions, should use the principles of marginal analysis. The retailer should allocate the budget to areas that will yield the greatest return. This approach for allocating a budget is sometimes referred to as the **high-assay principle.** Consider a miner who can spend his time digging on two claims. The value of the gold on one claim is assayed at $20 000 per tonne, whereas the assay value on the other claim is $10 000 per tonne. Should the miner spend two-thirds of his time at the first mine and one-third of his time at the other mine? Of course not! The miner should spend all of his time mining the first claim until the assay value of the ore mined drops to $10 000 a tonne, at which time he can divide his time equally between the claims.

Similarly, a retailer may find that its customers have a high awareness and very favourable attitude toward its women's clothing but may not know much about the store's men's clothing. In this situation, a dollar spent on advertising men's clothing might generate more sales than a dollar spent on women's clothing even though the sales of women's clothing are greater than the sales of men's clothing.

PLANNING, IMPLEMENTING, AND EVALUATING COMMUNICATION PROGRAMS—THREE ILLUSTRATIONS

The final stage in developing a retail communication program is implementation and evaluation (see Exhibit 16–1). In this final section of the chapter, we illustrate the planning and evaluation process for three communication programs—an advertising campaign by a small specialty retailer, a sales promotion opportunity confronting a supermarket chain, and a communication program emphasizing direct marketing undertaken by a large retail chain.

Advertising Campaign   South Gate West is one of several specialty import home furnishing stores competing for upscale shoppers. The store has the appearance of both a fine antique store and a traditional home furnishing shop, but most of its merchandise is new Asian imports.[24]

The owner realized that his communication budget was considerably less than the budget of the local Pier 1 store. (Pier 1 is a large international import home furnishings chain.) He decided to concentrate his limited budget on a specific segment and use highly distinctive copy and art in his advertising. His target market was experienced, sophisticated consumers of housewares and home decorative items. His experience indicated the importance of personal selling for more seasoned shoppers because they make large purchases and seek considerable information before making a decision. Thus, the retailer spent part of his communication budget on training his sales associates.

The advertising program that the retailer developed emphasized his store's distinctive image. He used the newspaper as his major vehicle. Competitive ads contained line drawings of furniture with prices. His ads emphasized the imagery associated with Asian furniture by featuring off-the-beaten-path scenes of Asian countries with unusual art objects. This theme was also reflected in the store's atmosphere.

To evaluate his communication program, the retailer needed to compare the results of his program with the objectives he developed during the first part of the planning process. To measure his campaign's effectiveness, he conducted an inexpensive tracking study. Telephone interviews were performed periodically with a representative sample of furniture customers in his store's trading area. Communication objectives were assessed using the following questions:

Communication Objective	Question
Awareness	What stores sell East Asian furniture?
Knowledge	Which stores would you rate outstanding on the following characteristics?
Attitude	On your next shopping trip for East Asian furniture, which store would you visit first?
Visit	Which of the following stores have you been to?

Here are the survey results for one year:

	Before Campaign	Six Months After	One Year After
Awareness (percentage mentioning store)	38%	46%	52%
Knowledge (percentage giving outstanding rating for sales assistance)	9	17	24
Attitude (percentage first choice)	13	15	19
Visit (percentage visited store)	8	15	19

The results show a steady increase in awareness, knowledge of the store, and choice of the store as a primary source of East Asian furniture. This research provides evidence that the advertising was conveying the intended message to the target audience.

Sales Promotion Opportunity   Many sales promotion opportunities undertaken by retailers are initiated by vendors. For example, Colgate-Palmolive might offer the following special promotion to Loblaws: During a one-week period, Loblaws can order Fab laundry detergent in the 2-kg size at 15 cents below the standard wholesale price. However, if Loblaws elects to buy Fab at the discounted price, the grocery chain must feature the 2-kg container of Fab in its Thursday newspaper ad at $1.59 (20 cents off the typical retail price). In addition, Loblaws must have an end-aisle display of Fab.

Before Loblaws decides whether to accept such a trade promotion and then promote Fab to its customers, it needs to assess the promotion's impact on its profitability. Such a promotion may be effective for the vendor but not for the retailer.

To evaluate a trade promotion, the retailer considers:

- the realized margin from the promotion
- the cost of the additional inventory carried due to buying more than the normal amount
- the potential increase in sales from the promoted merchandise

This end-aisle display of Fab is part of a special Colgate-Palmolive promotion in which the supermarket chain participated.

- the potential loss suffered when customers switch to the promoted merchandise from more profitable private-label brands

- the additional sales made to customers attracted to the store by the promotion.[25]

When Fab's price is reduced to $1.59, Loblaws will sell more Fab than it normally would. But Loblaws' margin on the Fab will be less because the required retail discount of 20 cents isn't offset by the wholesale discount of 15 cents. In addition, Loblaws might suffer losses because the promotion encourages customers to buy Fab, which has a lower margin than Loblaws' private-label detergent that customers might have bought. In fact, customers may stockpile Fab, buying several boxes, which will reduce sales of Loblaws' private-label detergent for some time after the special promotion ends. On the other hand, the promotion may attract customers who don't normally shop at Loblaws but who will visit to buy Fab at the discounted price. These customers might buy additional merchandise, providing a sales gain to the store that it wouldn't have realized if it hadn't promoted Fab.

Special Promotion Using a CRM/Campaign Management Tool   A national retailer with 580 store locations used its CRM/campaign management system to plan, design, evaluate, and implement a special Canada Day promotion.[26] The diagram of the system is shown in Exhibit 16–9. The retailer has a customer database with purchase information complemented with additional customer information acquired through external sources.

After an initial planning meeting, the retailer decided to use both direct-mail and e-mail communication channels with supporting in-store promotions and existing advertising. Customers would need to bring in a coupon to take advantage of the special promotion. The goal of the campaign was to generate a 10 percent increase in sales during the Canada Day period.

Using the campaign management tool in the system, the retailer examined a number of what-if scenarios enabling the team to chart out all of the tasks, costs, and related deadlines, to determine projected ROI. Initially, they wanted to target customers who had visited the stores and made a purchase within the last nine months. During the target market segmentation evaluation process, they determined that the counts were too low and increased the target criterion to customer purchases within the last 12 months. Using this criterion, the communication program would be directed to 2.6 million customers. A review of past holiday promotion programs suggested a response rate of 2.5 percent.

Based on the 2.5 percent response rate for 2.6 million customers, the number of people projected to visit the stores was 65 000. The special promotion was a $49 item, but the average sale once people were in the store was $99. On the basis of this information, the Canada Day event special promotion was targeted to generate gross sales between $3.1 million and $6.4 million.

The cost for the direct-mail piece was $0.65/piece and the e-mail piece was $0.03/e-mail. To mail and e-mail 2.6 million customers, the cost was $1 768 000. In

exhibit 16–9   CRM/Campaign Management System

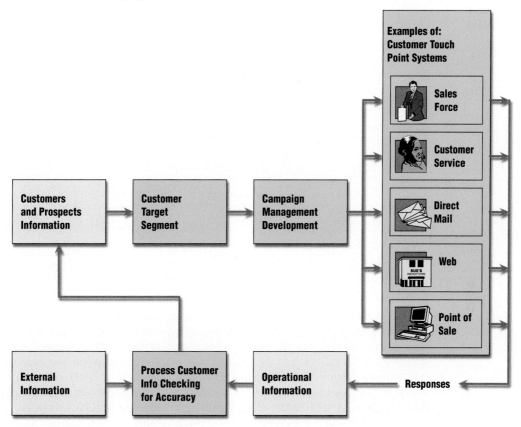

determining the product costs on the special promotion item, a 75 percent markup was used. The campaign profitability margin was projected to be between $600 000 and $3.1 million. The financial analysis developed by the planning tool is shown in Exhibit 16–10.

Once the what-if analysis was completed and the campaign plan was built with all of the details and responsibilities of each department, it was set into action. The action plan includes all the required steps in the campaign process, along with the costs, responsibilities, and deadlines on the marketing production schedule. By putting the plan into production, all of the tasks are sent to the people responsible for completing them, so that deadlines and costs are tracked. Each department would receive a series of tasks specific to that department's deliverables:

- The Creative Department was assigned the responsibility of designing the direct-mail piece with the coupon. It also designed the e-mail piece with a print coupon. Once the design process was completed and approved, the artwork was sent to the Print Vendor for printing and the Marketing Department for e-mail distribution.

- The Database Marketing Department was responsible for sending the list of customers in the target market analysis (the customers who had visited a store and made a purchase in the last 12 months) to the Mail Vendor. Each record in the customer database had a unique identifier so that the results of the campaign would be properly tracked and analyzed.

exhibit 16–10

Financial Analysis of Special Canada Day Promotion

CAMPAIGN PLANNING FINANCIALS			
Target Market Count		**Campaign Costs**	
Records in 12-month period	2.6 million	Direct mail ($0.65/piece)	$1 690 000
2.5% response rate		E-mail ($0.03/e-mail)	$ 78 000
Project response count	65 000	Total cost	$1 768 000
Gross Revenue		**Net Revenue (less product cost of 25%)**	
Special promotion $49/each	$3 185 000	$2 388 750	
Average sale $99/each	$6 435 000	$4 826 250	
Campaign Profitability			
	Special promotion	$620 750	
	Average sale	$3 058 250	

- The Store Promotions Department had to make sure that the in-store promotional materials were consistent with the message in the campaign. Media Services also had to verify consistency in all media with the campaign message.

During the entire campaign process, a management view of the financial information and campaign deliverables/deadline information was available. As the stores reported their customer sales, management's reports were automatically generated, and the response ROI was analyzed to determine if the marketing campaign was successful. The information from all of the customer touch points was collected, processed, and added to the customer database. The successful campaign was then templated for future use to save time in the planning phase for the next holiday campaign. The matrix solution allowed management to optimize resources and manage deadlines and deliverables, thus increasing productivity, efficiency, and ROI.

SUMMARY

In today's economy, where good news is often quickly matched by an equal portion of bad news, effectively competing and winning customers every day is vital to a retailer's success. The best retailers maintain their loyal customers and win new ones, pursuing larger market share by communicating through education, building brand awareness, and developing experiential involvement.

The communication program can be designed to achieve a variety of objectives for the retailer. Objectives include building a brand image of the retailer in the customer's mind, increasing sales and store traffic, providing information about the retailer's location and offering, and announcing special activities.

Retailers communicate with customers through advertising, sales promotions, Web sites, store atmo-

sphere, publicity, personal selling, e-mail, and word of mouth. These elements in the communication mix must be coordinated so customers will have a clear, distinct image of the retailer and won't be confused by conflicting information. Also, consumer rights requirements must be acknowledged and complied with.

Many retailers use rules of thumb to determine the size of the promotion budget. Marginal analysis (the most appropriate method for determining how much must be spent to accomplish the retailer's objectives) should be used to determine whether the level of spending maximizes the profits that could be generated by the communications mix.

The largest portion of a retailer's communication budget is typically spent on advertising and sales promotions. A wide array of media can be used for advertising. Each medium has its pros and cons. Newspaper advertising is effective for announcing sales, whereas TV ads are useful for developing an image. Sales promotions are typically used to achieve short-term objectives, such as increasing store traffic over a weekend. Most sales promotions are supported in part by promotions offered to the retailer by its vendors. Publicity and word of mouth are typically low-cost communications, but they are very difficult for retailers to control.

KEY TERMS

advertising, *476*
affordable budgeting method, *484*
aided recall, *470*
attitude branding, *468*
brand, *468*
brand associations, *470*
brand awareness, *470*
brand energy, *468*
brand equity, *469*
brand image, *471*
communication objectives, *473*
competitive parity method, *485*
contests, *476*
cooperative (co-op) advertising, *493*

cost per thousand (CPM), *479*
coupons, *476*
coverage, *479*
cumulative reach, *479*
e-mail, *477*
freestanding insert (FSI), *494*
frequency, *480*
high-assay principle, *486*
impact, *479*
integrated marketing communication program, *471*
magalogue, *472*
marginal analysis, *482*
objective-and-task method, *483*
percentage-of-sales method, *485*

personal selling, *477*
positioning statement, *473*
preprint, *494*
private-label brands, *468*
publicity, *477*
reach, *479*
rule-of-thumb methods, *484*
sales promotion, *476*
shopping guides, *496*
spot, *495*
store atmosphere, *477*
top-of-mind awareness, *470*
word of mouth, *477*

Get Out & Do It!

1. **INTERNET EXERCISE** Go to www.c3dsp.westjet.com and explain the success of West Jet ads in communicating to the customer.

2. **INTERNET EXERCISE** Go to www.campaignforrealbeauty.ca and describe how Dove has connected to the female consumer through emotional messages with their Real Beauty Campaign.

3. **INTERNET EXERCISE** Review the trends at www.trendwatching.com for a future focus on advertising and consumer directions.

4. **GO SHOPPING** Go to a retail store and make a list of all of the specific elements and information in the store that communicate the store's image and the merchandise it is offering to customers.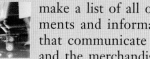

5. **GO SHOPPING** Look though the free-standing inserts in your Saturday newspaper. Evaluate the general use of FSIs, and select the FSIs that you think are most effective. Why are these FSIs more effective than the other ones?

6. **INTERNET EXERCISE** Visit the Consumers' Association of Canada at www.consumer.ca. Identify the nine consumer rights profiled on the site, and give a retail example of each.

7. INTERNET EXERCISE You can find more information about the use of radio as an advertising medium at the Radio Advertising Bureau site, www. rab.com. Based on this information, what types of retail messages can be delivered more effectively by radio compared to other media?

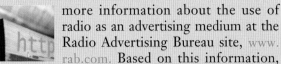

8. INTERNET EXERCISE Read the BusinessWeek online article entitled, "How In-store TVs Play to Shoppers," available at www. businessweek.com/bwdaily/dnflash/ nov2004/nf20041122_9652.htm. How are retailers using TV as an in-store communication tool? What are the key advantages of implementing in-store TV in the communications mix?

DISCUSSION QUESTIONS AND PROBLEMS

1. How do brands benefit consumers? Retailers?

2. How can advertising, personal selling, and promotion complement each other in an integrated marketing communications program?

3. As a means of communicating with customers, how does advertising differ from publicity?

4. Why is the newspaper the favourite medium used by retailers for advertising? What are the advantages and disadvantages of newspaper advertising? Why is the use of newspaper decreasing and use of direct mail increasing?

5. For which of the following growth opportunities do you think the retailer should use its brand name when pursuing the opportunity? Why?

   (a) McDonald's starts a new chain of restaurants to sell seafood in a sit-down environment competing with Red Lobster.

   (b) Sears starts a chain of stand-alone stores that sell just home appliances.

   (c) Blockbuster starts a chain of stores selling consumer electronics.

6. What factors should be considered in dividing up the budget among a store's different merchandise areas? Which of the following should receive the highest advertising budget: fashionable women's clothing, men's underwear, women's hosiery, or kitchen appliances? Why?

7. Outline some elements in a communcation program to achieve the following objectives:

   (a) Increase store loyalty by 20 percent.

   (b) Build awareness of the store by 10 percent.

   (c) Develop an image as a low-price retailer.

   How would you determine whether the communication program met the objective?

8. Some retailers direct their advertising efforts toward reaching as wide an audience as possible. Others try to expose the audience to an advertisement as many times as possible. When should a retailer concentrate on reach? When should a retailer concentrate on frequency?

9. A retailer plans to open a new store near a university. It will specialize in collegiate merchandise such as T-shirts, sweatshirts, and accessories. Develop an integrated communication program for the retailer. What specific advertising media should the new store use to capture the university market?

10. Cooperative (co-op) advertising is a good way for a retailer to extend an ad budget. Why is it not always in a retailer's best interests to rely extensively on co-op advertising?

APPENDIX 16A | Implementing Retail Advertising Programs

Implementing an ad program involves developing the message, choosing the specific media to convey the message, and determining the frequency and timing of the message. Let's look at each of these decisions.

Assistance in Advertising

Retailers get assistance in developing advertising campaigns from manufacturers through their co-op programs, advertising agencies, and media companies.

Co-op Programs **Cooperative (co-op) advertising** is a program undertaken by a manufacturer. The manufacturer pays for part of the retailer's advertising. But the manufacturer dictates some conditions for the advertising. For example, Sony may have a co-op program that pays for half of Best Buy's ads for Sony digital TVs.

Co-op advertising enables a retailer to increase its advertising budget. In the previous example, Best Buy only pays for half of its expenses (for ads including Sony digital TVs). In addition to lowering costs, co-op advertising enables a small retailer to associate its name with well-known national brands and use attractive artwork created by the national brand.

Co-op advertising programs are often used to support a manufacturer's effort to discourage retailers from discounting the manufacturer's products. For example, Estée Lauder might give its department store retailers 7 percent of sales for co-op advertising only if the retailers agree not to advertise a price below its suggested retail price.

Co-op advertising has other drawbacks. First, manufacturers want the ads to feature their products, whereas retailers are more interested in featuring their store's name, location, and assortment of merchandise and services offered. This conflict in goals can reduce the effectiveness of co-op advertising from the

> **refact**
>
> Co-op advertising accounts for approximately 50 percent of all department store and 75 percent of all grocery store advertising.[27]

retailer's perspective. In addition, ads developed by the vendor often are used by several competing retailers and may list the names and locations of all retailers offering their brands. Thus, co-op ads tend to blur any distinctions between retailers. Finally, restrictions the manufacturer places on the ads may further reduce their effectiveness for the retailer. For example, the manufacturer may restrict advertising to a period of time when the manufacturer's sales are depressed, but the retailer might not normally be advertising during this time frame.

In addition to co-op programs, retailers and manufacturers can work together as partners on a co-marketing program.

Agencies Many large retailers have a department that creates advertising for sales and special events. Advertising agencies are often used by large retailers to develop ads for store image campaigns. Many small retailers use local agencies to plan and create their advertising. These local agencies are often more skilled in planning and executing advertising than the retailer's employees are. Agencies also work on other aspects of the communication programs, such as contests, direct mail, and special promotions.

Media Companies Besides selling newspaper space and broadcast time, the advertising media offer services to local retailers ranging from planning an ad program to actually designing the ads. Media companies also do market research on their audiences and can provide information about shopping patterns in the local area.

CHOOSING THE MOST EFFECTIVE MEDIA

After developing the message, the next step is deciding what medium to use to communicate the message. The media used for retail advertising are newspapers, magazines, direct mail, radio, TV, outdoor billboards, the Internet, shopping guides, and the Yellow Pages. Exhibit 16–11 summarizes their characteristics.

exhibit 16–11
Media Capability

Media	Targeting	Timeliness	Information Presentation Capacity	Life	Cost
Newspapers	Good	Good	Modest	Short	Modest
Magazines	Modest	Poor	Modest	Modest	High
Direct mail	Excellent	Modest	High	Short	Modest
Television	Modest	Modest	Low	Short	Modest
Radio	Modest	Good	Low	Short	Low
Internet					
Banner	Excellent	Excellent	Low	Modest	High
Web site	Excellent	Excellent	High	Long	Modest
E-mail	Excellent	Excellent	Modest	Short	Low
Outdoor billboards	Modest	Poor	Very low	Long	Modest
Shopping guides	Modest	Modest	Low	Modest	Low
Yellow Pages	Modest	Poor	Low	Long	Low

Newspapers

Retailing and newspaper advertising grew up together over the past century. But the growth in retail newspaper advertising has slowed recently as retailers have begun using other media. Still, 16 of the nation's 25 largest newspaper advertisers are retailers.[28]

In addition to displaying ads with their editorial content, newspapers distribute freestanding inserts. A **freestanding insert (FSI)**, also called a **preprint**, is an ad printed at the retailer's expense and distributed as an insert in the newspaper.

Since newspapers are distributed in a well-defined local market area, they're effective at targeting retail advertising. Often the local market covered by a newspaper is similar to the market served by the retailer. Newspapers offer opportunities for small retailers to target their advertising through local area publications such as the *Barrie Advance*, in Barrie, Ontario.

Newspapers also offer quick response. There's only a short time between the deadline for receiving the ad and the time that the ad will appear. Thus, newspapers are useful for delivering messages on short notice.

Newspapers, like all print media, effectively convey a lot of detailed information. Readers can go through an ad at their own pace and refer back to part of the ad when they want to. In addition, consumers can save the ad and take it to the store with them. This makes newspaper ads effective at conveying information about the prices of sale items. But newspaper ads aren't effective for showing merchandise, particularly when it's important to illustrate colours, because of the poor reproduction quality.

Although newspapers are improving their printing facilities to provide better reproduction and colour in ads, retailers continue to rely on preprints to get good reproduction quality. Sears uses FSIs extensively, distributing them to newspaper readers weekly. However, FSIs are so popular that the insert from one retailer can be lost among the large number of inserts in the newspaper.

The life of a newspaper ad is short because the newspaper is usually discarded after it's read. In contrast, magazine advertising has a longer life since consumers tend to save magazines and read them several times during a week or month.

Finally, the cost of developing newspaper ads is very low. Newspaper ads can be developed by less experienced people and don't require expensive colour photography or typesetting. However, the cost of delivering the message may be high if the newspaper's circulation is broader than the retailer's target market, thus requiring the retailer to pay for exposures that won't generate sales.

Magazines

Retail magazine advertising is mostly done by national retailers such as Holt Renfrew and The

Gap. But magazine advertising is increasing with the growth of local magazines and regional editions of national magazines. Retailers tend to use this medium for image advertising because the reproduction quality is high.[30] Due to the lead time—the time between submitting the ad and publication—a major disadvantage is that the timing of a magazine ad is difficult to coordinate with special events and sales.

Direct Mail

Retailers frequently use data collected at POS terminals to target their advertising and sales promotions to specific customers using direct mail. For example, Holt Renfrew keeps a database of all purchases made by its credit card customers. With information on each customer's purchases, Holt Renfrew can target direct mail on a new perfume to customers with a history of purchasing such merchandise.

Retailers also can purchase a wide variety of lists for targeting consumers with specific demographics, interests, and lifestyles. For example, a home furnishings store could buy a list of subscribers to *Architectural Digest* in its trading area and then mail information about home furnishings to those upscale consumers. Finally, many retailers encourage their salespeople to maintain a preferred customer list and use it to mail personalized invitations and notes. Although direct mail can be very effective due to the ability to personalize the message, it's also costly. Many consumers ignore direct-mail advertising and treat it as junk mail.

Television

TV commercials tend to be expensive, but can be placed on a national network or a local station. A local television commercial is called a **spot**. Retailers typically use TV for image advertising.[31] They take advantage of the high reproduction quality and the opportunity to communicate through both visual images and sound. TV ads can also demonstrate product usage. For example, Canadian Tire's TV ad program is built around the theme of family activity, building or painting. The ads summarize the advantages of shopping at Canadian Tire on many levels: convenient location, available parking, broad assortment, and fast, easy checkout. Lifestyle ads connect Canadian Tire as a vital link to an active, healthy, reduced-stress lifestyle.

Besides high production costs, broadcast time for national TV advertising is expensive. Spots have relatively small audiences, but they may be economical for local retailers. To offset the high production costs, many vendors provide modular commercials, in which the retailer can insert its name or a "tag" after information about the vendor's merchandise.

Radio

Many retailers use radio advertising because messages can be targeted to a specific segment of the market.[33] Some radio stations' audiences are highly loyal to their announcers. When these announcers promote a retailer, listeners are impressed. The cost of developing and broadcasting radio commercials is quite low.

One disadvantage of radio advertising is that listeners generally treat the radio broadcast as background, which limits the attention they give the message. As with all broadcast media, consumers must get the information from a radio commercial when it's broadcast. They can't refer back to the ad for information they didn't hear or remember.

Internet

Three uses of the Internet by retailers to communicate with customers are banner ads and affiliate programs to generate awareness, Web sites to provide information about merchandise and special events, and e-mails to target messages.[35] Banner ads and affiliate programs are very effective for targeting communication, but they are not cost-effective for building awareness. Using information from a visitor's navigation and purchase behaviour and IP address, banner ads can be targeted to specific individuals. For example, Sportsline.com visitors who look at the box scores for Toronto Blue Jays baseball games are shown ads for Jays logo apparel and hats. DoubleClick, an Internet ad agency, downloads different banner ads from its server to host Web sites based on information it has on the specific visitor. However, Internet advertising is not cost-effective for building awareness because the large number of Web sites reduces the number of customers visiting a site and seeing a particular ad.

Although the Internet is not effective for building awareness, it is an excellent vehicle for conveying information to customers. In addition to selling merchandise for a Web site, retailers can provide a wide array of information ranging from the store locations to the availability and pricing of merchandise in specific stores. The interactivity of the Internet gives customers the opportunity to quickly sift through a vast amount of information. For example, visitors to the *Blacks Camera* Web site can find detailed information on specific digital camera models and generate a table comparing a select group of cameras on features of importance to the customer.

Finally, retailers can use the Internet to send e-mails to customers informing them of special events and new merchandise.

Outdoor Billboards

Billboards and other forms of outdoor advertising are effective vehicles for creating awareness and providing a very limited amount of information to a narrow audience. Thus, outdoor advertising has limited usefulness in providing information about sales. Outdoor advertising is typically used to remind customers about the retailer or to inform people in cars of nearby retail outlets.[36] La Senza used sexy images on billboards in the Toronto area to promote Christmas sales of lingerie.

Shopping Guides

Shopping guides are free papers delivered to all residents in a specific area. This medium is particularly useful for retailers that want to saturate a specific trading area. Shopping guides are cost-effective and assure the local retailer of 100 percent coverage in a specific area. In contrast, subscription newspapers typically offer only 30 to 50 percent coverage. An extension of the shopping guide concept is the coupon book or magazine. These media contain coupons offered by retailers for discounts. Shopping guides and coupon books make no pretense about providing news to consumers. They're simply delivery vehicles for ads and coupons.

Yellow Pages

The Yellow Pages are useful to retailers because they have a long life. The Yellow Pages are used as a reference by consumers who are interested in contacting a retailer and possibly making a purchase or arranging a needed service, such as roof repair or garden work.

SECTION V

cases

Case	Title	Chapter
1	eBay	3
2	Toys "R" Us Online	3
3	Sephora	4
4	American Eagle and Abercrombie & Fitch	4
5	Starbucks Coffee Company	5
6	Build-A-Bear Workshop	5
7	RadioShack and Best Buy	6
8	Rainforest Café	6
9	Stephanie's Boutique	6
10	Spence Diamonds	7
11	Lululemon	8
12	Home Depot	8
13	Ahold	8
14	Lindy's Bridal Shoppe	10
15	Hughe's	11
16	McFadden's Department Store	11
17	Capital Sportswear	12
18	Shopper's Drug Mart	13
19	Enterprise	14
20	Avon	14
21	Holt Renfrew	15
22	GoodLife Fitness Clubs	15
23	Nordstrom	15
24	Consumer Electronics	16

CASE 1   eBay: E-tailing Issues

The concept for eBay was born during a conversation between Pierre Omidyar and his wife, an avid Pez collector. (She has a collection of more than 400 dispensers.) She commented to Pierre how great it would be if she were able to collect Pez dispensers and interact with other collectors over the Internet. As an early Internet enthusiast, Pierre felt that many people like his wife needed a place to buy and sell unique items and to meet other users with similar interests. He started eBay in 1995 to fulfill this need.

Luckily for Pierre Omidyar, he was living in Silicon Valley when he got the idea for eBay. If Omidyar's family had stayed in France, his idea would never have gotten off the ground. It's not a lack of venture capital or Internet audience in France that would have stopped him; it was the law at that time. Under French regulations, only a few certified auctioneers are allowed to operate, so eBay could not have been opened for business in its founder's homeland back in 1995. Ten years later, eBay operated auctions in Argentina, Australia, Austria, Belgium, Brazil, Canada, China, France, Germany, Hong Kong, India, Ireland, Italy, Korea, Malaysia, Mexico, Netherlands, New Zealand, Philippines, Poland, Singapore, Spain, Sweden, Switzerland, Taiwan, and the U.K.

OFFERING TO CUSTOMERS

Most retailers follow the business-to-consumer sales model. eBay pioneered online person-to-person trading, also known as the consumer-to-consumer business model, by developing a Web-based community in which buyers and sellers are brought together using an efficient and entertaining auction format to buy and sell items. Initially, most of the items auctioned were collectibles such as antiques, coins, stamps, and memorabilia.

Many of the sellers on eBay are small mom-and-pop businesses that use the site as a sales channel. By 2003, most of the merchandise available on eBay had shifted from collectibles to practical items, such as power drills and computers. Now big businesses such as Disney and Sun Microsystems have discovered eBay. Retailers, manufacturers, and liquidators are using the site to unload returned merchandise, refurbished merchandise, and used products.

The eBay service permits sellers to list items for sale and enables buyers to bid on items of interest. All eBay users can browse through listed items in a fully automated, topically arranged, intuitive, and easy-to-use online service that is available 24 hours a day, seven days a week. However, even with automated bidding features, participating in an online auction requires more effort than buying fixed-price goods, and once the auction is over, most buyers have to send a cheque or money order and then get the merchandise up to two weeks later. Buyers have the option to purchase items in an auction-style format or at a fixed price through a feature called Buy It Now.

More than 500 million items are listed for sale each year. From Civil War to Star Wars items, from Beanie Babies to fine antiques, chances are that you'll find it among eBay's 45 000 categories of merchandise from 254 000 online sellers. "If you can't sell it on eBay, you might as well open up the window and throw it out in the backyard because it ain't worth a damn," says Bob Watts, an antique dealer in Fairfield, Virginia. The Web site has over 135 million registered users worldwide. People spend more time on eBay than any other online site, making it the most popular shopping destination on the Internet. Users often refer to eBay as a community—a group of people with similar interests. For example, Dr. Michael Levitt is by day a distinguished medical researcher at the Minneapolis Veterans Medical Centre, but at night he is an eBay warrior. Levitt is a collector of antique California Perfume Company bottles.

Every night he logs on to eBay to see if anything new is being offered. He has purchased hundreds of bottles through eBay simply because it's the most convenient way to connect with sellers. The Web site requires that all new sellers have a credit card on file, insurance, authentication, and escrow accounts.

Buyers and sellers can check the "reputation" of anyone using eBay. A Feedback Forum is provided through which eBay users can leave comments about their buying and selling experiences. If you're a bidder, you can check your seller's Feedback Profile before you place a bid to learn about the seller's reputation with previous buyers. If you're a seller, do the same with your bidders.

BUSINESS MODEL

Unlike most e-commerce companies, eBay has been profitable from the very beginning. Exhibit 1 shows net revenues, net income, employees, and net profit margin figures from 2000 to 2004. Most of the company's revenues come from fees and commissions (between 1.25 and 5.0 percent of the sale price) associated with online and traditional offline auction services.

Online revenues come from placement and success fees paid by sellers; eBay does not charge fees to buyers. Sellers pay a nominal placement fee, and by paying additional fees, sellers can have items featured in various ways. Sellers also

exhibit 1

Financial Overview for eBay

	2004	2003	2002	2001	2000
Net revenues ($ mil)	3271	2165	214	748	431
Net income ($ mil)	778	442	250	90	48
Employees	8100	6200	4000	2500	1927
Net profit margin	23.8%	20.4%	20.6%	12.1%	11.2%

pay a success fee based on the final purchase price. Online advertising on eBay has not made significant contributions to net revenues, and no significant revenue from advertising is expected in the near future.

Additional revenues come from auction-related services, including bidder registration fees and appraisal and authentication. Its online business model is significantly different from electronic retailers. Because individual sellers, rather than eBay, sell the items listed, the company has no procurement, carrying, or shipping costs and no inventory risk. The company's expenses are just personnel, advertising and promotion, and depreciation on site hardware and software.

COMPETITION

Due to the popularity of auctions with consumers, a number of e-businesses have entered the market. Some competing Internet auctions offering a broad range of products are Amazon.com, Yahoo!, uBid, and Overstock.com. In addition to these multicategory sites, there are vertical auction sites specializing in a single category of merchandise such as stamps or baseball cards.

Perhaps the most significant competitor is Amazon.com, which launched an auction site in 1999. Amazon has a well-known and highly regarded brand name and has substantial traffic on its Web site. (Amazon is the most widely known e-business, with eBay ranking third in brand awareness.) When Amazon launched its auction site, it offered some unique benefits to customers, including a no-deductible, no-haggle, no third-party money-back guarantee for purchases up to US$250 and a feature called Going, Going, Gone that extends the auction for 10 minutes if a bid is made in the last 10 minutes before closing. On eBay, it is common for items to be picked off in the closing minutes by vigilant consumers who make the last bid.

Amazon is known for the usability of its site. In response to Amazon's entry, eBay took steps to make buying and selling easier. It offers a Personal Shopper program that searches out specified products and My eBay, which gives users information about their current eBay activities, including bidding, selling, account balances, favourite categories, and recent feedback.

Finally, some Internet businesses have arisen that simply search and display summary information from many auction sites to enable comparison shopping. However, eBay sued one such site and has used technology to block access to another site to prevent them from gathering and displaying eBay auction data.

DISCUSSION QUESTIONS

1. What are the advantages and disadvantages from the buyer's and seller's perspectives of buying merchandise through Internet auctions such as eBay?

2. Will a significant amount of retail sales be made through Internet auctions such as eBay in the future? Why or why not?

3. What are eBay's competitive advantages? Will it be able to withstand the competition from other auction sites such as Yahoo and Amazon's auctions?

Source: This case was written by Barton Weitz, University of Florida.

CASE 2   Toys "R" Us Online

"How do I explain to my son that Santa is giving him a gift a week late?" said Michele Read on December 24, 1999, as she worried that the Leap Frog Learning toy she had ordered from Toysrus.com for her four-year-old son Tyler was not going to be under the Christmas tree the next day.

"This does nothing to appease a child on Christmas morning when he doesn't find his present," said Kevin Davitt, a customer who was still waiting for an order from Toysrus.com on December 23, 1999. "A six-year-old doesn't want a gift certificate, he wants his Nintendo or his Pokémon," said Davitt, who had ordered two video games for his six-year-old son on December 13, 1999, and agreed to pay US$19.90 for express shipping so that the gift would arrive within five days.

Michael Kinney, a customer from California, ordered a Chickaboom game for his son and was promised delivery within two weeks. After seven weeks, Kinney declared, "I'll never shop Toysrus.com again." During Christmas 1999, Toysrus.com employees faced a real siege. The company's "Black Sunday" came on Sunday, November 6, 1999, as 62 million advertising circulars were placed in local newspapers around the United States offering free shipping on Christmas toy orders placed over the Internet.

When Toysrus.com was unable to fulfill orders in time for Christmas, the firm received numerous consumer complaints and negative publicity from newspaper and magazine articles and TV news reports about the firm's problems. Toys "R" Us had the toys available in its warehouses, but was unable to pick, pack, and ship customer orders in a timely manner. Many employees worked for 49 straight days to fill orders, with some employees pulling sleeping bags out from under their desks to rest during the round-the-clock operation.

Despite the heroic efforts, customers were still displeased. "I have never been exposed to fouler language," explained Joel Anderson, a Toysrus.com vice-president, as he described the angry e-mails from unhappy customers.

In January 2000, John Eyler became the fourth CEO of the 53-year-old Toys "R" Us toy chain and parent of Toysrus.com. He came from being president of the much smaller FAO Schwarz toy chain and entered on the heels of the 18-month tenure of the previous CEO. He was immediately faced with the aftermath of the Christmas 1999 crisis and had less than 12 months to fix things for Christmas 2000.

TOYS "R" US TODAY

Toys "R" Us, Inc., headquartered in Paramus, New Jersey, is one of the largest retailers in the world, with 2002 sales over US$12 billion. The corporation consists of five businesses: (1) Toys "R" Us U.S., operating 701 toy stores, (2) Kids "R" Us, with 184 children's clothing stores, (3) Babies "R" Us, consisting of 165 infant–toddler stores, (4) Imaginarium, 42 educational specialty stores, and (5) Toys "R" Us, International, which operates, licenses, or franchises 507 toy stores in 28 countries outside the United States including many in Canada. In addition, the firm sells merchandise through Internet sites at www.toysrus.com, www.babiesrus.com, and www.imaginarium.com. Toys "R" Us stores carry everything from Crazy Bones at US$1.99 to Sony PlayStation at US$129.99.

The merchandise mix includes both children's and adults' toys and games, bicycles, sporting goods, small pools, infant and juvenile furniture, infant and toddler apparel, and children's books. An electronics section features video games, electronic handheld toys, videotapes and DVDs, audio CDs, and computer software, along with a smattering of small TVs, shelf stereos, and radios.

Most Toys "R" Us stores conform to a traditional big-box format, with stores averaging about 4278 square metres. Stores in smaller markets range between 1860 and 2910 square metres. In 1999, the company began converting stores to a new layout named the C3 (customer-driven, cost-effective concept) format store intended to make the Toys "R" Us stores easier to shop, with wider aisles, more feature opportunities and end caps, more shops, and logical category layouts.

THE TOY INDUSTRY

Bricks and Mortar The US$30 billion traditional toy industry has undergone significant changes during the last 10 years. Over this time period, the market share of general merchandise discount stores (mainly Wal-Mart) increased from 22 to 33.6 percent, while Toys "R" Us' market share decreased from 19.1 to 16.5 percent. In 1998, Wal-Mart overcame Toys "R" Us to become the top toy retailer.

Online Between 1999 and 2002, the share of the toy market purchased over the Internet increased significantly but still was less than 5 percent of total toy sales. In March 2001, with annual sales over US$200 million, eToys filed for bankruptcy. It was noted for its excellent customer service and user-friendly Web site. But its fixed costs were so high that its break-even sales volume escalated to US$750 million in annual sales.

THE NEW TOYS "R" US STRATEGY

Customers complained that the stores were ugly and untidy, that shopping was difficult, and that there were not enough sales personnel. To help regain its number-one place from Wal-Mart, Toys "R" Us developed a new corporate strategy and marketing plan. It hired a new marketing VP, Warren Kornblum, who immediately overhauled the company's whole marketing operation. In the past, Toys "R" Us had joined in small vendor promotions and managed scattered marketing efforts. Kornblum changed that around, deciding to do fewer but bigger promotions.

It did a promotional deal with Fox Kids Network and Walt Disney for the feature film Toy Story 2. As a result of these marketing efforts, sales increased from US$11.2 billion in 1998 to US$11.9 billion in 1999. For 2000–01, the company restructured its budget to allocate more money for marketing. It planned to continue with sports and movie entertainment themes for promotions.

Warren Kornblum's strategy seemed to work. He set up a "Scan and Win" promotion where shoppers held up UPC game pieces to scanners to see if they had won a prize. More than a million consumers were scanned in this promotion, making this one of the company's most successful store traffic improvement programs. The mountains of sweepstakes entries and packed venues, however, began causing inventory shortages in the all-important holiday period. Inventory mishaps were the main reason fourth-quarter 1999 sales stayed at a flat US$5 billion.

When John Eyler came in as the new CEO of Toys "R" Us in January 2000, he slashed expenses across the board, started efforts to provide better customer service, increased the number of employees in stores, and expanded store operating hours. All of the marketing activities were aimed at bringing customers into the chain's new store design and layout concept, C3. This easier-to-shop C3 format was installed in 75 percent of the stores by the end of 2000. Toys "R" Us hoped this new strategy would take market share back from Wal-Mart.

In addition to changing the layout of the stores, Toys "R" Us is opening boutique areas within the stores. For example, the Imaginarium area features educational toys and games, and the R-Zone areas offers video games targeting teenagers.

TOYSRUS.COM

Toys "R" Us arrived late to the e-business world with Toysrus.com in 1998, losing critical early battles to eToys.com and ceding some of the market to Amazon.com. The development, launch, and operation of Toysrus.com turned out to be both a corporate and public relations headache for almost a year. Things fell apart just as quickly as they came together. The investment deal with Benchmark Capital to fund the venture crumbled a few months after it was made as neither party could agree to the shares they would have.

Bob Moog, who was hired to run Toysrus.com, backed out of his employment deal in July 1999 three months after agreeing to come on board. With Christmas 1999 approaching, Toys "R" Us scrambled to put its Internet venture together. Hasbro executive John Barbour was hired as the new president for Toysrus.com in August 1999. He quickly developed a new plan, redesigned the site, and prepared for a holiday traffic onslaught.

The company began promoting online offers in its offline marketing efforts, the most ambitious of which dangled a US$10 discount for online purchases in the nationally distributed Toys "R" Us "holiday big book" coupon circulars. Toysrus.com also offered free shipping for the holiday season. The free shipping and "big book" coupon strategy worked, but a little too well for the logistics department of the company. Traffic exploded, and the site was buried in an avalanche of orders "beyond our most optimistic forecasts,"

said Barbour. The company was finally forced to announce that 5 percent of all online orders would not be fulfilled in time for Christmas. Embarrassed, Toys "R" Us issued a formal apology and issued $100 gift certificates to customers whose orders didn't make it under the tree. Toysrus.com declared revenues of US$49 million in 1999, US$39 million of which came during the holiday season.

Partnership with Amazon.com

Learning from the fiasco of Christmas 1999, when it failed to deliver goods in time, the company decided to go into a partnership with Amazon.com in 2000. Amazon.com took over the Toys "R" Us site operations, customer service, and fulfillment, while Toys "R" Us selected and bought the merchandise that it inventoried in Amazon warehouses.

Through this arrangement, Toysrus.com has realized a 40 percent reduction in operating costs, largely by outsourcing fulfillment activities. Its conversion rate, the percentage of site visitors who make purchases, doubled since the deal took effect in August 2000. In the critical 2000 holiday season, Toysrus.com boasted 99 percent on-time delivery amid a huge volume of orders, and sales volume more than tripled from the previous year, to US$124 million.

DISCUSSION QUESTIONS

1. Why was Wal-Mart able to take market share away from Toys "R" Us when they have not been as competitive with the consumer electronics category killers such as Future Shop and Best Buy?

2. How can Toys "R" Us regain its position as the number-one toy retailer?

3. How do Amazon.com and Toys "R" Us each benefit from their partnership?

4. What are the pros and cons of this relationship with Amazon.com from the Toys "R" Us perspective?

Source: This case was written by Professors Alan B. Eisner, Lubin School of Business, Pace University; Jerome C. Kuperman, Minnesota State University, Moorhead Department of Business Administration; Robert F. Dennehy, Lubin School of Business, Pace University; and John P. Dory, Lubin School of Business, Pace University. A full-length version of this case is forthcoming in the Journal of Behavioral and Applied Management. Special thanks to Margaret Ann deSouza-Lawrence for research assistance on this project. © 2002 Alan B. Eisner.

CASE 3 | Sephora: Consumer Behaviour

Sephora, a division of Moet Hennessy Louis Vuitton (LVMH), is an innovative retail concept from France that is changing the way cosmetics are sold. Sephora dares to be

different in its store design and product offerings. In fact, it designs the fashion retail concept to give its customers what they want: "freedom, beauty, and pleasure." Some of

Sephora's product offerings include makeup, fragrances, bath and body products, and skin care. There is no doubt every woman can find the products she desires at Sephora to pamper herself like a queen.

Sephora takes beauty offerings in a new, exciting direction, allowing the customer to choose her own level of service. The customer may opt for "an individual experience and reflection to detailed expert advice," whether it be in Sephora's store locations or on its highly interactive Web site.

Sephora has been taking the U.S. market by storm ever since it arrived in mid-1998 with its first two store locations in New York and Miami. Its flagship store that encompasses 1953 square metres opened in Rockefeller Center in New York City in October 1999. Now, Sephora operates more than 515 stores in 14 countries worldwide, with an expanding base of over 126 stores across North America. Sephora opened its first Canadian store in Toronto in 2004. (1)

Most fashion-oriented cosmetics are sold in department stores. The scent and cosmetics area in department stores consists of areas devoted to the products made by each manufacturer. Salespeople specializing in specific lines stand behind a counter and assist customers in selecting merchandise.

Sephora represents "the future of beauty," so it is no surprise that its store designs are a reflection of what to expect in the future. It lures customers into its stores with a bright red carpet that immediately induces an excitement and intrigue that cannot be matched. Once the customers enter the store, they are surrounded by what Sephora likes to call "the temple of beauty." Extraordinary assortments of products are arranged alphabetically and by category along the walls of the store. Customers are encouraged to sample the beauty products on their own from self-serve modules. The stores sell a tremendous variety of brands, including new lines, best-sellers, classics, and an exclusive Sephora collection.

Sephora has a strong presence throughout the United States; however, it also has stores in Canada, Czech Republic, England, France, Greece, Italy, Luxembourg, Monaco, Spain, Poland, Portugal, Romania, Russia, and Turkey. It decided to pull out of Japan and Germany because of financial concerns, having been unable to sell Japanese and German consumers on its unique retail concept.

Sephora offers its cosmetics online. There has been much speculation in recent years that beauty products cannot be displayed properly on a two-dimensional Web page. Many other retailers have attempted to make the transition, but they have been unsuccessful time and time again. On the other hand, Sephora has managed to set itself apart from other retailers once again by making it work while still yielding a profit.

Sephora offers over 250 classic and emerging brands, some that consumers have a difficult time finding in department stores, such as Philosophy, Bare Escentuals, and Lip Fusion. Women have been making purchases on the Sephora Web site because they cannot find these products in their hometown malls. To many customers' dismay, Sephora stores are not located in every regional mall across the country. For these customers, Sephora.com represents a one-stop shop for all of their beauty needs. They know that they can find the brands they love at a reasonable price with no hassles. What else can a person ask for?

Sephora continues to grow and expand, and in 2006 it joined forces with JC Penney in the U.S. to sell cosmetics in its stores. The JC Penney version of Sephora will be a "store within a store" concept and consumers will now have more choices to find their favourite Sephora products. (2)

Even though Sephora is the world's largest beauty retailer, it still recognizes the importance of giving back to the community. It has joined forces with Operation Smile, which provides reconstructive facial surgery for young children in developing countries and in the United States, to provide kids with a greater sense of confidence so that they can live a more normal life. Sephora committed itself to help improve the lives of children around the world. This joint effort allows children who would not normally be able to afford surgical procedures to get the help that they deserve to feel like a regular kid. The children have no reason to be self-conscious anymore because they are beautiful on the inside and outside. Sephora continues to make a difference by getting involved in the community even through its daily operations. Even though some women do not believe in the art of makeup, it is essential to recognize that it does allow many other women to feel more confident about their looks on a daily basis, and this contribution, in itself, is truly irreplaceable.

DISCUSSION QUESTIONS

1. What is Sephora's target market? What segment is attracted to its offerings?

2. Why do women prefer the self-service environment of Sephora to the service-oriented environment in department store cosmetic areas?

3. Why was Sephora unsuccessful in Japan and Germany when it has been so successful in other foreign countries? Explain.

4. How can a beauty retailer make a successful transition online? What makes Sephora's online site so successful?

Source: This case was written by Kristina Pacca, University of Florida.

(1) www.sephora.com Company Web site accessed online July 29, 2007.

(2) www.sephora.com Company Web site accessed online July 29, 2007.

CASE 4 | American Eagle and Abercrombie & Fitch

Jennifer Shaffer, a 17-year-old living in Newton, Massachusetts, used to shop at Abercrombie & Fitch (A&F) once a month. She thought the prices were high, but the brand name and image appealed to her. She says, "It's like I really had to have Abercrombie." Then an American Eagle store opened about 15 minutes from her home.

Now she shops at the American Eagle store about twice a month and rarely goes to the Abercrombie store. "They look the same, and they're both really cute," she says. "But American Eagle's prices are a little cheaper."

Both Abercrombie & Fitch and American Eagle are still growing into their present strategy of selling casual apparel to the teen/college market. A&F was established as an outdoor sporting goods retailer over 100 years ago. It sold the highest-quality hunting, fishing, and camping goods. A&F outfitted some of the greatest explorations in the early part of the twentieth century, including Robert Perry's expedition to the North Pole and Theodore Roosevelt's trips to the Amazon and Africa.

Over time, its tweedy image became less attractive to consumers. The chain experienced a significant decline in sales and profits, and, in 1977, it was forced to declare bankruptcy. The company, initially acquired by Oshman's Sporting Goods, did not experience a turnaround until The Limited Inc. acquired it in 1988. Initially, The Limited positioned A&F as a tailored clothing store for men.

In 1995, The Limited repositioned A&F to target both males and females in the teen and college market with an emphasis on casual American style and youth. In 1999, The Limited sold A&F, which now operates as a separate company. Currently, the company has over 970 Abercrombie & Fitch stores in the United States. There are 6 stores in Canada of which 3 are Hollister, a new, lower-priced chain of stores targeted at high school students. In 2007 a new flagship store was opened in London, England. There are more new stores planned for Japan and Canada. (1)

American Eagle, though not having the rich tradition of A&F, initially also was positioned as an outfitter when it started in 1977. Initially offering apparel only for men, American Eagle shifted its focus to teens and college students in 1995. In 2000, it acquired two Canadian specialty retail chains—Bluenotes/Thrifty's and Braemar. The Bluenotes chain was sold to another Canadian retailer and the Braemar locations were converted to American Eagle stores. (2) Today, American Eagle has over 840 stores in the United States and Canada. Even though A&F and American Eagle have evolved from their roots, there is still an outdoor, rugged aspect in their apparel. Both retail chains carry similar assortments of cargoes, tech pants, T-shirts, and sweaters, all private label.

A lot of the merchandise is athletically inspired. The rivalry between A&F and American Eagle is intense. A&F even filed a 1998 federal court lawsuit accusing American Eagle of copying its clothing styles and catalogue. The courts found that although the designs were similar, there was nothing inherently distinctive in Abercrombie's clothing designs that could be protected by a trademark. But the courts have ruled that Abercrombie's catalogue design and image are worthy of trade dress protection.

However, they also felt that American Eagle's catalogue had a different image that did not infringe upon the image of the A&F catalogue. A&F's catalogue, the A&F Quarterly, was discontinued in 2003, and replaced with the A&F Magazine, which played an important role in developing the company's brand image. (3) The photographs in the catalogue were sexually suggestive, featuring college-age girls and guys, sometimes partially nude. The chain's marketing has historically been controversial, particularly when it printed drink recipes in the Quarterly. Some people felt the recipes promoted binge drinking on college campuses.

But it was the Quarterly that first drew Jennifer to an A&F store a while ago. She recalls going through the catalogue with some girlfriends and looking at the muscular young men featured. "The guys in the magazine—that's what made us all go," she says. This young and sexy image is enhanced by store signage featuring scantily clad lacrosse players and young beachgoers.

Abercrombie & Fitch exploited this image by introducing a line of intimate apparel in 2001. Intimate apparel is now one of the best-selling merchandise categories in the stores. The image of American Eagle (www.ae.com) is more homecoming rather than hot tub. American Eagle sponsors a comedy competition for college students called the AE Campus Comedy Challenge and the grand prize is a trip to Cancun, Mexico. (4) It also has its apparel featured in various movies. Although its commercials are less suggestive than those of A&F, its "Get Together" commercials feature college- and high-school-age teens dancing and kissing.

Even though A&F devotes its advertising and marketing resources to reaching college-age consumers, many teenagers also patronize its stores. The company is concerned that the image of its stores will be negatively affected if they become a place for teenagers to hang out.

The development of the Hollister chain is one of the approaches that A&F has taken to preserve the A&F image while catering to the growing teenage market. The Hollister stores are unique. Their target market consists of consumers aged 14 to 18. The merchandise in the stores is 20 to 30 percent less expensive than A&F's merchandise.

The styling of the merchandise is also different. It has brighter colours and larger logos. However, many teenagers fail to recognize the subtle differences. They contend that it is essentially the same merchandise except at lower prices. Furthermore, Hollister stores are roughly 186 square metres smaller than A&F stores, and the store design is distinct.

A&F stores still convey an outdoor ruggedness in their décor; Hollister stores present a California beach-inspired theme. They want their customers to feel as though they are part of a beach party. This casual atmosphere provides young consumers with a more enjoyable shopping experience. The décor in the stores inspires and evokes memories of hot summer days at any time of the year.

DISCUSSION QUESTIONS

1. What, if any, are the differences in A&F's and American Eagle's retail strategies?

2. What are the brand images of A&F and American Eagle? What words and phrases are associated with each retailer's brand name?

3. Which retailer is in a stronger competitive position? Why?

4. Would you take a risk like A&F and pursue Hollister as a growth strategy? Why or why not?

Source: This case was written by Kristina Pacca, University of Florida.
(1) www.wikipedia.com accessed online on July 28, 2007
(2) www.ae.com Company Web site accessed online July 28, 2007
(3) www.abercrombie.com Company Web site accessed online July 28, 2007
(4) www.ae.com Company Web site accessed online July 28, 2007

CASE 5   Starbucks Coffee Company: Retail Successes and Challenges

Starbucks is the leading retailer of specialty coffee beverages and beans and related food and merchandise. Its annual sales in 2006 were US$7.8 billion and it employed 140 000 people in 39 countries. Starbucks owned and operated over 6000 retail stores and licensed additional supermarket and airport stores in the United States, Thailand, Australia, Great Britain, and Canada. (1)

In addition to its direct retailing activities, Starbucks had formed strategic alliances with Dreyer's Grand Ice Cream, Kraft Foods, Barnes & Noble Booksellers, Jim Beam, United Airlines, and PepsiCo to expand its product and distribution portfolios. Howard Schultz, chairman and CEO, and his senior management team were focusing on how to sustain their phenomenal growth and maintain their market leadership position.

THE COFFEE MARKET

The commercial market for coffee began in AD 1000 when Arab traders brought the coffee tree from its native Ethiopia to the Middle East. Over the next 200 years, coffee drinking spread through the Arab world and was eventually introduced in Europe in the 1500s by Italian traders.

By 1650, coffee houses emerged as popular meeting places in England and France. Well-known public figures would frequent London coffee houses to discuss political and literary issues. Coffee consumption flourished in the mid-twentieth century, aided by developments in manufacturing and cultivation. By 1940, large coffee processors such as Nestlé (Hills Bros. brand), Kraft General Foods (Maxwell House), and Procter & Gamble (Folgers) developed instant and decaffeinated coffee varieties in addition to their staple regular ground. Supermarkets emerged as the primary distribution channel for traditional coffee sales.

In the late 1980s, per capita coffee consumption fell slowly and steadily as consumers turned to soft drinks, bottled water, juices, and iced teas. The three major manufacturers—Procter & Gamble, Nestlé, and Kraft—fought for market share in a stagnant market. All of the major coffee brands were unprofitable. In an effort to regain profitability, the majors decreased historically high expenditures on image advertising, increased the use of robusta beans (as opposed to the high-quality arabica beans) to further reduce cost, and converted from 16-ounce cans to 13-ounce cans, claiming that the contents produced the same amount of coffee. Coupons and in-store promotions dominated manufacturer marketing plans as price warfare continued.

THE STARBUCKS COFFEE COMPANY: BACKGROUND

Inspiration for the present Starbucks concept came to Howard Schultz when he went to Italy on a buying trip in 1983. While wandering through the ancient piazzas of Milan, Schultz took particular note of the many cheerful espresso bars and cafés he passed. Italians, he felt, had captured the true romance of the beverage. Coffee drinking was an integral part of the Italian culture. Italians started their day at the espresso bar and returned there later on. "There's such a strong sense of community in those coffee bars," he mused. "People come together every single day and in many cases they don't even know each other's names. In Italy, coffee is the conduit to the social experience."

Schultz realized that Americans lacked the opportunity to savour a good cup of coffee while engaging in good conversation in a relaxed atmosphere. He returned to the United States convinced that Americans would find the Italian coffee house culture attractive. In 1987, Schultz bought Starbucks.

THE INITIAL YEARS
Retail Offering

Starbucks offers more than a cup of coffee. Scott Bedbury, the VP of marketing, elaborates:

> Our product is not just that which resides in the cup. The product is the store and the service you get in the store. We need to help people appreciate at a higher level why that coffee break feels the way it does, why it's worth the time it takes to prepare a good cup of coffee. I like to think that Starbucks is not so much food for thought, but brewed for thought. Coffee has for centuries been for thought. I have sometimes thought to myself, "Get out of this chair. You hit the wall." It's that private time for me between 2 and 3 PM when I walk down the Commons area here and make myself an Americano and think something through. I think that's maybe what Starbucks has to offer people: that safe harbour, that place to kind of make sense of the world. In the long run, what distinguishes us for our customers, what is the most enduring competitive advantage we have, is that we are able to give our customers an experience at the store level . . . better than any competitor out there, even the small ones. Starbucks should be a place, an experience, tied up in inspired thought.

Although designs vary in any particular store to match the local market, the typical Starbucks store works around a planned mix of organic and manufactured components: light wood tones at the counters and signage areas, brown bags, polished dark marble countertops, glass shelves, thin modern white track lighting, and pure white cups. Even the logo delivers the double organic/modern message: The Starbucks icon is earthy looking, yet rendered in a modern abstract form, in black and white with a band of colour around the centre only. The colours of the lamps, walls, and tables mimic coffee tones, from green (raw beans) to light and darker browns. Special package and cup designs are coordinated to create livelier, more colourful tones around holidays. Starbucks also keeps its look lively with rotating in-store variations based on timely themes.

Starbucks stores are spacious so that customers can wander around the store, drinking their coffee and considering the purchase of coffee paraphernalia ranging from coffee beans to brushes for cleaning coffee grinders to $1000 home cappuccino machines. Retail sales are composed of coffee beverages (58 percent), whole bean coffee by weight (17 percent), food items (16 percent), and coffee-related equipment (9 percent). Although coffee beverages are standardized across outlets, food offerings vary from store to store.

At Starbucks, espresso is brewed precisely 18 to 23 seconds and thrown away if it is not served within 10 seconds of brewing. Coffee beans are donated to charities seven days after coming out of their vacuum-sealed packs. Drip coffee is thrown away if it is not served within an hour of making it. Throughout the store there exists a keen attention to aroma: Employees are not allowed to wear colognes, stores use no scented cleaning products, and smoking is verboten.

Human Resource Management

The company, recognizing that its front-line employees are critical to providing "the perfect cup," has built an organizational culture based on two principles: (I) strict standards for how coffee should be prepared and delivered to customers and (II) a laid-back, supportive, and empowering attitude toward its employees.

All new hires, referred to as partners, go through a 24-hour training program that instills a sense of purpose, commitment, and enthusiasm for the job. New employees are treated with the dignity and respect that goes along with their title as baristas (Italian for bartender). To emphasize their responsibility in pleasing customers, baristas are presented with scenarios describing customers complaining about beans that were ground incorrectly.

The preferred response, baristas learn, is to replace the beans on the spot without checking with the manager or questioning the complaint. Baristas learn to customize each espresso drink and to explain the origins of different coffees and claim to be able to distinguish Sumatran from Ethiopian coffee by the way it "flows over the tongue."

Holding on to their motivated, well-trained employees is important, so all are eligible for health benefits and a stock option plan called "Bean Stock." Each employee is awarded stock options worth 12 percent of his or her annual base pay. (Starbucks now allows options at 14 percent of base pay in light of "good profits.") Employees are also given a free bag of coffee each week and a 30 percent discount on all retail offerings. Baristas know about and are encouraged to apply for promotion to store management positions.

Every quarter the company has open meetings at which company news, corporate values, and financial performance data are presented and discussed. Due to the training, empowerment, benefits, and growth opportunities, Starbucks' turnover is only 60 percent, considerably less than the 150 to 200 percent turnover at other firms in the food service business. "We treat our employees like true partners and our customers like stars," comments Schultz.

And stars they are. The average Starbucks customer visits the store 18 times a month; 10 percent visit twice a day. "I don't know of any retailer or restaurant chain that has that kind of loyalty," Schultz says.

Location Strategy

Starbucks' retail expansion strategy was sequential, based on conquering one area of a city or region at a time. Centralized cities served as hubs or regional centres for rollout expansion into nearby markets (e.g., Chicago as a hub for the Midwest). "Clustering" was also central to the strategy—major markets were saturated with stores before new markets were entered. For example, there were over 100 Starbucks outlets in the Seattle area before the company expanded to a new region. Having several stores in close proximity to each other generally increased overall revenues, though slowed growth in comparable store sales in saturated markets suggested sales were at the expense of some cannibalization of existing businesses.

Traffic was the major determinant in selecting cities and locations. "We want to be in highly visible locations," senior VP of real estate Jim Rubin explains, "with access to customers that value quality and great coffee. You want a store in the path of people's weekly shopping experience, their route to work, their way home from a movie. You want to be America's porch that no longer exists."

PHASE II GROWTH STRATEGY

Product Strategy

Starbucks has introduced a number of new products designed to capitalize on the company's strong brand name. "My plan is to bring the company and consequently the brand closer to consumers and to help unlock a greater potential for the brand while keeping its soul and integrity intact," explains Bedbury.

- Blue Note Blend. Blue Note Blend was introduced in conjunction with Capitol Records and its Blue Note label for jazz. "The combination of jazz music and coffees was consistent with the atmosphere of Starbucks," explained Bedbury.

- Frappuccino. The frappuccino beverage is a sweet, cold, creamy drink that combines milk, coffee, and ice. The product was very successful when introduced to cafés in 1995, so Starbucks entered a joint venture with PepsiCo to bottle a ready-to-drink (RTD) version.

Although canned or bottled coffee beverages had not been marketed in the United States, they were popular in Japan and other parts of the world. Coca-Cola was experimenting with a Nescafe RTD coffee beverage.

- MAZAGRAN. MAZAGRAN is a carbonated coffee RTD beverage. The product is manufactured, bottled, and distributed by PepsiCo, but Starbucks shared in the R&D and set flavour standards.

- Dreyer's Grand Ice Cream. Dreyer's Grand Ice Cream agreed to produce a line of premium ice cream products flavoured with Starbucks coffee. The first products in this line, five coffee-flavoured gourmet ice creams, were sold under the Starbucks name and distributed through supermarket outlets. Starbucks ice cream is the leading brand of gourmet coffee ice cream on the market.

- Kraft and supermarkets. Through an agreement with Kraft, the company also sells its branded coffee beans through supermarkets, which still command 80 percent of all coffee sales and generate nearly US$3 billion in sales annually. The company designed a line of specialty coffees just for supermarkets and opened Starbucks-operated kiosks in selected grocery chains. Kraft manages all distribution, marketing, advertising, and promotions for Starbucks whole bean and ground coffee in grocery and mass-merchandise stores. By the end of fiscal 2001, the company's whole bean and ground coffees were available throughout the United States in approximately 18 000 supermarkets.

- Jim Beam. Through a partnership with Jim Beam, a Starbucks coffee liqueur was developed.

Distribution Strategy

Several alternative channels have already been established, including the sale of whole beans through Nordstrom department stores and the sale of coffee by the cup in the cafés of Chapters and Barnes & Noble bookstores. Additional channels under consideration include distribution through service providers such as Holland America Cruise Lines, United Airlines, and Sheraton and Westin Hotels.

In addition to company-operated stores, Starbucks has entered into licensing and joint venture agreements involving 2800 stores in North America plus outlets in 15 countries, including Saudi Arabia, Switzerland, Israel, Japan, Taiwan, China, New Zealand, and South Korea.

Communication Strategy

Starbucks historically invested very little in advertising—less than US$100 million in its entire history. Explains Bedbury, "Our brand is at its best in the store."

DISCUSSION QUESTIONS

1. What is Starbucks' retail strategy? What is its target market and how does it try to develop an advantage over its competition?

2. Describe Starbucks' retail mix: location, merchandise assortment, pricing, advertising and promotion, store design and visual merchandising, customer service, and personal selling. How does its retail mix support its strategy?

3. What factors in the environment provided the opportunity for Starbucks to develop a new, successful retail chain? What demand and supply conditions prevailed in the U.S. coffee market when Howard Schultz purchased Starbucks in 1987? What insight did Schultz have that other players in the coffee market did not?

4. What were the principal drivers behind Starbucks' success in the marketplace? What does the Starbucks brand mean to consumers? How have the growth opportunities that Starbucks has pursued affected the value of its brand name?

5. What are the major challenges facing Starbucks as it goes forward? Is the brand advantage sustainable going forward? Can Starbucks defend its position against other specialty coffee retailers?

Source: This case was written by Susan Fournier, Harvard Business School, and Barton Weitz, University of Florida.
(1) www.starbucks.com/aboutus/company_factsheet.pdf accessed online July 30, 2007.

CASE 6   Build-A-Bear Workshop: Retailing Strategy

Today's consumers want good value, low prices, and convenience, but they also are attracted to a great shopping experience. Build-A-Bear Workshop, a chain with over 275 stores generating US$437 million in annual sales in 2006, is a teddy-bear-themed entertainment retailer whose stores are playgrounds for children. (1) They are located in the U.S., Canada, the U.K., and Ireland. They also have franchise stores in Europe, Asia, Africa, and Australia, making Build-A-Bear Workshop the leader in interactive retail. (2)

The stores are exactly what the name says: Customers choose an unstuffed animal and, working with the retailer's staff, move through eight "creation stations" to build their own bear. At the first station, the Stuffiteria, children can pick fluff from bins marked "Love," "Hugs and Kisses," "Friendship," and "Kindness." The stuffing is sent through a long, clear tube and into a machine. A sales associate holds the bear to a small tube while the builder pumps a foot pedal. In seconds, the bear takes its form. Before the stitching, builders must insert a heart. The builders follow the sales associate's instructions and rub the heart between their hands to make it warm. They then close their eyes, make a wish, and kiss the heart before putting it inside the bear. After selecting a name and having it stitched on the bear, builders take their bears to the Fluff Me station, where they brush their bears on a "bathtub" that features spigots blowing air. Finally they move to a computer station to create a birth certificate for their bear.

Bears are sent home in Club Condo boxes, which act as mini-houses complete with windows and doors. Besides adding value as playhouses, the boxes advertise Build-A-Bear to the child's friends. "[You] could buy a bear anywhere," says Maxine Clark, founder and Chief Executive Bear. "It's the experience that customers are looking for."

The experience is depicted on the retailer's Web site, www.buildabear.com. Maxine Clark has recently written a book called "The Bear Necessities of Business" to help people who have the dream of someday building their own companies. One hundred percent of the proceeds from the sales of the book will be donated to the Build-A-Bear Workshop Bear Hugs Foundation to fund programs that benefit children, families, and animals through financial support for community causes such as literacy and educational programs. Build-A-Bear Workshop also donates money to the World Wildlife Fund to help protect endangered species and their habitats. (3)

Customers pay about US$25 for the basic bear, but they can also buy sound, clothing, and accessories for their bear. To keep the experience fresh, Build-A-Bear regularly introduces new and limited-edition animals. Clothes and accessories are also updated to reflect current trends. Partners with Build-A-Bear include Limited Too fashion, Skechers shoes, Hello Kitty, Disney, and Harley Davidson. Officially licensed sports logos from the NBA and NHL are available in and Canada you can order either an Edmonton Oilers or Vancouver Canucks Hockey jersey for your bear. (4) There are also in-store birthday parties and an

refact

The origin of the teddy bear was a 1903 incident in which President Teddy Roosevelt refused to shoot a cub while bear hunting. The spared animal was thereafter referred to as the Teddy Bear.

official CD. To make sure that customers have a great experience every time they visit, all sales associates attend a three-week training program at "Bear University" and the firm offers incentive programs and bonuses. Build-A-Bear Workshops have recently expanded, and stores are now operating in Baseball stadiums in San Francisco and St. Louis, at the St. Louis Zoo and the St. Louis Science Center, and inside the Rainforest Café. (5). Build-A-Bear stores feature seasonal merchandise such as a Sweetheart Bear for Valentine's Day, a black cat with an orange nose for Halloween, and a penguin for Christmas.

DISCUSSION QUESTIONS

1. Is the Build-A-Bear concept a fad, or does it have staying power?
2. What can Build-A-Bear do to generate repeat visits to the store?

Source: This case was written by Barton Weitz, University of Florida.
(1) Company Web site fact sheet accessed online at www.buildabear.ca on July 25, 2007
(2) Company Web site
(3) Company Web site
(4) Company Web site

CASE 7 | RadioShack and Best Buy: Comparing Financial Performance

Both RadioShack and Best Buy/Future Shop sell consumer electronic merchandise; however, the companies have different retail strategies. RadioShack targets three family-oriented customer segments: (1) active suburban families with teenage children, (2) urban "flash" consumers with preteen kids, and (3) "small-town values" families with children of all ages.

exhibit 1   Financial Data for RadioShack and Best Buy

(all numbers in millions)	RADIOSHACK INCOME STATEMENT			BEST BUY INCOME STATEMENT		
	2004	2003	2002	2004	2003	2002
Net sales	$4 841	$4 649	$4 577	27 433	24 548	20 943
Cost of goods sold	2 407	2 334	2 339	20 938	18 677	15 998
Gross profit	2 434	2 315	2 238	6 495	5 871	4 945
Operating expenses Selling, general and administrative	1 775	1 740	1 729	5 053	4 567	3 935
Other expenses	101	92	83			
Total operating expenses	1 876	1 832	1,812	5 053	4 567	3 935
Net profit from operations	558	483	426	1 442	1 304	1 010
Number of employees	42 000	39 500	39,100	109,000	100 000	98 000
Selling space (square metres)	1 186 680	1 155 990	1 161 570	2 631 900	2 455 200	2 250 600
Growth in comparable store sales	3%	2%	−1%	4%	7%	3%

	RADIOSHACK BALANCE SHEET			BEST BUY BALANCE SHEET		
	2004	2003	2002	2004	2003	2002
Current assets						
Cash and equivalents	$438	$635	$447	$3 348	2 600	$1 914
Accounts receivable	241	182	208	375	343	312
Inventory	1 004	767	971	2 851	2 607	2 077
Other current assets	93	83	83	329	174	397
Total current assets	1 776	1 667	1 709	6 903	5 724	
Property, plant, equipment	652	513	422	2 464	2 244	3 089
Other assets	90	84	99	928	684	4 605
Total assets	2 518	2 264	2 230	10 295	8 652	7 694
Current liabilities	958	858	828	4 959	4 501	3 824
Long-term liabilities	637	618	672	887	729	1 140
Stockholder equity	923	788	730	4 449	3 422	2 730

SOURCE: SEC 10K filings at www.sec.gov.

These three demographic groups represent 38 percent of the U.S. population and 46 percent of the consumer electronics market. Through its stores, kiosks, and Web site, RadioShack provides families with accessories, consumer electronic solutions, and proprietary novelty products.

The customers in its target markets are willing to pay a reasonable price in return for convenience, selection, and simplicity in their shopping experience. The company provides excellent customer service that provides solutions for families' home electronic needs, as emphasized in its "You've Got Questions. We've Got Answers," branding campaign.

RadioShack has over 5000 stores in the United States, Puerto Rico, and the U.S. Virgin Islands. RadioShack used to operate nine stores in Canada but decided to close these stores in 2007. The stores, typically 232 square metres, are located in major malls and strip centres, as well as stand-alone locations. Each location carries a broad assortment of both private-label and national brand consumer electronics products. The product categories offered include mobile and wireless phones; direct-to-home satellite systems; computers and accessories; general and special purpose batteries; wire, cable, and connectivity products; digital cameras; radio-controlled cars and other toys; and satellite radios. In addition, RadioShack sells services provided by third parties, including cellular and PCS phone service, direct-to-home satellite activation, satellite radio service, and prepaid wireless airtime. The company also has a network of 2000 dealers servicing smaller markets, operates 500 kiosks located in Sam's Club stores, and owns four manufacturing plants producing its private-label merchandise.

In contrast to RadioShack's specialty store format, Best Buy operates 863 category-killer stores in the United States plus a Web site. There are 48 Best Buy stores in Canada and 122 Future Shop stores across all of Canada's provinces as of 2007. The stores, averaging 3996 square metres, are typically staffed by one general manager, four to five assistant managers, and 120 full- and part-time employees.

Best Buy/Future Shop's retail strategy focuses on bringing technology and consumers together in a retail environment that educates consumers on the features and benefits of technology and entertainment products. The stores offer merchandise in four product groups: consumer electronics, home office, entertainment software, and appliances. Consumer electronics, the largest product group, consists of televisions, digital cameras, DVD players, digital camcorders, MP3 players, car stereos, home theater audio systems, mobile electronics, and accessories. The home office product group includes desktop and notebook computers, telephones, networking, and accessories. Entertainment software products include DVDs, video game hardware and software, CDs, computer software, and subscriptions. The appliances product group includes major appliances, as well as vacuums, small electrics, and housewares.

exhibit 2   Strategic Profit Model

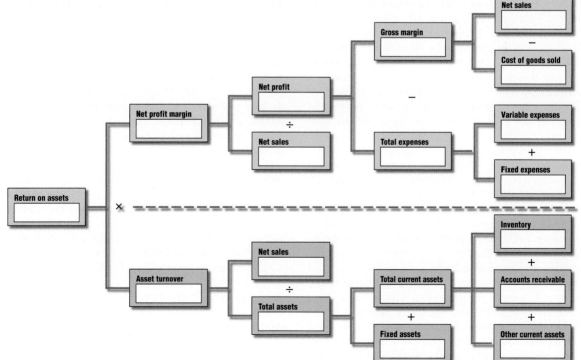

Best Buy/Future Shop also offers a variety of in-store and in-home services related to the merchandise offered within the four product groups. In-store services include computer setup, repair, and software installation, as well as the installation of mobile electronics. In-home services include computer setup, repair, software installation, and home networking, and the delivery and installation of appliances and home theatre systems. Although services were not a significant part of its revenue in fiscal 2004, it feels that service revenues will become a more significant component of its business.

DISCUSSION QUESTIONS

1. Using Exhibit 2, construct strategic profit models for RadioShack and Best Buy using data from the abbreviated income statements and balance sheets in Exhibit 1.

2. Explain, from a marketing perspective, why you would expect the gross margin percentage, expenses-to-sales ratio, net profit margin, inventory turnover, and asset turnover to be different for RadioShack and Best Buy.

3. Assess which chain has better overall financial performance. Why?

Source: This case was written by Barton Weitz, University of Florida.

CASE 8   Rainforest Café: Retailing Strategy

Steve Schussler opened the first Rainforest Café in the Mall of America, the largest enclosed mall in the world, in 1994. Before opening this unique retail store and theme restaurant, Schussler tested the concept for 12 years, eventually building a prototype in his home. It was not easy sharing a house with parrots, butterflies, tortoises, and tropical fish, but Schussler's creativity resulted in a highly profitable and fast-growing chain.

In 1996, the Rainforest Cafés (www.rainforestcafe.com), located in Chicago, Washington, DC, Fort Lauderdale, and Disney World in Orlando, Florida, in addition to the Mall of America in Minneapolis, Minnesota, generated US$48.7 million in sales and US$5.9 million in profits. They offer a unique and exciting atmosphere, recreating a tropical rainforest in 1860 to 2790 square metres. The cafés are divided into a restaurant seating 300 to 600 people and a retail store stocking 3000 SKUs of unique merchandise. Rainforest Cafés have since sprung up in various locations in Canada, including Toronto and Niagara Falls.

Retail merchandise accounts for 30 percent of the revenues generated by the cafés. Most theme restaurants stock fewer than 20 SKUs. The merchandise emphasizes eight proprietary jungle animals featured as animated characters in the restaurant. They include Bamba the gorilla, Cha Cha the tree frog, and Ozzie the orangutan. In addition to stuffed animals and toys, the characters are utilized on clothing and gifts and in animated films and children's books.

The cafés provide an environmentally conscious family adventure. The menu features dishes such as Rasta Pasta, Seafood Galapagos, Jamaica Me Crazy, and Eye of the Ocelot (meatloaf topped with sautéed mushrooms on a bed of caramelized onions). The restaurants have live tropical birds and fish plus animated crocodiles and monkeys, trumpeting elephants, gorillas beating their chests, cascading waterfalls surrounded by cool mist, simulated thunder and lightning, continuous tropical rainstorms, and huge mushroom canopies. As Schussler said, "Our cafés feature the sophistication of a Warner Brothers store with the animation of Disney."

Rainforest Cafés contribute to the local community through an outreach program. Over 300 000 schoolchildren visit the cafés each year to hear curators talk about the vanishing rainforests and endangered species. All coins dropped into the Wishing Pond and Parking Metre in the cafés are donated to causes involving endangered species and tropical deforestation.

Technology is used in the Rainforest Cafés to increase efficiency and profits. When a party enters the restaurant, the host (called a tour guide) enters the party's name in a computer, which prints a "passport" indicating the party's name, size, and estimated seating time. The party can then go shopping or sightseeing, knowing it will be ushered into the dining room within 5 to 10 minutes of the assigned seating time. When the party returns, the computer tells the "safari guide" the table at which the party will be seated. Tour and safari guides communicate with each other using headsets. This technology enables the Rainforest Cafés to turn tables five to six times a day compared to two to three turns in the typical restaurant.

The company expanded rapidly. By 2000, it had annual sales of US$200 million but earned only US$8 million in profits from 28 locations. Many of the locations were in regional malls rather than high-traffic entertainment centres at which the restaurants were initially located. As of 2005, Rainforest Café was the only restaurant concept at all three U.S. Disney locations. This restaurant can be found in 16 states and Canada, China, Japan, Mexico, and Europe. Two new restaurants are opening soon in Cairo, Egypt, and Istanbul, Turkey. (1)

After a protracted negotiation, Rainforest Café was acquired by Landry's Restaurant Inc.

Landry's which operates 311 restaurants in 36 states under the trade names of Joe's Crab Shack, Landry's Seafood House, Crab House, Charley's Crab, Chart House, Rainforest Café, and Saltgrass Steak House, generated 1.25 billion in revenue in 2005. (2) Tilman Fertitta, the founder and CEO of Landry's, explains his strategy for operating restaurants: "Our approach has always been simple. Put good concepts in good locations. Rainforest is a strong concept. The problem wasn't with sales. The worst stores do US$5 million a year. That's very different from other eatertainment chains like Planet Hollywood and Hard Rock Café. The major problem was poor locations in shopping centres with high lease costs." Following the acquisition, Landry's closed a number of Rainforest's mall locations but opened up new locations in London's Piccadilly Circus, Euro Disney outside Paris, Niagara

Falls, MGM Grand Hotel and Casino in Las Vegas, and Fisherman's Wharf in San Francisco.

DISCUSSION QUESTIONS

1. What is Rainforest Café's retail offering and target market?

2. Were malls good locations for Rainforest Cafés? Why or why not? What would be the best locations?

3. Many retailers have tried to make their stores more entertaining. In a number of cases, these efforts have failed. What are the pros and cons of providing a lot of entertainment in a retail store or restaurant?

Source: This case was written by Barton Weitz, University of Florida.
(1) www.rainforestcafe.com Company Web site accessed online July 25, 2007
(2) Spielberg, Susan, "Landry's rolls the dice on two fledgling concepts by Rainforest Café creator" Nation's Restaurant News, 3/13/2006, Vol. 40 Issue 11, p 4.

CASE 9   Stephanie's Boutique: Selecting a Store Location

Stephanie Wilson must decide where to open a ready-to-wear boutique she's been contemplating for several years. Now in her late 30s, she's been working in municipal government ever since leaving college, where she majored in fine arts. She's divorced with two children (ages five and eight) and wants her own business, at least partly to be able to spend more time with her children. She loves fashion, feels she has a flair for it, and has taken evening courses in fashion design and retail management.

Recently, she heard about a plan to rehabilitate an old arcade building in the downtown section of her city. This news crystallized her resolve to move now. She's considering three locations.

THE DOWNTOWN ARCADE

The city's central business district has been ailing for some time. The proposed arcade renovation is part of a master redevelopment plan, with a new department store and several office buildings already operating. Completion of the entire master plan is expected to take another six years.

Dating from 1912, the arcade building was once the centre of downtown trade, but it's been vacant for the past 15 years. The proposed renovation includes a three-level shopping facility, low-rate garage with validated parking, and convention centre complex. Forty shops are planned for the first (ground) floor, 28 more on the second, and a series of restaurants on the third.

The location Stephanie is considering is 84 square metres and situated near the main ground floor entrance. Rent is $220 per square metre, for an annual total of $18 480. If sales exceed $225 000, rent will be calculated at 8 percent of sales. She'll have to sign a three-year lease.

TENDERLOIN VILLAGE

The gentrified urban area of the city where Stephanie lives is nicknamed Tenderloin Village because of its lurid past. Today, however, the neat, well-kept brownstones and comfortable neighbourhood make it feel like a yuppie enclave. Many residents have done the remodelling work themselves and take great pride in their neighbourhood.

About 20 small retailers are now in an area of the Village adjacent to the convention centre complex. Most of them are trendy, affordable restaurants. There are also three small women's clothing stores. The site available to Stephanie is on the Village's main street on the ground floor of an old house. Its space is also about 84 square metres. Rent is $15 000 annually with no coverage clause. The landlord knows Stephanie and will require a two-year lease.

APPLETREE MALL

This suburban mall has been open for eight years. A successful regional centre, it has three department stores and 100 smaller shops just off a major highway about 10 kilometres from downtown. Of its nine women's clothing retailers, three are in a price category considerably higher than what Stephanie has in mind.

Appletree has captured the retail business in the city's southwest quadrant, though growth in that sector has slowed in the past year. Nevertheless, mall sales are still running 12 percent ahead of the previous year. Stephanie learned of plans to develop a second shopping centre east of town, which would be about the same size and character as Appletree Mall. But groundbreaking is still 18 months away, and no renting agent has begun to enlist tenants.

The store available to Stephanie in Appletree is two doors from the local department store chain's mall outlet. At 110 square metres, it's slightly larger than the other two possibilities. But it's long and narrow—7.3 metres in front by 15.2 metres deep. Rent is $262 per square metre ($28 820 annually).

In addition, on sales that exceed $411 500, rent is 7 percent of sales. There's an additional charge of 1 percent of sales to cover common-area maintenance and mall promotions. The mall's five-year lease includes an escape clause if sales don't reach $411 500 after two years.

DISCUSSION QUESTIONS

1. Give the pluses and minuses of each location.
2. What type of store would be most appropriate for each location?
3. If you were Stephanie, which location would you choose? Why?

Source: This case was prepared by Professor David Ehrlich, Marymount University.

CASE 10   Spence Diamonds—Innovation in Retail

Spence Diamonds is Canada's largest Canadian-owned diamond specialist, with nine different locations across Canada including Vancouver, Calgary, Edmonton, and Toronto. In 2006, the diamond industry was worth US$64 billion It is an old, mature industry run by large controlling companies such as De Beers. Spence Diamonds is breaking the traditional boundaries of diamond retail stores. Spence made retail history when it changed its approach to displaying diamonds. Instead of keeping the diamond jewellery behind glass as most other retailers do, Spence opens its display cases to customers, allowing them to handle and view up close high quality prototypes of its diamond jewellery. This gives customers the opportunity to browse without being pressured or intimidated by a salesperson. At Spence there are Diamond Consultants certified by the Diamond Council of America available to answer questions about any of the designs or the diamond quality. Consumers no longer have to look behind the glass and politely ask to see a diamond up close. Spence Diamonds breaks tradition by having the glass open to the customer side. This creates a relaxed, welcoming environment and aids in purchasing.

Founded in 1978 by Doug Spence, with its first location in Vancouver, British Columbia, the chain has grown to nine locations in British Columbia, Alberta, and Ontario. The goal of the company is to create a better diamond buying experience and, according to the company Web site (www.spencediamonds.com), that goal is the motivating force behind everything the company does. By specializing in diamonds alone, Spence is able to offer its customers better value, quality, and service. The company

manufactures the majority of its 4000 plus items of diamond jewellery in its Vancouver manufacturing facility.

Shopping for a diamond at Spence is different than at other retailers. The thousands of display rings are not real diamonds, but rather high quality prototypes that customers are freely encouraged to try on and examine on their own terms. This practice keeps the overhead costs of the stores low, and the savings are passed on to the customer. Through the company's high degree of vertical integration, Spence Diamonds can offer not only the best value to its customers but also the industry's most comprehensive guarantee.

The Spence Diamonds Guarantee is unique. They offer an unprecedented Buy-Back Policy and a 45-day return policy even on custom designs. The policy reads as follows: "At any time within five years from the time you purchase your Spence ring, we will buy your centre diamond back from you for exactly what you paid for it! This does not include setting fees, semi-mounts with other diamonds or sales tax. (We asked but the government won't give us back the tax!) Simply return your Spence ring in its original condition with your original invoice if you wish to take advantage of our Diamond Buy-Back policy. This offer applies to any purchase made on or after May 27, 2005." (1)

As a service to its customers, Spence offers large amounts of educational materials to help buyers make an informed purchase decision. There is information about diamond cuts and the 4C's of diamond quality. There is also a printable ring size guide available on the Web site so that every detail of a ring purchase can be researched before the customer even enters the showroom. There are videos on the site that help prepare customers for the showroom experience.

Sean Jones, the president of Spence Diamonds, says the best jewellers will not only explain the finer points of cut, clarity, carat, and colour, but will actually show a customer the difference, using proper diamontology instruments such as a proportion scope. "All diamonds look good under the lights of a jewellery store," says Jones, but the proof and the quality is in the stone's brilliance. And, Jones, says whether you want big, or beautiful, or rare, be sure to insist on the best cut, "and make sure the person is certified and has lots of trust and credibility behind them." (2)

Spence Diamonds is best known for its engagement rings, and it offers a wide range of designs including classic and modern solitaires, a variety of stone shapes including round, princess, and marquis styles. They offer carat sizes to suit any style and budget. Other diamond jewellery found at Spence includes diamond bracelets, earrings, necklaces, and right-hand rings. Spence employees have intimate knowledge of the complete process from importing and manufacturing to final sales which are all handled in house. All Spence Diamond Consultants are required to become DCA Certified Diamontologists to be able to provide information to buyers such as diamond care, diamond grades, and conflict diamonds. All Spence Diamonds are guaranteed conflict-free.

Advertising for Spence includes radio ads that are witty and targeted towards a young male audience. Doug Spence, the founder of Spence Diamonds, produced his own radio ads for over 20 years before he retired. Now the ads are produced by an advertising agency in Vancouver who, on a limited budget, need to produce 60 spots a year in which they mention the word "diamond" at least 10 times in every spot. The ads run for approximately 50 weeks every year. The ads talk to young men but they don't exclude the women who really help to drive the sales of diamonds. During one campaign every ad opened with the line, "It's not easy making sense out of matters of the heart. Thank goodness there's a store that makes sense out of diamonds," and closed with the line "Give a diamond with all your heart, but use your head to buy one." (3)

More and more consumers are taking a look at Spence Diamonds as they consider one of the most important and expensive purchases of their life. The company's original approach to diamond retailing has helped make them the largest Canadian-owned diamond retailer in the country and they continue to grow their business with a new tagline, "*Visibly* better diamonds, *Obviously* better prices." There is even a DJ at a popular club in Toronto who has adopted the company's name as his own stage name: DJ Spence Diamonds.

DISCUSSION QUESTIONS

1. What steps does Spence Diamonds take to implement its strategy of providing an outstanding customer experience in their store?

2. How do these activities enable Spence to reduce the gaps between perceived service and customer expectations, as described in Chapter 15?

3. What are the pros and cons of Spence's approach to developing a competitive advantage through customer service?

Sources for Quotes:
(1) http://www.aboutus.org/SpenceDiamonds.com accessed online August 8, 2007.
(2) Shelley Fralic, Wedding Rings: From cut to colour, it takes homework and a reputable jeweller to find the right rock. *The Vancouver Sun*, Tuesday February 21, 2006. pg C.4
(3) Mary Birchard, How to replace a pitchman: when Doug Spence retired as Spence Diamond's radio voice, Grey Worldwide Northwest rose to the challenge. *Marketing Magazine*, Toronto, July 22, 2002. Vol. 107, Iss. 29 pg. 9

Sources:
(4) Spence Diamonds Complete Profile at www.strategis.ic.gc.ca accessed online August 8, 2007
(5) Darrell Zahorsky, Diamond Difference, Small Business Information, Thursday August 10, 2006. accessed online at www.sbinformation.about.com August 8, 2007
(6) Melissa Mayntz, engagementrings.lovetoknow.com/wiki/Spence_Diamonds - 21k - 2007-06-15 accessed online at www.lovetoknow.com August 8, 2007.
(7) Grey to handle Spence radio ads, *Marketing Magazine*, Toronto, Oct 1, 2001, Vol. 106, Iss. 39, pg. 3.
(8) David Menzies, The Great Diamond Caper, *Marketing*, Toronto, May 28, 2007. Vol. 112, Iss. 10, pg. 34.
(9) Spence Diamonds company Web site accessed online at www.spencediamonds.com on August 8, 2007.

CASE 11   Lululemon—Can Canadian Yoga Wear Go Global?

What does it take to make a tiny underground yoga-inspired clothing line into a worldwide success? Take a look at Lululemon Athletica, the Vancouver-based yoga wear retail phenomenon and you will find out the answers.

Lululemon's first store opened in 1998 in the beach area of Kitsilano in Vancouver and it operated as a yoga studio at night to help pay the rent. "My original goal was to have one store in Kitsilano, and never grow beyond that," says Chip Wilson, Lululemon's founder, who was also the entrepreneur behind the surf and snowboard clothing company Westbeach which Wilson sold in 1997. "But then I surround myself with great twenty-five to thirty-five-year-old people. And they want a future and a family and a mortgage. In order to keep these people, I had to expand." (1)

Lululemon now has 59 stores, with the majority in Canada, 10 in the United States, two in Japan, and one in Melbourne, Australia. Sales exceeded US$148.9 million in 2006 after tripling in the last three years. In fiscal 2006, Canada represented 87.1 percent of Lululemon's revenues, 11.7 percent came from the U.S. and 1.2 percent came from Australia and Japan. At stores open for at least a year, sales were up 25 percent and the company posted average sales of US$16 000 per square metre. This makes its average sales among the best in the apparel retail sector. Plans for further expansion include adding 200 more stores in the U.S. and 40 to 45 more units in Canada over the next five years.

Most of the company's sales come from women's athletic apparel, and Lululemon believes that its focus on women differentiates it and positions Lululemon Athletica to address a void in the market. It is also focusing on men's apparel, which represented 11 percent of sales in 2006, and accessories, which accounted for 9 percent of sales.

It is not just athletes who are wearing Lululemon. Since the pants are credited with flattering a woman's backside, everyone from female fashionistas to soccer mom's and even professionals are wearing them. Men often buy them for gifts for their girlfriends or wives.

Secrets of Success

Yoga participation more than doubled among adults between 2001 and 2006, according to an MRI Sports Trend study. Lululemon has been able to ride the wave of this trend because of to its innovative styling and designs that cater to the yoga crowd. More than 200 styles per year are developed at Lululemon. In-store assortments are changed every 45 days and news styles added every 21 days. The product line caters to active women and men with creative designs and uses innovative technical fabrics such as Silverscent, an antibacterial textile. Lululemon's patented high-tech fabric called Luon (86 percent nylon, 14 percent lycra) is used for the solid-coloured yoga pants which retail for around $84 and feature a variety of waistbands and lengths. Sleeveless wrap tops retail for $44 and logo gym bags sell for $64. The company is constantly experimenting with new textiles, and current fabrics incorporate organic ingredients such as seaweed and vitamin B.

To stay ahead of rapid growth, Lululemon needed to integrate its product development, sourcing, manufacturing, and wholesale distribution process. "Rather than becoming a Gap—"this is our summer line and we've got lots of it"—Lululemon will have more products but with a shorter lifecycle. "Less depth but more breadth," says Christopher Ng, chief supply chain officer. (2) This solution means that more unique styles and colours can be produced in smaller quantities with a shorter demand cycle. One goal of the shortened cycle is to encourage customers to visit the stores more frequently because they will find new styles every three weeks. Another goal is to encourage them to buy on the spot because they know the product will disappear quickly.

What Is in a Name?

According to the company Web site www.lululemon.com, the Lululemon name was chosen in a survey of 100 people from a list of 20 brand names and 20 logos. The logo represents a stylized "A" that was the first letter in the name "athletically hip," a name which failed to make the cut. Another source says the name originally came from Chip Wilson when he first worked with the Japanese market in his dealings with the Westbeach stores. During that time, he learned that Japanese marketing companies would never come up with a name that had an L in it. The letter L is very difficult for the Japanese to pronounce as it is not part of their vocabulary. He thought that if he ever ran another company, he would make a name with three L's in it and see if he could make three times the money. He was playing with the L's and came up with the name Lululemon. It's a brand name that is kind of exotic for the Japanese and Chip says that it is funny to try and watch them say it.

Buzz Marketing

Lululemon's unique brand name has helped it to grow without any traditional advertising or marketing. There are no television commercials, no radio ads, and no national newspaper campaigns. Lululemon has always relied heavily on word of mouth. It generates buzz by supplying free clothing to yoga teachers and fitness instructors. It then asks these "ambassadors" to spread the word. The idea is for individual stores to be active in their own communities. Some stores sponsor programs such as yoga on the beach.

People

The staff training division is very active since management considers a product-savvy staff key to making sales. There are seven full-time employees on the training and development team, making it almost as large as the design team. Lululemon pays for its employees to take up to two yoga classes as week at approved studios. This has helped to keep staff happy and healthy, while at the same time increasing Lululemon's profile with its target market. Staff turnover at Lululemon is less than half the retail average.

Although sales are booming for Lululemon, it does have its critics. Some yogis prefer natural fibres over Lululemon's rather pricey gear. Other yoga practitioners are simply offended by the idea of paying nearly $100 for a pair of workout pants. Some employees have refused to take the Landmark Education courses that are strongly encouraged as part of management training. The three-day workshop "designed to bring about positive and permanent shifts in the quality of your life" has been accused of being a cult.

International Expansion

In 2003, encouraged by success at home, the first U.S. Lululemon store opened in Santa Monica, California. It is estimated that Americans spend $US2.95 billion on yoga gear annually. Nine other stores have opened in the U.S. since then, but it has not been easy expanding into the U.S. market. Challenges include securing good real estate locations. For example, the Santa Monica store is big and bright but doesn't get the foot traffic it would if it were located a few blocks over in a pedestrian mall.

In order to capture more of the lucrative U.S. market, Chip Wilson sold 48% of Lululemon to venture capital firms in Massachusetts. The result was a new CEO named Robert Meers who used to work for Reebok International. While at Reebok, Meers helped the company expand to 120 different countries. The goal at Lululemon is to expand globally, and Meers has the experience to help make the dream a reality. Wilson remains as the company's chairman.

A new Beverly Hills Lululemon store opened in the fall of 2006. It is 409 square metres and is located on high-traffic Beverly Boulevard. It is the third retail location to open in Southern California and it is almost double the size of the company's two other U.S. stores located in Santa Monica and Santa Barbara. Robert Meers, the new CEO, says, "Beverly Hills has a marquee address and reputation. The Southern California woman is very committed to fitness and exercise and stress reduction. The tourist trade that walks Beverly Drive is looking for similar innovative products."(3) Meers said the company looks for three elements when scouting new retail locations. The first is heavy foot traffic, followed by close proximity to yoga studios and health and fitness centres, and finally, spaces that are in lifestyle centres such as open-air mall environments. Future plans in the U.S. include expansion into Chicago, New York City, and Boston.

Asian Expansion—The Big Prize?

The new playing field for athletic apparel companies such as Lululemon is Asia. The Asian region as a whole contributes only one-tenth to one-third of sales for most companies, but industry experts predict that growth will outpace the more mature European and North American markets in the future.

China is the big target, with more than 1.3 billion people. Japan is considered the second most important market with the world's second largest economy and a per capita income of about $30 000. South Korea is next, followed by India. Many executives say, "India is the next China." (4) The populations in these countries are huge and young, and discretionary incomes are growing. These young consumers particularly like American things, and there is a big focus on having brands exactly like they are in the U.S.

The Asian market is different and presents some unique challenges for Lululemon. Robert Meers believes that "you need someone with local market knowledge" in order to be successful. (5) Another issue is sizing. More than a third of Lululemon's Asian sales are XXS, XS, and S, although those contribute only a tiny fraction to North American sales. Lululemon customizes 20 percent of its styles in local design and colour to take advantage of different trends. One trend which appears to be the same so far is that exercise in general has always been a big part of the Asian culture. Yoga, exercise, diet, well-being, and stress reduction seem to be international ideals. There are plans to open four more Lululemon stores in Tokyo, followed by further Asian expansion in the future. This expansion will ultimately change the corporate culture of Lululemon as it operates today, but change is what the future is all about, and the Lululemon's company slogan reminds us all to "Do It Now!"

DISCUSSION QUESTIONS

1. What is Lululemon's retail strategy? What is its target market and how does it try to develop an advantage over its competition?

2. Describe Lululemon's retail mix: location, merchandise assortment, pricing, advertising and promotion, store design and visual merchandising, customer service, and personal selling. How does its retail mix support its strategy?

3. What were the principal drivers behind Lululemon's success in the marketplace? What does the Lululemon brand mean to consumers? How have the growth opportunities that Lululemon has pursued affected the value of its brand name?

4. What are the major challenges facing Lululemon as it goes forward? Is the brand advantage sustainable going forward? Can Lululemon defend its position against other women's active apparel retailers?

Sources for Quotes:
(1) Bogomolny, L (2006, April 24) Toned and Ready, *Canadian Business*, 79 (9) 59–63. Accessed online Aug 2, 2007 from Business Source Database.
(2) Kusterbeck, S. (2006, June) Lululemon Closes the Loop, *Apparel Magazine*, 47(10) 36-40, accessed online Aug 2, 2007.
(3) Vesilind, E. (2006, October 20). Lululemon Expansion Plan sees 240 Units in 5 Years. *WWD: Women's Wear Daily*, 192(84). Accessed online on Aug 2, 2007 from Business Source Database.

(4) Beckett, W. (2006 November 8) Active Firms Compete on Asian Playing Field. *WWW Women's Wear Daily*, 192(98) p. 6 Accessed online August 2, 2007.

(5) Beckett, W. (2006 November 8) Active Firms Compete on Asian Playing Field. *WWW Women's Wear Daily*, 192(98) p. 6 Accessed online August 2, 2007.

Sources:

(6) Lululemon Plans Public Offering in the U.S. (2007, June) SGB, retrieved Aug 2, 2007, from Business Source Premier Database.

(7) Chip Wilson, Entrepreneur of the Year, Lululemon Athletica Inc, *National Post Business Magazine*, December 2004. pg 72-77.

(8) Schiffman, K. (2005 November). Chip Wilson. *Profit*, 24(5), p. 15. Accessed online at Business Source Premier August 2, 2007.

(9) Beckett, W. (2006 November 8) Active Firms Compete on Asian Playing Field. *WWW Women's Wear Daily*, 192(98) p. 6 Accessed online August 2, 2007.

(10) www.lululemon.com Company Web site accessed Aug 2, 2007

(11) Kane, M. Lululemon Shares Soar 55 percent, *The Vancouver Sun*, July 28, 2007 G1.

(12) Young, V. (2007, July 16) Lululemon Releases New IPO Prospectus. *WWD. Women's Wear Daily*, 194(10), p. 20. Accessed online August 2, 2007

(13) Lazarus, E. (2006 November 20) Stretching Its Influence, *Marketing Magazine*, 111(36), p. 25 Accessed online August 2, 2007.

(14) Anderson, D. (2006, May). Stretching for Success. *Business 2.0*, 7(4) 58-60. Accessed online Aug 2, 2007.

CASE 12   Home Depot: Retailing Strategy

Founded in Atlanta, Georgia, Home Depot has grown into the world's largest home improvement specialty retailer. Twenty years of consistent growth is quite an achievement for any retailer; however, due to this growth, Home Depot is a much different company than it was when it was founded by Bernard Marcus and Arthur Blank in 1978. Changes in the company, put into motion by the former CEO, Bob Nardelli, are shaking up the way Home Depot does business. In 2006 Home Depot reported sales of US$90.8 billion, an increase of 10%. However, it dropped three spots to #17 on the 2007 Fortune magazine's Fortune 500 list. It was #13 in 2005 and #14 in 2006. (1)

HISTORY AND CULTURE OF THE COMPANY

During Home Depot's first 20 years, Bernard Marcus was CEO. In 1997, Arthur Blank succeeded his partner at the top of the company. In founding Home Depot, the partnership of Marcus and Blank revolutionized home improvement shopping by creating a different kind of store. Warehouse is a better term for the stores' layout; each location stocks large volumes of goods that enable the company to compete by maintaining low prices. Because Home Depot's primary customer is the individual homeowner or small contractor, the stores also offer knowledgeable customer service to assist those in need of a little direction. In fact, the company took this further by offering how-to clinics and longer four-week courses in its Home Depot University to educate customers about various home improvement projects such as laying tile and caulking bathrooms. Thus, Home Depot effectively combined the strategies of low price and high service, not commonly seen in retailing.

Home Depot's "do-it-yourself" slogan was not just aimed at customers. This philosophy was fostered by the founders and trickled down through the entire company. Home Depot grew, not as a part of a complex plan, but as a result of a good business idea, good people, and some experimentation with new projects such as the Expo home decorating stores. Home Depot's corporate structure was very decentralized; many typical corporate policies were nonexistent in the firm. Each store manager was also a do-it-yourselfer and had a significant amount of control in making decisions pertaining to such areas as merchandising, advertising, and inventory selection for a particular area. Thus, Home Depot stores tended to be less homogeneous in their merchandise offerings than many other national retail chains.

But this decentralization of decision making allows managers to feel a stronger sense of ownership in a store's business. Associates of the company demonstrate a great deal of loyalty and pride in the company. Many store associates are hired with strong background experience in home improvement and are able to pass their knowledge along to customers. By building an enthusiastic staff, Home Depot has been able to deliver its promise of exceptional customer service.

LEADERSHIP CHANGES

In 1999, with well over 900 stores, market share of 24 percent, and several growth initiatives, Home Depot exuded success. However, historical success and future success are different concepts. Home Depot's board of directors was becoming increasingly unhappy. The company's performance at the time was faltering, with a sharp drop in stock price in October of 2000. After disputes about strategy, stores, and people, Home Depot's directors finally took action and so set out to find a leader capable, in their view, of continuing the firm's growth in sales and profits.

The board found their man in Bob Nardelli. At the time, Nardelli was vying for Jack Welch's position as CEO of GE but lost the battle to Jeff Immelt. Although he was passed up at GE, Bob Nardelli's career has been impressive, to say the least. From playing football at Western Illinois University to starting as a manufacturing engineer at GE. Nardelli's attitude was one of persistence and relentless hard work. Nardelli managed to work up through GE to the position of manufacturing VP, left to join the equipment maker Case as an executive vice-president, and then returned to GE to run the Canadian appliance business.

He then continued to prove himself at GE as the head of GE Transportation and CEO of GE Power Systems. Throughout his career at GE, Nardelli was recognized for his ability to improve operations and execute, but, unfortunately, he was not viewed as a strong strategic leader. Believing he was finally in the right position to succeed Welch, Nardelli was very disappointed at the announcement of Immelt's appointment. Home Depot quickly snatched Nardelli up, placing him as CEO of Home Depot in December of 2000. Nardelli redirected his energy into a mission to develop Home Depot.

In January 2007, Home Depot and Robert Nardelli mutually agreed on his resignation after six years in the CEO position. There were complaints about Nardelli's heavy-handed management and whether his pay package of $123.7 million, excluding stock options, over the past five years was excessive. Compared to the major competitor Lowe's in the U.S., the Home Depot stock had performed poorly. Nardelli received a golden parachute severance of $210 million despite the fact that stock went down. His successor is Frank Blake, who served as the vice chairman of the board and executive vice president at Home Depot since 2002. (2)

CHANGES AT HOME DEPOT

Since Nardelli took the lead at Home Depot, the company has experienced significant changes. Home Depot is shifting toward a more centralized organization, one that can more efficiently handle the operations of a 2500 store company in Canada, Mexico, and the United States. For example, buying, once handled by nine regional offices, is now located at corporate headquarters in Atlanta. The company as a whole benefits from consolidation; buyers can get larger quantities of goods at lower costs, but how does this affect the do-it-yourself store manager? Nardelli,

always a relentless workaholic, expected those around him to have the same attitude, holding frequent meetings and treating weekends like any other day of business.

Changes are not just affecting Home Depot's associates. In the past, Home Depot's customer return policy was simply to give cash back, no matter what. Although this was fantastic customer service, without receipt restrictions abuse of the policy was out of control. Home Depot will now save more than US$10 million annually with a new return policy of only store credit without a receipt.

Nardelli applied the GE mindset, one characterized by strict measurement emphasizing efficiency, to his new company. Home Depot is now using GE's Six Sigma quality control method and is quickly increasing the company's use of the Internet. Another new focus is associate training and evaluation. Pre-Nardelli, Home Depot had 157 different associate appraisal forms. All 295 000 associates are now reviewed using just two different forms.

These changes do not mean that the company is less interested in developing its people; in fact, Home Depot is trying to create an environment that will best highlight individuals' abilities. At the headquarters in Atlanta, the company is forming a leadership institute offering courses on leadership, merchandising, store planning, financial operations, and Six Sigma to executives with high potential.

Nardelli wanted to create a "coaching environment" that promoted succession planning and avoided the recent incident of having to hire a CEO from outside the company. Despite Nardelli's efforts, the market has not been kind to Home Depot. In Nardelli's first six months, the stock price rose from US$39 to US$53 but then, curiously, fell 10 percent after a first-quarter announcement of 35 percent profits growth. Quarterly earnings continue to grow as in the past, but, unfortunately, Home Depot's stock price is not reflecting this trend.

COMPETITION AND GROWTH POTENTIAL

As Home Depot struggles with its own growing pains, the company must also consider the ever-increasing competition from Lowe's in the U.S. and Canadian Tire and Rona in Canada. By placing stores in directly competing areas, Lowe's is definitely a factor in future planning. Lowe's best advantage is that its stores are designed with less of a "warehouse" feel, having wider aisles and better lighting.

Store appearance may not be a crucial factor, but it is definitely a differentiating feature for a female shopper. And women are increasingly doing a greater percentage of home improvement shopping. Canadian Tire is a well-established Canadian retailer that has recently completed major renovations to its stores and added unique customer services, such as the Celebration Station and convenience stores connected to its gas bars. Home Depot is trying to address issues by cleaning up and modernizing its store look with lower shelving and different product mixes.

Extending its already strong business targeted at individual customers, Home Depot is now opening several professional stores for contractors, developers, and superintendent or maintenance people. The firm is also looking to expand through purchases of European home improvement companies.

DISCUSSION QUESTIONS

1. What are the differences between Home Depot, Canadian Tire, and Rona?

2. What is the best way for Home Depot to continue to grow?

3. Can Home Depot maintain its current market position with its new policies and increasing competition?

4. How successful was Home Depot in targeting the female market? What changes did it make in its retail marketing mix to appeal to the female target?

5. How might the shifts in corporate culture affect executives, management, and associates?

Source: This case was written by Cynthia Wongsuwan, University of Florida.
(1) www.wikipedia.com
(2) www.homedepot.com Company Web site accessed online July 28, 2007.

CASE 13   Ahold: International Retailing Strategy

In 1887, 22-year-old Albert Heijn took over his father's small grocery store near Zaandam, West Holland. His strategy for growing the family business was to offer quality products with excellent customer service at the lowest prices. Now, 120 years later, Ahold (an abbreviation of Albert Heijn Holding) is the world's second-largest food retailer.

It operates 1600 stores in 27 countries, with 2003 sales greater than US$56 billion. But its name is not on a single store it owns. Ahold operates under 26 different names in Europe, America, Asia, and Latin America. It uses 10 different formats for its stores, ranging from tiny gas station outlets in the Netherlands to 13 950 square metre hypermarkets in Northern Brazil. The company refers to its strategy as "multilocal, multiformat, multichannel." "Our culture is first and foremost the culture of the local operating company," says Cees van der Hoeven, Ahold's 54-year-old CEO. "What makes Ahold unique is that we're perceived by our customers as the local guy." Very few customers at a Bruno's supermarket in Alabama or a Disco store in Argentina realize that their store is part of global retail giant headquartered in the Netherlands.

Wal-Mart and Carrefour, the first- and third-largest food retailers, use a different approach. From Paris to Shanghai, all Carrefour stores look the same and have identical layouts (to reach the deli counter, for example, you always turn left at the entrance). Wal-Mart also uses its name on most of its stores across the world. Three years ago, it acquired the Asada chain in the U.K. and still operates the stores under the Asada name. But when it bought the Wertkauf chain and some Spar stores in Germany, it converted the stores to Wal-Marts. The British and German stores are expected to conform to the cost-conscious, customer-oriented Wal-Mart culture.

Ahold is a food retailer. Food sales account for 90 percent of its revenues. Recognizing the lifestyle trend toward more out-of-home food consumption, Ahold is attempting to increase its share of the stomach through its acquisition of food-service companies. In contrast, Wal-Mart and Carrefour focus on operating larger supercentres or hypermarkets that offer general merchandise as well as food.

Another difference between Ahold and its major international competitors is its growth strategy. Although Wal-Mart has made some acquisitions, most of its international growth, and all of Carrefour's, has been internally generated. In contrast, Ahold has grown primarily through acquisitions. More than 50 percent of Ahold's revenue now comes from the U.S. supermarket chains it acquired.

Its first acquisition in the United States, in 1977, was BI-LO, a South Carolina–based grocery store chain operating about 450 stores in South Carolina, Georgia, Tennessee, Florida, and Alabama. Then it acquired Stop & Shop, with 320 stores stretching from Massachusetts to Eastern New Jersey; Giant Landover of Maryland in

Maryland, Washington, DC, Delaware, Southern New Jersey, and Northern Virginia; Giant Carlisle in Pennsylvania; Tops in New York; and Bruno in Alabama, the Florida Panhandle, and Mississippi. With 1400 stores in the United States, Ahold is the largest food retailer in the eastern part of the country and the fourth biggest in the whole U.S.

In 1999, the company bought U.S. Foodservice, America's second-largest supplier of ready-made meals, prepared foods, and ingredients to restaurants, hotels, and other institutions. Ahold rescued Peapod, one of the first Internet grocers, from bankruptcy in 2000 by taking a majority stake in the company. Peapod now operates out of Stop & Shop and Giant stores in the Boston, New York, and Washington, DC, areas, as well as on its own in its home base of Chicago.

No other European retailer has been as successful in entering the U.S. market as Ahold. For example, Carrefour opened two stores in suburban Philadelphia in the late 1980s but gave up quickly when it faced labour problems and the loyalty customers had to their local supermarket chains. The profit margin for Ahold's U.S. division is 5.7 percent, whereas the profit margin for the European division is only 3.9 percent of sales.

Van der Hoeven has a vision of a future in which Ahold's stores in Guatemala would offer tips on pricing to their colleagues in the United States and the flooring for every Ahold supermarket from Boston to São Paulo would be ordered from the same supplier. The payoff from this networked global juggernaut would be the ability to leverage its size to get rock-bottom prices from its vendors on everything from corn flakes to oranges.

Meanwhile, Ahold's companies in Europe, America, Asia, and Latin America would lower their costs by using the same trucks, sharing the same accountants, and exchanging ideas over the corporate intranet. But this global network would be invisible to the 20 million customers who pass through Ahold stores every week. Ahold has yet to realize this vision. Although Ahold has now centralized the procurement of fresh and chilled products across its six U.S. chains, only 5 percent of all merchandise in Ahold's stores is ordered on a cross-continental basis, about the same as Wal-Mart and Carrefour.

Ahold's U.S. managers are just beginning to exchange best practices with their counterparts overseas. For example, Stop & Shop and Peapod are trying to improve their fulfillment accuracy by learning how Ahold's Scandinavian Internet home-delivery service has achieved its successes in performing these activities. However, Ahold's goal is to bring the same supply chain efficiencies achieved by Wal-Mart and Carrefour in general merchandise distribution to food distribution.

DISCUSSION QUESTIONS

1. What are the advantages and disadvantages of the growth strategies pursued by Ahold, Carrefour, and Wal-Mart?

2. Should Ahold use its name on all of its stores like Wal-Mart and Carrefour? Why or why not?

3. What are the advantages and disadvantages of Wal-Mart and Carrefour's more centralized decision making compared to Ahold's decentralized decision making?

Source: This case was written by Barton Weitz, University of Florida.

CASE 14   Lindy's Bridal Shoppe

Located in Lake City (population 80 000), Lindy's Bridal Shoppe, a small bridal store, sells bridal gowns, prom gowns, accessories, and silk flowers. It also rents men's formal wear and performs various alteration services. Lindy Armstrong, age 33, has owned the store since its founding in March 1997. She's married to a high school teacher and is the mother of three young children. A former nurse, she found the demands of hospital schedules left too little time for her young family. An energetic, active woman with many interests, she wanted to continue to work but also have time with her children.

The silk flowers market enabled Lindy to combine an in-home career with child rearing. She started Lindy's Silk Flowers with $75 of flower inventory in Vernon, a small town of about 10 000 people 10 kilometres from Lake City. Working out of her home, she depended on word-of-mouth communication among her customers, mainly brides, to bring in business. As Lindy's Silk Flowers prospered, a room was added onto the house to provide more space for the business. Lindy was still making all the flowers herself.

Her flower-making schedule kept her extremely busy. Long hours were the norm. Lindy was approached by a young photographer named Dan Morgan, who proposed establishing a one-stop bridal shop. In this new business, Dan would provide photography, Lindy would provide silk flowers, and another partner, Karen Ross (who had expertise in the bridal market), would provide gowns and accessories. The new store would be located in Vernon in a rented structure. Shortly before the store was to open, Dan and Karen decided not to become partners and Lindy became the sole owner. She knew nothing about the bridal business. Having no merchandise or equipment, Lindy was drawn to an ad announcing that a bridal store in a major city was going out of business.

She immediately called and arranged to meet the owner. Subsequently, she bought all his stock (mannequins, racks, and carpet) for $4000. The owner also gave her a crash course in the bridal business. From March 1997 to December 2006, Lindy owned and operated a bridal gown and silk flowers store named Lindy's Bridal Shoppe in Vernon. The location was chosen primarily because it was close to her home. Although Vernon is a very small town, Lindy felt that location wasn't a critical factor in her store's success. She maintained that people would travel some distance to make a purchase as important as a bridal gown. Rent was $250 per month plus utilities. Parking was a problem.

During this period, Lindy's Bridal Shoppe grew. Bridal gowns and accessories as well as prom dresses sold well. As the time approached for Lindy to renew her lease, she wondered about the importance of location. A move to Lake City might be advisable. A much larger town than Vernon, Lake City is the site of a university. Lindy decided to move.

GENERAL BUSINESS DESCRIPTION

The majority of Lindy's Bridal Shoppe's current sales are made to individuals who order bridal gowns off the rack or from the catalogues of three major suppliers. At the time of the order, the customer pays a deposit, usually half of the purchase price. The balance is due in 30 days. Lindy would like payment in full at the time of ordering regardless of the delivery date. But payment is often delayed until delivery. Once ordered, a gown must be taken and the bill paid when delivered.

No tuxedos are carried in the store, so customers must order from catalogues. Fitting jackets and shoes are provided to help patrons size their purchases. Lindy's Bridal Shoppe rents its men's formal wear from suppliers. Payment from the customer is due on delivery. Certain times of the year see more formal events than others. Many school proms are held during late April and May, and June, July, and August are big months for weddings.

Since traditional dates for weddings are followed less and less closely, Lindy believes that the business is becoming less seasonal, though January and February are quite slow.

PROMOTION PRACTICES

Lindy's Bridal Shoppe engages in various promotional activities but is constrained by her limited finances. The firm has no operating budget, which prevents any formal appropriation for advertising expenses. Newspaper ads constitute the primary promotional medium, though radio is occasionally used. Ads for prom dresses are run only during prom season. These ads usually feature a photograph of a local high school student in a Lindy's Bridal Shoppe gown plus a brief description of the student's activities.

Other promotional activities include bridal shows at a local mall. Lindy feels these have been very successful, though they're a lot of work. A recent prom show in a local high school used students as models. This proved to be an excellent way to stimulate sales. Lindy hopes to go into several other area high schools during the next prom season, though this will demand much planning.

PERSONNEL

Lindy, the sole owner and also the manager of the firm, finds it hard to maintain a capable workforce. As a small company, Lindy's Bridal Shoppe can't offer premium salaries for its few positions. There's one full-time salesperson. The part-time staff includes a salesperson, alterations person, bookkeeper, and custodian. Lindy handles all the paperwork. Her responsibilities include paying bills, ordering merchandise and supplies, hiring and firing personnel, fitting customers, and selling various items. She makes all the major decisions that directly affect the firm's operations. She also makes all the silk flowers herself. It's time-consuming, but she isn't satisfied with how anyone else makes them.

MERCHANDISE OFFERINGS

Lindy's Bridal Shoppe's major product lines are new wedding, prom, and party gowns. No used gowns are sold. Discontinued styles or gowns that have been on the rack for a year are sold at reduced prices, primarily because discoloration is a major problem. Gowns tend to yellow after hanging on the racks for a year. A wide variety of accessories are provided. Lindy believes it's important that her customers not have to go anywhere else for them. These accessories include shoes, veils, headpieces, jewellery, and foundations. Slips may be rented instead of purchased. One room of Lindy's Bridal Shoppe is used only to prepare silk flowers.

SERVICE OFFERINGS

Lindy's Bridal Shoppe's major service offering is fitting and alteration. Most gowns must be altered, for which there's a nominal charge. Lindy feels that personal attention and personal service set her apart from her competitors. Emphasizing customer satisfaction, she works hard to please each customer. This isn't always easy. Customers can be picky, and it takes time to deal with unhappy people.

LOCATION

Lindy's Bridal Shoppe is located at the end of Lake City's main through street. Initially Lindy didn't think location was important to her bridal store's success, but she's changed her mind. Whereas business was good in Vernon, it's booming in Lake City. Vehicular traffic is high, and there's adequate, if not excess, parking. Lindy's Bridal Shoppe has a 12-year lease. Rent ($1800 per month) includes heat and water, but Lindy's Bridal Shoppe must pay for interior decoration. The physical facility is generally attractive, with open and inviting interior display areas. But some areas both inside and outside the store have an unfinished look.

Some storage areas require doors or screens to enhance the interior's appearance. The fitting room ceilings are unfinished, and the carpeting inside the front door may be unsafe. One other interior problem is insufficient space. There seems to be inadequate space for supporting activities such as flower preparation, customer fittings, and merchandise storage, which gives the store a cluttered look.

Several external problems exist. The signs are ineffective, and there's a strong glare on the front windows. This detracts from the effectiveness of the overall appearance and interior window displays. The parking lot needs minor maintenance. Parking lines should be painted and curbs must be repaired. Much should be done to add colour and atmosphere through basic landscaping.

COMPETITION

Lindy's Bridal Shoppe is the only bridal shop in Lake City. Lindy believes she has four main competitors. Whitney's Bridal Shoppe is 5 km from Lake City; Ender's Brides, a new shop with a good operation, is in Spartan City, 80 km away; Carole's is a large, established bridal shop in Smithtown, 110 km distant; and Gowns-n-Such is in Andersonville, 120 km away. A new store in Yorktown (25 km away) is selling used gowns and discontinued styles at reduced prices. Lindy watches this new- and used-gown store closely.

Some of her potential customers are buying wedding gowns from electronic retailers such as the Knot (www.theknot.com) and the Wedding Channel (www.weddingchannel.com). Although these electronic retailers are not making significant sales in her trading area now, Lindy is concerned that some of the services offered by these electronic retailers (such as gift registries, e-mail notices, wedding planning, and wedding picture displays) will attract her customers.

FINANCIAL CONSIDERATIONS

Basic financial information includes:

1. Markup: 50 percent.
2. 2007 sales: $200 000 (estimated).
3. Average inventory: $70 000.
4. Turnover: 3.0 (approximately).
5. Annual expenses are:
   Rent: $19 200.
   Labour: $24 000.
   Utilities: $7000.
   Supplies: $12 000.
   Equipment: $4000.
   Miscellaneous: $4000.
6. Estimated total costs ($200 000 sales): $170 200.
7. Implied profit including owner's salary: $29 800.
8. Capital invested (equipment, $8000; inventory, $70 000): $78 000.
9. ROI: $5800/$78 000 = 7.4 percent. (Assume owner salary of $24 000 per year.)

THE FUTURE

Lindy Armstrong is uncertain about the future. She enjoys the business, but feels that she's working very hard and not making much money. During all the years of Lindy's Bridal Shoppe's operation, she hasn't taken a salary. She works 60 hours or more a week. Business is excellent and growing, but she's tired. She has even discussed selling the business and returning to nursing.

DISCUSSION QUESTIONS

1. Could Lindy change the emphasis of her merchandise mix to increase her sales?
2. Which products should have more emphasis? Which should have less?
3. What personnel decisions must Lindy face to improve her business?
4. How could someone like Lindy Armstrong balance the demands of her family and her business?
5. If one of Lindy's competitors were to offer her $150 000 for her business, should she sell?

Source: This case was prepared by Linda F. Felicetti and Joseph P. Grunewald, Clarion University of Pennsylvania.

CASE 15   Hughe's: Developing a Buying Plan

In this hypothetical case, a well-established, medium-sized Canadian department store, Hughe's reflects consumers' needs by featuring popular names in fashion for the individual consumer, family, and home. It tries to offer a distinctive, wide assortment of quality merchandise with personalized customer service. The many customer services include personal shoppers; credit with in-house charge, MasterCard, and Visa; and an interior design studio. Hughe's pricing policy permits it to draw customers from several income brackets. Moderate-income consumers seeking value and fashion-predictable soft goods are target customers, as are upscale customers with a special interest in fashion.

The department store is implementing new marketing strategies to prepare for continuing growth and expansion. Hughe's merchandising philosophy is to attract the discerning middle-market customer who comprises 70 percent of the population as well as sophisticated fashion-conscious consumers who expect to buy high-quality, brand-name merchandise at competitive prices.

One portion of Hughe's buying staff is responsible for the Oriental rug department within home furnishings. The open-to-buy figure for this classification within the home furnishings division will be based on last year's sales history (Exhibit 1).

exhibit 1
Last Year's Fall/Winter Sales Results for Oriental Rugs

Sales volume	$120 000			
Markup	51.5%			
Size	Percentage of Sales		Fabrication	Percentage of Sales
3′ × 5′	20%		Silk	15%
4′ × 6′	40		Cotton	25
6′ × 9′	15		Wool	60
8′ × 10′	10			
9′ × 12′	15			

It has been projected that a 15 percent increase over last year's sales volume can be attained due to oriental rugs' continued popularity. This year's open-to-buy for fall/winter will be $66 200. The buying staff will be making its purchases for fall/winter in Amritsar, India, a city known for top-quality carpets. Ghuman Export Private, Ltd., of Amritsar, Punjab, India, is the manufacturer the buyers will contact.

Exhibit 2 shows information about Ghuman to use in the decision-making process.

DISCUSSION QUESTION

1. Work up a buying plan to use when buying from Ghuman. Decide how to distribute the allotted open-to-buy dollars among the available sizes, colours, and fabrications. Since it's an overseas manufacturer, consider additional costs such as duty and shipping, which also need to be covered by the allocated open-to-buy dollars.

This case was prepared by Professor Ann Fairhurst, Indiana University.

exhibit 2
Ghuman's Wholesale Price List

	FABRICATION		
Size	Silk	Wool	Cotton
3′ × 5′	$400	$250	—
4′ × 6′	700	500	$200
6′ × 9′	850	700	275
8′ × 10′	1200	1000	350
9′ × 12′	1400	1300	500

Colours: Background colours available are navy, burgundy, black, and cream.

Quantities required for purchase: No minimum orders required.

Payment plan: Payment can be made in Canadian dollars or Indian rupees. Letter of credit needs to be established prior to market trip.

Delivery: Air freight—10 to 14 days, delivery time; cost is usually 25 percent of total order.

Ocean freight—39 days plus inland time is necessary; cost is usually 8–10 percent of total order.

Customer loyalty: Loyalty to customers is exceptional. Damaged shipments can be returned. Ghuman's philosophy is to help the retailers obtain a profit on their product lines.

CASE 16 — McFadden's Department Store: Preparation of a Merchandise Budget Plan

In this hypothetical case, McFadden's Department Store in Canada has been a profitable family-owned business since its beginning in 1910. Last year's sales volume was $180 million. More recently, however, many of its departments have been losing ground to national stores moving into the area. To complicate this problem, a recession equalling a 6.5 percent drop in sales in the coming year is predicted.

Department 121 is one of the more profitable departments in the store, maintaining a gross margin of 55 percent. Its basic merchandise is young men's clothing. Last year sales reached $2 780 750 for the July–December season.

The highest sales period is the back-to-school period in August, when autumn fashions are supported by strong promotional advertising. Reductions (including markdowns, discounts to employees, and shrinkage) typically run 20 percent of sales. The percentage of reductions is spread throughout the season as follows:

July	August	September	October	November	December
10	20	15	10	10	35

exhibit 1   Form for Merchandise Budget Plan

By month, the percentages of annual sales for Department 121 within this six-month period had been distributed as follows:

	July	August	September	October	November	December
2003	3.6	10.1	9.2	6.4	4.8	9.1
2004	3.5	10.3	9.6	6.8	5.3	8.8
2005	3.5	10.5	9.6	6.2	5.5	8.2
2006	3.0	10.3	9.8	6.6	5.5	8.0

A pre-Christmas sale has been planned in an attempt to counterbalance the slackened sales period following the first of the year. The buyer has decided to bring in some new merchandise for the sale to go along with the remaining fall fashion merchandise. The buyer expects that this will increase December's percentage of annual sales to 30 percent above what it would be without the sale. Top management has emphasized that the department achieve a gross margin return on investment (GMROI) of 250 percent.

Forecasted ending stock level in December is $758 000. Additional information is available on the historical stock-to-sales ratio for this type of department. This information is taken from a similar department in another store that happens to have a lower average stock-to-sales ratio.

July	August	September	October	November	December
3.0	1.9	2.1	2.4	2.5	2.2

DISCUSSION QUESTION

1. Your task is to prepare a merchandise budget plan by using the form in Exhibit 1.

Source: This case was prepared by Michael Levy, Babson College, and Harold Koenig, Oregon State University.

CASE 17   Capital Sportswear: Buying

"We need to have vendors who can take this burden off of us," said Ken Joynes, Capital Sportswear inventory manager. "We have had a sales increase of 20 percent over the last two years and my people can't keep up with it anymore."

In this hypothetical case, Keith Wilson, general manager of Capital Sportswear, reviewed the colourful chart showing the sales trend and replied, "I never thought I would have to complain about a sales increase, but it is obvious that the sales are well beyond our control. Something has to be done and that is why we are meeting today."

Capital Sportswear was founded by George Wilson in 1963 in a major metropolitan area. For years, Capital Sportswear has been successful in the sportswear market. In 2000, George Wilson retired, and his son, Keith Wilson, was appointed general manager. From the beginning, Keith Wilson has been a real go-getter. Recently completing his MBA, he has wasted no time in locating new markets for Capital Sportswear. He immediately contacted major universities and colleges and gained four-year exclusive contracts for apparel purchases made by the sports teams of their athletic departments.

Soon after, Capital's sportswear became popular among students. This growing demand for the company's products motivated Wilson to open two more retail stores. During the fall of 2006, the sales had increased beyond expectations. Although the company achieved a successful reputation in the marketplace, sales growth has generated major problems.

In the beginning, operations were fairly smooth and the company's inventory control department updated most of its procedures. Joynes emphasized the crucial role of routinization in the overall inventory maintenance process to keep up with the increasing turnover. The sales increase was 20 percent, as opposed to the 12 percent that had been forecasted for 2007. It was this increase that initiated a series of problems in the inventory control department. To temporarily alleviate the backlog, Wilson authorized Joynes to lease an additional warehouse (see the replenishment level for July 2006 in Exhibit 1). It was decided that a maximum of 16 percent of the total inventory carrying costs was going to be dedicated to the off-premise inventory.

Worrying about not being able to meet demand on time, Joynes met with suppliers and asked them to provide more timely delivery schedules to Capital Sportswear. When he stated that the company was not going to tolerate any reasons for future delays, two major suppliers expressed their concerns about his lack of flexibility and requested price concessions. They simply indicated that Joynes's demand had to be supported by providing cash or reducing quantity discounts. Joynes ignored these comments and indicated how serious he really was by stating that Capital Sportswear could always find new suppliers.

By the end of a long discussion, arguments were beyond the manageable point and the two large suppliers decided to quit dealing with the company. After the meeting, Joynes received a memo from Wilson. Wilson was very concerned about the potential reactions of the rest of the

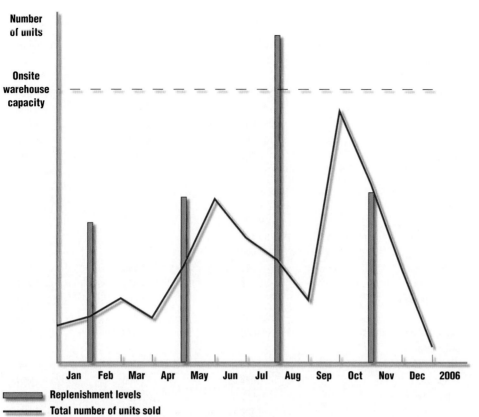

exhibit 1

Sales for Capital
Sportswear in 2006

Number of units

Onsite warehouse capacity

Jan Feb Mar Apr May Jun Jul Aug Sep Oct Nov Dec 2006

▬ Replenishment levels
──── Total number of units sold

vendors. He stated in his memo that since Capital Sportswear was continuously growing, it was expected to present a more supportive attitude to its suppliers. He expressed his belief that the company needed a cohesive atmosphere with the rest of the channel members, especially with its vendors.

During the next six months, Joynes had limited success in locating one or more large suppliers that would be able to deliver the products to Capital Sportswear on a timely basis. Faced with growing demand from the surrounding colleges and universities, he had to accumulate excess stock to avoid possible shortages. At the end of the six-month period, a memo from the accounting department of the company indicated the financial significance of the problem. In his memo, accounting manager Roger Boles simply addressed the high costs of inventory maintenance/security functions (for details, see Exhibit 2). He advised finding a substitute inventory policy to lower these cost figures.

Specifically, he stated that the rental cost for the additional warehouse had levelled off at 16 percent, well beyond the maximum. Keith Wilson immediately scheduled a meeting and asked the top managers to come up with the alternative plans to eliminate this problem. "I

should have never let those suppliers quit," said Joynes. "It had a negative effect on our image, and now we all see the results." "It's too late to worry about that," admonished Wilson. "Instead, we have to come up with a strategy to meet the demand effectively without increasing our costs to the detriment of profits. You realize that the university contracts will expire at the end of the year."

"That's the crucial fact," said Boles. "We simply cannot afford to stock up beyond the current level; it is just too expensive. It is well beyond the funds we have had even from the increased sales."

"In other words, the elimination of the excess inventory is necessary. Who are the vendors that we have at the moment?" asked Wilson. "There are only three suppliers remaining after the last meeting," replied Joynes. "They are fairly small businesses, but we've been dealing with them for quite some time. They have been successful in keeping up with us, and the details of their operations are summarized in their report."

"It seems like we have a good selection here," said Wilson, after looking at the report in front of him. "If they mostly work with us, we should be able to influence the future direction of their operations. In other words, it should

exhibit 2

Comparative Statement of Profit and Loss for Years Ended December 31

	2007 (forecast)	2006	2005
Net sales	$165 000	$120 000	$100 000
Cost of sales			
Beginning inventory	7 000	6 000	4 000
Purchases (net)	140 000	92 000	62 000
	147 000	98 000	66 000
Ending inventory	9 000	7 000	6 000
	138 000	91 000	61 000
Gross profit	27 000	29 000	39 000
Expenses			
Stock maintenance	7 500	5 250	750
Rent	2 500	1 250	250
Insurance	4 500	3 500	1 500
Interest	4 500	2 500	1 000
Selling	3 500	2 500	2 000
Promotion	7 500	5 500	4 000
Supplies	2 750	1 500	250
Miscellaneous	2 250	1 500	250
	35 000	23 500	10 000
Net profit from operations	(8 000)	5 500	29 000
Other income			
Dividends	925	750	450
Interest	825	600	350
Miscellaneous	650	400	200
	2 400	1 750	1 000
Net profit before taxes	(5 600)	7 250	130 000
Provision for income taxes	1 008	1 305	8 100
Net profit after taxes	(4 592)	5 945	21 900

not be difficult to convince them that they need to upgrade their deliveries in such a way that we can eliminate our excess inventory."

"That would cut down the rental costs that we incur from the additional warehouse," said Boles. "Obviously!" Wilson replied impatiently. "We will probably need to provide those vendors with a comprehensive support program. If we can convert the floor space of the warehouse from storage to sales, we will have additional funds in retail operations. We can invest a portion of these funds in supporting our vendors and improve our image by forming a cohesive network with them. Of course, there will be a limit to this support. After all, it will be expensive for us to make the transition, too. Therefore, I would like you to come up with an analysis for converting the existing system to a more efficient one. I would like to know what we can do and how we can do it. To be very honest, gentlemen, I do not want to increase the sales if we do not know how to handle that increase."

DISCUSSION QUESTIONS

1. What is relationship management?

2. Explain how relationship management can benefit both retailer and supplier?

3. How might the use of a quick response system affect the financial performance of Capital Sportswear?

4. What problems would Wilson have implementing a quick response system with vendors?

Source: This case was prepared by S. Alton Erdem, University of Minnesota–Duluth.

CASE 18 — Shoppers Drug Mart: Category Management

Shoppers Drug Mart is a full-service retailer that offers shoppers the convenience of one-stop shopping at its drug/cosmetic/food combo stores. The chain features a variety of high-quality products at competitive prices but uses promotional pricing as well. Historically, Shoppers has enjoyed great success in its markets and had led the region for several years. In this hypothetical case, one winter morning Robert Ignacio, the director of strategic planning, had a more immediate concern. The wire services had reported a few weeks ago that the Valumart grocery chain had announced plans for the construction of 10 new food-and-drug combo centres throughout Shoppers' markets. After poring over current research and financial results, a decision had been made to examine category management as a defence against the encroachment of Valumart.

A decision was also made to pilot test category management in some categories before implementing a systemwide rollout. One of the categories chosen for the test was shampoo. Robert's immediate assignment was to review the product category and report back to management with an initial recommendation. Robert reviewed the events of the past few weeks and the information that he had obtained on the shampoo category. He had several third-party reports (Exhibits 1, 2, and 3) that provided background information about national trends in the shampoo category and trends in supermarkets. Another report (Exhibit 4) provided him with information on how Shoppers' shampoo sales compared to the rest of the market.

However, these reports did not provide Robert with information on how Shoppers stacked up against the competition in terms of its assortment and pricing. After some checking around, Robert found that he could order reports from third-party vendors that would provide him with an analysis of Shoppers and the competition on product mix and pricing. He had placed an urgent order for these analyses, which arrived via courier (Exhibits 5, 6, and 7).

exhibit 1

Total Supermarket Dynamics: Shampoo— Aerosol, Liquid, Lotion, and Powder

52 Weeks	# Active UPCs	% New UPCs	# UPCs Handled	UPC Dollar Velocity
Category	1974	15%	235	$1.64
Brands	1714	16	229	1.65
Private label	241	12	5	1.33
Generic	19	—	1	1.00

exhibit 2

Shampoo Dollar Share

Trade Channel	12 Months Last Year	12 Months This Year
Food	51.7%	50.5%
Drug	25.6	25.0
Mass merchant	22.7	24.5

exhibit 3

Shampoo Growth

Trade Channel	Dollar Sales % Change versus a Year Ago
Food	0.9%
Drug	4.2
Mass merchant	8.1

exhibit 4

Dollar Sales: Percent Change versus a Year Ago

	MARKET		SHOPPERS	
	13 Weeks	52 Weeks	13 Weeks	52 Weeks
Total dollar sales	+0.1	+1.2	−10.6	−4.5
HBA department	+1.5	+4.2	−8.5	−4.3
Shampoo category	−3.5	+0.7	−19.6	−9.7

exhibit 5

Competitive Price Comparison for Shampoo: Counts of Items Showing Differences from the Base Zone (Shoppers Drug Mart)

	Shoppers	Food #1	Mass Merch.	Chain Drug	Food #2
Competition is higher	0	87	0	101	0
Competition is same	103	0	0	0	59
Competition is lower	0	16	103	2	44
Competition does not carry	0	0	0	0	0

Here are explanations of a few terms in the analyses:

UPC	Supermarket terminology for SKU (stock-keeping unit)
UPCs handled	Average number of UPCs stocked by food stores
UPC dollar velocity	Revenue per UPC per store per week
HBA	Health and beauty aids
Market	All food stores
Remaining market	All food stores excluding Shoppers

As Robert headed for the water cooler, feeling upbeat in the thought that he had a handle on the shampoo category, he ran into Hal Jeffreys, who was a longtime veteran of Shoppers and a vice-president of information systems. Knowing that Hal had at one time managed Health and Beauty Aids at Shoppers, Robert mentioned his review of the shampoo category and the category management initiative. Hal said that for years he had a simple approach for category management: he would begin by generating a list of slow sellers in the category and then try to replace these slow sellers with new products or by increasing the shelf space for existing products. With the new information systems that Shoppers had installed in the past year,

exhibit 6　Brand Importance Report for Shampoo: Shoppers Drug Mart versus Remaining Market for 13 Weeks

Description	Chain Sales	Chain Rank	Rem. Mkt. Rank	Rem. Mkt. Sales	Chain Mkt. Share	Chain Category Impt.	Rem. Mkt. Cat. Impt.
Clean & Soft	$108 826	1	1	$512 345	17.5%	14.5	13.0
1st Impressions	77 672	2	3	370 341	17.3	10.3	9.4
Mane Tame	64 446	3	4	244 160	20.9	8.6	6.2
Bargain Bubbles	56 864	4	2	433 300	11.6	7.6	11.0
Silky Style	43 198	5	6	147 773	22.6	5.8	3.7
Elegance	30 869	6	5	181 075	14.6	4.1	4.6

exhibit 7　Product Mix Summary Report: Shampoo Dollar Sales—13 Weeks

	Clean & Soft	1st Impressions	Mane Tame	Bargain Bubbles	Silky Style	Elegance	Private Label
Items carried							
Shoppers	25	25	15	21	13	5	7
Rem. mkt.	25	39	28	42	20	16	28
Sizes carried							
Shoppers	6	6	6	2	4	1	4
Rem. mkt.	7	10	11	3	5	4	6
Types carried							
Shoppers	6	7	6	19	4	5	6
Rem. mkt.	6	10	8	32	5	7	21

exhibit 8　Slow Seller Report: Shampoo for Shoppers Drug Mart, 13 Weeks versus a Year Ago

Item	Chain Sales	Chain Mkt. Shr.	Chain Subcat Impt.	Rem. Mkt. Growth	Chain Growth	Chain Avg. % Stores Selling
Golden JJB Lq T 3 oz.	$ 3	9.9%	0.0	−51.2	−50.0	0%
1st Imprs. DF ND Lot. 11 oz.	10	0.7	0.0	−59.4	−99.4	0
Gentle GLD Lq. 11 oz.	11	100.0	0.0	−100.0	9.6	0
Golden AV Lq. T 3 oz.	12	22.4	0.0	13.2	−69.2	1
Suds PB Lq. 8 oz.	14	6	0.0	107.1	2.9	0
Sikly Style X-B Lq. 18 oz.	14	1.6	0.0	−65.6	−99.5	0

Case 19   Enterprise: Human Resource Strategy

531

generating a slow seller list was very easy. To prove his point Hal walked back with Robert to his office and, using his PC, generated a slow seller report for the shampoo category (Exhibit 8). "See, technology has made this a real cinch," said Hal and wondered whether the expense and effort of category management would produce net improvements over and above this very simple "knock off the slow seller" approach. "I'll try to come to your presentation tomorrow," said Hal as he left Robert's office.

As Hal left his office, Robert sank back into his chair with a knot in his stomach. He felt that he had jumped the gun in thinking that he had a handle on the shampoo category. Things seemed to be more complicated than they had appeared earlier in the day. Robert wondered whether the shampoo category seemed so difficult because it was the first attempt at category management. In any case, his immediate concern was to prepare for his presentation tomorrow. Since Hal Jeffreys would be in the audience, he knew that he would have to address the "knock out the slow sellers" perspective.

DISCUSSION QUESTIONS

1. In this hypothetical case of Shoppers Drug Mart, what are the national sales trends in the shampoo category?

2. What are the differences in shampoo sales trends at Shoppers compared to the national trends?

3. What could be causing these differences?

4. Suggest a plan of action.

Source: This case was written by Professor Kirthi Kalyanam, Retail Management Institute, Santa Clara University. © Dr. Kirthi Kalyanam.

(1) www.shoppersdrugmart.ca Company Web site accessed online July 29, 2007.

CASE 19   Enterprise: Human Resource Strategy

When most people think of car rental firms, they think of Hertz or Avis, but Enterprise is the largest and most profitable U.S. car rental business. The worldwide revenue in 2006 was US$9.0 billion. There were 711 000 rental car vehicles in service and more than 6900 offices located conveniently where people live and work. More than 6000 of these offices are in the U.S alone, and there are currently more than 900 offices in Canada, the United Kingdom, Germany, and Ireland. (1) In 1957, Jack Taylor started Enterprise with a unique strategy. Most car rental firms targeted business and leisure travel customers who arrived at an airport and needed to rent a car for local transportation.

Taylor decided to target a different segment—individuals whose own cars are being repaired, who are driving on vacation, or who for some other reason simply need an extra car for a few days. Today, Enterprise offers rental cars to consumers who need a car because of an accident, mechanical repair, or theft. (2) The traditional car rental companies have to charge relatively high daily rates because their locations in or near airports are expensive. In addition, their business customers are price-insensitive because the rental expenses are paid for by their companies. Although the airport locations are convenient for customers travelling by air, they are inconvenient for people seeking a replacement car while theirs is in the shop or an extra car to drive for a few days. So Enterprise locates its rental offices in downtown and suburban areas, where much of its target market lives and works. The firm provides local pickup and delivery service at no cost in most areas. They have offices within 15 miles of 90 percent

of the U.S. population, which is part of their outstanding service strategy. (3)

Enterprise's human resource strategy is a key to its success. The firm hires university graduates for its management trainee positions because it feels that a university degree demonstrates intelligence and motivation. Rather than recruiting the best students, it focuses on hiring people who were athletes or actively involved in campus social activities. Enterprise wants people who were social directors or high-ranking officers of social organizations such as fraternities, sororities, and clubs because they typically have good interpersonal skills needed to effectively deal with Enterprise's customers.

Jack Taylor's growth strategy was based on providing high-quality, personalized service so that customers would return to Enterprise when they needed to rent a car again. But operating managers were compensated on the basis of

exhibit 1
Financial Overview for Enterprise Rental Car

	2006	2005	2004	2003	2002
Worldwide Revenue ($ billions)	9.0	8.2	7.4	6.9	6.5
Rental Car Vehicles in Service	711 000	667 000	602 000	560 000	533 000

sales growth initially, not customer satisfaction. So service quality declined.

The first step Enterprise took to improve customer service was to develop a customer satisfaction measure. The questionnaire, called the Enterprise Service Quality Index, was developed on the basis of input from the operating managers. Thus, the managers felt ownership of the measurement tool. As the index gained legitimacy, Enterprise made a big deal about it. It posted the scores for each location prominently in its monthly operating reports—right next to the net profit numbers that determined managers' pay.

The operating managers were able to track how they were doing and how all their peers were doing, because all of the locations were ranked. To increase the motivation of managers to improve the service at their location, Enterprise announced that managers could be promoted only if their customer satisfaction scores were above the company average. Then it demonstrated that it would abide by this policy by refusing to promote some star performers who had achieved good growth and profit numbers but had below-average satisfaction scores.

To provide a high level of service, new employees generally work long, gruelling hours for what many see as relatively low pay. They, like all Enterprise managers, are expected to jump in and help wash or vacuum cars when the agency gets backed up. But all this hard work can pay off. The firm does not hire outsiders for other than entry-level jobs—every position is filled by promoting someone already inside the company. Thus, Enterprise employees know that if they work hard and do their best, they may very well succeed in moving up the corporate ladder and earn a significant income. The results of this strategy are impressive and they include many accolades and awards for Enterprise. They ranked in the top 10 of *BusinessWeek's* first-ever list of "Customer Service Champs" and they were ranked no. 5 by *BusinessWeek* as one of the "50 Best Places to Launch a Career." (4)

DISCUSSION QUESTIONS

1. What are the pros and cons of Enterprise's human resource management strategy?

2. Would you want to work for Enterprise? Why or why not?

3. How does its human resource strategy complement the quality of customer service delivered by its representatives?

Source: This case was written by Barton Weitz, University of Florida.

(1) www.enterprise.com Company Web site accessed online July 29, 2007.

(2) www.enterprise.com

(3) www.enterprise.com

(4) www.enterprise.com

CASE 20   Avon: Human Resource Management

Women have always played an important role at Avon, the largest cosmetics firm in the North America. Mrs. P. F. Albee of Winchester, New Hampshire, pioneered the company's now-famous direct-selling method. Women have been selling Avon since 1886. Today, with sales representatives numbering 5 million, Avon products are sold in more than 100 countries around the world. (1)

Although most of Avon's employees and customers are women, until recently the company has been run by men. However, a series of poor strategic decisions in the 1980s led the company to aggressively increase the number of women and minorities in its executive ranks. This decision to increase diversity in its managers was a major factor in Avon's improved financial performance.

Now Avon is recognized as a leader in management diversity. It has more women in management positions (86 percent) than any other Fortune 500 company. Almost half of the members of its board of directors are women. The company has undertaken a number of programs to ensure that women and minorities have opportunities for development and advancement.

In the United States, Canada, and elsewhere, Avon has internal networks of associates, including a parents' network, a Hispanic network, a black professional association, an Asian network, and a gay and lesbian network. The networks act as liaisons between associates and management to bring their voice to critical issues that affect the workplace and the marketplace.

Avon's problems started in the 1970s when its top management team, all men, tried to change the firm's strategy. First the management ignored its own marketing research indicating that more women were entering the workforce and seeking professional careers, that their cosmetic needs would change, and that new approaches for selling products to them were needed. Then sales growth slowed, and the company reacted by seeking growth through unrelated diversifications. Finally, as the firm was on the brink of bankruptcy, a new top management team was brought in.

Led by CEO Jim Preston, Avon refocused itself on its roots and began again to market cosmetics to a female, but very different, market. Preston realized that Avon's customers needed to be represented in senior management.

He enacted policies to quickly promote more women into higher-level positions. In addition, Preston shifted the firm's organization culture to be more accommodating to all its employees. For example, the firm dropped its season-ticket purchases to Knicks and Yankees games and replaced them with season tickets for the New York City Ballet and the New York Philharmonic.

Avon has also turned to foreign markets for additional growth. Preston credits several key female executives for championing the international push and for making sure that it was done right. Now many new managers come from international operations.

Preston's vision is reflected in Avon's senior management. Andrea Jung is chairman and CEO, and Geralyn R. Breig is senior vice-president and global brand president. (2) Almost half of the members of the executive committee, the senior management of the firm, are women.

Clearly, Avon is a firm that has changed its own culture and that appreciates the power of diversity and multiculturalism. The new management team has launched a number of growth initiatives building on Avon's strong brand name and distribution channel through its customer representative network. Avon's products fall into three product categories: "Beauty," which consists of cosmetics, fragrance and toiletries; "Beauty Plus," which consists of jewellery, watches, and apparel and accessories; and "Beyond Beauty," which consists of home products, gifts, decorative, and candles.

In addition to expanding its product line, Avon participates in many events to increase awareness of its powerful brand name. In 2007 Avon started the Avon Hello Tomorrow Fund where every week for a year $5000 will be awarded to an individual to help realize a program, project, or idea to empower women. Also in 2007, Avon hosted the Global Summit for a Better Tomorrow to raise awareness of International Women's Day. In Canada, Avon has raised more than $12 million in 12 years for breast cancer research. Avon Canada is the country's leading corporate contributor to this vital cause. (3)

Finally, Avon is using technology to support the efforts of its 450 000 customer representatives. An electronic ordering system allows the representatives to run their businesses more efficiently and improve order processing accuracy. Now Avon representatives use the Internet to manage their business electronically. In North America, Avon representatives use a new online marketing tool called youravon.com. The site helps representatives build their own Avon business by enabling them to sell online through their own personalized Web pages, developed in partnership with Avon.

Avon e-representatives are able to promote special products, target specific groups of customers, place and track orders online, and capitalize on e-mail to share product information, selling tips, and marketing incentives.

DISCUSSION QUESTIONS

1. How has Avon adapted to changing lifestyles of women since 1886?

2. Why is Avon so committed to diversity?

3. How has increasing diversity been beneficial to Avon as it develops new strategies?

4. Evaluate the new opportunities that Avon is pursuing. Should Avon begin targeting men?

Source: This case was written by Barton Weitz, University of Florida.
(1) www.avoncompany.com Company Web site accessed online July 29, 2007
(2) www.avoncompany.com Company Web site accessed online July 29, 2007
(3) www.avon.ca Web site accessed online July 29, 2007

CASE 21   Holt Renfrew: Ultimate Customer Service

Holt Renfrew is one of the top luxury retailers in Canada. They are considered to be one of the world's leading fashion and lifestyle shopping experiences. They carry top designer labels from the world's most prestigious brands as well as cosmetics and fragrances from London to New York to Paris to Milan. They have recently spent over $30 million dollars on their Vancouver store to double its size and remodel it to attract a wider audience and build customer loyalty in the competitive luxury retail market.

Holt Renfrew started out as a hat shop in Quebec City, Canada, in 1837 run by an Irishman named William Samuel Henderson. In 1849 William started selling furs and then sold the shop to his brother John. In 1860 G.R. Renfrew became a partner and Henderson, Renfrew & Co. was formed. In 1867, John Holt joined the company and Holt Renfrew officially came into being in 1908. Holt Renfrew became famous for their furs and they became the Furrier-in-Ordinary to Queen Victoria and subsequent British Monarchs.

In the 1930s and 1940s international designers were added and the contract with Christian Dior that is still in effect today was established in order to showcase his haute couture furs in Canada. In 1986, after ten years of foreign ownership, Holt Renfrew resumed its Canadian ownership under Galen Weston, one of Canada's top entrepreneurs. Today there are nine Holt Renfrew stores across Canada including Quebec City, Montreal, Ottawa, Toronto (three), Calgary, Edmonton, and Vancouver.

The new store in Vancouver is 12 555 square metres, more than double the size of the former space. It has many features that highlight the Holt Renfrew commitment to superior customer service. There are 23 personal shoppers at the nine different stores across Canada. Building a relationship with their customers is paramount to Holt Renfrew and some of the different ways they provide the ultimate shopping experience are evident in the new Vancouver store.

Image that you pull up to the valet station in the underground parkade and throw your keys to the valet who will arrange for your car to be detailed while you shop. Then you enter the store and pass through the men's department with its reclaimed flooring and its Ralph Lauren, Dior, and Ferragamo boutiques. You ride the escalator up the main floor and pass through the full-service spa for a facial or touch-up manicure. The onsite concierge can find you tickets to the theatre in New York for your weekend trip or can book you a dog walker. Also on the main floor are the purses, shoes, and other accessories. At the new cosmetics department you can indulge in more than 45 different product lines arranged by colour not brand. Finally, in the fragrance section you can enter Canada's first Frederic Malle glass and steel, phone-booth-like cylinders where you can test pure samples of perfume.

When you move up to the second floor you will find women's designer labels including big names such as Chanel, Marc Jacobs, Dolce & Gabbana, Gucci, and Prada. You can book into one of the five new personal shopping suites and let a personal shopper work for you. When you are ready to move on to the rooftop restaurant, which opens onto a beautiful landscaped terrace decorated in green and gold, you can enjoy the floating, elliptical bar and order your favourite cocktail. Gary Balaski, the general manager of Holt Renfrew in Vancouver, says, "It's all those things that will make this store worth coming to. It's a place of escape, of entertainment. Because nowadays retail is not just about buying a shirt, you know. It's about buying an experience." (1)

To ensure the ultimate shopping experience for its customers, Holt Renfrew has enlisted top architects and designers to remodel the store. Unique features in the store include quilted glass on the second floor and the main entrance designed for the store by local craftsman. There is an installation of over 100 pendulum lights from Vancouver designer Omer Arbel that is topped by an enormous skylight. There is also a glass façade at the street level that allows shoppers to look inside while reflecting the colours and lights of the city on the outside.

Holt Renfrew appears to be appealing to a more mid-market consumer with its new store. They are trying to target The Bay and Sears' customers and move them up market. David Gray, a Vancouver-based retail consultant, says, "but to get all those new shoppers in the front doors, they'll have to change their image of being snobby and inaccessible, and become attainable to a larger market. It will be interesting to see how they pull it off." (2)

It seems as though Generation Y are the ones that are fuelling the interest in brand names in retail today. The under-35 crowd is heavily influenced by what celebrities are buying and they have both the cash and credit to buy the big brands. Things certainly have changed in the past 10 years since the book "No Logo" was published. Even the Baby Boomers are not choosing to spend their discretionary income on brands anymore, preferring experiences such as the spa or high-end luxury travel instead. It is the younger group that is driving the demand for brand-name fashion and products.

One of the changes evident in the luxury market today is that most luxury stores have added entry-level products in order to make the big brands more accessible. Some say a "democratization of luxury" is happening in retail, and Holt Renfrew is helping to drive this new idea. Holt Renfrew is the only successful department store in Canada at the moment and hopefully their strategy will pay off. Their personal shopping program is key to their continued success. The program started in Toronto 15 years ago, and in 2006 every Holt store exceeded its sales targets and the strongest year to date in sales was recorded. Before the remodel, the old Vancouver store had the highest sales per square metre of any store in Canada. "At Holt Renfrew, we want to be internationally recognized for our gorgeous fashion, amazing service, and exciting stores," says Caryn Lerner, president of Holt Renfrew. (3) By pampering their customers and building relationships with them, Holt Renfrew hopes to continue its retail success across Canada.

DISCUSSION QUESTIONS

1. How does Holt Renfrew build loyalty for Holt Renfrew customers versus other upscale retailers (such as Leone and Hills Department Stores)?

2. How effective is the Holt Renfrew Personal Shopping program in developing customer loyalty?

3. Toward whom should Holt Renfrew target the Personal Shopping program?

4. Has Holt Renfrew overestimated the luxury market in Canada? How could more customers be targeted?

Sources for Quotes:
(1) Rebecca Philip, Attention Shoppers, *Vancouver Magazine*, Volume 40, No.5, June 2007. pg. 40.
(2) Ibid., pg. 42.
(3) Alison Embrey Madina, A Sofa Sanctuary, *Display & Design Ideas*, October 2006, Vol. 18, Issue 10 pg. 50.

Sources:
(4) Holt Renfrew Company Web site accessed online at www. holtrenfrew.com July 24, 2007.
(5) Zena Olinjnyk, Betting on the Glitz, *Canadian Business*. 10/9/2006, Vol. 79 Issue 20, pg. 104–108.
(6) Fashion Scoops, *WWD, Women's Wear Daily*, 2/16/2007, Vol. 193, Issue 37, pg. 7.
(7) Janet Groeber, Couture Club, *Display & Design Ideas*, May 2007, Vol. 19, Issue 5, pg. 20–22.

CASE 22   GoodLife Fitness Clubs: Customer Loyalty

"These retention rates are poor. I need to do a better job of keeping members," thought Krista Swain, manager of the GoodLife Fitness Club in Kitchener, Ontario, as she reviewed her retention rates for the 2005–2006 fiscal year. As she was analyzing the report, Maureen Hagan, vice president of the chain entered her office. Krista looked up and said, "Hi Maureen. I've just been looking over the retention rates for the clubs. I'm not happy with my numbers."

"Neither is head office," Maureen replied, "and that's why I'm here today. You run one of our best clubs, and yet your retention rates are around 60 percent, the average for the 140 GoodLife Clubs. We lose 40 percent of our members each year."

"I agree," said Krista. "We have to figure out how to keep the members enthused and show that the club offers them value."

"That's what I wanted to hear," replied Maureen. "As a first step, let's both think about this and meet again next week with some ideas. Then I'd like you to prepare a retention plan that will be the model for all the clubs."

HEAD OFFICE

In March 1979, David Patchell-Evans established Good-Life as a sole proprietorship. Canadian fitness clubs were largely cash- and sales-oriented, with little emphasis on scientific fitness or member retention. By 2007, "Patch" had built this privately owned fitness company to over 140 clubs from coast to coast in Canada. GoodLife had the largest group of fitness clubs in Canada, with over 300 000 members and it employed 4000 associates across the country. (1)

The head office was located at the Galleria Mall Fitness Club in London, Ontario. Head office personnel numbered approximately 40, led by Patch and Maureen Hagan (vice president). The head office's main role was to provide leadership and support for the franchisees and company-owned clubs. One of Maureen Hagan's responsibilities was the design and management of GoodLife University, where each month 50 to 60 new associates went through a one-week program. The training included an orientation to GoodLife (basic knowledge of GoodLife and its philosophy), personal training (skills required to assist members as a personal trainer), and computer program training. When club managers hired the associates, they typically spent their first few weeks learning the ropes at the club and then attended the University program. Maureen led some of the training sessions and evaluation of the participants, some of whom failed and left GoodLife.

GOODLIFE KITCHENER

After a remodel, the GoodLife Kitchener Club reopened on the second floor of an indoor mall in downtown Kitchener, Ontario. Prior to that it was located two blocks away in a relatively small (1116 square metres) and poorly designed facility. The new facility was larger (2790 square metres) and had an open concept design and an extensive range of equipment and programs. Over the next 18 months, membership increased dramatically under Krista Swain's guidance. As of May 2006, the club had 3500 members, an increase of 2300 over the original 1200 members who moved from the old club. In early 2006, the Kitchener club was signing up over 230 new members per month (Exhibit 1). At the same time, the club was losing about 100 members per month, for a net gain of about 130 members. On an annual basis, the club was losing 40 percent of its members. Overall, the rapid growth in membership had a very positive effect on revenues, which increased by over 60 percent between June 2005 and March 2006 (Exhibit 2).

The Kitchener club's 40 associates (10 full-time, 30 part-time) worked in four groups: sales, customer service, personal training, and service.

- The four sales associates (all full-time) were responsible for getting new members.

- Customer service employees, who were primarily part-time, worked the front desk.

- Personal trainers worked with individual club members on fitness programs.

- Service employees introduced new members to the club and its philosophy through a series of programs on fitness and equipment use.

All employees were involved in selling. Although the sales associates were dedicated to selling new memberships, the personal trainers spent time encouraging members to sign up for personal training. The customer service employees would sell tanning programs and other services to members. Typically, each group or individual had sales targets and earned bonuses and commissions based on meeting those targets.

Most of the employees earned a base salary of $8.00 per hour plus bonuses if they achieved the weekly targets. As an example, a sales associate might have a target of eight new members per week. If he or she achieved or exceeded the target, the associate could earn $1250 or more every two weeks. Customer service staff could earn up to $25 per week if they met targets, which included phoning members to remind them of upcoming events, encouraging them to use the club, and selling various club products and services

exhibit 1   GoodLife Kitchener Club—Membership by Month

Month	Members Lost during Month	Members Gained during Month	Net Members Gained during Month	Members (at end of month)	Retention Rate per Year (%)	Loss Rate per Month (%)
March 2005	—	—	—	1900	—	—
April 2005	58*	163	105	2005	63.5**	3.0
May 2005	61	158	97	2102	64.0	3.0
June 2005	73	156	83	2185	59.4	3.4
July 2005	75	155	80	2263	60.9	3.3
August 2005	68	150	82	2341	65.2	2.9
September 2005	70	168	98	2423	64.8	2.9
October 2005	108	196	88	2521	48.5	4.3
November 2005	91	220	129	2609	57.9	3.5
December 2005	90	223	133	2738	60.1	3.3
January 2006	103	244	141	2871	56.4	3.6
February 2006	99	238	139	3012	60.1	3.3
March 2006	113	234	121	3151	56.4	3.6
Annual average					59.8†	3.4

*At the beginning of April, the club had 1900 members. The monthly loss rate for April is 3.0 percent (based on a yearly retention rate for April of 63.5 percent which is a yearly loss rate of 36.5 percent). The club lost 1900 × 0.03 = 58 members in April.

**About 63.5 percent of the members as of April 2004 were still members as of April 2005; 36.5 percent were no longer members.

†The average retention rate for the year shown is 59.8 percent; average loss rate per month is 3.4 percent (1 − 0.598 = 0.402/12).

Source: GoodLife Fitness Clubs.

exhibit 2   GoodLife Kitchener Club—Selected Revenues and Expenses

	June 30, 2005 Month	June 30, 2005 YTD (12 months)	March 31, 2006 Month	March 31, 2006 YTD (9 months)
Revenues	(%)	(%)	(%)	(%)
Membership	89.9	88.2	86.9	83.3
Services*	9.3	10.2	11.9	15.5
Other	1.8	1.6	1.2	1.2
Total revenues	100.0	100.0	100.0	100.0
Expenses				
Sales wages and commissions**	10.5	12.1	8.3	8.9
Service wages and commissions†	9.0	7.1	5.3	12.3
Service and other††	19.4	28.6	20.4	17.1
Total direct expenses	38.9	47.8	34.0	38.3
Manager controlled‡	9.2	15.6	4.8	10.4
Administrative‡‡	31.8	31.1	26.3	32.6
Total expenses§	79.9	94.4	65.0	81.3
Members	2 200		3 200	
Total revenue ($)	120 000	1 004 000	195 000	1 177 000

*Includes personal training, specialty programs, tanning, and pro shop.

**Related to new membership sales.

†Includes personal training and member services.

††Includes service staff wages and expenses.

‡Includes utilities, supplies, and services.

‡‡Includes advertising, administrative management, rent, realty taxes, and equipment leasing.

§Not included are depreciation, amortization, interest, and taxes.

such as tanning. Personal trainers could make up to $27.00 per hour for personal training in addition to their base pay of $8.00 per hour. The more members the trainer signed up, the more hours he or she spent in personal training.

Through these incentive programs GoodLife encouraged its staff, particularly the sales associates, to be entrepreneurial. As Krista often said, "The staff have to make things happen; they can't wait for them to happen. Both GoodLife and the staff do better when they make things happen." As noted, GoodLife had formal training programs for new employees. In addition, Krista spent time with the new employees teaching them the technical side of the job and establishing the norms and culture of the club. By emphasizing what was important to her, Krista hoped they would understand the importance of excellent customer service: "If I can show the new employees what's important to me, and get them to trust me, they come on board and are part of the team. For example, we hold weekly staff meetings where we discuss a number of issues, including how to improve the club. People don't miss the meetings. Every once in a while, a new associate decides not to come to the meetings. The team lets him or her know that's not acceptable. Those people either become part of the team or decide to leave GoodLife."

Employee turnover at the Kitchener GoodLife Club was slightly better than the average across all the GoodLife clubs. In the past year, Krista had a turnover of about 35 percent, with the rate for full-time slightly lower than for part-time. Part-time turnover was higher, in part, because many of the part-time employees were students who left to go to university or left after completing their degree programs.

Like Maureen Hagan, Krista was concerned about employee turnover, but she wasn't sure what actions could improve the situation. She had noticed that some new employees were surprised at the amount of selling involved in their positions. She also felt that some employees were not satisfied with the base salary of $8.00 per hour.

Typically, when an employee left, Krista needed to hire a new associate relatively quickly. She would place an ad in the local paper, the *Record*; get some applications; conduct interviews; and hire the individual she felt was most suited for the position. With full-time employees, Krista was not always happy with the pool of applicants she interviewed; but there was always the pressure of filling the job, which had to be balanced against the quality of the applicants. With the economy improving and a low local unemployment rate, it was sometimes difficult to attract high-quality applicants.

THE MEMBERS

Most new members joined the club through referrals. When an individual asked about joining the club, a sales associate would show him or her the club and discuss the benefits of membership and the GoodLife philosophy. If the individual decided to join, the sales associate would ask if he or she had any friends who might also be interested in joining the club; any such referrals would receive a free membership for one week. Typically, the associate tried to get five referrals. The associate would then contact these people, offer the free one-week membership and set up a meeting with them if they accepted. The cycle was repeated with each new member. On average, the sales associates converted between one and two of the five contacts to new members. Referrals generated between 60 percent and 80 percent of all new members.

The price for a new membership varied depending on the promotion option. The two main options were (1) a $199 initiation fee and the first six months free and $40 per four weeks after that, or (2) the initiation fee was waived and the member paid $40 per four weeks. Payments were on a biweekly basis through an automatic payment plan that the member signed. The new member also paid a total of $54 for the membership card ($15) and a processing fee ($39). A new member could also decide to join for a three-month period for $180. Members could also decide to pay once a year and not use the automatic payment plan.

When an individual joined the club, an associate from the service group would take the new member through three programs as an introduction to the club and the GoodLife approach to a healthy lifestyle. The three programs were (I) Fit Fix 1—an introduction to strength training; (II) Cardio—basic information about cardiovascular training principles; and (III) Fit Fix 2—adding exercises to an existing program. Any new member could also have a fitness assessment (resting heart rate, body-fat measurements, and so forth). After six weeks, the new member could also have a second fitness assessment to track his or her progress.

A problem common to most of the GoodLife Clubs was referred to as the "20–20–60 phenomenon." Twenty percent of the club members were hard-core fitness and health people. These members came three or more times a week, were serious about their training, and would tolerate a lot (e.g., uneven service) as long as it didn't interfere with their training. The second 20 percent were the new members.

They were enthusiastic and wanted to get fit; and over time they either became committed or not. The largest group, the remaining 60 percent, were those members who came on an irregular basis. The club staff didn't know their names, these members often were not sure about how the equipment worked or what they should be doing, and they often wouldn't ask for help. Even when they stopped coming, this group kept their membership for a period until they decided to cancel. When one came to cancel, an associate tried to get her or him to stay, usually with little success.

Krista and other associates at GoodLife felt that getting members to feel that they were part of the GoodLife Club was important in retaining them. Krista believed that many of the 60 percent probably never felt they were part of the club because they didn't know many or any of the other members or the staff. Krista remembered that although many of the 1200 members from the old club liked the new facility (open, spacious, more equipment, and so forth), they felt that the club was more impersonal. In particular, as the membership grew, the "original" members felt less at home. Krista estimated that, within a year, about 50 percent of these members had left the club.

CUSTOMER RETENTION

As Krista prepared for the meeting with Maureen, she knew that improved customer retention rates were possible but was uncertain as to what actions would be most effective. She identified three major areas that she could address: employee turnover, a new bonus system, and swipe card technology. Employee turnover, at over 40 percent, created a lack of stability at the club. Every time a new employee started, he or she didn't know any members and then over time would learn the members' names (often those who visited frequently). If the employee left, so did the knowledge.

Krista had always felt that members would have a greater sense of "belonging" to the club if the front-desk staff could greet them by name. Although many of the front-desk staff knew some of the members by name (most of these members were the hard-core regulars who came frequently), most of the front-desk staff were part-time associates or had recently joined GoodLife; therefore, they knew relatively few members by name.

Krista had two ideas for reducing employee turnover, both based on increasing wages. Increasing the hourly base rate from $8.00 to $9.00 for most employees, excluding managers and sales associates, would add about $4000 per month to wage costs. The problem was that, although she knew that employee turnover would decline, she didn't know by how much, nor did she know the effect on retention rates. A second option was to focus only on the front-desk employees who greeted members. Increasing their rate to $9.00 would increase monthly wage costs by about $1000.

Next, Krista considered introducing a bonus plan for increasing customer retention. Virtually all the targets and bonuses at GoodLife focused on increasing sales, reflecting, in part, Patch's aggressive growth targets. Although she didn't have a specific plan in mind, Krista felt that an allocation of at least $1000 to bonuses for increased retention was feasible. Her initial idea was that for every percent increase in retention rates per month (e.g., from 60 percent to 61 percent), staff would receive $200 in bonuses.

Where Krista was uncertain was how the target should be set—on an individual or group basis. The front-desk staff had the most contact with members, but potentially all the employees could be involved. Krista felt that better use of the swipe card information could improve retention. Members swiped their membership card when they visited the club. A valid card allowed a member to go through a turnstile; an invalid card (because it had expired) did not release the turnstile. Krista knew that other information (e.g., number of member visits and so on) was available, but no one at the club or head office had developed a software program to track member visits. Krista contacted two software companies, one of which offered a membership management program that would provide interface with swipe scanners and provide reports on members' frequency of visits, along with a host of other member information. The cost ranged from $3500 for a licence for five sites up to $8500 for unlimited site use.

One of the targets for the front-desk associates was to make "motivation" calls to members each week. Associates would call a specified number of members to reach their target. The associates would begin anywhere on the member list and begin calling members to encourage them to use the facilities or inform them of special events. After the call, the associate would record the date called and his or her name next to the member's name. Ideally, all members were called once every six weeks, but this didn't always happen.

With the new software system, reports could identify members who had not visited the club for a particular period. Staff could then contact members who had not visited for a specific time period (e.g., three weeks, four weeks, and so forth). Krista felt that this would substantially improve the existing approach and would improve member retention rates.

Krista knew that there were other available approaches or tactics to improve retention rates. In particular, any activities that built a greater sense of community would increase interaction between members and a sense of belonging. But it was difficult to find the time to figure it out. Managing a club with 3500 members kept her busy making sure everything was running smoothly, and she spent most of her time "doing" not "planning."

A week later, Maureen met Krista in her office. Maureen started the conversation. "Let me review the situation. As I mentioned last week, if we could improve your club's retention rates from 60 to 65 percent, based on last year's numbers, gross revenues would increase by over $35 000. In this business most of the costs tend to be fixed, probably about 60 percent of revenues, so most of the revenue would be profits. If we could do that for all the clubs, it would be great for business and I think we would have more satisfied members. And just to put this in perspective, on average, we have about 2000 members per club."

Maureen continued: "In the past year, the story has been about the same for most of our clubs. For every 100 new members signed up each month, we have about 40 people who don't renew or cancel their membership. We spend a lot on marketing to get them in the door. Then we spend time with them setting up an exercise or training program. They are enthusiastic to begin with, then they stop coming to classes or exercise. Then they cancel or don't renew when their membership comes up. When they cancel, we ask them why they are leaving. The most common reasons are that they don't have enough time or they can't fit it in to their schedule. I think that about 30 percent of the time they have a good reason for leaving, such as they are moving out of town. I think that 70 percent of the time we could have done something to keep them with the club."

DISCUSSION QUESTIONS

1. Evaluate the strengths and weaknesses of GoodLife's customer acquisition and retention strategies.

2. Calculate the revenues and net profits at GoodLife Kitchener if retention rates were 65 percent and 70 percent versus 60 percent in the past year.

3. What is the average long-term value of a member at GoodLife in terms of total revenue at 60 percent, 70 percent, and 80 percent retention rates?

4. Evaluate the major options considered by Krista, assuming an average GoodLife Club with 2000 members. What overall plan would you recommend that GoodLife pursue in increasing customer retention rates? Be specific in your recommendations and be prepared to justify them.

Source: This case was written by Dr. Gordon H. G. McDougall, Professor of Marketing in the School of Business and Economics, Wilfrid Laurier University, Waterloo, Ontario, Canada.
(1) www.goodlifefitness.com Company Web site accessed online July 30, 2007

CASE 23   Nordstrom: Customer Service and Relationship Management

Nordstrom's unwavering customer-focused philosophy traces its roots to founder Johan Nordstrom's values. Johan Nordstrom believed in people and realized that consistently exceeding their expectations led to success and a good conscience. He built his organization around a customer-oriented philosophy. The organization focuses on people, and its policies and selections are designed to satisfy people. As simple as this philosophy sounds, few of Nordstrom's competitors have truly been able to grasp it. Many retailers in Canada have tried to copy the simple Nordstrom way but so far none has been able to duplicate it.

A FOCUS ON PEOPLE

Nordstrom employees treat customers like royalty. Employees are instructed to do whatever is in the customer's best interest. Customer delight drives the values of the company. Customers are taken seriously and are at the heart of the business. Customers are even at the top of Nordstrom's so-called organization chart, which is an inverted pyramid.

Following customers from the top of the inverted pyramid are the salespeople, department managers, and general managers. Finally, at the bottom is the board of directors. All lower levels work toward supporting the salespeople, who in turn, work to serve the customer. Employee incentives are tied to customer service. Salespeople are given personalized business cards to help them build relationships with customers.

Uniquely, salespeople are not tied to their respective departments, but to the customer. Salespeople can travel from department to department within the store to assist their customer, if that is needed. For example, a Nordstrom salesperson assisting a woman shopping for business apparel helps her shop for suits, blouses, shoes, hosiery, and accessories. The salesperson becomes the "personal shopper" of the customer to show her merchandise and provide fashion expertise. This is also conducive to the building of a long-term relationship with the customer, as over time, the salesperson understands the customer's fashion sense and personality.

The opportunity to sell across departments enables salespeople to maximize sales and commissions, while providing superior customer service. As noted on a *60 Minutes* segment, "[Nordstrom's service is] not service like it used to be, but service that never was." Despite the obsession with customer service at Nordstrom, ironically the "customer comes second." Nordstrom understands that customers will be treated well by their employees, only if the employees themselves are treated well by the company. Nordstrom employees are treated almost like the extended Nordstrom family, and employee satisfaction is a closely watched business variable.

Nordstrom is known for promoting employees from within its ranks. The fundamental traits of a successful Nordstrom salesperson (such as a commitment to excellence and customer service) are the same traits emphasized in successful Nordstrom executives. Nordstrom hires people with a positive attitude, a sense of ownership, initiative, heroism, and the ability to handle high expectations. This sense of ownership is reflected in Nordstrom's low rate of shrinkage. Shrinkage, loss due to theft and record-keeping errors, at Nordstrom is under 1.5 percent of sales, roughly half the industry average.

The low shrinkage can be attributed in large part to the diligence of salespeople caring for the merchandise as if it were their own. Employees at all levels are treated like businesspeople, and empowered to make independent decisions. They are given the latitude to do whatever they believe is the right thing, with the customers' best interests at heart. All employees are given the tools and authority to do whatever is necessary to satisfy customers, and management almost always backs subordinates' decisions.

In summary, Nordstrom's product is its people. The loyal Nordstrom shopper goes to Nordstrom for the service received—not necessarily the products. Of course, Nordstrom does offer quality merchandise, but that is secondary for many customers.

CUSTOMER-FOCUSED POLICIES

One of the most famous examples of Nordstrom's customer service occurred in 1975 when a Nordstrom salesperson gladly took back a set of used automobile tires and gave the customer a refund, even though Nordstrom had never sold tires! The customer had purchased the tires from a Northern Commercial Company store, whose retail space Nordstrom had since acquired. Not wanting the customer to leave the Nordstrom store unhappy, the salesperson refunded the price of the tires.

Nordstrom's policies focus on the concept of the "Lifetime Value of the Customer." Although little money is made on the first sale, when the lifetime value of a customer is calculated, the positive dollar amount of a loyal customer is staggering. The lifetime value of a customer is the sum of all sales generated from that customer, directly or indirectly. To keep its customers for a "lifetime," Nordstrom employees go to incredible lengths.

In a Nordstrom store in Seattle, a customer wanted to buy a pair of brand-name slacks that had gone on sale. The store was out of her size and the salesperson was unable to locate a pair at other Nordstrom stores. Knowing that the same slacks were available at a competitor nearby, the sales clerk went to the rival, purchased the slacks at full price using petty cash from her department, and sold the slacks to the customer at Nordstrom's sale price. Although this sale resulted in an immediate loss for the store, the investment in promoting the loyalty of the happy customer went a long way.

Nordstrom's employees try to "Never Say No" to the customer. Nordstrom has an unconditional return policy. If a customer is not completely satisfied, he or she can return the new and generally even heavily used merchandise at any time for a full refund. Ironically, this is not a company policy; rather it is implemented at the discretion of the salesperson to maximize customer satisfaction. Nordstrom's advice to its employees is simply, "Use good judgment in all situations." Employees are given the freedom, support, and resources to make the best decisions to enhance customer satisfaction. The cost of Nordstrom's high service, such as its return policy, coupled with its competitive pricing would, on the surface, seem to cut into profit margins. This cost, however, is recouped through increased sales from repeat customers, rare markdowns, and, if necessary, the "squeezing" of suppliers.

Nordstrom's up-channel policies also focus on maximizing customer satisfaction. According to former CEO Bruce Nordstrom, "[Vendors] know that we are liberal with our customers. And if you're going to do business with us, then there should be a liberal influence on their return policies. If somebody has worn a shoe and it doesn't wear satisfactorily for them, and we think that person is being honest about it, then we will send it back." Nordstrom realizes some customers will abuse the unconditional return policy, but refuses to impose that abuse back onto its vendors. Here again, the rule of "doing what is right" comes into play.

Nordstrom's merchandising and purchasing policies are also extremely customer-focused. A full selection of merchandise in a wide variety of sizes is seen as a measure of customer service. An average Nordstrom store carries roughly 150 000 pairs of shoes with a variety of sizes, widths, colours, and models. Typical shoe sizes for women range from 2 1/2 to 14, in widths of A to EEE. Nordstrom is fanatical about stocking only high-quality merchandise.

Once, when the upper parts of some women's shoes were separating from the soles, every shoe from that delivery was shipped back to the manufacturer.

DISCUSSION QUESTIONS

1. What steps does Nordstrom take to implement its strategy of providing outstanding customer service? How can their customer service be taken to the next level? Outline a process to engage staff, suppliers, and customers.

2. How do these activities enable Nordstrom to reduce the gaps between perceived service and customer expectations?

3. What are the pros and cons of Nordstrom's approach to developing a competitive advantage through customer service?

Source: This case was written by Alicia Lueddemann, the Management Mind Group; and Sunil Erevelles, University of North Carolina, Charlotte. The authors relied substantially on the following references in the preparation of this case: Sunil Erevelles and Alicia Lueddemann, "Why Winners Win," unpublished manuscript, 2002; and Robert Spector and Patrick D. McCarthy, *The Nordstrom Way: The Inside Story of America's #1 Customer Service Company* (New York: John Wiley and Sons, 1995).

CASE 24 Consumer Electronics: Advertising Strategy

A consumer electronics chain in the Winnipeg, Manitoba, area is planning a big sale in its suburban warehouse over the three-day Victoria Day weekend (Saturday through Monday). The sale will include nearly $2 million worth of consumer electronics products, 50 percent of the merchandise sold in the store. The company hopes to realize at least $900 000 in sales during the three days. In the retailer's past experience:

- The first day's sales were 50 percent of the total. The second day's were 35 percent, and the last day's, 15 percent.

- One of every two customers who came made a purchase.

It's known further that large numbers of people always flock to such sales, some driving as far as 100 kilometres. They come from all economic strata, but all are confirmed bargain hunters. You're the assistant to the general merchandise manager, who has asked you to plan the event's marketing campaign. You have the following information:

1. A full-page Winnipeg Free Press ad costs $10 000; a half-page ad costs $6000; and a quarter-page ad costs $3500. To get the maximum value from a newspaper campaign, it's company policy to always run two ads (not necessarily the same size) for such events.

2. The local Winnipeg community paper is printed weekly and distributed free to some 15 000 households. It costs $700 for a full page and $400 for a half page.

3. To get adequate TV coverage, at least three channels must be used, with a minimum of eight 30-second spots on each at $500 per spot, spread over three or more days. Producing a TV spot costs $3000.

4. The store has contracts with three radio stations. One appeals to a broad general audience aged 25 to 34. One is popular with the 18-to-25 group. A classical music station has a small but wealthy audience. Minimum costs for a saturation radio campaign, including production, on the three stations are $8000, $5000, and $3000, respectively.

5. To produce and mail a full-colour flyer to the store's 80 000 charge customers costs $10 000. When the company used such a mailing piece before, about 3 percent responded.

DISCUSSION QUESTIONS

1. Knowing that the company wants a mixed-media ad campaign to support this event, prepare an ad plan for the general merchandise manager that costs no more than $40 000.

2. Work out the daily scheduling of all advertising.

3. Work out the dollars to be devoted to each medium.

4. Justify your plan.

Source: This case was prepared by David Ehrlich, Marymount University.

Glossary

ABC   See *activity-based costing*.

***ABC* analysis**   An analysis that rank orders SKUs by a profitability measure to determine which items should never be out of stock, which should be allowed to be out of stock occasionally, and which should be deleted from the stock selection.

abilities   The aptitude and skills of an employee.

accessibility   (1) The degree to which customers can easily get into and out of a shopping centre; (2) ability of the retailer to deliver the appropriate retail mix to the customers in the segment.

accessories   Merchandise in apparel, department, and specialty stores used to complement apparel outfits. Examples include gloves, hosiery, handbags, jewellery, handkerchiefs, and scarves.

accordion theory   A cyclical theory of retailer evolution suggesting that changes in retail institutions are explained in terms of depth versus breadth of assortment. Retail institutions cycle from high-depth/low-breadth to low-depth/high-breadth stores and back again.

account opener   A premium or special promotion item offered to induce the opening of a new account, especially in financial institutions and stores operating on an installment credit basis.

accounts payable   The amount of money owed to vendors, primarily for merchandise inventory.

accounts receivable   The amount of money due to the retailer from selling merchandise on credit.

accrued liabilities   Liabilities that accumulate daily but are paid only at the end of a period.

ACORN (A Classification of Residential Neighbourhoods)   A market segmentation system that classifies neighbourhoods in the United States into distinctive consumer groups, or market segments.

acquisition   A strategic growth activity in which one firm acquires another firm, usually resulting in a *merger*. See also *leveraged buyout*.

actionability   Means that the definition of a market segment must clearly indicate what the retailer should do to satisfy its needs.

activity-based costing (ABC)   A financial management tool in which all major activities within a cost centre are identified, calculated, and then charged to cost objects, such as stores, product categories, product lines, specific products, customers, and suppliers.

adaptability   A company's recognition of cultural differences and adaptation of its core strategy to the needs of local markets.

adaptive selling   An approach to personal selling in which selling behaviours are altered based on information about the customer and the buying situation.

additional markup   An increase in retail price after and in addition to original markup.

additional markup cancellation   The percentage by which the retail price is lowered after a markup is taken.

additional markup percentage   The addition of a further markup to the original markup as a percentage of net sales.

add-on selling   Selling additional new products and services to existing customers, such as a bank encouraging a customer with a chequing account to also apply for a home improvement loan from the bank.

administered vertical marketing system   A form of vertical marketing system designed to control a line or classification of merchandise as opposed to an entire store's operation. Such systems involve the development of comprehensive programs for specified lines of merchandise. The vertically aligned companies—manufacturer or wholesaler—even though in a nonownership position, may work together to reduce the total systems cost of such activities as advertising, transportation, and data processing. (See also *contractual vertical marketing system* and *corporate vertical marketing system*.)

advanced shipping notice (ASN)   An electronic document received by the retailer's computer from a supplier in advance of a shipment.

advertising   Paid communications delivered to customers through nonpersonal mass media such as newspapers, television, radio, direct mail, and the Internet.

advertising manager   A retail manager who manages advertising activities such as determining the advertising budget, allocating the budget, developing ads, selecting media, and monitoring advertising effectiveness.

advertising reach   See *reach*. The percentage of customers in the target market exposed to an ad at least once.

affinity marketing   Marketing activities that enable consumers to express their identification with an organization. An example is offering credit cards tied to reference groups such as the consumer's university or an NFL team.

affordable budgeting method   A budgeting method in which a retailer first sets a budget for every element of the retail mix except promotion and then allocates the leftover funds to a promotional budget.

agent   (1) A business unit that negotiates purchases, sales, or both but does not take title to the goods in which it deals; (2) a person who represents the principal (who, in the case of retailing, is the store or merchant) and who acts under authority, whether in buying or in bringing the principal into business relations with third parties.

aging   The length of time merchandise has been in stock.

aided recall   When consumers indicate they know the brand when the name is presented to them.

alteration costs   Expenses incurred to change the appearance or fit, to assemble, or to repair merchandise.

alternative dispute resolution   A provision included in a contract between retailer and vendor to help avoid litigation in the case of a dispute. Can include methods of settling the dispute that the parties agree upon, such as mediation, arbitration, or med-arb.

amount and quality of parking facilities   A store's having enough parking spaces, close enough to the building, that the store is ideally accessible to customers, but not so many open spaces that the store is viewed as being unpopular. A standard rule of thumb is 5.9 spaces per 100 square metres of retail store space.

analogue approach A method of trade area analysis also known as the similar store or mapping approach. The analysis is divided into four steps: (1) describing the current trade areas through the technique of customer spotting; (2) plotting the customers on a map; (3) defining the primary, secondary, and tertiary area zones; and (4) matching the characteristics of stores in the trade areas with the potential new store to estimate its sales potential.

anchors Major retailers located in a shopping centre.

anchor store A large, well-known retail operation located in a shopping centre or mall and serving as an attracting force for consumers to the centre.

ancillary services Services such as layaway, gift wrap, and credit that are not directly related to the actual sale of a specific product within the store.

anticipation discount A discount offered by a vendor to a retailer in addition to the cash discount or dating, if the retailer pays the invoice before the end of the cash discount period.

anticompetitive leasing arrangement A lease that limits the type and amount of competition a particular retailer faces within a trading area.

antitrust legislation A set of laws directed at preventing unreasonable restraint of trade or unfair trade practices. Aim is to foster a competitive environment. See also *restraint of trade*.

application form A form used for information on a job applicant's education, employment experience, hobbies, and references.

arbitration Used in the case of a dispute between retailer and vendor that involves the appointment of a neutral party—the arbitrator—who considers the arguments of both sides and then makes a decision that is usually agreed upon in advance as binding.

artificial barriers In site evaluations for accessibility, barriers such as railroad tracks, major highways, or parks.

assets Economic resources, such as inventory or store fixtures, owned or controlled by an enterprise as a result of past transactions or events.

asset turnover Net sales divided by total assets.

assortment The number of SKUs within a merchandise category. Also called *depth of merchandise and depth of stock*.

assortment plan A list of merchandise that indicates in very general terms what should be carried in a particular merchandise category.

atmospherics The design of an environment via visual communications, lighting, colours, music, and scent to stimulate customers' perceptual and emotional responses and ultimately to affect their purchase behaviour.

attitude branding The choice of a symbol which represents a feeling that is not necessarily connected with the product or retailer.

auction A market in which goods are sold to the highest bidder; usually well publicized in advance or held at specific times that are well known in the trade. Auctions are very popular on the Internet.

autocratic leader A manager who makes all decisions on his or her own and then announces them to employees.

automatic reordering system A system for ordering staple merchandise using a predetermined minimum quantity of goods in stock. An automatic reorder can be generated by a computer on the basis of a perpetual inventory system and reorder point calculations.

average BOM stock-to-sales ratio The number of months in the period divided by planned inventory turnover for the period.

average inventory The sum of inventory on hand at several periods in time divided by the number of periods.

baby boomer The generational cohort of people born between 1946 and 1964.

back order A part of an order that the vendor has not filled completely and that the vendor intends to ship as soon as the goods in question are available.

backup stock The inventory used to guard against going out of stock when demand exceeds forecasts or when merchandise is delayed. Also called *safety stock* or *buffer stock*.

backward integration A form of vertical integration in which a retailer owns some or all of its suppliers.

bait-and-switch An unlawful, deceptive practice that lures customers into a store by advertising a product at lower than usual prices (the bait), then induces the customers to switch to a higher-price model (the switch).

balance sheet The summary of a retailer's financial resources and claims against the resources at a particular date; indicates the relationship between assets, liabilities, and owners' equity.

bank card Credit card issued by a bank, such as Visa and MasterCard.

bar code See *Universal Product Code (UPC)*.

bargaining power of vendors A competitive factor that makes a market unattractive when a few vendors control the merchandise sold in it. In these situations, vendors have an opportunity to dictate prices and other terms, reducing retailer's profits.

barriers to entry Conditions in a retail market that make it difficult for firms to enter the market.

base stock See *cycle stock*.

basic merchandise See *staple merchandise*.

basic stock list The descriptive and recordkeeping function of an inventory control system; includes the stock number, item description, number of units on hand and on order, and sales for the previous periods.

basic stock method An inventory management method used to determine the beginning-of-month (BOM) inventory by considering both the forecast sales for the month and the safety stock.

benchmarking The practice of evaluating performance by comparing one retailer's performance with that of other retailers using a similar retail strategy.

benefits The customer's specific needs that are satisfied when the customer buys a product.

benefit segmentation A method of segmenting a retail market on the basis of similar benefits sought in merchandise or services.

black market The availability of merchandise at a high price when it is difficult or impossible to purchase under normal market circumstances; commonly involves illegal transactions.

blog A Web site where entries are written in chronological order and displayed.

bonus Additional compensation awarded periodically, based on a subjective evaluation of the employee's performance.

book inventory system See *retail inventory method.*

bootleg The sale of imitation goods where there is little or no attempt at hiding the fact that the product is counterfeit.

bottom-up planning When goals are set at the bottom of the organization and filter up through the operating levels.

boutique (1) Departments in a store designed to resemble small, self-contained stores; (2) a relatively small specialty store.

boutique layout See *free-form layout.*

brand A distinguishing name or symbol (such as a logo, design, symbol, or trademark) that identifies the products or services offered by a seller and differentiates those products and services from the offerings of competitors.

brand association Anything linked to or connected with the brand name in a consumer's memory.

brand awareness The ability of a potential customer to recognize or recall that a particular brand name belongs to a retailer or product/service.

brand building The design and implementation of a retail communication program to create an image in the customer's mind of the retailer relative to its competitors. Also called *positioning.*

brand energy The concept that links the idea that a brand creates value through meaningful experiences rather than a focus on generating profits.

brand equity The value that brand image offers retailers.

brand image Set of associations consumers have about a brand that are usually organized around some meaningful themes.

breadth See *variety.*

breadth of stock See *variety.*

break-even analysis A technique that evaluates the relationship between total revenue and total cost to determine profitability at various sales levels.

break-even point (BEP) The quantity at which total revenue equals total cost and beyond which profit occurs.

breaking bulk A function performed by retailers or wholesalers in which they receive large quantities of merchandise and sell them in smaller quantities.

breaking sizes Running out of stock on particular sizes.

brick and click A retailer that uses the Internet to promote its goods and services but also maintains a traditional physical retail storefront.

broker A middleman that serves as a go-between for the buyer or seller; assumes no title risks, does not usually have physical custody of products, and is not looked upon as a permanent representative of either the buyer or seller.

buffer stock Merchandise inventory used as a safety cushion for cycle stock so the retailer won't run out of stock if demand exceeds the sales forecast. Also called *safety stock.*

building codes Legal restrictions describing the size and type of building, signs, type of parking lot, and so on that can be used at a particular location.

bulk fixture See *rounder.*

buyback A strategy vendors and retailers use to get products into retail stores, either when a retailer allows a vendor to create space for goods by "buying back" a competitor's inventory and removing it from a retailer's system, or when the retailer forces a vendor to buy back slow-moving merchandise.

buyer Person in a retailing organization responsible for the purchase and profitability of a merchandise category. Similar to *category manager.*

buyer's market Market occurring in economic conditions that favour the position of the retail buyer (or merchandiser) rather than the vendor; in other words, economic conditions are such that the retailer can demand and usually get concessions from suppliers in terms of price, delivery, and other market advantages. Opposite of a seller's market.

buyer's report Information on the velocity of sales, availability of inventory, amount of order, inventory turnover, forecast sales, and, most important, the quantity that should be ordered for each SKU.

buying behaviour The activities customers undertake when purchasing a good or service.

buying calendar A plan of a store buyer's market activities, generally covering a six-month merchandising season based on a selling calendar that indicates planned promotional events.

buying committee A committee that has the authority for final judgment and decision making on such matters as adding or eliminating new products.

buying power The customer's financial resources available for making purchases.

buying situation segmentation A method of segmenting a retail market based on customer needs in a specific buying situation such as a fill-in shopping trip versus a weekly shopping trip.

buzz Genuine, street-level excitement about a hot new product.

call system A system of equalizing sales among salespersons—for example, some stores rotate salespeople, giving each an equal opportunity to meet customers.

capacity fixture See *rounder.*

career path The set of positions to which management employees are promoted within a particular organization as their careers progress.

cash Money on hand.

cash discounts Reductions in the invoice cost that the vendor allows the retailer for paying the invoice prior to the end of the discount period.

cash-wrap areas The places in a store where customers can purchase merchandise and have it "wrapped"—placed in a bag.

catalogue retailer A nonstore retailer that communicates directly with customers using catalogues sent through the mail.

catalogue retailing Nonstore retail format in which the retail offering is communicated to a customer through a catalogue.

catalogue showroom A type of retailer that uses a showroom to display merchandise combined with an adjacent warehouse; typically specializes in hard goods such as housewares.

category An assortment of items (SKUs) the customer sees as reasonable substitutes for each other.

category captain A supplier that forms an alliance with a retailer to help gain consumer insight, satisfy consumer needs, and improve the performance and profit potential across the entire category.

category killer A discount retailer that offers a complete assortment in a category and thus dominates a category from the customers' perspective. Also called a *category specialist*.

category life cycle A merchandise category's sales pattern over time.

category management The process of managing a retail business with the objective of maximizing the sales and profits of a category.

category manager See *buyer*.

category specialist See *category killer*.

caveat emptor Latin term for "let the buyer beware."

census tracts Subdivisions of a Metropolitan Statistical Area (MSA), with an average population of 4000.

central business district (CBD) The traditional downtown business area of a city or town.

centralization The degree to which authority for making retail decisions is delegated to corporate managers rather than to geographically dispersed regional, district, and store management.

centralized buying A situation in which a retailer makes all purchase decisions at one location, typically the firm's headquarters.

central market See *market*.

central place A centre of retailing activity such as a town or city.

central place theory Christaller's theory of retail location suggesting that retailers tend to locate in a central place. As more retailers locate together, more customers are attracted to the central place. See also *central place*.

chain discount A number of different discounts taken sequentially from the suggested retail price.

chargeback A practice used by retailers in which they deduct money from the amount they owe a vendor.

chat room Location in an Internet site at which customers can engage in interactive, real-time, text-based discussions.

checking The process of going through goods upon receipt to make sure that they arrived undamaged and that the merchandise received matches the merchandise ordered.

checkout areas The places in a store where customers can purchase merchandise and have it "wrapped"—placed in a bag.

cherry picking Customers visiting a store and buying only merchandise sold at big discounts or buying only the best styles or colours.

classic A merchandise category that has both a high level and a long duration of acceptance.

classification A group of items or SKUs for the same type of merchandise, such as pants (as opposed to jackets or suits), supplied by different vendors.

classification dominance An assortment so broad that customers should be able to satisfy all of their consumption needs for a particular category by visiting one retailer.

classification merchandising Divisions of departments into related types of merchandise for reporting and control purposes.

clearance sale An end-of-season sale to make room for new goods; also pushing the sale of slow-moving, shopworn, and demonstration model goods.

closeout (1) An offer at a reduced price to sell a group of slow-moving or incomplete stock; (2) an incomplete assortment, the remainder of a line of merchandise that is to be discontinued and so is offered at a low price to ensure immediate sale.

closeout retailer Off-price retailer that sells a broad but inconsistent assortment of general merchandise as well as apparel and soft home goods, obtained through retail liquidations and bankruptcy proceedings.

coaching The activity of supporting people to achieve their goals by goal setting, training, advising, encouraging, and rewarding their successes.

cocooning A term that describes a behavioural pattern of consumers who increasingly turn to the safe, familiar environment of their homes to spend their limited leisure time.

COD (cash on delivery) Purchase terms in which payment for a product is collected at the time of delivery.

collaboration, planning, forecasting, and replenishment (CPFR) A collaborative inventory management system in which a retailer shares information with vendors. CPFR software uses the data to construct a computer-generated replenishment forecast that is shared by the retailer and vendor before it's executed.

combination store A retailer that sells both food and nonfood items.

commercial bribery A vendor's offer of money or gifts to a retailer's employee for the purpose of influencing purchasing decisions.

commission Compensation based on a fixed formula, such as percentage of sales.

committee buying The situation whenever the buying decision is made by a group of people rather than by a single buyer. A multiunit operation is usually the type of firm that uses this procedure.

common stock The type of stock most frequently issued by corporations. Owners of common stock usually have voting rights in the retail corporation.

communication gap The difference between the actual service provided to customers and the service promised in the retailer's promotion program. This factor is one of the four factors identified by the gaps model for improving service quality.

communication objectives Specific goals for a communication program related to the effects of the communication program on the customer's decision-making process.

comparative price advertising A common retailing practice that compares the price of merchandise offered for sale with a higher "regular" price or a manufacturer's list price.

comparison shopping A market research method in which retailers shop at competitive stores, comparing the merchandise, pricing, visual display, and service to their own offering.

compatibility The degree to which the fashion is consistent with existing norms, values, and behaviours.

compensation Monetary payments including salary, commission, and bonuses; also, paid vacations, health and insurance benefits, and a retirement plan.

competition-oriented method A pricing method in which a retailer uses competitors' prices, rather than demand or cost considerations, as guides.

competitive parity method An approach for setting a promotion budget so that the retailer's share of promotion expenses is equal to its market share.

competitive rivalry The frequency and intensity of reactions to actions undertaken by competitors.

competitor analysis An examination of the strategic direction that competitors are likely to pursue and their ability to implement their strategy successfully.

complexity Refers to how easy it is to understand and use a new fashion. Consumers have to learn how to incorporate a new fashion into their lifestyle for it to be successful.

composite segmentation A method of segmenting a retail market using multiple variables, including benefits sought, lifestyles, and demographics.

computerized checkout See *point-of-sale (POS) terminal*.

conditional sales agreement An agreement that passes title of goods to the consumer, conditional on full payment.

conditions of sale See *terms of sale*.

conflict of interest A situation in which a decision maker's personal interest influences or has the potential to influence his or her professional decision.

congestion The amount of crowding of either cars or people.

consignment goods Items not paid for by the retailer until they are sold. The retailer can return unsold merchandise; however, the retailer does not take title until final sale is made.

consortium exchange A retail exchange that is owned by several firms within one industry.

consumer cooperative Customers own and operate this type of retail establishment. Customers have ownership shares, hire full-time managers, and share in the store's profits through price reductions or dividends.

consumerism The activities of government, business, and independent organizations designed to protect individuals from practices that infringe upon their rights as consumers.

contests Promotional activities in which customers compete for rewards through games of chance. Contests can also be used to motivate retail employees.

contract distribution service company Firm that performs all of the distribution functions for retailers or vendors, including transportation to the contract company's distribution centre, merchandise processing, storage, and transportation to retailers.

contractual vertical marketing system A form of vertical marketing system in which independent firms at different levels in the channel operate contractually to obtain the economies and market impacts that could not be obtained by unilateral action. Under this system, the identity of the individual firm and its autonomy of operations remain intact. See also *administered vertical marketing system* and *corporate vertical marketing system*.

contribution margin Gross margin less any expense that can be directly assigned to the merchandise.

convenience centre A shopping centre that typically includes such stores as a convenience market, a dry cleaner, or a liquor store.

convenience goods Products that the consumer is not willing to spend the effort to evaluate prior to purchase, such as milk or bread.

convenience store A store that provides a limited variety and assortment of merchandise at a convenient location in a 186 to 279 square metre store with speedy checkout.

conventional supermarket A self-service food store that offers groceries, meat, and produce with limited sales of nonfood items, such as health and beauty aids and general merchandise.

cookies Computer text files that identify visitors when they return to a Web site, so that customers do not have to identify themselves or use passwords every time they visit the site. Cookies also collect information about other sites the person has visited and what pages have been downloaded.

cooperative buying When a group of independent retailers work together to make large purchases from a single supplier.

cooperative (co-op) An establishment owned by an association of customers. In general, the distinguishing features of a cooperative are patronage dividends based on the volume of expenditures by the members and a limitation of one vote per member regardless of the amount of stock owned.

cooperative (co-op) advertising A program undertaken by a vendor in which the vendor agrees to pay all or part of a promotion for its products. Enables a retailer to associate its name with well-known national brands and use attractive artwork created by the national brand. Also a method a retailer uses of sharing the cost of advertising with a vendor.

copy The text in an advertisement.

copycat branding A branding strategy that imitates the manufacturer brand in appearance and trade dress but generally is perceived as lower quality and is offered at a lower price.

copyright A regulation that protects original works of authors, painters, sculptors, musicians, and others who produce works of artistic or intellectual merit.

core assortment A relatively large proportion of the total assortment that is carried by each store in the chain, regardless of size.

corporate vertical marketing system A form of vertical marketing system in which all of the functions from production to distribution are at least partially owned and controlled by a single enterprise. Corporate systems typically operate manufacturing plants, warehouse facilities, and retail outlets. See also *administered vertical marketing system* and *contractual vertical marketing system*.

corporation A firm that is formally incorporated under law and that is a different legal entity from shareholders and employees.

cost code The item cost information indicated on price tickets in code. A common method of coding is the use of letters from an easily remembered word or expression with nonrepeating letters corresponding to numerals. For example:

y o u n g b l a d e
1 2 3 4 5 6 7 8 9 0

cost complement The percentage of net sales represented by the cost of goods sold.

cost method of accounting A method in which retailers record the cost of every item on an accounting sheet or include a cost code on the price tag or merchandise container. When a physical inventory is conducted, the cost of each item must be determined, the quantity in stock is counted, and the total inventory value at cost is calculated. See *retail inventory method*.

cost multiplier The cumulative markup multiplied by 100 percent minus cumulative markup percentage.

cost-oriented method A method for determining the retail price by adding a fixed percentage to the cost of the merchandise; also known as cost-plus pricing.

cost per thousand (CPM) A measure that is often used to compare media. CPM is calculated by dividing an ad's cost by its reach.

counterfeit merchandise Goods that are made and sold without permission of the owner of a trademark, a copyright, or a patented invention that is legally protected in the country where it is marketed.

coupons Documents that entitle the holder to a reduced price or some number of cents off the actual price of a product or service.

courtesy days The days on which stores extend to loyalty club customers the privilege of making purchases at sale prices in advance of public sale.

coverage The theoretical number of potential customers in the retailer's target market that could be exposed to an ad in a given medium.

CPFR See *collaboration, planning, forecasting,* and *replenishment*.

credit Money placed at a consumer's disposal by a retailer or financial or other institution. For purchases made on credit, payment is due in the future.

credit limit The quantitative limit that indicates the maximum amount of credit that may be allowed to be outstanding on each individual customer account.

CRM See *customer relationship management*.

cross-docking distribution centre A warehouse at which merchandise is delivered to one side of the facility by vendors, is unloaded, and is immediately reloaded onto trucks that deliver merchandise to the stores. With cross-docking, merchandise spends very little time in the warehouse.

cross-selling When sales associates in one department attempt to sell complementary merchandise from other departments to their customers.

culture The meaning and values shared by most members of a society.

cumulative attraction The principle that a cluster of similar and complementary retailing activities will generally have greater drawing power than isolated stores that engage in the same retailing activities.

cumulative markup The average percentage markup for the period; the total retail price minus cost, divided by retail price.

cumulative quantity discounts Discounts earned by retailers when purchasing certain quantities over a specified period of time.

cumulative reach The cumulative number of potential customers that would see an ad that runs several times.

current assets Cash or any assets that can normally be converted into cash within one year.

current liabilities Debts that are expected to be paid in less than one year.

customer allowance An additional price reduction given to the customer.

customer buying process The stages a customer goes through in purchasing a good or service. Stages include need recognition, information search, evaluation and choice of alternatives, purchase, and postpurchase evaluation.

customer database See *data warehouse*.

customer data warehouse See *data warehouse*.

customer loyalty Customers' commitment to shopping at a store.

customer relationship management (CRM) A business philosophy and set of strategies, programs, and systems that focuses on identifying and building loyalty with a retailer's most valued customers.

customer returns The value of merchandise that customers return because it is damaged, doesn't fit, and so forth.

customer service The set of retail activities that increase the value customers receive when they shop and purchase merchandise.

customer service department The department in a retail organization that handles customer inquiries and complaints.

customer spotting A technique used in trade area analysis that "spots" (locates) residences of customers for a store or shopping centre.

customization approach An approach used by retailers to provide customer service that is tailored to meet each customer's personal needs.

cycle stock Inventory that results from the replenishment process and is required to meet demand when the retailer can predict demand and replenishment times (lead times) perfectly.

cyclical theories Theories of institutional change based on the premise that retail institutions change on the basis of cycles. See also *wheel of retailing* and *accordion theory*.

databased retailing The development and implementation of retailing programs to build store loyalty utilizing a computerized file (data warehouse) of customer profiles and purchase patterns.

data mining Technique used to identify patterns in data found in data warehouses, typically patterns that the analyst is unaware of prior to searching through the data.

data warehouse The coordinated and periodic copying of data from various sources, both inside and outside the enterprise, into an environment ready for analytical and informational processing. It contains all of the data the firm has collected about its customers and is the foundation for subsequent CRM activities.

dating A series of options that tells retailers when discounts can be taken from vendors and when the full invoice amount is due.

deal period A limited time period allowed by manufacturers for retailers to purchase merchandise at a special price.

debit card A card that resembles a credit card but allows the retailer to subtract payments automatically from a customer's chequing account at the time of sale.

decentralization When authority for retail decisions is made at lower levels in the organization.

deceptive advertising Any advertisement that contains a false statement or misrepresents a product or service.

decile analysis A method of identifying customers in a CRM program that breaks customers into ten deciles based on their LTV (lifetime customer value). When using decile analysis, the top 10 percent of the customers would be the most-valued group.

deep pockets Considerable financial resources that enable companies to make strategic decisions, such as expansion into international markets, requiring significant and ongoing financial commitment, often at the expense of short-term profit.

deferred billing An arrangement that enables customers to buy merchandise and not pay for it for several months, with no interest charge.

delivery gap The difference between the retailer's service standards and the actual service provided to customers. This factor is one of the four factors identified by the gaps model for improving service quality.

demalling The activity of revitalizing a mall by demolishing a mall's small shops, scrapping its common space and food courts, enlarging the sites once occupied by department stores, and adding more entrances to the parking lot.

demand/destination area Department or area in a store in which demand for the products or services offered is created before customers get to their destination.

demand-oriented method A method of setting prices based on what the customers would expect or be willing to pay.

democratic leader A store manager who seeks information and opinions from employees and bases decisions on this information.

demographics Vital statistics about populations such as age, sex, and income.

demographic segmentation A method of segmenting a retail market that groups consumers on the basis of easily measured, objective characteristics such as age, sex, income, and education.

department A segment of a store with merchandise that represents a group of classifications the consumer views as being complementary.

department store A retailer that carries a wide variety and deep assortment, offers considerable customer services, and is organized into separate departments for displaying merchandise.

departmentalization An organizational design in which employees are grouped into departments that perform specific activities to achieve operating efficiencies through specialization.

depth See *assortment*.

depth interview An unstructured personal interview in which the interviewer uses extensive probing to get individual respondents to talk in detail about a subject.

depth of stock See *assortment*.

deseasonalized demand The forecast demand without the influence of seasonality.

destination store A retail store in which the merchandise, selection, presentation, pricing, or other unique feature acts as a magnet for customers.

dialectic theory An evolutionary theory based on the premise that retail institutions evolve. The theory suggests that new retail formats emerge by adopting characteristics from other forms of retailers in much the same way that a child is the product of the pooled genes of two very different parents.

direct investment The investment and ownership by a retail firm or a division or subsidiary that builds and operates stores in a foreign country.

direct-mail catalogue retailer A retailer offering merchandise or services through catalogues mailed directly to customers.

direct-mail retailer A nonstore retailer that communicates directly with customers using mail brochures and pamphlets to sell a specific product or service to customers at one point in time.

direct marketing A form of nonstore retailing in which customers are exposed to merchandise through print or electronic media and then purchase the merchandise by telephone, mail, or over the Internet.

direct product profitability (DPP) The profit associated with each category or unit of merchandise. DPP is equal to the per-unit gross margin less all variable costs associated with the merchandise such as procurement, distribution, sales, and the cost of carrying the assets.

direct-response advertising Advertisements on TV and radio that describe products and provide an opportunity for customers to order them.

direct retailing See *nonstore retailing*.

direct selling A retail format in which a salesperson, frequently an independent distributor, contacts a customer directly in a convenient location (either at a customer's home or at work) and demonstrates merchandise benefits, takes an order, and delivers the merchandise to the customer.

disability Any physical or mental impairment that substantially limits one or more of an individual's major life activities or any condition that is regarded as being such an impairment.

disclosure of confidential information An unethical situation in which a retail employee discloses proprietary or confidential information about the firm's business to anyone outside the firm.

discount   A reduction in the original retail price granted to store employees as a special benefit or to customers under certain circumstances.

discount-oriented centre   See *promotional centre*.

discount store   A general merchandise retailer that offers a wide variety of merchandise, limited service, and low prices.

discrimination   An illegal action of a company or its managers that results when a member of a protected class (women, minorities, etc.) is treated differently from nonmembers of that class (see *disparate treatment*) or when an apparently neutral rule has an unjustified discriminatory effect (see *disparate impact*).

disintermediation   When a manufacturer sells directly to consumers, thus competing directly with its retailers.

disparate impact   In the case of discrimination, when an apparently neutral rule has an unjustified discriminatory effect, such as when a retailer requires high school graduation for all its employees, thereby excluding a larger proportion of disdvantaged minorities, when at least some of the jobs (e.g., custodian) could be performed just as well by people who did not graduate from high school.

disparate treatment   In the case of discrimination, when members of a protected class are treated differently than nonmembers of that class, such as when a qualified woman (protected class) does not receive a promotion given to a less qualified man.

dispatcher   A person who coordinates deliveries from the vendor to the distribution centre or stores, or from the distribution centre to stores.

display stock   Merchandise placed on various display fixtures for customers to examine.

distribution   See *logistics*.

distribution centre   A warehouse that receives merchandise from multiple vendors and distributes it to multiple stores.

distribution channel   A set of firms that facilitate the movement of products from the point of production to the point of sale to the ultimate consumer.

distribution intensity   The number of retailers carrying a particular category.

distributive fairness   Exists when outcomes received are viewed as fair with respect to outcomes received by others.

distributive justice   Exists when outcomes received are viewed as fair with respect to outcomes received by others.

diversification opportunity   A strategic investment opportunity that involves an entirely new retail format directed toward a market segment not presently being served.

diversionary pricing   A practice sometimes used by retailers in which a low price is stated for one or a few goods or services (emphasized in promotion) to give the illusion that all of the retailer's prices are low.

diverted merchandise   Merchandise that is diverted from its legitimate channel of distribution; similar to grey-market merchandise except there need not be distribution across international boundaries.

diverter   A firm that buys diverted merchandise from retailers and manufacturers and then resells the merchandise to other retailers. See *diverted merchandise*.

double-coupon   A retail promotion that allows the customer to double the face value of a coupon.

downtown location   The central business district located in the traditional shopping area of smaller towns, or a secondary business district in a suburb or within a larger city, generally featuring lower occupancy costs, fewer people, fewer stores, smaller overall selection of goods or services, and fewer entertainment and recreational activities than more successful primary central business districts.

drawing account   A method of sales compensation in which salespeople receive a weekly cheque based on their estimated annual income.

drugstore   Specialty retail store that concentrates on pharmaceuticals and health and personal grooming merchandise.

duty   See *tariff*.

EAS   See *electronic article surveillance system*.

e-commerce   The distribution, buying, selling, marketing, and servicing of products over the Internet.

economic order quantity (EOQ)   The order quantity that minimizes the total cost of processing orders and holding inventory.

EDI   See *electronic data interchange*.

EDLP   See *everyday low pricing*.

80–20 rule   A general management principle stating that 80 percent of the sales or profits come from 20 percent of the customers.

electronic agent   Computer program that locates and selects alternatives based on some predetermined characteristics.

electronic article surveillance system (EAS)   A loss-prevention system in which special tags placed on merchandise in retail stores are deactivated when the merchandise is purchased. The tags are used to discourage shoplifting.

electronic data interchange (EDI)   The computer-to-computer exchange of business documents from retailer to vendor, and back.

electronic retailing   A retail format in which the retailers communicate with customers and offer products and services for sale over the Internet. Also called *e-tailing*.

e-mail   A paid personal communication vehicle that involves sending messages to customers over the Internet.

emotional support   Supporting retail service providers with the understanding and positive regard to enable them to deal with the emotional stress created by disgruntled customers.

employee discount   A discount from retail price offered by most retailers to employees.

employee productivity   Output generated by employee activities. One measure of employee productivity is the retailer's sales or profit divided by its employee costs.

employee turnover   The number of employees occupying a set of positions during a period (usually a year) divided by the number of positions.

empowerment   The process of managers sharing power and decision-making authority with employees.

empty nest   A stage in a family life cycle in which children have grown up and left home.

empty nester   Household in which all children are grown and have left home.

end cap   Display fixture located at the end of an aisle.

end-of-month (EOM) dating   A method of dating in which the discount period starts at the end of the month in which the invoice is dated (except when the invoice is dated the 25th or later).

energy management   The coordination of heating, air conditioning, and lighting to improve efficiencies and reduce energy costs.

environmental apparel   Merchandise produced with few or no harmful effects on the environment.

EOQ   See *economic order quantity.*

escape clause   A clause in a lease that allows the retailer to terminate its lease if sales don't reach a certain level after a specified number of years or if a specific co-tenant in the centre terminates its lease.

e-tailing   See *electronic retailing.*

ethics   A system or code of conduct based on universal moral duties and obligations that indicate how one should behave.

evaluation of alternatives   The stage in the buying process in which the customer compares the benefits offered by various retailers.

everyday low pricing (EDLP)   A pricing strategy that stresses continuity of retail prices at a level somewhere between the regular nonsale price and the deep-discount sale price of the retailer's competitors.

evolutionary theories   Theories of institutional change based on the premise that retail institutions evolve. See *dialectic theory* and *natural selection.*

exclusive dealing agreement   Restriction a manufacturer or wholesaler places on a retailer to carry only its products and no competing vendors' products.

exclusive geographic territory   A policy in which only one retailer in a certain territory is allowed to sell a particular brand.

exclusive use clause   A clause in a lease that prohibits the landlord from leasing to retailers selling competing products.

executive training program (ETP)   A training program for retail supervisors, managers, and executives.

expenses   Costs incurred in the normal course of doing business to generate revenues.

experiment   A research method in which a variable is manipulated under controlled conditions.

expert system   Computer program that incorporates knowledge of experts in a particular field. Expert systems are used to aid in decision making and problem solving.

exponential smoothing   A sales forecasting technique in which sales in previous time periods are weighted to develop a forecast for future periods.

express warranty   A guarantee supplied by either the retailer or the manufacturer that details the terms of the warranty in simple, easily understood language so customers know what is and what is not covered by the warranty.

extra dating   A discount offered by a vendor in which the retailer receives extra time to pay the invoice and still take the cash discount.

extranet   A collaborative network that uses Internet technology to link businesses with their suppliers, customers, or other businesses.

extrinsic reward   Reward (such as money, promotion, and recognition) given to employees by their manager or the firm.

factoring   A specialized financial function whereby manufacturers, wholesalers, or retailers sell accounts receivable to financial institutions, including factors or banks.

factory outlet   Outlet store owned by a manufacturer.

fad   A merchandise category that generates a lot of sales for a relatively short time—often less than a season.

fair trade laws   See *resale price maintenance laws.*

fashion   Category of merchandise that typically lasts several seasons; sales can vary dramatically from one season to the next.

fashion/specialty centre   A shopping centre that is composed mainly of upscale apparel shops, boutiques, and gift shops carrying selected fashions or unique merchandise of high quality and price.

feature area   Area designed to get the customer's attention that includes end caps, promotional aisles or areas, freestanding fixtures, and mannequins that introduce a soft goods department, windows, and point-of-sale areas.

feature fixture   See *four-way fixture.*

features   The qualities or characteristics of a product that provide benefits to customers.

fill rate   The percentage of an order that is shipped by the vendor.

financial leverage   A financial measure based on the relationship between the retailer's liabilities and owners' equity that indicates financial stability of the firm.

first-degree price discrimination   Charging customers different prices based on their willingness to pay.

fixed assets   Assets that require more than a year to convert to cash.

fixed cost   A cost that is stable and doesn't change with the quantity of product that's produced and sold.

fixed expenses   Expenses that remain constant for a given period of time regardless of the sales volume.

fixed-rate lease   A lease that requires the retailer to pay a fixed amount per month over the life of the lease.

flattening the organization   A reduction in the number of management levels.

flexible pricing   A pricing strategy that allows consumers to bargain over selling prices.

flextime   A job scheduling system that enables employees to choose the times they work.

floor-ready merchandise   Merchandise received at the store ready to be sold, without the need for any additional preparation by retail employees.

FOB (free-on-board) destination   A term of sale designating that the shipper owns the merchandise until it is delivered to the retailer and is therefore responsible for transportation and any damage claims.

FOB (free-on-board) origin   A term of sale designating that the retailer takes ownership of the merchandise at the point of origin and is therefore responsible for transportation and any damage claims.

focus group A marketing research technique in which a small group of respondents is interviewed by a moderator using a loosely structured format.

forward buy An opportunity to purchase at an extra discount more merchandise than the retailer normally needs to fill demand.

forward integration A form of vertical integration in which a manufacturer owns wholesalers or retailers.

four-way fixture A fixture with two cross-bars that sit perpendicular to each other on a pedestal.

franchisee The owner of an individual store in a franchise agreement.

franchising A contractual agreement between a franchisor and a franchisee that allows the franchisee to operate a retail outlet using a name and format developed and supported by the franchisor.

franchisor The owner of a franchise in a franchise agreement.

free-form layout A store design, used primarily in small specialty stores or within the boutiques of large stores, that arranges fixtures and aisles asymmetrically. Also called *boutique layout*.

freestanding fixture Fixtures and mannequins located on aisles that are designed primarily to get customers' attention and bring them into a department.

freestanding insert (FSI) An ad printed at a retailer's expense and distributed with a newspaper. Also called a *preprint*.

freestanding site A retail location that is not connected to other retailers.

free trade zone A special area within a country that can be used for warehousing, packaging, inspection, labelling, exhibition, assembly, fabrication, or transshipment of imports without being subject to that country's tariffs.

freight collect When the retailer pays the freight.

freight forwarders Companies that purchase transport services. They then consolidate small shipments from a number of shippers into large shipments that move at a lower freight rate.

freight prepaid When the freight is paid by the vendor.

frequency The number of times a potential customer is exposed to an ad.

frequent shopper program A reward and communication program used by a retailer to encourage continued purchases from the retailer's best customers. See *loyalty program*.

fringe trade area See *tertiary zone*.

frontal presentation A method of displaying merchandise in which the retailer exposes as much of the product as possible to catch the customer's eye.

full-line forcing When a supplier requires a retailer to carry the supplier's full line of products if the retailer wants to carry any part of that line.

full warranty A guarantee provided by either the retailer or manufacturer to repair or replace merchandise without charge and within a reasonable amount of time in the event of a defect.

functional discount See *trade discount*.

functional product grouping Categorizing and displaying merchandise by common end uses.

functional relationships A series of one-time market exchanges linked together over time.

future dating A method of dating that allows the buyer additional time to take advantage of the cash discount or to pay the net amount of the invoice.

gaps model A conceptual model that indicates what retailers need to do to provide high-quality customer service. When customers' expectations are greater than their perceptions of the delivered service, customers are dissatisfied and feel the quality of the retailer's service is poor. Thus, retailers need to reduce the service gap—the difference between customers' expectations and perceptions of customer service to improve customers' satisfaction with their service.

general merchandise catalogue retailers Nonstore retailers that offer a broad variety of merchandise in catalogues that are periodically mailed to their customers.

generational cohort People within the same generation who have similar purchase behaviours because they have shared experiences and are in the same stage of life.

Generation X The generational cohort of people born between 1965 and 1976.

Generation Y The generational cohort of people born between 1977 and 1995.

generic brand Unbranded, unadvertised merchandise found mainly in drug, grocery, and discount stores.

gentrification A process in which old buildings are torn down or are restored to create new offices, housing developments, and retailers.

geodemographic segmentation A market segmentation system that uses both geographic and demographic characteristics to classify consumers.

geographic information system (GIS) A computerized system that enables analysts to visualize information about their customers' demographics, buying behaviour, and other data in a map format.

geographic segmentation Segmentation of potential customers by where they live. A retail market can be segmented by countries, provinces, cities, and neighbourhoods.

glass ceiling A figurative barrier that makes it difficult for minorities and women to be promoted beyond a certain level.

global culture A company's embracing a multicultural perspective and developing an infrastructure that makes maximal use of local management.

global strategy Replicating a retailer's standard retail format and centralized management throughout the world in each new market.

globally sustainable competitive advantage One of the characteristics of retailers that have successfully exploited international growth opportunities.

gondola An island type of self-service counter with tiers of shelves, bins, or pegs.

graduated lease A lease that requires rent to increase by a fixed amount over a specified period of time.

limited warranty   A type of guarantee in which any limitations must be stated conspicuously so that customers are not misled.

local links   A way to help customers get around a Web site on the Internet by using links that are internal to a Web site.

logistics   Part of the supply chain process that plans, implements, and controls the efficient, effective flow and storage of goods, services, and related information from the point of origin to the point of consumption in order to meet customers' requirements.

long-term liabilities   Debts that will be paid after one year.

loop   See *racetrack layout*.

loss leader   An item priced near or below cost to attract customer traffic into the store.

low-price guarantee policy   A policy that guarantees that the retailer will have the lowest possible price for a product or group of products, and usually promises to match or better any lower price found in the local market.

loyalty program   A program set up to reward customers with incentives such as discounts on purchases, free food, gifts, or even cruises or trips in return for their repeated business.

macro-environment   The external environment that the retailer cannot control, including competition, economic stability of the trade area, the technology that will make retailing more efficient, the regulatory and ethical environment in which the business operates, and the social trends including consumer behaviour and lifestyle and demographic trends.

magalogue   A combination magazine and catalogue.

mail-order retailer   See *direct-mail catalogue retailer*.

Main Street   The central business district located in the traditional shopping area of smaller towns, or a secondary business district in a suburb or within a larger city.

maintained markup   The amount of markup the retailer wishes to maintain on a particular category of merchandise; net sales minus cost of goods sold.

maintenance-increase-recoupment lease   A provision of a lease that can be used with either a percentage or straight lease. This type of lease allows the landlord to increase the rent if insurance, property taxes, or utility bills increase beyond a certain point.

mall   A shopping centre with a pedestrian focus where customers park in outlying areas and walk to the stores.

management   A strategic approach of an organization to achieve its objectives by developing policies and plans for allocating resources.

management by objectives   A popular method for linking the goals of a firm to goals for each employee and providing information to employees about their role.

managing diversity   A set of human resource management programs designed to realize the benefits of a diverse workforce.

manufacturer brand   A line of products designed, produced, and marketed by a vendor. Also called a national brand.

manufacturer's agent   An agent who generally operates on an extended contractual basis; often sells within an exclusive territory; handles noncompeting but related lines of goods; and possesses limited authority with regard to prices and terms of sale.

manufacturer's outlet store   A discount retail store owned and operated by a manufacturer.

maquiladoras   Manufacturing plants in Mexico that make goods and parts or process food for export to the United States.

marginal analysis   A method of analysis used in setting a promotional budget or allocating retail space, based on the economic principle that firms should increase expenditures as long as each additional dollar spent generates more than a dollar of additional contribution.

markdown   The percentage reduction in the initial retail price.

markdown cancellation   The percentage increase in the retail price after a markdown is taken.

markdown money   Funds provided by a vendor to a retailer to cover decreased gross margin from markdowns and other merchandising issues.

market   A group of vendors in a concentrated geographic location or even under one roof or over the Internet; also known as a *central market*.

market attractiveness/competitive position matrix   A method for analyzing opportunities that explicitly considers the capabilities of the retailer and the attractiveness of retail markets.

market basket analysis   Specific type of data analysis that focuses on the composition of the basket (or bundle) of products purchased by a household during a single shopping occasion.

market development   See *market penetration opportunity*.

market expansion opportunity   A strategic investment opportunity that employs the existing retailing format in new market segments.

marketing segmentation   The process of dividing a retail market into homogeneous groups. See *retail market segment*.

market penetration opportunity   An investment opportunity strategy that focuses on increasing sales to present customers using the present retailing format.

market potential index (MPI)   Measures the likely demand for a product or service in a country, postal code or zip code, or other trade area.

market research   The systematic collection and analysis of information about a retail market.

market share   A retailer's sales divided by the sales of all competitors within the same market.

market week   See *trade show*.

markup   The increase in the retail price of an item after the initial markup percentage has been applied but before the item is placed on the selling floor.

marquee   A sign used to display a store's name or logo.

mass customization   The production of individually customized products at costs similar to mass-produced products.

mass-market theory   A theory of how fashion spreads that suggests that each social class has its own fashion leaders who play a key role in their own social networks. Fashion information trickles across social classes rather than down from the upper classes to the lower classes.

mass merchandiser   See *discount store*.

Mazur plan A method of retail organization in which all retail activities fall into four functional areas: merchandising, publicity, store management, and accounting and control.

med-arb Used in the case of a dispute between retailer and vendor that involves an initial attempt at mediation followed by binding arbitration if the mediation is unsuccessful. See *mediation* and *arbitration*.

media coverage The theoretical number of potential customers in a retailer's market who could be exposed to an ad.

mediation Used in the case of a dispute between retailer and vendor that involves selecting a neutral party—the mediator—to assist the parties in reaching a mutually agreeable settlement.

memorandum purchases Items not paid for by a retailer until they are sold. The retailer can return unsold merchandise; however, the retailer takes title on delivery and is responsible for damages. See *consignment goods*.

mentoring program The assigning of higher-level managers to help lower-level managers learn the firm's values and meet other senior executives.

merchandise category See *category*.

merchandise classification See *classification*.

merchandise group A group within an organization managed by the senior vice-presidents of merchandise and responsible for several departments.

merchandise management The process by which a retailer attempts to offer the right quantity of the right merchandise in the right place at the right time while meeting the company's financial goal.

merchandise plan A plan used by buyers to determine how much money to spend in each month on a particular fashion merchandise category, given the firm's sales forecast, inventory turnover, and profit goals.

merchandise show See *trade show*.

merchandising See *merchandise management*.

merchandising optimization software Set of algorithms (computer programs) that monitors merchandise sales, promotions, competitors' actions, and other factors to determine the optimal (most profitable) price and timing for merchandising activities, especially markdowns.

merchandising planner A retail employee responsible for allocating merchandise and tailoring the assortment in several categories for specific stores in a geographic area.

merger A financial strategy in which one larger firm acquires a smaller firm. This term is used interchangeably with acquisition. See also *leveraged buyout*.

message board Location in an Internet site at which customers can post comments.

Metropolitan Statistical Area (MSA) A city with 50 000 or more inhabitants or an urbanized area of at least 50 000 inhabitants and a total MSA population of at least 100 000 (75 000 in New England).

micro-environment All of the things within the retailer's control, including the retail product that will be sold, the price for the product, the store location, the promotion and visual image of the store, and the store management decisions.

mission statement A broad description of the scope of activities a business plans to undertake.

mixed-use development (MXD) Development that combines several uses in one complex—for example, shopping centre, office tower, hotel, residential complex, civic centre, and convention centre.

model stock list A list of fashion merchandise that indicates in very general terms (product lines, colours, and size distributions) what should be carried in a particular merchandise category; also known as model stock plan.

monthly additions to stock The amount to be ordered for delivery in each month, given the firm's turnover and sales objectives.

multichannel retailer Retailer that sells merchandise or services through more than one channel.

multilevel direct selling A form of direct selling in which people sell directly to customers, serve as master distributors, and recruit other people to become distributors in their network. The master distributors either buy merchandise from the firm and resell it to their distributors or receive a commission on all merchandise purchased by the distributors in their network.

multilevel network A retail format in which people serve as master distributors, recruiting other people to become distributors in their network.

multinational strategy A strategy that involves changing a retailer's products and image to reflect the international marketplace, using a decentralized format, learning about the country's culture, and changing the retail concept to adapt to cultural differences and cater to local market demands.

multiple-unit pricing Practice of offering two or more similar products or services for sale at one price.

mystery shopper Professional shopper who "shops" a store to assess the service provided by store employees.

NAICS (North American Industry Classification System) Classification of retail firms into a hierarchical set of six-digit codes.

national brand See *manufacturer brand*.

natural barrier A barrier, such as a river or mountain, that affects accessibility to a site.

natural selection A theory of retail evolution that argues that those institutions best able to adapt to changes in customers, technology, competition, and legal environments have the greatest chance for success.

needs The basic psychological forces that motivate customers to act.

negligence A product liability suit that occurs if a retailer or a retail employee fails to exercise the care that a prudent person usually would.

negotiation An interaction between two or more parties to reach an agreement.

neighbourhood centre A shopping centre that includes a supermarket, drugstore, home improvement centre, or variety store. Neighbourhood centres often include small stores, such as apparel, shoe, camera, and other shopping goods stores.

net invoice price The net value of the invoice or the total invoice minus all other discounts.

net lease   A lease that requires all maintenance expenses such as heat, insurance, and interior repairs to be paid by the retailer.

net profit   A measure of the overall performance of a firm; revenues (sales) minus expenses and losses for the period.

net profit margin   The profit (after tax) a firm makes divided by its net sales.

net sales   The total number of dollars received by a retailer after all refunds have been paid to customers for returned merchandise.

network direct selling   See *multilevel direct selling*.

net worth   See *owners' equity*.

never-out list   A list of key items or best-sellers that are separately planned and controlled. These items account for large sales volume and are stocked in a manner so they are always available. These are A items in an ABC analysis.

noncumulative quantity discount   Discount offered to retailers as an incentive to purchase more merchandise on a single order.

nondurable   Perishable product consumed in one or a few uses.

nonstore retailing   A form of retailing to ultimate consumers that is not store-based. Nonstore retailing is conducted through the Internet, vending machines, mail, direct selling, and direct marketing.

notes payable   Current liabilities representing principal and interest the retailer owes to financial institutions (banks) that are due and payable in less than a year.

objective-and-task method   A method for setting a promotion budget in which the retailer first establishes a set of communication objectives and then determines the necessary tasks and their costs.

observability   The degree to which a new fashion is visible and easily communicated to others in a social group.

observation   A type of market research in which customer behaviour is observed and recorded.

odd pricing   The practice of ending prices with an odd number (such as 69 cents) or just under a round number (such as $98 instead of $100).

off-price retailer   A retailer that offers an inconsistent assortment of brand-name, fashion-oriented soft goods at low prices.

off-the-job training   Training conducted in centralized classrooms away from the employee's work environment.

one hundred percent location   The retail site in a major business district or mall that has the greatest exposure to a retail store's target market customers.

one-price policy   A policy that, at a given time, all customers pay the same price for any given item of merchandise.

one-price retailer   A store that offers all merchandise at a single fixed price.

1-to-1 retailing   Developing retail programs for small groups or individual customers.

on-the-job training   A decentralized approach in which job training occurs in the work environment where employees perform their jobs.

open-to-buy   The plan that keeps track of how much is spent in each month, and how much is left to spend.

opinion leader   Person whose attitudes, opinions, preferences, and actions influence those of others.

opportunity cost of capital   The rate available on the next-best use of the capital invested in the project at hand. The opportunity cost should be no lower than the rate at which a firm borrows funds, since one alternative is to pay back borrowed money. It can be higher, however, depending on the range of other opportunities available. Typically, the opportunity cost rises with investment risk.

optical character recognition (OCR)   An industrywide classification system for coding information onto merchandise; enables retailers to record information on each SKU when it is sold and to transmit the information to a computer.

opt in   A customer privacy issue prevalent in the European Union. Takes the perspective that consumers "own" their personal information. Retailers must get consumers to explicitly agree to share this personal information.

option credit account   A revolving account that allows partial payments without interest charges if a bill is paid in full when due.

option-term revolving credit   A credit arrangement that offers customers two payment options: (1) pay the full amount within a specified number of days and avoid any finance charges, or (2) make a minimum payment and be assessed finance charges on the unpaid balance.

opt out   A customer privacy issue prevalent in the United States. Takes the perspective that personal information is generally viewed as being in the public domain and retailers can use it in any way they desire. Consumers must explicitly tell retailers not to use their personal information.

order form   When signed by both parties, a legally binding contract specifying the terms and conditions under which a purchase transaction is to be conducted.

order point   The amount of inventory below which the quantity available shouldn't go or the item will be out of stock before the next order arrives.

organization chart   A graphic that displays the reporting relationships within a firm.

organization culture   A firm's set of values, traditions, and customs that guide employee behaviour.

organization structure   A plan that identifies the activities to be performed by specific employees and determines the lines of authority and responsibility in the firm.

outlet centre   Typically features stores owned by retail chains or manufacturers that sell excess and out-of-season merchandise at reduced prices.

outlet store   Off-price retailer owned by a manufacturer or a department or specialty store chain.

outparcel   A building or kiosk that is in the parking lot of a shopping centre but isn't physically attached to a shopping centre.

output measure   Measure that assesses the results of retailers' investment decisions.

outshopping   Customers shopping in other areas because their needs are not being met locally.

outsourcing Obtaining a service from outside the company that had previously been done by the firm itself.

overstored trade area An area having so many stores selling a specific good or service that some stores will fail.

owners' equity The amount of assets belonging to the owners of the retail firm after all obligations (liabilities) have been met; also known as net worth and shareholders' equity.

pallet A platform, usually made of wood, that provides stable support for several cartons. Pallets are used to help move and store merchandise.

parallel branding A branding strategy that represents a private label that closely imitates the trade dress (packaging) and product attributes of leading manufacturer brands but with a clearly articulated "invitation to compare" in its merchandising approach and on its product label.

partnering relationship See *strategic relationship*.

party plan system Salespeople encourage people to act as hosts and invite friends or co-workers to a "party" at which the merchandise is demonstrated. The host or hostess receives a gift or commission for arranging the meeting.

patent A law that gives the owner of a patent control of the right to make, sell, and use a product for a period of 17 years (14 years for a design).

penetration A low-pricing strategy for newly introduced categories.

percentage lease A lease in which rent is based on a percentage of sales.

percentage lease with specified maximum A lease that pays the lessor, or landlord, a percentage of sales up to a maximum amount.

percentage lease with specified minimum The retailer must pay a minimum rent no matter how low sales are.

percentage-of-sales method A method for setting a promotion budget based on a fixed percentage of forecast sales.

percentage variation method An inventory planning method wherein the actual stock on hand during any month varies from average planned monthly stock by only half of the month's variation from average estimated monthly sales.

periodic reordering system An inventory management system in which the review time is a fixed period (e.g., two weeks), but the order quantity can vary.

perpetual book inventory See *retail inventory method*.

perpetual ordering system The stock level is monitored perpetually and a fixed quantity, known as EOQ (economic order quantity), is purchased when the inventory available reaches a prescribed level.

personal selling A communication process in which salespeople assist customers in satisfying their needs through face-to-face exchange of information.

physical inventory A method of gathering stock information by using an actual physical count and inspection of the merchandise items.

pick ticket A document that tells the order filler how much of each item to get from the storage area.

pilferage The stealing of a store's merchandise. See also *shoplifting*.

planogram A diagram created from photographs, computer output, or artists' renderings that illustrates exactly where every SKU should be placed.

point-of-purchase (POP) area See *point-of-sale area*.

point-of-sale area An area where the customer waits at checkout. This area can be the most valuable piece of real estate in the store, because the customer is almost held captive in that spot.

point-of-sale (POS) terminal A cash register that can electronically scan a UPC code with a laser and electronically record a sale; also known as *computerized checkout*.

polygon Trade area whose boundaries conform to streets and other map features rather than being concentric circles.

popping the merchandise Focusing spotlights on special feature areas and items.

population density The number of people per unit area (usually square kilometre) who live within a geographic area.

positioning The design and implementation of a retail mix to create in the customer's mind an image of the retailer relative to its competitors. Also called *brand building*.

positioning statement A statement that explains how the retailer's product or service is different from key competitors'.

poverty of time A condition in which greater affluence results in less, rather than more, free time because the alternatives competing for customers' time increase.

power centre Shopping centre that is dominated by several large anchors, including discount stores (Target), off-price stores (Marshalls), warehouse clubs (Costco), or category specialists such as Home Depot, Office Depot, Circuit City, Sports Authority, Best Buy, and Toys "R" Us.

power retailer See *category killer* or *category specialist*.

power shopping centre An open-air shopping centre with the majority of space leased to several well-known anchor retail tenants—category specialists.

predatory pricing A method for establishing merchandise prices for the purpose of driving competition from the marketplace.

preferred client High-purchasing customers with whom salespeople communicate regularly, sending notes about new merchandise and sales in the department, and making appointments with for special presentations of merchandise.

premarking Marking of the price by the manufacturer or other supplier before goods are shipped to a retail store. Also called *prepricing*.

premium branding A branding strategy that offers the consumer a private label at a comparable manufacturer-brand quality, usually with a modest price savings.

premium merchandise Offered at a reduced price, or free, as an incentive for a customer to make a purchase.

prepricing See *premarking*.

preprint An advertisement printed at the retailer's expense and distributed as a freestanding insert in a newspaper. Also called a freestanding insert (FSI).

press conference A meeting with representatives of the news media that is called by a retailer.

press release A statement of facts or opinions that the retailer would like to see published by the news media.

prestige pricing A system of pricing based on the assumption that consumers will not buy goods and services at prices they feel are too low.

price bundling The practice of offering two or more different products or services for sale at one price.

price comparison A comparison of the price of merchandise offered for sale with a higher "regular" price or a manufacturer's list price.

price discrimination An illegal practice in which a vendor sells the same product to two or more customers at different prices. See *first-degree price discrimination* and *second-degree price discrimination*.

price elasticity of demand A measure of the effect a price change has on consumer demand; percentage change in demand divided by percentage change in price.

price-fixing An illegal pricing activity in which several marketing channel members establish a fixed retail selling price for a product line within a market area. See *vertical price-fixing* and *horizontal price-fixing*.

price lining A pricing policy in which a retailer offers a limited number of predetermined price points within a classification.

pricing experiment An experiment in which a retailer actually changes the price of an item in a systematic manner to observe changes in customers' purchases or purchase intentions.

primary data Marketing research information collected through surveys, observations, and experiments to address a problem confronting a retailer.

primary trade area See *primary zone*.

primary zone The geographic area from which the store or shopping centre derives 60 to 65 percent of its customers. Also called primary trade area.

private exchanges Exchanges that are operated for the exclusive use of a single firm.

private-label brands Products developed and marketed by a retailer and only available for sale by that retailer. Also called *store brands*.

private-label store credit card system A system in which credit cards have the store's name on them, but the accounts receivable are sold to a financial institution.

procedural fairness The perceived fairness of the process used to resolve customer complaints.

procedural justice An employee's perception of fairness (how he or she is treated) that is based on the process used to determine the outcome.

product attributes Characteristics of a product that affect customer evaluations.

product availability A measurement of the percentage of demand for a particular SKU that is satisfied.

productivity measure The ratio of an output to an input determining how effectively a firm uses a resource.

product liability A tort (or wrong) that occurs when an injury results from the use of a product.

product line A group of related products.

profitability A company's ability to generate revenues in excess of the costs incurred in producing those revenues.

profit margin Net profit after taxes divided by net sales.

prohibited use clause A clause in a lease that keeps a landlord from leasing to certain kinds of tenants.

promotion Activities undertaken by a retailer to provide consumers with information about a retailer's store and its retail mix.

promotional aisle or area Aisle or area of a store designed to get the customer's attention. An example might be a special "trim-the-tree" department that seems magically to appear right after Halloween every year for the Christmas holidays.

promotional allowance An allowance given by vendors to retailers to compensate the latter for money spent in advertising a particular item.

promotional centre A type of specialty shopping centre that contains one or more discount stores plus smaller retail tenants. Also called *discount-oriented centre*.

promotional department store A department store that concentrates on apparel and sells a substantial portion of its merchandise on weekly promotion.

promotional stock A retailer's stock of goods offered at an unusually attractive price in order to obtain sales volume; it often represents special purchases from vendors.

promotion from within A staffing policy that involves hiring new employees only for positions at the lowest level in the job hierarchy and then promoting employees for openings at higher levels in the hierarchy.

promotion mix A communication program made up of advertising, sales promotions, Web sites, store atmosphere, publicity, personal selling, and word of mouth.

proprietary store credit card system A system in which credit cards have the store's name on them and the accounts receivable are administered by the retailer; also known as an *in-house credit system*.

providing assortments A function performed by retailers that enables customers to choose from a selection of brands, designs, sizes, and prices at one location.

psychographics Refers to how people live, how they spend their time and money, what activities they pursue, and their attitudes and opinions about the world.

publicity Communications through significant unpaid presentations about the retailer (usually a news story) in impersonal media.

public warehouse Warehouse that is owned and operated by a third party.

puffing An advertising or personal selling practice in which a retailer simply exaggerates the benefits or quality of a product in very broad terms.

pull distribution strategy Strategy in which orders for merchandise are generated at the store level on the basis of demand data captured by point-of-sale terminals.

purchase visibility curve A display technique in which the retailer tilts low shelves so more merchandise is in direct view.

pure play e-tailer An e-tailer that uses the Internet as its primary means of retailing.

push distribution strategy Strategy in which merchandise is allocated to stores based on historical demand, the inventory position at the distribution centre, as well as the stores' needs.

push money (PM) An incentive for retail salespeople provided by a vendor to promote, or push, a particular product; also known as *spiff*.

pyramid scheme When the firm and its program are designed to sell merchandise and services to other distributors rather than to end users.

quantity discount The policy of granting lower prices for higher quantities.

quick response (QR) delivery system System designed to reduce the lead time for receiving merchandise, thereby lowering inventory investment, improving customer service levels, and reducing distribution expenses; also known as a just-in-time inventory management system.

quota Target level used to motivate and evaluate performance.

quotas–bonus plan Compensation plan that has a performance goal or objective established to evaluate employee performance, such as sales per hour for salespeople and maintained margin and turnover for buyers.

racetrack layout A type of store layout that provides a major aisle to facilitate customer traffic that has access to the store's multiple entrances. Also known as a *loop*.

Radio Frequency Identification (RFID) technology A technology that provides real-time data collection and detection of product via automated messages received by an antenna which reads radio frequency tags on product.

rain check When sale merchandise is out of stock, a written promise to customers to sell them that merchandise at the sale price when it arrives.

reach The actual number of customers in the target market exposed to an advertising medium. See *advertising reach*.

rebate Money returned to the buyer in the form of cash based on a portion of the purchase price.

receipt of goods (ROG) dating A dating policy in which the cash discount period starts on the day the merchandise is received.

receiving The process of filling out paperwork to record the receipt of merchandise that arrives at a store or distribution centre.

recruitment Activity performed by a retailer to generate job applicants.

reduction Markdown; discount to employees and customers; and inventory shrinkage due to shoplifting, breakage, or loss.

reference group One or more people whom a person uses as a basis of comparison for his beliefs, feelings, and behaviours.

reference price A price point in the consumer's memory for a good or service that can consist of the price last paid, the price most frequently paid, or the average of all prices customers have paid for similar offerings. A benchmark for what consumers believe the "real" price of the merchandise should be.

refusal to deal A legal issue in which either a vendor or a retailer reserves the right to deal or refuses to deal with anyone it chooses.

region In retail location analysis, refers to the part of the country, a particular city, or Census Metropolitan Area (CMA).

regional centre Shopping mall that provides general merchandise (a large percentage of which is apparel) and services in full depth and variety.

regression analysis A statistical approach based on the assumption that factors that affect the sales of existing stores in a chain will have the same impact on stores located at new sites.

Reilly's law A model used in trade area analysis to define the relative abilities of two cities to attract customers from the area between them.

related diversification opportunity A diversification opportunity strategy in which the retailer's present offering and market share something in common with the market and format being considered.

relational partnership Long-term business relationship in which the buyer and vendor have a close, trusting interpersonal relationship.

remarking The practice of changing the price label or identification tag on merchandise due to price changes, lost or mutilated tickets, or customer returns.

reorder point The stock level at which a new order is placed.

resale price maintenance laws Laws enacted in the U.S. in the early 1900s to curb vertical price-fixing. These laws were designed to help protect small retailers by prohibiting retailers from selling below the manufacturer's suggested retail price. Also called *fair trade laws*. In 1975 these laws were repealed by the *Consumer Goods Pricing Act*.

resident buying office An organization located in a major buying centre that provides services to help retailers buy merchandise.

restraint of trade Any contract that tends to eliminate or stifle competition, create a monopoly, artificially maintain prices, or otherwise hamper or obstruct the course of trade and commerce as it would be carried on if left to the control of natural forces; also known as unfair trade practices.

retail audit See *situation audit*.

retail chain A firm that consists of multiple retail units under common ownership and usually has some centralization of decision making in defining and implementing its strategy.

retailer A business that sells products and services to consumers for their personal or family use.

retail exchanges Electronic marketplaces operated by organizations that facilitate the buying and selling of merchandise using the Internet.

retail format The retailers' type of retail mix (nature of merchandise and services offered, pricing policy, advertising and promotion program, approach to store design and visual merchandising, and typical location).

retail format development opportunity An investment opportunity strategy in which a retailer offers a new retail format—a format involving a different retail mix—to the same target market.

retail information system System that provides the information needed by retail managers by collecting, organizing, and storing relevant data continuously and directing the information to the appropriate managers.

retailing A set of business activities that adds value to the products and services sold to consumers for their personal or family use.

retailing concept A management orientation that holds that the key task of a retailer is to determine the needs and wants of its target markets and to direct the firm toward satisfying those needs and wants more effectively and efficiently than competitors do.

retail inventory method (RIM) An accounting procedure whose objectives are to maintain a perpetual or book inventory in retail dollar amounts and to maintain records that make it possible to determine the cost value of the inventory at any time without taking a physical inventory; also known as *book inventory system* or *perpetual book inventory*.

retail market A group of consumers with similar needs (a market segment) and a group of retailers using a similar retail format to satisfy those consumer needs.

retail market segment A group of customers whose needs will be satisfied by the same retail offering because they have similar needs and go through similar buying processes.

retail-sponsored cooperative An organization owned and operated by small, independent retailers to improve operating efficiency and buying power. Typically, the retail-sponsored cooperative operates a wholesale buying and distribution system and requires its members to concentrate their purchases from the cooperative wholesale operation.

retail strategy A statement that indicates (1) the target market toward which a retailer plans to commit its resources, (2) the nature of the retail offering that the retailer plans to use to satisfy the needs of the target market, and (3) the bases upon which the retailer will attempt to build a sustainable competitive advantage over competitors.

retained earnings The portion of owners' equity that has accumulated over time through profits but has not been paid out in dividends to owners.

return on assets Net profit after taxes divided by total assets.

return on owners' equity Net profit after taxes divided by owners' equity; also known as return on net worth.

reverse auction Auction conducted by retailer buyers. Known as a reverse auction because there is one buyer and many potential sellers. In reverse auctions, retail buyers provide a specification for what they want to a group of potential vendors. The competing vendors then bid down the price at which they are willing to sell until the buyer accepts a bid.

reverse logistics A flow back of merchandise through the channel, from the customer to the store, distribution centre, and vendor, for customer returns.

review time The period of time between reviews of a line for purchase decisions.

revolving credit A consumer credit plan that combines the convenience of a continuous charge account and the privileges of installment payment.

RFM (Recency, Frequency, Monetary) Analysis Often used by catalogue retailers and direct marketers, is a scheme for segmenting customers based on how recently they have made a purchase, how frequently they make purchases, and how much they have bought.

ribbon centre See *strip centre*.

road condition Includes the age, number of lanes, number of stoplights, congestion, and general state of repair of roads in a trade area.

road pattern A consideration used in measuring the accessibility of a retail location via major arteries, freeways, or roads.

rounder A round fixture that sits on a pedestal. Smaller than the straight rack, it is designed to hold a maximum amount of merchandise. Also known as a *bulk fixture* or *capacity fixture*.

routine decision making See *habitual decision making*.

rule-of-thumb method A type of approach for setting a promotion budget that uses past sales and communication activity to determine the present communications budget.

safety stock See *buffer stock*.

sale-leaseback The practice in which retailers build new stores and sell them to real estate investors who then lease the buildings back to the retailers on a long-term basis.

sales associate The same as a salesperson. The term is used to recognize the importance and professional nature of the sales function and avoids the negative image sometimes linked with the term "salesperson."

sales consultant See *sales associate*.

sales per cubic metre A measure of space productivity appropriate for stores such as wholesale clubs that use multiple layers of merchandise.

sales per linear metre A measure of space productivity used when most merchandise is displayed on multiple shelves of long gondolas, such as in grocery stores.

sales per square metre A measure of space productivity used by most retailers since rent and land purchases are assessed on a per-square-metre basis.

sales promotions Paid impersonal communication activities that offer extra value and incentives to customers to visit a store or purchase merchandise during a specific period of time.

saturated trade area A trade area that offers customers a good selection of goods and services, while allowing competing retailers to make good profits.

scale economies Cost advantages due to the size of a retailer.

scanning The process in point-of-sale systems wherein the input into the terminal is accomplished by passing a coded ticket over a reader or having a hand-held wand pass over the ticket.

scrambled merchandising The offering of merchandise not typically associated with the store type, such as clothing in a drugstore.

search engines Computer programs that simply search for and provide a listing of all Internet sites selling a product category or brand with the price of the merchandise offered. Also called *shopping bots*.

seasonal discount Discount offered as an incentive to retailers to place orders for merchandise in advance of the normal buying season.

seasonal merchandise Inventory whose sales fluctuate dramatically according to the time of the year.

secondary data Market research information previously gathered for purposes other than solving the current problem under investigation.

secondary trade area See *secondary zone*.

secondary zone The geographic area of secondary importance in terms of customer sales, generating about 20 percent of a store's sales. Also called *secondary trade area*.

second-degree price discrimination Charging different prices to different people on the basis of the nature of the offering.

security An operating unit within a retail organization that is responsible for protecting merchandise and other assets from pilferage (internal or external). Those working in security may be employees or outside agency people.

security policy Set of rules that apply to activities in the computer and communications resources that belong to an organization.

self-analysis An internally focused examination of a business's strengths and weaknesses.

self-service retailer A retailer that offers minimal customer service.

selling agent An agent who operates on an extended contractual basis; the agent sells all of a specified line of merchandise or the entire output of the principal, and usually has full authority with regard to prices, terms, and other conditions of sale. The agent occasionally renders financial aid to the principal.

selling process A set of activities that salespeople undertake to facilitate the customer's buying decision.

selling space The area set aside for displays of merchandise, interactions between sales personnel and customers, demonstrations, and so on.

sell-through analysis A comparison of actual and planned sales to determine whether early markdowns are required or whether more merchandise is needed to satisfy demand.

seniors The generational cohort of people aged 65 and over.

service gap The difference between customers' expectations and perceptions of customer service, assessed in order to improve customers' satisfaction with their service.

service level A measure used in inventory management to define the level of support or level of product availability; the number of items sold divided by the number of items demanded. Service level should not be confused with customer service. See *customer service*.

services retailer Organization that offers consumers services rather than merchandise. Examples include banks, hospitals, health spas, doctors, legal clinics, entertainment firms, and universities.

sexual harassment Unwelcome sexual advances, requests for sexual favours, or other verbal or physical conduct with sexual elements.

shareholders' equity See *owners' equity*.

share of wallet The percentage of total purchases made by a customer in a store.

shoplifting The act of stealing merchandise from a store by customers or people posing as customers.

shopping bots See *search engines*.

shopping centre A group of retail and other commercial establishments that is planned, developed, owned, and managed as a single property.

shopping guide Free paper delivered to all residents in a specific area.

shopping mall Generally more planned than a strip centre and with more pedestrian activity, it can be either open-air or enclosed.

shortage See *shrinkage*.

shrinkage An inventory reduction that is caused by shoplifting by employees or customers, by merchandise being misplaced or damaged, or by poor bookkeeping.

single-price retailer Close-out stores that sell all their merchandise at a single price, such as $1.

situation audit An analysis of the opportunities and threats in the retail environment and the strengths and weaknesses of the retail business relative to its competitors.

skimming A high-pricing strategy for newly introduced categories.

SKU See *stock keeping unit*.

sliding scale A part of some leases that stipulates how much the percentage of sales paid as rent will decrease as sales go up.

slotting allowance Fee paid by a vendor for space in a retail store. Also called *slotting fee*.

slotting fee See *slotting allowance*.

socialization The steps taken to transform new employees into effective, committed members of the firm.

sole proprietorship An arrangement in which an unincorporated retail firm is owned by one person.

span of control The number of subordinates reporting to a manager.

specialization The organizational structure in which employees are typically responsible for only one or two tasks rather than performing all tasks. This enables employees to develop expertise and increase productivity.

specialty catalogue retailer A nonstore retailer that focuses on specific categories of merchandise, such as fruit (Harry and David), gardening tools (Smith & Hawken), and seeds and plants (Burpee).

specialty department store A store with a department store format that focuses primarily on apparel and soft home goods (such as Neiman Marcus or Saks Fifth Avenue).

specialty product A product for which the customer will expend considerable effort to buy.

specialty store Store concentrating on a limited number of complementary merchandise categories and providing a high level of service in an area typically under 764 square metres.

spending potential index (SPI) Compares the average expenditure in a particular area for a product to the amount spent on that product nationally.

spiff See *push money*.

split shipment A vendor ships part of a shipment to a retailer and back orders the remainder because the entire shipment could not be shipped at the same time.

spot A local television commercial.

spot check Used particularly in receiving operations when goods come in for reshipping to branch stores in packing cartons. Certain cartons are opened in the receiving area of the central distribution point and spot-checked for quality and quantity.

spotting technique   See *analogue approach*.

staging area   Area in which merchandise is accumulated from different parts of the distribution centre and prepared for shipment to stores.

standardization   Involves requiring service providers to follow a set of rules and procedures when providing service.

standardization approach   An approach used by retailers to provide customer service by using a set of rules and procedures so that all customers consistently receive the same service.

standards gap   The difference between the retailer's perceptions of customers' expectations and the customer service standards it sets. This factor is one of four factors identified by the gaps model for improving service quality.

staple merchandise   Inventory that has continuous demand by customers over an extended period of time. Also known as *basic merchandise*.

stock balance   Trade-offs associated with determining variety, assortment, and product availablity.

stock keeping unit (SKU)   The smallest unit available for keeping inventory control. In soft goods merchandise, an SKU usually means size, colour, and style.

stocklift   See *buyback*.

stock overage   The amount by which a retail book inventory figure exceeds a physical ending inventory.

stock-to-sales ratio   Specifies the amount of inventory that should be on hand at the beginning of the month to support the sales forecast and maintain the inventory turnover objective. The beginning-of-month (BOM) inventory divided by sales for the month. The average stock-to-sales ratio is 12 divided by planned inventory turnover. This ratio is an integral component of the merchandise budget plan.

store atmosphere   The combination of the store's physical characteristics (such as architecture, layout, signs and displays, colours, lighting, temperature, sounds, and smells), which together create an image in the customer's mind. See *atmospherics*.

store brand   See *private-label brand*.

store image   The way a store is defined in a shopper's mind. The store image is based on the store's physical characteristics, its retail mix, and a set of psychological attributes.

store maintenance   The activities involved with managing the exterior and interior physical facilities associated with the store.

straight commission   A form of salesperson's compensation in which the amount paid is based on a percentage of sales made minus merchandise returned.

straight lease   A type of lease in which the retailer pays a fixed amount per month over the life of the lease.

straight rack   A type of fixture that consists of a long pipe suspended with supports going to the floor or attached to a wall.

straight salary compensation   A compensation plan in which salespeople or managers receive a fixed amount of compensation for each hour or week they work.

strategic alliance   Collaborative relationship between independent firms. For example, a foreign retailer might enter an international market through direct investment but develop an alliance with a local firm to perform logistical and warehousing activities.

strategic profit model (SPM)   A tool used for planning a retailer's financial strategy based on both margin management (net profit margin), asset management (asset turnover), and financial leverage management (financial leverage ratio). Using the SPM, a retailer's objective is to achieve a target return on owners' equity.

strategic relationship   Long-term relationship in which partners make significant investments to improve both parties' profitability.

strategic retail planning process   The steps a retailer goes through to develop a strategic retail plan. It describes how retailers select target market segments, determine the appropriate retail format, and build sustainable competitive advantages.

strengths and weaknesses analysis   A critical aspect of the situation audit in which a retailer determines its unique capabilities—its strengths and weaknesses relative to its competition.

strict product liability   A product liability suit in which the injury to the customer may not have been intentional or under the retailer's control.

strip centre   A shopping centre that usually has parking directly in front of the stores and does not have enclosed walkways linking the stores.

style   The characteristic or distinctive form, outline, or shape of a product.

subculture   A distinctive group of people within a culture. Members of a subculture share some customs and norms with the overall society but also have some unique perspectives.

subculture theory   A theory of how fashion spreads that suggests that subcultures of mostly young and less affluent consumers, such as motorcycle riders and urban rappers, have started fashions for such things as colourful fabrics, T-shirts, sneakers, jeans, black leather jackets, and surplus military clothing.

subjective employee evaluation   Assessment of employee performance based on a supervisor's ratings rather than on objective measures such as sales per hour.

supercentre   Large store (13 950 to 18 600 square metres) combining a discount store with a supermarket.

superregional centre   Shopping centre that is similar to a regional centre; but because of its larger size, it has more anchors and a deeper selection of merchandise, and it draws from a larger population base

superstore   A large supermarket between 1860 and 4650 square metres in size.

supply chain management   The integration of business processes from end user through original suppliers that provides products, services, and information that add value for customers.

survey   A method of data collection, using telephone, personal interview, mail, or any combination thereof.

sustainable competitive advantage   A distinct competency of a retailer relative to its competitors that can be maintained over a considerable time period.

sweepstake A promotion in which customers win prizes based on chance.

SWOT analysis An analysis of strengths, weaknesses, opportunities, and threats, designed to assess both the micro- and macro-environments and their relation to the retailer.

symbiotic store A store that does not create its own traffic and whose trade area is determined by the dominant retailer in the shopping centre or retail area. Also called a parasite store.

target market The market segment(s) toward which the retailer plans to focus its resources and retail mix.

tariff A tax placed by a government upon imports.

task performance behaviours Planning, organizing, motivating, evaluating, and coordinating store employees' activities.

television home shopping A retail format in which customers watch a TV program demonstrating merchandise and then place orders for the merchandise by phone.

terms of purchase Conditions in a purchase agreement with a vendor that include the type(s) of discounts available and responsibility for transportation costs.

terms of sale Conditions in a sales contract with customers including such issues as charges for alterations, delivery, or gift wrapping, or the store's exchange policies.

tertiary zone The outermost ring of a trade area; includes customers who occasionally shop at the store or shopping centre. Also called tertiary trade area.

theme centre A shopping centre that tries to replicate a historical place and typically contains tenants similar to those in specialty centres, except there usually is no large specialty store or department store as an anchor. See *historical centre*.

third-party logistics company Firm that facilitates the movement of merchandise from manufacturer to retailer but is independently owned.

thrift store A retail format offering used merchandise.

ticketing and marking Procedures for making price labels and placing them on the merchandise.

tie-in An approach used to attract attention to a store's offering by associating the offering with an event.

tonnage merchandising A display technique in which large quantities of merchandise are displayed together.

top-down planning One side of the process of developing an overall retail strategy where goals are set at the top of the organization and filter down through the operating levels.

top-of-mind awareness The highest level of brand awareness; arises when consumers mention a brand name first when they are asked about a type of retailer, a merchandise category, or a type of service.

trade area A geographic sector that contains potential customers for a particular retailer or shopping centre.

trade discount Reduction in a retailer's suggested retail price granted to wholesalers and retailers; also known as a functional discount.

trade dress A product's physical appearance, including its size, shape, colour, design, and texture. For instance, the shape and colour of a Coca-Cola bottle is its trade dress.

trademark Any mark, work, picture, or design associated with a particular line of merchandise or product.

trade show A temporary concentration of vendors that provides retailers opportunities to place orders and view what is available in the marketplace; also known as a merchandise show or market week.

traditional distribution centre Warehouse in which merchandise is unloaded from trucks and placed on racks or shelves for storage.

traditional strip centre A shopping centre that is designed to provide convenience shopping for the day-to-day needs of consumers in their immediate neighbourhood.

traffic appliance Small portable appliance.

traffic flow The balance between a substantial number of cars and not so many that congestion impedes access to the store.

transformational leader A leader who gets people to transcend their personal needs for the sake of realizing the group goal.

transportation cost The expense a retailer incurs if it pays the cost of shipping merchandise from the vendor to the stores.

travel time contours Used in trade area analysis to define the rings around a particular site based on travel time instead of distances.

trialability The costs and commitment required to initially adopt a fashion.

trickle-down theory A theory of how fashion spreads that suggests that the fashion leaders are consumers with the highest social status—wealthy, well-educated consumers. After they adopt a fashion, the fashion trickles down to consumers in lower social classes. When the fashion is accepted in the lowest social class, it is no longer acceptable to the fashion leaders in the highest social class.

triple-coupon promotion A retail promotion that allows the customer triple the face value of the coupon.

trust A belief that a partner is honest (reliable, stands by its word, sincere, fulfills obligations) and is benevolent (concerned about the other party's welfare).

tying contract An agreement between a vendor and a retailer requiring the retailer to take a product it does not necessarily desire (the tied product) to ensure that it can buy a product it does desire (the tying product).

ultimate consumers Individuals who purchase goods and services for their own personal use or for use by members of their household.

undercover shopper Person hired by or working for a retailer who poses as a customer to observe the activities and performance of employees. See *mystery shopper*.

understored trade area An area that has too few stores selling a specific good or service to satisfy the needs of the population.

unit pricing The practice of expressing price in terms of both the total price of an item and the price per unit of measure.

Universal Product Code (UPC) The black-and-white bar code found on most merchandise; used to collect sales information at the point of sale using computer terminals that read the code. This information is transmitted computer-to-computer to buyers, then distribution centres, and then to vendors, who in turn quickly ship replenishment merchandise.

unrelated diversification Diversification in which there is no commonality between the present business and the new business.

UPC code See *Universal Product Code.*

URL (uniform resource locator) The standard address format for a page on the World Wide Web (e.g., http://www.canadiantire.ca/intro/homepage.jsp), consisting of the access protocol (http), the domain name (www.canadian tire.ca), and optionally, the path to a file or resource residing on that server (intro/homepage.jsp).

value Relationship of what a customer gets (goods/services) to what he or she has to pay for it.

value added network (VAN) A third-party logistics company that facilitates electronic data interchange (EDI) by making computer systems between vendors and retailers compatible.

value retailers General merchandise discount stores that are found in either low-income urban or rural areas and are much smaller than traditional discount stores, less than 837 square metres.

variable cost A cost that varies with the level of sales and that can be applied directly to the decision in question.

variable pricing Charging different prices in different stores, markets, or zones.

variety The number of different merchandise categories within a store or department.

vending machine retailing A nonstore format in which merchandise or services are stored in a machine and dispensed to customers when they deposit cash or use a credit card.

vendor Any firm from which a retailer obtains merchandise.

vertical integration An example of diversification by retailers involving investments by retailers in wholesaling or manufacturing merchandise.

vertical merchandising A method whereby merchandise is organized to follow the eye's natural up-and-down movement.

vertical price-fixing Agreements to fix prices between parties at different levels of the same marketing channel (for example, retailers and their vendors).

virtual community A network of people who seek information, products, and services and communicate with each other about specific issues.

virtual mall A group of retailers and service providers that can be accessed over the Internet at one location.

visibility The customers' ability to see the store and enter the parking lot safely.

visual communications The act of providing information to customers through graphics, signs, and theatrical effects—both in the store and in windows—to help boost sales by providing information on products and by suggesting items or special purchases.

want book Information collected by retail salespeople to record out-of-stock or requested merchandise. Similar to a want slip.

warehouse club A retailer that offers a limited assortment of food and general merchandise with little service and low prices to ultimate consumers and small businesses.

Web site A page or series of pages on the Internet, identified by a unique address (*URL*), that can provide information or facilitate electronic commerce.

Weeks of inventory The number of months of supply times four weeks.

wheel of retailing A cyclical theory of retail evolution whose premise is that retailing institutions evolve from low-price/service to higher-price/service operations.

wholesaler A merchant establishment operated by a concern that is primarily engaged in buying, taking title to, usually storing, and physically handling goods in large quantities, and reselling the goods (usually in smaller quantities) to retailers or to industrial or business users.

wholesale-sponsored voluntary cooperative group An organization operated by a wholesaler offering a merchandising program to small, independent retailers on a voluntary basis.

word of mouth Communications between people about a retailer.

zone pricing Charging different prices for the same merchandise in different geographic locations to be competitive in local markets.

zoning The regulation of the construction and use of buildings in certain areas of a municipality.

Endnotes

Chapter 1

1. John Stanton, "You Can Do It," *CIBC Run: Training Guide*, 2003.
2. Conseil Quebecois du Commerce de Detail (CQCD). "Vive la difference!" *Canadian Retailer*, March/April, 2004.
3. For a more detailed discussion of distribution channels, see Louis W. Stern, Adel I. El-Ansary, Erin Anderson, and Anne T. Coughlan, *Marketing Channels* (Englewood Cliffs, NJ: Prentice Hall, 2002).
4. Conseil Quebecois du Commerce de Detail (CQCD). "Vive la difference!" *Canadian Retailer*, March/April, 2004.
5. Carolyn Green, "London Drugs: A Prescription for Success," *Canadian Retailer*, July/August, 2003.
6. Carolyn Green, "John Forzani on Top of his Game," *Canadian Retailer*, July/August 2001; Marina Strauss, "Forzani Close to Settling Dispute," *Globe and Mail*, March 26, 2004.

Chapter 2

1. "Retail Industry Factsheet," National Retail Federation, www.nrf.com.
2. Michael Levy and Dhruv Grewal, "So Long, Kmart Shoppers," *The Wall Street Journal*, January 28, 2000, www.wsj.com.
3. Larry Greenberg, "Hudson's Bay Faces Challenge from Southern Rival," *The Wall Street Journal*, May 24, 1996, p. B4.
4. Carlta Vitzthum, "Just-in-Time Fashion—Spanish Retailer Zara Makes Low-Cost Lines in Weeks by Running Its Own Show," *The Wall Street Journal*, May 18, 2001, p. B1; and Benjamin Jones, "Madrid: Zara Pioneers Fashion on Demand," *Europe*, September 2001. pp. 43-44
5. Marianne Wilson, "Disposable Chic at H&M," *Chain Store Age*, May 2000, pp. 64-66.
6. Ken Jones and Michael Doucet, "The Impact of Big Box Development on Toronto's Retail Structure," *CSCA Publications*, January 1999.
7. Nancy Carr, "Major Expansion in Rona's Game Plan," *The National Post*, April 7, 2004.
8. Hollie Shaw, "Landlord Rivalries at Root of Store Wars," *The National Post*, July 16, 2003.
9. "Lowe's Widens Its Growth Focus," *National Home Center News*, September 8, 1997, p. 7.
10. David P. Schulz, "Triversity Top 100 Retailers: The Nation's Biggest Retail Companies," www.stores.org, 2001.
11. Amy Merrick, Jeffrey A. Trachtenberg, and Ann Zimmerman, "Department Stores Fight to Save a Model That May Be Outdated," *The Wall Street Journal*, March 12, 2002, p. 1. Research by Chris Ohlinger, chief executive of Service Industry Research Systems Inc. of Highland Heights, KY.
12. "Wal-Mart Stores, Inc.," Hoovers Online, 2002, www.hoovers.com.
13. Tracie Rozhon, "Main Street's Latest Threat," *New York Times*, June 14, 1999, p. A25; "Annual Report of Categories," *Drug Store News*, May 17, 1999; and "Annual Report on Drug Chains," *Drug Store News*, April 26, 1999.
14. Susan Reda, "Redefining Pharmacy's Role," *Stores*, April 1997, pp. 34-36.
15. Hollie Shaw, "Spending Spree Will Continue." *The National Post*, January 6, 2003.
16. Leanne Delap, "Hard-Core Winners Addicts Tell All," *Globe and Mail*, February 28, 2004.
17. *HomeStyle Magazine*, September/October, 2003.
18. Debby Garbato Stankevich, "More Value to a Dollar: With Traditional Discounters Concentrating Market," *Retail Merchandiser*, October 2001, pp. 21-23.
19. Ira Kalish, "The World's Leading Food Retailers," *Global Retail Intelligencer*, (Columbus, OH: Retail Forward, Inc., August 2001), p. 1.
20. Hollie Shaw. "Supermarket Offers Health Club," *Canadian Press Newswire*, November 8, 1999.
21. *Language of the Food Industry* (Washington, DC: Food Marketing Institute, 1998).
22. "Roaring 20s Ends in Depression," *Chain Store Age Executive*, June 1994, p. 49.
23. "Markets in Motion," in "66th Annual Report of the Grocery Industry," Progressive Grocer, April 1999, p. 31.
24. Hollie Shaw, "Supermarket Offers Health Club," *Canadian Press Newswire*, November 8, 1999.
25. *Language of the Food Industry*.
26. "Food for Thought," forecast by PricewaterhouseCoopers LLP.
27. Personal communication, Bryan Gildenberg, M. Ventures, February 2002.
28. Sandra J. Skrovan, "Industry Brief: Warehouse Clubs," PricewaterhouseCoopers, June 2001, p. 7.
29. George Strachan, Keith Wills, and Yukihiro Moroe, "Retail Surprises: A Look Back from 2005," Goldman Sachs, December 2000, pp. 9-10.
30. www.eatzis.com.
31. "A *Supermarket Business* Survey of Consumers Shows That the More Prepared Foods They Buy, the Bigger the Ring at the Checkout," *Supermarket Business*, July 15, 2001, pp. 37, 40+.
32. Personal communication, Jo Natale, Wegmans, February 2002.
33. www.marks-and-spencer.co.uk.
34. "Consumer Direct Channel Will Account for 12% of U.S. Retail Sales by 2010," *Retail Industry*, June 28, 2000, http://retailindustry.about.com/library/bl/bl_net0628.htm?terms=catalogs.
35. Joanna Barsh, Blair Crawford, and Chris Grosso, "How E-Retailing Can Rise from the Ashes," *McKinsey Quarterly*, 2000.
36. "Lessons from the Top 25," *Internet Retailer*, January 2002, pp. 3-7.
37. Carolyn Green, "Canadian Tire: Bucking the Status Quo," *Canadian Retailer*, March/April 2002.
38. "Internet Generates 13 Percent of Catalog Sales," *Retail Industry*, January 2002, http://retailindustry.about.com/library/bl/q2/bl_dma060401b.htm.
39. "2001 State of the Vending Industry Report," *Automatic Merchandiser*, www.amonline.com/current/industryreports.shtml.
40. Ibid., chap. 2

41. "Japanese Retailing—Marketplace Is Alive and Kicking," *Retail Week*, April 27, 2001, p. 16.

42. Valarie Zeithaml, A. Parasuraman, and Leonard Berry, "Problems and Strategies in Services Marketing," *Journal of Marketing* 49 (Spring 1985), pp. 33-46; and Stephen W. Brown and Mary Jo Bitner, "Services Marketing," *AMA Management Handbook*, 3rd ed. (New York: AMACOM Books, 1994), pp. 15-5-15-15.

43. Dun and Bradstreet Corporate Starts (New York: Dun and Bradstreet, 1998).

44. Bill Quinn, *How Wal-Mart Is Destroying America (and the World): And What You Can Do about It* (Ten Speed Press, 2000).

45. This section is based on material in Lyda Hyde, "Multi-Channel Integration: The New Retail Battleground," PricewaterhouseCoopers, 2001; and Joseph Alba, John Lynch, Barton Weitz, Chris Janiszewski, Richard Lutz, Alan Sawyer, and Stacy Woods, "Interactive Home Shopping: Consumer, Retailer, and Manufacturers Incentives to Participate in Electronic Markets," *Journal of Marketing* 61 (July 1997), pp. 38-53.

46. *Surveying the Digital Future: UCLA Internet Project Report 2001*, UCLA Center for Communication Policy, 2001, p. 38, www.ccp.ucla.edu/pdf/UCLA-Internet-Report-2001.pdf.

47. Mitch Moxley, "Mountain Co-op Adding to City Locations," *National Post*, June 18, 2004.

48. David Moin, "Getting Personal," *Women's Wear Daily* Internet Supplement, May 2000, pp. 10-17.

49. Reid Claxton, "Customer Safety: Direct Marketing's Undermarketed Advantage," *Journal of Direct Marketing* 9 (Winter 1995), pp. 67-78.

Chapter 3

1. Jared Sandberg, "It Isn't Entertainment That Makes the Web Shine: It's Dull Data," *The Wall Street Journal*, July 20, 1998, pp. A1, A6.

2. Phil Patton, "Buy Here, and We'll Teach You What You Like," *New York Times*, Electronic Commerce Special Section, September 22, 1999, p. 5; and Pattie Maes, "Smart Commerce: The Future of Intelligent Agents in Cyberspace," *Journal of Interactive Marketing* 3 (Summer 1999), pp. 66-76.

3. Pui-Wing Tam, "Surfing for Wedding Help," *The Wall Street Journal*, November 12, 2001, p. B1; Eric Wilson, "Bridal Firms Waltz with the Net," *WWD*, August 10, 1999, pp. 10-11; and Ellen Neuborne, "Weddings and the Web: A Marriage Made in Cyber Heaven," *Business Week*, February 15, 1999, p. 45

4. "E-tailing Group Reviewed 100 Retail Sites," E-Retailing Group, November 2001, www.e-tailing.com.

5. Geoff Wissman "Where's the Growth?" *E-Retailing -Intelligence Update* (Columbus, OH: Retail Forward, February 2002), p. 6.

6. Everett Rogers, *Diffusion of Innovations*, 4th ed. (New York: Free Press, 1995).

7. Mark Evans, "Canada Leads Global Pack in Internet Use," *National Post*, January 22, 2004.

8. Ipsos-Reid. "eConfidence Growing in Canada," *Globe and Mail*, November 29, 2003.

9. www.nua.com/surveys/how_many_online/index.html, February 2002.

10. "Meeting Generation Y," *NUA*, July 19, 1999; and "Young Consumers Have Internalized the Net," Forrester Research, August 11, 1999.

11. Bob Tedeschi, "Credit Card Companies Go to Great Lengths Online to Develop Products That Will Corral Teenage Consumers," *New York Times*, January 14, 2002, p. C6.

12. Karen Thomas, "Rocketcash Makes Allowances for Kids," *USA Today*, December 10, 2000, p. 3D.

13. Warren Caragata, "An Overview of Electronic Commerce," *Prism*, July 12, 1999, pp. 32-38.

14. Valerie Seckler, "E-Tailing Sales: Data Privacy Is Seen as Key," *WWD*, August 25, 1999, p. 5.

15. Timothy Mullaney, "Taking in the Travel Sites," *Business Week*, July 26, 1999, p. EB68; "Travel Special Report," *The Industry Standard*, June 14, 1999, pp. 52-74; and "E-Com Fly with Me," *New Media Age*, March 11, 1999, pp. 12-14.

16. Andrew Osterland, "Nothing but Net," *Business Week*, August 2, 1999, p. 72; Bill Orr, "E-Banks or E-Branches?" *ABA Banking Journal*, July 1999, pp. 32-42; Alex Sheshunoff, "The Wait Is Over for Internet Banking," *ABA Banking Journal*, June 1999, pp. 18-20; "Financial Services On-Line," *The Industry Standard*, May 17, 1999, pp. 44-80; and "Banking in Cyberspace," *International Journal of Retail & Distribution Management* 26 (February-March 1998), pp. 128-30.

17. Nancy Carr, "Cash No Longer King for Holiday Shoppers," *The Toronto Star*, November 27, 2003.

18. Rachel Ledford, "The Connected Customer," *E-Retailing Intelligence Update* (Columbus, OH: Retail Forward, December 2001), p. 6.

19. John Lynch Jr. and Daniel Arliey, "Wine Online: Search Costs and Competition on Price, Quality and Distribution," *Marketing Science* 19, no. 1, pp. 83-103.

20. Xing Pan, Brian Ratchford, and Venkatesh Sankar, "Why Aren't the Prices for the Same Items the Same at Me.com and You.com? Drivers of Price Dispersion among E-Tailers," working paper, Robert H. Smith Business School, University of Maryland, 2001; and Erik Brynjolfsson and Michael Smith, "Frictionless Commerce? A Comparison of Internet and Conventional Retailers," *Management Science* 46, no. 4 (April 2000), pp. 563-85.

21. Rachel Ledford, "The Connected Customer," *E-Retailing Intelligence Update* (Columbus, OH: Retail Forward, November 2001), p. 3.

22. Ellen Neuborne, "Happy Returns: How to Deal with Rejected Web Purchases," *Business Week*, October 8, 2001, p. SB12.

23. 10-K405 report filed with SEC by CDNOW, Inc., on March 16, 1999.

24. Gerald Lohse and Peter Spiller, "Electronic Shopping," *Communications of the ACM* 41 (July 1998), pp. 81-88; and Donna Hoffman and Thomas Novak, "Marketing in Hypermedia Computer-Mediated Environments: Conceptual Foundations," *Journal of Marketing* 60 (Summer 1996), pp. 50-63.

25. Paul Barker, "Swimming Lessons," *The National Post*, June 10, 2002.

26. Princeton Survey Research Associates for Consumer WebWatch, January 2002.

27. James Crawford, *Getting the Retail Technology Advantage* (Cambridge, MA: Forrester Research, April 2002), p. 3.

28. David Chalk, "Drawing Traffic to Your Web Site," *The Costco Connection*, Technology, January/February 2003.

29. Megan Barnett, "Why Macys.com Won't Sell Levi's," *The Industry Standard*, November 30, 1998, p. 22.

30. Rachel Ledford, "The Connected Customer," *E-Retailing Intelligence Update* (Columbus, OH: Retail Forward, November 2001), p. 6.

31. Kenneth Clow, David Kurtz, John Ozment, and Beng Soo Ong, "The Antecedents of Consumer Expectations of Services: An Empirical Study across Four Industries," *Journal of Services Marketing* 11 (May-June 1997), pp. 230-48; and Ann Marie Thompson and Peter Kaminski, "Psychographic and Lifestyle Antecedents of Service Quality Expectations," *Journal of Services Marketing* 7 (1993), pp. 53-61.

32. Susan Stellin, "Online Customer Service Found Lacking," *New York Times*, January 3, 2002, p. C1.

33. Mary Jo Bittner, "Self-Service Technologies: What Do Customers Expect? In This High-Tech World, Customers Haven't Changed—They Still Want Good Service," *Marketing Management*, Spring 2001, pp. 10-15.

34. Timothy Keiningham and Terry Vavra, *The Customer Delight Principle* (Chicago: American Marketing Association, 2002).

35. The following discussion of the gaps model and its implications is based on Deon Nel and Leyland Pitt, "Service Quality in a Retail Environment: Closing the Gaps," *Journal of General Management* 18 (Spring 1993), pp. 37-57; Valarie Zeithaml, A. Parasuraman, and Leonard Berry, *Delivering Quality Customer Service* (New York: Free Press, 1990); and Valarie Zeithaml, Leonard Berry, and A. Parasuraman, "Communication and Control Processes in the Delivery of Service Quality," *Journal of Marketing* 52 (April 1988), pp. 35-48.

36. A. Parsuraman and Valarie Zeithaml, "Understanding and Improving Service Quality: A Literature Review and Research Agenda," in B. Weitz and R. Wensley, eds., *Handbook of Marketing* (London: Sage, 2002).

37. Michael Harline and O. C. Ferrell, "The Management of Customer-Contact Service Employees: An Empirical Investigation," *Journal of Marketing* 60 (October 1996), pp. 52-70; and Lois Mohr and Mary Jo Bittner, "The Role of Employee Effort in Satisfaction with Service Transactions," *Journal of Business Research* 32 (March 1995, pp. 239-52.

38. Paul Lima, "Instant Gratification," *Profit*, April 2002, p. 56. Sandra Guy, "Stores Juggle Service with High-Tech Savvy," *Chicago Sun-Times*, July 1, 2002, p. B12; Julie Clark, "The Importance of Kiosks in Retail Has Grown," *Display and Design Ideas*, September 2001, p. 18; and Ken Clark, Confused about Kiosks," *Chain Store Age*, November 1, 2000, p. 96.

39. http://retailindustry.about.com, April 4, 2001.

40. Bob Tedeschi, "Bricks-and-Mortar Merchants Struggling to Assess Web Sidelines," *New York Times*, September 3, 2001, p. C3.

41. Mark Evans, "Canada Leads Global Pack in Internet Use," *National Post*, January 22, 2004.

42. Tyler Hamilton, "Future Shop Repudiates Discount," *Toronto Star*, January 15, 2004.

43. Lyda Hyde, "Multi-Channel Integration: The New Retail Battleground," *PricewaterhouseCoopers*, 2001, pp. 28-35.

44. Hillary Stauth, "Retail and the Internet," *Canadian Retailer*, January/February, 2004.

45. Mitch Betts, "Turning Browsers into Buyers," *Sloan -Management Review* 42 (Winter 2000), p. 8.

Chapter 4

1. For a detailed discussion of customer behaviour, see J. Paul Peter and Jerry C. Olson, *Consumer Behavior and Marketing Strategy*, 6th ed. (New York: McGraw-Hill, 2002); and Michael R. Solomon, *Consumer Behavior: Buying, Having, and Being*, 5th ed. (Upper Saddle River, NJ: Prentice Hall, 2002).

2. Steve Maich, "Only the Nimblest Survive Store Wars," *The National Post*, December 17, 2003.

3. Cyndee Miller, "Top Marketers Take a Bolder Approach in Targeting Gays," *Marketing News*, July 4, 1994, pp. 1-2.

4. Geng Cui, "The Different Faces of the Chinese Consumer," *China Business Review*, July 1997, pp. 34-42.

5. Robert Verdisco, "Gender-Specific Shopping," *Chain Store Age*, February 1999, pp. 26-28; Matthew Klein, "He Shops, She Shops," *American Demographics*, March 1998, pp. 34-40; and Suein Hwang, "From Choices to Checkout, the Genders Behave Very Differently in Supermarkets," *The Wall Street Journal*, March 22, 1994, pp. A1, A4.

6. Faith Popcorn, *Evolution* (New York: Hyperion Press, 2000); David Foot and Daniel Stoffman, *Boom Bust & Echo 2000* (Toronto: Macfarlane Walter & Ross, 1998); Oliver Bertin, "Harley-Davison's Great Ride to the Top," *Globe and Mail*, July 4, 2003; Don Tapscott, *Growing Up Digital* (New York: McGraw-Hill, 1998); Brad Adgate, "Everything You'd Care to Know about Teens," *Horizon Media*, October 29, 2003.

7. Michael J. Weiss, *The Clustered World* (Boston: Little, Brown, 2000).

8. GD Sourcing, "Research and Retrieval," *The Business Newsletter*, June 26, 2003, gdsourcing.com; Michael Adams, *Better Rich than Happy* (Toronto: Penguin Books, 2000).

9. "Let's Play Shopping," *Marketing Week*, November 22, 2001, pp. 45-47; Conway Lachman and John Lanasa, "Family Decision-Making Theory: An Overview and Assessment," *Psychology & Marketing* 10 (March-April 1993), pp. 81-94; and Robert Boutlier, "Pulling the Family Strings," *American Demographics*, August 1993, pp. 44-48.

10. Jean Darian, "Parent–Child Decision Making in Children's Clothing Stores," *International Journal of Retail & Distribution Management* 26 (October 1998), pp. 421-32; Kay Palaland and Robert Wilkes, "Adolescent-Parent Interaction in Family Decision Making," *Journal of Consumer Research* 24 (September 1997), pp. 159–71; Christy Fisher, "Kidding around Makes Sense," *Advertising Age*, June 27, 1994, pp. 34, 37; and Sharon Beatty and Salil Talpade, "Adolescent Influence in Family Decision Making: A Replication with Extension," *Journal of Consumer Research* 31 (September 1994), pp. 332-41.

11. "Bring the Family ... Bring the Kids," *Travel Agent Caribbean and Bahamas Supplement*, April 7, 1997.

12. Dianne Pogoda, "It's a Matter of Time: Stores Keep Traffic Moving, Cash Flowing," *Women's Wear Daily*, April 9, 1996, pp. 1, 8.

13. Judy Waytiuk, "Discounter Diversity," *Marketing Magazine*, May 19, 2003; David Chow, "Reaching New Canadians," *Strategy Magazine*, September 22, 2003; Natalie Rivard, "Reaching Tween Girls in Quebec," *Strategy Magazine*, December 1, 2003.

14. Soyeon Shim and Mary Ann Eastwick, "The Hierarchical Influence of Personal Values on Mall Shopping Attitudes and Behaviors," *Journal of Retailing* 74 (Spring 1998), pp. 139-60.

15. Bruce Little, "Economic Woes Seen as Temporary," *Globe and Mail*, September 19, 2003.

16. For additional information about fashion and the fashion industry, see Giannino Malossi, ed., *The Style Engine: Spectacle, Identity, Design and Business: How the Fashion Industry Uses Style to Create Wealth* (New York: Monacelli Press, 1998); Jeannette Jarnow and Kitty G. Dickerson, *Inside the Fashion Business*, 6th ed. (Upper Saddle River, NJ: Merrill, 1997); and Mike Easey, ed., *Fashion Marketing* (Oxford, England: Blackwell, 1995).

17. "Millennium Timeline: Ideas," *The Wall Street Journal*, January 11, 1999, p. R14.

18. "Millennium Timeline: Ideas," *The Wall Street Journal*, January 11, 1999, p. R14.

19. Tina Cassidy, "How Fashions That Models Wear in Milan or Paris Find Their Way to a Mall Near You," *Boston Globe*, March 14, 2002, p. D1.

20. Rich Marin and Sarah Van Boven, "The Buzz Machine," *Newsweek*, July 27, 1998, p. 22.

21. J. Freedom du Lac, "Entering the World of Goth," *Sacramento Bee*, March 9, 1999, p. C1; and "Dressed to Express and Impress," *Women's Wear Daily Echo Boomers Supplement*, February 19, 1998, pp. 26-27.

22. "The Fashion Innovators," *WWD*, March 20, 1997, p. 2.

23. Paul Brent, "Targeting Spendthrifts: The Young Male Market," *National Post*, April 26, 2004.

Chapter 5

1. See David Aaker, *Strategic Market Management*, 6th ed. (New York: John Wiley, 2001); and A. Coskun Samli, *Strategic Marketing for Success in Retailing* (Westport, CT: Quorum Books, 1998).

2. Roger Evered, "So What Is Strategy?" *Long Range Planning* 16 (Fall 1983), p. 120.

3. Michael Porter, *On Competition* (Boston: Harvard Business School Press, 1998); and Michael Porter, "What Is Strategy?" *Harvard Business Review*, November-December 1996, pp. 61-78.

4. Bridget Finn and Gary Heavin, "How to Grow a Chain That's Already Everywhere." *Business 2.0*, March 2005, p. 52; Clarke Canfield, "No-Frills Fitness Club Takes Its Alternative Route to Small Towns," *Los Angeles Times*, November 26, 2004, p. C.4.

5. Kevin Keller, "Managing Brands for the Long Run: Effective Brand Reinforcement and Revitalization Strategies," *California Management Review* 41 (March 1999), pp. 102-21.

6. Donald Lehman and Russell Winer, *Analysis for Marketing Planning*, 5th. ed. (Burr Ridge, IL: McGraw-Hill/Irwin, 2001).

7. Andrew Campbell, "Mission Statements," *Long Range Planning* 30 (December 1997), pp. 931-33.

8. Alfred Rappaport, *Creating Shareholder Value: The New Standard for Business Performance* (New York: Wiley, 1988); Robert C. Higgins and Roger A. Kerin, "Managing the Growth-Financial Policy Nexus in Retailing," *Journal of Retailing* 59, no. 3 (Fall 1983), pp. 19-47; and Roger Kerin, Vijay Mahajan, and P. Rajan Varadarajan, *Contemporary Perspectives on Strategic Market Planning* (Boston: Allyn & Bacon, 1991), Ch. 6.

9. David Aaker, *Strategic Market Management*, 6th ed. (New York: John Wiley, 2001).

10. Michael Porter, "Strategy and the Internet," *Harvard Business Review*, March 2001, pp. 63-78; and Michael Porter, *Competitive Strategy* (New York: Free Press, 1980).

11. "The Estée Lauder Companies Inc.," *Hoovers Online*, 2002, www.hoovers.com/premium/profile/8/0,2147,40148,00.html.

12. "L'Oréal SA," Hoovers Online, 2002, www.hoovers.com/premium/profile/2/0,2147,41772,00.html.

13. Terry Clark, P. Rajan Varadarajan, and William M. Pride, "Environmental Management: The Construct and Research Propositions," *Journal of Business Research* 29, no. 1 (January 1994), pp. 23-39; James Lang, Roger Calantone, and Donald Gudmundson, "Small Firm Information Seeking as a Response to Environmental Threats and Opportunities," *Journal of Small Business Management*, January 1997, pp. 11-29; and Masoud Yasai-Ardekani and Paul Nystrom, "Designs for Environmental Scanning Systems: Tests of a Contingency Theory," *Management Science* 42 (February 1996), pp. 187-204.

14. Bill Quinn, *How Wal-Mart Is Destroying America (and the World): And What You Can Do About It* (Ten Speed Press, 2000).

15. Erin White, "Retail Brand Buys Brooks Brothers from Marks & Spencer for $225 Million," *The Wall Street Journal*, November 23, 2001, wsj.com; and Andrew Ross Sorkin, "Owner of Casual Corner Chain in Deal for Brooks Brothers," *New York Times*, November 23, 2001. NYTimes.com

16. David Aaker, *Strategic Market Management*, 6th ed. (New York: John Wiley, 2001); G. Stalk, "Competing on Capabilities: The New Rules of Corporate Strategy," *Harvard Business Review*, March-April 1992, pp. 51-69; and Donna Cartwright, Paul Boughton, and Stephen Miller, "Competitive Intelligence Systems: Relationships to Strategic Orientation and Perceived Usefulness," *Journal of Managerial Issues* 7 (Winter 1995), pp. 420-34.

17. Mary Teresa Bitti, "Not the Biggest But the Best," *National Post*, January 12, 2004.

18. Marina Strauss, "Laura Secord Put on the Selling Block Again," *Globe and Mail*, May 7, 2004.

19. Ian Karleff, "For Retailers, There's Mastercard," *National Post*, May 7, 2004.

20. Anthony Boardman and Aidan Vining, "Defining Your Business Using Product–Customer Matrices," *Long Range Planning* 29 (February 1996), pp. 38-48; and R.L. Rothschild, *How to Gain and Maintain Competitive Advantage in Business* (New York: McGraw-Hill, 1984).

21. Cynthia Montgomery, "Creating Corporate Advantage," *Harvard Business Review*, May-June 1998, pp. 71-80; Shelby Hunt and Robert Morgan, "The Comparative Advantage Theory of Competition," *Journal of Marketing* 59 (April 1995), pp. 1-15; Kathleen Conner and C.K. Prahalad, "A Resource-Based Theory of the Firm: Knowledge versus Opportunism," *Organizational Science* 7 (September-October 1996), pp. 477-501; David Collins and Cynthia Montgomery, "Competing on Resources: Strategy for the 1990s," *Harvard Business Review* 73 (July-August 1995), pp. 118-28; William Werther and Jeffrey Kerr, "The Shifting Sands of Competitive Advantage," *Business Horizons* 38 (May-June 1995), pp. 11-17; "10 Quick Wins to Turn Your Supply Chain into a Competitive Advantage," January 2002, http://retailindustry.about.com/library/bl/bl_ksa0112.htm?terms=competitive+advantage; and "Multi-Channel Integration: The New Retail Battleground," *Retail Forward, Inc.*, March 2001, www.pwcris.com.

22. Gerrard Macintosh and Lawrence Lockshin, "Retail Relationships and Store Loyalty: A Multi-Level Perspective,"

International Journal of Research in Marketing 14 (1997), pp. 487-97.

23. Jo Marney, "Bringing Consumers back for More," *Marketing Magazine*, September 10, 2001, p. 33; Kathleen Seiders and Douglas Tigert, "Impact of Market Entry and Competitive Structure on Store Switching/Store Loyalty," *International Review of Retail, Distribution and Consumer Research* 7, no. 3 (1997), pp. 234-56; and Niren Sirohi, Edward McLaughlin, and Dick Wittink, "A Model of Consumer Perceptions and Store Loyalty Intentions for a Supermarket Retailer," *Journal of Retailing* 74 (June 1998), pp. 223-47.

24. Richard Czerniawski and Michael Maloney, *Creating Brand Loyalty: The Management of Brand Positioning and Really Great Advertising* (New York: AMACOM, 1999); S. Chandrasekhar, Vinod Sawhney, Rafique Malik, S. Ramesh Kumar, and Pranab Dutta, "The Case of Brand Positioning," *Business Today*, June 7, 1999, pp. 131-40; Bernard Schmitt, Alex Simonson, and Joshua Marcus, "Managing Corporate Image and Identity," *Long Range Planning* 28 (October 1995), pp. 82-92; Tim Ambler, "Category Management Is Best Deployed for Brand Positioning," *Marketing*, p. 18 November 29, 2001; and Harriet Marsh, "Why New Look Must Take Stock," *Marketing*, March 29, 2001. p. 17

25. Amy Merrick, "Tired of Trendiness, Former Shoppers Leave Gap, Defect to Competitors," *The Wall Street Journal*, December 6, 2001. p. B-1

26. S.A. Shaw and J. Gibbs, "Procurement Strategies of Small Retailers Faced with Uncertainty: An Analysis of Channel Choice and Behaviour," *International Review of Retail, Distribution and Consumer Research* 9, no. 1 (1999), pp. 61–75.

27. "Global Brands Face up to International Retailing," *Marketing Week*, October 26, 2000, p. 32.

28. Mary Jo Bitner, "Self-Service Technologies: What Do Customers Expect?" *Marketing Management*, Spring 2001; Mary Jo Bitner, Steven W. Brown, and Matthew L. Meuter, "Technology Infusion in Service Encounters," *Journal of the Academy of Marketing Science*, March 2000; Mary Jo Bitner and Valerie Zeithaml, *Services Marketing*, 2nd ed. (Burr Ridge, IL: McGraw-Hill/Irwin, 1999); Leonard Berry, "Relationship Marketing of Services Growing Interest: Emerging Perspectives," *Journal of the Academy of Marketing Science* 23 (Fall 1995), pp. 236-45; and Mary Jo Bitner, "Building Service Relationships: It's All about Promises," *Journal of the Academy of Marketing Science* 23 (Fall 1995), pp. 246-51.

29. Werther and Kerr, "The Shifting Sands of Competitive Advantage."

30. Roger Kerin, Vijay Mahajan, and P. Rajan Varadarajan, *Contemporary Perspectives on Strategic Market Planning* (Boston: Allyn & Bacon, 1991), Ch. 6. See also Susan Mudambi, "A Topology of Strategic Choice in Retailing," *International Journal of Retail & Distribution Management*, 1994, pp. 22–25.

31. Ian Murphy, "Marketers Ponder P-O-P in Stores of the Future," *Marketing News*, May 26, 1997. p. 2.

32. Marina Strauss, "HBC Unveils Bold Plan to Triple Profit, Boost Sales in Five Years," *Globe and Mail*, September 26, 2003.

33. Erin White, "Abercrombie Seeks to Send Teeny--Boppers Packing," *The Wall Street Journal*, August 30, 2001, pp. B1, B4.

34. Sarah Ellison, "Carrefour Finds It Difficult to Build Single Global Brand," *The Wall Street Journal*, August 30, 2001. www.wsj.com

35. Tara Murphy, "Foot Locker Poised to Perform," March 26, 2002, www.forbes.com.

36. Anita McGahan, "Sustaining Superior Profits: Customer and Supplier Relationships," *Harvard Business Online*, http://harvardbusinessonline.hbsp.harvard.edu March 1, 1999, pp. 1-7; and Randolph Beard, "Regulation, Vertical Integration and Sabotage," *Journal of Industrial Economics* 49, no. 3, (2001), pp. 319-33.

37. Geoff Wissman, "Critical Issues: The Top 100 Retailers Worldwide 2000," *Retail Forward, Inc.*, August 2001, p. 16.

Chapter 6

1. Connie Robbins Gentry, "Site Unseen," *Chain Store Age*, October 1, 2000, p. 153.

2. Michael E. Porter, *Competitive Strategy: Techniques for Analyzing Industries and Competitors* (Simon & Schuster Trade, 1998).

3. *The SCORE: Shopping Center Operations, Revenues, and Expenses*, New York: International Council of Shopping Centres, 2004.

4. "Back to the Future," *New York Times Magazine*, April 6, 1997, pp. 48-49.

5. Eddie Baeb, "A Mall Struggles to Defend Its Glitz," *Crain's Chicago Business* 23, no. 9 (February 29, 2000), p. 3; Elin Schoen Brockman, "As Malls Die, the Next Generation Re-Creates the Past," *New York Times*, August 8, 1999, p. 4; Kevin Kenyon, "Power Moves: New Formats Help Developers Rejuvenate Enclosed Centers," *Shopping Centers Today*, October 8, 1999; and Herb Greenberg, "Dead Mall Walking," *Fortune* 141, no. 9 (May 1, 2000), p. 304.

6. Kelly Green, "Once-Mighty Avondale Closes Its Doors After Losing Battle against Discounters," *The Wall Street Journal*, December 12, 2001; based on research by National Research Bureau of Chicago and the U.S. Census, and Michael Beyard, Urban Land Institute.

7. Debra Hazel, "Demalling for Dollars," *Shopping Centers Today*, January 2, 2001; and Suzette Hill, "To De-Mall or E-Mall? Shaping Web Shopping," *Apparel Industry Magazine* 61, no. 2 (February 2000), pp. 36-38.

8. Patricia Williams, "$355M Vaughan Mall Built on Themes: Innovative Design Reflects Canadian Culture," *Daily Commercial News and Construction Record*, Vol. 76: June 19, 2003; and Rebecca Sullivan, "Construction Begins on Vaughan Mills," *Canada Newswire*. Ottawa: June 16, 2003.

9. Kevin Kenyon, "Mall of America Turns Trash into Cash," *Shopping Centers Today*, www.icsc.org/srch/sctl. October 1997, pp. 5-6.

10. Julie Elliott, "Retail Gets a Breath of Fresh Air," *The National Post*, November 3, 2003.

11. Edmund Mander, "Defining a Hot Concept Lifestyle Centers Elude Classification," *Shopping Centers Today*, August 2001, pp. 1, 44-45.

12. Lois Huff and Stephanie Shamroski, "Outlet Centers: The Search for Value," *Retail Forward, Inc.*, May 2001.

13. Ray A. Smith, "Outlet Centers in the U.S. Turn Upmarket in Amenities," *The Asian Wall Street Journal*, June 8, 3002, p. 11.

14. Jennifer Steinhauser, "It's a Mall ..., It's an Airport," *New York Times*, June 10, 1998, pp. C1, C4.

15. "Airport 2000," *VM & SD*, December 2000, pp. 40, 42, 44; research attributed to Aviation Consumer Action Project.

16. Mark Blaxil and Jean Mixer, "The Business Case for Pursuing Retail Opportunities in the Inner City," *The Boston Consulting Group*, June 1998, pp. 1-31.

17. Connie Robbins Gentry, "The Rebirth of City Development," *Chain Store Age*, May 2000, pp. 83-90.

18. Robert W. Buckner, *Site Selection: New Advancements in Methods and Technology* (New York: Lebhar-Friedman Books, 1998), p. 18.

19. Karen A. Machleit, Sevgin A. Eroglu, and Susan Powell Mantel, "Perceived Retail Crowding and Shopping Satisfaction: What Modifies This Relationship?" *Journal of Consumer Psychology* 9, no. 1 (2000), p. 29.

20. Robert W. Buckner, *Site Selection: New Advancements in Methods and Technology* (New York: Lebhar-Friedman Books, 1998), pp. 31-32.

21. Robert W. Buckner, *Site Selection: New Advancements in Methods and Technology* (New York: Lebhar-Friedman Books, 1998), Ch. 15; and Christian Harder, *GIS Means Business* (Redlands, CA: Environmental Systems Research Institute, Inc., 1997).

22. Christian Harder, *GIS Means Business* (Redlands, CA: Environmental Systems Research Institute, Inc., 1997), p. 1.

23. Robert W. Buckner, *Site Selection: New Advancements in Methods and Technology* (New York: Lebhar-Friedman Books, 1998).

24. David L. Huff, "Defining and Estimating a Trade Area," *Journal of Marketing* 28 (1964), pp. 34-38; and David L. Huff and William Black, "The Huff Model in Retrospect," *Applied Geographic Studies* 1, no. 2 (1997), pp. 22-34.

25. Tammy Drezner and Zvi Dressner, "Validating the Gravity-Based Competitive Location Model Using Inferred Attractiveness," *Annals of Operations Research* 111 (March 2002), pp. 227-41.

26. Robert W. Buckner, *Site Selection: New Advancements in Methods and Technology* (New York: Lebhar-Friedman Books, 1998), Ch. 15.

27. Conseil Quebecois du Commerce de Detail (CQCD). "Vive la difference!" *Canadian Retailer*, March/April, 2004.

Chapter 7

1. Mitchell Mauk, "The Store as Story," *VM & SD*, October 2000, pp. 23, 25.

2. M. Joseph Sirgy, Dhruv Grewal, and Tamara Mangleburg, "Retail Environment, Self-Congruity, and Retail Patronage: An Integrative Model and a Research Agenda," *Journal of Business Research* 49, no. 2 (August 2000), pp. 127-38.

3. Kathleen Purvis, "It's Scary: Your Supermarket Shopping Is Done by Design," *Seattle Times*, June 19, 2002, based on research by Kevin Kelly.

4. Julie Baker, A. Parasuraman, Dhruv Grewal, and Glen Voss, "The Influence of Multiple Store Environment Cues on Perceived Merchandise Value and Patronage Intentions," *Journal of Marketing* 66 (April 2002), pp. 120-41; Barry J. Babin and Jill S. Attaway, "Atmospheric Affect as a Tool for Creating Value and Gaining Share of Customer," *Journal of Business Research* 49, no. 2 (August 2000), pp. 91-101; Alain d'Astous, "Irritating Aspects of the Shopping Environment," *Journal of Business Research* 49, no. 2 August 2000, pp. 149-57; Karen A Machleit and Sevgin A. Eroglu, "Describing and Measuring Emotional Response to Shopping Experience," *Journal of Business Research* 49, no. 2 (August 2000), pp. 101-11; Elaine Sherman, Anil Mathur, and Ruth Belk Smith, "Store Environment and Consumer Purchase Behavior: Mediating Role of Consumer Emotions," *Psychology and Marketing*, July 1997, pp. 361-78; and Teresa A. Summers and Paulette R. Hebert, "Shedding Some Light on Store Atmospherics: Influence of Illumination on Consumer Behaviors," *Journal of Business Research* 54, no. 2 (November 2001), pp. 145-150.

5. Joseph Weishar, "Moving Targets." *Visual Merchandising and Store Design*, September 1990.

6. "International Interior Store Design Competition," *Visual Merchandising and Store Design*, February 1996, pp. 35-76.

7. Lorrie Grant, "Department Stores Ring up Centralized Checkouts; Cost-Cutting, Success of Kohl's Help Drive Trend," www.plainvanillashell.com, *Retail and Development News*, June 6, 2002; and Eileen Smith, "Retail Giants Change Checkouts," www.courierpostonline.com, June 13, 2002.

8. Joseph Weishar, "The Business of — the Wall," *Visual Merchandising and Store Design*, October 1985.

9. Paco Underhill, *Why We Buy: The Science of Shopping* (New York: Simon & Schuster, 2000).

10. Four of the most popular planogram programs are Marketmax (www.marketmax.com), Apollo (www.metirimensus.com), Pegman (www.wellingtoninc.com), and Spaceman (www.acnielsen.com).

11. Raymond R. Burke, "Virtual Shopping: Breakthrough in Marketing Research," *Harvard Business Review*, March-April 1996, pp. 120-34.

12. "The Need for Speed," *WWD*, November 5, 1998, p. 2.

13. S. Silcoff, "One of the Few Labels to Succeed Internationally," *National Post*, April 24, 2004.

14. "Five Easy Steps," *VM&SD*, June 2000, pp. 42-43.

15. The concept of atmospherics was introduced by Philip Kotler in "Atmosphere as a Marketing Tool," *Journal of Retailing* 49 (Winter 1973), pp. 48-64. The definition is adapted from Richard Yalch and Eric Spangenberg, "Effects of Store Music on Shopping Behavior," *Journal of Service Marketing* 4, no. 1 (Winter 1990), pp. 31-39.

16. Anna S. Mattila and Jochen Wirtz, "Congruency of Scent and Music as a Driver of In-Store Evaluations and Behavior," *Journal of Retailing* 77, no. 2 (Summer 2001), pp. 273-89.

17. Teresa A. Summers and Paulette R. Hebert, "Shedding Some Light on Store Atmospherics; Influence of Illumination on Consumer Behavior," *Journal of Business Research* 54, no. 2 (November 2001), pp. 145-50.

18. Susan Franke, "Architects, Experts Say Proper Design Can Propel Shoppers into Stores," *Pittsburgh Business Times*, July 12, 2002.

19. For a review of this research, see Joseph A. Bellizzi and Robert E. Hite, "Environmental Color, Consumer Feelings, and Purchase Likelihood," *Psychology and Marketing* 9, no. 5 (September-October 1992), pp. 347-63.

20. J. Duncan Herrington and Louis Capella, "Effects of Music in Service Environments: A Field Study," *Journal of Services Marketing* 10, no. 2 (1996), pp. 26-41.

21. Richard F. Yalch and Eric R. Spangenberg, "The Effects of Music in a Retail Setting on Real and Perceived Shopping Times," *Journal of Business Research* 49, no. 2 (August 2000), pp. 139-48; Michael Hui, Laurette Dube, and Jean-Charles Chebat, "The Impact of Music on Consumers' Reactions to Waiting for Services," *Journal of Retailing* 73, no. 1, (1997), pp. 87-104; and Julie Baker, Dhruv Grewal, and Michael

Levy, "An Experimental Approach to Making Retail Store Environmental Decisions," *Journal of Retailing* 68 (Winter 1992), pp. 445-60.

22. Maxine Wilkie, "Scent of a Market," *American Demographics*, August 1995, pp. 40-49.

23. Anna S. Mattila and Jochen Wirtz, "Congruency of Scent and Music as a Driver of In-Store Evaluations and Behavior," *Journal of Retailing* 77, no. 2 (Summer 2001), pp. 273-90.

24. Cathleen McCarthy, "Aromatic Merchandising: Leading Customers by the Nose," *Visual Merchandising and Store Design*, April 1992, pp. 85-87.

Chapter 8

1. Lawrence Stevenson, Joseph Shlesinger, and Michael Pearce, *Power Retail*, McGraw-Hill Ryerson, Toronto: 1999; and Jonathan Reynolds and Christine Cuthbertson, *Retail Strategy: The View from the Bridge*, Elsevier, Amsterdam: 2004.

2. Geoff Wissman, "Critical Issues: The Top 100 Retailers Worldwide 2000," *Retail Forward, Inc.*, August 2001, p. 16.

3. Sarah Raper, "Gap's Tour de Force," *WWD*, July 1, 1999, p. 3.

4. Brenda Sternquist, *International Retailing*, ABC Media Inc., 1998; "A Tiger, Falling behind a Dragon," *The Economist*, June 21, 2003; "Two Systems, One Grand Rivalry," *The Economist*, June 21, 2003.

5. Jane Barrett, "Designer Heralds Upturn as Retail Sales Rise 9%," *The National Post*, April 14, 2004.

6. Bernard Wysocki, Jr., "In Developing Nations, Many Youth Are Big Spenders," *The Wall Street Journal*, June 26, 1997, pp. A1, A11.

7. Elisabeth Rosenthal, "Buicks, Starbucks and Fried Chicken. Still China?" *New York Times*, February 25, 2002. www.NYTimes.com

8. David Woodruff, "For French Retailers, a Weapon against Wal-Mart," *The Wall Street Journal*, September 27, 1999, pp. B1, B4; and David Woodruff, "Carrefour Is Mounting a Push into Japanese Markets," *The Wall Street Journal*, June 15, 1999, p. B7.

9. "Retailers Are Trying to Go Global," *The Economist Newspaper* (U.S. ed.), June 19, 1999, p. 1.

10. Geoff Wissman, "Critical Issues: The Top 100 Retailers Worldwide 2000," *Retail Forward, Inc.*, August 2001, p. 16.

11. "The World Is Not Their Oyster," *Chain Store Age*, May, 2001, p. 60.

12. This section is adapted from "Winning Moves on a Global Chessboard: Wal-Mart and Costco in a Global Context," Goldman Sachs Investment Research, May 12, 2000.

13. "East 57th Street Again Tops Retail List Highest Rents in the World," *New York Times*, www.nytimes.com, December 9, 2001.

14. Geoff Wissman, "Critical Issues: The Top 100 Retailers Worldwide 2000," *Retail Forward, Inc.*, August 2001, p. 16.

15. Lisa Penaloza and Mary Gilly, "Marketer Acculturation: The Changer and the Changed," *Journal of Marketing* 63 (Summer 1999), pp. 84-95.

16. Sarah Ellison, "Carrefour Finds It Difficult to Build Single Global Brand," *The Wall Street Journal*, August 30, 2001. www.wsj.com.

17. Erik Gordon, "Taking the Plunge?" *Chain Store Age Supplement*, December 1997, pp. 14-23; and "Shopping the World," *The Economist Newspaper*, June 18, 1999, pp. 1-2.

18. "Handcuffs on High Street," *The Economist*, May 13, 2000, p. 62.

19. "Handcuffs on High Street," *The Economist*, May 13, 2000, p. 62.

20. "Handcuffs on High Street," *The Economist*, May 13, 2000, p. 62.

21. Jean-Pierre Jeannet and H. David Hennessey, *Global Marketing Strategies*, 5th ed., (Boston: Houghton Mifflin, 2000); and "What's the Best Way to Set up Shop?" *Chain Store Age Global Retailing Supplement*, December 1997, pp. 32-35.

22. Greg Silverman and David Wasserman, "Retailing in Latin America," *Global Retail Forward*, July 2001, p. 13; Stephanie Shamroski, "Retailing in Turkey," *Global Retail Forward*, January 2000, p. 6; Ira Kalish and Stephanie Shamroski, "Global Retail Intelligencer," *Global Retail Forward*, April 2001, p. 2; Philip Walker, "Retailing in India," *Global Retail Forward*, March 2000, p. 12; Lois Huff and Stephanie Shamroski, "Retailing in the United Kingdom," *Global Retail Forward*, December 2000, p. 17; and Marianne Wilson, "Thinking Big," *Chain Store Age*, July 1, 2001, p. 47.

23. "An Opening Door Policy," *Chain Store Age*, January 2000, pp. 62-63.

24. www.marksandspencer.com.

25. David Barboza, "In Roaring China, Sweaters are West of Sock City," *New York Times*, December 24, 2004, p. C2.

26. Ted Fishman, "The Chinese Century," *New York Times Magazine*, July 4, 2004, p. 26.

27. "Wal around the World," *The Economist*, December 8, 2001, p. 8; and "Pooled Assests," *Chain Store Age*, June 1, 2001, p. 50.

28. Rob Deloney, "McDonald's Banks on Franchising in China," *The National Post*, September 9, 2003.

29. Alex Gillis, "Spanish Armada," *The National Post*, October 1, 1999.

30. Erik Gordon, "Taking the Plunge?" *Chain Store Age Global Retailing Supplement*, Ernst & Young, December 1997, pp. 14-23.

31. "Company Profile," Hoovers Online, June 2002, www.hoovers.com.

32. Dana Flavelle, "Swedish Gap Poised to Enter the Canadian Clothing Market," *Toronto Star*, January 15, 2004.

33. Barbara Hogan Galvin, "Outlet Center Challenge," *Shopping Centers Today*, June 2001, pp. 25-28.

34. "Global 200 Highlights," *Stores*, January 2002, p. G7.

35. Bernadette Morra, "H & M Is Almost Here," *Toronto Star*, January 22, 2004.

36. Jeet Heer and Steve Penfold, "McFelafels, McHuevos, McLuks," *National Post*, February 15, 2003.

37. Jacqueline Thorpe, "India the Jewel in Global Market," *National Post*, April 16, 2004.

38. Mitch Moxley, "Mountain Co-op Adding to City Locations," *National Post*, June 18, 2004.]

39. See Aaker, *Strategic Market Management*, Ch. 7; and Kerin, Mahajan, and Varadarajan, *Contemporary Perspectives*, Ch. 3. Another matrix that is often used in strategic planning is the Boston Consulting Group (BCG) market growth/market share matrix. Rather than considering all of the factors that determine market attractiveness and competitive position, the

BCG matrix focuses on just two factors: market growth and market share. Research indicates that concentrating on these two factors may result in poor strategic decisions. See Robin Wensley, "Strategic Marketing: Betas, Boxes, and Basics," *Journal of Marketing* 45 (Summer 1981), pp. 173-82, for a critical analysis of these approaches.

40. "Global Retailing: Asian Assignment," *Chain Store Age Executive*, January 1995, sect. 2, p. 5.

Chapter 9

1. Patrick Dunne and Robert Lusch, *Retailing*, 5th ed. (Mason, OH: Southwest, 2000) pp. 39-40.

2. "Diversity at MacDonald's: A Way of Life," *Nation's Restaurant News*, January, 2005, pp.92-95.

3. "Harper's Index," *Harpers*, February 1994, p. 13.

4. Robert D. Hof and Heather Green, "How Amazon Cleared the Hurdle," *Business Week*, February 4, 2002.

5. "Top 100 Retailers," 2001, www.stores.org; and www.freeedgar.com.

6. Average retail inventory is estimated from the balance sheet inventory. Assume the end-of-year inventory on the balance sheet is average cost inventory. Average retail inventory = Average cost inventory/(1 – Gross margin percent (expressed as a decimal)).

7. James Surowiecki, "The Most Devasting Retailer in the World," *The New Yorker*, September 18, 2000, p. 74.

8. Although the use of asset turnover presented here is helpful for gaining appreciation of the performance ratio, capital budgeting or present value analyses are more appropriate for determining the long-term return of a fixed asset.

9. Bryan Gildenberg, Mventures, personal communication, February 2002.

10. All categories of shares, including preferred shares, paid-in capital, and treasury shares, are included with common shares for simplicity.

11. "A Strong and Useful Light," *Harvard Business Review* 80, no. 5 (May 2002), p. 12.; John D. Sterman and Nelson P. Repenning, "Nobody Ever Gets Credit for Fixing Problems That Never Happened: Creating and Sustaining Process Improvement," *Harvard Business Online*, July 1, 2001; Loren Gary, "The Right Kind of Failure," *Harvard Management*, update article, January 1, 2002; Gary Sutton, *The Six-Month Fix: Adventures in Rescuing Failing Companies* (New York: John Wiley & Sons, November 2001); and Bernard Salanie, *The Microeconomics of Market Failures* (Boston: MIT Press, November 2000).

12. Daniel J. Sweeney, "Improving the Profitability of Retail Merchandising Decisions," *Journal of Marketing*, January 1973, pp. 60-68.

`13. To illustrate, suppose Net sales = $50,000 and Average inventory at retail = $10,000; Inventory turnover = $50,000 ÷ $10,000 = 5. To convert inventory turnover expressed at retail to turnover at cost, we multiply by the cost complement, which is the percentage of net sales represented by the cost of goods sold. If the gross margin is 40 percent, the cost complement is 60 percent (100% – 40%). By multiplying the numerator and denominator by 60 percent, the result is cost of goods sold divided by the average inventory at cost. Thus, inventory turnover is 5 whether it is calculated using retail or cost figures.

14. The rationale behind this equation is as follows: The sales-to-stock ratio is expressed with the numerator at retail and the denominator at cost. To get inventory turnover, both numerator and denominator must be at either retail or cost. 100% – Gross margin % is the percentage of net sales represented by the cost of goods sold (also known as the cost complement). By multiplying the sales-to-stock ratio by the cost complement we, in essence, convert the numerator (sales) to the cost of goods sold and therefore have numerator and denominator both expressed at cost.

15. This section is adapted from William R. Davidson, Daniel J. Sweeney, and Ronald W. Stampfl, *Retailing Management*, 5th ed. (New York: John Wiley & Sons, 1984).

Chapter 10

1. The concept of category management began in the grocery business but has spread rapidly to general merchandise, home furnishings, books, and recordings. In fact, the Food Marketing Institute, the primary trade organization in the grocery industry, has published a book on the subject: Robert C. Blattberg and Edward J. Fox, *Category Management* (Washington, DC: Food Marketing Institute and the Center for Retail Management, Northwestern University, 1995).

2. Brandon Copple, "Shelf-Determination," Forbes.com, April 15, 2002.

3. Anna Rominger and Subir Bandyopadyay, "Investigating Antitrust Issues in Category Management," presentation made at the 2002 Research Workshop on Marketing Competitive Conduct and Antitrust Policy, University of Notre Dame, May 2–4, 2002.

4. Walter S. Mossberg, "Palm's New Hand-Held Goes Mano a Mano with BlackBerry," *The Wall Street Journal*, January 31, 2002, p. B1.

5. Richard A. Kreuger and Mary Anne Casey, *Focus Groups*, 3rd ed. (Thousand Oaks, CA: Sage Publications: April 2000).

6. This section was developed with the assistance of KhiMetrics.

7. *Chain Store Age*/Cap Gemini Ernst & Young U.S.L.L.C, 2001.

8. Dan Scheraga, "Penney's Net Advantage," *Chain Store Age*, September 2000, pp. 114-18.

9. David Moin, "Macy's Web Site Gets a Major Apparel Upload," *WWD*, November 19, 1998.

Chapter 11

1. Don Berezowski, "Protect Your Assets," *Canadian Retailer*, March/April, 2004; "Robbery, Employee Theft, Leading Causes of Supermarket Losses," *Chain Store Age*, August 1998, p. 84; based on the Food Marketing Institute's annual security survey.

2. Murali Mantrala, "Allocating Marketing Resources," in *Handbook of Marketing*, Barton Weitz and Robin Wensley, eds. (London: Sage publications, 2002).

3. These issues were taken from Janet Wagner, Richard Ettenson, and Jean Parrish, "Vendor Selection among Retail Buyers: An Analysis by Merchandise Division," *Journal of Retailing* 65, no. 1 (Spring 1989), pp. 58-79.

4. Douglas M. Lambert, Martha C. Cooper, and Janus D. Pagh, "Supply Chain Management: Implementation Issues and Research Opportunities," *International Journal of Logistics Management* 9, no. 2 (1998), p. 1.

5. "Hoovers Company Capsule," Hoovers Online, May 2002, www.hoovers.com.

6. William H. Inmon, *Building the Datawarehouse* (New York: John Wiley & Sons, Inc., 2002).

7. Don Berezowski, "Protect Your Assets," *Canadian Retailer*, March/April, 2004.

8. Liz Parks, "Transforming the Supply Chain with Technology," *Drug Store News*, July 19, 1999, p. 10.

9. Presented at the annual business meeting, Council of Logistics Management, Anaheim, CA, October 1998. The definition is posted at the CLM's homepage, www.CLM1.org.

10. Martha C. Cooper, Douglas M. Lambert, and Janus D. Pagh, "Supply Chain Management: More Than a New Name for Logistics," *International Journal of Logistics Management* 8, no. 1 (1997), pp. 1-14.

11. Alan Goldstein, "Logistics Goes High-Tech to Figure Demand in Dallas Area," *Knight Ridder Tribune Business News*, April 21, 2002, p. 1.

12. "Flow-Through DC Yields Savings for Fred Meyer," *Chain Store Age*, October 1995, pp. 64-66; quote by Mary Sammons, senior vice-president, Fred Meyer.

13. Barbara E. Kahn and Leigh McAlister, *Grocery Revolution: The New Focus on the Consumer* (Reading, MA: Longman, Addison-Wesley, 1997).

14. James Surowiecki, "The Most Devastating Retailer in the World," *The New Yorker*, September 18, 2000, p. 74; and William Echikson, "The Mark of Zara," *Business Week*, May 29, 2000, p. 98.

15. Ken Clark, "Coping with Returns," *Chain Store Age*, November 1, 2000, p. 124; based on focus group research conducted by the Reverse Logistics Executive Council and the University of Nevada's Center for Logistics Management.

16. Laurie Joan Aron, "Delivering on E-Commerce," *Chain Store Age*, June 1999, pp. 130-31.

Chapter 12

1. Stephen B. Shepard, "The Best Global Brands," *Business Week*, August 6, 2001, p. 12.

2. www.federated-fds.com/home.asp.

3. Robin Rusch, "Private Labels: Does Branding Matter?" Brandchannel.com, May 13, 2002; www.brandchannel. com/ ;features-effect.asp?id=94 based on research by John Stanley of John Stanley Associates.

4. Robin Rusch, "Private Labels: Does Branding Matter?" Brandchannel.com, May 13, 2002; www.brandchannel. com/ ;features-effect.asp?id=94 based on research by John Stanley of John Stanley Associates.

5. John Stanley, "Brands versus Private Labels," *About Retailing Industry Newsletter*, January 2, 2002. retailindustry.about.com

6. Michael Harvey, "The Trade Dress Controversy: A Case of Strategic Cross-Brand Cannibalization," *Journal of Marketing Theory and Practice* 6, no. 2 (Spring 1998), pp. 1-15.

7. Bruce C Brown, "Wages and Employment in the U.S. Apparel Industry," *Contemporary Economic Policy* 19, no. 4 (October 2001), pp. 454-64.

8. Sherrie E. Zhan, "Made in the USA," *World Trade*, April 1, 1999, pp. 32–46.

9. Export tariffs are used in some less developed countries to generate additional revenue. For instance, the Argentine government may impose an export tariff on wool that is exported.

An export tariff actually lowers the competitive ability of domestic manufacturers, rather than protecting them, as is the case with import tariffs.

10. "Border Battles," *The Economist*, October 3, 1998, p. 6.

11. "Moore Pledges to Build on Doha Success in 2000," *WTO News: 2002*, press release, January 2, 2002.

12. "FAS BACKGROUNDER: Benefits of NAFTA," FASonline, July 2001, www.fas.usda.gov.

13. Personal communication, David Gunter, director of corporate communications, Coldwater Creek, July 2002.

14. "Sweatshops under the American Flag," *New York Times*, May 10, 2002, p. A34.

15. Steven Greenhouse, "18 Major Retailers and Apparel Makers Are Accused of Using Sweatshops," *New York Times*, January 14, 1999, p. A9.

16. Shawn McCarthy, "Gap Pressures Other Retailers with First Report on Sweat Shops," *Globe and Mail*, May 13, 2004.

17. "Labor Forces Review," *Daily News*, April 26, 1998.

18. www.fashioncenter.com

19. www.dallasmarketcenter.com

20. www.dallasmarketcenter.com

21. Silver, Erin. "Fashion Week in Toronto: A Day for the New Guys," *Toronto Fashion*, March 21, 2002.

22. "One-stop-shop!" CGTA Gift Show, 2002.

23. Dan Scheraga, "Collaboration Evolves," *Chain Store Age*, July 2005, p.58.

24. Janet Adamy, "Retail Exchanges Plan Merger to Vie with Wal-Mart," *The Wall Street Journal*, April 26, 2005, p. B7.

25. Sandy Jap, "Online Reverse Auctions: Issues, Themes, and Prospects for the Future," *Journal of the Academy of Marketing Science* 30, no. 4 (Fall 2002); forthcoming M.L. Emiliani, "Business-to-Business Online Auctions: Key Issues for Purchasing Process Improvement," *Supply Chain Management: An International Journal* 5, no. 4 (2000), pp. 176-86.

26. Richard Wise and David Morrison, "Beyond the Exchange: The Future of B2B," *Harvard Business Review*, November-December 2000, pp. 86-96.

27. Stephanie Williams and Noah Rothbaum, "Returns: All That Glitters Isn't Gold—Ten Secrets of the Trade Your Jeweler Will Probably Never Tell You," *Asian Wall Street Journal*, February 22, 2002, p. W2.

28. Tim Laseter, Brian Long, and Chris Capers, "B2B Benchmark: The State of Electronic Exchanges," *strategy+business*, 4th quarter, 2001. http://www.strategy-business.com/ search/ archives

29. Tim Laseter, Brian Long, and Chris Capers, "B2B Benchmark: The State of Electronic Exchanges," *strategy+business*, 4th quarter, 2001. http://www.strategy-business.com/ search/ archives

30. Adapted from, V. Kasturi Rangan, "FreeMarkets Online," Harvard Business School case #9-598-109, February 1999.

31. Barton Weitz and Sandy Jap, "Relationship Marketing and Distribution Channels," *Journal of the Academy of Marketing Sciences* 23 (Fall 1995), pp. 305-20; and F. Robert Dwyer, Paul Shurr, and Sejo Oh, "Developing Buyer-Seller Relationships," *Journal of Marketing* 51 (April 1987), pp. 11-27.

32. Nirmalya Kumar, "The Power of Trust in Manufacturer–Retailer Relationships," *Harvard Business Review*, November-December 1996, pp. 92-106.

33. Jim Yardley, "Vendorville," *New York Times Magazine*, March 8, 1998, p. 62.

34. Erin Anderson and Anne Coughlan, "Structure, Governance, and Relationship Management," in *Handbook of Marketing*, eds. B. Weitz and R. Wensley (London: Sage, 2002).

35. Erin Anderson and Barton Weitz, "The Use of Pledges to Build and Sustain Commitment in Distribution Channels," *Journal of Marketing Research* 29 (February 1992), pp. 18-34.

36. Erin Anderson and Barton Weitz, "The Use of Pledges to Build and Sustain Commitment in Distribution Channels," *Journal of Marketing Research* 29 (February 1992), pp. 18-34.

37. Mitch Moxley, "Mountain Co-op Adding to City Locations," *National Post*, June 18, 2004.

38. Peter Brieger, "Celebrity Lines Lift Sears Canada," *National Post*, April 22, 2004.

39. Thomas J. Ryan, "Financial Forum: Chargeback Debate Roars on as Practice Remains Fact of Life," *WWD*, June 1, 1998, pp. 14, 16.

40. Similar types of fees charged to vendors are display fees (paid for special merchandising and display of products) and pay-to-stay fees (paid to continue stocking and displaying a product).

41. Ramarao Desiraju, "New Product Introductions, Slotting Allowances, and Retailer Discretion," *Journal of Retailing* 77, no. 3 (Fall 2001), p. 335. Estimate taken from *Advertising Age*, March 13, 2000, p. 75.

42. Ramarao Desiraju, "New Product Introductions, Slotting Allowances, and Retailer Discretion," *Journal of Retailing* 77, no. 3 (Fall 2001), p. 335. Estimate taken from *Advertising Age*, March 13, 2000, p. 75.

43. Stephanie Thompson, "Wal-Mart Stomps to Top of Supermarket Heap," AdAge.com, April 29, 2002. http:// www. adage.com/news.cms?newsid=34573

44. Conwood Company, LLP v United States Tobacco Co., 2002 Fed App/0171P (6th Cir. 2002).

45. Federal Trade Commission, "World's Largest Manufacturer of Spice and Seasoning Products Agrees to Settle Price Discrimination Charges," FTC press release, March 8, 2000.

46. Ken Bensinger, "Can You Spot the Fake?" *The Wall Street Journal*, February 16, 2001, www.wsj.com

47. "Software Piracy," *The Economist*, June 27, 1998, p. 108.

48. This section draws from Michael R. Czinkota and Ilkka A. Ronkainen, *International Marketing*, 6th ed. (Cincinnati: South-Western, 2000).

49. Kmart Corp. v. Cartier, Inc., 486 U.S. 281 (1988).

50. Sebao Inc. v. GB Unic. SA, 1999 E.T.M.R. 681.

51. Irvine Clarke III and Margaret Owens, "Trademark Rights in Gray Markets," *International Marketing Review* 17, no. 2/3 (2000), p. 272.

52. Suein L. Hwant, "Tobacco: As Cigarette Prices Soar, a Gray Market Booms," *The Wall Street Journal*, January 28, 1999, p. B1.

53. Southern Card & Novelty v. Lawson Mardon Label, 138 F.3d 869 (1998).

54. In re Toys R Us Antitrust Litigation, 191 F.R.D. 347 (E.D.N.Y. 2000).

55. Itzhak Sharav, "Cost Justification under the *Robinson-Patman Act*," *Management Accounting*, July 1978, pp. 15-22.

56. For different perspectives on determining a quantity discount pricing policy, see Abel P. Jeuland and Steven M. Shugan, "Managing Channel Profits," *Marketing Science* 2 (Summer 1983), pp. 239-72; Rajiv Lal and Richard Staelin, "An Approach for Developing an Optimal Discount Pricing Policy," *Management Science* 30 (December 1984), pp. 1524-39; Michael Levy, William Cron, and Robert Novack, "A Decision Support System for Determining a Quantity Discount Pricing Policy," *Journal of Business Logistics* 6, no. 2 (1985), pp. 110-41; James Monahan, "A Quantity Discount Pricing Model to Increase Vendor Profits," *Management Science* 30 (June 1984), pp. 720-27; Kent B. Monroe and Albert J. Della Bitta, "Models for Pricing Decisions," *Journal of Marketing Research* 15 (August 1990), pp. 413-28; James B. Wilcox, Roy D. Howell, Paul Kuzdrall, and Robert Britney, "Price Quantity Discounts: Some Implications for Buyers and Sellers," *Journal of Marketing* 51, no. 3 (July 1987), pp. 60-71; and Pinhas Zusman and Michael Etgar, "The Marketing Channel as an Equilibrium Set of Contracts," *Management Science* 27 (March 1981), pp. 284-302.

57. Michael Levy and Michael van Breda, "A Financial Perspective on the Shift of Marketing Functions," *Journal of Retailing* 60, no. 4 (Winter 1984), pp. 23-42.

Chapter 13

1. *Chain Store Age*/Cap Gemini Ernst & Young U.S. L.L.C, 2001.

2. Christopher S. Tang, David R. Bell, and Teck-Hua Ho, "Store Choice and Shopping Behavior: How Price Format Works," *California Management Review* 43, no. 2 (Winter 2001), pp. 56-74; and Alan Sawyer and Peter Dickson, "Everyday Low Prices vs. Sale Price," *Retailing Review* 1, no. 2 (1993), pp. 1-2, 8.

3. Christopher S. Tang, David R. Bell, and Teck-Hua Ho, "Store Choice and Shopping Behavior: How Price Format Works," *California Management Review* 43, no. 2 (Winter 2001).

4. "Survey Reveals Shoppers' Peeves," *Chain Store Age*, May 2000, p. 54.

5. In some rare situations, retail price and initial markup as a percentage of cost are known, and the retailer is seeking to determine the cost. In this case the following formula applies:

Initial markup as a % of retail = Initial markup as a % of cost 100% + Initial markup as a % of cost

6. This section was developed with the assistance of KhiMetrics.

7. This section is based on Thomas T. Nagle and Reed K. Holden, *The Strategy and Tactics of Pricing: A Guide to Profitable Decision Making* (Prentice Hall, 2002).

8. Amy Merrick, "Priced to Move: Retailers Try to Get Leg Up on Markdowns with New Software," *The Wall Street Journal*, August 7, 2001, p. A1.

9. D. Soman, "Does Holding on to a Product Result in Increased Consumption Rates?" *Advances in Consumer Research* 24 (1997), pp. 33-35; Brian Wansink, "Do We Use More When We Buy More? The Effects of Stockpiling on Product Consumption," *Advances in Consumer Research* 25 (1998), pp. 21-22; and Valerie S. Folkes, Ingrid M. Martin, and Kamal Gupta, "When to Say When: Effects of Supply on Usage," *Journal of Consumer Research* 20, no. 3, (December 1992), pp. 467-77.

10. William M. Bulkeley, "Rebates' Big Appeal: Many People Neglect to Redeem Them," *The Wall Street Journal*, February 10, 1998, pp. B1-B2.

11. Carl Shapiro, Carol Shapiro, and Hal R. Varian, *Information Rules: A Strategic Guide to the Network Economy* (Harvard Business School Publishing, 1998).

12. This section was developed with the assistance of KhiMetrics.

13. "Levi Strauss Reacquires a Pair of Jeans, at Markup," *The Wall Street Journal*, May 29, 2001, p. B.13A.

14. Dan Scheraga, "One Price Doesn't Fit All," *Chain Store Age*, March 2001, pp. 104-5; taken from research by Mark Husson, who tracks the supermarket sector for Merrill Lynch.

15. Itamar Simonson, "Shoppers Easily Influenced Choices," *New York Times*, November 6, 1994, p. 311; based on research by Itamar Simonson and Amos Tversky, www.nytimes.com

16. This section was developed with the assistance of KhiMetrics.

17. This discussion has been going on for at least 70 years; see Louis Bader and James De. Weinland, "Do Odd Prices Earn Money?" *Journal of Retailing* 8 (1932), pp. 102-4. For recent research in this area, see Karen Gedenk and Henrik Sattler, "The Impact of Price Thresholds on Profit Contribution—Should Retailers Set Nine-Ending Prices?" *Journal of Retailing* 75, no. 1 (1999), pp. 33-57; Robert M. Schindler and Patrick N. Kirby, "Patterns of Rightmost Digits Used in Advertised Prices: Implications for Nine-Ending Effects," *Journal of Consumer Research* 24 (September 1997), p. 192-201; and Mark Stiving and Russell S. Winer, "An Empirical Analysis of Price Endings with Scanner Data," *Journal of Consumer Research* 24 (June 1997), pp. 57-67.

18. Michelle Rafter, "Cheap, Cheaper, Cheapest," *The Industry Standard*, January 11, 1999, pp. 50-52; George Anders, "Comparison Shopping Is the Web's Virtue—Unless You're a Seller," *The Wall Street Journal*, July 23, 1998, pp. A1, A8.

19. Rebecca Quick, "Web's Robot Shoppers Don't Roam Free," *The Wall Street Journal*, September 3, 1998, pp. B1, B8.

20. Xing Pan, Brian Ratchford and Venkatesh Sankar, "Why Aren't the Prices for the Same Items the Same at Me.com and You.com? Drivers of Price Dispersion among E-Tailers," working paper, Robert H. Smith Business School, University of Maryland, 2001; Erik Brynjolfson and Michael Smith, "Frictionless Commerce? A Comparison of Internet and Conventional Retailer," *Management Science* 46, no. 4 April 200), pp. 563-85.

21. Borden Co v. FTC, 381 F.2d 175 (5th Cir. 1967).

22. "Booksellers Swear Anti-trust," *Discount Store News*, April 6, 1998, p. 8; and John Accola, "Tattered Cover Takes Aim," *Rocky Mountain News*, March 19, 1998, p. B1.

23. Dianna Marder, "Study Finds Gender Bias in Philadelphia Merchants Pricing," *Philadelphia Inquirer*, March 5, 1999.

24. Bob Ortega, "Suit over Wal-Mart's Pricing Practices Goes to Trial Today in Arkansas Court," *The Wall Street Journal*, August 23, 1993, p. A3; and Pete Hisey, "Ark. Supreme Court Rules Wal-Mart's No Predator: Lack of Proof Overturns Price Conviction," *Discount Store News*, February 6, 1995, pp. 3, 89.

25. "Nine West Settles State and Federal Price Fixing Charges," FTC press release, March 6, 2000.

26. Melody Petersen, "Treading a Contentious Line," *New York Times*, January 13, 1999, pp. C1-C2.

27. State Oil v. Kahn, 522 U.S. 3 (1997).

28. Larry D. Compeau, Dhruv Grewal, and Diana S. Grewal, "Adjudicating Claims of Deceptive Advertised Reference Prices: The Use of Empirical Evidence," *Journal of Public Policy & Marketing* 14 (Fall 1994); Dhruv Grewal, Diana S. Grewal, and Larry D. Compeau, "States' Crackdown on Deceptive Price Advertising: Retail and Public Policy Implications," *Pricing Strategy & Practice: An International Journal* 1, no. 2 (1993), pp. 33-40; Dhruv Grewal and Larry D. Compeau, "Comparative Price Advertising: Informative or Deceptive?" *Journal of Public Policy & Marketing* 11 (Spring 1992), pp. 52-62; Robert N. Corley and O. Lee Reed, *The Legal Environment*, 7th ed. (New York; McGraw-Hill, 1987); Teri Agins, "Low Prices or Low Practice? Regulators Cast Wary Eye on Retailers' Many Sales," *The Wall Street Journal*, February 13, 1990, pp. B1, B7; and *Do's and Don'ts in Advertising Copy* (Council of Better Business Bureaus, 1987).

29. "Price Check II Shows Scanner Accuracy Has Improved Since 1996," FTC press release, December 16, 1998.

Chapter 14

1. Susan Jackson and Randall Schuler, *Managing Human Resources through Strategic Relationships*, 8th ed. (Mason, OH: Southwestern, 2003); p. 5.

2. H. John Bernardin, *Human Resource Management: An Experiential Approach*, 4th ed. (Burr Ridge, IL: McGraw-Hill, 2006); Raymond Noe, John Hollenbeck, Barry Gerhart, and Patrick Wright, *Fundamentals of Human Resource Management*, 2nd ed. (Burr Ridge, IL: McGraw-Hill, 2006).

3. *Merchandising and Operations Costs Report* (New York: Fairchild Publications, 1999).

4. Michael Bergdal, "Our 'People' Culture Is a Major Competitive Asset," *Stores*, April 1999, pp. 114–15; Raphael Amit, "Human Resources Management Processes: A Value-Creating Source of Competitive Advantage," *European Management Journal*, April 1999, pp. 174–82; Tim Ambler, "Valuing Human Assets," *Business Strategy Review* 10 (Spring 1999), pp. 57–58; Tony Grundy, "How Are Corporate Strategy and Human Resources Strategy Linked?" *Journal of General Management* 23 (Spring 1998), pp. 49–73; and Gerard Farias, "High Performance Work Systems: What We Know and What We Need to Know," *Human Resource Planning* 21 (June 1998), pp. 50–55.

5. Anthony Rucci, Steven Kirn, and Richard T. Quinn, "The Employee–Customer–Profit Chain at Sears," *Harvard Business Review*, January–February 1998, pp. 82–97.

6. Jeffrey Pfeffer, *The Human Equation* (Boston: Harvard Business School Press, 1998), pp. 26–28.

7. D. Roth, "My Job at the Container Store," *Fortune*, January 10, 2000, pp. 74–78.

8. "Helping the World One Employee at a Time," *Canadian Retailer*, November/December 2003.

9. *Retailing: Mirror on America* (Washington, DC: National Retailer Federation, 2002).

10. Susan Jackson and Randall Schuler, *Managing Human Resources through Strategic Relationships*, 8th ed. (Mason, OH: Southwestern, 2003); p. 69.

11. John A. Challenger, "The Changing Workforce," *Vital Speeches*, September 15, 2001, pp. 721–25; and JoAnn Greco, "America's Changing Workforce," *Journal of Business Strategy* 19 (March–April 1998), pp. 43–47.

12. James Fitzsimmons and Mona Fitzsimmons, *Service Development: Creating Memorable Experiences* (Thousand Oaks, CA.: Sage Publications, 2000); and Suzanne Barry Osborn, "Is Your Customer Being SERVED?" *Chain Store Age*, November 1, 2000, p. 52.

13. Michael Gold and Andrew Campbell, "Do You Have a Well-Designed Organization?" *Harvard Business Review*, March 2002, pp. 117–25; and Richard L. Daft, *Essentials of Organization Theory and Design*, 2nd ed. (Cincinnati: South-Western College Publishing, 2000).

14. Dave Crisp, "Human Resources Keeps Evolving," *Canadian Retailer*, November/December 2003.

15. "Business Antiquities," *The Wall Street Journal*, November 17, 1999, p. B1.

16. Walter Loeb, "Unbundling or Centralize: What Is the Answer?" *Retailing Issues Letter* (College Station: Center for Retailing Studies, Texas A&M University, May 1992).

17. Carol Sansone and Judith M. Harackiewicz, *Intrinsic and Extrinsic Motivation: The Search for Optimal Motivation and Performance* (San Diego: Academic Press, 2000).

18. "Retailers among the Best," *Canadian Retailer*, January/February 2004.

19. Patrica Sellers, "Can Home Depot Fix Its Sagging Stock?" *Fortune*, March 4, 1996, pp. 139–45; and Bob Ortega, "What Does Wal-Mart Do If Stock Drop Cuts into Workers' Morale?" *The Wall Street Journal*, January 4, 1995, pp. A1, A5.

20. Susan Jackson and Randall Schuler, *Managing Human Resources through Strategic Relationships*, 8th ed. (Mason, OH: Southwestern, 2003); p. 405.

21. Susan Jackson and Randall Schuler, *Managing Human Resources through Strategic Relationships*, 8th ed. (Mason, OH: Southwestern, 2003); p. 525.

22. David Good and Charles Schwepker, "Sales Quotas: Critical Interpretations and Implications," *Review of Business* 22 (Spring-Summer 2001), pp. 32-37.

23. Todd Zenger and C. R. Marshall, "Determinants of Incentive Intensity in Group-Based Rewards, " *Academy of Management Journal* 43 (April 2000), pp. 149-63.

24. William Bliss, "Why Is Corporate Culture Important?" *Workforce* 78 (February 1999), pp. W8–W10; W. Matthew Juechter, "Five Conditions for High-Performance Cultures," *Training & Development* 52 (May 1998), pp. 63–68; and Andrew Chan, "Corporate Culture of a Clan Organization," *Management Decision*, January–February 1997, pp. 94–100.

25. Susan Jackson and Randall Schuler, *Managing Human Resources through Strategic Relationships*, 8th ed. (Mason, OH: Southwestern, 2003); p. 141.

26. Beverly Kaye and Betsy Jacobson, "True Tales and Tall Tales: The Power of Organizational Storytelling," *Training & Development* (March 1999), pp. 44–51; and Nancy L. Breuer, "The Power of Storytelling," *Workforce* (December 1998); pp. 36–42.

27. Aaron Bernstein, "Too Many Workers? Not for Long," *Business Week*, May 20, 2002, p. 126.

28. Debby Stankevich, "Retailers Focus on Optimizing Technology," *Retailer Merchandiser*, March 2002, pp. 55–58; Ginger Koloszyc, "Tight Labor Market Spurs High-Tech Employment Screening," *Stores*, July 1998, pp. 77–81; and David Schulz, "Small Retailers Turn to Pre-Employment Screening Services," *Stores*, May 1998, pp. 72–74.

29. Sarah Fister, "Separating Hires from Liars," *Training*, July 1999, pp. 22–24.

30. Susan Jackson and Randall Schuler, *Managing Human Resource through Strategic Relationships*, 8th ed. (Mason, OH: South-Western, 2003), p. 328.

31. Jane Bahls, "Available Upon Request," *HR Magazine*, January 1999, pp. S2–S7.

32. John Bernardin and Donna Cooke, "Validity of an Honesty Test in Predicting Theft among Convenience Store Employees," *Academy of Management Journal* 36 (October 1993), pp. 1097–1099.

33. Kal Lifson, "Turn Down Turnover to Turn Up Profits," *Chain Store Age*, November 1, 1996, pp. 64–66.

34. Susan Jackson and Randall Schuler, *Managing Human Resources through Strategic Relationships*, 8th ed. (Mason, OH: South-Western, 2003), p. 330.

35. Richard Hollinger and Jason Davis, *2001 National Retail Security Survey* (Gainesville, FL: Security Research Project, Department of Sociology, University of Florida, 1998), p. 8, web.soc.ufl.edu/SRP/NRSS_2001.pdf.

36. Paul Taylor, "Providing Structure to Interviews and Reference Checks," *Workforce, Workforce Tools Supplement*, May 1999, pp. S11–S55; and Allen Huffcutt and David Woehr, "Further Analysis of Employment Interview Validity: A Quantitative Evaluation of Interviewer-Related Structuring Methods," *Journal of Organizational Behavior* 20 (July 1999), pp. 549–56.

37. John Bible, "Discrimination in Job Applications and Interviews," *Supervision*, November 1998, pp. 9–12; Laura Williamson, James Campion, Mark Roehling, Stanley Malos, and Michael Campion, "Employment Interview on Trial: Linking Interview Structure with Litigation Outcomes," *Journal of Applied Psychology* 82 (December 1997; pp. 900–13; and Peter Burgess, "How Those 'Innermost Thoughts' Are Revealed," *Grocer*, March 9, 1996, pp. 60–62.

38. Lucette Comer and Tanya Drollinger, "Active Empathetic Listening and Selling Success: A Conceptual Framework," *Journal of Personal Selling and Sales Management* 9 (Winter 1999), pp. 15–29; and C. David Sheppard, Stephen Castleberry, and Rick Ridnour, "Linking Effective Listening with Sales Performance: An Exploratory Investigation," *Journal of Business and Industrial Marketing* 12 (1997), pp. 315–21.

39. John McKinnon, "Retailers Beware!" *Florida Trend*, June 1996, pp. 20–21.

40. This section is based on Chapter 3 in Jeffrey Pfeffer, *The Human Equation* (Boston: Harvard Business School Press, 1998).

41. Gary Dessler, "How to Earn Your Employees' Commitment," *Academy of Management Executive* 13 (May 1999), pp. 58–59; Deb McCusker, "Loyalty in the Eyes of Employers and Employees," *Workforce*, November 1998, pp. 23–28; and David L. Stum, "Five Ingredients for an Employee Retention Formula," *HR Focus*, September 1998, pp. S9–S11

42. Shari Caudron, "How HR Drives Profits: Academic Research and Real-World Experience Show How HR Practices Affect the Bottom Line," *Workforce*, December 2001, pp. 26–30; and "HR's New Role: Creating Value," *HR Focus*, January 2000, pp. 1–4.

43. "Workers Are Seeking Employers of Choice," *Chain Store Age*, October 1998, p. 72.

44. Ling Sing Chee, "Singapore Airlines: Strategic Human Resource Initiatives," in International Human Resource Management: Think Globally and Act Locally, ed. Derek Torrington (New York: Prentice Hall, 1994), pp. 314–330.

45. "State of the Industry Operational Management," *Chain Store Age*, August 1, 1998, p. 17A.

46. Daniel Cable and Charles Parson, "Socialization Tactics and Person-Organization Fit," *Personnel Psychology* 54 (Spring 2001), pp. 1–24; and Cheri Young and Craig Lundberg, "Creating a First Day on the Job," *Cornell Hotel and Restaurant Administration Journal*, December 1996, pp. 26–29.

47. John Wanous and Arnon Rechers, "New Employee Orientation Program," *Human Resource Management Review* 10 (Winter 2000), pp. 435–52; and Charlotte Garvey, "The Whirland of a New Job," *HR Magazine* 46 (June 2001), pp. 110–16.

48. Bert Versloot, Jan Jong, and Jo Thijssen, "Organisational Context of Structured on-the-Job Training," *International Journal of Training and Development* 5 (March 2001), pp. 2–23.

49. Graham L. Bradley and Beverley A. Sparks, "Customer Reactions to Staff Empowerment: Mediators and Moderators," *Journal of Applied Social Psychology*, May 2000, pp. 991–1003; Martin Beirne, "Managing to Empower? A Healthy Review of Resources and Constraints," *European Management Journal*, April 1999, pp. 218–26; and Mohammed Rafiq, "A Customer-Oriented Framework for Empowering Service Employees," *Journal of Services Marketing* 12 (May–June 1998), pp. 379–97.

50. Shankar Ganesan and Barton Weitz, "The Impact of Staffing Policies on Retail Buyer Job Attitudes and Behaviors," *Journal of Retailing*, Spring 1996, pp. 231–45.

51. Janet Wiscombe, "Flex Appeal—Not Just for Moms," *Workforce*, March 2002, p. 18; Leslie Faught, "At Eddie Bauer You Can Work and Have a Life," *Workforce*, April 1997, pp. 83–88; and Davan Maharaj, "A Suitable Schedule: Flextime Gains as Employers Agree There's More to Life than Work," *Los Angeles Times*, July 10, 1998, p. D2.

52. Charles J. Hobson, Linda Delunas, and Dawn Kesic, "Compelling Evidence of the Need for Corporate Work/Life Balance Initiatives: Results from a National Survey of Stressful Life-Events," *Journal of Employment Counseling*, March 2001, pp. 38–42; and Jeffrey Hill, Alan J. Hawkins, Maria Ferris, and Michelle Weitzman, "Finding an Extra Day a Week: The Positive Influence of Perceived Job Flexibility on Work and Family Life Balance," *Family Relations*, January 2001, pp. 49–57.

53. R. Roosevelt Thomas, "From Affirmative Action to Diversity," *Harvard Business Review*, March–April 1990, pp. 107–17.

54. Michael Petrou, "Employment Equity Is about Hiring the Best," *The Ottawa Citizen*, December 21, 2003.

55. Kathleen Iverson, "Managing for Effective Workforce Diversity," *Cornell Hotel & Restaurant Administration Quarterly*, April 2000, pp. 2–7; Parshotam Dass, "Strategies for Managing Human Resource Diversity: From Resistance to Learning," *Academy of Management Executive* 13 (May 1999), pp. 68–69; and Philip Rosenzweig, "Strategies for Managing Diversity," *Financial Times*, March 6, 1998, pp. 6–9.

56. Audrey J. Murrell, Faye J. Crosby, and Robin J. Ely, eds., *Mentoring Dilemmas: Developmental Relationships within Multicultural Organizations* (Mahwah, NJ: Erlbaum, 1999); Max Messmer, "Mentoring: Building Your Company's Intellectual Capital," *HR Focus*, September 1998, pp. S11–S13; and Erik Van Slyke, "Mentoring: A Results-Oriented Approach," *HR Focus*, February 1998, pp. 14–15.

57. Sharon Maloney, "RCC and the Government Agenda," *Canadian Retailer*, November/December 2003.

58. "Helping the World One Employee at a Time," *Canadian Retailer*, November/December 2003.

59. "Helping the World One Employee at a Time," *Canadian Retailer*, November/December 2003.

60. Linda Wirth, *Breaking through the Glass Ceiling: Women in Management* (Washington DC: International Labour Office, 2001); Sheila Wellington, "Cracking the Ceiling," *Time*, December 7, 1998, p. 187; Alison Maitland, "Cracks Appear in Glass Ceiling," *Financial Times*, April 8, 1999, p. 22; and Tammy Reiss, "More Cracks in the Glass Ceiling," *Business Week*, August 10, 1998, p. 6.

61. Ontario Federation of Labour, *Employment Standards Act*, October 2000.

62. Gary Dessler, Nina Cole, Patricia Goodman, and Virginia Sutherland, *Fundamentals of Human Resources Management in Canada*, Toronto: Pearson, 2004.

63. "Helping the World One Employee at a Time," *Canadian Retailer*, November/December 2003.

64. Mary Wagner, "Don't Call Us," *Internet Retailer*, June 2002, pp. 8–9.

65. A. Colquitt, "On the Dimensionality of Organizational Justice: A Construct Validation of a Measure," *Journal of Applied Psychology* 86 (2001), pp. 386–400.

66. "Combating Shrink at the Source," *Chain Store Age*, December 2000, p. 152.

67. Ginger Koloszyc, "Supermarkets Find Growing Payoff in EAS Anti-Shoplifting Systems," *Stores*, February 1999, pp. 28–30; and "Sales Up, Shrink Down with Source Tagging," *Chain Store Age*, August 1998, p. 84.

68. Timothy Henderson, "Loss Prevention Software Aids in Retail Fight against Costly Employee Theft," *Stores*, March 2001, pp. 68–72.

69. Paul M. Mazur, *Principles of Organization Applied to Modern Retailing* (New York: Harper & Brothers, 1927).

70. Data for 2000 from www.federated-fds.com/retail/ rlg_1_3.asp.

71. Dave Crisp, "Human Resources Keeps Evolving," *Canadian Retailer*, November/December 2003.

Chapter 15

1. A. Parsuraman and Valarie Zeithaml, "Understanding and Improving Service Quality: A Literature Review and Research Agenda," in eds. B. Weitz and R. Wensley, *Handbook of Marketing* (London: Sage, 2002).

2. Michael Hartline and O.C. Ferrell, "The Management of Customer-Contact Service Employees: An Empirical Investigation," *Journal of Marketing* 60 (October 1996), pp. 52-70; and Lois Mohr and Mary Jo Bitner, "The Role of Employee Effort in Satisfaction with Service Transactions," *Journal of Business Research* 32 (March 1995), pp. 239-52.

3. Fredrick Reichfeld, *The Loyalty Effect* (Cambridge, MA: Harvard Business School Press, 1996).

4. See Stephanie Coyles and Timothy Gokey, "Customer Retention Is Not Enough," *McKinsey Quarterly* 2 (2002), pp. 3-14.

5. Anna S. Mattila, "Emotional Bonding and Restaurant Loyalty," *Cornell Hotel and Restaurant Administration Quarterly*, December 2001, pp. 73-80; and Susan Fournier, Susan Dobscha, and David Glen Mick, "Preventing the Premature Death of Relationship Marketing," *Harvard Business Review*, January-February 1998, pp. 42-50.

6. B. Joseph Pine and James Gilmore, *Experience Economy: Work Is Theatre and Every Business a Stage* (Boston: Harvard -Business Press, 1999).

7. Frank Badillo, *Retail Perspectives on Customer Relationship Management* (Columbus, OH: Retail Forward, February 2001), p. 33.

8. CyberAtlas, January 23, 2002, www.cyberatlas.internet.com.

9. "Cooking Up a Deep-Dish Database," *Business Week*, November 20, 1995, p. 160.

10. Lorie Grant, "Why Do Cashiers Want Your Digits?" *USA Today*, April 23, 2002, p. B1.

11. Doris Hajewski, "Small Grocer Keeps Pace by Marketing Loyalty," *Milwaukee Journal Sentinel*, May 1, 2002, p. B1.

12. George Milne, "Privacy and Ethical Issues in Database/Interactive Marketing and Public Policy: A Research Framework and Overview of the Special Issue," *Journal of Public Policy and Marketing* 19 (Spring 2000), pp. 1-7.

13. Dan Scheraga, "Courting the Customer," *Chain Store Age*, January 2000, p. 88; Ro Panepinto, "Preventative Customer Care," *Response*, October 1999, pp. 46-53; and Steve Larsen, "Personalization Without Privacy Won't Sell: Build Trust by Keeping Customers Informed," *Internet Retailer*, November 1999, p. 70.

14. Jill Clayton, "Employers Brace for Privacy Law," *National Post*, December 15, 2003; Matthew McClearn, "Full Disclosure," *Canadian Business*, Vol. 76, November/December 2003; "New Privacy Law Takes Effect January 1, 2004," Canada NewsWire, Ottawa: December 1, 2003; and Amanda Maltby, "Adapting to Canada's New Privacy Rules," *Marketing Magazine*, November 3, 2003.

15. Christopher Robertson and Ravi Sarathy, "Digital Privacy: A Pragmatic Guide for Senior Managers Charged with Developing a Strategic Policy for Handling Privacy Issues," *Business Horizons* 45 (January-February 2002), pp. 2-6.

16. Jill Dyche, *The CRM Handbook* (Upper Saddle River, NJ.: Addison-Wesley, 2002), pp. 134-5.

17. "Data Mining/CRM: Search for an ROI," *Chain Store Age*, October 1, 2001, p. 24.

18. Frank Badillo, *Retail Perspectives on Customer Relationship Management* (Columbus, OH: Retail Forward, February 2001), p. 25.

19. Valarie Zeithaml, Roland Rust, and Katherine Lemon, "The Customer Pyramid: Creating and Serving Profitable Customers," *California Management Review* 43 (Summer 2001), p. 124.

20. "Retailers Plan to Invest in CRM in 2002," CyberAtlas, January 23, 2002, www.cyberatlas.internet.com.

21. See Werner Reinartz and V. Kumar, "On the Profitability of Long-Life Customers in a Noncontractual Setting: An Empirical Investigation and Implications for Marketing," *Journal of Marketing* 64 (October 2000).

22. James Cigliano, Margaret Georgladis, Darren Pleasance, and Susan Whalley, "The Price of Loyalty," *McKinsey Quarterly* 4 (2000), p. 69. pp. 17-33, for an examination of programs designed to develop long-term relationships.

23. James Cigliano, Margaret Georgladis, Darren Pleasance, and Susan Whalley, "The Price of Loyalty," *McKinsey Quarterly* 4 (2000), p. 73.

24. Graham Dowling and Mark Uncles, "Do Customer Loyalty Programs Really Work?" *Sloan Management Review* 38 (Summer 1997), pp. 71-82.

25. James Cigliano, Margaret Georgladis, Darren Pleasance, and Susan Whalley, "The Price of Loyalty," *McKinsey Quarterly* 4 (2000), p. 70.

26. "Loyalty: At What Cost?" *Marketing*, May 16, 2002, pp. 48-50.

27. "Why Service Stinks," *Business Week Online*, October 23, 2000.

28. Ken Gofton, "Pinpointing Loyalty," *Marketing*, January 21, 1999, p. 65.

29. Roland Rust, Valarie Zeithaml, and Katherine Lemon, *Driving Customer Equity* (New York: Free Press, 2002), Ch. 13.

30. Frank Badillo, *Retail Perspectives on Customer Relationship Management* (Columbus, OH: Retail Forward, February 2001), pp. 33-34.

31. Roland Rust, Valarie Zeithaml, and Katherine Lemon, *Driving Customer Equity* (New York: Free Press, 2002), Ch.. 13.

32. "Retail IT 2001," *Chain Store Age*, October 1, 2001, p. 24.

33. Valarie Zeithaml, Leonard Berry, and A. Parasuraman, "The Behavioral Consequences of Service Quality," *Journal of Marketing* 60 (April 1996), pp. 31-46.

34. Robert Spector and Patrick McCarthy, *The Nordstrom Way: The Inside Story of America's #1 Customer Service Company*, 2nd ed. (New York: John Wiley, 2001).

35. Murray Raphael, "Tell Me What You Want and the Answer Is Yes," *Direct Marketing*, October 1996, p. 22.

36. "Driving Customers Away," *Chain Store Age*, June 2001, p. 39.

37. G. Odekerken-Schroder, K. De Wulf, H. Kasper, M. Kleijnen, J. Hoekstra, and H. Commandeur, "The Impact of Quality on Store Loyalty: A Contingency Approach," *Total Quality Management* 12 (May 2001), pp. 307-22; and Benjamin Schneider and David Bowen, *Winning the Service Game* (Boston: Harvard Business School Press, 1995).

38. Banwari Mittal and Walfried Lassar, "The Role of Personalization in Service Encounters," *Journal of Retailing* 72 (Spring 1996), pp. 95-109.

39. Roger Bennett, "Queues, Customer Characteristics and Policies for Managing Waiting-Lines in Supermarkets," *International Journal of Retail and Distribution Management* 26 (February–March 1998), pp. 78–88; and Julie Baker and Michaelle Cameron, "The Effects of the Service Environment on Affect and Consumer Perceptions of Waiting Time: An Integrative Review and Research Propositions," *Journal of the Academy of Marketing Science* 24 (Fall 1996), pp. 338–49.

40. "Retailers Join the War Effort," *Chain Store Age*, June 1994, p. 15

40. Cha, "Finding Fewer Happy Returns."

41. William Parsons, "Give the Lady What She Wants," *Chain Store Age*, November 1995, pp. 86-87.

42. Rebecca Eckler, "Sometimes ... You Have to Test Drive It," *National Post*, August 26, 2003; and Deirdre McMurdy, "Returns Rethink," *National Post*, December 21, 2002.

43. Martha McNeil Hamilton and Dina El Boghdady, "The Spirit of Giving Back; Shoppers Discover Stricter Policies for Returning Gifts," *Washington Post*, December 27, 2001, p. E01; and "Retailers Get Strict on Merchandise Returns," *St. Louis Post-Dispatch*, May 17, 2002, p. C1.

44. "Retailers Get Strict on Merchandise Returns," *St. Louis Post-Dispatch*, May 17, 2002, p. C1.

45. A. Parsuraman and Valarie Zeithaml, "Understanding and Improving Service Quality: A Literature Review and Research Agenda," in eds. B. Weitz and R. Wensley, *Handbook of*

Marketing (London: Sage, 2002); and Praveen Kopalle and Donald Lehmann, "Strategic Management of Expectations: The Role of Disconfirmation Sensitivity and Perfectionism," *Journal of Marketing Research*, August 2001, pp. 386-401.

46. Kenneth Clow, David Kurtz, John Ozment, and Beng Soo Ong, "The Antecedents of Consumer Expectations of Services: An Empirical Study across Four Industries," *Journal of Services Marketing* 11 (May-June 1997), pp. 230-48; and Ann Marie Thompson and Peter Kaminski, "Psychographic and Lifestyle Antecedents of Service Quality Expectations," *Journal of Services Marketing* 7 (1993), pp. 53-61.

47. Mary Jo Bitner, "Self-Service Technologies: What Do Customers Expect? In This High-Tech World, Customers Haven't Changed—They Still Want Good Service," *Marketing Management*, Spring 2001, pp. 10-15.

48. Susan Stellin, "Online Customer Service Found Lacking," *New York Times*, January 3, 2002, p. C1.

49. Timothy Keiningham and Terry Vavra, *The Customer Delight Principle* (Chicago: American Marketing Association, 2002).

50. The following discussion of the gaps model and its implications is based on Deon Nel and Leyland Pitt, "Service Quality in a Retail Environment: Closing the Gaps," *Journal of General Management* 18 (Spring 1993), pp. 37-57; Valarie Zeithaml, A. Parasuraman, and Leonard Berry, *Delivering Quality Customer Service* (New York: Free Press, 1990); and Valarie Zeithaml, Leonard Berry, and A. Parasuraman, "Communication and Control Processes in the Delivery of Service Quality," *Journal of Marketing* 52 (April 1988), pp. 35-48.

51. http://retailindustry.about.com, April 4, 2001.

52. "Merchant Prince: Stanley Marcus," *Inc.*, June 1987, pp. 41-44.

53. U. Chapman and George Argyros, "An Investigation into Whether Complaining Can Cause Increased Consumer Satisfaction," *Journal of Consumer Marketing* 17, 2000, pp. 9-19; Tibbett L. Speer, "They Complain Because They Care," *American Demographics*, May 1996, pp. 13-15; and Jagdip Singh and Robert Wilkes, "When Customers Complain: A Path Analysis of Key Antecedents of Customer Complaint Response Analysis," *Journal of the Academy of Marketing Science* 24 (Fall 1996), pp. 350-65.

54. "Driving Customers Away," *Chain Store Age*, June 2001, p. 39.

55. www.llbean.com.

56. Sandra Guy, "Stores Juggle Service with High-Tech Savvy," *Chicago Sun-Times*, July 1, 2002, p. B12; Julie Clark, "The Importance of Kiosks in Retail Has Grown," *Display and Design Ideas*, September 2001, p. 18; and Ken Clark, "Confused about Kiosks," *Chain Store Age*, November 1, 2000, p. 96.

57. Paul Hemp, "My Week as a Room-Service Waiter at the Ritz," *Harvard Business Review*, June 2002, pp. 50-62; and Len Berry, *On Great Customer Service* (New York: Free Press, 1995), pp. 73-74.

58. See Chuck Chakrapani, *How to Measure Service Quality and Customer Satisfaction: The Informal Field Guide for Tools and Techniques* (Chicago: American Marketing Association, 1998).

59. David Lipke, "Mystery Shoppers," *American Demographics*, December 2000, pp. 41-44; and "Mystery Shopping's Lightweight Reputation Undeserved," *International Journal of Retail and Distribution Management* 27 (February-March 1999), pp. 114-17; Rachel Miller, "Undercover Shoppers," *Marketing*, May 28, 1998, pp. 27-30; and Jennifer Steinhauer,

"The Undercover Shoppers," *New York Times*, February 4, 1998, p. D1.

60. See Jim Poisant, *Creating and Sustaining a Superior Customer Service Organization: A Book about Taking Care of the People Who Take Care of the Customers* (Westport, CT: Quorum Books, 2002); "People-Focused HR Policies Seen as Vital to Customer Service Improvement," *Store*, January 2001, p. 60; Michael Brady and J. Joseph Cronin, "Customer Orientation: Effects on Customer Service Perceptions and Outcome Behaviors," *Journal of Service Research*, February 2001, pp. 241-51; and Michael Hartline, James Maxham III, and Daryl McKee, "Corridors of Influence in the Dissemination of Customer-Oriented Strategy to Customer Contact Service Employees," *Journal of Marketing* 64 (April 2000), pp. 25-41.

61. Disney Institute and Michael Eisner, *Be Our Guest: Perfecting the Art of Customer Service* (New York: Disney Editions, 2001).

62. Alicia Grandey and Analea Brauburger, "The Emotion Regulation behind the Customer Service Smile," in *Emotions in the Workplace: Understanding the Structure and Role of Emotions in Organizational Behavior*, eds. R. Lord, R. Klimoski, and R. Kanfer (San Francisco: Jossey-Bass, 2002); and Mara Adelman and Aaron Ahuvia, "Social Support in the Service Sector: The Antecedents, Processes, and Consequences of Social Support in an Introductory Service," *Journal of Business Research* 32 (March 1995), pp. 273-82.

63. Moria Cotlier, "Adieu to Abandoned Carts," *Catalog Age*, October 2001, p. 39.

64. Mark Johlke and Dale Duhan, "Supervisor Communication Practices and Service Employee Job Outcomes," *Journal of Service Research*, November 2000, pp. 154-65.

65. Conrad Lashley, *Empowerment: HR Strategies for Service Excellence* (Boston: Butterworth/Heinemann, 2001).

66. Alan Randolph, and Marshall Sashkin, "Can Organizational Empowerment Work in Multinational Settings?" *Academy of Management Executive* 16 (February 2002), pp. 102-16; and Graham Bradley and Beverly Sparks, "Customer Reactions to Staff Empowerment: Mediators and Moderators," *Group and Organization Management*, 26 (March 2001), pp. 53-68.

67. Alan Randolph, and Marshall Sashkin, "Can Organizational Empowerment Work in Multinational Settings?" *Academy of Management Executive* 16 (February 2002), pp. 102-16.

68. Piyush Kumar, Manohar Kalawani, and Makbool Dada, "The Impact of Waiting Time Guarantees on Customers' Waiting Experiences," *Marketing Science* 16, no. 4 (1999), pp. 676-785.

69. James Maxham, "Service Recovery's Influence on Consumer Satisfaction, Positive Word-of-Mouth, and Purchase Intentions," *Journal of Business Research*, October 2001, pp. 11-24; and Michael McCollough, Leonard Berry, and Manjit Yadav, "An Empirical Investigation of Customer Satisfaction after Service Failure and Recovery," *Journal of Service Research*, November 2000, pp. 121-37.

70. "Correcting Store Blunders Seen as Key Customer Service Opportunity," *Stores*, January 2001, pp. 60-64; Stephen W. Brown, "Practicing Best-in-Class Service Recovery: Forward-Thinking Firms Leverage Service Recovery to Increase Loyalty and Profits," *Marketing Management*, Summer 2000, pp. 8-10; Stephen Tax, Stephen Brown, and Murali Chandrashekaran, "Customer Evaluations of Service Complaint Experience: Implications for Relationship Marketing," *Journal of Marketing* 62 (April 1998), pp. 60-76; and Amy Smith and

Ruth Bolton, "An Experimental Investigation of Customer Reactions to Service Failures and Recovery Encounters: Paradox or Peril?" *Journal of Services Research* 1 (August 1998), pp. 23-36; and Cynthia Webster and D.S. Sundaram, "Service Consumption Criticality in Failure Recovery," *Journal of Business Research* 41 (February 1998), pp. 153-59.

71. Marina Strauss, "Mining Customer Feedback, Firms Go Undercover and Online," *Globe and Mail*, May 13, 2004.

72. Ko de Ruyter and Martin Wetsel, "The Impact of Perceived Listening Behaviour in Voice-to-Voice Service Encounters," *Journal of Service Research*, February 2000, pp. 276-84.

Chapter 16

1. "Retail's Best Brands: 10 Stores with the Strongest Brand Image," *Display & Design Ideas*, September 15, 2001, p. 10.

2. Linda Hyde and Elaine Pollack, *What's in a Name?* (Columbus, OH: Retail Forward, Inc., June 1999), p. 9.

3. Stephanie Gordon and Michael Szego, "A Road Map for Retail Marketers," *Marketing Magazine*, February 24, 2003.

4. Denise Deveau, "Spreading the Good Word through Sponsorships," *Canadian Retailer*, March/April 2004.

5. "History in the Making: A Look at 16 Campaigns That Helped Redefine Promotion Marketing," *Promo*, March 2002, p. 23.

6. "The Return of SEX," May 13, 2002, p. 34; Amy Barrett, "To Reach the Unreachable Teen," *Business Week*, September 18, 2000, p. 78; and Terilyn Henderson and Elizabeth Mihas, "Building Retail Brands," *McKinsey Quarterly*, Summer 2000, pp. 110-15.

7. Molly Prior, "TRU Launches *RZone Magazine* for Teen Pop-Culture Enthusiasts," *DSN Retailing Today*, July 8, 2002, p. 4.

8. Peter Childs, Suzanne Heywood, and Michael Kliger, "Do Retail Brands Travel?" *McKinsey Quarterly* 1 (2001), pp. 12-16.

9. Consumers' Association of Canada, *Consumer Rights*, 2004.

10. Sara Owens, "The Price Is Righter; The Rewards of In-Store Sampling Are Greater than You Think," *Promo*, September 2001, p. 10.

11. Gabriella Stern, "With Sampling, There Is Too a Free Lunch," *The Wall Street Journal*, March 11, 1994, p. B1.

12. See A. Coskun Samli, "Store Image Definition, Dimensions, Measurement, and Management," in *Retail Market Strategy*, ed. A. Samli (New York: Quorum, 1989).

13. "State of Couponing," *Brandmarketing*, April 2002, p. 8.

14. Joe Dysart, "E-Mail Marketing Grows Up," *Chain Store Age*, June 2001, pp. 91-92

15. Frederick Reichheld, "Loyalty-Based Management," *Harvard Business Review*, March-April 1993, p. 65.

16. W. Glynn Mangold, Fred Miller, and Gary Brockway, "Word-of-Mouth Communication in the Service Marketplace," *Journal of Services Marketing* 13 (January-February 1999), pp. 73-77; "Word of Mouth Still Works," *Discount Store News*, June 22, 1998, p. 17; George Silverman, "How to Harness the Awesome Power of Word of Mouth," *Direct Marketing*, November 1997, pp. 32-38; and Chip Walker, "Word of Mouth," *American Demographics*, July 1995, pp. 38-43.

17. Donald Ziccardi and David Moin, *Master Minding the Store: Advertising, Sales Promotion, and the New Marketing Reality* (New York: Wiley, 1997); John McCann, Ali Tadlaqui, and

John Gallagher, "Knowledge Systems in Merchandising: Advertising Design," *Journal of Retailing*, Fall 1990, pp. 257-77; and Meryl Gardner and Michael Houston, "The Effects of Visual and Verbal Components of Retail Communications," *Journal of Retailing*, Summer 1986, pp. 65-78.

18. Gary Witkin, "Effective Use of Retail Data Bases," *Direct Marketing*, December 1995, pp. 32-35.

19. "Whom Do You Trust?" *Chain Store Age*, July 2, 2002, p. 36.

20. Ken Clark, "Play Ball," *Chain Store Age*, July 2002, p. 39.

21. Stephen Smith, Narendra Agrawal, and Shelby McIntyre, "A Discrete Optimization Model for Seasonal Merchandise Planning," *Journal of Retailing* 74 (Summer 1998), pp. 193-222; Scott Neslin and John Quilt, "Developing Models for Planning Retailer Sales Promotions: An Application to Automobile Dealerships," *Journal of Retailing* 63 (Winter 1987), pp. 333-64; and Arthur Allaway, J. Barry Mason, and Gene Brown, "An Optimal Decision Support Model for Department-Level Promotion Mix Planning," *Journal of Retailing* 63 (Fall 1987), pp. 216-41.

22. George Belch and Michael Belch, *Advertising and Promotion*, 5th ed. (New York: McGraw-Hill, 2001), pp. 227-28.

23. Murali Mantralla, "Allocating Marketing Resources," in eds. Barton Weitz and Robin Wensely, *Handbook of Marketing* (London: Sage, 2002), pp. 409-435.

24. This example is adapted by William R. Swinyard, professor of business management, Brigham Young University, from the "Overseas Airlines Service" case.

25. Ronald Curhan and Robert Kopp, "Obtaining Retailer Support for Trade Deals: Key Success Factors," *Journal of Advertising Research* 27 (December 1987-January 1988), pp. 51-60.

26. This illustration was provided by Kathy Perry, senior vice-president, Matrix Technology Group, Inc., www.mxtg.net.

27. "Top 100 Advertisers," *Advertising Age*, September 17, 1999, p. 16.

28. "Top 100 Advertisers," *Advertising Age*, September 17, 1999, p. 31.

29. "Top 100 Advertisers," *Advertising Age*, September 17, 1999, p. 16.

30. James Fredrick and Allene Symons, "Building an Image," *Drug Store News*, November 18, 1996, p. 9.

31. Joe Dysart, "E-Mail Marketing Grows Up," *Chain Store Age*, June 2001, pp. 91-92

32. Tony Case, "A Rocky Road Predicted for Newspaper Advertising," *Editor and Publisher*, September 23, 1995, p. 27.

33. "Maximizing the Potential of Audio Advertising," *Chain Store Age*, March 1995, p. B13.

34. Gabriella Stern, "With Sampling, There Is Too a Free Lunch," *The Wall Street Journal*, March 11, 1994, p. B1.

35. Susan Reda, "Retailers Use Affiliate Programs to Drive Internet Traffic and Sales," *Stores*, May 1998, pp. 46-49; Greg Notess, "Intricacies of Advertisement Information on the Web," *Online Magazine*, November 1999, pp. 79-81; and "Retooling for Interactivity," *Response*, November 1999, pp. 28-31.

36. Cyndee Miller, "Outdoors Gets a Makeover," *Marketing News*, April, 10, 1995, pp. 1, 26; and Teresa Andreoli, "From Retailers to Consumers: Billboards Drive the Message Home," *Discount Store News*, September 19, 1994, p. 14.

Credits

Name Index

Company Index

Subject Index

global location decisions, 208–210
importance of, 125
levels of, 126
lifestyle characteristics, 128
locational advantages within a centre, 143–144
site selection. *See* site selection
span of managerial control, 129
logistics
costs of, 312
defined, 312
electronic retailing, 316
quick response (QR) delivery systems, 313–316
reduction of expenses, 315
long-term liabilities, 236
loop, 169–170
loss leaders, 373
low price guarantee policy, 356–357
loyalty. *See* customer loyalty
loyalty programs, 113, 431

macro-environment
analysis of, 104–105
described, 109
global growth opportunities, and, 198–199
magalogue, 472
magazines, 494–495
maintained markup, 359–361
malls
advantages of, 134–135
defined, 132
demalling, 136
disadvantages of, 135–136
external environment, lack of worries about, 135
fashion/specialty centre, 137
lifestyle centre, 136–137
outlet centres, 137
management, 388
See also retail management
customer relationship management. *See* customer relationship management
financial management. *See* financial management
human resource management. *See* human resource management
international sourcing decisions, 329–330
merchandise management. *See* merchandise management
supply chain management. *See* supply chain management
managing diversity
career development and promotions, 413–414
described, 412
diversity training, 413
fundamental principle, 413
mentoring programs, 413
support groups, 413
manufacturer brands, 322–323, 322*f*
manufacturer's suggested retail price (MSRP), 380
manufacturers
disintermediation, and, 64–66
retailers, as, 326
maquiladoras, 328
marginal analysis, 482–483

markdown adjustments, 31*f*
markdown money, 369
markdowns
defined, 367
forecasting of, 293
inventory turnover, and, 244
liquidation of markdown merchandise, 369–370
markdown money, 369
merchandising optimization software, 368
optimizing markdown decisions, 368
price discrimination, and, 370
reasons for, 367
working with vendors to reduce markdowns, 369
market, 331
market analysis. *See* situation audit
market attractiveness/competitive position matrix, 215–217
market basket analysis, 434
market expansion opportunity, 118
market factors, and situation audit, 103
market penetration opportunity, 117
market segmentation
accessibility, 77–78
actionability, 76–77
benefit segmentation, 85
buying situation segmentation, 84–85
composite segmentation, 85
demographic segmentation, 79–81
evaluation criteria, 76–78
geodemographic segmentation, 82–83
geographic segmentation, 78–79
identifiability, 77
lifestyle segmentation, 83–84
methods for, 77*f*, 79–81
retail market segment, 76
size, 78
market segments, identification of, 434–435
market size, 213
market weeks, 332
market, from retail perspective, 332
markup opportunities, 337
mass-market theory, 91
med-arb, 344
media. *See* advertising media
media companies, 493
mediation, 344
men
shopping and, 79
young males, and fashion, 92
mentoring programs, 413
merchandise
assortment. *See* assortment
basic merchandise, 266
breadth of stock, 24
complementary merchandise and services, 60
e-tailing, in, 58–59
highlighting, 186
kiosks, 138
management, coordination with, 398–399
physical characteristics, 176
popping the merchandise, 186
presentation of, on websites, 61
pull distribution strategy, 301
push distribution strategy, 301
returns, 313

seasonal merchandise, 266
staple merchandise, 266
type of, 24
unique merchandise, 60, 114
variety of, 24
merchandise allocation, 300–301
merchandise budget plan
BOM (beginning-of-month) stock-to-sales ratio, 294–297
BOM stock, 296–297
described, 290
EOM (end-of-month) stock, 297
evaluation of, 297–298
fashion merchandise, 290–298
monthly additions to stock, 297
monthly reductions, 293
monthly reductions percent distribution to season, 293–294
monthly sales, 293
monthly sales percent distribution to season, 292
sample, 291*f*
merchandise classification scheme, 259*f*
merchandise division, 423
merchandise flows, 308*f*, 313*f*
See also logistics
merchandise group, 258
merchandise in motion, 241
merchandise inventory, 232–234
merchandise kiosks, 138
merchandise management
allocation to stores, 300–301
assortment plan, 258, 279–280
assortment planning process, 271–279
category captain, 262
category life cycles, 262–266
category management, 261
category, the, 260–270
defined, 257
information flows, 308*f*, 309–321
issues, 258*f*, 286*f*
logistics, 312–316
merchandise budget plan (fashion merchandise), 290–298
merchandise performance analysis, 301–305
merchandise plan, 271
objectives for merchandise plan, 271
open-to-buy, 298–299
replenishment order, 306
staple merchandise buying systems, 286–290
supply chain management, 306
merchandise mix, profitability of, 275
merchandise performance analysis
ABC analysis, 301–303, 303*f*
multiattribute method, 304–305
sell-through analysis, 304
weighted average approach, 305*f*
merchandise plan, 271
merchandise presentation techniques, 179–184
colour presentation, 180
consistency of display, 179
display design principles, 191–193
fixtures, 183–184
frontal presentation, 182
idea-oriented presentation, 180
issues, 179

right-entry pattern, 167
risks, perceived, in e-tailing, 58
road condition, 142
road pattern, 142
Robinson-Patman Act, 380
ROG dating, 350
rounder, 183–184
rule-of-thumb methods, 484–485

safety, 46
safety stock, 277, 287
sales, 358
sales forecasting
    category life cycles, and, 262
    category-level forecasts, information for, 266–268
    demand, 285
    developing a sales forecast, 266–267
    factors influencing, 270*f*
    season, procedure for, by, 267
    staple items, for, 288–290
    store-level forecasting, 269
sales margin per square metre measures, 303
sales per linear metre, 179
sales per square metre, 179
sales promotions, 476
sales-to-stock ratio, 239
salesperson morale, 244
SARS, impact of, 88–89
saturated trade area, 129
saturation stage, 93
scale economies, 103, 127, 201
scanned vs. posted prices, 382
scent, 187
scrambled merchandising, 12
screening process, 403, 418
search engines, 59, 64, 375
seasonal discounts, 350
seasonal merchandise, 266
seasonal needs, 175
seasonality, and sales forecasts, 270*f*
second-degree price discrimination, 370
secondary zone, 144
security. *See* store security management
security management. *See* store security management
security measures, 417, 418*f*
security policy, 312
selection, and retail exchanges, 331
self-service grocery stores, 33–34
sell-through analysis, 301, 304
service gap, 450
    communications gap, 450, 459
    defined, 450
    delivery gap, 450, 456–458
    knowledge gap, 450, 451–453
    standards gap, 453–456
service level, 274
    See also product availability
service providers, role of, 455
service quality. *See* customer service
service recovery
    distributive fairness, 461
    fair solutions, 461
    listening to customers, 460–461
    procedural fairness, 461
    quick problem resolution, 461
service retailers
    assortment planning, 274

demand and supply, matching, 42
described, 40
inconsistency, 42
intangibility, 41
merchandise retailers, vs., 41–42
merchandise/service continuum, 41*f*
perishability, 42
simultaneous production and consumption, 41–42
variety of, 40
services
    complementary merchandise and, 60
    cost of, 26
    customer services, 24–25
    increasing value of, 8
    industrialization of, 42
    provided by retailers, 8
sexual harassment, 415
shallow assortment, 272
share of wallet, 66, 427, 428, 441
shared goals, 340–341
shareholders' equity, 230, 236–237
shipping terms and conditions, 351–352
shoes, assortment plan for, 280
shoplifting, 294, 417
shopping bots, 59, 375
shopping carts, 446
shopping centres
    cumulative attraction, 144
    defined, 132
    definitions, 133*f*
    described, 129–130
    first shopping centre, 134
    locational advantages, assessment of, 143–144
    malls, 132, 134–138
    power centre, 133
    regional multilevel, 143
    strip centres, 132–134
    traditional strip centre, 132
shopping guides, 496
shopping in the future, 72
shopping malls. *See* malls
showcase, 338
shrinkage, 294, 361
signs, 184–185
similar store approach, 148–157
simultaneous production and consumption, 41–42
single-store retailers, 42–43, 395–396
site decisions. *See* location decisions
site selection. *See also* location decisions
    accessibility, 142–143
    attractiveness of site, factors affecting, 142
    cumulative attraction, 144
    demand for new location, estimate of. *See* estimating demand
    macro analysis, 142
    micro analysis, 142–143
    trade area, defining, 144–145
situation audit
    competitive factors, 103–104
    defined, 102
    elements in, 103*f*
    macro-environment, 104–105
    market factors, 103
    strengths and weaknesses analysis, 105
size of target segment, 78

SKU (stock keeping unit)
    ABC analysis, and, 301
    buying organization, 259–260
    described, 24
    product availability, and, 277
    rank ordering of, 302–303
    retail exchanges, on, 333–334
    sales forecasting, and, 269
    slotting allowances, and, 345
slotting allowances or fees, 345
social experience, 46
social influences on buying, 85–88
social responsibility concerns, 331
socialization, 408
space planning. *See also* store layout
    adjacent departments, 176
    butt-brush effect, 177
    demand/destination areas, 175
    departmental layout, evaluation of, 177
    described, 173
    easy access, 177
    floor space allocation, 174*f*
    grocery stores, 176
    impulse products, 175
    location of departments, 173–174
    merchandise within departments, 177–179
    physical characteristics of merchandise, 176
    planograms, 177–179
    relative location advantages, 175
    sales per linear metre, 179
    sales per square metre, 179
    seasonal needs, 175
    transition zone, 177
span of managerial control, 129
spatial allocation models, 157
specialization, 393
specialty catalogue retailers, 37
specialty store retailing issues, 27–28
specialty stores, 27
specific objectives, establishment of, 106
square assortment planning, 274
staffing. *See* recruitment
standardization approach, 446
standards gap, 450
    closing, 453
    commitment to service quality, 454
    described, 453
    innovative approaches, 454
    service goals, 455–456
    service performance, measurement of, 456
    service providers, role of, 455
    solutions to service problems, 454–455
    technology and, 454–455
staple merchandise, 266
staple merchandise buying systems
    backup stock, 289
    basic stock list, 288–289
    described, 286
    functions of, 288
    inventory management report, 288–290
    inventory turnover, 289
    order point, 290
    order quantity, 290
    product availability, 289
    sales forecast, 290
Statistics Canada, 146

terms of purchase
anticipation discounts, 351
cash discounts, 350–351
functional discounts, 349
negotiation of, 337
quantity discounts, 349
seasonal discounts, 350
shipping terms and conditions, 351–352
trade discounts, 349
tertiary zone, 144
testing, 404
Textile Labelling Act, 475
texture, 191
theatrical effects, 185
Third World labour conditions, 331
timing of advertising, 480
tonnage merchandising, 182
top-of-mind awareness, 470
touching products, 45
town locations, 139
trade area
business climate, 128
cannibalization, 127
census information, 146
competition, 129
competition, measurement of, 147
customer spotting technique, 146
defined, 144
defining, 144–145
demographic characteristics, 128
demographic data, 146–147
described, 126
destination stores, and, 145
driving time, 144
economies of scale, 127
factors affecting demand, 126, 127f
factors in defining, 144–145
geographic information systems (GIS),
146–147
lifestyle characteristics, 128
overstored trade area, 129
polygons, 144
primary zone, 144
saturated trade area, 129
secondary zone, 144
size, 144–145
sources of information for defining,
145–147
span of managerial control, 129
symbiotic store, and, 145
tertiary zone, 144
understored trade area, 129
trade discounts, 349, 379
trade shows, 332
trademark, 346
traditional strip centre, 132
traffic appliances, 368
traffic flow, 142–143, 209
traffic patterns, 167
transition zone, 177
transportation costs, 329, 337, 351–352
trends
attractiveness of retail markets, and,
104–105
retail trends. *See* retail trends
trialability, 92
trickle-down theory, 91
trust, 340
trustworthy reputation, 60, 340

turnover path
accounts payable, 236
accounts receivable, 231–232
accrued liabilities, 236
asset turnover, 235
assets, 230
cash, 234
current assets, 231
current liabilities, 235
described, 224
fixed assets, 234
liabilities, 230, 235–237
long-term liabilities, 236
merchandise inventory, 232–234
notes payable, 236
owners' equity, 230–231, 236–237
retained earnings, 237
shareholders' equity, 230, 236–237
tween generation, 81
tying contract, 348

understored trade area, 129
unique merchandise, 60–61, 114
uniqueness of retail offering, 131
United States
aging population, 198
American territories overseas, 331
Canadian retail failure in, 196–198
distribution system in, 212
products, in other countries, 327
retailing success in Canada, 195–196
top global retailers, 212
universal product code (UPC), 306
unpaid impersonal communications, 477
unpaid personal communications, 477
unprofitable customers, 442–443
unrelated diversification, 118
unusual events, and sales forecasts, 270f
UPCs (Universal Product Codes), 14, 313

value
described, 355
store design elements, of, 165
value retailers, 32
Vancouver Canadian demographic 2004,
148f–150
variable costs, 366
variable pricing, 372–373
variety, 12, 24, 271–272, 275–276
vending machine retailing, 39
vendors
bargaining power of, 104
buying offices, 332
category-level forecast, information
source for, 268
chargebacks, and, 344
connection with, 331–336
evaluation, with weighted average
approach, 305f
negotiations with, 336–339
relations, and sustainable competitive
advantage, 114–115
resident buying offices, 332
retail exchanges, 333–335
reverse auctions, 334
strategic relationships, 339–341
trade shows, 332
wholesale market centres, 331
vertical integration, 7, 119

vertical merchandising, 181–182, 182f
vertical price-fixing, 380
virtual communities, 56
visibility, 142
visual communications
appropriate typefaces, 185
coordination with store image, 185
described, 185
freshness of displays, 185
graphics, 184–185
informing the customer, 185
limit copy on signs, 185
props, signs and graphics as, 184
signs, 184–185
theatrical effects, 185
visual merchandising strategies. *See* store
planning
visual presentation, quality of, 46

walls, 172–173
warehouse clubs, 35
weather, and sales forecasts, 270f
websites
availability of merchandise, information
on, 66
communication method, as, 477
designs, 64
development of, 62–64
information, presentation of, 61
layout, and assortment planning, 276
merchandise, presentation of, 61
product, as, 64
standardization approach, and, 446
top 50 retail websites designs, 64
weekly store visits, 117
weeks of inventory, 294
weeks of supply, 294
weighted average approach, 305f
Weights and Measures Act, 475
wholesale market centres, 331
wholesale-sponsored voluntary cooperative
group, 43
windows, 171
wireless mobility technology, 32
women
career development and promotions,
413–414
clothing ideas, and store displays, 180
discrimination, and, 406
gender-based price discrimination, 379
glass ceiling, 413–414
home improvement store purchases, 29
merchandise returns, 313
shopping and, 79–80
word of mouth, 477
work-family balance, 412
World Trade Organization (WTO),
328–329
world's largest, 209f

Yellow Pages, 496
young people
living with parents, 93
online shopping, 57
young males, and fashion, 92

zigzag display, 191
zone pricing, 372–373